CW01483751

TWO YEAR OLDS
OF 1998

Fourteenth Edition

STEVE TAPLIN

ISBN 1 901570 04 5

Price £5.99

This Edition First Published in 1998
by
Portway Press Limited

CONTENTS

Two Year Olds of 1998

Cover photograph by Laurie Morton—

Henry Cecil is pictured with author Steve Taplin at Warren Place; the horse is Richmond Stakes and Champagne Stakes winner Daggers Drawn, pinpointed last year in 'Two Year Olds' when Henry told readers: 'I'm very pleased with the colt . . . he's certainly one to watch out for'.

FOREWORD

I am delighted to accept Steve Taplin's invitation to write the foreword to the latest edition of 'Two Year Olds'. The book is now in its fourteenth year and anyone who works as hard as Steve deserves the success he has had.

'Two Year Olds' is firmly established among the standard works on flat racing, providing a unique source of reference to each season's fresh crop of two-year-olds. In the hands of the punter it's dynamite—'The Early Types' section highlighting the two-year-olds likely to be of most immediate interest and 'The Premier Section' providing appraisals of the potential future stars.

'Two Year Olds' is compiled with the full co-operation of all the trainers featured. I, for one, look forward to Steve's annual visit to Warren Place and always feel that our discussions are fruitful. Readers of 'Two Year Olds' certainly have a pretty good idea of the identity of my most promising young horses!

Steve's newly-introduced 'Fifty To Follow' section produced a healthy profit last year when 'Two Year Olds' was enhanced for the first time by the addition of tables showing the leading trainers of two-year-olds (yours truly figuring prominently, I'm pleased to say) and the top sires of juveniles.

In short, 'Two Year Olds' is a mine of information which I'm sure you'll find invaluable.

Henry Cecil

INTRODUCTION

One of the more fascinating aspects of each Flat Racing season is the emergence of a new crop of young racehorses to represent the hopes of aspirations of their owners and trainers. Some of these two-year-olds will excite us with their speed and precocity, whilst others will show us a glimpse of greater things to come.

Between them, the last two editions of this book have selected over 260 individual 2-y-o winners. This year, with the continued enthusiastic help of trainers, I have been able to include many more horses than in any previous year, topping the 1,000-mark for the first time and giving the reader an even greater insight into the best two-year-olds trained in Britain, Ireland and France in 1998.

Despite the success I have had with my selections, the intention of this book is not simply to provide the punter with two-year-old winners alone. My equally important aim is to highlight the very best from each racing crop, many of which will only begin to excel as three-year-olds when the Classics and other Group One events will become the target. For example, the previous ten editions of "Two-Year-Olds" have highlighted eight King George winners, whilst the countless numbers of Classic winners to have emerged include the recent stars Always Loyal, Bosra Sham, Dance Design, Entrepreneur, Reams of Verse, Sleepytime, Spinning World and Ta Rib.

The book is divided into six distinct sections :-

    a) Fifty To Follow. An elite group of two-year-olds particularly highly regarded by their trainers.

    b) The Premier Section devoted to the finest bred young racehorses in Europe.

    c) The Early Types, focusing on horses expected by their trainers to win races in the early months of the season.

    d) The Stallion Reference, detailing the racing and stud careers of each sire with representatives in part (b).

    e) Two-year-old Race Trends. A statistical analysis of those juvenile events which regularly highlight the stars of the future.

    f) Timeform Statistical Review.

My selections this year include the full brothers or sisters to the top-class racehorses Air Express, Carmine Lake, Carnegie, Cezanne, Classic Cliché, Danehill, Entrepreneur, Generous, Grand Lodge, Mister Baileys, Shadayid, Tenby, Timber Country, User Friendly, Vettori and Wandesta.

Readers will also discover the whereabouts of the first foals of the high-class racemares Coup de Genie, Culture Vulture, Dalara, East of the Moon, Gold Splash, Hatoof, Kissing Cousin, Las Meninas, Mehthaaf, Nicer, Prophecy, Talented and Urban Sea.

Moreover, there are half-brothers or sisters to a great number of Group 1 winners, most notably Arazi, Be My Chief, Celtic Swing, Dr Devious, Erhaab, Hernando, Iktamal, In The Wings, Lady Carla, Last Tycoon, Mystiko, Peintre Celebre, Pennekamp, Pilsudski, Revoque, Salsabil, Sayyedati, Sheikh Albadou, Sleepytime, Snow Bride, Spinning World, Subotica, Ta Rib, Turtle Island and Zafonic.

I would like to thank John Ingles of Timeform for his help, all the racing and stud secretaries for their kindness and good humour, and of course the trainers for their invaluable advice and assistance.

Researched and compiled by Steve Taplin BA

Statistical Review by the kind consent of Timeform

FIFTY TO FOLLOW

Daggers Drawn (right) and Docksider, pictured fighting out the finish of the Champagne Stakes at Doncaster, were both in last year's 'fifty'

FIFTY TO FOLLOW

Take extra note of these young horses. This is a choice selection of two-year-olds of whom their trainers have high expectations this year.

ALL TO EASY (IRE)
b.f. Alzao - Easy To Copy (Affirmed).

"A big filly and a really nice type, All to Easy will be one to follow in the second half of the season. She's one of my best two-year-olds and I expect her to be decent. She just could be well named!". Dermot Weld

ASLEY (IRE)
b.c. Danehill - Ausherra (Diesis).

"We like this colt and he's certainly one to watch. He'll be out in May - probably over six furlongs - and shows speed". Marcus Tregoning

ATLANTIC PRINCE (IRE)
b.c. Fairy King - Idle Chat (Assert).

"Going extremely well, Atlantic Prince will be an early runner for the yard". Mark Johnston

BELASCO
ch.c. Gone West - Musicale (The Minstrel).

"A bit later than some of my two-year-olds, but he's done everything right and goes nicely. He'll make a two-year-old and everyone at Manton likes him". Peter Chapple-Hyam

BINT ALLAYL
b.f. Green Desert - Society Lady (Mr Prospector).

"A lovely filly with plenty of size and scope. She should be out in May and will certainly make a two-year-old". Mick Channon

BLUE SNAKE (USA)
b.c. Gone West - Dabaweyaa (Shareef Dancer).

"A very nice colt, very athletic and with a good attitude, he'll be out by mid-summer if not earlier and is a promising individual". Godolphin

BREAD WINNER
b.c. Reprimand - Khubza (Green Desert).

"This colt looks like being a nice two-year-old. A good-looking horse, he'll be out around June time over five or six furlongs". Ian Balding

BURMA BABY (USA)
ch.c. Woodman - Rangoon Ruby (Sallust).

"A big horse, but not that backward, he'll be suited by seven furlongs eventually. A lovely stamp of a horse, he has a good temperament and shows a lot of promise". Barry Hills

CABALLERO
b.c. Cadeaux Genereux - On Tiptoes (Shareef Dancer).

"A very nice horse that shows speed and he looks like being one of our better two-year-olds - possibly a Middle Park type". Clive Brittain

DALIAPOUR (IRE)
b.c. Sadler's Wells - Dalara (Doyoun).

"Daliapour could be a very nice colt indeed, he's very good-looking and has a touch of class. He's going pretty well at the moment, is strong and well-forward". Luca Cumani

DANE FRIENDLY
b.c. Danehill - Always Friendly (High Line).

"This colt may take a bit of time, but look out for him because he'll be a nice horse come mid-season". Peter Chapple-Hyam

DEHOUSH (USA)
ch.c. Diesis - Dream Play (Blushing Groom).

Dehoush is a nice horse and a very good mover. He enjoys his work, is a medium-sized, good sort of colt and he's going to be a two-year-old alright". Alec Stewart

EL MOBASHERR (USA)
b.c. Machiavellian - Sheroog (Shareef Dancer).

"A leggy colt (and thus very much like his dam), this is a well-grown, free-moving colt. A really nice type, he should be out by August or September". Michael Jarvis

EXIT
b.f. Exbourne - Meteoric (High Line).

"Very much liked by everyone in the yard. A very powerful mover, he could start off in a six furlong maiden in mid-May at Newmarket. One to follow". Michael Bell

FAIR FLIGHT
b.c. Green Desert - Barari (Blushing Groom).

"Fair Flight has always been quite a colty little horse but he goes well and has done nothing wrong. He looks precocious and should be a horse we can crack on with fairly soon". Ed Dunlop

FRAGRANT OASIS (USA)
ch.f. Rahy - Raahia (Vice Regent).

"A most beautiful looking filly, Fragrant Oasis has a lovely temperament and she moves very well. Going nicely at the moment, she's well developed and should make a nice two-year-old". Ed Dunlop

FULL PITCH
ch.c. Cadeaux Genereux - Tricky Note (Song).

"Full Pitch is a nice colt, quite backward now but when he strengthens he'll be a seriously nice horse. He'll be out by mid-summer and I don't think he'll be slow!". William Haggas

GOODBYE (IRE)
b.c. Thatching - Itqan (Sadler's Wells).

"A neat, good-actioned, straightforward colt, he's likely to be an early runner and is similar to his half-brother, Hello, who was campaigned from this yard". John Dunlop

HULA ANGEL (USA)
br.f. Woodman - Jode (Danzig).

"This is a lovely two-year-old. She should be out by June, has a good temperament and is a classy-looking filly. She's doing extremely well and is a good mover". Barry Hills

HYPERACTIVE (IRE)
b.c. Perugino - Hyannis (Esprit du Nord).

"This is a nice little horse. Quite mature, I would imagine he'd be one of the first of my two-year-olds to run - probably towards the end of May. He looks a quick type". Alec Stewart

IFTITAH (USA)
ch.c. Gone West - Mur Taasha (Riverman).

"This is a horse I like a lot. He looks a really nice sort, won't be too early, but is a quality two-year-old". Godolphin

INFLITE
b.c. Indian Ridge - Nightitude (Night Shift).

"Inflite is a horse I just hope will be ready for Royal Ascot. He'll be a really good horse, shows plenty of ability and should be a five or six furlong type". Willie Muir

JERYAAN (IRE)
b.c. Fairy King - Moonshine Lake (Kris).

"We like this colt particularly well. He has a wonderful temperament and a smooth, easy action for such a big-topped colt". Marcus Tregoning

KILLER INSTINCT
b.c. Zafonic - Rappa Tap Tap (Tap On Wood).

"A big horse, watch out for him later this year. I expect him to be a good two-year-old". Henry Cecil

KING OBERON (IRE)
b.c. Fairy King - Annenberg (Slip Anchor).

"A very nice horse and sharp too. I'll be aiming him for the Gimcrack - a race I've always wanted to win". William Haggas

LIGHTHOUSE
br.f. Warning - Valika (Valiyar).

"This is a nice filly. She's still growing a bit and will make a good two-year-old later on. A good mover, I do like her". Henry Cecil

MINNESOTA
b.c. Danehill - Santi Sana (Formidable).

"A very, very nice horse. He looks the part, does everything well, is on the big side but certainly not backward. At this stage he's giving me the same sort of feel that Danehill Dancer did". Neville Callaghan

MODUS OPERANDI (USA)
b.c. Known Fact - Proud Lou (Proud Clarion).

"A good sort and an active colt, he's a good mover and is one to keep an eye on". Henry Cecil

MOTHER OF PEARL
b.f. Sadler's Wells - Sisania (High Top).

"Mother Of Pearl won't be early, but I'm really pleased with her. Probably my best two-year-old, she's really attractive, quite a big filly and walks around as if she owned the place. She'll certainly make a nice two-year-old but will be even better next year". Peter Chapple-Hyam

MUTAAHAB (CAN)
b.c. Dixieland Band - Serene Nobility (His Majesty).

Not very big, but fairly level, this colt will be a two-year-old alright. He carries a lot of condition and certainly seems to be going the right way". Ed Dunlop

MUTAFAWEQ (USA)
b.c. Silver Hawk - The Caretaker (Caerleon).

"This is a very nice colt and next year he'll be a smart middle-distance horse. He has enough speed to win as a two-year-old from mid-summer onwards and is a colt with a lot of potential". Godolphin

NASHEED (USA)
b.br.f. Riverman - Thawakib (Sadler's Wells).

"This is a good-actioned, quality filly. She is taller than her half-sister Alharir and appears to have a little more scope". John Dunlop

PEACE OF MIND
ch.c. Nashwan - De Stael (Nijinsky).

"Peace Of Mind is a very nice horse and a very good mover. An exciting horse at this stage, if you didn't know his family you'd expect him to be early. As it is, I'd expect him to be out by July at the earliest...I like him a lot". Roger Charlton

RAS SHAIKH (USA)
b.f. Sheikh Albadou - Aneesati (Kris).

"This is a very nice filly, rangy and showing all the right signs. She'll be out by June and should be one to follow". Barry Hills

RED SEA
b.c. Barathea - Up Anchor (Slip Anchor).

"A very strong colt, not over big, he'll be out in mid-summer. I like him a lot". Paul Cole

RING THE RELATIVES
b.f. Bering - Relatively Special (Alzao).

Although she came into the yard rather late, this filly is from a family I know very well and I expect her to be a good sort". Luca Cumani

ROSE OF TARA (IRE)
ch.f. Generous - Flame Of Tara (Artaius).

"A filly with a lot of quality, she's the image of her sire. Strong, deep-bodied with a good temperament and not over-big, she's a bit backward but has plenty of scope and depth" Michael Grassick

ROSSELLI
b.c. Puissance - Miss Rossi (Artaius).

"A colt with a real future. A beautiful looking horse, he's got all the hallmarks of a real racehorse and is the nearest thing to Mind Games that I've seen". Jack Berry

ROYAL COMMAND (IRE)
b.c. Green Desert - Elegance in Design (Habitat).

A bit more backward than one might expect, but this is a nice colt that will make a two-year-old by September or October. One to follow". Dermot Weld

ROYAL FLAME
b.f. Royal Academy - Samnaun (Stop The Music).

"Of all my fillies up to now, I suppose Royal Flame would be my favourite. She won't be out until the mid-summer but she's got a lot of quality about her, has a beautiful action and does everything really easily. I like her a lot". John Hills

SARHAN (USA)
b.br.c. Gone West - My Song For You (Seattle Song).

"Sarhan could come to hand quite quickly as he's training very nicely and we like him a lot.

He has a lot of presence and we'll probably start him over six furlongs". Godolphin

SINGLE CURRENCY
b.c. Barathea - Kithanga (Darshaan).

"A bit backward now, he'll be a middle-distance colt next year, but Single Currency is a very nice horse that will start over seven furlongs in late-summer. A very big, scopey colt with a good attitude and good legs, he's certainly one to follow". Paul Cole

SUPER DOLLAR (USA)
ch.c. Great Commotion - L'Americaine (Verbatim).

"Definitely a two-year-old type, this colt goes well and is very athletic". Paul Cole

TAMGEED (USA)
ch.f. Woodman - Toujours Elle (Lyphard).

"A quality filly. Very athletic with a top-class pedigree, she has the action and conformation to match". John Dunlop

TIME MILL
b.c. Shirley Heights - Not Before Time (Polish Precedent).

"A lovely, quality colt, he's very much for the end of the season and for next year. But he's got a beautiful action and has a lot of quality about him. A colt that does everything extremely easily...at the moment of all my two-year-olds he's giving me the best feel". John Hills

TRANQUIL LIFE (USA)
b.f. Dayjur - Sanctuary (Welsh Pageant).

"A very nice filly, she looks like she could be fairly early and we really like her". Godolphin

TYLER'S TOAST
ch.c. Grand Lodge - Catawba (Mill Reef).

"A lovely colt, very similar to his sire and although he may not turn out so good, he's a strong, good-looking horse that catches the eye. He's got a good attitude and we have high hopes for him". William Jarvis

WAHOO
br.c. Warning - Jubilee Trail (Shareef Dancer).

"This colt has a good action, the right attitude and looks to be a very nice two-year-old". John Gosden

WESTERN FOLLY
ch.c. Gone West - Nimble Folly (Cyane).

"Western Folly won't be too early, but he's an active colt and I like him. A nice horse and one to follow". Henry Cecil

WAR CABINET
b.c. Rainbow Quest - Balleta (Lyphard).

"War Cabinet is a horse I like quite a bit. He's a nice colt that will make a decent two-year-old". Henry Cecil

PREMIER SECTION

Henry Cecil and Peter Chapple-Hyam have trained the most 2-y-o's rated 100+ by Timeform in the past three years

Robert Armstrong

1 - ADMIRAL'S PLACE (IRE) ch.c. Perugino - Royal Daughter (High Top).
April 21. 28,000Y. Tattersalls October.
Half-brother to the quite useful 2-y-o 6f winners Love Of The Arts (by Tate Gallery) and Lime Street Blues (by Digamist), to a winner in Italy and Germany by Magical Wonder and a winner over hurdles by Glenstal. The dam was placed once over 12f and is a half-sister to 4 winners including the Goodwood Cup winner Tug Of War. The second dam, Pirate Queen (by Pirate King), was placed once over 7f at 2 yrs. (Mr C G Donovan). *"A nice horse and good-looking with plenty of bone, Admiral's Place is a sensible colt and he covers a lot of ground. He'll be out by June and will be suited by six furlongs to start with"* Robert advises me.

2 - AHDAAB (USA) ch.f. Rahy - Dish Dash (Bustino).
May 13.
Half-sister to the 3-y-o Dahomey (by Dayjur), to the 1994 Group 1 1m Queen Elizabeth II Stakes winner Maroof (by Danzig), the useful 1995 2-y-o triple 7f winner Mawwal (by Elmaamul), the useful 1987 2-y-o 7f winner Arrasas (by Irish River), the quite useful 1993 2-y-o 6f winner Fawaakeh, the fair 1992 3-y-o 10f winner Mayaasa (both by Lyphard), the minor French winner White Mantle and also the maiden Sabaah (both by Nureyev) - dam of the Irish 2,000 Guineas and Irish Derby winner Desert King. The dam, a smart filly, won once over 6f at 2 yrs and over 1m and 12f at 3, the latter event being the Group 2 Ribblesdale Stakes at Royal Ascot. She is a half-sister to 6 winners including Canterbury Tale, Silk and Satin, Feliciano and Smuggly - all at least very useful. The second dam, Loose Cover (by Venture VII), was a useful miler and a winner of 4 races. (Hamdan Al Maktoum). *"Quite a small filly, she's a very good mover and covers a lot of ground".*

3 - KINAN (USA) b.c. Dixieland Band - Alsharta (Mr Prospector).
January 31. First foal.
The dam is an unraced half-sister to the fairly useful 2-y-o 7f winner Mashhaer. The second dam, Life's Magic (by Cox's Ridge), a Champion 3-y-o filly and Champion older mare in the USA won five Grade 1 events including the Breeders Cup Distaff and is a half-sister to the very useful US colt Housebuster. (Hamdan Al Maktoum). *"I like this colt very much - he's a natural athlete and should be running at the Guineas meeting over six furlongs".*

4 - MALAAH (IRE) gr.c. Pips Pride - Lingdale Lass (Petong).
February 9. Second foal. 26,000Y. Tattersalls October.
Brother to the modest 1997 5f placed 2-y-o Blue Shadow. The dam, a modest 2-y-o 6f winner, is a half-sister to 4 minor winners. The second dam, Our Mother (by Bold Lad, Ire), was a useful dual 5f winner at 2 yrs. (Hamdan Al Maktoum). *"Still growing at the moment, he's a nice colt but will take some time to come to hand".*

5 - ONE QUICK LION b.c. Lion Cavern - One Quick Bid (Commemorate).
March 11. Second foal. 38,000Y. Tattersalls Houghton.
Half-brother to the quite useful 1997 2-y-o 6f winner Swift Alliance (by Belong To Me). The dam, a minor winning 4-y-o sprinter in the USA, is a half-sister to 6 winners including the very smart Group 3 Rose Of Lancaster Stakes winner Tamayaz and the US Grade 2 winner Star Standing. The second dam, Minstrelsy (by The Minstrel), is a winning half-sister to the Kentucky Oaks winner Sweet Alliance (the dam of Shareef Dancer). (Mr R J Arculli). *"I like this colt. He's a good mover, does everything right and has a good temperament. He'll take a bit of time, but may be ready to run in mid-summer"* says Robert.

6 - ZIENAT (USA) ch.f. Woodman - Ice Folly (Icecapade).
April 25. Fourth foal. $260,000Y. Keeneland September.
Half-sister to the minor US winner of 6 races from 2 to 4 yrs Gallinaccia (by Hansel). The dam won 4 races in the USA including the listed Debutante Stakes and is a half-sister to 8 winners including the minor US 2-y-o 6f stakes winner Lomax. The second dam, River Guide (by Drone), is an unraced half-sister to 2 US stakes winners. (Hamdan Al Maktoum). *"Zienat is a lovely filly and I like her a lot. She should be a decent two-year-old at Newmarket's July meeting".*

7 - UNNAMED b.c. Pips Pride - Classic Ring (Auction Ring).
March 4. Third foal. IR32,000Y. Goffs Challenge.
Half-brother to the 1997 unplaced 2-y-o Classic Silver (by Silver Kite). The dam, a 2-y-o 7f seller winner, is a half-sister to 3 winners. The second dam, Classic Choice (by Patch), is an unraced half-sister to 8 winners including the Group 3 White Rose Stakes placed River Beauty. *"A very attractive horse with a good temperament, he should be out in June over six furlongs".*

Ian Balding

8 - BLUES BROTHER b.c. Bluebird - Manx Millenium (Habitat).
March 23.
Sister to the very useful filly Blue Siren, a winner of three races from 5f to 7f and disqualified from first place in two more, notably the Group 1 5f Nunthorpe Stakes (the winner on merit) and half-sister to several winners including the quite useful 9f winner Northern Habit (by Salmon Leap) and the 1996 3-y-o 7f and 1m winner Bandit Girl (by Robellino). The dam was placed over 1m and is a half-sister to several winners. The second dam, Daphne (by Acropolis), was useful at up to 12f. (Mr J C Smith). *"Blues Brother looks like he'll be a nice mid-summer two-year-old" says Ian. "He's medium-sized, strong and a good mover".*

9 - BREAD WINNER b.c. Reprimand - Khubza (Green Desert).
March 20. Second foal. 64,000Y. Doncaster St Leger.
Half-brother to the very useful 1997 2-y-o Trans Island (by Selkirk), winner of 3 races from 6f to 7f including a listed event at Deauville. The dam, a quite useful 3-y-o 7f winner, is a half-sister to the listed Harry Rosebery Challenge Trophy winner Heard A Whisper. The second dam, Breadcrumb (by Final Straw), was a very useful winner of 3 races at 3 yrs over 6f and 7f and is a half-sister to the high-class sprinter College Chapel. (Al Muallim Partnership). *"This colt looks like being a nice two-year-old. A good-looking horse, he'll be out around June time over five or six furlongs" Ian informs me.*

10 - CARMARTHEN ch.c. Hamas - Solar Attraction (Salt Dome).
March 4. First foal. IR45,000Y. Fairyhouse September.
The dam was placed once over 5f in Ireland at 2 yrs and is a half-sister to 6 winners including the Irish listed winners Bufalino and Maledetto. The second dam, Croglin Water (by Monsanto), is an unplaced half-sister to the smart sprinter Governor General. (Elite Racing Club). *"The earliest of my two-year-olds, he should be out before your book is published. He's quite sharp, small, strong and speedy".*

11 - DORISSIO b.f. Efisio - Floralia (Auction Ring).
March 18. Second living foal. 24,000Y. Tattersalls October.
Half-sister to the French trained 3-y-o Flavinia (by Cadeaux Genereux). The dam, a quite useful 3-y-o 7f and 8.9f winner, is a half-sister to 4 winners including the listed Easter Stakes winner Ultimo Imperatore. The second dam, Norpella (by Northfields), was a fairly useful 10f and 12f winner and a daughter of a half-sister to Teenoso. (Miss A V Hill). *"This is quite a nice filly. She's sharp and early, wants five furlongs and is therefore a typical two-year-old type".*

12 - HOH HOH SEVEN b.c. College Chapel - Fighting Run (Runnett).
May 10. 35,000Y. Tattersalls October.
Half-brother to the 3-y-o Royal Arrow (by Royal Academy), to the fair 1993 3-y-o 7.6f winner Croire (by Lomond) and a winner in Russia by Caerleon. The dam is an unraced half-sister to the useful 6f and 1m winner Leipzig (herself dam of the listed winner Pfalz), to the dams of the Group winners Adam Smith, Braashee, Ghariba, Careafolie, Gouriev and Run And Gun, and to the American Grade 1 third Stop The Fighting. The second dam, Fighting (by Aggressor), won over 1m at 3 yrs and is a half-sister to the dams of Hadeer, Bay Street, Rose of Montreaux, Glancing and Bassenthwaite. (Mr D F Allport & Hoh Supply Ltd). *"A handsome horse, he looks like he'll be a nice two-year-old and I should think I'll be looking for a race over six furlongs in June to start him off".*

13 - RIMATARA ch.c. Selkirk - Humble Pie (Known Fact).
March 20. 115,000Y. Tattersalls Houghton.
Half-brother to the 3-y-o Lower Chapel, to the Group 3 5f Premio Omenoni winner and Group 2 Diadem Stakes second Leap For Joy (both by Sharpo), the 1996 3-y-o 7f winner West Humble (by Pharly) and the 1993 3-y-o 6f winner and subsequent French winner Waffle On (by Chief Singer) - both fairly useful. The dam, a fairly useful 2-y-o 6f winner, is a half-sister to 5 winners including the high-class sprinter

College Chapel. The second dam, Scarcely Blessed (by So Blessed), won the Group 3 5f King George Stakes and is out of the July Cup winner Parsimony. (Mr R Hitchins). *"A nice, back-end type two-year-old, he should get a mile this year. Very much like his sire to look at, with a big white face".*

14 - SARANGANI
b.c. Polish Precedent - Height of Folly (Shirley Heights).
February 7. 94,000Y. Tattersalls October.
Half-brother to the 3-y-o Act Of Folly (by Midyan), to the fairly useful 1993 2-y-o 7.5f and 8.1f winner Charity Crusader (by Rousillon), the fair 1997 9.7f and 10f winner Opalette (by Sharrood) and the fair 1994 2-y-o 7.1f winner Opaline (by Salse). The dam, a quite useful stayer, won 3 races and is a half-sister to 3 minor winners. The second dam, Criminelle (by Crepello), is an unplaced half-sister to the dams of Ragstone (Ascot Gold Cup), Castle Keep (Group 1 Grand Prix Prince Rose) and Assez Cuite (French listed winner and dam of the French St Leger winner El Cuite). (Mr R Hitchins). *"A very nice horse and entered in the Derby, Sarangani looks a nice back-end two-year-old. He's a medium-sized, handsome horse with a lot of quality" Ian tells me.*

15 - SOLE SINGER (GER)
b.c. Slip Anchor - Singer On The Roof (Chief Singer).
February 4. First foal.
The dam was a modest 3-y-o winner over 1m and is a half-sister to the Group 1 Prix Saint-Alary winner Aie de Rien. The second dam, On The Tiles (by Thatch), won over 10f in Ireland. (Mr J C Smith). *"A decent sized horse, Sole Singer looks a really nice type. I'll start him off at seven furlongs this year".*

16 - SULU (IRE)
b.c. Elbio - Foxy Fairy (Fairy King).
February 14. Second foal. 22,000Y. Doncaster St Leger.
The dam is an unplaced half-sister to the Irish sprinter Fundraiser, a winner of three races including two listed events and herself dam of the French listed winner Clever Caption. The second dam, Secret Story (by Pry), won four races at 6 yrs on the flat and three races over hurdles. (Mr R Hitchins). *"A bit backward, he might well make a nice two-year-old later on over five or six furlongs".*

17 - TARAWAN
ch.c. Nashwan - Soluce (Junius).
April 2. 45,000Y. Tattersalls Houghton.
Half-brother to the 3-y-o Prima Facie (by Primo Dominie), to the useful listed 6f Abernant Stakes winner Splice, the quite useful 5f and 6f winner Splicing (both by Sharpo), the fairly useful 1m winner and subsequent Italian winner Alfujairah (by Diesis), the modest 1m winner Solo Sail (by Slip Anchor) and a winner abroad by Cadeaux Genereux. The dam won the Group 3 Irish 1,000 Guineas Trial and is a half-sister to 3 winners. The second dam, Amatrice (by Appiani II), won at 3 yrs and is a half-sister to the Lingfield Oaks Trial winner Gift Wrapped (herself dam of the Royal Lodge Stakes winner Reach). (Mr R Hitchins). *"A nice horse and similar in type to another of my two-year-olds, Sarangani, he's also entered in the Derby and would want seven furlongs to start this year. A good-sized horse, he's not unlike his sire Nashwan to look at".*

Pascal Bary

18 - CHRISTOPHENE
b.c. Kingmambo - Miss Summer (Luthier).
March 2.
Half-brother to the 1987 French 2-y-o listed 1m Prix de Lieurey winner and Group 1 Prix de la Salamandre and Group 1 Grand Criterium placed Most Precious, to the very useful 1996 3-y-o dual 7f winner High Summer (both by Nureyev), the French and US winner Ofanto (by Lyphard), the 1994 French 3-y-o 10.5f winner Summer Groom (by Blushing Groom) and the 1994 2-y-o 7f winner - on her only start - Private Line (by Private Account). The dam won the listed 1m Prix de Saint-Cyr and is a half-sister to the Group 2 Prix Hocquart winner Mot d'Or, the Group 1 Gran Premio de Milano winner Lydian, the Group 2 Ribblesdale Stakes winner Ballinderry (herself dam of Sanglamore) and the French 2,000 Guineas second Sharpman. The second dam, Miss Manon (by Bon Mot III), was a good winner of three races at around 10f and was fourth in the French Oaks. (Khaled Abdulla).

19 - LA JOIE (USA)
b.f. Kingmambo - La Tritona (Touching Wood).
Fourth foal.
Closely related to the French-trained 3-y-o La Petite Danseuse (by Woodman) and half-sister to the smart Group 1 9f Prix Jean Prat winner Le Triton (by El Gran Senor). The dam won from 10f to 12.5f in France including a Group 3 event and is a half-sister to the Japan Cup and Washington D C International winner Le Glorieux and to Lucaya (dam of the Group 1 Premio Parioli winner Lucratif).

The second dam, La Mirande (by Le Fabuleux), won twice in France, was third in the Group 3 12.5f Prix de Royallieu and is a sister to the Oaks third La Manille. (Mrs O'Reilly).

---

20 - MARIA DE LA LUZ b.f. Machiavellian - Light Of Hope (Lyphard).
March 8.
Half-sister to the French trained 3-y-o Happy Heart (by Exit To Nowhere), to the modest 1996 3-y-o 12f all-weather winner Harbet House (by Bikala) and the quite useful 1993 3-y-o 10.3f winner Savoy Truffle (by Law Society). The dam, a useful 3-y-o dual 10f winner, is a sister to the smart 1m to 10f winner and sire Alzao. The second dam, Lady Rebecca (by Sir Ivor), was a very useful French middle-distance winner and a half-sister to two good American horses in Tom Rolfe and Chieftain. (Mme R G Ehrnrooth).

---

21 - RAINBOWAIN (FR) b.c. Unfuwain - Rainbow Reliance (Rainbow Quest).
April 19. First foal. FF400,000. Deauville August.
The dam ran once unplaced and is a half-sister to the Group 1 Prix de la Foret and Grade 1 Hollywood Derby winner Procida. The second dam, With Distinction (by Distinctive), won 7 races in the USA, was third in the Grade 3 Signature Stakes and is a half-sister to the US Grade 1 winner Country Queen. (J C Seroul).

---

22 - WATERSTONE b.c. Riverman - Lovealoch (Lomond).
April 12. First foal. 100,000Y. Tattersalls Houghton.
The dam, a very useful 7f (at 2 yrs) and 9f winner here and placed in the Group 2 Falmouth Stakes and the Group 2 Premio Lydia Tesio, subsequently won once in the USA. She is a half-sister to 3 minor winners out of the very useful 12f winner and Park Hill Stakes fourth Civility, herself a half-sister to the smart 1976 2-y-o Piney Ridge. (Grundy Bloodstock Ltd).

---

23 - UNNAMED gr.c. Nureyev - Ancient Regime (Olden Times).
April 21. 460,000 Y. Tattersalls Houghton.
Closely related to the very smart 5f Prix Yacowlef winner and Group 1 5f Prix de l'Abbaye second La Grande Epoque (by Lyphard) - herself dam of the very useful 6f to 7f winner Matelot and to the very useful 1990 2-y-o Group 3 6.5f Prix Eclipse winner Crack Regiment (by El Gran Senor) and half-brother to the very useful 6f and 7f winner and Group 2 Queen Anne Stakes second Rami (by Riverman) and the minor 1995 French 3-y-o winner Trois Graces (by Alysheba). The dam, winner of the Group 1 6f Prix Morny, was the champion French 2-y-o filly of 1980, is a sister to the Group 2 6.5f Prix Maurice de Gheest winner Cricket Ball and the American stakes winner Olden, and a half-sister to the US Grade 3 winner Mug Punter. The second dam, Caterina II (by Princely Gift), won 4 races notably the 5f Nunthorpe Stakes and was a half-sister to the Eclipse winner Scottish Rifle. (Wafic Said).

Michael Bell

---

24 - AFFIDAVIT b.f. Slip Anchor - Lady Barrister (Law Society).
February 16.
Sister to the fairly useful 1994 2-y-o Italian 1m listed winner Edipo Re and half-sister to the fairly useful 1997 2-y-o 5.9f winner Eloquent (by Polar Falcon) and the modest 1995 2-y-o 7f winner Stately (by Be My Chief). The dam is an unraced daughter of a sister to the top-class miler Kings Lake and a half-sister to the high-class middle-distance colt Salmon Leap. *"A stoutly-bred filly, Affidavit covers the ground well but is a back-end type two-year-old"*. *Michael has more two-year-olds in the Early Types section.*

---

25 - CHAMELEON b.f. Green Desert - Old Domesday Book (High Top).
May 23. IR300,000Y. Goffs Orby.
Sister to the high-class Group 1 6f July Cup, Group 2 6f Moet and Chandon Rennen, Group 3 6f Cork and Orrery Stakes and Group 3 6f Duke of York Stakes winner Owington (by Green Desert) and half-sister to the quite useful 3-y-o 7.3f winner Great Inquest (by Shernazar), the fair 1m (at 2 yrs) and 12f winner Common Council (by Siberian Express) and the fair 1997 3-y-o 6f winner Midnight Shift (by Night Shift). The dam, a fairly useful 3-y-o 10.4f winner, was third in the listed 10f Sir Charles Clore Memorial Stakes. The second dam, Broken Record (by Busted), was a useful winner of four races from

12f to 15f, was third in the Jockey Club Gold Cup and fourth in the Tote Ebor Handicap. *"She won't be an early two-year-old, but she's done very well and looks a potentially smart filly. An autumn type"*.

John Benstead

26 - MEHMAAS
b.c. Distant Relative - Guest List (Be My Guest).
February 5. Fifth foal. 30,000Y. Tattersalls October.
Half-brother to the quite useful 1994 2-y-o 7f all-weather winner Dangerous Guest (by Deploy), to the modest 1m and 8.5f winner Backstabber (by Flash Of Steel) and the German winner Juschika (by Salse). The dam, a quite useful 6f (at 2 yrs) and 7f winner, is a half-sister to the high-class Prix de la Foret and Prix du Moulin winner Sanedtki. The second dam, Fortlin (by Fortino II), won 4 races and was a fairly useful 2-y-o sprinter. (Hamdan Al Maktoum). *"Mehmaas is quite a nice two-year-old. Not forward, he won't be out until mid-summer, probably over five or six furlongs"*.

27 - TAMMAM (IRE)
b.c. Priolo - Bristle (Thatch).
February 16. 30,000Y. Tattersalls October.
Half-brother to the 1997 3-y-o 10f and 12f winner Aerleon Pete (by Caerleon), to the 6f (at 2 yrs) to 1m winner Big Leap (by Auction Ring) - both fairly useful, the fair 1997 4-y-o 10f winner Premier Generation (by Cadeaux Genereux), the Italian winner of 6 races Speedy Wind (by Law Society) and the quite useful 7f gelding Rakis (by Alzao) - a winner of 10 races on turf and the all-weather. The dam, a fairly useful Irish 2-y-o 8.5f winner, was fourth in the Group 3 Silken Glider Stakes and is a half-sister to 8 winners. The second dam, Queen Of The Brush (by Averof), won once at 3 yrs and is a half-sister to the Prix Royal-Oak and Italian Derby winner Old Country. (Hamdan Al Maktoum). *"A very active horse, Tammam is likely to be out in May over five furlongs. A nice sort of colt"* says John.

28 - ZAIDAAN
b.c. Ezzoud - River Maiden (Riverman).
May 14. First foal. 40,000Y. Tattersalls October.
The dam won once at 2 yrs in France and is a half-sister to 4 winners including the German Group 3 winner Tout Est Permis and the useful 1997 1m listed winner Jafn. The second dam, Harold's Girl (by Northfields), won over 6f at 2 yrs in France. (Hamdan Al Maktoum). *"Another nice colt of Sheikh Hamdan's, he's bigger than Tammam but will also be relatively early"*.

Jim Bolger

Jim is particularly pleased with his young horses this year, but explained that most of them will not be out until the second half of the year.

29 - AERAIOCHT (IRE)
b.f. Tenby - Direct Lady (Fools Holme).
May 25. Second foal. IR20,000Y. Fairyhouse September.
Half-sister to the 3-y-o Direct Project (by Project Manager). The dam, a winner of three races at 3 yrs over 11f and 12f and also three races over hurdles, is a half-sister to the Group 1 Heinz "57" Phoenix Stakes winner Eva Luna and the Group 3 Futurity Stakes winner Cois Na Tine. The second dam, Guess Again (by Stradavinsky), won over 1m at 3 yrs and is out of a half-sister to the high-class sprinter Double Form and the Lupe Stakes winner Scimitarra. *"This filly ran third on her debut on bad ground and will improve"*.

30 - ASPIRATION (IRE)
b.f. Sadler's Wells - La Meilleure (Lord Gayle).
May 28.
Half-sister to the useful listed 7f Athasi Stakes and listed 1m Derrinstown Stud 1,000 Guineas Trial winner Zavaleta (by Kahyasi), to the useful 6f and 7f winner Nordic Fox and the fairly useful 2-y-o 5f winner and Molecomb Stakes second Raghida (both by Nordico). The dam, a quite useful 7f and 1m winner in Ireland, is from the family of Double Form and Scimitarra.

31 - BARAVELLI (IRE)
b.c. Barathea - Savelli (Vision).
February 23. Second living foal. IR67,000Y. Goffs Orby.
Half-brother to the Irish-trained 3-y-o Signore Savelli (by Alzao). The dam, a minor Irish 2-y-o 9f winner, is a half-sister to 8 winners including the Irish 2-y-o listed winner Nordic Soprano. The second dam, Angor (by Lorenzaccio), won at 3 yrs and is a half-sister to the top-class sprinter Double Form, the Lupe Stakes winner Scimitarra and to the dam of the Group 1 Phoenix Stakes winner Eva Luna.

32 - BERENGARIUS b.br.c. Grand Lodge - Special Display (Welsh Pageant).
March 14. 50,000Y. Tattersalls October.
Half-brother to 4 winners in Ireland by Nordico including the listed 7f Garnet Stakes winner Nordic Pageant, to the minor Irish winner of 6 races at up to 14f Diamond Display (by Shardari) and the Irish 10f winner and listed 1m Brownstown Stakes second Special Pageant (by Ahonoora). The dam won twice in Ireland and is a half-sister to 3 minor winners on the Flat and 2 more over jumps. The second dam, Refifi (by Reform), won once at 3 yrs.

33 - CASTLE QUEST (IRE) b.f. Grand Lodge - In Unison (Bellypha).
March 24. Fourth foal. IR80,000Y. Goffs Orby.
Half-sister to the 1997 Irish 2-y-o 7f winner Diya (by Hamas), to the fairly useful 6f (at 2 yrs) and 7f winner Iblis (by Danehill) and the minor 1996 3-y-o winner Easy To Remember (by Mujtahid). The dam won over 1m at 3 yrs and is a half-sister to the Group 1 6f Haydock Park Sprint Cup winner Cherokee Rose. The second dam, Celtic Assembly (by Secretariat), a quite useful 3-y-o 10.6f winner, is a sister to the US stakes winner Subjective and a half-sister to the Group 1 Prix du Cadran winner Molesnes and the Group 3 Horris Hill Stakes winner Celtic Air.

34 - DANCING SEA (IRE) b.f. Storm Cat - Coral Dance (Green Dancer).
May 18.
Half-sister to the top-class 2,000 Guineas, Dewhurst Stakes and Prix de la Salamandre winner Pennekamp (by Bering), to the smart Group 2 12f Prix Hocquart winner Nasr El Arab - subsequently a high class winner of four Grade 1 events in the United States, the minor French winner Furiant (both by Al Nasr), the French listed 10.5f winner Shaal (by Lear Fan) and the dual French 1m winner Foyer (by Forli). The dam was a very useful winner at up to 1m in France and the USA and was placed in the Prix Marcel Boussac and the Prix d'Aumale. The second dam, Carvinia (by Diatome), a useful French middle-distance winner, was a half-sister to the high class colt Carvin. *"A well-developed filly that will stay a mile"*.

35 - DAZZLING PARK (IRE) br.f. Warning - Park Express (Ahonoora).
April 22.
Half-sister to the 1993 French 3-y-o 7f winner Lady Express (by Soviet Star), to the 1994 French 2-y-o 7f winner Tycoon King (by Last Tycoon) and the 1995 Japanese 3-y-o winner Shinko Forest (by Green Desert). The dam won 5 races including the Group 1 10f Phoenix Champion Stakes, the Group 2 10f Nassau Stakes and the Group 3 12f Lancashire Oaks and is a half-sister to numerous winners including the listed 6f Firth of Clyde Stakes winner Myra's Best. The second dam, Matcher (by Match III), ran unplaced twice and was a half-sister to 4 winners including a minor stakes winner in the USA. *"A good-sized filly, she'll stay ten furlongs"*.

36 - FARDUS (IRE) b.f. Danehill - Easy To Please (What a Guest).
May 11.
Sister to the useful 1996 Irish 2-y-o dual 6f listed winner Azra and half-sister to the fair Irish 2-y-o 5f winner Capellino (by Imperial Frontier). The dam, a useful Irish 2-y-o 1m winner, trained on to win the Queen Alexandra Stakes. *"A strong, well-developed filly that should be out by June over six furlongs"*.

37 - GAELIC PROJECT (IRE) br.f. Project Manager - Gayle Gal (Lord Gayle).
March 2. Sixth foal.
Sister to the Irish 10f winner Canadian Project and half-sister to the useful Irish 6f to 9f winner Celladonia (by Green Desert). The dam won the Moyglare Stud Stakes. The second dam, Best Gal (by Bonne Noel), won over 9f in Ireland. *"A strong, well-developed filly that should be out by June"*.

38 - GRANDIOSE IDEA (IRE) b.f. Danehill - Gorgeoso (Damascus).
April 21. Fourth living foal. IR65,000Y. Goffs Orby.
Half-sister to the fair 1996 3-y-o 9f and 10f winner Elashath (by El Gran Senor). The dam was placed twice in the USA and is a half-sister to 3 winners including the US Grade 2 placed Country Store. The second dam, Geraldine's Store (by Exclusive Native), won 13 races including the Grade 2 Diana Handicap and is a half-sister to the Irish 1,000 Guineas and Coronation Stakes winner Al Bahathri.

39 - GURKHA WARRIOR (USA) ch.c. St Jovite - Contredance (Danzig).

Half-brother to a stakes-placed winner in Japan by Gulch and to 3 minor winners in the USA by Private Account (2) and Forty Niner. The dam won the Grade 1 Washington Lassie Stakes in the USA, is a sister to the listed Roses Stakes winner Old Alliance and to the dam of the very smart colt Eltish and a half-sister to the Group winners Shotiche and Skimble. The second dam, Nimble Folly (by Cyane), is an unraced sister to the very useful Group 3 winner and Group 1 third Misgivings.

40 - OVAZIONE
ch.f. Seeking The Gold - O'Slewmova (Seattle Slew).
April 7. Fifth foal. 74,000Y. Tattersalls Houghton.
Half-sister to the useful 1995 French 2-y-o 6.5f winner and Group 2 Criterium des 2 Ans third Seattle Special (by Nureyev) and to a minor winner in the USA by Mt Livermore. The dam was placed twice in the USA, is a sister to the Prix de la Foret winner Septieme Ciel and a half-sister to the Prix Marcel Boussac winner Macoumba, the US Grade 3 winner Maxigroom and the French listed winners Balchaia and Manureva. The second dam, Maximova (by Green Dancer), won 7 races including the Prix de la Salamandre and is a half-sister to the French Group winners Vilikaia and Navratilovna. *"A beautiful, strong filly, I hope she'll live up to her pedigree" says Jim.*

41 - QUEEN'S LOVE (USA)
b.f. Kingmambo - Wiedniu (Danzig Connection).
Second foal.
The dam, a very useful maiden, was placed in the Coronation Stakes, the Falmouth Stakes and the Fred Darling Stakes before an injury forced her retirement. She is closely related to the very useful 5f (at 2 yrs) to 8.5f winner Batzushka and a half-sister to the useful 7f and 1m winner Cielamour. The second dam, Nicole Mon Amour (by Bold Bidder), won twice at up to 10f and is a half-sister to the US Grade 1 winners Stephan's Odyssey and Lotka.

42 - STEFANOVA (IRE)
b.c. Project Manager - Ivory Home (Home Guard).
March 29. April 17.
Half-brother to the 1997 unplaced 2-y-o Ivory Isle (by Erin's Isle) and to several winners in Ireland including the smart 7f (at 2 yrs) to 10f winner Upward Trend (by Salmon Leap), the 1996 2-y-o 7f winner Sadler's Home (by Sadler's Wells) and the useful 6f (at 2 yrs) and 1m winner Ivory Frontier (by Imperial Frontier). The unraced dam is from the family of Gorytus and Glad Rags.

43 - WHATS THE NEWS
ch.c. Grand Lodge - Belle Epoque (Habitat).
April 7. 25,000Y. Tattersalls October.
Half-brother to the 1989 2-y-o Group 3 5f Curragh Stakes winner Aminata (herself dam of the Irish listed winner Swift Gulliver) and to the quite useful 1990 2-y-o 6f winner Vassileva (by Gorytus). The dam, a modest maiden who stayed 7f, was placed 7 times and is a sister to the high-class sprinter Double Form and a half-sister to the Lupe Stakes winner Scimitarra. The second dam, Fanghorn (by Crocket), won 2 races at 2 yrs and was third in the French 1,000 Guineas.

Clive Brittain

44 - ALONSA (IRE)
b.f. Trempolino - Alimana (Akarad).
May 4. Fifth foal. 28,000Y. Tattersalls Houghton.
Sister to the French 3-y-o Alwiyda and half-sister to the minor French winners Alampour (by Shahrastani) and Alkami (by Alleged). The dam, a fair 2-y-o 9f winner, only ran once. She is a full or half-sister to 7 winners including the disqualified Oaks winner Aliysa (herself dam of the Group 3 Craven Stakes winner Desert Story) and Aleema (dam of the French Group winners Altayan and Altashar). The second dam, Alannya (by Relko), a very smart French 1m listed winner, is a half-sister to the dam of the Group 1 winners Nishapour and Nassipour. (Mr Saeed Manana). *"A filly for the second half of the season, probably over seven furlongs or more. The type to make a good three-year-old".*

45 - ARDECHE (USA)
ch.c. Bien Bien - Ardisia (Affirmed).
April 3. Second foal. 37,000Y. Tattersalls Houghton.
Half-brother to the 7.1f (at 2 yrs) to 12.4f placed Dark Green (by Green Dancer). The dam, a quite useful winner of 3 races at around 10f, is a half-sister to 8 winners including Ausherra (Lingfield Oaks Trial) and the useful middle-distance colt Royal Scimitar. The second dam, Princess Of Man (by Green God), won three races including the Group 3 Musidora Stakes. (Prince Abdul Aziz bin Saud). *"A very nice colt, he's just doing cantering work now. He'll probably start off at six furlongs and might be good enough to go to Royal Ascot".*

46 - ASSURED MOVEMENTS (USA)
b.c. Northern Flagship - Love At Dawn (Grey Dawn II).
April 22. Third foal. IR34,000Y. Goffs Orby.
Brother to the 3-y-o Carte Blanc. The dam, a minor winner at 3 yrs in the USA, is a half-sister to 6 winners including Tiltalating, winner of the Grade 1 Spinaway Stakes and the Grade 2 Sorority Stakes.

The second dam, Linda Cubanita (by Proudest Roman), won twice in the USA. (Mr Peter A Head). *"A smart looking 2-y-o that shows a bit of speed, he'll be out in May" informs Clive.*

47 - BELLEFONTE (IRE)

b.c. Scenic - La Bella Fontana (Lafontine).
May 2. Sixth foal. 32,000Y. Tattersalls Houghton.
Half-brother to the 3-y-o Northumbrian Belle (by Distinctly North), to the 1996 Champion 2-y-o Revoque, winner of the Group 1 Grand Critrium and the Group 1 Prix dela Salamandre, the modest 1m and 9.7f winner Swinging Sixties (both by Fairy King) and the hurdles winner Barsal (by Absalom). The dam was unplaced on her only start and is a half-sister to the Group 3 7f Hungerford Stakes winner Abuzz and to the dam of the Group 3 Phoenix Sprint Stakes winner Point Of Light. The second dam, Sorebelle (by La Belle), was a useful winner of 3 races at up to 1m and was second in the listed Bunbury Cup. (Saeed Manana). *"Bellefonte has grown quite a bit since we bought him and won't be out until the second half of the season" Clive informs me.*

48 - CABALLERO

b.c. Cadeaux Genereux - On Tiptoes (Shareef Dancer).
March 5. Third foal. 115,000Y. Tattersalls Houghton.
Half-brother to the fair 1997 5f placed 2-y-o Odette (by Pursuit Of Love). The dam was a useful winner of 5 races at around 5f including the Group 3 Queen Mary Stakes and is a half-sister to the useful 6f and 7f winner Penny Candle (by Be My Guest). The second dam, Pennyweight (by Troy), is an unplaced half-sister to the Irish 2,000 Guineas and Lockinge Stakes winner Wassl out of the Molecomb Stakes winner Hayloft. (Sheikh Marwan Al Maktoum). *"A very nice horse that shows speed and he looks like being one of our better two-year-olds - possibly a Middle Park type".*

49 - COMPREHENSION (USA)

b.f. Diesis - Je Comprend (Caerleon).
April 1. Fifth foal. 40,000Y. Tattersalls Houghton.
Closely related to the US stakes winner Krigeorj's Gold (by Kris) and half-sister to the 1998 3-y-o French Wood (by Woodman). The dam, a modest fourth over 12f at 3 yrs in Ireland, is a sister to the very useful Australian Grade 2 and Italian Group 3 winner Alquoz and a half-sister to 6 winners including the US Grade 3 winner Ayman and the Australian Grade 3 winner Seeker's Gold. The second dam, I Understand (by Dr Fager), won 4 races in the USA and is a half-sister to the Grade 1 winner Royal And Regal, to the Grade 3 winner Regal And Royal and to the dam of the Group 1 winners Dowsing and Fire The Groom. (Saeed Manana). *"A very nice filly, not over-expensive and she's done very well. She'll be up for the better fillies' races at the back-end".*

50 - CONFLICT (FR)

b.c. Warning - La Dama Bonita (El Gran Senor).
April 17. Third foal. FF700,000. Deauville August.
Half-brother to the 3-y-o La Isla Bonita (by Lion Cavern) and to the 1997 French placed 3-y-o Army Of One (by Machiavellian). The dam, a quite useful 2-y-o 5f and 3-y-o 7.3f winner, is closely related to the Group 1 6f Ladbroke Sprint Cup and Group 2 7f Juddmonte Lockinge Stakes winner Polar Falcon. The second dam, Marie d'Argonne (by Jefferson), won 3 races in France and the USA, was third in the Grade 2 9f Black Helen Handicap and is a half-sister to the Group 2 Prix de Pomone winner Marie de Litz. (Sheikh Marwan Al Maktoum). *"Conflict is another nice horse, not early, but I would hope he'd be running by mid-summer".*

51 - LYRIST

gr.f. Cozzene - La Llave (Risen Star).
March 6. First foal. 25,000Y. Tattersalls Houghton.
The dam was placed once in the USA and is a half-sister to 4 winners including the Irish 2,000 Guineas winner Prince Of Birds and the dam of the US Grade 2 winner Special Happening. The second dam, Special Key (by Key To The Mint), is an unraced half-sister to the French listed winner Palace Dancer out of the US winner Better Begin (a half-sister to Gorytus). (Saeed Manana). *"Lyrist could have been very well bought. She shows speed and will certainly get a mile this year. Another interesting one for good races at the back-end".*

52 - MAGDA (IRE)

b.f. Turtle Island - Pennine Drive (Pennine Walk).
February 18. Fourth living foal. IR40,000Y. Goffs Challenge.
Half-sister to the 1997 2-y-o 6f winner and Fred Darling Stakes second Wenda and to the useful Irish 12f winner Carnelly (both by Priolo). The dam, an Irish 12f winner, is closely related to the Irish listed winner Diamond Seal (dam of the French Group winners Diamond Dance and Diamond Mix). The second dam, Panserina (by Sovereign Path), ran once unplaced and is a half-sister to the Irish 2,000 Guineas winner Pampapaul. (Mr B H Voak). *"This filly is still growing and is a little bit up behind, so we'll take our time with her".*

53 - RESPECTFUL (IRE)   b.f. College Chapel - Congress Lady (General Assembly).
March 6. 20,000Y. Tattersalls Houghton.
Half-sister to 7 winners (two of them over hurdles) including the fairly useful 1997 3-y-o 1m to 10f winner Ganga (by Generous), the Scandinavian listed winner Senador (by Alzao) and the Irish 6f to 8.5f winner Sadlers Congress (by Sadler's Wells). The dam, a fairly useful French 8.5f winner, was listed placed and is a half-sister to 9 winners including the Group 2 Pretty Polly Stakes winner Mariel (dam of the Irish 1,000 Guineas winner Sarah Siddons). (Saeed Manana). *"This filly is showing speed and she should be out in May. A good-sized filly that has done well since we bought her, she'll be a better filly next year".*

---

54 - ROSE BAY   b.f. Shareef Dancer - Cormorant Bay (Don't Forget Me).
March 21. Third foal. 24,000Y. Tattersalls October.
Half-sister to the modest 1997 6f to 9f placed 3-y-o Glen Ogil (by Thatching). The dam, a moderate maiden, stayed 10f and is a half-sister to the top-class filly Cormorant Wood, winner of the Benson And Hedges Gold Cup and the Dubai Champion Stakes and herself dam of the high-class middle-distance stayer Rock Hopper. The second dam, Quarry Wood (by Super Sam), won four races from 12f to 14f and is a half-sister to 5 winners including the Great Metropolitan Handicap winner Cullen. (Saeed Manana). *"Very backward at the sales but she's improved tremendously. Definitely more of a 3-y-o type however"* warns Clive.

---

55 - ROYAL DANCE (USA)   b.c. Trempolino - Rosey Ramble (Chieftain II).
April 1. 60,000Y. Tattersalls Houghton.
Half-brother to the very useful Group 3 7f Jersey Stakes winner Cliveden (by Valdez), to the US Grade 3 Modesty Handicap winner Assert Oneself (by Affirmed), the minor US 2-y-o 6f stakes winner Go Not A'Ramblin (by Huguenot), the Irish and French winner of 6 races La Cote Fleurie (by L'Emigrant) and minor winners in the USA by Blushing John and Pia Star. The dam is an unraced half-sister to the dual US Grade 2 winner Fleet Velvet and to the dam of the US Grade 2 winners Ramblin Guy and Sword Blade. The second dam, Velvet Rose (by Round Table), won once in the USA and is a half-sister to 11 winners. (Jaber Abdullah). *"This is a really nice horse that shows enough speed to warrant him running over six furlongs in May".*

---

56 - SILVER SNAKE (IRE)   b.c. Salse - Ibtisamm (Caucasus).
February 24. IR70,000Y. Goffs Orby.
Brother to the high-class miler Air Express, winner of the Group 1 Queen Elizabeth II Stakes, the Group 2 German 2,000 Guineas and the Group 2 Italian 2,000 Guineas and half-brother to the useful 10f to 11.9f winner Aljazzaf (by Mtoto), the fair 7f winner Al Sadi (by Sharpo), the modest 8.3f winner Rubbiyati (by Cadeaux Genereux) and the poor 6f winner Dosha (by Touching Wood). The dam, a fair 3-y-o 1m winner, is a half-sister to 4 winners including the Grade 3 British Columbia Oaks winner Au Printemps (herself dam of the Grade 1 Breeders Cup Juvenile winner Success Express). The second dam, Lorgnette (by High Hat), was placed in the 7f Park Stakes in Ireland and is a half-sister to the Irish 1,000 Guineas second Lovely Gale. (Mohamed Obaida).

---

57 - TANUSIUS   b.c. Warning - Tanz (Sadler's Wells).
February 1. Fourth foal. 74,000Y. Tattersalls October.
Half-brother to the 3-y-o Please (by Kris), to the fair 12f winner Tarxien (by Kendor) and the French winner La Militaire (by General Holme). The dam, a fair 12.2f winner, is a sister to the very useful middle-distance filly Spring and closely related to the top-class middle-distance colt Pentire. The second dam, Gull Nook (by Mill Reef), a smart filly and winner of the Group 2 12f Ribblesdale Stakes, is a sister to the useful 12f winner Primrose Valley, closely related to the Group 3 12f Princess Royal Stakes winner Banket and a half-sister to the Group 3 13.5f Ormonde Stakes winner Mr Pintips. (Abdullah Saeed bul Hab).

---

58 - THUNDER SKY   b.c. Zafonic - Overcast (Caerleon).
February 18. Second foal. 100,000Y. Tattersalls Houghton.
Brother to the French-trained 3-y-o Hidden Costs. The dam, a winner over 1m at 3 yrs in Ireland, is closely related to the Group 2 Derrinstown Stud Derby Trial and dual US Grade 2 winner Phantom Breeze and a half-sister to 4 winners. The second dam, Ask The Wind (by Run The Gantlet), won the listed 9f Hard Fought Stakes and was fourth in the Ribblesdale Stakes. (Ali Saeed).

59 - WHO CARES WINS　　　　　　　　　　　　　　　　　　ch.c. Kris - Anne Bonny (Ajdal).
February 27. First living foal. 52,000 Y. Tattersalls Houghton.
The dam, a winner of 2 races over 1m and 10f, was third in the Group 3 12f Princess Royal Stakes and is a half-sister to the 3-y-o 7f winner Sveltana and the 3-y-o 11.5f winner Scorpius - both quite useful. The second dam, Sally Brown (by Posse), was a smart filly and winner of three races over middle-distances including the Group 1 12f Yorkshire Oaks and the Group 2 Ribblesdale Stakes. She is a half-sister to Untold, winner of the Yorkshire Oaks and Hoover Fillies Mile and placed in the Oaks, the Irish Oaks and the St Leger. (Khalifa Dasmal).

---

60 - UNNAMED　　　　　　　　　　　　　　　　　b.br.f. Woodman - Dawn Deal (Grey Dawn II).
March 3. First foal. 30,000Y. Tattersalls Houghton.
The dam, a winner of 2 minor races in the USA, is a half-sister to 9 winners including the US Grade 3 8.5f winner Wolf Brigade. The second dam, March On He Said (by Stop The Music), is an unraced half-sister to the US Grade 1 winner Rest Your Case and to the dams of the US Grade 1 winners Bates Motel, Hatim and Optimistic Gal. (Mr C Brittain). *"Not over-big at first, but she's certainly grown since then. She shows speed, is a nice mover and should be out before early June".*

---

61 - UNNAMED　　　　　　　　　　　　　b.c. Perugino - Love With Honey (Full Pocket).
March 20. Fourth foal. IR180,000Y. Goffs Orby.
Half-brother to the 3-y-o Lovely Memories (by Sharp Victor). The dam, a minor winner in the USA, is a half-sister to 8 winners including the Royal Lodge Stakes second Samoan. The second dam, Pago Dancer (by Pago Pago), a stakes-placed winner of 7 races in the USA, is a half-sister to the Grade 2 winner Our Dancing Girl and to the dam of Island Whirl (three Grade 1 wins in the USA). (Mr C Brittain). *"Probably one of the loveliest looking yearlings I saw at the sales and he's followed on that way. I should think that he's a horse that could go all the way".*

---

62 - UNNAMED　　　　　　　　　　　　　　　　gr.c. Zilzal - Silver Glitz (Grey Dawn II).
May 8. Fourth foal. IR45,000Y. Goffs Orby.
Half-brother to a placed 2-y-o in the USA by Proper Reality. The dam won 3 races in the USA, was third in the listed 1m Magnolia Stakes and is a half-sister to 3 winners. The second dam, Flaunter (by High Echelon), won a stakes event over middle-distances in the USA and is a half-sister to the very smart Italian Group 1 and Lingfield Derby Trial winner Jalmood. (Mr C Brittain). *"This colt was a little bit light at the sales when we bought him but this last month he's really started to develop and we could well end up with an Ascot 2-y-o".*

Gerard Butler

---

63 - COMPTON ADMIRAL　　　　　　　　　　　　　b.c. Suave Dancer - Sumoto (Mtoto).
January 11. Second foal. 21,000Y. Tattersalls October.
Half-brother to the 3-y-o Princess Deya (by Be My Guest), unplaced in both her starts at 2 yrs. The dam, a useful 6f (at 2 yrs) and 7f winner, is a half-sister to 3 winners including the useful listed Princess Elizabeth Stakes third Sumonda. The second dam, Soemba (by General Assembly), was a quite useful 9f winner and a half-sister to 4 minor winners here and abroad. (Mr E Penser). *First season trainer Gerard has worked for D Wayne-Lukas in America, Colin Hayes in Australia and for John Dunlop - not a bad apprenticeship! Regarding this two-year-old, Compton Admiral, Gerard tells me that "he'll be early enough but will want seven furlongs this year. A nice horse and quite mature, he does everything easily and should be out by the end of May. Hopefully, he'll prove good enough for the Chesham Stakes at Royal Ascot". The stable has two more young horses in the Early Types section.*

---

64 - COMPTON AMBER　　　　　　　　　　　　　　b.f. Puissance - Amber Mill (Doulab).
February 28. Third foal. 25,000Y. Doncaster St Leger.
Half-sister to the quite useful 1997 2-y-o dual 5f winner Salamanca (by Paris House). The dam, a useful winner over 5f (twice) and 6f, is a half-sister to the listed Cock of the North Stakes winner Tenacity. The second dam, Millaine (by Formidable), a half-sister to the Italian dual Group 1 winner Svelt, was placed once at 4 yrs and stayed 12f. (Mr E Penser). *"Compton Amber is a very nice filly and our little star! She does all her work nicely, should be out over five furlongs in May and is the apple of my eye!".*

65 - COMPTON ANGEL (IRE) b.f. Fairy King - Embla (Dominion).
March 11. IR45,000Y. Goffs Orby.
Closely related to the French 3-y-o 9f winner Nordic Myth (by Shareef Dancer) and half-sister to the 3-y-o 7f winner Ghost Tree (by Caerleon) and the 3-y-o 10f winner Enriched (by Generous) - both quite useful. The dam, a high-class winner of the Group 1 6f Cheveley Park Stakes and second in the Group 1 1m Coronation Stakes, is a half-sister to 4 winners. The second dam, Kaftan (by Kashmir II), won over 10f at 3 yrs and is a half-sister to the good sprinter Blue Cashmere. (Mr E Penser). *"A nice filly with a nice way of going, she'll be racing from mid-summer onwards"*.

66 - COMPTON ASTORIA (USA) ch.f. Lion Cavern - Perfolia (Nodouble).
May 16. Second foal. IR38,000Y. Goffs Orby.
The dam, a useful winner of 4 races over 7f, is a half-sister to the French 1,000 Guineas, Fillies Mile and Prix Marcel Boussac winner Culture Vulture. The second dam, Perfect Example (by Far North), is an unraced half-sister to the dams of the Grade/Group 1 winners Awe Inspiring, Polish Precedent and Zilzal. (Mr E Penser). *"Quite a tall, heavy-topped filly, she won't be racing until the back-end of the season"*.

Neville Callaghan

67 - BLACK AMBER (IRE) b.c. College Chapel - Flying Diva (Chief Singer).
May 26. Fourth foal. IR34,000Y. Goffs Challenge.
Half-brother to Hoh Navigator (by Common Grounds), placed over 5f on his only start at 2 yrs and to the fair 6f (at 2 yrs) and 10f winner White Plains (by Nordico). The dam, a useful 2-y-o 6f and 7f winner, was placed at up to 10f at 3 yrs. The second dam, Flying Fantasy (by Habitat), was an unplaced sister to the 1,000 Guineas and Champion Stakes winner Flying Water. (Mrs J Magnier & Mr M Tabor). *"A late foal, but Black Amber will still be a nice two-year-old. He'll probably start over six furlongs and he really is a nice horse. It remains to be seen if College Chapel (a son of Sharpo) sires horses that need a bit of give in the ground"* explained Neville.

68 - CASTARA BEACH (IRE) b.f. Danehill - Sea Harrier (Grundy).
March 11. 100,000Y. Tattersalls Houghton.
Sister to the useful Group 3 7f Criterion Stakes winner Hill Hopper and half-sister to the Australian Grade 1 West End Adelaide Cup winner Water Boatman (by Main Reef), the quite useful 10f winner Glendera (by Glenstal), the fair 2-y-o 7f winner Classic Flyer and the fairly useful 1997 3-y-o 12f winner Prairie Falcon (both by Alzao). The dam ran twice unplaced and is a half-sister to 5 winners including the Group 2 12f King Edward VII Stakes winner Sea Anchor. The second dam, Anchor (by Major Portion), won the Nell Gwyn Stakes and is a half-sister to 8 winners including the Oaks winner Bireme, the Coronation Cup winner Buoy and the Duke Of York Stakes winner Fluke. (Mrs J Magnier & Mr M Tabor). *"A very nice filly, she'll be out in May or June and she'll make a two-year-old alright"*.

69 - MINNESOTA b.c. Danehill - Santi Sana (Formidable).
March 29. Second foal. 170,000Y. Tattersalls Houghton.
The dam, a quite useful 3-y-o 7f winner, is a sister to the very smart Group 1 Premio Emilio Turati winner and good sire Efisio and a half-sister to 3 winners including the Grade 1 Santa Barbara Handicap and Grade 2 San Gorgonio Handicap winner Mountain Bear (by Welsh Pageant). The second dam, Eldoret (by High Top), was a useful 6f and 1m winner and was second in the listed Virginia Stakes. (Mrs J Magnier & Mr M Tabor). *"A very, very nice horse. He looks the part, does everything well and is on the big side but certainly not backward. At this stage he's giving me the same sort of feel that Danehill Dancer did. Watch out for him, he'll be running by mid-summer at the latest"*.

Henry Candy

70 - FLAVIAN b.f. Catrail - Fatah Flare (Alydar).
March 16. 36,000Y. Tattersalls December.
Closely related to the useful triple 3-y-o 7f winner Mata Cara (by Storm Bird) - herself dam of a French listed winner - and half-sister to the fair 1997 7f and 1m placed 2-y-o Fly By Night (by Night Shift), the fairly useful 3-y-o 10f winner Refugio (by Reference Point) and the fair 2-y-o 6f winner Fire and Shade (by Shadeed). The dam, a 2-y-o 6f winner, was placed in both the Princess Margaret Stakes and the Waterford Candelabra Stakes before winning the Group 3 10.5f Musidora Stakes at 3 yrs. She is a

27

half-sister to Sabin, a dual US Grade 1 winner over 9f and 10f, and to the useful 2-y-o 6f winner Soughaan. The second dam, Beaconaire (by Vaguely Noble), a winner of 3 races at up to 10f in France including a stakes event, is a half-sister to the Grade 2 winner Kittiwake (dam of the multiple Grade 1 winner Miss Oceana, the Prix Jean Prat winner Kitwood and the Grade 2 winner Larida - herself dam of the Coronation Stakes winner Magic of Life). (Major M G Wyatt). *"This is a nice filly, very tall but pretty active. She'll start in mid-season over six furlongs"* says the trainer.

71 - ROLLER
b.c. Bluebird - Tight Spin (High Top).
March 9. Sixth foal. 65,000Y. Tattersalls October.
Half-brother to the promising 1997 10f placed 3-y-o Vicious Circle (by Lahib) and the modest 6f winner Girl Next Door (by Local Suitor). The dam ran once unplaced and is a half-sister to 5 winners. The second dam, Petty Purse (by Petingo), was a smart winner of 4 races from 5f to 7f including the listed Strensall Stakes and is a half-sister to the very useful sprinter Scarcely Blessed (dam of the smart sprinter College Chapel). (Prince Fahd Salman). *"A bit backward at the sales, I'd still expect him to be racing by June or July over five furlongs. He has very strong quarters and shows plenty of speed".* Henry has an earlier two-year-old in the next section of the book.

Henry Cecil

When I spoke to Henry in early April, he had yet to ask any serious questions of his two-year-olds. Any of the horses listed below could turn out to be stars of the future, but the ones really taking the trainer's eye at the moment are the colts Attack, Killer Instinct, Modus Operandi, Touch 'n' Fly, War Cabinet and Western Folly, whilst the Cadeaux Genereux colt Voracious will be earlier than most. Amongst the fillies, the pick of the bunch would seem to be Brighter, Easy To Love, Flame Cutter, Lighthouse and Royal Highness.

72 - ADELPHI (IRE)
b.c. Sadler's Wells - Societe Royale (Milford).
April 10. IR120,000Y. Goffs Orby.
Half-brother to the 1997 6f and 7f placed Irish 2-y-o Coconut Creek, to the fair 1m winner Razinah (both by Danehill), the 1997 Irish 3-y-o 7f and 1m winner Royale and the Hong Kong Kong winner Banker's Delight (both by Royal Academy). The dam is an unraced half-sister to 7 winners including the high-class sprinter Double Form (winner of the Kings Stand Stakes and the Vernons Sprint Cup) and the Lupe Stakes winner Scimitarra. The second dam, Fanghorn (by Crocket), was a useful 2-y-o 5f and 7f winner and was third in the French 1,000 Guineas. (Mr M Tabor, Mrs J Magnier and Dr T Ryan). *"Very backward, but a nice mover and really active".*

73 - ANUSKHA (IRE)
ch.f. Indian Ridge - Shaping Up (Storm Bird).
February 2. Second foal. 45,000Y. Tattersalls Houghton.
Half-sister to the 1997 Irish 3-y-o 9f winner Islamorada (by Persian Bold). The dam, a quite useful 5.7f winner at 2 yrs, is a half-sister to 3 winners. The second dam, Manicure Kit (by J O Tobin), won a 6f stakes event in the USA at 2 yrs and is a half-sister to 8 winners including the dam of Interco (four Grade 1 wins in the USA). (Clark Industrial Services Partnership).

74 - ARABIS
ch.f. Arazi - Mill On The Floss (Mill Reef).
February 19.
Half-sister to the very useful 1994 3-y-o 10f winner Milly Ha Ha (by Dancing Brave), the useful 1992 3-y-o 10.2f winner Hatta's Mill (by Green Desert), the useful 7f (at 2 yrs) and 10.3f winner Yeltsin (by Soviet Star), the 1997 3-y-o 12f winner Milly Of The Vally (by Caerleon) and the 10.2f and 12f winner Top Mill (by High Top) - both fairly useful. The dam, a winner over 7f at 2 yrs and the Group 3 12f Lingfield Oaks Trial at 3 yrs, was second in both the Ribblesdale Stakes and the Princess Royal Stakes, is closely related to the useful Queen Alexandra Stakes winner Overdrive and a half-sister to the very useful Sun Chariot Stakes second Kashmir Lass and to the dam of the smart Park Hill Stakes winner Madame Dubois. The second dam, Milly Moss (by Crepello), won the Cheshire Oaks and is a sister to the very smart Park Hill Stakes winner Mil's Bomb. (Cliveden Stud).

75 - ATTACK
gr.c. Sabrehill - Butsova (Formidable).
April 18. 160,000Y. Tattersalls October.
Brother to the unplaced 1997 2-y-o Sabre Butt and half-brother to the fairly useful 1992 3-y-o 11.1f winner Bustinetta (by Bustino). The dam, a fairly useful 3-y-o 6f winner, is a half-sister to 7 winners including Terimon (Group 1 Juddmonte International winner and Epsom Derby second). The second

dam, Nicholas Grey (by Track Spare), won 8 races including 3 Italian listed events. (Prince Fahd Salman). *"A nice, active sort, this colt will make a two-year-old later on".*

76 - AZOUZ PASHA (USA)
b.c. Lyphard - Empress Club (Farnesio).
January 10. First foal. $380,000. Keeneland July.
The dam, a champion at 2, 3 and 4 yrs in South Africa, won 15 races including two Grade 1 events. She is a half-sister to the South African Grade 1 winners Ecurie and Epoque, and to the dam of the Argentinian 2-y-o Grade 1 winner Espaciado. The second dam, Elysee (by El Gran Capitan), is a half-sister to another Grade 1 winner in Argentina. (Wafic Said). *"This colt was cheeky earlier on but he's growing up now. He's quite well-made and I like him".*

77 - BALLET MASTER (USA)
ch.c. Kingmambo - Danse Royale (Caerleon).
April 9. Second foal. IR180,000Y. Goffs Orby.
Closely related to the H Cecil trained 3-y-o Twickenham (by Woodman). The dam, a very useful filly, won 3 races including the Group 3 10f Prix de Psyche and the listed 7f Derrinstown 1,000 Guineas Trial and was third in the Irish 1,000 Guineas. She is closely related to the Group 3 6f Railway Stakes winner Flame of Athens and a half-sister to 6 winners including the brilliant filly Salsabil, winner of the 1,000 Guineas, Oaks, Irish Derby and Prix Vermeille, the high-class Group 1 St James's Palace Stakes winner Marju, the smart 1995 3-y-o dual 12f winner Song of Tara and the very useful 1989 3-y-o 10f and 10.5f winner Nearctic Flame (herself dam of the Irish Group 3 winner Blushing Flame). The second dam, Flame of Tara (by Artaius), won 8 races including the Group 2 1m Coronation Stakes and the Group 2 Pretty Polly Stakes and was second in the Champion Stakes. She is a half-sister to Fruition - dam of both the Breeders Cup Turf winner Northern Spur and the high-class stayer Kneller. (Mr M Tabor & Partners).

78 - BIONIC
br.f. Zafonic - Bonash (Rainbow Quest).
March 5. First foal.
The dam, a very useful filly, won 4 races in France from 1m to 12f including the Prix d'Aumale, the Prix Vanteaux and the Prix de Malleret. The second dam, Sky Love (by Nijinsky), a fairly useful 10f winner, is a half-sister to the high-class Prix de la Cote Normande winner Raft. (Khaled Abdulla).

79 - BONDOSAN
b.c. Barathea - Fern (Shirley Heights).
February 16. Third foal. 140,000Y. Tattersalls Houghton.
Half-brother to the quite useful 1997 2-y-o 7f winner Frond (by Alzao) and to the 3-y-o German 1m winner Flying Heights (by Kris). The dam, a useful 3-y-o 11.9f winner and third in the listed 10f Lupe Stakes, is a half-sister to the Group 1 Fillies Mile winner and Oaks second Shamshir. The second dam, Free Guest (by Be My Guest), won 9 races including the Group 2 Sun Chariot Stakes (twice) and the Group 2 Nassau Stakes and is a half-sister to the Group 2 Blandford Stakes winner and Oaks second Royal Ballerina. (Wafic Said). *"A well-made colt and active, he's a nice mover and looks like making a decent sort of two-year-old".*

80 - BRIGHTER (USA)
ch.f. Gone West - Top Trestle (Nijinsky).
April 2. Third living foal.
The dam, a minor stakes winner at around 1m in the USA, is a half-sister to the Grade 1 Alabama Stakes, Ashland Stakes and Gazelle Handicap winner Classy Cathy (by Private Account), herself dam of the Prince Of Wales's Stakes winner Placerville. The second dam, Trestle (by Tom Rolfe), is an unraced half-sister to the US Grade 3 winner Edge. (Prince Fahd Salman). *"I quite like this filly, she's a nice, active two-year-old".*

81 - BRIGHTEST STAR
b.f. Unfuwain - Shirley Superstar (Shirley Heights).
April 29. 280,000Y. Tattersalls Houghton.
Closely related to the 3-y-o Startreck (by Night Shift) and half-sister to the high-class 1996 Oaks winner Lady Carla (by Caerleon), to the quite useful 1997 9f winner Azores (by Polish Precedent) and the modest 7f (at 2 yrs) to 16.4f placed Chita Rivera (by Chief Singer). The dam, a fairly useful 2-y-o 7f winner, is a half-sister to the Duke of York Stakes third Si Signor and the Hungerford Stakes third Moviegoer. The second dam, Odeon (by Royal and Regal), won the listed 12f Galtres Stakes at York and was placed in eight Group races. (Helena Springfield Ltd).

82 - CAERAU
ch.f. Nashwan - Charming Life (Habitat).
February 2. 110,000Y. Tattersalls Houghton.
Half-sister to the Group 3 5f Prix du Petit-Couvert winner Run And Gun (by Lomond), to the quite useful 1990 3-y-o 8.2f winner Saddle Bow (by Sadler's Wells) and to 2 winners in Japan by In The Wings and

Green Desert. The dam, a quite useful 4-y-o 7f winner, is a half-sister to the listed winner Leipzig and the dams of the Group winners Adam Smith, Braashee, Ghariba, Careafolie and Gouriev. The second dam, Fighting (by Aggressor), won over 1m at 3 yrs and is a half-sister to the dams of the Group winners Bassenthwaite, Bay Street, Glancing, Hadeer, Monaasib and Rose Of Montreaux.

---

83 - COMMANDER
b.c. Puissance - Tarkhana (Dancing Brave).
February 19. First reported foal. 72,000Y. Tattersalls October.
The dam, a minor winner over 1m 5f in Ireland at 4 yrs, is a half-sister to the French winner and Group 3 Prix Vanteaux second Tashiriya. The second dam, Tashtiya (by Shergar), won the Group 3 Princess Royal Stakes and is a half-sister to 8 winners including Tassmoun (Group 3 Prix Messidor) and Tashkourgan (Group 3 Premio Carlo Porta). (Prince Fahd Salman). *"A big, quite good-looking horse, he's had sore shins but will make a two-year-old later on".*

---

84 - CONFIDENTIAL
ch.f. Generous - Just You Wait (Nonoalco).
February 6.
Half-sister to the very smart Group 2 9.7f Prix Dollar winner Wiorno (by Wassl), to the very smart Trusthouse Forte Mile, Gimcrack Stakes and Earl of Sefton Stakes winner Reprimand (by Mummy's Pet), the very useful 1m winner and Irish 1,000 Guineas fourth Distant Oasis (by Green Desert), the useful 2-y-o 7.6f winner and middle-distance placed 3-y-o Waiting (by Polish Precedent) and the minor winning sprinter Another Rhythm (by Music Boy). The dam is an unraced half-sister to the good broodmares Little Loch Broom (dam of the very useful Fawzi and the Group 3 Prix de la Jonchere winner Soft Currency) and Kristana (dam of the Group 1 Prix Robert Papin winner Ozone Friendly). The second dam, Sleat (by Santa Claus), won the Sun Chariot Stakes and is a half-sister to the St Leger winner Athens Wood. (Prince Fahd Salman).

---

85 - COSH
b.f. A.P.Indy - Jolypha (Lyphard).
January 29. Second foal.
Half-sister to the 3-y-o Eaton Square (by Nureyev). The dam was a top-class winner of the Group 1 10.5f Prix de Diane and the Group 1 12f Prix Vermeille and was placed in the Grade 1 Breeders Cup Classic and the Grade 1 Beverley Hills Handicap. She is a sister to the great Dancing Brave, winner of the Prix de l'Arc de Triomphe, the King George VI and Queen Elizabeth Diamond Stakes and the 2,000 Guineas etc. The second dam, Navajo Princess (by Drone), a good winner of 16 races at up to 1m including the Grade 2 Molly Pitcher Handicap and the Grade 3 Falls City Handicap, is a sister to the stakes winner Passamaquoddy (herself dam of 5 winners) and a half-sister to the Grade 3 winner Soldier Boy. (Khaled Abdulla).

---

86 - COUNTESS PARKER
ch.f. First Trump - Hoist (Bluebird).
March 24. First foal. 22,000Y. Tattersalls October.
The dam, a fair 4-y-o 6f all-weather winner, is a half-sister to winners including the Group 3 Prix de Royaumont third Elite Guest. The second dam, Elevate (by Ela Mana Mou), a fairly useful dual 3-y-o 12f winner, was third in the listed Ballymacoll Stud Stakes and is a half-sister to the top-class winners Sun Princess and Saddlers Hall. (Angus Dundee plc).

---

87 - EASY TO LOVE (USA)
b.f. Diesis - La Sky (Law Society).
February 5. Third foal.
Half-sister to the French 12f winner Laurentine and to a minor winner in the USA (both by Private Account). The dam, a useful 10f winner and second in the Lancashire Oaks, is closely related to the Champion Stakes winner Legal Case. The second dam, Maryinsky (by Northern Dancer), won twice at up to 9f in the USA and is a half-sister to the US Grade 3 winners Bold Place and Card Table and to the unraced dam of the Italian Group 1 winner Malevic. (Mr T F Harris). *"This is another two-year-old I like at this early stage. She moves well and looks racy".*

---

88 - EMERALD CUT
ch.f. Rainbow Quest - Hatton Gardens (Auction Ring).
January 5. 180,000Y. Tattersalls Houghton.
Sister to the 3-y-o Diamond Quest and half-sister to the South African Grade 1 winner Kundalini, the US stakes winner Pixie Spirit, the Irish 2-y-o 7f winner Marshad - subsequently a winner of 13 minor races in the USA - (all by El Gran Senor) and the useful 7.1f (at 2 yrs) and 10.4f winner Ludgate (by Lyphard). The dam, a fairly useful Irish 6f to 1m winner, including a listed event, is a half-sister to the Coronation Stakes, Eclipse Stakes and Irish 1,000 Guineas winner Kooyonga. The second dam, Anjuli (by Northfields), is a half-sister to the 2,000 Guineas winner Roland Gardens. (Wafic Said).

89 - ENDORSEMENT b.f. Warning - Overdrive (Shirley Heights).
May 21. Fourth living foal.
Half-sister to the fairly useful dual 6f winner Zugudi (by Night Shift) and the fair 1992 2-y-o 1m winner Dakar Rally (by Green Desert). The dam, a useful middle-distance stayer, won the Queen Alexandra Stakes, is closely related to the Lingfield Oaks Trial winner Mill On The Floss (herself dam of numerous winners) and a half-sister to the Sun Chariot Stakes second Kashmir Lass and the Lancashire Oaks second Shadywood (dam of the smart Park Hill Stakes winner Madame Dubois). The second dam, Milly Moss (by Crepello), won the Cheshire Oaks and was a sister to the very smart Park Hill Stakes winner Mil's Bomb. (Cliveden Stud).

90 - ENEMY ACTION (USA) b.f. Forty Niner - Sun And Shade (Ajdal).
April 6. Second foal.
Half-sister to the smart 1997 2-y-o Daggers Drawn (by Diesis), winner of the Group 2 6f Richmond Stakes and the Group 2 7f Laurent Perrier Rose Champagne Stakes. The dam, a useful 2-y-o 6f winner, is a half-sister to the very smart Madame Dubois, winner of five of her seven starts at 3 yrs from 9f to 14.6f including the Group 2 Park Hill Stakes, the Group 2 Prix de Royallieu and the Galtres Stakes. The second dam, Shadywood (by Habitat), a useful 10f winner, was second in the Lancashire Oaks and is a half-sister to the very useful fillies Kashmir Lass and Mill on the Floss (dam of the useful winners Hatta's Mill, Milly Ha Ha and Yeltsin). (Cliveden Stud). *"Enemy Action will certainly make a two-year-old. She moves well, I like her and she's one to watch".*

91 - ENRIQUE b.c. Barathea - Gwydion (Raise a Cup).
April 29.
Closely related to the listed 11f La Coupe de Marseille winner Synergetic (by Sadler's Wells) and half-brother to the 1997 Irish placed 2-y-o Eljamil (by Night Shift) and the minor French winners Box Card (by Top Ville) and Keanu (by Kris). The dam won 4 races including the Group 3 5f Queen Mary Stakes and was placed in the July Cup, the King's Stand Stakes and the William Hill Sprint Championship - all Group 1 events. She is a half-sister to 5 winners including the dam of the listed winner Chipaya out of the placed Papamiento (by Blade) - herself a half-sister to 6 winners including Armistice III (Grand Prix de Paris) and Twice Worthy (Grade 1 Suburban Handicap). (Niarchos Family). *"This colt is quite nice. He'll make a two-year-old and I like him. He's active and has plenty of scope".*

92 - ESPERIS (IRE) gr.f. Warning - Trikymia (Final Straw).
May 15.
Half-sister to the useful 6f (at 2 yrs) and 7f listed winner Epagris (by Zalazl), the useful 10f winner Ismaros (by Selkirk), the quite useful 10f winner Graegos (by Shareef Dancer) and the quite useful 5.8f to 1m winner Wave Hill (by Sizzling Melody). The dam was placed third over 5f at 2 yrs on her only outing and is a half-sister to the Irish Derby winner Tyrnavos, the champion 2-y-o Tromos, the Coronation Stakes winner Tolmi and the Middle Park Stakes winner Tachypous. The second dam, the celebrated broodmare Stilvi (by Derring Do), won the 5f King George Stakes and the 6f Duke of York Stakes. (Mr L Marinopoulos).

93 - FLAME CUTTER (USA) ch.f. Miswaki - Flaming Torch (Rousillon).
February 8.
Half-sister to the quite useful 1996 2-y-o 7f winner Flaming West (by Gone West). The dam, a winner over 1m at 2 yrs in France, subsequently won a Grade 3 11f event at 4 yrs in the USA and is a half-sister to the fair 1m and 12f winner Peace King. The second dam, Flaming Peace (by Lyphard), was a disappointing half-sister to numerous winners including the good middle distance performers Peacetime and Quiet Fling and the Cambridgeshire winner Intermission - herself dam of the very useful filly Interval. (Khaled Abdulla). *"A nice, active filly, Flame Cutter is the type to win races as a two-year-old".*

94 - GALETTE b.f. Caerleon - Madame Dubois (Legend Of France).
May 2.
Half-sister to the 3-y-o Nuance (by Rainbow Quest), to the useful 1996 3-y-o 11.8f and 12f winner Place de l'Opera (by Sadlers Wells) and the quite useful 1995 3-y-o 12f winner Richelieu (by Kris). The dam, a very smart filly, won five of her seven starts at 3 yrs from 9f to 14.6f including the Group 2 Park Hill Stakes, the Group 2 Prix de Royallieu and the Galtres Stakes. The second dam, Shadywood (by Habitat), a useful 10f winner, was second in the Lancashire Oaks and is a half-sister to the very useful fillies Kashmir Lass and Mill on the Floss (dam of the useful winners Hatta's Mill, Milly Ha Ha and Yeltsin). (Cliveden Stud).

95 - HARVARD KID
b.c. Warning - Sistabelle (Bellypha).
February 2. 420,000Y. Tattersalls Houghton.
Brother to the very useful Torch Rouge, a winner from 5f to 1m here and the Grade 2 1m Arlington
Handicap in the USA and half-brother to the quite useful 10f winner Filmore West (by In The Wings)
and the hurdles winner Volunteer (by Midyan). The dam is an unraced sister to the Group 2 Prix de
l'Opera and Group 3 Waterford Candelabra Stakes winner Bella Colora - herself dam of the high-class
Prince of Wales's Stakes winner Stagecraft - and a half-sister to the Irish Champion Stakes winner
Cezanne and the Irish Oaks winner Colorspin (dam of the King George winner Opera House). The
second dam, Reprocolor (by Jimmy Reppin), won the Lingfield Oaks Trial, Lancashire Oaks and Pretty
Polly Stakes. (Wafic Said).

96 - INITIATIVE
ch.c. Arazi - Dance Quest (Green Dancer).
February 13.
Closely related to the high-class colt Pursuit of Love, winner of the 7f Free Handicap, the 6.5f Prix
Maurice de Gheest and the 7f Kiveton Park Stakes and placed in the 2,000 Guineas and July Cup and
to the fairly useful 1996 2-y-o 7f winner Courtship (both by Groom Dancer) and half-brother to the
smart Prix d'Arenburg, Prix de Ris-Oranges and Prix du Gros Chene winner Divine Danse and the
quite useful dual 3-y-o 7f winner Divine Quest (both by Kris). The dam was a smart French 2-y-o
sprinter and a half-sister to the high class 2-y-o Noblequest, winner of the Prix de la Salamandre. The
second dam, Polyponder (by Barbizon), won from 5f to 1m including four Group 3 events in France.
(Lord Howard de Walden).

97 - INSINUATE (USA)
ch.f. Mr Prospector - All At Sea (Riverman).
March 7. Second foal.
Half-sister to the useful 6f and 7f winner and listed-placed Imroz (by Nureyev). The dam was a high-class
filly and winner of 5 races from 1m to 10.4f including the Group 1 Prix du Moulin, the Musidora Stakes
and the Pretty Polly Stakes and was second in the Oaks, the Juddmonte International and the Nassau
Stakes. She is a half-sister to the Free Handicap winner Over the Ocean, the listed 10f winner Quandary
and the US stakes winner Full Virtue. The second dam, Lost Virtue (by Cloudy Dawn), an unraced
half-sister to the US Grade 2 Shuvee Handicap winner Anti-Lib, is out of a half-sister to Damascus.
(Khaled Abdulla).

98 - INTERVENE
ch.f. Zafonic - Interval (Habitat).
March 7.
Sister to the 3-y-o Imbalala and half-sister to the fair 1992 3-y-o 10f winner Intent (by Kris) and the
1994 French 3-y-o 1m listed winner Cheyenne Dream (by Dancing Brave). The dam was a high-class
sprinting winner of four races from 5f to 1m including the Group 2 Prix Maurice de Gheest, was third
in the 1,000 Guineas to Miesque and is a half-sister to the very useful 1994 3-y-o 1m and 10f winner
Interim and to the unraced Welcome Break, herself dam of the Hoover Fillies Mile winner Invited Guest.
The second dam, Intermission (by Stage Door Johnny), won the Cambridgeshire Handicap and is a
half-sister to 7 winners including the high-class middle-distance colts Peacetime and Quiet Fling.
(Khaled Abdulla).

99 - IPSO FACTO (IRE)
b.br.c. Sunday Silence - Lingerie (Shirley Heights).
April 29. Third foal. 280,000Y. Tattersalls Houghton.
The dam, placed 7 times in France, is a half-sister to 4 winners including the French listed placed
Evocatrice. The second dam, Northern Trick (by Northern Dancer), won the Prix de Diane and the Prix
Vermeille, was second in the Prix de l'Arc de Triomphe and is a half-sister to the US Grade 1 Jockey
Club Gold Cup winner On The Sly. (Niarchos Family). *"A tall, narrow horse, he moves fine but is a bit
backward mentally at the moment".*

100 - KILLER INSTINCT
b.c. Zafonic - Rappa Tap Tap (Tap On Wood).
April 18. 260,000Y. Tattersalls Houghton.
Half-brother to the 3-y-o Glorious, to the 1996 Irish 3-y-o 1m winner and listed-placed Oriane (both by
Nashwan), the very useful 1988 2-y-o 7f winner and Group 1 Hoover Fillies Mile second Pick of the
Pops (by High Top), the fairly useful 1993 3-y-o dual 10f winner Tap on Air (by Caerleon) and the fair
1995 Irish 3-y-o 9f winner Winger (by In the Wings). The dam was a useful winner of 3 races from 6f
to 1m including the Blue Seal Stakes and is a half-sister to the Irish Oaks winner Colorspin (herself
dam of the top-class colt Opera House), to the Group 2 Prix de l'Opera winner Bella Colora (dam of
the high-class colt Stagecraft) and to the Irish Champion Stakes winner Cezanne. The second dam,

Reprocolor (by Jimmy Reppin), won the Lingfield Oaks Trial and the Lancashire Oaks in 1979. (The Thoroughbred Corporation). *"A big horse, watch out for him later this year. I expect him to be a good two-year-old"*.

---

101 - LIGHTHOUSE

br.f. Warning - Valika (Valiyar).
April 2. 220,000Y. Tattersalls Houghton.

Half-sister to the fair 1997 7f placed North Ofthe Border, to the very smart 1993 2-y-o First Trump, a winner of 5 races over 6f including the Group 1 Middle Park Stakes, the Group 3 July Stakes and the Group 3 Richmond Stakes, the quite useful 1993 3-y-o 7f winner First Veil (all by Primo Dominie), the Australian winner Keyhinge Boy and the fairly useful 1995 2-y-o 5f winner and 1m listed-placed 3-y-o Prancing (both by Prince Sabo). The dam was placed three times from 1m to 12f at 3 yrs and is a half-sister to the high-class sprinter Mr Brooks and to the smart 3-y-o dual 7f winner Larionov. The second dam, Double Finesse (by Double Jump), was a fairly useful winner over 6f (at 2 yrs), 7f and 1m (at 4 yrs). (Lord Lloyd-Webber). *"This is a nice filly. She's still growing a bit and will make a good two-year-old later on. A good mover, I do like her"*.

---

102 - LUCONIC

br.c. Zafonic - Felucca (Green Desert).
February 1. First foal.

The dam, a fairly useful 2-y-o 6f winner, was placed over 7f at 3 yrs. The second dam, Bloudan (by Damascus), is an unraced half-sister to the high-class Irish 1,000 Guineas and Coronation Stakes winner Al Bahathri. (Khaled Abdulla).

---

103 - MAKE RINGS

b.f. Rainbow Quest - Guillem (Nijinsky).
February 26. Third foal.

The dam, a fair 11.4f placed 3-y-o on her only outing, is closely related to the smart winner at up to 12f Lydian and to the useful 10f winner Pride Of Araby and a half-sister to the Ribblesdale Stakes winner Ballinderry (herself dam of the French Derby winner Sanglamore) and the French Derby third Sharpman. The second dam, Miss Manon (by Bon Mot III), was a smart French middle-distance performer. (Khaled Abdulla).

---

104 - MODUS OPERANDI (USA)

b.c. Known Fact - Proud Lou (Proud Clarion).
February 8.

Brother to the 1996 French 3-y-o 1m winner Proud Fact and half-brother to the French 1,000 Guineas and Prix de la Grotte winner Houseproud (by Riverman). The dam, winner of the Grade 1 1m Frizette Stakes at 2 yrs in the USA, is a half-sister to 5 winners. The second dam, Baby Louise (by Exclusive Native), won a 2-y-o stakes event in the USA. (Khaled Abdulla). *"A good sort and an active colt, he's a good mover and is one to keep an eye on"*.

---

105 - MY MICHELINE

ch.f. Lion Cavern - Mariakova (The Minstrel).
February 16. 90,000Y. Tattersalls Houghton.

Closely related to the modest 7f all-weather placed Dixie Eyes Blazing (by Gone West) and half-sister to the useful 2-y-o 5f and 3-y-o 1m winner Well Beyond (by Don't Forget Me) and to the fair 12f all-weather winner Society Ball (by Law Society). The dam was placed over 6f at 2 yrs and 1m at 3 yrs, is a sister to the smart filly Zaizafon (dam of Zafonic) and a half-sister to the unraced Modena (dam of Elmaamul and Reams of Verse). The second dam, Mofida (by Right Tack), won 8 races at up to 7f and was placed in the Duke of York Stakes. (Wafic Said). *"This is a nice, active filly with a touch of class"*.

---

106 - NUCLEAR FREEZE

b.c. Danzig - Razyana (His Majesty).
March 28.

Brother to the top-class sprinter and sire Danehill, winner of the Group 1 6f Ladbroke Sprint Cup, the 6f Cork and Orrery Stakes and the 7f Ladbroke European Free Handicap and to the French 2-y-o 5f winners Anziyan and Eagle Eyed. The dam, placed over 7f at 2 yrs and 10f at 3 yrs, is out of Spring Adieu (by Buckpasser), a winner of three small sprint races at 3 yrs and a half-sister to Northern Dancer. (Khaled Abdulla).

---

107 - PURSE

b.f. Pursuit Of Love - Rose Noble (Vaguely Noble).
February 29. Second foal.

Closely related to the fairly useful 1997 2-y-o 1m winner Dower House (by Groom Dancer). The dam, a modest 3-y-o 11.5f winner, is a half-sister to the Champion two-year-old Grand Lodge, winner of the St James's Palace Stakes and the Dewhurst Stakes. The second dam, La Papagena (by Habitat), is an unraced half-sister to the listed Scottish Derby winner Eagling and to the Gallinule Stakes second and South African listed winner Lost Chord. (Lord Howard de Walden). *"Purse is a good-looking filly and she's doing well in her work".*

108 - ROYAL HIGHNESS
b.f. Shirley Heights - Royal Ballet (Sadler's Wells). February 14. First foal.
The dam ran unplaced twice over 10f at 3 yrs, is a sister to the top-class colt King's Theatre, winner of the Group 1 Racing Post Trophy, the Group 1 King George VI and Queen Elizabeth Diamond Stakes and second in both the Epsom Derby and the Irish Derby and a half-sister to the champion 2-y-o colt High Estate (by Shirley Heights) and the smart 1m (at 2 yrs) and 10f winner King's Loch (by Salmon Leap). The second dam, Regal Beauty (by Princely Native), was unplaced in two starts and is a half-sister to 8 minor winners. (Michael Poland). *"This is quite an active filly, I like her and feel that she'll make a nice two-year-old later on this year".*

109 - SAMOA
b.f. Rainbow Quest - Sardegna (Pharly). March 7. Third foal.
Half-sister to the useful listed 10f winner Sardonic and the fair 1997 10f placed 3-y-o Serpentara (both by Kris). The dam was a very useful 2-y-o 7f and 3-y-o 10f Pretty Polly Stakes winner and is a half-sister to the smart middle distance colt Sebastian. The second dam, the Lancashire Oaks winner Sandy Island (by Mill Reef), is a half-sister to the Derby winner Slip Anchor. (Lady Howard de Walden).

110 - SEA OF GOD (USA)
b.c. Gone West - Yemanja (Alleged). May 24. Third living foal. IR40,000Y. Goffs Orby.
Half-brother to the 3-y-o Molokai (by Nureyev). The dam is an unplaced half-sister to the Champion Stakes and 1,000 Guineas winner Bosra Sham and the French 2,000 Guineas winners Hector Protector and Shanghai. The second dam, Korveya (by Riverman), was a useful winner of the Group 3 9f Prix Chloe and is a half-sister to the high-class 6f to 7f filly Proskona. The third dam, Konafa (by Damascus), was second in the 1,000 Guineas and is a half-sister to the Yorkshire Oaks winner Awaasif - herself dam of the Oaks winner Snow Bride and thus grandam of Derby winner Lammtarra. (Niarchos Family). *"A lovely horse but big and slightly immature. He'll take a bit of time but one day he'll be quite nice. I like him".*

111 - SHIKASTA (IRE)
ch.f. Kris - India Atlanta (Ahonoora). February 14. Fifth foal. 75,000Y. Tattersalls Houghton.
Half-sister to the French trained 3-y-o Fairy Hoof (by Fairy King), to the smart US Grade 2 1m Colonel F W Koester Handicap and German Group 3 1m Ostermann Pokal winner Ventiquattrofogli (by Persian Bold), the German 1997 3-y-o listed winner Irish Fighter (by Persian Heights) and the Italian 2-y-o winner Suspiria (by Glenstal). The dam is an unraced half-sister to 4 winners including the German Group 3 1m winner Sinyar. The second dam, Place Of Honour (by Be My Guest), won once at 3 yrs and is out of the Coronation Stakes winner Sutton Place. (Mr L Marinopoulos).

112 - SOLIDUS (USA)
b.c. Irish River - Shirley Valentine (Shirley Heights). March 19. Third foal.
Half-brother to the very useful 1997 dual 10f winner Memorise (by Lyphard). The dam, a useful 11.8f winner, was fourth in the Park Hill Stakes and the Lancashire Oaks. She is a sister to the high class 10.6f and 12f winner and Irish Derby second Deploy and a half-sister to several winners including the Epsom Derby and Irish Derby winner Commander in Chief, the Champion 2-y-o and miler Warning (by Known Fact), the Great Voltigeur Stakes winner Dushyantor and the Grade 1 10f Flower Bowl Invitational Handicap winner Yashmak. The second dam, Slightly Dangerous (by Roberto), a very smart filly and winner of the 7.3f Fred Darling Stakes, was second in the Oaks to Time Charter and is a half-sister to the dams of the Arc winner and top class sire Rainbow Quest and the Dewhurst Stakes dead-heater Scenic. (Khaled Abdulla).

113 - SPICY MANNER (USA)
b.f. Cryptoclearance - Mangala (Sharpen Up). April 26.
Half-sister to the high-class colt Allied Forces (by Miswaki), winner of the Group 2 1m Queen Anne Stakes here and four Graded stakes events on turf in the USA, to Barraq (by Crystal Glitters), a winner of 6 minor races in France and the USA and to a minor US winner by Siberian Express. The dam, a winner over 7f and 1m in France, is a half-sister to several winners including the French listed stakes winner Nureyev's Best and the Park Hill Stakes third Allegedly Blue - herself dam of the listed winner

Hawait Al Barr. The second dam, Meadow Blue (by Raise a Native), is an unraced sister to the Champion 2-y-o Crowned Prince and the Kentucky Derby winner Majestic Prince and a half-sister to the dam of the French Derby winner Caracolero. (Buckram Oak Holdings).

---

114 - SPRY
b.f. Suave Dancer - Sandy Island (Mill Reef).
February 9.
Half-sister to the 3-y-o Spa, to the smart triple 12f winner Sebastian (both by Sadler's Wells), the very useful 10f Newmarket Pretty Polly Stakes winner Sardegna (by Pharly), the fair 2-y-o 7f winner and 12f placed 3-y-o Subterfuge (by Machiavellian) and to 4 disappointing animals by Pharly, Dancing Brave, Shareef Dancer and Green Desert. The dam, a very useful filly, won the Group 3 12f Lancashire Oaks and the 10f Pretty Polly Stakes. She is closely related to Slip Anchor and a half-sister to the German 2,000 Guineas winner Swazi. The second dam, Sayonara (by Birkhahn), won 5 races at up to 10.5f and was second in the German Oaks. (Lord Howard de Walden).

---

115 - TONGARIRO (USA)
ch.c. Trempolino - Air de Noblesse (Vaguely Noble).
February 12. Fourth foal. 150,000 Y. Tattersalls Houghton.
Half-brother to the 3-y-o L'Arrosee (by Woodman) and the minor US winner Diamond Accessory (by Soviet Star). The dam, placed 5 times in France, is a half-sister to the Group 3 winners Rami and Crack Regiment and the listed winner La Grande Epoque. The second dam, Ancient Regime (by Olden Times), the Champion French 2-y-o filly of 1980, won the Group 1 6f Prix Morny and is a sister to the Group 2 6.5f Prix Maurice de Gheest winner Cricket Ball. (Prince Fahd Salman).

---

116 - TOUCH 'N' FLY
b.c. Catrail - Menominee (Soviet Star).
January 19. Second foal. IR210,000Y. Goffs Orby.
Half-brother to the 3-y-o Count de Money (by Last Tycoon). The dam is an unraced half-sister to the smart Group 1 10f Prix Saint-Alary and Group 3 10.5f Prix Penelope winner Muncie (by Sadler's Wells), to the smart Group 1 15.5f Prix Royal-Oak winner Mersey (by Crystal Palace) and the placed Madame du Barry (dam of both the Group 3 C L Weld Park Stakes winner Morcote and the listed winner Miami Sands). The second dam, Martingale (by Luthier), was a useful winner of 2 races over 1m at 3 yrs and is a half-sister to the Prix du Moulin winner Mount Hagen and the French 1,000 Guineas winner Madelia (herself dam of the Prix Saint-Alary winner Moonlight Dance). (The Thoroughbred Corporation). *"I feel this colt will be a nice two-year-old. A big horse, he's a good mover and is one to look out for".*

---

117 - VARIETY SHOP (USA)
b.f. Mr Prospector - Nimble Feet (Danzig).
February 12.
Closely related to the useful 1996 3-y-o 8.3f winner Yamuna (by Forty Niner) and half-sister to the very smart Eltish (by Cox's Ridge), winner of the 7f Lanson Champagne Stakes and 1m Royal Lodge Stakes and runner-up to Timber Country in the Grade 1 8.5f Breeders Cup Juvenile, to the useful 5f and 6f winner Forest Gazelle (by Green Forest), the fairly useful 1996 2-y-o 7f winner Fleet River (by Riverman) and the French 3-y-o listed 10f winner Souplesse (by Majestic Light). The dam, a quite useful 2-y-o 5f winner, is a sister to the Grade 1 Washington Lassie Stakes winner Contredance and to the listed Roses Stakes winner Old Alliance and a half-sister to the Group winners Shotiche and Skimble. The second dam, Nimble Folly (by Cyane), is an unraced sister to the very useful Group 3 winner and Group 1 third Misgivings. (Khaled Abdulla).

---

118 - VORACIOUS
b.c. Cadeaux Genereux - Victoriana (Storm Bird).
January 25. Fifth foal.
Half-brother to Victorian Style (by Nashwan), winner of 2 races at around 1m and to the winning stayer Sea Victor (by Slip Anchor) - both quite useful. The dam won over 5f in France and is a half-sister to the Champion 1997 2-y-o Xaar. The second dam, Monroe (by Sir Ivor), a useful Irish 5f and 6f winner, is a sister to the good 2-y-o Gielgud and to the very smart Malinowski, and a half-sister to the dual Grade 1 winner Blush With Pride and to Sex Appeal - the dam of El Gran Senor and Try My Best. (Khaled Abdulla). *"A good mover, this colt will be one of my earliest two-year-olds".*

---

119 - WAR CABINET
b.c. Rainbow Quest - Balleta (Lyphard).
April 3. Fourth foal.
Brother to the French 3-y-o Colour Dance and half-brother to the very useful 6f (at 2 yrs) and 1m listed winner Barricade (by Riverman). The dam, a quite useful 3-y-o 10f winner, also won 3 races in the USA, is a sister to the great 'Arc' and 'King George' winner Dancing Brave and to Jolypha (winner of the Group 1 Prix Vermeille and Group 1 Prix de Diane). The second dam, Navajo Princess (by Drone),

won 16 races at up to 8.5f including the Grade 2 Molly Pitcher Handicap and the Grade 3 Falls City Handicap, is a sister to the stakes winner Passamaquoddy (herself dam of five winners) and a half-sister to the Grade 3 winner Soldier Boy. (Khaled Abdulla). *"War Cabinet is a horse I like. He's a nice colt that will make a two-year-old".*

---

120 - WELLS FARGO
b.f. Sadler's Wells - Cruising Height (Shirley Heights).
April 14.
Half-sister to the very useful 11.9f to 14.6f winner Corradini (by Rainbow Quest). The dam, a very useful 10.6f and 12.2f winner, is a half-sister to the Park Hill Stakes winner Trampship. The second dam, Nomadic Pleasure (by Habitat), was a fairly useful 9f winner and a half-sister to the Prix Vermeille winner Paulista. (Khaled Abdulla).

---

121 - WESTERN FOLLY (USA)
ch.c. Gone West - Nimble Folly (Cyane).
May 11.
Half-brother to the Grade 1 Washington Lassie Stakes winner Contredance, to the quite useful 2-y-o 5f winner Nimble Feet (dam of the very smart colt Eltish), the listed Roses Stakes winner Old Alliance (all by Danzig) and the Graded stakes winners Shotiche (by Northern Dancer) and Skimble (by Lyphard). The second dam, Nimble Folly (by Cyane), is an unraced sister to the very useful 2-y-o Group 3 winner and Group 1 third Misgivings. (Khaled Abdulla). *"Western Folly won't be too early, but he's an active colt and I like him. A nice horse and one to follow".*

---

122 - WINCE
b.f. Selkirk - Flit (Lyphard).
April 26.
Half-sister to the 1997 Group 1 Prix Saint-Alary second Fleeting Glimpse (by Rainbow Quest). The dam, a fair 3-y-o 10f winner, is a sister to Skimble (a US winner of 7 stakes races) and is closely related to the Grade 1 Washington Lassie Stakes winner Contredance, the listed Roses Stakes winner Old Alliance and to the dam of the Lanson Champagne Stakes winner Eltish. The second dam, Nimble Folly (by Cyane), is an unraced sister to the very useful 2-y-o Group 3 winner and Group 1 third Misgivings. (Khaled Abdulla).

---

123 - YARALINO
b.c. Caerleon - Wemyss Bight (Dancing Brave).
March 20. Second foal.
Half-brother to the 3-y-o Wemyss Quest (by Rainbow Quest). The dam, a very smart filly, won 5 races including a maiden race over 9f (at 2 yrs), the Group 1 12f Irish Oaks, the Group 2 12f Prix de Malleret, the Group 3 10.5f Prix Cleopatre and the Group 3 10.5f Prix Penelope. The second dam, Bahamian (by Mill Reef), a very useful winner of the Group 3 Lingfield Oaks Trial and placed in the Prix de l'Esperance (disqualified from first place), the Prix de Pomone, the Park Hill Stakes and the Princess Royal Stakes, is a half-sister to the very useful winners Captivator, Eileen Jenny and Kasmayo. The third dam, Sorbus (by Busted), was disqualified after winning the Irish Oaks and was placed in the Irish 1,000 Guineas, the Irish St Leger and the Yorkshire Oaks. (Khaled Abdulla).

---

124 - UNNAMED
b.f. Green Desert - Alidiva (Chief Singer).
April 19. Fifth foal.
Half-sister to the 3-y-o Anytime (by Fairy King) and to three high-class racehorses - the 1,000 Guineas winner Sleepytime, the Group 1 1m Sussex Stakes winner Ali Royal (both by Royal Academy) and the Group 1 12f Europa Preis and Group 1 10f Premio Roma winner Taipan (by Last Tycoon). The dam, a useful winner of 3 races from 6f to 1m, including a listed event, is a half-sister to the Group 2 Prix Greffulhe winner Croco Rouge. The second dam, Alligatrix (by Alleged), a very useful 2-y-o 7f winner, was third in the Hoover Fillies Mile. (Greenbay Stables Ltd).

---

125 - UNNAMED
b.f. Royal Academy - Alligatrix (Alleged).
June 2.
Half-sister to the 1998 Group 2 10.5f Prix Greffulhe winner Croco Rouge (by Rainbow Quest), to the useful 10f winner Tom Waller, the useful 7f listed Oak Tree Stakes winner Alidiva (by Chief Singer) - herself the dam of Sleepytime, Ali-Royal and Taipan - to the useful 6f winner and subsequent US stakes winner Persianelli (by Persian Bold), the useful 2-y-o 5f winner Carbon Steel (by Sure Blade) and the fair 1m all-weather winner Galatrix (by Be My Guest). The dam was a very useful 2-y-o 7f winner, was third in the Group 1 Fillies Mile and is a half-sister to 6 winners. The second dam, Shore (by Round

Table), won 6 races including a stakes event in the USA and is a half-sister to three good US stakes winners and to the dam of the Prix de l'Abbaye winner Polonia. (Greenbay Stables Ltd).

Julie Cecil

126 - ARBUCKLE
ch.c. Grand Lodge - Little Change (Grundy).
February 3. 37,000Y. Tattersalls October.
Half-brother to the 3-y-o Donna Grazio (by Sharpo), to the fairly useful 1m to 12f and subsequent Australian winner Forfun (by Jalmood), the modest winner of 6 races at up to 12f Mr Wishing Well (by Dunbeath), the modest 7f and 12f winner Spring Sixpence (by Dowsing) and minor winners in France and Germany by Robellino and Simply Great. The dam, a fair 5f placed 2-y-o, is a half-sister to 9 winners including the Cheveley Park Stakes fourth Penny Blessing. The second dam, Pennycuick (by Celtic Ash) was a sprint winner of 2 races and a half-sister to Mummy's Pet and the July Cup winner Parsimony. (Mr Michael Sears & Partners). *"A strong colt, Arbuckle is coming along fine and should be a relatively early two-year-old" says Julie.*

127 - CUSIN
ch.c. Arazi - Fairy Tern (Mill Reef).
May 3. 40,000Y. Tattersalls Houghton.
Closely related to the minor US winner Scherbo (by Blushing Groom) and to the fair 3-y-o 7.6f winner Fairy Fortune (by Rainbow Quest) and half-brother to 7 winners including the US stakes winner Way Of The World (by Dance Of Life), the very useful 6f and 1m winner Hoy (by Habitat), the useful 1996 2-y-o 7f winner Papua (by Green Dancer), the fairly useful 3-y-o 6f winner Fairy Flax (by Dancing Brave) and minor winners by Greinton, Teenoso and High Top. The dam, a very useful 5f and 7f winner, is a full or half-sister to 8 winners including the Group 2 Tattersalls Rogers Gold Cup winner Elegant Air. The second dam, Elegant Tern (by Sea Bird II), won three races including the Group 3 12f Princess Royal Stakes. (Mrs M Slater). *"A fine, bonny colt, he'll be quite early and would want five or six furlongs to start with this year".*

128 - KIRK
b.f. Selkirk - Sancta (So Blessed).
May 14.
Closely related to the smart 7f Houghton Stakes and 3-y-o 10f winner Carmelite House (by Diesis), to the fair 10f winner Khrisma (by Kris) and the 1998 3-y-o Shaveling (by Sharpo) and half-sister to the very useful John Smith's Magnet Cup winner Wolsey (by Our Native), the useful 2m winner Saint Keyne and the quite useful 14f to 18.2f winner Well Beloved (both by Sadler's Wells). The dam, a useful winner of 3 races over 1m (twice) and 10f, is a half-sister to the outstanding broodmare Doubly Sure (the dam of Kris and Diesis). The second dam, Soft Angels (by Crepello), was a high-class 2-y-o winner of the Royal Lodge Stakes. (Lord Howard de Walden). *"A tall and rather narrow filly, Kirk is a late foal and will take time but she's a nice filly for the late summer".*

129 - WAQUAAS
b.c. Green Desert - Hamaya (Mr Prospector).
January 19. Third foal.
Half-brother to the 3-y-o Thaayer (by Wolfhound). The dam, placed fourth over 7f at 3 yrs on her only outing, is closely related to the US Grade 1 9f Flamingo Stakes winner Talinum and a half-sister to the dam of the Group 2 Park Hill Stakes winner Noble Rose. The second dam, Water Lily (by Riverman), a half-sister to the Group 2 Grand Prix de Deauville winner First Prayer, was a very useful filly herself and winner of the 5f Prix Yacowlef at 2 yrs in France and a Grade 3 Handicap in the USA. (Hamdan Al Maktoum). *"Waquaas came into the yard late but he's a grand little horse that will hopefully be out in mid-summer".*

Peter Chapple-Hyam

130 - ATLANTIC CHARTER (USA)
b.c. Gone West - Silk Slippers (Nureyev).
January 22. Third foal. $475.000. Keeneland July.
Closely related to the fairly useful 6f (at 2 yrs), 1m and subsequent US winner Silk Masque (by Woodman). The dam was a useful filly and winner of the Group 2 Hoover Fillies Mile. The second dam, Nalee's Fantasy (by Graustark), won at up to 10f in the USA, was Grade 3 placed and is a half-sister to numerous winners including the Irish St Leger winner Meneval. (Mr R Sangster). *"A biggish horse, he'll take a bit of time to come to hand and will be more of a three-year-old type. This year I'll probably start him off in August over seven furlongs" says Peter.*

131 - BASSANELLO (USA)   ch.f. Nureyev - Feminine Wiles (Ahonoora).
April 3. Second reported foal.
Sister to the promising 1997 7f placed 2-y-o Connoisseur Bay. The dam, a very useful 1m (at 2 yrs) and 10f listed winner, is out of the minor US winner Instinctive Move (by Nijinsky), herself a half-sister to Legal Bid and Law Society. (Mr R Sangster). *"A really nice filly this, she's coming on well and will be out in the mid-summer".*

132 - BELASCO (USA)   ch.c. Gone West - Musicale (The Minstrel).
February 4. Third foal.
Closely related to the very promising 1997 6f placed 2-y-o Musical Twist (by Woodman). The dam was a very useful winner of the Group 3 6f Cherry Hinton Stakes and the 7f Rockfel Stakes at 2 yrs and the Group 3 7.3f Gainsborough Stud Fred Darling Stakes at 3 yrs. The second dam, Gossiping (by Chati), won over 6f in the USA and is a half-sister to the high-class sprinter Committed, winner of the Prix de l'Abbaye and the William Hill Sprint Championship. (Mr R Sangster). *"A bit later than some of my two-year-olds, but he's done everything right so far and goes nicely. He'll make a two-year-old and everyone at Manton likes him".*

133 - BELLAMONT FOREST (USA)   b.br.c. Hermitage - Teresa's Spirit (Master Derby).
May 20. $82,000Y. Keeneland September.
Half-brother to 5 winners including the US stakes-placed Rejoui (by Mighty Adversary). The dam won at 2 yrs in the USA and is a sister to a stakes-placed winner. The second dam, Damascus Betty (by Damascus), won twice at 3 yrs in the USA. (Mr R Sangster & Mrs J Magnier). *"Bellamont Forest is coming along very nicely. He's good-bodied, will be ready to run by July time and looks a nice colt".*

134 - BLANKENBERGE (IRE)   ch.c. Pips Pride - Renata's Ring (Auction Ring).
April 14. Third foal. 42,000Y. Doncaster St Leger.
Brother to the minor 1997 7f placed 2-y-o Bodfari Pride and half-brother to the fairly useful 1996 2-y-o 5f winner Joint Venture (by Common Grounds). The dam was placed over 7f in Ireland and is a half-sister to 5 winners. The second dam, Maria Renata (by Jaazeiro), is a placed sister to the very useful Irish chaser Rust Never Sleeps and a half-sister to the French listed winner Interdit and to the dam of the Middle Park Stakes winner Balla Cove. (Mr R Sangster). *"Another that will be much better as a three-year-old, but he's a nice colt that does everything we ask. He's cantering well at the moment and is coming along nicely".*

135 - BRANCASTER (USA)   b.br.c. Riverman - Aseltine's Angels (Fappiano).
April 6. Fourth foal. $95,000Y. Keeneland September.
Half-brother to Angel's Reward (by Half A Year), a minor winner of 4 races in the USA. The dam is a placed daughter of Honor Tricks (by Bold Bidder), herself an unraced half-sister to the champion filly and mare Tosmah, the US Grade 1 winner and good sire Halo and to Queen Sucree (dam of the Kentucky Derby winner Cannonade). (Royal Ascot Racing Club). *"More of a three-year-old in type, he's coming along nicely, has done everything we ask and I'm pleased with him".*

136 - BUTTERFLY BAY (USA)   b.f. Dehere - Face The Facts (Lomond).
April 15. Fourth foal.
Half-sister to the quite useful 1996 2-y-o 5.2f winner Raven Master (by Shalford). The dam, placed once at 2 yrs in Ireland, is closely related to the high class Epsom Oaks and Prix Vermeille winner Intrepidity and to the smart 5f and 6f winner Acushla and a half-sister to the useful 6f winner River Prince and the useful 1m and 10f winner Calandra. The second dam, Intrepid Lady (by Bold Ruler), won over 12f in France at 3 yrs and is a sister to the US stakes winner Big Advance and a half-sister to the US stakes winners Progressing and High Bid - the latter also dam of the champion sire Bold Bidder. (Mr R Sangster & Mrs J Magnier). *"A filly that looks quite sharp but will probably be suited by six furlongs to start with, Butterfly Bay is very strong and I'm really pleased with her. She should be out in June or July and I think she'll be a nice filly".*

137 - CALADASA (USA)   b.f. Nureyev - Aunt Pearl (Seattle Slew).
February 8. Second reported foal.
Sister to the fairly useful 1997 2-y-o dual 6f winner Social Charter. The dam, a winner at up to 7f in the USA, is out of a sister to Prospector's Fire (dam of the Vernon's Sprint Cup winner Dowsing) and a half-sister to the smart US colts Royal And Regal and Regal And Royal. (Mr R Sangster). *"A February foal and although she'll be an early two-year-old, she'll be better over six furlongs than five. She may make her debut at Chester in May".*

138 - CAIRDE NUA b.f. Mukaddamah - Bourbon Topsy (Ile de Bourbon). February 12. Fifth foal. 32,000Y. Doncaster St Leger.
Half-sister to the fair 1995 3-y-o 12f and 2m (all-weather) winner Anjou (by saumarez). The dam, a useful winner of four races at 3 yrs from 11.5f to 2m and third in the Group 3 Lancashire Oaks, is a half-sister to 7 winners including the high-class colt and useful sire Most Welcome. The second dam, Topsy (by Habitat), won the Sun Chariot Stakes and is a half-sister to Teenoso. (Mr S Muiryan) *"This filly may need time to mature, but I do think she's going to be sharp one day"*.

139 - CASINO QUEEN (IRE) ch.f. Royal Academy - Castilian Queen (Diesis). March 8. Third foal.
Sister to the high-class 1997 3-y-o Group 1 5f Prix de l'Abbaye winner Carmine Lake (by Royal Academy) and half-sister to the fair 1997 2-y-o 6.9f winner Star Of Grosvenor (by Last Tycoon). The dam, a fair 2-y-o 6f winner, is a half-sister to the useful 6f and 7f winner and Diomed Stakes third Regal Sabre. The second dam, Royal Heroine (by Lypheor), won ten races in England, France and the USA including the 6f Princess Margaret Stakes (at 2 yrs) followed by the Group 2 9.2f Prix de l'Opera, the Group 3 1m Child Stakes and the 9f Hollywood Derby, 9f Matriarch Stakes and the Breeders Cup Mile (all Grade 1 events). (Mr R Sangster). *"Very weak still, she was small when we first got her and is still growing. She'll be a five or six furlong filly but will take a bit of time"*.

140 - COLONIAL STATE (USA) b.c. Pleasant Colony - Star Pastures (Northfields). May 24.
Half-brother to the 3-y-o Marcus Maximus, to the useful 2-y-o 7f winner Monza (both by Woodman), to the useful Irish 7f to 13f winner Esprit d'Etoile (by Spectacular Bid), the fairly useful 10f winner Lord Justice (by Alleged), the fair 3-y-o 7f winner Turbulent River (by Riverman), the minor French winner of 3 races at 4 yrs Emir Albadou (by Bering), the 1996 German 3-y-o winner Rassoul Al Arab (by Risen Star) and the minor American winner Stellarina (by Pleasant Colony). The dam was a high-class filly at up to 10f, winning 5 races including the Group 3 Child Stakes and is a half-sister to 6 winners including the very useful 7f to 10f winner Pixie Erin and the good middle-distance colt Skaramanga. The second dam, Spirit in the Sky (by Tudor Melody), won 3 races from 6f to 12f and was third in the Group 2 Nassau Stakes. (Mr R. Sangster). *"A very big horse, he'll take time and will be much more of a three-year-old. I like him though and he does everything asked of him"*.

141 - COMMANDER COLLINS (IRE) b.c. Sadler's Wells - Kanmary (Kenmare). April 8.
Brother to the 3-y-o Flying Kiss, closely related to Lit de Justice, winner of the 1996 Grade 1 Breeders Cup Sprint, to the very smart 7f Washington Singer Stakes winner and 2,000 Guineas, Derby and Irish Derby placed Colonel Collins, the useful 1997 3-y-o 6f and 7f winner Captain Collins (all by El Gran Senor) and the fair 2-y-o 5f winner Stormswept (by Storm Bird). The dam, a smart French 2-y-o 5f winner, stayed 9f and is a half-sister to numerous winners including the Prix de Royallieu winner Passionaria. The second dam, Djallybrook (by Djakao), was a minor French 11f winner. (Mr R Sangster). *"A colt from a family I know well, he's much more of a three-year-old type and won't run this year until the back-end. Coming along nicely though"* mused Peter.

142 - DANE FRIENDLY b.c. Danehill - Always Friendly (High Line). April 8. First foal. 130,000 Y. Tattersalls Houghton.
The dam, a very useful filly, won 3 races invluding the Group 3 12f Princess Royal Stakes and was placed in the Prix Royal-Oak and Gran Premio de Milano. The second dam, Wise Speculation (by Mr Prospector), was unplaced and bred four other minor winners. (Mr L Gaucci). *"This colt may take a bit of time, but look out for him because he'll be a nice horse come mid-season. We'll probably start him off over six furlongs but I should think he'd get further"*.

143 - DAY COURAGE (USA) b.c. Dayjur - Badge Of Courage (Well Decorated). March 31.
Half-brother to the fair 1997 1m placed 2-y-o Brave Noble (by Woodman), to the very useful 1993 Group 3 10f winner True Hero (by The Minstrel), the minor US 4-y-o winner Raayaat (by Phone Trick) and the Irish 2-y-o 7f and 1m winner Patently Clear (by Miswaki) - herself dam of a stakes winner in Japan. The dam is an unraced half-sister to the 2,000 Guineas winner and very useful sire Known Fact, to the US Grade 1 winner Tentam, the US Grade 2 winner Terete and the high-class broodmares Secrettame (dam of Gone West and Lion Cavern) and Taminette (dam of Grade 1 winner Tappiano). The second dam, Tamerett (by Tim Tam), won 4 races in the USA. (Mr L Gaucci). *"Quite a sharp little colt, he's forward in his work, would want five or six furlongs and is certainly a two-year-old type"*.

144 - ENTERTAINER b.c. Be My Guest - Green Wings (General Assembly).
February 4. Sixth foal. 44,000Y. Tattersalls October.
Half-brother to the Italian winner of 4 races Paris Texas (by Salt Dome), to the French 3-y-o 9f winner Ballymount (by Doulab) and the 1995 2-y-o 1m all-weather seller winner Addie Pray (by Great Commotion). The dam, a winner over middle-distances in Ireland at 4 yrs, is a half-sister to 2 winners including the Group 3 5f King George Stakes second Golden Green. The second dam, Kentucky Green (by One For All), won 4 races and is a half-sister to the Phoenix Stakes second Saratosa Star. (Royal Ascot Racing Club). *"More of a three-year-old but he's an early foal and everything comes easily to him. He'll be out in mid-summer, has a very sharp attitude and is a horse I like".*

145 - FIRST NIGHT (IRE) b.f. Sadler's Wells - Morning Devotion (Affirmed).
January 22.
Closely related to the top-class filly Balanchine, winner of the 1994 Oaks and Irish Derby, to the minor US winner Storm Centre (both by Storm Bird), the smart Group 3 10f Rose Of Lancaster Stakes winner and Derby third Romanov and the very useful 2-y-o 7f and Group 2 10.5f Sun Chariot Stakes winner Red Slippers (both by Nureyev). The dam, a useful winner over 6f at 2 yrs and third in the Fillies Mile, was fourth in the 12f Lancashire Oaks at 3 yrs. The second dam, Morning Has Broken (by Prince John), only ran twice but is a half-sister to the joint champion US 2-y-o filly of 1978 It's In The Air. (Mr R Sangster). *"She'll take a bit of time and will probably have one nice run at the back-end. I'm really pleased with her however, she's very similar to Romanov, but seemingly not as early".*

146 - FISHERMAN'S SONG (IRE) b.c. Fairy King - Rose Of Jericho (Alleged).
May 9.
Brother to Shinko King, a listed winner in Japan, closely related to the smart Group 3 13.4f Ormonde Stakes winner Royal Court (by Sadler's Wells) and half-brother to the top-class Epsom Derby, Irish Champion Stakes and Dewhurst Stakes winner Dr Devious (by Ahonoora) and the very useful 6f Greenlands Stakes winner Archway (by Thatching). The dam is an unraced daughter of Rose Red (by Northern Dancer), a minor Irish 2-y-o 6f winner and herself a half-sister to the high-class middle-distance colt Critique and to Cambretta (herself dam of the smart French 1m to 10f winner Pluralisme and of the very useful winners Singletta and Classic Tale). (Mr R Sangster & Mrs J Magnier). *"A lovely horse, although not really like his half-brother Dr Devious, this colt will be better next year but should still make a two-year-old around August time".*

147 - J.R. STEVENSON (USA) ch.c. Lyphard - While It Lasts (Foolish Pleasure).
March 22. Fifth foal. $140,000. Keeneland September.
Half-brother to a placed horse in the USA by Buckfinder. The dam, a fair 3-y-o 11f and 11.5f winner, is a full or half-sister to 7 winners including the US stakes winner Special Weekend. The second dam, Prom Date (by Arts And Letters), is an unraced half-sister to the Champion 3-y-o Stage Door Johnny. (Mr R Sangster & Mr B Sangster). *"J R goes along really nicely, not very big, he'll be a six furlong horse to start with but will get further in time. He'll be running in May or June, has a nice attitude and is very sharp".*

148 - KISS ME GOODNIGHT b.f. First Trump - Flitteriss Park (Beldale Flutter).
February 9. Sixth foal. 45,000Y. Tattersalls Houghton.
Half-sister to the smart Group 3 Cork And Orrery Stakes and Grade 3 Jaipur Stakes winner Atraf (by Clantime), to the useful 1992 Group 2 Richmond Stakes winner Son Pardo (by Petong), the useful 6f winner Emerging Market and the quite usefl 6f winner Whittle Woods Girl (both by Emarati). The dam, a modest 1m winner, is a half-sister to 5 winners including the South African Grade 3 winner Lady Of Habits and the 2-y-o listed winner Snipe Hall. The second dam, Geopelia (by Raffingora), was a very useful sprinter and a winner of 6 races. (Mr D Clee). *"Quite a small filly, she'll be a sprinter, will be out in May and definitely has races in her. Coming along well".*

149 - MIDDELKERKE b.c. College Chapel - Andbell (Trojen Fen).
February 29. Sixth foal. 40,000 Y. Tattersalls Houghton.
Brother to the 3-y-o Sandia Point and half-brother to the Norwegian winner Milly Molly Mango (by Mango Express). The dam, unplaced in all three of her races, is a half-sister to 4 winners including the useful listed Irish 1,000 Guineas Trial winner Bell Tower and the US stakes-placed winner Rock Crystal. The second dam, Ring The Changes (by Auction Ring), won once at 3 yrs over 5f and is a full or half-sister to 10 winners including Blue Star, Pearl Star, Portese, Seadiver (all listed winners) and Flying Melody (dam of the Group 1 winners Lyric Fantasy, Royal Applause and In Command). (Mr R Sangster). *"A big colt that will require a bit of cut in the ground, he looks like a sprinter with his huge back-end".*

150 - MIRBECK (USA) b.f. Gone West - Oakmead (Lomond).
First foal.
The dam, a smart filly, won the Lingfield Oaks Trial, was third in the Oaks and is a half-sister to the Grade 1 Yellow Ribbon Stakes winner Delighter (by Lypheor). The second dam, Amazer (by Vaguely Noble), won the Prix de Royallieu and the Yellow Ribbon Stakes and is a sister to the William Hill Futurity Stakes winner Sporting Yankee. (Mr R Sangster). *"A really nice filly, she'll be big just like her mum, is coming on really nicely and should be out around August".*

151 - MOTHER OF PEARL (IRE) b.f. Sadler's Wells - Sisania (High Top).
January 14.
Closely related to the high-class colt Turtle Island (by Fairy King), winner of the Group 1 6f Heinz "57" Phoenix Stakes, the Group 2 6f Gimcrack Stakes and the Irish 2,000 Guineas. The dam won two races in Italy at around 10f and is a half-sister to 3 winners. The second dam, Targo's Delight (by Targowice), was an unraced half-sister to the Observer Gold Cup second Sea Break. (Mr R Sangster & Mrs J Magnier). *"Mother Of Pearl won't be early, but I'm really pleased with her. Probably my best two-year-old, she's really attractive, quite a big filly and walks around as if she owned the place. She'll certainly make a nice two-year-old but will be even better next year".*

152 - MUSICAL TREAT (IRE) ch.f. Royal Academy - Mountain Ash (Dominion).
February 12. Second foal.
The dam won over 7f twice at 2 yrs and subsequently was a very useful Italian Group 3 and listed winner over 7f and 1m. She is a half-sister to several winners including the very useful 1m to 10.5f winner New Barry. The second dam, Red Berry (by Great Nephew), was second in the Cheveley Park Stakes. (Mr R Sangster). *"Musical Treat is coming along nicely and will be running in May. I like her a lot"* says the trainer.

153 - OUTER LIMIT (IRE) b.c. Caerleon - Lady Liberty (Noble Bijou).
March 2. Fifth foal.
Closely related to the very useful 1996 2-y-o 1m Curragh Futurity Stakes winner Equal Rights and half-brother to 2 winners in Australasia, including a Grade 2 winner by Bluebird. The dam won the Grade 1 12f Australian Oaks. (Mr R Sangster). *"Really taking the eye at the moment, this is a horse I like a lot"* Peter tells me.

154 - SOCIAL SCENE (IRE) ch.f. Grand Lodge - Ardmelody (Law Society).
April 14. Sixth foal. IR58,000Y. Goffs Orby.
Half-sister to the Grade 2 12f Orchid Handicap and Grade 3 9f Bewitch Stakes winner Memories (by Don't Forget Me) - previously a listed winner in Ireland, to the very useful 1997 4-y-o 9f to 10f winner Danish Rhapsody, the very useful 1997 3-y-o 10f winner Garuda (both by Danehill) and a winner in Japan by Last Tycoon. The dam is an unraced half-sister to 7 winners out of Thistlewood (by Kalamoun) - herself a half-sister to Ardross. (Mr R Sangster & Mr B Sangster). *"A nice big filly that will take time. She'll be out in mid-summer, will want fast ground and she'll be a decent two-year-old, probably over seven furlongs to start".*

155 - STORMHILL (IRE) b.c. Caerleon - Jackie Berry (Connaught).
February 18.
Brother to the 2-y-o 7f winner and smart middle-distance placed Pencader and to the 4-y-o Gulf Harbour and half-brother to the useful 7f (at 2 yrs) to 12f winner Coneybury and the 7f and 10f winner Juniper Berry (by Last Tycoon). The dam, a fairly useful Irish 7f and 8.5f winner, is out of a sister to the very smart Sun Chariot Stakes winner Cranberry Sauce. (Mr R Sangster). *"This is a two-year-old to look out for. Like another Caerleon colt I have, Outer Limit, this is a nice horse I like very much".*

156 - STRING QUARTET (IRE) b.f. Sadler's Wells - Fleur Royale (Mill Reef).
May 1. IR85,000Y. Goffs Orby.
Sister to the 1997 Irish listed 10f winner Casey Tibbs, to the fairly useful 1996 3-y-o 12.3f and 14f winner Flamands and the 1995 Irish 3-y-o 11f winner Heaven's Gable and closely related to the 1992 Irish 2-y-o 7f winner Oiseau de Feu (by Nijinsky) and the 1990 Irish listed-placed 2-y-o African Dance (by El Gran Senor). The dam, a very useful filly, won the Group 2 10f Pretty Polly Stakes, was second in the Irish Oaks and is a half-sister to the dam of the smart colts Nomrood, Alleging and Monastery. The second dam, Sweet Mimosa (by Le Levenstell), was a smart winner of the French Oaks and a sister to the top class colts Levmoss and Le Moss. (Mr R Sangster). *"Quite immature, he'll take time and will want a trip".*

157 - VALENCAY (IRE) b.f. Sadler's Wells - Detroit (Riverman).
May 24.
Sister to the top-class colt Carnegie, winner of the Prix de l'Arc de Triomphe, Grand Prix de Saint-Cloud, Prix Foy etc., to the useful 1995 5-y-o 10f and 12f winner Wayne County and the useful 3-y-o listed 13.5f winner Honfleur, closely related to the smart Group 2 10f Prix Guillaume d'Ornano winner Antisaar (by Northern Dancer) and half-sister to the smart Group 3 St Simon Stakes winner Lake Erie (by Kings Lake). The dam won the 1980 Prix de l'Arc de Triomphe (beating Argument, Ela Mana Mou and Three Troikas) and is a half-sister to the Cheveley Park Stakes winner Durtal (herself dam of the Ascot Gold Cup winner Gildoran). The second dam, Derna II (by Sunny Boy III), was placed from 10f to 13f in France. (Mr R Sangster). *"A little bit small, she does all her work well but needs to mature"* Peter explained.

158 - VANILLE (IRE) b.f. Selkirk - Stormswept (Storm Bird).
May 1. Third foal. 38,000Y. Tattersalls Houghton.
Half-sister to the 3-y-o Cavell (by Lion Cavern) and to the modest 1m all-weather winner Amico (by Efisio). The dam, a fair 2-y-o 5f winner, is closely related to the Grade 1 Breeders Cup Sprint winner Lit de Justice and the Derby, Irish Derby and 2,000 Guineas third Colonel Collins. The second dam, Kanmary (by Kenmare), won the Group 3 5f Prix du Bois at 2 yrs, was second in the Group 3 Prix Chloe and third in the Group 1 Prix Robert Papin. (Mr J Steinmann & Mr P Deel). *"Vanille has a good attitude, goes nicely and is a filly I like. I have high hopes for her"*.

159 - WATERFRONT (IRE) b.c. Turtle Island - Rising Tide (Red Alert).
March 7. IR38,000Y. Goffs Orby.
Closely related to the Irish 1997 2-y-o 6f winner Fairy Flight and to the useful dual 6f winner King Of The East (both by Fairy King) and half-brother to the French listed 10.5f winner Titled Ascent (by Sir Ivor), the Irish listed winning sprinter Northern Tide (by Northern Pole) and a winner in Malaysia by Gregorian. The dam was a useful 2-y-o 5f winner and a half-sister to 5 winners including the Group 1 Heinz "57" Phoenix Stakes winner King Persian. The second dam, Naiad Queen (by Pampered King), a fairly useful winner of 2 races at up to 7f in Ireland, is a half-sister to the dam of the Irish Group 2 and US Grade 2 winner Just a Game. (Mr R Sangster). *"Six furlongs in May or June should suit Waterfront to begin with. I'm hoping this is going to be a really nice horse"*.

160 - WORLD ALERT (IRE) b.c. Alzao - Steady The Buffs (Balidar).
April 14.
Brother to the very useful filly Aldbourne, a winner from 6f (at 2 yrs) to 8.5f and placed in the English and Irish 1,000 Guineas and to the useful 1993 2-y-o Group 3 1m Beresford Stakes winner Sheridan. The dam, a modest 7f to 10f placed 3-y-o, is out of Dinant (by Abernant), a very useful winning sister to the 1,000 Guineas winner Abermaid. (Mr R Sangster). *"A mid-season type two-year-old, I have high hopes for World Alert. A colt that's well put together, I like him"*.

Roger Charlton

161 - AGITANDO b.c. Tenby - Crown Rose (Dara Monarch).
April 25. Third foal. IR66,000Y. Goffs Orby.
Half-brother to the 1997 Irish 6.5f placed 3-y-o Moon Rose (by Imperial Frontier). The dam ran unplaced twice and is a half-sister to 7 winners including the Irish dual listed winner and Group placed Lord Bud - subsequently a winner and Graded stakes-placed in the USA. The second dam, Darling Bud (by Whistling Wind), won the listed Waterford Glass Nursery Handicap at 2 yrs. (Khaled Abdulla). *"An attractive horse, he's growing now although he looked at one stage as though he'd be early. He shows a bit of speed and should be running over six or seven furlongs in June or July"*.

162 - AMUSEMENT ch.c. Mystiko - Jolies Eaux (Shirley Heights).
April 15. Third foal. 25,000Y. Tattersalls October.
Half-brother to the 3-y-o Minnehaha (by Be My Chief) and the 1995 Irish 2-y-o 7f winner Slide By (by Aragon). The dam is an unplaced half-sister to the Galtres Stakes winners Deadly Serious (dam of the Australian Grade 1 winner Runyon) and Sans Blague. The second dam, Joking Apart (by Jimmy Reppin), won the listed Strensall Stakes and was third in the 1,000 Guineas. *"Always an early type, even at the sales he was quite mature"* Roger was telling me. *"An attractive colt, he'll be out by the end of May over six furlongs"*.

163 - ANALYTICAL   b.c. Pursuit Of Love - Risha Flower (Kris).
April 7. Fourth foal. 35,000Y. Tattersalls October.
Half-brother to the 3-y-o Karriba (by Rudimentary) and to 2 winners in Italy by Persian Bold and Persian Heights. The dam, a quite useful 1m winner, is a half-sister to 7 winners including the useful 6f to 1m winner Tatsfield. The second dam, Sephira (by Luthier), won in France over 1m and is a sister to the Prix de l'Abbaye winner Sigy (dam of the Group 3 winners Sicyos and Radjasi and the very useful sprinter King's Signet) and the Group 3 winning sprinter Sonoma (dam of the smart French winners Funambule and Sarmatie). *"An attractive horse and still growing, he'll be out in July at the earliest. I'll start him at six or seven furlongs".*

164 - BOATMAN (USA)   ch.c. Irish River - Peplum (Nijinsky).
March 16. Fourth foal.
Half-brother to the 1996 2-y-o 7f winner Palisade (by Gone West) and to the 9f to 10.4f placed maiden Pep Talk (by Lyphard) - both quite useful. The dam, a useful winner of the listed 11.3f Cheshire Oaks, was third in the 12f Princess Royal Stakes and fourth in the 10.5f Prix de Flore. She is a half-sister to the top class filly Al Bahathri, winner of the 1,000 Guineas and the Coronation Stakes and to the US stakes winner Geraldines Store. The second dam, Chain Store (by Nodouble), won 8 races at up to 9f including a stakes event and is out of a half-sister to the high class middle distance colt General Holme. (Khaled Abdulla). *"This is a big horse and very much a three-year-old type".*

165 - DOVIRI (USA)   ch.f. Irish River - Storm Dove (Storm Bird).
March 17. Second foal.
Closely related to the quite promising 1997 1m placed 2-y-o Storm River (by Riverman). The dam, a 2-y-o 6f and useful 3-y-o listed 7f winner at Goodwood, was placed in the Group 3 Kiveton Park Stakes and is a half-sister to a minor stakes-placed winner. The second dam, Daeltown (by Dictus), a smart French filly, won at up to 10f. (Khaled Abdulla). *"Bigger than her mother, she looks to me like she'll be a nice two-year-old. She moves nicely and will hopefully be out in mid-summer".*

166 - DUCK OVER   b.f. Warning - Waterfowl Creek (Be My Guest).
April 3. Third foal.
Half-sister to the 3-y-o Hulls Beat (by Belmez) and to the useful 1997 3-y-o 10f listed winner Maid Of Camelot (by Caerleon). The dam, a quite useful 3-y-o dual 1m winner, is a sister to the very useful dual 1m winner Guest Artiste, closely related to the very useful Inchmurrin - winner of 6 races including the Group 2 Child Stakes and herself dam of the very smart colt Inchinor - and a half-sister to numerous winners including the very useful 2-y-o Group 2 6f Mill Reef Stakes winner Welney. The second dam, On Show (by Welsh Pageant), a fairly useful 3-y-o 10f winner, is out of the Park Hill Stakes winner African Dancer. *"This athletic filly is taller than her half-sister Maid Of Camelot. She'll be ready for the racecourse by July and be suited by six furlongs initially".*

167 - ENGLAND'S ROSE   b.f. Alzao - Gold Tear (Tejano).
April 13. Second foal. IR120,000Y. Goffs Orby.
The dam, a winner of 2 races in France at 3 yrs, is a half-sister to the Prix Lupin winner Galetto, the Prix de la Foret winner Gabina and to the dam of the Grand Criterium winner Goldmark. The second dam, Gold Bird (by Rheingold), won a listed event in France over 10.5f and is a half-sister to the Prix Chloe winner Gaelic Bird. *"A nice filly and a very good mover that will be suited by seven furlongs this year"*

168 - FAIRY GODMOTHER   b.f. Fairy King - Highbrow (Shirley Heights).
April 1.
Half-sister to the 1997 unplaced 2-y-o Blueprint (by Generous), to the 1997 12f winner Ghillies Ball (by Groom Dancer) and the 10f and 12f winner Beyond Doubt (by Belmez), both fairly useful. The dam, a very useful 2-y-o 1m winner and Group 2 12f Ribblesdale Stakes second, is closely related to the good middle-distance colt Milford and a half-sister to the Princess of Wales's Stakes winner Height of Fashion - herself dam of Nashwan and Unfuwain, and to the dam of the Epsom Oaks second Wind in Her Hair. The second dam, Highclere (by Queens Hussar), won the 1,000 Guineas and French Oaks in 1973. (The Queen). *"Quite a nice, scopey filly, she'll be out in late summer over seven furlongs".*

169 - MAHONIA   b.f. Rainbow Quest - Danthonia (Northern Dancer).
February 26.
Half-sister to the 3-y-o Zante (by Zafonic). The dam, a quite useful 2-y-o 5f winner, is closely related to the Group 3 1m Prix Quincey winner Masterclass (by The Minstrel), the useful triple 6f winner Didicoy

(by Danzig) and the French 3-y-o 5f winner Victoriana (by Storm Bird) and a half-sister to the champion 1997 2-y-o Xaar (by Zafonic), the Group 3 10.5f Prix Corrida winner Diese (by Diesis) and the useful 4-y-o 1m and 10.4f winner Esquire (by High Line). The second dam, Monroe (by Sir Ivor), a useful Irish 5f and 6f winner, is a sister to the good 2-y-o Gielgud and to the very smart Malinowski, and a half-sister to the dual Grade 1 winner Blush With Pride and to Sex Appeal - the dam of El Gran Senor and Try My Best. (Khaled Abdulla).

170 - MIGRATION
b.c. Rainbow Quest - Armeria (Northern Dancer).
March 5.

Brother to the 3-y-o Beleaguer, to the top-class 1992 2-y-o Group 1 1m Racing Post Trophy winner Armiger, (a somewhat disappointing 3-y-o despite winning the Chester Vase and finishing second in the Prix Lupin and St Leger), the useful 1996 2-y-o 8.1f and 8.5f winner and Group 1 Racing Post Trophy fourth Besiege and the useful 1996 3-y-o 10f winner Quota. The dam, a fair 3-y-o 10f winner at Windsor, is a half-sister to the Park Hill Stakes winner I Want To Be. The second dam, Frontonian (by Buckpasser), was placed third once over 10f in France and is a half-sister to Diomedia (dam of Media Starguest), Crown Treasure (dam of Glint of Gold and Diamond Shoal) and Carefully Hidden (dam of Ensconse). (Khaled Abdulla). *"A nice horse and a typical Rainbow Quest, he's quite well grown and will be a back-end two-year-old"* Roger informs me.

171 - OATH (IRE)
b.c. Fairy King - Sheer Audacity (Troy).
April 22. IR450,000Y. Goffs Orby.

Closely related to the top-class colt Pelder (by Be My Guest), winner of the Group 1 1m Gran Criterium, the Group 1 1m Premio Parioli and the Group 1 10.5f Prix Ganay and to the 1997 Irish 12f winner Night Raider (by Night Shift) and half-brother to the fairly useful 1m to 10.4f winner Sheer Danzig (by Roi Danzig) and the Italian seven-time winner El Rashid (by Jareer). The dam, placed twice in Italy, is closely related to the Ribblesdale Stakes winner Miss Petard - herself dam of 9 winners including the Park Hill Stakes winner Rejuvenate. The second dam, Miss Upward (by Alcide), won at 10f. *"A strong, medium-sized colt and a typical Fairy King, he should come to hand by late May. I'll start his career over six or seven furlongs"* Roger tells me.

172 - PEACE OF MIND
ch.c. Nashwan - De Stael (Nijinsky).
April 25.

Brother to the smart 12f listed Newmarket winner and subsequent Grade 1 Santa Ana Handicap and Grade 1 Santa Barbara Handicap winner Wandesta, closely related to the 1998 3-y-o Conical, the 1995 3-y-o Group 2 12f Prix du Conseil de Paris winner De Quest and the useful 10.3f to 14f winner Source of Light (all by Rainbow Quest) and half-brother to the smart French 10f to 15f winner Turners Hill (by Top Ville) and the fairly useful 1996 3-y-o 12f winner Fine Detail (by Shirley Heights). The dam, a fairly useful dual 7f winner at 2 yrs, is a sister to the high-class middle-distance colts Peacetime and Quiet Fling and a half-sister to the Cambridgeshire winner Intermission - herself dam of the good sprinter Interval . The second dam, Peace (by Klairon), won the 6f Blue Seal Stakes at 2 yrs and was second in the 1,000 Guineas Trial. (Khaled Abdulla). *"Peace Of Mind is a very nice horse and a very good mover. An exciting horse at this stage, if you didn't know his family you'd expect him to be early. As it is, I'd expect him to be out by July at the earliest. He is similar to Source Of Light regarding build and I like him a lot".*

173 - PORT MEADOW (IRE)
b.c. Common Grounds - Kharimata (Kahyasi).
March 14. Second foal. 45,000Y. Tattersalls October.

The dam, a minor winner at 3 yrs at Deauville, is a half-sister to 2 winners including the Group 3 15f Prix Berteux placed Kharizmi. The second dam, Khariyda (by Shakapour), won 5 races in France, Italy and America including the Group 1 Premio Lydia Tesio and the Grade 2 E P Taylor Stakes. *"This colt has a bit of a knee action and so may want soft ground. Although he's a late foal he looks quite mature. Nevertheless I should think he'll be an autumn two-year-old".*

174 - RUSTIC
b.f. Grand Lodge - Style Of Life (The Minstrel).
March 18. Sixth foal. IR100,000Y. Goffs Orby.

Half-sister to the 1997 Irish 7f and 9f winner Yudrik (by Lahib) and to the fairly useful 6f winner and Group 3 7f Criterion Stakes third Stylish Ways (by Thatching). The dam won over 6f and 7f in Ireland and is a sister to the listed 7f Ballycorus Stakes winner and Group 3 placed Seasonal Pickup. The second dam, Bubinka (by Nashua), won a Group 3 event over 1m in Italy. (Khaled Abdulla). *"A nice filly that will be reasonably early, she's quite mature, is going nicely at this stage and will be out in late May over six furlongs".*

175 - SHEBA SPRING (IRE)　　　　　　　　　b.f. Brief Truce - Shebasis (General Holme).
February 14. Sixth foal. 40,000Y. Tattersalls October.
Half-sister to the 3-y-o Bank House (by Zafonic), to the US winner of 2 races Busheto (by Be My Guest) and to a winner in Sweden by Bluebird. The dam is an unraced half-sister to 5 minor winners in the USA. The second dam, Annie Aaron (by Buffalo Lark), won twice in the USA and is a half-sister to the outstanding colt Alysheba (11 wins including nine Grade 1 stakes). *"This filly will start over seven furlongs. She's grown a lot and won't run until the back-end".*

176 - SMART SAVANNAH　　　　　　　　　b.c. Primo Dominie - High Savannah (Rousillon).
March 26. Third foal. 64,000Y. Tattersalls Houghton.
Half-brother to the useful 1997 2-y-o listed 6f Empress Stakes winner Lady In Waiting (by Kylian) and to the quite useful 1996 2-y-o 5.7f winner Sabina (by Prince Sabo). The dam, a fair middle-distance placed maiden, is a half-sister to the useful sprinters Maid For The Hills and Maid For Walking. The second dam, Stinging Nettle (by Sharpen Up), won the listed 6f Duke Of Edinburgh Stakes at 2 yrs and is a half-sister to the Royal Lodge Stakes winner Gairloch. *"A colt that hasn't been in my yard very long, he's a big, strong horse and a good mover"* says the trainer.

177 - TRELLIS BAY　　　　　　　　　b.f. Sadler's Wells - Bahamian (Mill Reef).
March 17.
Sister to the 1997 3-y-o New Abbey and half-sister to the very smart 1993 3-y-o filly Wemyss Bight (by Dancing Brave), a winner of five races from 9f (at 2 yrs) to 12f including the Group 1 Irish Oaks, Group 2 Prix de Malleret, Group 3 Prix Cleopatre and Group 3 Prix Penelope. The dam was a very useful winner of the Group 3 12f Lingfield Oaks Trial and was placed in the Prix de l'Esperance (disqualified from first place), Prix de Pomone, Park Hill Stakes and Princess Royal Stakes. She is a half-sister to the very useful winners Captivator, Eileen Jenny and Kasmayo. The second dam, Sorbus (by Busted), was disqualified after winning the Irish Oaks and was second in the Irish 1,000 Guineas, the Irish St Leger and the Yorkshire Oaks. (Khaled Abdulla). *"A filly very much for the end of the season and for next year".*

Paul Cole

178 - BORN FREE　　　　　　　　　ch.f. Caerleon - Culture Vulture (Timeless Moment).
February 1. First foal.
The dam, a very smart filly, won the Fillies Mile, the Prix Marcel Boussac and the French 1,000 Guineas - all Group 1 events. The second dam, Perfect Example (by Far North), is an unraced half-sister to the dams of the Group/Grade 1 winners Zilzal, Polish Precedent and Awe Inspiring. *"Small and sharp, she's not very big or scopey, but hopefully she'll be tough like her mother was"* says her trainer.

179 - CHAMBOLLE MUSIGNY (USA)　　　　　　b.f. Majestic Light - Bridal Up (Sharpen Up).
February 5. Fifth foal. $75,000Y. Keeneland September.
Sister to the US winner of 2 races Majestic Groom. The dam won 2 minor races in the USA at 3 yrs and is a half-sister to Alwuhush (Group 1 winner in Italy and the USA), Simply Majestic (seven Graded stakes wins in the USA), Husband and Pia Bride (listed winners in France). The second dam, Beaming Bride (by King Emperor), won 2 races at up to 9f at 4 yrs in the USA. (Prince Fahd Salman).

180 - CHICAGO BEAR (IRE)　　　　　　　ch.c. Night Shift - Last Drama (Last Tycoon).
May 6. Third foal. 50,000Y. Tattersalls October.
The dam, a winner of 3 races at 3 yrs in France and listed placed over 1m and 10f, is a sister to the US Grade 3 Selima Stakes winner Tycoon's Drama and a half-sister to 3 winners. The second dam, Drama (by Sir Ivor), won the Group 3 6f Greenlands Stakes at the Curragh. (Mr C Wright & Mrs J M Corbett) *"This is a nice, strong, medium-sized colt. He'll be out in late summer over six furlongs".*

181 - COPIOUS (IRE)　　　　　　　　ch.f. Generous - Flood (Riverman).
April 5. Sixth living foal.
Closely related to the very useful 1m (at 2 yrs) and 11.6f winner King Sound (by Caerleon) and half-sister to the Japanese winner of 3 races Trideed (by Shadeed) and the quite useful 1992 3-y-o 12f winner Mr Flood (by Al Nasr). The dam won once over 6f in the USA and is a half-sister to the Grade 1 Californian Stakes winner and Breeders Cup Mile second Sabona. The second dam, Hail Maggie (by Hail to Reason), was unplaced in her only race and is a sister to the top-class mare Trillion (dam of Triptych) and a half-sister to the dam of the Derby winner Generous. (Prince Fahd Salman).

45

182 - DIVORCE ACTION　　　　　　b.c. Common Grounds - Overdue Reaction (Be My Guest).
February 24. IR50,000Y. Goffs Orby.
Half-brother to the US stakes-placed winner Instant Strike (by Strike Gold), to the minor US winner Glo
Of Eden (by Far Out East), the German listed-placed winner Don't Go Crazy (by Houston), the modest
11.6f winner Atlantic Mist (by Elmaamul) and a winner in Hong Kong by Pursuit Of Love. The dam was
placed fourth once in the USA and is a half-sister to 5 winners including the US Grade 2 9f Bay
Meadows Handicap winner Wait Till Monday, the Triumph Hurdle winner Rare Holiday and the Group
3 C L Weld Park Stakes winner Token Gesture. The second dam, Temporary Lull (by Super Concorde),
is an unraced sister to the Nell Gwyn Stakes winner Martha Stevens. (Mr Frank Stella). *"An attractive
sort of horse that carries plenty of condition, he should make a two-year-old"*.

---

183 - FOCUS　　　　　　　　　　　　b.c. First Trump - Glimpse (Night Shift).
February 13. First foal. 47,000Y. Tattersalls October.
The dam, a fair 2-y-o 6f winner, is a half-sister to 3 minor winners here and abroad. The second dam,
Lovers Light (by Grundy), is an unplaced half-sister to the good broodmare Lady Moon (dam of the
Group winners Moon Cactus and Shining Steel). The third dam, Moonlight Night, won the Musidora
Stakes and was third in the Oaks. (Highclere Thoroughbred Racing Ltd). *"A nicely balanced colt, I like
him. He's got a good attitude and temperament"*.

---

184 - MADAM JIRY (USA)　　　　　　　　b.f. Rahy - Free Thinker (Shadeed).
April 7. Fourth foal. $130,000Y. Keeneland September.
Half-sister to the minor US 3-y-o winner Check Raise (by Wild Again). The dam, a useful 3-y-o 1m
winner in England and Italy, was second in the listed Derrinstown Stud 1,000 Guineas Trial and is a
half-sister to 3 winners. The second dam, Top Hope (by High Top), a very useful 2-y-o 7f winner and
second in the Group 3 12f Lancashire Oaks, is a half-sister to the smart colt Wylfa and to the Italian
Group 3 winner Pretty Pol - herself dam of the listed winner Polka Dancer. (Lord Lloyd-Webber). *"A bit
temperamental, but this filly goes very well and she'll be out in mid-summer"*.

---

185 - FREETOWN (IRE)　　　　　　b.c. Shirley Heights - Pageantry (Welsh Pageant).
April 25. IR120,000Y. Goffs Orby.
Closely related to the very useful Group 3 12f St Simon Stakes winner Up Anchor and half-brother to
the 1998 3-y-o Generosity (by Generous), the fair 10.8f winner Allegation and the triple US Grade 3
winner at around 8.5f Just Class (both by Dominion). The dam, a quite useful 5f and 6f placed 2-y-o,
is a half-sister to 4 winners including the Italian Derby winner Welnor. The second dam, Norfolk Light
(by Blakeney), was a quite useful 2-y-o 7f winner and stayed 12f. (Prince Fahd Salman).

---

186 - GREATER (USA)　　　　　　　　b.c. Dayjur - Nicer (Pennine Walk).
March 25. First foal.
The dam, winner of the Irish 1,000 Guineas and third in the Group 1 Premio Vittorio di Capua, is a
half-sister to 9 winners and to the unraced dam of the Group 2 Prix du Conseil de Paris winner Passing
Sale. The second dam, Everything Nice (by Sovereign Path), won the Group 3 Cherry Hinton Stakes
and the Group 3 Musidora Stakes. (Prince Fahd Salman).

---

187 - JAQUENETTA　　　　　　　　　b.f. Manila - Jadeeda (Silver Hawk).
March 19. First foal. 18,000Y. Tattersalls Houghton.
The dam, a winner of 6 races in the USA including a listed stakes, is a half-sister to 4 minor winners
in the USA. The second dam, Farasha (by Bay Express), won once at 2 yrs here and once in the USA.
(Sir George Meyrick & Lady Sondes). *"Jaquenetta goes well, would probably want six furlongs this
year and is more likely to win than not as a two-year-old"* says Paul.

---

188 - JIG (IRE)　　　　　　　　　　b.c. Catrail - River Jig (Irish River).
March 25. Sixth foal. 80,000Y. Tattersalls Houghton.
Half-brother to the very useful Group 3 5f Queen Mary Stakes and Group 3 7.3f Fred Darling Stakes
winner Dance Parade, to the fairly useful 1m winner Western Reel (both by Gone West) and the Grade
3 9f Bay Meadows Derby winner Ocean Queen (by Zilzal). The dam, a useful 2-y-o 9f winner here,
also won over 12f in Italy and is a half-sister to 5 winners including the dam of the Prix Gladiateur
winner Always Aloof. The second dam, Baronova (by Nijinsky), won once at 3 yrs. (Prince Fahd
Salman). *"A rather tall, leggy filly but she moves well and I like her"*.

189 - LENNOX
b.c. Bustino - Ivory Gull (Storm Bird).
February 5. Sixth foal. 21,000Y. Tattersalls October.
Half-brother to the US stakes-placed winner Mogul Madness (by Local Suitor) and the fair 3-y-o 11.1f winner Mister Kite (by Damister). The dam, a quite useful 2-y-o 6f winner, is a sister to the high-class sprinter Bluebird, winner of the Group 1 Kings Stand Stakes. The second dam, Ivory Dawn (by Sir Ivor), is an unraced half-sister to Javamine, dam of the top-class US colt Java Gold and of the Group 3 Doncaster Cup winner Spicy Story. (Sir George Meyrick, J Wates & P Cole). *"A nice horse, but a three-year-old type. He's big and growing into his frame".*

190 - LILA
b.f. Zafonic - Bint Pasha (Affirmed).
February 5. Sixth foal.
Half-sister to the very useful winner of 7 races - including the Group 3 10f Gran Premio Citta di Napoli - Revere (by Dancing Brave), to the fairly useful 1996 2-y-o 7f winner Ovation (by Generous) and the fairly useful 3-y-o dual 12f winner Monarch (by Sadlers Wells). The dam, a high class filly, won the Group 1 12f Yorkshire Oaks, Group 1 12f Prix Vermeille and the Group 2 10f Curragh Pretty Polly Stakes. She is the only foal of her dam, Icely Polite (by Graustark), a minor stakes winner at up to 1m and a half-sister to the dual Grade 1 stakes winner Taisez Vous. (Prince Fahd Salman). *"A very nice filly. Not an early two-year-old, but she's a big, long-striding filly".*

191 - LS LOWRY (USA)
b.c. Thorn Dance - Queluz (Saratoga Six).
February 1. Third foal. 40,000Y. Tattersalls October.
Half-brother to the quite useful 1997 2-y-o dual 6f winner Burlington House (by Housebuster). The dam was placed over 7f here and won twice at up to 9f in the USA. The second dam, Mariella (by Roberto), a useful middle-distance filly, won 3 races and was Group-placed both here and in the USA. She is a half-sister to 10 winners including the dams of the US Grade 1 winner Too Chic (herself dam of two US Grade 1 winners), the Gold Cup winner Sadeem and the Champion Stakes second Prima Voce. (Richard Green (Fine Paintings)). *"He's had a slight setback, but physically he looks a very nice type of colt".*

192 - MAGNO (USA)
b.c. El Gran Senor - Nice Noble (Vaguely Noble).
May 4. $100,000Y. Keeneland September.
Closely related to the minor US winner of 3 races Landholder (by Dixieland Band) and half-brother to 6 winners including the stakes-placed winner of 6 races Nice Cresta (by Cresta Rider). The dam, a winner in Italy, is a half-sister to 9 winners including the Irish 1,000 Guineas winner Nicer and to the unraced dam of the Prix du Conseil de Paris winner Passing Sale. The second dam, Everything Nice (by Sovereign Path), won the Cherry Hinton Stakes and the Musidora Stakes. (Prince Fahd Salman). *"A big, strong horse with scope, he'll be a back-end two-year-old".*

193 - MARKAN (USA)
ch.c. Affirmed - Norma (Procida).
March 24. First foal. 170,000Y. Tattersalls Houghton.
The dam, a minor winner of 9 races in the USA, is a half-sister to 5 winners including the Grade 1 9f Gamely Handicap and listed 1m Prix Coronation winner Metamorphose. The second dam, Normia (by Northfields), won in France and was third in the listed 1m Prix de la Calonne and is a half-sister to 5 winners including the US Grade 2 San Luis Obispo Handicap winner Regal Bearing. (Prince Fahd Salman). *"This colt goes well, I like him and he'll be a nice horse in mid-summer over seven furlongs and a mile".*

194 - MENTEITH (USA)
b.c. Dehere - Bunka Bunka (Raja Baba).
February 20. Third foal. $60,000Y. Keeneland September.
The dam, a winner of 6 races in the USA including a stakes event over 6f at 3 yrs, is a sister to the US Grade 3 winner Far Out East and to 2 stakes-placed winners and a half-sister to 10 winners. The second dam, Bambar (by Ambehaving), is a half-sister to Goofed (the dam of Lyphard and Nobiliary). (Sir George Meyrick). *"A very big, strong and scopey colt, he'll make a two-year-old by mid-season".*

195 - NEWSCASTER
b.c. Bluebird - Sharp Girl (Sharpman).
May 3. 30,000Y. Tattersalls October.
Half-brother to the fair 1997 7f placed 2-y-o Robsart (by Robellino), to the quite useful 8.5f all-weather (at 2 yrs) and 11.4f winner Tart (by Tragic Role), the fair winner of 12 races from 9.2f to 12f Gold Blade, the French 1m and 10.6f winner Razor's Edge (both by Rousillon) and the French and US winner Lodoiska (by Polish Precedent). The dam won over 10f in France and stayed 10f, was second in the

Group 3 Prix Minerve and is a full or half-sister to 7 winners including the Group 3 Prix du Calvados winner Arousal. The second dam, Model Girl (by Lyphard), won twice in France and is a half-sister to 7 winners including the dams of the King George winner Belmez and the Prix de Diane winner Lypharita. *"He's had a slight setback and is only cantering at the moment, but he's a two-year-old type alright"* Paul tells me.

196 - PRESENT LAUGHTER
b.c. Cadeaux Genereux - Ever Genial (Brigadier Gerard).
April 19. 28,000Y. Tattersalls October.
Half-brother to Receptionist (by Reference Point), a winner of 3 races at 3 yrs at up to 18.2f and to the 10f winners Highly Praised (by Shirley Heights) and Evert (by Kris) - all quite useful. The dam was a smart filly and a winner of 4 races at up to 1m including the Group 3 Hungerford Stakes and the Group 3 May Hill Stakes. The second dam, Shorthouse (by Habitat), won twice at 2 yrs including the listed 7f Sandleford Priory Stakes and is a sister to the Group 3 Princess Royal Stakes winner One Way Street (herself dam of the Group winners Red Route, Grape Tree Road and Windsor Castle). (Lord Portman). *" He won't be early but this is a nice, big, very strong colt with plenty of scope"* the trainer asserts.

197 - RED SEA
b.c. Barathea - Up Anchor (Slip Anchor).
February 9. Second foal. 170,000Y. Tattersalls Houghton.
Half-brother to the extremely promising 1997 2-y-o 7.1f winner Fleetwood (by Groom Dancer). The dam won four races including the Group 3 12f St Simon Stakes, was third in the Italian Oaks and is a half-sister to Just Class, a useful winner over 7f and 1m here and subsequently winner of three Grade 3 events in the USA at around 8.5f. The second dam, Pageantry (by Welsh Pageant), was placed over 5f and 6f at 2 yrs, her only season to race, and is a sister to the Italian Derby winner Welnor. (Prince Fahd Salman). *"A very strong colt, not over big, he'll be out in mid-summer. I like him a lot".*

198 - SILVER APPLE (IRE)
gr.c. Danehill - Moon Festival (Be My Guest).
May 3. Third living foal. IR80,000Y. Goffs Orby.
Half-brother to the 1997 9f placed 2-y-o Moonlight Truce (by Brief Truce). The dam, a fair 10f and 12f placed maiden, is a sister to the fair middle-distance winner Moon Carnival and a half-sister to 6 winners including Moon Madness (St Leger and Grand Prix de Saint-Cloud), Sheriff's Star (Coronation Cup and Grand Prix de Saint-Cloud) and Lucky Moon (Goodwood Cup). The second dam, Castle Moon (by Kalamoun), won from 1m to 13f, is a sister to the very smart middle-distance stayer Castle Keep and a half-sister to the Ascot Gold Cup winner Ragstone. (Mr Anthony Speelman). *"A big, strong, scopey horse, I'm pleased with him. He won't be early, but he has a good action and is a nice individual".*

199 - SINGLE CURRENCY
b.c. Barathea - Kithanga (Darshaan).
February 3. First foal. 160,000Y. Tattersalls Houghton.
The dam was a smart winner of 3 races including the Group 3 12f St Simon Stakes and the listed 11.9f Galtres Stakes. The second dam, Kalata (by Assert), ran once unplaced in France and is a half-sister to the Group 3 Premio Roma Vecchia winner Karkisiya and to the dams of the Derby winner Kahyasi, the Yorkshire Oaks winner Key Change and the Prix Cleopatre winner Kalajana. (Mrs S Arbib & Lady Harris). *"A bit backward now, he'll be a middle-distance colt next year, but Single Currency is a very nice horse that will start over seven furlongs in late-summer. A very big, scopey colt with a good attitude and good legs, he's certainly one to follow".*

200 - STRATEGIC COURSE (USA)
b.c. Alleged - Danlu (Danzig).
April 3.
Brother to the high-class Group 1 14f Irish St Leger, Group 1 12f Gran Premio di Milano, Group 2 12.5f Grand Prix de Deauville and Group 3 12f John Porter Stakes winner Strategic Choice (by Alleged) and half-brother to the 3-y-o Sure Dancer (by Affirmed), the 1m all-weather winner Suvalu (by Woodman) and the fairly useful 1995 2-y-o 7f winner Swift Fandango (by Lear Fan). The dam won over 1m at 2 yrs and 8.5f at 3 yrs in Ireland and is a sister to the Group 2 6f Goldene Peitsche winner Nicholas and the listed 1m Schwarzgold Rennen winner Arbusha. The second dam, Lulu Mon Amour (by Tom Rolfe), won twice at around 1m in the USA and is a half-sister to the smart winners Nordance and Shudance. (Mr M Arbib). *"A very big and backward colt, he'll just have the one run at the back-end".*

201 - STRIKE A BLOW (USA)
b.c. Red Ransom - Lilian Bayliss ((Sadler's Wells).
March 31. Fourth foal. $97,000Y. Keeneland September.
Half-brother to the 1997 Italian 3-y-o winner Pariofige (by Alleged). The dam, a useful 7f (at 2 yrs) and 9f winner, was third in the Group 3 Nell Gwyn Stakes, is a sister to the very useful French 2-y-o 6f

winner Ernani and a half-sister to 12 winners including the high-class Prix Eclipse and Prix Quincey winner Phydilla (by Lyphard) and the Irish Derby second Observation Post (by Shirley Heights). The second dam, Godzilla (by Gyr), a useful winner of 5 races in Italy at up to 7.5f, is a half-sister to 8 winners including the dam of the Group 1 Gran Criterium winner Grease. (Mr J S Gutkin). *"This is a precocious two-year-old type that goes well and is very sharp".*

---

202 - SUNDAE GIRL (USA)

b.f. Green Dancer - Charmie Carmie (Lyphard).
May 19.

Half-sister to the quite useful 6f and 7f winner Himmah (by Habitat) and to the Peruvian Champion Faaz (by Fappiano). The dam was placed 9 times in the USA and is a half-sister to numerous winners including the triple Grade 1 winner Chris Evert (the grandam of Chief's Crown) and All Rainbows (dam of the Kentucky Derby winner Winning Colors). The second dam, Miss Carmie (by T.V. Lark), won 3 races in the USA including a stakes event over 6f at 2 yrs. (Mr C Wright). *"A very attractive filly and well balanced, Sundae Girl will come to hand early and be suited by six furlongs to start with".*

---

203 - SUPER DOLLAR (IRE)

ch.c. Great Commotion - L'Americaine (Verbatim).
March 30. 62,000Y. Tattersalls October.

Half-brother to the 1997 French 3-y-o winner and listed-placed Libria (by Bering), to minor winners in France by Fools Holme, Night Shift, Priolo and Valiyar and to a winner in Belgium by Tirol. The dam won a minor event in France at 3 yrs and is a half-sister to 10 winners. The second dam, La Francaise (by Jim French), was placed in the USA and is a half-sister to the Group 3 winner and smart sire Alzao. (Mrs S Arbib & Lady Harris). *"Definitely a two-year-old type, this colt goes well and is very athletic".*

---

204 - TOP ORDER (USA)

b.f. Dayjur - Victoria Cross (Spectacular Bid).
May 3.

Half-sister to the 1992 2-y-o Grade 3 6f Tremont Breeders Cup Stakes winner and Grade 1 6.5f Hopeful Stakes third England Expects (by Topsider) and the fairly useful 1997 13.8f and 14f winner Valagalore (by Generous). The dam is an unraced half-sister to 6 stakes winners in the USA including the Grade 1 winners Hero's Honor and Sea Hero and the Grade 2 winners Glowing Honor and Wild Applause - the latter also dam of the Grade 1 winner Eastern Echo. The second dam, Glowing Tribute (by Graustark), won 9 races in the USA including the Grade 2 9f Diana Handicap (twice) and is a half-sister to the dam of the Group 2 Blandford Stakes winner Magesterial. (Prince Fahd Salman). *"A decent sized filly, she's had a slight setback but I like her. She's very racy and I think she'll do well as a two-year-old".*

---

205 - WORSHIP (USA)

ch.f. Irish River - Pedestal (High Line).
March 28. Fifth foal. 100,000Y. Tattersalls Houghton.

Half-sister to the French-trained 3-y-o Kowtow (by Shadeed), to the quite useful 7f winner Lionize (by Storm Cat) and the modest 10f and hurdles winner Plinth (by Dowsing). The dam, unplaced in her only race, is a half-sister to the Queen Mary Stakes winner Pushy (herself dam of the smart fillies Bluebook and Myself), to the Japan Cup winner Jupiter Island and the high-class 2-y-o Precocious. The second dam, Mrs Moss (by Reform), won over 5f at 2 yrs. (Lord Lloyd-Webber). *"We like this filly. Not over-big but quite strong, she goes well and would want six furlongs to start".*

Robert Collet

---

206 - TENDER IS THE NIGHT (IRE)

b.f. Barathea - Mill Princess (Mill Reef).
April 23.

Closely related to the quite useful 1993 2-y-o 6f winner Flowerdrum and to the Irish 1m (at 2 yrs) and 10f winner Moon Flower (both by Sadlers Wells) and half-sister to numerous winners including the top-class colt and good sire Last Tycoon, winner of the Grade 1 Breeders Cup Mile, the Group 1 Kings Stand Stakes and the Group 1 William Hill Sprint Championship, the useful Group 3 5f Prix du Bois winner The Perfect Life (both by Try My Best) and the very useful Group 2 6f Premio Melton and Group 3 6f Goldene Peitsche winner Astronef. The dam won over 10f at 2 yrs in France and is a half-sister to the Irish Sweeps Derby winner Irish Ball and the top-class broodmare Irish Bird, dam of the classic winners Assert, Bikala and Eurobird. The second dam, Irish Lass II (by Sayajirao), won the 12f Prix de Minerve and was a sister to the Irish Oaks, Irish St Leger and Yorkshire Oaks winner Lynchris.

207 - THE GOOD LIFE (IRE)   b.f. Rainbow Quest - Once In My Life (Lomond).
February 18. Third foal.
Half-sister to the modest 1997 8.5f all-weather placed Genius (by Lycius). The dam, a very useful filly, won three races in France at 2 and 3 yrs including the Group 3 1m Prix de Sandringham and was placed in the Group 2 1m Prix d'Astarte and the Grade 2 All Along Stakes in the USA. She is closely related to 2 winners including the French 2,000 Guineas winner No Pass No Sale and a half-sister to 4 winners. The second dam, No Disgrace (by Djakao), won once in France at 2 yrs over 7.5f, was fourth in the Group 3 Prix Chloe and the Group 3 Prix Cleopatre and is a half-sister to the dam of the US Grade 2 San Bernardino Handicap and Group 2 Supreme Stakes winner Anshan.

Con Collins

208 - DELPHI (IRE)   ch.c. Grand Lodge - Euridice (Woodman).
March 4. First foal. IR35,000Y. Goffs Orby.
The dam, a modest 3-y-o 9.7f winner, is a half-sister to 3 winners. The second dam, Arctic Kite (by North Stoke), won 2 races at 3 yrs in the USA at up to 7f and is a half-sister to 12 minor winners. *"A big, strong colt, he'll be out in late summer and would be suited by a mile this year".*

209 - DELRAY (IRE)   b.c. Wolfhound - Euromill (Shirley Heights).
March 16. Sixth foal. IR45,000Y. Goffs Orby.
Half-brother to the 1997 2-y-o Tadwiga, winner of the 6.3f Goffs £100,000 Challenge and to the useful Irish 2-y-o listed 7f Orby Stakes winner and Group 2 Premio Ribot fourth Bartok (both by Fairy King). The dam, a middle-distance stayer, won twice in Ireland and is a half-sister to 6 winners including the Group 2 placed Luchiroverte. The second dam, Green Lucia (by Green Dancer), won a listed race in Ireland, was placed in the Yorkshire Oaks and the Irish Oaks and is a half-sister to the top-class middle-distance colt Old Vic. *"Delray will be out in late spring, is a stocky looking colt and will want six furlongs to start with"* says his trainer.

210 - SERINA   ch.f. Rainbow Quest - Green Lucia (Green Dancer).
February 23. 30,000Y. Tattersalls Houghton.
Half-sister to the smart 12f colt Luchiroverte, to the fairly useful 3-y-o 11.8f to 14.6f winner Acanthus (both by Slip Anchor), the very useful 2-y-o 7f Houghton Stakes winner Muthaiga (by Kalaglow), the 14.1f winner Ela-Yie-Mou, the 1996 2-y-o 7f winner Kris Green, the 12f winner Korambi - all fairly useful - (all by Kris) and minor winners by Habitat and Shirley Heights. The dam, a half-sister to the outstanding middle-distance colt Old Vic, won over 6f and 10f, was second in the Group 1 Yorkshire Oaks and third in the Irish Oaks. The second dam, Cockade (by Derring-Do), won over 1m, is a sister to High Top and Camden Town and has also bred the smart colt Splash of Colour. *"This is a very nice filly and despite her stout pedigree I think she'll make a two-year-old alright".*

Luca Cumani

211 - AEGEAN DREAM (IRE)   b.f. Royal Academy - L'Ideale (Alysheba).
January 26. First foal. 25,000Y. Tattersalls Houghton.
The dam, unplaced twice in France, is a half-sister to the Group 1 Grand Criterium winner Loup Solitaire and to the French 2,000 Guineas second Loup Sauvage. The second dam, Louveterie (by Nureyev), won the Group 3 9.5f Prix Vanteaux, was second in the Prix de Diane and the Prix Saint-Alary and is a half-sister to the French Group 2 winner Lascaux and the Group 3 winners Leonardo da Vinci, L'ile du Reve and Legend Of France. (Theobalds Stud). *"Pretty backward at the moment (early April) Aegean Dream is a sweet enough filly but she may only have the one run at the back-end of the season" Luca informs me. In addition to the horses in this section, he also has three two-year-olds amongst the 'Early Types'.*

212 - AVEBURY   b.c. Fairy King - Circle Of Chalk (Kris).
March 5. 54,000Y. Tattersalls Houghton.
Half-brother to the fair 1997 7f placed 2-y-o Wandering Wolf (by Wolfhound). The dam was a fair 3-y-o 10.7f winner in the French provinces and is a sister to the useful 1994 3-y-o French listed 12f winner From Beyond. The second dam, Magic of Life (by Seattle Slew), was a smart winner of 3 races from 5f to 1m at 3 yrs including the Group 1 Coronation Stakes and is out of the US Grade 2 winner Larida - herself a half-sister to Miss Oceana (winner of six Grade 1 races in the USA). (Sackville Syndicate).

"A likeable sort, Avebury should be running by mid-summer. He's a medium-sized, classy-looking horse and I think he'll do well from August onwards. I'll probably start him over six furlongs" says Luca.

213 - CAJOLE (IRE)
ch.f. Barathea - Friendly Persuasion (General Assembly).
March 14. Third foal. 80,000Y. Tattersalls December.
Half-sister to the fair 1997 7f placed 2-y-o Anemos (by Be My Guest) and to the minor 1996 Irish 3-y-o 12f winner Friendly Bird (by Bluebird). The dam won five races in Ireland including the listed 12f Trigo Stakes and is a half-sister to 4 minor winners. The second dam, Cri de Coeur (by Lyphard), won once at 2 yrs. (Sackville Syndicate). *"A nice filly but very big and backward, Cajole may just have the odd run in the autumn".*

214 - CINDESTI (IRE)
b.c. Barathea - Niamh Cinn Oir (King Of Clubs).
March 25. Fourth foal. IR77,000Y. Goffs Orby.
Half-brother to a 3-y-o in Hong Kong by Wolfhound. The dam won over 12f and 14f in Ireland and is a half-sister to 5 winners including the Sun Chariot Stakes winner Home on the Range - herself the dam of the outstanding colt Reference Point. The second dam, Great Guns (by Busted), won 6 races at 3 yrs. (Sheikh Mohammed). *"Cindesti is quite a good-looking horse, rather big and similar to his sire in make and shape. He should be ready to run by August over seven furlongs".*

215 - CRISIS (IRE)
b.c. Second Set - Special Offer (Shy Groom).
April 26. First foal. 33,000Y. Tattersalls October.
The dam was placed three times over 10f in Ireland and is a half-sister to 4 winners including the Group 2 10f Tattersalls Rogers Gold Cup winner Cockney Lass. The second dam, Big Bugs Bomb (by Skymaster), won 4 races and was listed-placed in Ireland. (Mrs Angie Silver). *"Not a bad looking type, Crisis should be suited by six or seven furlongs and be ready to run in late summer".*

216 - DALIAPOUR (IRE)
b.c. Sadler's Wells - Dalara (Doyoun).
March 10.
The dam, a smart filly and winner of the Group 2 12.5f Prix de Royallieu, is a half-sister to the French Derby winner and high-class sire Darshaan and to the Prix Vermeille winner Darara. The second dam, Delsy (by Abdos), won over 12f and was third in the Prix de Pomone. (H H Aga Khan). *Luca seems to like this colt a lot. "Daliapour could be a very nice colt indeed, he's very good-looking and has a touch of class. He's going pretty well at the moment, is strong and well-forward".*

217 - DANCING KING (IRE)
b.c. Fairy King - Zariysha (Darshaan).
January 24. First foal. IR95,000Y. Goffs Orby.
The dam is an unraced sister to the Group 3 Greenham Stakes winner Zayyani and a half-sister to 3 winners including the dam of the listed Ballyroan Stakes winner Zafzala. The second dam, Zariya (by Blushing Groom), won twice over 7f at 2 yrs. (Mrs M J Dawson). *"A good-looking colt but sidelined at the moment due to an injury".*

218 - DARK VICTOR
b.c. Cadeaux Genereux - Dimmer (Kalaglow).
March 25. Fifth foal. 28,000Y. Tattersalls Houghton.
Half-brother to the 3-y-o Fairer (by Fairy King). The dam, a useful filly, won 2 races at 3 yrs over 10f including the listed Atalanta Stakes and is a half-sister to 5 winners including the Group 1 International Stakes and Group 2 Tattersalls Rogers Gold Cup winner Shady Heights. The second dam, Vaguely, (by Bold Lad, Ire), was a fairly useful 1m and 10f winner. (Umm Qarn Racing). *"Pretty backward, he's from a staying family and despite being by Cadeaux Genereux I don't expect him to be a sprinter. He'll have a run or two later on this year".*

219 - DRIFT OF SANDS
b.c. Exit To Nowhere - Douceur (Shadeed).
May 11. Fifth foal. 20,000Y. Tattersalls October.
Half-brother to the 3-y-o Mach One (by Sanglamore) and to the modest 1996 4-y-o 10f winner It'sthebusiness (by Most Welcome). The dam, a winner at 3 yrs in France over 9.5f, is a half-sister to 7 winners. The second dam, Jamila (by Sir Gaylord), is a placed half-sister to the Prix Lupin winner No Lute and the French 1,000 Guineas winner River Lady. (Mr M Marchetti). *"Quite a nice colt but pretty big and backward, Drift Of Sands won't be ready to run until the autumn".*

220 - EDEN
b.f. Polish Precedent - Isle Of Flame (Shirley Heights).
March 21. First foal. 72,000Y. Tattersalls October.
The dam is an unraced daughter of the minor US stakes winner and Group 3 Irish 1,000 Guineas Trial second Burning Issue (by Persian Bold), herself a half-sister to the Middle Park Stakes winner Balla

Cove and the Irish listed winners Blasted Heath and Tribal Rite. (Mr L Marinopoulos). *"Polish Precedent's don't make 2-y-o's usually and although this filly is likeable enough she won't be ready until the back-end", says her trainer.*

---

221 - ERMINE
ch.f. Cadeaux Genereux - Nibbs Point (Sure Blade).
February 6. Third foal.

Half-sister to the useful 1997 2-y-o 1m and 3-y-o 9f winner Border Arrow (by Selkirk) and the modest 2m winner Pen Friend (by Robellino). The dam, a very useful filly, won the listed 11.9f Galtres Stakes at York and is a half-sister to the useful 2-y-o 7f and 1m winner Prince Ibrahim. The second dam, Fanny's Cove (by Mill Reef), was a fairly useful 10f winner of her only start. (Lord Halifax). *"Ermine is quite a likeable filly. On pedigree it's difficult to know what her trip will be but she should be running by mid-summer".*

---

222 - FRENZY
b.f. Zafonic - Free Guest (Be My Guest).
April 15.

Half-sister to the very useful filly Shamshir, winner of the Group 1 Brent Walker Fillies Mile and placed in the Oaks, Yorkshire Oaks, Nassau Stakes and Musidora Stakes, to the fair 1997 3-y-o 9f winner Behind the Scenes (both by Kris), the useful 1996 1m to 12f winner Freequent (by Rainbow Quest), the useful 1992 3-y-o 12f winner and Lupe Stakes third Fern and the hurdles winner French (by Rousillon). The dam was a high-class winner of nine races from 2 to 4 yrs and from 7f to 12f, notably the Sun Chariot Stakes (twice), the Nassau Stakes and the Princess Royal Stakes. The second dam, Fremanche (by Jim French), won over 9f in Italy on her only outing. (Fittocks Stud). *"This is the first time Free Guest has produced something that can be described as big and backward. She won't be running for some considerable time".*

---

223 - KUSTER
b.c. Indian Ridge - Ustka (Lomond).
January 21. Third foal. 170,000Y. Tattersalls Houghton.

Half-brother to the 3-y-o Yajree (by Selkirk) and to the quite useful 10f and 12f winner Travelmate (by Persian Bold). The dam, a modest 3-y-o 7f winner, is closely related to the smart Prix Royal-Oak, Yorkshire Cup and Ormonde Stakes winner Braashee and to the US Grade 3 winner Adam Smith and a half-sister to the Nell Gwyn Stakes winner Ghariba - both very useful. The second dam, Krakow (by Malinowski), won twice over 7f at 3 yrs and is a half-sister to 6 winners including the listed winner Leipzig and the dams of the Group 3 winners Caerefolie, Gouriev and Run And Gun. (Lord Vestey). *"A good-looking horse and though slightly immature he should be running as a 2-y-o".*

---

224 - MOVIE STAR (IRE)
b.f. Barathea - Mary Astor (Groom Dancer).
March 5. First foal. FF680,000. Deauville August.

The dam, a minor winner of 4 races at 3 yrs in France, is a half-sister to 10 winners including the Group 2 Prix de Royallieu winner Passionaria and the Group 3 Prix du Bois winner Kanmary (herself dam of the Breeders Cup Sprint winner Lit de Justice and the Derby third Colonel Collins). The second dam, Djallybrook (by Djakao), a minor French 11f winner, is a half-sister to the dam of the Prix du Cadran winner Trebrook. (Mr Robert H Smith). *"Movie Star is a nice sort of filly that should be running by August or September. I quite like her" says Luca.*

---

225 - NEUTRALITY (IRE)
ch.f. Common Grounds - Azallya (Habitat).
February 19. FF380,000. Deauville August.

Half-sister to the 1992 2-y-o 6f winner Serious (by Shadeed). The dam, a French 8.3f winner at 3 yrs, is a half-sister to the Group 3 12f Prix Minerve winner Anitra's Dance - herself dam of the Group 3 Prix Fille de l'Air winner Solveig. The second dam, Azurella (by High Hat), won the Group 3 Prix de Malleret and the Group 3 Prix de Royaumont. (Mr Robert H Smith). *"Quite a nice filly that should be running over six or seven furlongs this summer".*

---

226 - PARABLE
b.c. Midyan - Top Table (Shirley Heights).
May 28. Third foal. 53,000Y. Doncaster St Leger.

Half-brother to the fairly useful 1997 2-y-o 6f winner Krispy Knight (by Kris). The dam, a modest 12f placed maiden, is a half-sister to the very smart 1m listed winner and Group 2 Queen Anne Stakes second Centre Stalls. The second dam, Lora's Guest (by Be My Guest), was a useful 7f winner and a sister to the 1,000 Guineas and Sussex Stakes winner On The House. (Sackville Syndicate). *"Parable is a very good-looking horse that should be running by September. I think he'll want a mile to start with".*

227 - PRESTIGEOUS (USA)   ch.f. Rainbow Quest - Danseur Fabuleux (Northern Dancer). March 29.

Closely related to the great 1991 2-y-o Arazi (by Blushing Groom), winner of the Breeders Cup Juvenile, Prix Robert Papin, Prix Morny, Prix de la Salamandre and Ciga Grand Criterium - all Group 1 events between 5f and 8.5f, and subsequently winner of the 1m Prix Omnium and 1m Prix du Rond-Point at 3 yrs and half-sister to the fairly useful 1993 2-y-o Evry 1m winner Columbus Day (by Mr Prospector), the French 2-y-o 7.5f winner Fortrose (by Forty Niner) and the French 2-y-o 6f winner River Sunset (by Irish River). The dam was placed in the Group 3 12f Prix de Minerve and is closely related to the very useful 12f winner Fabulous Dancer. The second dam, Fabuleux Jane (by Le Fabuleux), won 4 races including the Group 3 Prix de Pomone and is a half-sister to Formidable and Ajdal. (Sheikh Mohammed).

---

228 - QUESTABELLE   ch.f. Rainbow Quest - Bella Colora (Bellypha). 470,000 Y. Tattersalls Houghton.

Sister to the modest 1997 10f placed 3-y-o Arco Colora (by Rainbow Quest) and half-sister to the high-class Group 2 10f Prince of Wales's Stakes and Group 3 10f Brigadier Gerard Stakes winner Stagecraft, the useful 1997 4-y-o listed 9f winner Balalaika, the quite useful 1993 3-y-o 9f winner Bella Ballerina (all by Sadlers Wells) and the very useful dual 3-y-o 1m listed stakes winner Hyabella (by Shirley Heights). The dam, from an excellent family, won four races including the Group 2, 9.2f Prix de l'Opera and the Group 3, 7f Waterford Candelabra Stakes and was a very close third in the 1,000 Guineas. She is a half-sister to the Irish Oaks winner Colorspin, herself dam of the top-class middle-distance colt Opera House, to the Irish Champion Stakes winner Cezanne and to the very useful filly Rappa Tap Tap. The second dam, Reprocolor (by Jimmy Reppin), was a very useful winner of the 12f Lingfield Oaks Trial, the Lancashire Oaks and the Pretty Polly Stakes. (Helena Springfield Ltd). *Questabelle was very backward and still not in the yard in early April.*

---

229 - REDONES (USA)   b.c. Seeking The Gold - Red Slippers (Nureyev). April 11.

Half-sister to the 4-y-o Redbridge (by Alleged), a very promising third over 11f on his only start at 3 yrs. The dam, a very useful 7f (at 2 yrs) and Group 2 10f Sun Chariot Stakes winner, is a sister to the smart Derby third Romanov and is closely related to the Oaks and Irish Derby winner Balanchine. The second dam, Morning Devotion (by Affirmed), was a useful 2-y-o 6f winner and was third in the Hoover Fillies Mile. (Sheikh Mohammed). *"Redones seems OK at this stage" (early April) says Luca. "A likeable colt, he's a bit weak but should be ready to run by August or September over seven furlongs or a mile".*

---

230 - RING THE RELATIVES   b.f. Bering - Relatively Special (Alzao). February 2. First foal. 50,000Y. Tattersalls Houghton.

The dam won the Group 3 7f Rockfel Stakes at 2 yrs and was placed in the Irish 1,000 Guineas, the Nassau Stakes and the Sun Chariot Stakes. She is a half-sister to the Dante Stakes winner Alnasr Alwasheek and the Sun Chariot Stakes winner One So Wonderful. The second dam, Someone Special (by Habitat), a useful 3-y-o 7f winner, was third in the Coronation Stakes and is a sister to the top-class miler Milligram. (Helena Springfield Ltd). *"Although she came into the yard rather late, this filly is from a family I know very well and I expect her to be a good sort" Luca tells me.*

---

231 - SALLIGRAM   b.f. Salse - Alligram (Alysheba). April 17. 20,000Y. Tattersalls October.

Half-sister to the 3-y-o Kissogram (by Caerleon). The dam ran three times unplaced from 7f to 8.2f at 3 yrs and is a half-sister to the moderate 3-y-o 7f winner Footlight Fantasy. The second dam, the top-class filly Milligram (by Mill Reef), winner of the Group 1 1m Queen Elizabeth II Stakes, the Group 2 1m Coronation Stakes and the Group 2 Waterford Crystal Mile, is a half-sister to the Coronation Stakes placed Someone Special - herself dam of the Group winners Alnasr Alwasheek and Relatively Special. The third dam, One in a Million (by Rarity), won the 1,000 Guineas and the Coronation Stakes. (Fittocks Stud). *"Quite a decent sort, Salligram will probably be running by September-October time over seven furlongs or a mile".*

---

232 - SEEK   br.c. Rainbow Quest - Souk (Ahonoora). April 5. Fourth foal. 50,000Y. Tattersalls Houghton.

Half-brother to the 3-y-o Cellini (by Caerleon), to the quite useful 1997 3-y-o 10.5f winner Shouk (by Shirley Heights) and the very useful 10f and 12f listed winner Puce (by Darshaan). The dam, a fairly useful 7f winner, was listed placed over 1m and is a half-sister to 3 winners. The second dam, Soumana (by Pharly), is an unraced half-sister to the French 1,000 Guineas winner Dumka (dam of the Group winners Doyoun, Dalsaan, Dolpour and Dafayna). (Fittocks Stud). *"A nice-enough horse, though backward, Seek is much more a horse for the future. The family does better as three or four-year-olds".*

233 - SIGNIFY
b.c. Marju - Windmill Princess (Gorytus).
April 4. Fourth foal. IR21,000Y. Goffs Orby.
Half-brother to the fair 1997 2-y-o 6f winner Cosmic Countess (by Lahib) and the fairly useful dual 7f winner Cosmic Prince (by Teenoso). The dam, a poor 1m and 11f placed maiden, is a half-sister to 4 winners and to the unraced dam of the September Stakes winner Spartan Shareef. The second dam, Cley (by Exbury), was a quite useful 12f winner and a half-sister to the Derby winners Blakeney and Morston. (Mr M J Dawson). *"A likeable sort, if quite big and a bit weak. He'll be a better 3-y-o but should run once or twice this year".*

234 - SILVER ROBIN
b.c. Silver Hawk - Wedge Musical (What A Guest).
May 10. Fifth foal. 55,000Y. Tattersalls Houghton.
Brother to the useful Group 3 2m Queens Vase winner Silver Wedge and half-brother to the 3-y-o Wandering Man (by Leo Castelli). The dam won over 6.5f in France and 1m in the USA. The second dam, Musical Soul (by Youth), won twice in France and is a half-sister to 5 minor winners in France and the USA. (W V, M W & Mrs E S Robins). *"Quite a nice colt, he's a staying type but should be running as a two-year-old in August or September".*

235 - SINGLE SHOT (USA)
b.c. Hermitage - Bourbon Miss (Smile).
January 21. First foal. 82,000Y. Tattersalls October.
The dam is an unraced half-sister to four minor winners in the USA. The second dam, Pointe du Jour (by Invested Power), won 3 races in Venezuela and is a sister to the Venezuelan Grade 2 winner Invested Gail. (Sackville Syndicate). *"Single Shot is a nice individual that should be on the racetrack by July".*

236 - SIVA
ch.f. Cadeaux Genereux - Toast (Be My Guest).
April 17. Third foal. 36,000Y. Tattersalls October.
Half-sister to the poor 12f and 14f placed Action Stations (by High Estate). The dam is an unplaced sister to the Group 2 10f Prix Eugene Adam and Group 3 1m Prix de la Jonchere winner What A Guest and a half-sister to the Group 3 Dee Stakes winner Infantry. The second dam, Princess Tiara (by Crowned Prince), won the listed 7f Somerville Tattersall Stakes at 2 yrs and is a half-sister to 8 minor winners. (Mr L Marinopoulos). *"A nice filly, Siva has grown a lot, is a bit leggy and needs to strengthen but she should be running by August" says Luca.*

237 - ST TRINITY
b.f. Distant Relative - Bint Secreto (Secreto).
March 12. Fifth foal. 22,000Y. Tattersalls October.
Half-sister to the minor 1994 French 3-y-o winner Secreto Slip (by Slip Anchor) and the minor 1995 French dual 2-y-o winner Secreto Bold (by Never So Bold). The dam was placed twice in France and is a half-sister to 7 winners including the US stakes winner of 10 races Full Tigress - herself dam of the US dual Grade 1 winner Over All. The second dam, Miss Fullhouse (by Poker), won 3 races in the USA and is a half-sister to the dam of the champion US 3-y-o colt Conquistador Cielo. (Mr Paolo Ricardi). *"A fairly speedy filly, St Trinity should be running by mid-summer over six or seven furlongs".*

238 - TARADIYA (IRE)
b.f. Danehill - Tarakana (Shahrastani).
March 17. Second foal.
Half-sister to the 3-y-o Tarakan (by Doyoun). The dam won 9f in Ireland at 3 yrs and was placed in four listed events from 7f to 12f. The second dam, Tarafa (by Akarad), was a fairly useful dual 12f winner and a half-sister to the Princess Royal Stakes winner Tashtiya, the Prix Messidor winner Tassmoun and the Premio Carlo Porta winner Tashkourgan. (H H Aga Khan). *"A strong, very good-looking filly from a staying family, she should be one to look out for in the late summer over seven furlongs or a mile" informs Luca.*

239 - TENOR BELL (IRE)
b.br.c. Tenby - Top Bloom (Thatch).
May 8. Sixth foal. 45,000Y. Tattersalls October.
Half-brother to the 1997 unplaced 2-y-o Static Power (by Statoblest), to the quite useful 2-y-o 5f and 6f winner Serious Option (by Reprimand) and the modest 2-y-o 5f winner Thorny Flat (by Precocious). The dam ran twice unplaced and is a half-sister to 6 winners including the Coventry Stakes second and subsequent US Grade 3 winner Hegemony and the Irish listed winner Mr Iconoclast. The second

dam, Second Bloom (by Double Jump), was placed at 2 yrs. (Mrs E H Vestey). *"This is a good-looking colt that goes well. He won't be very early, but he should be running by August, probably over seven furlongs or a mile".*

---

240 - UNNAMED b.f. Wolfhound - Myth (Troy).
May 7. 22,000Y. Tattersalls October.
Half-sister to the smart middle-distance colt Midnight Legend (by Night Shift), a winner of 3 listed events, to the fairly useful 10f and 12f winner Spillo (by Midyan), the quite useful 12.3f winner Hard Task (by Formidable), the modest middle-distance winner of 6 races Supertop (by High Top) and a winner in Germany by Be My Chief. The dam, a fairly useful 12f and 13f winner, is a half-sister to 7 winners including the dam of the very useful 1997 2-y-o filly Crazee Mental. The second dam, Hay Reef (by Mill Reef), a fair 10f winner at 3 yrs, is a half-sister to the dam of Wassl. (The Speculators). *"Probably not a sprinter and not particularly early, but she's a good-looking filly I expect to be running as a two-year-old".*

---

241 - UNNAMED b.c. Hermitage - Social Missy (Raised Socially).
February 7. First foal. IR30,000Y. Goffs Orby.
The dam is an unraced half-sister to 3 winners including the US dual Grade 3 winner Appealing Missy. The second dam, Out of Joint (by Quack), is a placed half-sister to 5 winners including the US stakes winner Dancing School. *"This is a good-looking horse I would expect to be running in July. I think you should add him to your list"* Luca was telling me.

Ed Dunlop

---

242 - ABLA b.f. Robellino - Sans Blague (The Minstrel).
April 11. 125,000Y. Tattersalls October.
Half-sister to the 3-y-o Princess Sceptre (by Cadeaux Genereux), to the useful 1986 2-y-o listed 7f winner Nettle (by Kris), the fairly useful 10f winner Humourless (by Nashwan), the 12f winner Quip (by High Line), the 2-y-o 5f winner Fiction (by Dominion) and the 11.7f winner Galejade (by Sharrood) - all 3 only modest. The dam, a useful winner of the listed 12f Galtres Stakes, is a half-sister to 4 winners including the Galtres Stakes winner Deadly Serious - dam of the Australian Grade 1 winner Runyan. The second dam, Joking Apart (by Jimmy Reppin), won the listed Strensall Stakes and was third in the 1,000 Guineas. (Hamdan Al Maktoum). *"This is a nice filly who has developed very well"* Ed tells me. *"She has great depth and although she won't be rushed, she's going nicely on the gallops".*

---

243 - AL NABA (USA) ch.c. Mr Prospector - Forest Flower (Green Forest).
February 11. Sixth foal. $300,000. Keeneland July.
Half-brother to the Italian winner Eastwood Hall (by Reference Point), to the 1997 Japanese 3-y-o winner Flower Arch (by Nashwan), the 1995 Irish 2-y-o 8.5f winner Flaming Feather and the quite useful gelding Hill of Dreams (both by Shirley Heights), a winner of four races from 11.8f to 14f. The dam was a high class winner of the Irish 1,000 Guineas, Mill Reef Stakes, Queen Mary Stakes and Cherry Hinton Stakes. The second dam, Leap Lively (by Nijinsky), was a smart filly herself and won 3 races including the Hoover Fillies Mile and the Lingfield Oaks Trial and was third in the Oaks behind Blue Wind. (Hamdan Al Maktoum). *"A beautifully-bred colt with the most wonderful temperament, Al Naba is relatively precocious but I won't push him too soon. He's an adequate mover without being startling and I would hope to give him a race or two later in the season"* says trainer Ed Dunlop.

---

244 - CANDLERIGGS ch.c. Indian Ridge - Ridge Pool (Bluebird).
January 8. First foal. IR46,000Y. Goffs Orby.
The dam won over 6f in Ireland at 2 yrs and is a half-sister to a winner in Ireland and Italy. The second dam, Casting Couch (by Thatching), won at 2 yrs and is a half-sister to the US Grade 3 Selima Stakes winner Tycoon's Drama out of the Group 3 Greenlands Stakes winner Drama. (Mr A. Ferguson). *"Quite backward at the moment, Candleriggs is taking longer than I expected. He's not over-big but he's a short, compact, powerful little colt".*

---

245 - COPS (IRE) ch.c. Grand Lodge - Gentle Guest (Be My Guest).
February 28. Fifth foal. 85,000Y. Tattersalls Houghton.
Half-brother to the fair 1997 8.2f winner Freedom Chance (by Lahib) and to the modest 1995 5f and 6f placed 2-y-o Bearnaise (by Cyrano de Bergerac). The dam is an unraced half-sister to 6 minor winners. The second dam, Relkalim (by Relko), is a winning half-sister to the Irish 1,000 Guineas

winner Lacquer, the Coronation Stakes winner Sovereign and the Cambridgeshire Handicap winner and top-class broodmare Violetta III (the dam or grandam of numerous Group 1 winners including Teenoso). (Abdullah Ali). *"Cops has a wonderful temperament but, due to a minor setback, he's a little bit behind some of my other 2-y-o's at the moment. Not over-big, he should make a 2-y-o".*

---

246 - DATE
b.c. Cadeaux Genereux - Faribole (Esprit du Nord).
February 23. First living foal. 120,000Y. Tattersalls Houghton.
The dam, a useful French 3-y-o 10f winner, was third in the Group 3 Prix Chloe and the Group 3 Prix de Psyche. The second dam, Sandbank (by Riverman), won 3 races in France from 1m to 11f including the listed Prix Coronation. (Abdullah Ali). *"Date is more of a backward type then some of my 2-y-o's. He's done a lot of growing since we've had him and is quite a weak horse at the moment".*

---

247 - DEVIL'S IMP (IRE)
ch.f. Cadeaux Genereux - High Spirited (Shirley Heights).
April 15. Fifth foal. 210,000Y. Tattersalls Houghton.
Half-sister to the 3-y-o Spring Easy (by Alzao), to the very useful 1996 3-y-o Group 2 12f King Edward VII Stakes winner Amfortas (by Caerleon), the 1997 3-y-o Group 3 10.5f Prix de Royaumont winner Legend Maker and the useful 1995 3-y-o 10.4f winner Motakabber (both by Sadler's Wells). The dam was quite useful and won two of her seven races over 14f and 16f at 3 yrs. She is a sister to the Premio Roma, Ribblesdale Stakes and Park Hill Stakes winner High Hawk - herself dam of the Breeders Cup Turf winner In the Wings, and a half-sister to the 1m winner Seriema - dam of the Rothmans International winner Infamy. The second dam, Sunbittern (by High Hawk II), was a very useful 2-y-o 6f and 7f winner. (Maktoum Al Maktoum). *"Devil's Imp is a nice filly. She's some way behind at the moment (early April) having arrived here late, but has flourished enormously. She's done tremendously well, has a good pedigree, good looks and is a lovely, balanced filly whilst cantering. A nice filly for the future"* says the trainer.

---

248 - DIRECT DEAL
b.c. Rainbow Quest - Al Najah (Topsider).
March 3. Fifth foal.
Half-brother to the 3-y-o Shanjah (by Darshaan), to the useful 1994 3-y-o dual 6f winner Tabook (by Cadeaux Genereux) and a winner in Sweden by Mujtahid. The dam, a quite useful 8.5f winner at 3 yrs, is out of the US placed Personal Attention (by Alydar), herself a half-sister to 3 winners in the USA. The second dam, B Thoughtful (by Don B), won 9 races including the Grade 1 La Canada Stakes, the Grade 2 Oak Leaf Stakes and the Grade 2 Hollywood Lassie Stakes.(Maktoum Al Maktoum). *"Not a particularly precocious horse, but he's going very nicely. A good-looking, good-moving son of Rainbow Quest".*

---

249 - EBINZAYD (IRE)
b.c. Tenby - Sharakawa (Darshaan).
March 24. Second foal. FF400,000. Deauville August.
Half-brother to the extremely promising 1997 2-y-o dual 7f winner Rabi (by Alzao). The dam is an unraced half-sister to the fairly useful 3-y-o 9.6f winner Sharadiya (by Akarad). The second dam, Sharaya (by Youth), won the Group 1 Prix Vermeille and the Group 3 Prix de la Nonette and is a half-sister to the Group 2 Grand Prix d'Evry winner Sharaniya and the US Grade 3 Nijana Stakes winner Shannkara. (Hamdan Al Maktoum). *"Ebinzayd was very backward at the sales and was a sick horse shortly after. We're just feeling our way with him and although he canters very well, he's very much at the growing stage and we won't be rushing him this year".*

---

250 - FAIR FLIGHT
b.c. Green Desert - Barari (Blushing Groom).
March 11.
Brother to the 3-y-o White Heart and to the useful 6f to 7.5f winner Green Barries (by Green Desert) and half-brother to the fairly useful 1997 3-y-o 12f winner Generous Gift (by Generous) and the Belgian winner Zahabi (by Jareer). The dam is an unraced half-sister to the Canadian Grade 1 winner Rainbows For Life and to the Group 2 Prix de l'Opera winner Colour Chart. The second dam, Rainbow Connection (by Halo), a champion 2-y-o and 3-y-o filly in Canada, is a half-sister to 3 stakes winners including the Canadian Grade 1 winners Archdeacon and Hangin' on a Star. (Maktoum Al Maktoum). *"Fair Flight has always been quite a colty little horse but he goes well and has done nothing wrong. He looks precocious and should be a horse we can crack on with fairly soon".* Clearly, Ed feels this is a horse to watch out for in the early months of the season.

251 - FOLLOW THAT DREAM   b.f. Darshaan - Try To Catch Me (Shareef Dancer).
February 27. Fourth foal.
Sister to the 3-y-o Sandrella and half-sister to the fairly useful 11f to 13f winner Desert Frolic (by Persian Bold) and the fair 1993 2-y-o 7f winner Nawafell (by Kris). The dam won once over 1m at 3 yrs in France, is closely related to the US stakes winner Air Dancer and a half-sister to the Group 2 Criterium de Maisons-Laffitte winner Bitooh and the listed Virginia Stakes winner Monaassabaat. The second dam, It's In The Air (by Mr Prospector), was a Champion 2-y-o filly and winner of the Vanity Handicap (twice), the Ruffian Handicap, the Alabama Stakes and the Delaware Oaks (all Grade 1 events). (Maktoum Al Maktoum). *"This filly is bred to stay. She's a nice, good-bodied type of filly and seems to be going nicely. She'll probably make her first appearance over seven furlongs".*

252 - FRAGRANT OASIS (USA)   ch.f. Rahy - Raahia (Vice Regent).
February 2.
Closely related to the modest 1993 3-y-o 7f winner Mithi Al Gamar (by Blushing Groom) and half-sister to the 2-y-o 7f winner Wakeel (by Gulch) and the 3-y-o 1m winner Top Guide (by Diesis) - both quite useful. The dam, a fairly useful 2-y-o 6f winner, was third in the Group 3 7f Nell Gwyn Stakes and is a half-sister to 2 winners. The second dam, Full Marks (by Round Table), won twice in the USA and is a half-sister to 6 winners. (Maktoum Al Maktoum). *"A most beautiful-looking filly, Fragrant Oasis has a lovely temperament and she moves very well. Going nicely at the moment, she's well developed and should make a nice 2-y-o".*

253 - GHAAZI   ch.c. Lahib - Shurooq (Affirmed).
March 7. Sixth foal.
Half-brother to the quite useful 5f and 6f winner Maraatib (by Green Desert), to the quite useful 2-y-o 5f and subsequent Dubai winner Shati (by Last Tycoon), the fair 2-y-o 1m winner Hafafah (by Shirley Heights) and two winners in Dubai by Unfuwain. The dam, a fairly useful 2-y-o 6f and 7f winner, stayed 12f at 3 yrs and is a a half-sister to numerous winners including Smasher, winner of the Grade 2 San Felipe Handicap in the USA. The second dam, Frolic and Fun (by Jester), was an unraced half-sister to 10 winners. (Hamdan Al Maktoum). *"Ghaazi is the most beautiful-looking horse. He came into the yard late and is a bit behind some of the others at the moment but he's catching up quite well. I like what I see"* Ed tells me.

254 - HISHMAH   b.f. Nashwan - Na-Ayim (Shirley Heights).
April 21. Second foal.
Half-sister to the fair 1997 7f and 8.2f placed 2-y-o Tajawuz (by Kris). The dam was a modest 2-y-o 6f winner, is closely related to a winner by Slip Anchor and a half-sister to 2 winners by Nashwan (the sire of this filly). The second dam, Christabelle (by Northern Dancer), was placed at 2 yrs in Ireland and is a half-sister to the outstanding broodmare Slightly Dangerous (dam of Commander In Chief, Warning, Dushyantor, Deploy and Yashmak) and to the dams of Rainbow Quest and Scenic. (Hamdan Al Maktoum). *"A beautiful filly, not very precocious but she's done particularly well since she came into the yard. A nice filly for the future".*

255 - I PLEDGE ALLEGIANCE (USA)   b.c. Alleged - Yafill (Nureyev).
April 15. Fourth foal.
Half-brother to the 3-y-o Parmian (by Shadeed) and to the minor 1996 US 3-y-o winner Fillycap (by Capote). The dam, a quite useful 2-y-o 6f winner, is a half-sister to the 1996 US stakes winner Naughty Notions. The second dam, Tara's Charmer (by Majestic Light), won twice in the USA at up to 7f and is a half-sister to Zilzal and to the Irish listed winner Charmante. (Hamdan Al Maktoum). *"I know Alleged horses need plenty of time and this colt does have a little bit of a rounded knee-action, but he's got a very good temperament and is going nicely. From what I've seen so far, I like him".*

256 - KHIBRAH (IRE)   br.f. Lahib - Sabayik (Unfuwain).
February 5. First foal.
The dam was a fairly useful 3-y-o 1m winner and stayed 10f. She is a half-sister to 5 winners including the Doncaster Cup third Haitham out of the fairly useful Group 3 6f Premio Primi Passi winner Balqis (by Advocator), herself a half-sister to the dam of the Holywood Derby winner Slew The Dragon. (Hamdan Al Maktoum). *"A small filly, Khibrah was particularly so when she came in but she's grown and developed. She's been going extremely well and will certainly make a two-year-old".*

257 - MABSHUSH (IRE) b.c. Mujtahid - Just a Mirage (Green Desert).
May 4. Third foal.
Half-brother to the very promising 1997 7f placed 2-y-o Doomna and to the smart Group 2 7f Challenge Stakes winner Kahal (both by Machiavellian). The dam, a fair maiden, was placed at up to 1m, is a sister to the very useful miler Distant Oasis, closely related to the Group 2 Prix Dollar winner Wiorno and a half-sister to the Gimcrack Stakes and Trusthouse Forte Mile winner Reprimand. The second dam, Just You Wait (by Nonoalco), is an unraced half-sister to the dams of Ozone Friendly (Prix Robert Papin winner), Ardkinglass (Jersey Stakes winner), Soft Currency (Prix de la Jonchere) and Fawzi (Mill Reef Stakes second). (Hamdan Al Maktoum). *"A nice horse, though big and backward, he's showing a lot of speed but he's more of a three-year-old type".*

---

258 - MIZHAR (USA) b.br.c. Dayjur - Futuh (Diesis).
April 17. Fourth foal.
Brother to the smart 1997 2-y-o Group 1 6f Middle Park Stakes winner Hayil and half-brother to the fairly useful 1995 2-y-o 6f and subsequent Dubai 10f winner Tamhid (by Gulch). The dam, a fairly useful 2-y-o 6f winner, is a half-sister to the Canadian Selene Stakes winner Rose Park (herself the dam of the smart 1997 US 3-y-o Grade 2 winner Wild Rush). The second dam, Hardship (by Drone), won 4 races at up to 1m and was third in the Grade 1 Frizette Stakes. (Hamdan Al Maktoum). *"Mizhar seems more precocious than his brother Hayil apparently was, but nevertheless he won't be early. He has a good temperament and is a good-looking horse".*

---

259 - MUTAAHAB (CAN) b.c. Dixieland Band - Serene Nobility (His Majesty).
January 20. Second foal. $190,000F. Keeneland November.
Closely related to the 3-y-o Gypsy Baron (by Dixie Brass). The dam won 9 races including 3 stakes events in the USA and is a half-sister to 4 winners including the US stakes winner Corax. The second dam, Peaceful Snow (by Hold Your Peace), won once at 3 yrs in the USA and is a half-sister to 7 winners including the Grade 2 winner Hold Your Tricks. (Hamdan Al Maktoum). *"Not very big, but fairly level, this colt will be a 2-y-o alright. He carries a lot of condition and certainly seems to be going the right way. Again, I like what I see",* Ed was telling me.

---

260 - MY ENIGMA b.f. Rainbow Quest - Zawaahy (El Gran Senor).
May 4. Third foal.
Closely related to As Friendly (by Arazi), a winner over 7f and 1m in Dubai and half-sister to Bay Of Delight (by Cadeaux Genereux), unplaced twice over 7f at 2 yrs in 1997. The dam, a fairly useful 1m winner, was placed at up to 11.5f and is closely related to the Derby winner Golden Fleece. The second dam, Exotic Treat (by Vaguely Noble), is an unraced half-sister to the champion filly What a Treat - herself the dam of Be My Guest. (Maktoum Al Maktoum). *This filly was still at stud in Ireland in early April.*

---

261 - PAY THE PIED PIPER (USA) b.c. Red Ransom - Fife (Lomond).
April 26. Fourth foal.
Half-brother to the 3-y-o Hudood (by Gone West) and to the useful 1995 2-y-o 6f and 7f winner Witch of Fife (by Lear Fan). The dam, a fairly useful 1m winner, stayed 12f and is a half-sister to the smart stayer El Conquistador. The second dam, Fiddle Faddle (by Silly Season), a quite useful 12f and 16f winner, is a half-sister to the Irish St Leger winner Mountain Lodge. (Maktoum Al Maktoum). *"A lovely, big horse who moves and behaves very well. I really like him. He's big and backward but well balanced for his size. Very much an autumn type 2-y-o and he should be better still at 3 yrs".*

---

262 - RAIN RAIN GO AWAY (USA) ch.c. Miswaki - Stormagain (Storm Cat).
March 24. Second foal. $190,000Y. Keeneland September.
The dam won in France and in the USA and was placed in the 5f Prix d'Arenburg, the 6.5f Prix du Calvados and the 7f Prix Eclipse (all 2-y-o Group 3 events). She is closely related to the French winner and Group 3 placed After the Sun and a half-sister to 6 winners including the German 2,000 Guineas winner Royal Abjar. The second dam, Encorelle (by Arctic Tern), is an unraced sister to the Prix de Diane winner Escaline. (Maktoum Al Maktoum). *"Quite backward, he looked a neat little colt at the sales but he's grown and has got a little coarser. He seems to be very much at a changing stage and is going to take more time than most of the others".*

263 - SECRET DELL b.c. Doyoun - Summer Silence (Stop The Music).
March 7. IR47,000Y. Goffs Orby.
Brother to the Irish trained 3-y-o Malvadilla, unplaced twice at 2 yrs, and half-brother to the quite useful 9f winner Shaarid, subsequently a winner over jumps. The dam won a minor event over 7f in the USA at 4 yrs and is a half-sister to 5 winners including the German Group 3 winner and Premio Lydia Tesio fourth Fields Of Spring. The second dam, Memory Lane (by Never Bend), won the Group 3 Princess Elizabeth Stakes and is a sister to Mill Reef. (Ahmed Ali). *"Secret Dell is a nice horse who had a little problem which caused him to lose a couple of weeks. He wouldn't cover an enormous amount of ground, is a little bit highly strung, but all the lads who have ridden him seem to like him. A little bit behind some of the others, but he looks relatively precocious and I would hope he'd make a 2-y-o".*

264 - SEDRAH (USA) ch.f. Dixieland Band - Madame Secretary (Secretariat).
April 18.
Closely related to the useful 2-y-o 6f listed Firth of Clyde Stakes and 3-y-o 1m winner Tabdea (by Topsider), to the fair 2-y-o 1m winner Hawl (by Lyphard) and half-sister to the smart 1996 French 1,000 Guineas winner and Falmouth Stakes second Ta Rib (by Mr Prospector), the fair 1995 3-y-o 7f winner Itab (by Dayjur) and the minor US winner Top Hat White Tie (by Saratoga Six). The dam won 2 races in America at around 1m including a minor stakes and is a half-sister to 4 winners including the useful stayer Zero Watt and the Stewards Cup winner Green Ruby. The second dam, Ruby Tuesday (by T.V.Lark), was placed at 3 yrs and is a half-sister to the very smart French colt Cresta Rider. (Hamdan Al Maktoum). *"This is a big, powerful filly, very much like a colt to look at her" says Ed. "She seems to have a very good temperament, is very laid back and although she'll take a bit of time she could be a very nice filly in the future".*

265 - SIR LEGEND (USA) b.br.c. El Gran Senor - Tadkiyra (Darshaan).
June 4. Second foal. $100,000. Keeneland September.
The dam won at 3 yrs in France and is a half-sister to 9 winners including the Group 3 12f Princess Royal Stakes winner Tashtiya and the Group 3 1m Prix Messidor winner Tassmoun. The second dam, Tremogia (by Silver Shark), is an unraced daughter of the Prix Saint-Alary winner Tonnera. (Maktoum Al Maktoum). *"Very much a June foal, very backward and still growing at the moment (early April), Sir Legend is very much a 3-y-o type. However, I do like what I've seen of him so far".*

266 - SURPRISE ENCOUNTER ch.c. Cadeaux Genereux - Scandalette (Niniski).
February 7. 110,000Y. Tattersalls Houghton.
Half-brother to the quite useful 1997 2-y-o 7f winner Night Flyer (by Midyan). The dam is an unraced half-sister to 7 winners including the Group 1 July Cup winner Polish Patriot and the Italian listed winner Grand Cayman. The second dam, Maria Waleska (by Filiberto), won the Group 1 Gran Premio d'Italia and the Group 1 Oaks d'Italia. (Ahmed Ali). *"Surprise Encounter is a nice horse and he will be a 2-y-o. A very good-looking horse, he's precocious and although he's only just beginning serious work, from what we've seen so far he looks nice".*

267 - ZAAJER (USA) ch.c. Silver Hawk - Crown Quest (Chief's Crown).
March 21. Fifth foal. $430,000Y. Keeneland September.
Half-brother to the modest 1997 3-y-o 7f winner Shoumatara (by Seeking The Gold) and to the US 2-y-o sprint winner Misohapi (by Majestic Light). The dam won a minor stakes event and was second in the Grade 2 8.5f Tempted Stakes at 2 yrs in the USA. The second dam, Glorious Quest (by Hawaii), won at 3 yrs and is a half-sister to the Champion 2-y-o filly Heavenly Cause and to the dam of the Grade 1 winner Bounding Basque. (Hamdan Al Maktoum). *"Zaajer is a big horse and is quite long but well-balanced. Not an obvious 2-y-o type - he's all of 16 hands now - but those who have ridden him rather like him"* Ed informs me.

268 - UNNAMED b.c. Indian Ridge - Mercy Bien (Be My Guest).
January 18. First foal. 95,000Y. Tattersalls Houghton.
The dam, a modest 7f and 10f placed maiden, is a half-sister to the listed Sceptre Stakes winner Arjuzah and the Irish listed winner Ormsby. The second dam, Saving Mercy (by Lord Gayle), won the 1m Lincoln Handicap and is a half-sister to the dam of the US Grade 1 winners Anka Germania and Mourjane. (Sultan Ahmed Shah). *"This is a nice horse and very good-looking. He has a bit of a workmanlike action but he's good-bodied and will be nice in time. Quite big but relatively precocious".*

John Dunlop

269 - ADNAAN (IRE) ch.c. Nashwan - Whakilyric (Miswaki).
March 10. IR900,000Y. Goffs Orby.
Closely related to the French trained 3-y-o Res Judicata (by Rainbow Quest) and half-brother to the the top-class middle-distance colt Hernando (by Niniski), a winner of seven races notably the Group 1

Prix du Jockey Club and Group 1 Prix Lupin and second in the Prix de l'Arc de Triomphe, the very useful Group 1 10.5f Prix Lupin and US Grade 2 1m winner Johann Quatz and the smart French 10.5f to 13.5f listed winner Walter Willy (both by Sadlers Wells). The dam won over 5.5f and the Group 3 7f Prix du Calvados, was third in the Prix de la Salamandre (all at 2 yrs) and in the Group 1 7f Prix de la Foret and is a half-sister to the Prix Daphnis winner Bricassar. The second dam, Lyrism (by Lyphard), was an unraced daughter of the very useful miler and subsequent smart American middle-distance performer Pass a Glance. (Hamdan Al Maktoum). *"This colt, a half-brother to Hernando, has wintered in Dubai and has yet to arrive at Arundel" John tells me.*

---

270 - ALABAQ (USA) b.br.f. Riverman - Salsabil (Sadler's Wells).
April 1. Fifth foal.
Half-sister to the fairly useful 1997 2-y-o 1m winner Muhaba, to the very useful 1996 2-y-o 6f and 7f winner Sahm (both by Mr Prospector) and to the very useful 6f, 7f (both at 2 yrs) and 10f winner Bint Salsabil (by Nashwan). The dam won two of her three races as a two-year-old - notably the Group 1 1m Prix Marcel Boussac - and trained on to become a top class 3-y-o, winning the 1,000 Guineas, the Irish Derby, the Epsom Oaks and the Prix Vermeille - all Group 1 events. She is a half-sister to the high class colt Marju, winner of the St James's Palace Stakes and the Craven Stakes, and to the very useful Prix de Psyche winner Danse Royale. The second dam, Flame of Tara (by Artaius), won the Coronation Stakes and the Curragh Pretty Polly Stakes, was second in the Champion Stakes and is a half-sister to Fruition - dam of both the Breeders Cup Turf winner Northern Spur and the high-class stayer Kneller. (Hamdan Al Maktoum). *"The last foal of Salsabil, Alabaq is a good-moving, athletic filly".*

---

271 - AL SAQIYA (USA) b.f. Woodman - Augusta Springs (Nijinsky).
January 28. Second foal. $200,000. Keeneland September.
The dam, a minor stakes-placed winner of 3 races at 3 yrs in the USA, is a half-sister to the Grade 1 Hollywood Starlet Stakes winner Cuddles and to the dam of the Grade 2 San Fernando Breeders Cup Stakes winner Northern Afleet. The second dam, Stellarette (by Tentam), won the Grade 3 7f Barbara Fritchie Handicap in the USA at 3 yrs and is a half-sister to the US Grade 1 winner Love Smitten (the dam of Swain) and to the Canadian Oaks winner Kamar (dam of the Grade 1 winners Gorgeous and Seaside Attraction). (Hamdan Al Maktoum). *"A good-actioned filly, but she appears to be backward and is unlikely to debut until the autumn".*

---

272 - BARAFAMY gr.f. Barathea - Infamy (Shirley Heights).
April 21. Sixth foal. 42,000Y. Tattersalls Houghton.
Half-sister to the 3-y-o Innuendo, to the quite useful 1997 3-y-o 12f winner Badge Of Fame (both by Caerleon), the quite useful 1993 2-y-o 14f winner Kamikaze and the Italian 11f winner Simy (both by Kris). The dam, a very smart 10f to 12f filly, won the Grade 1 Rothmans International, the Group 2 Sun Chariot Stakes and the Group 3 Gordon Richards Stakes. The second dam, Seriema (by Petingo), a minor 1m winner at 3 yrs, is a half-sister to the high-class filly High Hawk (by Shirley Heights) - dam of the top-class middle-distance colt In the Wings. (Mr G Pinchen). *"A nice sort of filly from a good family, she should be making her debut in mid-summer".*

---

273 - COME ON GEORGE (IRE) b.c. Barathea - Lacovia (Majestic Light).
February 28. 150,000Y. Tattersalls Houghton.
Half-brother to the French trained 3-y-o Otavalo (by Diesis), to the French 3-y-o winner and listed-placed Lambada (by Lyphard) and the minor French winners Obelisco (by Chief's Crown) and Cirino (by Gone West). The dam won the Group 1 10.5f Prix de Diane and the Group 1 10f Prix Saint-Alary and is a half-sister to 3 winners. The second dam, Hope For All (by Secretariat), was placed from 6f to 8.3f in the USA and is a half-sister to Miswaki and to the listed winner Northern Eternity (dam of the US Grade 1 winner Eternity Star). *"A backward, heavy type of colt".*

---

274 - DARK ALBATROSS (USA) b.br.f. Sheikh Albadou - Rossard (Glacial).
January 16. 29,000Y. Tattersalls October.
Half-sister to the Irish 1m and 9f listed winner Unusual Heat (by Nureyev), to the minor US winner Danish Prospector (by Miswaki) and a winner in Panama by Shahrastani. The dam won 14 races in Scandinavia and the USA including the Grade 1 10f Flower Bowl Handicap and is a half-sister to 4 winners. The second dam, Peas-Blossom (by Midsummer Night II), is a placed half-sister to the Prix Gladiateur winner Hickleton. (Mrs S Abbott). *"A tall, strong filly with a fair action".*

275 - DEBAAJ
ch.c. Indian Ridge - Gold Bracelet (Golden Fleece).
April 23. Sixth living foal. 30,000Y. Tattersalls October.
Half-brother to the useful Irish 1m (at 2 yrs) and 12f winner Lake Kariba (by Persian Bold) and the fairly useful 1992 7.1f 2-y-o winner Mukhamedov (by Robellino). The dam is an unplaced half-sister to the top-class sprinter Thatching. The second dam, Abella (by Abernant), won 3 races and was second in the Group 3 7f Challenge Stakes. (Kuwait Racing Syndicate). *"A good-actioned colt and a typical Indian Ridge, Debaaj is likely to be one of my earlier two-year-old runners".*

276 - EL KARIM (USA)
ch.c. Storm Cat - Gmaasha (Kris).
February 1. Third foal.
Half-brother to the fair 1997 6f placed 3-y-o Malabi (by Danzig) and to Sinan (by Mr Prospector), unplaced twice at 2 yrs in 1997. The dam is an unraced sister to the smart 7f and 1m winner Hasbah and a half-sister to the useful dual 6f winner Za-Im. The second dam, Al Bahathri (by Blushing Groom), was a high-class winner of 6 races from 6f to 1m, notably the Irish 1,000 Guineas, Coronation Stakes, Child Stakes and Lowther Stakes. (Hamdan Al Maktoum). *"A big, very backward colt and a very laid-back character, he's unlikely to run before the end of the season".*

277 - ELLE QUESTRO
b.f. Rainbow Quest - Lady Be Mine (Sir Ivor).
March 8.
Half-sister to the 3-y-o My Career (by Caerleon), to the champion 2-y-o of 1989 Be My Chief, winner of the Group 1 1m Racing Post Trophy, the Solario Stakes and the Lanson Champagne Stakes etc., the fairly useful 1995 4-y-o 9f to 14.6f winner Chief Bee (both by Chief's Crown), the fair 2-y-o 5f winner Run Little Lady (by J.O.Tobin), the fair 3-y-o 1m winner Albemine (by Al Nasr) and the 1997 4-y-o 11.8f winner Kota (by Kris). The dam, a minor 3-y-o 1m winner at Yarmouth, is a half-sister to Mixed Applause, dam of the high-class miler Shavian and the Gold Cup winner Paean. The second dam, My Advantage (by Princely Gift), won over 5f at 2 yrs and is a half-sister to the dam of Marwell. (Mrs M Burrell). *"A tall, backward filly, she needs time despite being a half-sister to Be My Chief and she appears to follow Chief Bee in this respect".*

278 - ELM DUST
ch.f. Elmaamul - Galaxie Dust (Blushing Groom).
April 26.
Half-sister to the fair 1997 7f placed 2-y-o Saeedah, to the very useful Group 3 7.3f Gainsborough Stud Fred Darling Stakes and listed 10f Lupe Stakes winner Bulaxie (both by Bustino), the very smart 6.5f to 12f winner Zimzalabim, the fair 3-y-o 1m and 10f winner Galactic Miss (both by Damister), the very smart 1997 Group 3 10f Prix de la Nonette winner Dust Dancer (by Suave Dancer) and the 1996 German 3-y-o winner Smoke Dancer (by Formidable). The dam, a quite useful 2-y-o 6f winner, is a half-sister to 2 minor winners out of High Galaxie (by Blushing Groom) - a winner of 10 races in Puerto Rico and the USA. (Hesmonds Stud Ltd). *"A tall, leggy, good-actioned filly, she'll probably follow her half-sisters Bulaxie and Dust Dancer in that she's unlikely to run until the second half of the year".*

279 - ETIZAAZ (USA)
b.f. Diesis - Alamosa (Alydar).
February 15. Third foal. 500,000Y. Tattersalls Houghton.
Half-sister to the US Grade 3 7f Lafayette Stakes winner Trafalger (by Storm Bird) and the minor US 3-y-o winner Omara (by Storm Cat). The dam is an unraced half-sister to the King George VI and Queen Elizabeth Diamond Stakes winner Swain. The second dam, Love Smitten (by Key To The Minstrel), won the Grade 1 Apple Blossom Handicap and the Grade 2 Santa Maria Handicap and is a sister to the top-class mare Kamar - winner of the Kentucky Oaks and dam of Key To The Moon , Gorgeous and Seaside Attraction - all Grade 1 winners. (Hamdan Al Maktoum). *"Etizaaz is a long, backward filly. Likely to debut in the second half of the season".*

280 - FNAN
b.c. Generous - Rafha (Kris).
February 28. Fourth foal. 70,000Y. Tattersalls Houghton.
Half-brother to the very promising 1997 2-y-o 7.6f winner Sadian (by Shirley Heights) and to the useful dual 1m (at 2 yrs) and 11.8f winner Al Widyan (by Slip Anchor). The dam, a very smart winner from 6f (at 2 yrs) to 11.5f including the Group 1 Prix de Diane, the Group 3 Lingfield Oaks Trial and the Group 3 May Hill Stakes, is a half-sister to the 2-y-o 7f winner Fayfa and to the middle-distance winners Alkhafji and Sarawat - all fairly useful. The second dam, Eljazzi (by Artaius), a fairly useful 2-y-o 7f winner, is a half-sister to the good miler Pitcairn and to Dingle Bay (dam of the smart stayer Assessor) out of the Yorkshire Oaks and Park Hill Stakes second Eljazzi. *"A nice sort of colt and a strong type. He'll need a bit of time".* (Prince A A Faisal).

281 - GHITA (IRE)   ch.f. Zilzal - Sabria (Miswaki).
March 14. First foal. 25,000Y. Tattersalls October.
The dam is an unraced half-sister to 3 winners including the very useful Grand Criterium third King Sound. The second dam, Flood (by Riverman), won over 6f in the USA and is a half-sister to the US Grade 1 Californian Stakes winner Sabona. The third dam, Hail Maggie, is a half-sister to the top-class racemare Trillion (the dam of Triptych) and to the dam of Generous. (Mr R J McAulay). *"A small, good actioned, sharp sort, one of the more forward members of the string. Likely to be an early runner" says John.*

---

282 - GOODBYE (IRE)   b.c. Thatching - Itqan (Sadler's Wells).
April 1. Third foal. 75,000Y. Tattersalls Houghton.
Half-brother to the smart 1996 2-y-o Group 1 1m Gran Criterium winner Hello (by Lycius), subsequently a winner in America and third in the Grade 1 Santa Anita Derby. The dam, a fairly useful winner of 3 races from 11.9f to 14.8f, is a half-sister to 3 winners out of the quite useful 1m and 9f winner Photo (by Blakeney), herself a daughter of the 1,000 Guineas second Photo Flash. (Mr I D Cameron). *"A neat, good-actioned, straightforward colt, he's likely to be an early runner and is similar to his half-brother Hello".*

---

283 - GOODWOOD JAZZ (IRE)   b.f. Night Shift - Wood Violet (Riverman).
April 26. 20,000Y. Tattersalls October.
Half-sister to the 1997 Irish 2-y-o 6f and 7f winner Viola Royale (by Royal Academy), to the fairly useful 10f winner Shaleel, the modest 10f and 12f all-weather winner No Speeches (by Last Tycoon) and the Italian 2-y-o winner Golden Lomond (by Lomond). The dam is an unraced half-sister to 4 minor winners. The second dam, Honor Tricks (by Bold Bidder), is an unraced half-sister to 9 winners including the US Grade 1 winner and high-class sire Halo, the good stakes winners Tosmah and Maribeau and the dam of the Kentucky Derby winner Cannonade. (Goodwood Racehorse Owners Group). *"A small, sharp-actioned filly and a relatively early sort who will hopefully be making her debut in the first half of the season".*

---

284 - GRAND MAITRE (USA)   gr.c. Gone West - La Grand Epoque (Lyphard).
April 17.
Half-brother to the very useful French listed 6f and 7f winner and Jersey Stakes second Matelot (by Riverman). The dam, a very smart filly, won the 5f Prix Yacowlef and was second in the Group 1 5f Prix de l'Abbaye and is a half-sister to the Group 3 winners Rami and Crack Regiment. The second dam, Ancient Regime (by Olden Times), a winner of the Group 1 Prix Morny and the best 2-y-o filly of her year in France, is a sister to the smart French colt Cricket Ball out of the Nunthorpe Stakes winner Caterina II. (Mr Robin Scully). *"A colt from a late-maturing, very fast family".*

---

285 - HAWRIYAH (USA)   b.br.f. Dayjur - Lady Cutlass (Cutlass).
April 4.
Sister to the smart 1994 2-y-o 6f winner and Group 3 1m Craven Stakes third Nwaamis and half-sister to the top-class Group 1 1m Queen Elizabeth II Stakes and Group 2 1m Queen Anne Stakes winner Lahib, the useful 1997 10f winner Eshtiaal (both by Riverman), the very useful US miler Maceo (by Nodouble), the fairly useful 7f and 1m winner Sajjaya (by Blushing Groom) and minor winners by Halo and Northern Baby. The dam won three races from 5f to 7f in the USA and was stakes placed. She is a half-sister to 10 winners including the high-class French middle distance colt General Holme, the Del Mar Oaks and Vanity Handicap winner Commisary and General Store - grandam of Al Bahathri. (Hamdan Al Maktoum). *"A good-actioned, light-framed filly, she's unlikely to debut until the second half of the season".*

---

286 - INTIZAA (USA)   b.f. Mr Prospector - Oumaldaaya (Nureyev).
March 15. Third foal.
Half-sister to the useful 1997 2-y-o listed 7f Somerville Tattersall Stakes winner Haami and to the fairly useful 1996 2-y-o 1m winner Asas (both by Nashwan). The dam, a very useful filly, won over 7f at 2yrs and the Group 2 10f Premio Lydia Tesio and listed 10f Lupe Stakes at 3 yrs. She is a half-sister to the 1994 Derby winner Erhaab out of the French 10.5f winner Histoire (by Riverman), herself a half-sister to the smart Group 3 Prix de Porte Maillot winner Hamanda. (Hamdan Al Maktoum). *"A very well-bred filly who will be getting all the time she needs".*

287 - LIGHTNING ARROW (USA) b.c. Silver Hawk - Strait Lane (Chieftain). March 9.

Brother to the US triple Grade 1 winner Hawkster, the Group 3 Prix de la Grotte winner and Irish Oaks third Silver Lane and the French 6f and 1m listed winner and Prix de la Salamandre third Silver Kite and half-brother to 5 minor winners including the modest 11f and 12f winner Explosive Speed (by Exceller). The dam is an unraced half-sister to 2 stakes winners in the USA. The second dam, Level Sands (by Mahmoud), was stakes-placed winner of 4 races at 2 yrs and a half-sister to Washington D C International winner Fisherman. *"A full-brother to the top American performer Hawkster, this is a nice colt who will not be rushed"*.

288 - LUCKY LINDA b.f. Bluebird - Spectacular Dawn (Spectacular Bid). April 8. Second foal. IR35,000Y. Goffs Orby.

Half-sister to the 3-y-o Harbiya (by Salse). The dam, a fair winner of 4 races from 10f to 17.2f, is a half-sister to 6 winners including the Group 1 St Leger winner and Derby second Silver Patriarch, the Group 3 Henry II Stakes winner My Patriarch and the useful sprinter Silver Singing. The second dam, Early Rising (by Grey Dawn II), a minor winner in the USA at around 1m, is a half-sister to the Group 3 Gilltown Stud Stakes winner Clare Bridge and the listed Winter Hill Stakes winner Song Of Sixpence. The third dam, Gliding By (by Tom Rolfe), was a winning half-sister to the champion US horses Fort Marcy and Key To The Mint. (Mr Peter Winfield). *"A good-actioned filly with an interesting, active pedigree"*.

289 - MAZAYA (IRE) b.f. Sadler's Wells - Sharaniya (Alleged). May 8. 150,000Y. Tattersalls Houghton.

Closely related to the French 1m winner and listed placed Shamsiya (by The Minstrel) and half-sister to the 3-y-o Divvinayshan (by Darshaan), to the useful Irish 12f to 2m winner Sharazan (by Akarad) and 2 minor winners in France by Shahrastani. The dam was a smart winner of the Group 2 12f Grand Prix d'Evry, the Group 3 12f Prix Minerve and the Group 3 12.5f Prix de Royallieu and is a half-sister to the Prix Vermeille winner Sharaya and the US Grade 3 winner Shannkara. The second dam, Shanizadeh (by Baldric II), was a useful French 6f and 1m winner. (Hamdan Al Maktoum). *"Mazaya is a very nice, good-actioned filly, with a stature typical of Sadler's Wells"*.

290 - NASHEED (USA) b.br.f. Riverman - Thawakib (Sadler's Wells). February 20. Second foal.

Half-sister to the fairly useful 1997 2-y-o 7f winner Alharir (by Zafonic). The dam, a useful filly, won twice over 7f (at 2 yrs) and the Group 2 12f Ribblesdale Stakes. She is a half-sister to numerous winners including the top-class middle-distance colt Celestial Storm - winner of the Group 2 Princess of Wales's Stakes - and to the placed dam of the Group 1 Rothmans International winner River Memories. The second dam, Tobira Celeste (by Ribot), won twice at up to 9f in France, was third in the Group 3 12f Prix de Minerve and is a half-sister to the smart French filly A Thousand Stars. (Hamdan Al Maktoum). *"This is a good-actioned, quality filly. She is taller than her half-sister Alharir and appears to have a little more scope"* John explained.

291 - NOWHERE TO EXIT b.c. Exit to Nowhere - Tromond (Lomond). March 14. First foal. 65,000Y. Tattersalls Houghton.

The dam, a fairly useful 9f winner, was second in the listed 10f Ballymacoll Stud Stakes at Newbury. The second dam, Troyes (by Troy), a quite useful 12f winner, is a sister to the winner and Group 2 King Edward VII Stakes second New Trojan and a half-sister to 6 winners including the Yorkshire Oaks winner Hellenic (herself dam of the Aston Park Stakes winner Election Day). *"From a stout, middle-distance family, the sort likely to have a run in the latter half of the season"*.

292 - OSOOL (USA) b.c. Danzig - Histoire (Riverman). March 29.

Closely related to the 1994 Derby winner Erhaab (by Chief's Crown) and half-sister to the very useful Group 2 10f Premio Lydia Tesio and Lupe Stakes winner Oumaldaaya, the quite useful 1995 2-y-o 7f winner Samim (both by Nureyev), the fairly useful French 1m and 9f winner Hispaniola (by Kris), the minor French winner Historique (by Rainbow Quest) and to Hittias (by Touching Wood), a winner in France and the USA and third in the Grade 3 13f Seneca Handicap. The dam won once in France over 10.5f and is a half-sister to the Group 3 7f Prix de la Porte Maillot winner Hamanda. The second dam, Helvetie (by Klairon), won once in France over 1m. (Hamdan Al Maktoum). *"A tall, very backward half-brother to Erhaab who appears to need a great deal of time"*.

293 - RAAQI
b.c. Nashwan - Mehthaaf (Nureyev).
February 7. First foal.
The dam, a high-class filly and winner of the Irish 1,000 Guineas, the Tripleprint Celebration Mile and the Nell Gwyn Stakes, is closely related to the Diadem Stakes winner Elnadim and to the French 2-y-o 7.5f winner Only Seule (herself dam of the Group 3 Prix des Reservoirs winner Occupandiste). The second dam, Elle Seule (by Exclusive Native), a very smart winner of the Group 3 1m Prix d'Astarte, is a half-sister to the Group/Grade 1 winners Fort Wood, Hamas and Timber Country and to the Group winners Northern Aspen, Colorado Dancer and Mazzacano. The third dam, the clearly outstanding broodmare Fall Aspen (by Pretense), won the Grade 1 7f Matron Stakes. (Hamdan Al Maktoum). *"A strong sort of colt, Raaqi seems to have taken after the sire rather than the dam physically and he has a good, sound temperament".*

294 - RAHAYEB
b.f. Arazi - Bashayer (Mr Prospector).
March 3. First foal.
The dam, a dual 1m winner, is a sister to 1m and 10.4f winner Wijdan and the 1997 3-y-o 10.1f listed winner Sarayir - all useful - and a half-sister to the Derby, King George, Eclipse and 2,000 Guineas winner Nashwan and the Princess Of Wales's Stakes winner Unfuwain. The second dam, Height Of Fashion (by Bustino), a high-class winner of 5 races from 7f to 12f including the Princess of Wales's Stakes, is a half-sister to the good middle-distance colt Milford. The third dam, Highclere (by Queens Hussar), won the 1,000 Guineas and the Prix de Diane. (Hamdan Al Maktoum). *"A tall, good-actioned filly and a late-maturing type".*

295 - SAABIKAH (USA)
b.br.f. Dayjur - Sajjaya (Blushing Groom).
April 7. Fourth living foal.
Closely related to the 1997 2-y-o 6f winner Shuhrah (by Danzig) and half-sister to the fairly useful 10f winner Raased (by Unfuwain) - both fairly useful. The dam, a useful 2-y-o 7f and 3-y-o 1m winner, is a half-sister to the top-class Group 1 1m Queen Elizabeth II Stakes and Group 2 1m Queen Anne Stakes winner Lahib, to the smart 2-y-o 7f winner and Group 3 1m Craven Stakes third Nwaamis and the very useful American miler Maceo. The second dam, Lady Cutlass (by Cutlass), won 3 races from 5f to 7f in the USA, was stakes placed and is a half-sister to 10 winners including the high-class French middle-distance colt General Holme and the Del Mar Oaks and Vanity Handicap winner Commisary. (Hamdan Al Maktoum). *"A neat filly, Saabikah is likely to be one of the yard's earlier runners".*

296 - SAKHA
ch.f. Wolfhound - Harmless Albatross (Pas de Seul).
March 29.
Closely related to the very smart French 6f (at 2 yrs) to 10f winner and Grade 1 Rothmans International and Group 1 Prix de la Salamandre placed Volochine (by Soviet Star) and half-sister to the promising 1997 2-y-o 1m winner Kahtan (by Nashwan), the very useful 1997 3-y-o middle-distance winner Ghataas (by Sadler's Wells) and the fairly useful 1995 3-y-o 12f winner Haniya (by Caerleon). The dam, a very useful French filly, won the Group 3 1m Prix des Chenes at 2 yrs and a 1m listed event at 3 yrs. She is a half-sister to the Group 2 10f Prix d'Harcourt winner Fortune's Wheel and the very useful French 5.5f (at 2 yrs) and 1m winner Libertine. The second dam, North Forland (by Northfields), a useful 3-y-o 10f winner and second in the Ribblesdale Stakes, is a half-sister to the Prix Ganay winner Infra Green (herself dam of 4 good winners and grandam of the St Leger winner Toulon). (Hamdan Al Maktoum). *"A stocky, sharp-actioned half-sister to the yard's three-year-old Khatan".*

297 - SARRAIA
b.br.f. Formidable - Lili Cup. (Fabulous Dancer).
April 15. Third foal. 22,000Y. Tattersalls October.
Half-sister to the Italian winner of 4 races Uruk (by Efisio). The dam is an unraced half-sister to 4 winners including the Franch listed 5.5f winner Charme Slave. The second dam, Irish Arms (by Irish River), won in France and is a half-sister to 9 winners. (Kuwait Racing Syndicate). *"Sarraia has a good action, is well-grown and will be an early type".*

298 - SECOND NATURE
b.c. Second Set - Tittlemouse (Castle Keep).
February 12. Sixth foal. 26,000Y. Tattersalls October.
Half-brother to the unplaced 1997 2-y-o Sumbawa (by Magic Ring), to the modest 9.7f and 11f winner Jemima Puddleduck (by Tate Galery) and the French 10f and 10.5f winner Midy Mouse (by Midyan). The dam, a quite useful 10f winner, is a half-sister to the Group 3 Guardian Classic Trial winner and Dewhurst Stakes second Gordian - subsequently Grade 1 placed in the USA. The second dam, Mrs Tiggywinkle (by Silly Season), was a very useful winner of the listed 5f Rous Memorial Stakes and was third in the 1,000 Guineas. (Hesmonds Stud Ltd). *"Likely to be one of the earlier runners".*

299 - SPANISH LADY (IRE) b.f. Bering - Belle Arrivee (Bustino).
February 23. Fifth foal. 220,000 Y. Tattersalls Houghton.
Half-sister to the useful 1996 3-y-o 10f winner Berenice (by Groom Dancer) and the fair 1995 3-y-o 7f winner Kafani Al Widd (by Royal Academy). The dam, a quite useful 3-y-o 10f winner, is closely related to the King George VI and Queen Elizabeth Diamond Stakes and Coral-Eclipse Stakes winner Mtoto and a half-sister to 13 other winners including Savoureuse Lady (Group 3 Prix Fille de l'Air) and the dam of the smart sprinter Lugana Beach. The second dam, Amazer (by Mincio), won over 6f at 2 yrs in France. (Windflower Overseas Holdings Inc). *"A very backward, quality filly"*.

300 - TAMGEED (USA) ch.f. Woodman - Toujours Elle (Lyphard).
May 12. Third foal. 430,000Y. Tattersalls October.
Half-sister to the 3-y-o Toto Le Heros (by Saumarez). The dam is an unplaced three-parts sister to the Irish 1,000 Guineas winner Mehthaaf. The second dam, Elle Seule (by Exclusive Native), won the Group 2 Prix d'Astarte and is a half-sister to the Grade/Group 1 winners Timber Country, Hamas, Northern Aspen and Fort Wood, to the Goodwood Cup winner Mazzacano, the Prix de Pomone winner Colorado Dancer, the Kentucky Derby third Prince Of Thieves and the unraced Dance Of Leaves (dam of Charnwood Forest and Medaaly). (Hamdan Al Maktoum). *"A quality filly. Very athletic with a top-class pedigree, she has the action and conformation to match"*.

301 - TAYIL b.c. Caerleon - Desert Bluebell (Kalaglow).
March 15. Fourth foal. 250,000Y. Tattersalls Houghton.
Brother to the useful 1997 2-y-o 1m winner Distant Mirage and half-brother to the useful 1996 3-y-o 1m and subsequent US winner Roses In The Snow (by Be My Guest), the Italian 4-y-o winner Barbara Frietchie (by Try My Best) and the hurdles winner Scud Missile (by Persian Heights). The dam was placed 3 times at 3 yrs and stayed 13.6f and is a sister to the Group 3 Solario Stakes winner Shining Water (herself dam of the Grand Criterium and Dante Stakes winner Tenby). The second dam, Idle Waters (by Mill Reef), won the Group 2 Park Hill Stakes. (Hamdan Al Maktoum). *"Very closely related to Tenby, this is a well-made colt but unlikely to be out until the autumn"*.

302 - TRICOLORE b.f. Sadler's Wells - Tricorne (Green Desert).
February 15. First foal. 77,000Y. Tattersalls Houghton.
The dam was a fairly useful 2-y-o 6f winner and stayed 1m at 3 yrs. She is a sister to the useful 8.5f winner Papaha and a half-sister to the listed Fern Hill Stakes winner Barboukh. The second dam, Turban (by Glint Of Gold), a fair 10f and 11.7f winner, is a half-sister to the top-class middle-distance colt Old Vic, the dual Group 3 winner Splash Of Colour and the listed winners Bobinski and Green Lucia. (Mr M L Page). *"A small, backward filly at the moment"*.

303 - TRIPLE GREEN b.f. Green Desert - Triple Reef (Mill Reef).
May 28.
Half-sister to the unplaced 1997 2-y-o Trinity Reef, to the very useful Group 2 10f Sun Chariot Stakes winner Talented (both by Bustino), the useful 12f to 14.8f winner Trifolio (by Touching Wood), the useful 6f and 7f all-weather winner Triple Joy (by Most Welcome), the quite useful 13f to 14.9f winner Trazl (by Zalazl), the minor French 3-y-o winner Triple Entente (by Mummy's Pet) and the minor Irish 2-y-o winner Swift Chorus (by Music Boy). The dam is an unraced half-sister to the smart middle-distance winners Maysoon, Richard of York, Three Tails (dam of the high-class middle-distance colt Tamure) and Third Watch. The second dam, Triple First (by High Top), won the Group 2 10f Nassau Stakes and the Group 2 10f Sun Chariot Stakes. (Hesmonds Stud Ltd). *"A late foal and so backward at the moment"*.

304 - TRUMPET BLUES (USA) b.c. Dayjur - Iosifa (Top Ville).
January 27. 26,000Y. Tattersalls December.
Half-brother to the 1993 3-y-o 15.4f winner Elburg (by Ela Mana Mou) and to the staying winner of 9 races Iota (by Niniski) - both quite useful. The dam, a very useful 2-y-o 7f winner, was second in the listed Lingfield Oaks Trial. The second dam, Cojean (by Prince John), was a quite useful 2-y-o 5f winner. (Mr Bob Lalement). *"This is an early colt. He's well-grown and likely to debut in May"*.

305 - TURTLE VALLEY (IRE) b.c. Turtle Island - Primrose Valley (Mill Reef).
February 10. Sixth living foal. 34,000Y. Tattersalls October.
Half-brother to the Italian listed winner Prime Glade (by Green Forest), to the 1997 French 3-y-o winner Veiled Threat (by Be My Guest), the US winner of 10 minor races Tanis Valley (by Shahrastani) and a winner in Belgium by Danzig Connection. The dam, a useful 3-y-o 12f winner, is a sister to the

Ribblesdale Stakes winner Gull Nook (dam of the top-class middle-distance colt Pentire) and a half-sister to several good winners including the Group 3 winners Banket and Mr Pintips. The second dam, Bempton (by Blakeney), is a placed half-sister to Shirley Heights. (Hesmonds Stud Ltd). *"A compact, sharp sort of colt. On the small side, he's likely to be early".*

306 - UNNAMED
b.c. Storm Bird - Croquetallie (Alydar).
April 3. Third foal. IR300,000Y. Goffs Orby.
The dam, a minor winner at 4 yrs in the USA, is a half-sister to the Canadian Grade 3 8.5f Eclipse Stakes and Grade 3 10f Dominion Day Handicap winner Gold Alert. The second dam, Croquis (by Arts And Letters), won 6 races in the USA including a stakes event, was placed in the Grade 1 CCA Oaks and the Grade 1 Delaware Handicap and is a half-sister to the Grade 1 winner Linkage.

307 - UNNAMED
ch.c. Elmaamul - Lovers Light (Grundy).
April 19. IR33,000Y. Goffs Orby.
Half-brother to the 1997 unplaced 2-y-o Flicker (by Unfuwain), to the fair 1993 2-y-o 6f winner Glimpse (by Night Shift), the fair 3-y-o 12f winner Eliki (by Nishapour) and to a winner abroad by Mashhor Dancer. The dam is an unplaced half-sister to the good broodmare Lady Moon (dam of the Group winners Shining Steel and Moon Cactus). The second dam, Moonlight Night (by Levmoss), won the Musidora Stakes, was third in the Oaks and is a half-sister to the July Stakes and Cumberland Lodge Stakes winner Main Reef. (British Land Co.). *"A three-year-old in the making, he's a nice sort of horse who will get the time he needs".*

Mick Easterby

308 - DOONAREE (IRE)
b.c. Sadler's Wells - Rosananti (Blushing Groom).
January 12. IR200,000Y. Goffs Orby.
Half-brother to the very useful 14.8f winner and St Leger fourth Rubicund, to the 1997 French 12f listed winner Rosabella (both by Niniski), the Irish 2-y-o 6f winner Wedding Gallery (by Royal Academy), the modest 1m winner Persian Emperor (by Persepolis) and the poor 6f all-weather and 7f winner First Flush (by Precocious). The dam was a useful filly and a winner of 3 races from 6f to 1m including the Group 1 Premio Regina Elena and was second in the Group 1 12f Italian Oaks. She is a half-sister to 7 winners including Claddagh (a winner of 13 races here and in Europe), the Group 3 Berteux winner Sharnfold and the dam of the Princess Of Wales's Stakes winner Sapience. (MP Burke's 5th Family Settlement). *"A nice, big horse, he'll be out around June time and would want six or seven furlongs to start with".*

309 - MARNOR (USA)
b.c. Diesis - Love's Reward (Nonoalco).
March 3. Sixth foal. 140,000Y. Tattersalls Houghton.
Brother to the very promising 1997 2-y-o 7f winner Altibr, to the very smart Group 1 5f Prix de l'Abbaye winner Keen Hunter and the minor 4-y-o 7f winner Shedad and half-brother to the quite useful 3-y-o 14f winner Amoodi (by Forli) and the modest 1995 2-y-o 8.5f all-weather winner Kissing Gate (by Easy Goer). The dam is an unplaced half-sister to the Group 1 Middle Park Stakes winner Bassenthwaite and the very useful 2-y-o 5f and 6f winner Glancing. The second dam, Splashing (by Petingo), won the Cornwallis Stakes and is a half-sister to the dams of the Group winners Hadeer, Bay Street and Rose of Montreaux. (MP Burke's 5th Family Settlement). *"A big horse and just cantering at the moment, he'll be a decent sort and will be running by August".*

310 - MAYO
b.c. Nashwan - Nuryana (Nureyev).
March 11. Sixth foal. 220,000Y. Tattersalls Houghton.
Closely related to the quite useful 1991 2-y-o 1m winner Mystic Park (by Rainbow Quest) and half-brother to the high-class Group 1 1m Coronation Stakes winner Rebecca Sharp (by Machiavellian), the smart Group 3 11.5f Lingfield Derby Trial winner Mystic Knight (by Caerleon), the fairly useful middle-distance winner of 4 races Mystic Hill (by Shirley Heights) and the quite useful 2-y-o 6f winner Nuryandra (by Reference Point). The dam was a useful winner of 2 races over 1m including the listed Grand Metropolitan Stakes and is a half-sister to 5 winners including the dam of the useful Laurent-Perrier Champagne Stakes, Gimcrack Stakes and July Stakes placed 2-y-o Take A Left. The second dam, Loralane (by Habitat), was a quite useful 3-y-o 7f winner and a half-sister to the 1,000 Guineas and Sussex Stakes winner On The House. (MP Burke's 5th Family Settlement). *"Seven furlongs in July should be this colt's starting point as a two-year-old".*

311 - PAT THE FIDDLER (IRE)   b.c. Night Shift - Lucky Song (Seattle Song).
March 30. Fourth foal. IR41,000Y. Goffs Orby.
Half-brother to the smart listed 10f winner and Group 3 Brigadier Gerard Stakes second Lucky Di (by
Diesis) and to the minor US 3-y-o winner Baywood (by Woodman). The dam, a very smart filly, won
the Group 2 Park Hill Stakes and is a half-sister to 6 winners including the US Grade 3 winner Pollocks
Luck. The second dam, Lucky Us (by Nijinsky), is an unraced half-sister to the dam of the Champion
Canadian 3-y-o filly La Lorgnette. (MP Burke's 5th Family Settlement). *"A nice type of horse, and very
correct, he'll be running in May over five furlongs"*.

312 - PEAJAY (USA)   b.c. Dehere - Petroleuse (Habitat).
May 1. IR395,000Y. Goffs Orby.
Half-brother to the Grade 2 12f Long Island Handicap and listed 10f Prix Charles Laffitte winner Peinture
Bleue (by Alydar) - herself dam of the Prix de l'Arc de Triomphe winner Peintre Celebre, to the US
Grade 3 1m William P Kyne Handicap winner Provins and the Group 3 11f Andre Baboin winner Parme.
The dam won the Group 3 8.5f Princess Elizabeth Stakes and the Blue Seal Stakes and is a half-sister
to Pawneese (winner of the King George VI and Queen Elizabeth Stakes, the Oaks and the Prix de
Diane). The second dam, Plencia (by Le Haar), won the listed Prix de l'Elevage and is a half-sister to
the King George winner Montaval. (MP Burke's 5th Family Settlement). *"A handy type of horse and
very correct, we won't see him on the racecourse until August"*.

313 - STANLEY WIGFIELD (USA)   b.c. Woodman - Las Meninas (Glenstal).
April 16. First foal. IR110,000Y. Goffs Orby.
The dam won 2 races including the 1,000 Guineas and was second in the Irish 1,000 Guineas and the
Group 1 Heinz '57' Phoenix Stakes. She is a sister to Head Of The Abbey (a winner of 7 races in
Ireland and the USA) and a half-sister to 3 winners. The second dam, Spanish Habit (by Habitat), is
an unraced half-sister to 5 winners out of the Group 2 Player-Wills Stakes winner Donna Cressida.
(MP Burke's 5th Family Settlement). *"This colt should be out in May, he's quite sharp and rangy"*.

314 - TISSIFER   b.c. Polish Precedent - Ingozi (Warning).
March 26. First foal. 120,000Y. Tattersalls Houghton.
The dam, a fairly useful winner over 7f and 8.1f at 3 yrs including a listed event at Sandown Park, is a
half-sister to the very smart and tough 7f Greenham Stakes, 7f Criterion Stakes and 7.3f Hungerford
Stakes (all Group 3 events) winner Inchinor (by Ahonoora). The second dam, Inchmurrin (by Lomond),
a very useful winner of 6 races from 5f to 1m including the Child Stakes and second in the Coronation
Stakes, is closely related to the very useful 1m winner Guest Artiste and a half-sister to the Mill Reef
Stakes winner Welney. (MP Burke's 5th Family Settlement). *"A strong colt, he'll be out over seven
furlongs in mid-summer"*.

Tim Easterby

315 - MARTON MERE   ch.c. Cadeaux Genereux - Hyatti (Habitat).
April 25. 30,000Y. Tattersalls October.
Half-brother to the 3-y-o Roxy (by Rock City), to the fair 5f (at 2 yrs) and 6f all-weather winner Most
Uppitty (by Absalom), the fair Memsahb (by Prince Sabo), a winner of four races over 5f at 2 and 3 yrs
and the useful maiden and Irish 1,000 Guineas second Goodnight Kiss (by Night Shift). The dam, a
fair 3-y-o 9f placed maiden, is a half-sister to 3 minor winners in France and Germany. The second
dam, Cutie Kiss (by Luthier), is an unraced half-sister to the Group 2 Premio Ribot winner Costly Wave
(herself dam of Great Lakes, Inishdalla, Severn Bore and Swept Away - all at least useful). (Mr T H
Bennett). *"Marton Mere might want six furlongs to start with. He's a good-looking, sensible colt with a
bit of size and I like him at the moment"*. Tim has several other two-year-olds in the Early Types section
of the book.

316 - MIXSTERTHETRIXTER (USA)   b.c. Alleged - Parliament House (General Assembly).
January 24. Third foal. 38,000Y. Tattersalls Houghton.
The dam, a minor winner in the USA, is closely related to the US stakes winner Subjective and to the
Lupe Stakes second Celtic Assembly (dam of the Group 1 Haydock Park Sprint winner Cherokee
Rose) and a half-sister to 9 other winners including Molesnes (Group 1 Prix du Cadran) and Celtic Heir
(Group 3 Horris Hill Stakes). The second dam, Welsh Garden (by Welsh Saint), won 5 races including
the listed Waterford Glass Nursery Handicap and is a half-sister to the Grade 1 Man O'War Stakes and
Grade 1 Sunset Handicap winner Galaxy Libra and the Group 2 Prix du Conseil de Paris winner Garden

Of Heaven. (MP Burke's 5th Family Settlement). *"Seven furlongs or a mile should suit this colt this year. He's a good sort and a very good mover"* the trainer tells me.

---

317 - PROSPERITY
b.c. Catrail - Bequeath (Lyphard).
March 16. Sixth foal. 27,000Y. Tattersalls December.
Half-brother to the very smart Group 2 1m Prix du Rond-Point and Group 3 7f Hungerford Stakes winner Decorated Hero, to the German 2-y-o winner Give Warning (both by Warning), the 1997 7f placed 2-y-o Mubrik (by Lahib) and the fair handicapper Beneficiary (by Jalmood), a winner of 6 races at up to 7f. The dam, a minor French 3-y-o 9f winner, is a half-sister to 3 winners out of the US winner and Grade 2 placed Bequa (by Never Bend), herself a half-sister to 6 winners. (R Griffin Syndicate). *"A mid-summer type two-year-old, Prosperity has done well physically over the winter".*

---

318 - RUM POINTER
b.c. Turtle Island - Osmunda (Mill Reef).
April 24. IR50,000Y. Goffs Orby.
Half-brother to the 1997 Irish 7f placed 2-y-o Broken Promise (by Brief Truce), to the fairly useful 12f and 16.5f winner Icecapped, the Irish 10f and hurdles winner Padiord (both by Caerleon), the Irish 12f winner Jury Service (by Law Society) and the modest 1996 3-y-o 10f winner El Bardador (by Thatching). The dam, a winner in Ireland over 10f and fourth in the Group 2 Pretty Polly Stakes, is a half-sister to the Group 2 Beresford Stakes winner Icelandic and the Group 2 Sun Chariot Stakes winner Snow. The second dam, Arctic Walk (by Arctic Slave), won over 12f and 2m. (MP Burke's 5th Family Settlement). *"A very good-bodied horse, he's not going to be as early as we first thought. A tough colt and very laid-back, he looks very much like his sire".*

David Elsworth

319 - DEADLY NIGHTSHADE (IRE)
b.f. Night Shift - Dead Certain (Absalom).
March 13. Fifth foal.
Closely related to the useful 1996 Irish 3-y-o 7f and 10f winner Hamad and the quite useful 1997 3-y-o 11.6f winner Dead Aim (both by Sadler's Wells). The dam was a very smart filly and winner of the Group 1 6f Cheveley Park Stakes, the Queen Mary Stakes and the Lowther Stakes at 2 yrs, and the Group 2 6.5f Prix Maurice de Gheest as a three-year-old when she was also second in the Cork and Orrery Stakes. Dead Certain is a half-sister to 6 winners, including the fairly useful 10f handicapper Fire Top, out of the French 1m to 10f winner Sirnelta (by Sir Tor) - herself a daughter of a half-sister to the French Derby winner Sanctus II. (Exors of the late Commander G G Martin). *David has given me these three particularly nice two-year-olds to watch out for this year. "Deadly Nightshade came into the yard late but she could still make a two-year-old. To start with, a Salisbury maiden over five or six furlongs could be on the cards for her". The two colts below are both useful types we should keep an eye on.*

---

320 - ISLAND SANDS
br.c. Turtle Island - Tiavanita (J O Tobin).
January 27. IR18,000Y. Goffs Orby. Fourth foal.
Half-brother to the 3-y-o Ruby Affair (by Night Shift), to the quite useful 1995 3-y-o 8.2f and 10f winner Muferr (by Groom Dancer) and a winner in Sweden by Polish Patriot. The dam is an unraced half-sister to 8 winners including the Great Voltigeur Stakes and Lingfield Derby Trial winner Corrupt. The second dam, Nirvanita (by Right Royal), is an unraced half-sister to the Prix d'Ispahan and Prix Jacques le Marois winner Nadjar.

---

321 - WOLF TOOTH
ch.c. Wolfhound - Collide (High Line).
March 28. 32,000Y. Tattersalls October.
Closely realated to the 3-y-o Starwort (by Soviet Star). The dam, a useful dual 1m winner at 3 yrs, is a sister to the winning Irish stayer Carricero and a half-sister to 8 winners. The second dam, Collapse (by Busted), was a very useful winner of 5 races from 5f to 1m and was listed placed.

Andre Fabre

322 - ARIUS
ch.c. Royal Academy - Ville Eternelle (Slew O'Gold).
March 12. Fourth foal.
Half-brother to the French trained 3-y-o Villa Franca (by In The Wings). The dam is a half-sister to the high-class colts Mill Native (by Exclusive Native), winner of the Grade 1 10f Arlington Million and French Stress (by Sham), winner of the Group 3 1m Prix du Chemin de Fer du Nord and the Group 3 1m Prix

Edmond Blanc, to the very useful Group 3 10.5f Prix de Flore winner Sporades (by Vaguely Noble) and the 2-y-o 5f Prix du Bois winner American Stress (by Sham). The second dam, Stresa (by Mill Reef), won over 10f at 3 yrs at Deauville and is a half-sister to Terreno and Antrona - both very smart.

323 - ASTORIA
b.c. Sadler's Wells - Penza (Soviet Star).
March 16. First foal. 140,000Y. Tattersalls Houghton.
The dam, placed once over 10f at 3 yrs in Ireland, is a half-sister to the Italian Derby winner White Muzzle and the listed Diamond Stakes winner Elfaslah. The second dam, Fair Of The Furze (by Ela-Mana-Mou), won 4 races including the Group 2 Tattersalls Rogers Gold Cup and is a half-sister to the listed winners Norman Style, Proconsular, Majestic Role and Supreme Commander.

324 - BLUE CLOUD (IRE)
ch.f. Nashwan - Batave (Posse).
January 31.
Half-brother to the high class Group 1 1m Queen Elizabeth II Stakes, Group 1 9.3f Prix d'Ispahan and Group 1 7f Prix de la Foret winner Bigstone, to the 1990 2-y-o 6f listed Prix Yacowlef winner Bague Bleue (both by Last Tycoon) and the French 1m winner and Group 3 Prix Quincey third Bakari (by Lomond),. The dam, a dual 3-y-o 6f winner at Newmarket and Kempton, subsequently won in France and was placed in both the Group 3 6f Prix de Meautry and Goup 3 5f Prix de Saint-Georges and is a half-sister to the good French hurdler Beaux Arts. The second dam, Bon Appetit (by Major Portion), was a useful winner of the Group 3 Prix Vanteaux.

325 - CARNAC (FR)
b.br.c. Royal Academy - La Consaca (Konigsstuhl).
April 2. Second foal. FF2,300,000. Deauville August.
The dam was placed once at 3 yrs in Germany, is a sister to the German Group 2 winner Lorado and a half-sister to the Group 1 Grosser Preis Von Baden winner Lomitas. The second dam, La Colorada (by Surumu), won a Group 3 event over 10.5f in Germany. (Sheikh Mohammed).

326 - CHEVIOT HILLS (USA)
b.f. Gulch - Chateaubaby (Nureyev).
May 2. Fifth foal. $350,000Y. Keeneland September.
Half-sister to Fantastic Fellow (by Lear Fan), a winner from 7f (at 2 yrs) to 8.5f including the listed Prix Djebel and two Grade 3 events in the USA and to the minor French 2-y-o 5.5f winner Chateau La Riviere (by Irish River). The dam, a modest 5f and 7f placed 2-y-o, is a half-sister to the Derby winner Henbit and to the dam of the US Grade 1 winners Mr Purple and Queens Court Queen. The second dam, Chateaucreek (by Chateaugay), won 6 races in the USA including a stakes event. (Sheikh Mohammed).

327 - CHOICE SPIRIT (USA)
b.f. Danzig - Zaizafon (The Minstrel).
March 25.
Half-sister to the French trained 3-y-o Zagruhta, to the Champion 1992 2-y-o and 1993 3-y-o Zafonic, winner of the 2,000 Guineas, the Dewhurst Stakes, the Prix de la Salamandre and the Prix Morny, the smart 1996 French 2-y-o Zamindar (all by Gone West), winner of the Group 3 6f Prix de Cabourg and second in the Prix Morny, the minor US 4-y-o winner Botanic (by Mr Prospector), the 1994 French 2-y-o 6f winner Bold Empress (by Diesis) and the 1993 French 2-y-o dual 1m winner Press Baron (by Private Account). The dam won twice over 7f at 2 yrs and was a smart 3-y-o, being placed in the Group 1 1m Queen Elizabeth II Stakes and the Group 3 1m Child Stakes. She is a half-sister to the unraced Modena, herself dam of the high class Eclipse Stakes and Phoenix Champion Stakes winner Elmaamul. The second dam, Mofida (by Right Tack), was a very useful winner of 8 races at up to 7.2f and was placed in the Duke of York Stakes. She was very tough too, running no less than 41 times from 2 to 4 yrs. This filly is inbred 2x3 to Northern Dancer. (Khaled Abdulla).

328 - COLCHICA
b.f. Machiavellian - Ivrea (Sadler's Wells).
February 26. Third foal.
Closely related to the quite useful 1994 2-y-o 7f winner and 1m placed 3-y-o Hedera (by Woodman) and the modest 1997 3-y-o 13.8f winner Itatinga (by Riverman). The dam, a very useful 2-y-o 7f winner, was placed in the Group 2 12f Ribblesdale Stakes and the Group 3 10.5f Musidora Stakes at 3 yrs, is a sister to the useful 2-y-o 6f winner Iviza (also placed in the Musidora and Ribblesdale) and a half-sister to the very useful Irish 2-y-o 1m and 3-y-o Group 1 12f Italian Oaks winner Ivyanna (by Reference Point). The second dam, Ivy (by Sir Ivor), placed twice at 2 yrs in the USA, is a full or half-sister to 11 winners including the Grade 1 Santa Anita Derby winner An Act and the Grade 2 winner Sarsar. (Sheikh Mohammed).

329 - DANCING FIRE (USA) b.f. Dayjur - Danseuse du Soir (Thatching).

Third foal.

Half-sister to the French trained 3-y-o Dircret Amour (by Riverman). The dam was a smart sprinter and a winner of five races including the Group 2 Prix du Gros Chene, the Group 2 Prix du Ris-Orangis, the Group 3 Prix de Seine et Oise and the Group 3 Prix d'Arenburg. She is a half-sister to the high-class colt Pursuit of Love, winner of the Group 2 Prix Maurice de Gheest and second in the July Cup. The second dam, Dance Quest (by Green Dancer), was also a smart sprinter - particularly at 2 yrs - and is a half-sister to the Prix de la Salamandre winner Noblequest.

330 - DANZARI ch.f. Arazi - Dangora (Sovereign Dancer).

March 10. Fourth foal.

Half-sister to the quite useful 1996 2-y-o 7f winner Corsini (by Machiavellian) and the 1995 French 2-y-o 6f winner Delegate (by Polish Precedent). The dam, a very useful 2-y-o, won twice over 6f and was second in the Group 2 Lowther Stakes. She is closely related to the smart filly Zaizafon (dam of Zafonic) and a half-sister to the unraced Modena (dam of Elmaamul). Second dam, Mofida (by Right Tack), won 8 races at up to 7f and was placed in the Duke of York Stakes. (Khaled Abdulla).

331 - DHARMA (USA) b.f. Zilzal - Encorelle (Arctic Tern).

Half-sister to the 3-y-o Come Up Smiling, to the very smart German Group 2 winning miler Royal Abjar, the fairly useful 1996 2-y-o 7f winner Sunbeam Dance (all by Gone West), the useful French 1m (at 2 yrs) and 10f winner After The Sun (by Storm Bird), the French 2-y-o winner and Group 3 placed Stormagain (by Storm Cat), the French listed winner Encoremoi (by Assert) and minor winners in France and the USA by Storm Bird and Clever Trick. The dam is an unraced sister to the Group 1 Prix de Diane winner Escaline and a half-sister to the Group 3 Premio Carlo Porta winner Esdale. The second dam, Esdee (by Hail To Reason), was placed at 3 yrs in France and is a half-sister to 6 winners. (Maktoum Al Maktoum).

332 - FIRST MAGNITUDE (IRE) ch.c. Arazi - Crystal Cup (Nijinsky).

April 17. 115,000Y. Tattersalls Houghton.

Half-brother to the high-class colt Iktamal (by Danzig Connection), winner of the Group 1 6f Haydock Sprint Cup and the Group 3 7f Beeswing Stakes and to the US Grade 2 9f Arkansas Derby winner Rockamundo (by Key to the Mint), the quite useful 11.7f to 14f winner Crystal Cross (by Roberto), the fair 1997 2-y-o 6f all-weather winner Roi Brisbane (by Roi Danzig) and the 2-y-o Japanese winner Suspense Queen (by Woodman). The dam ran unplaced twice in the USA but is a half-sister to 8 winners including the Group 3 Gladness Stakes winner Rose Reef and the listed winners Golden Bowl and Rokeby. The second dam, Rose Bowl (by Habitat), a half-sister to Ile de Bourbon, was a champion filly and winner of 6 races including the Champion Stakes and the Queen Elizabeth II Stakes (twice).

333 - GRACIOSO (USA) ch.c. Nureyev - Don't Sulk (Graustark).

May 16. $385,000. Keeneland July.

Sister to the very useful French 1993 3-y-o 1m listed stakes winner and subsequent US Grade 2 Bay Meadows Handicap winner Caesour, to the useful 12f listed Galtres Stakes winner Professional Girl, the useful 7f (at 2 yrs) and 8.5f winner Dragonada and the minor French 3-y-o winner Tragic Role, closely related to the minor French 12f winner Boudeuse (by Nijinsky) and half-sister to the minor winner Provocatrice (by Irish River). The dam won 3 races including the Group 3 12f Prix de Royallieu, is a sister to the US Grade 1 winner Jim French and a half-sister to the good middle-distance colt Triomphe and to Native Partner (the dam of Ajdal and Formidable). The second dam, Dinner Partner (by Tom Fool), won 4 races including 2 minor stakes and bred a total of 12 winners. (Sheikh Mohammed).

334 - GRAZALEMA (USA) b.c. Storm Bird - Dellagrazia (Trempolino).

April 5. First foal. FF2,200,000. Deauville August.

The dam, a minor winner in France, is a half-sister to 7 winners including the Group 2 Tattersalls Rogers Gold Cup winner Fair Of The Furze (dam of the Italian Derby winner White Muzzle) and the listed winners Norman Style, Proconsular, Majestic Role and Supreme Commander. The second dam, Autocratic (by Tyrant), won once in Ireland and is a half-sister to 6 winners including the US Grade 3 winner Flightish. (Sheikh Mohammed).

335 - GREAT SPIRIT (USA)　　　　　　　　　　　b.c. Irish River - Gold Bird (Rheingold).

Half-brother to the Group 1 Prix Lupin winner Galetto, the Group 1 Prix de la Foret winner Gabina (both by Caro) and the minor French 10.5f winner and listed placed Gold Rose (by Noblequest) - herself dam of the smart 1994 2-y-o Group 1 1m Grand Criterium winner Goldmark. The dam won a listed event over 10.5f in France and is out of Orange Bird, a winning half-sister to the Premio Roma winner Duke of Marmalade and to the dam of the high-class American colt Cryptoclearance.

336 - HALL OF HEROES (USA)　　　　　　b.c. Gone West - Personal Glory (Danzig).
　　　　　　　　　　　　　　　　April 2. Fifth foal. $300,000. Keeneland July.
Brother to the US 2-y-o Grade 2 8.5f Norfolk Stakes winner Supremo and half-sister to the German listed winner Personal Love. The dam is an unraced half-sister to the Grade 2 Jersey Derby and Grade 2 Discovery Handicap winner Dynaformer. The second dam, Andover Way (by His Majesty), won the US Grade 1 Top Flight Handicap and is a half-sister to the US Grade 2 winner Darby Creek Road. (Sheikh Mohammed).

337 - HEALING HANDS　　　　　　　　　br.f. Zafonic - One Life (L'Emigrant).
　　　　　　　　　　　　　　　　April 8. Sixth foal. 160,000Y. Tattersalls Houghton.
Half-sister to the quite useful 7.5f to 12f winner Tenorio (by Law Society), to the French 3-y-o winner of 7 races from 7f to 9f Lithuania (by Ti King) and the minor French winner No Rehearsal (by Baillamont). The unraced dam is closely related to the outstanding filly Miesque (herself dam of the Group 1 winners Kingmambo and East of the Moon). The second dam, Pasadoble (by Prove It), won four races in France including two stakes events over 1m and is a half-sister to the US Grade 1 winner Silver Supreme. (Maktoum Al Maktoum).

338 - JOIE DE VIVRE (IRE)　　　　　　ch.f. Be My Guest - Secretary Bird (Kris).
　　　　　　　　　　　　　　　　February 13. Third foal. IR350,000Y. Goffs Orby.
Half-sister to the 3-y-o Mama Carmen (by Ela-Mana-Mou). The dam is an unraced half-sister to the classic winners Assert (French and Irish Derby), Bikala (French Derby) and Eurobird (Irish St Leger). The second dam, Irish Bird (by Sea Bird II), won over 11f in France and is a half-sister to the Irish Derby winner Irish Ball and to Mill Princess, dam of the top-class colt Last Tycoon.

339 - LOTHAIR (USA)　　　　　　　　　b.br.c. Kingmambo - Lotka (Danzig).
　　　　　　　　　　　　　　　　February 29. $350,000. Keeneland July.
Closely related to the US Grade 3 8.5f Affectionately Handicap winner Lotta Dancing (by Alydar) and to the minor US 3-y-o winner Kossakowna (by Mr Prospector). The dam won 10 races including the Grade 1 1m Acorn Stakes and the Grade 2 9f Black Helen Handicap and is a sister to the Grade 1 Hollywood Futurity and Dwyer Stakes winner Stephan's Odyssey. The second dam, Kennelot (by Gallant Man), won 3 races in the USA and is a half-sister to the Kentucky Derby winner Cannonade. (Sheikh Mohammed).

340 - LOUP DES NEIGES (IRE)　　　　　b.c. Rainbow Quest - Louve Romaine (Alydar).
　　　　　　　　　　　　　　　　April 18. Third foal.
Half-sister to the French trained 3-y-o Lune de Mai (by Kenmare). The dam was a smart French 10f winner and was placed in the Group 1 Prix de Diane and the Group 1 Prix Saint-Alary. She is a half-sister to the very smart 1m winners Legend of France and Louveterie (herself dam of the Group 1 Grand Criterium winner Loup Solitaire) and the very useful 10f winner and Prix Saint-Alary second Louve Bleue. The second dam, Lupe (by Primera), won the 1970 Oaks and the Coronation Cup.

341 - LOUVE (USA)　　　　　　　　　　b.f. Irish River - Louveterie (Nureyev).
　　　　　　　　　　　　　　　　Fifth foal.
Closely related to the very smart 1997 Group 3 10f Prix du Prince d'Orange winner and Irish Derby third Loup Sauvage and the promising 1997 French 2-y-o 7.5f winner Loudeac (both by Riverman) and half-sister to the Group 1 1m Grand Criterium winner and Group 1 10.5f Prix Lupin second Loup Solitaire (by Lear Fan). The dam won the Group 3 8.2f Prix Vanteaux and was second in the Prix de Diane. She is closely related to the good miler Legend of France and a half-sister to the good winners Leonardo de Vinci, Louve Bleue and Louve Romaine. The second dam, Lupe (by Primera), won the Oaks, the Coronation Cup and the Yorkshire Oaks.

342 - MARINA CAY br.c. Zafonic - Dockage (Riverman).
February 24.
Brother to the promising 1997 2-y-o 7f winner Pontoon and half-brother to the very useful 1992 2-y-o Group 3 6f July Stakes and 3-y-o listed 9f winner Wharf (by Storm Bird), the 1994 2-y-o 7f winner Shapely and the fairly useful 1993 2-y-o 1m winner Colza (both by Alleged). The dam, a winner over 1m at 2 yrs and a 9f listed event at 3 yrs in France, is out of Golden Alibi (by Empery), a three-parts sister to the brilliant mare Dahlia. (Khaled Abdulla).

---

343 - MOUNTAIN SPIRIT (IRE) b.f. Royal Academy - Martingale (Luthier).
March 11.
Half-sister to the smart Group 1 10f Prix Saint-Alary and Group 3 10.5f Prix Penelope winner Muncie (by Sadler's Wells), to the smart Group 1 15.5f Prix Royal-Oak winner Mersey (by Crystal Palace) and the placed Madame du Barry (dam of both the Group 3 C L Weld Park Stakes winner Morcote and the listed winner Miami Sands). The dam was a useful winner of 2 races over 1m at 3 yrs and is a half-sister to the Prix du Moulin winner Mount Hagen and the French 1,000 Guineas winner Madelia (herself dam of the Prix Saint-Alary winner Moonlight Dance). The second dam, Moonmadness (by Luthier), was placed in the USA.

---

344 - NOCONA (FR) b.f. Fairy King - Eclat Nocturne (Majestic Light).
January 18. Fourth foal. FF900,000. Deauville August.
The dam is an unraced daughter of the 1983 2-y-o listed 7.5f Criterium de Bernay winner and dual Group 3 placed Perdomi (by Persian Bold), herself a half-sister to the Prix du Lutece and Prix de Barbeville winner Mardonius. (Sheikh Mohammed).

---

345 - PACE STALKER (USA) b.c. Lear Fan - In The Habit (Lyphard).
April 20. Sixth foal. $340,000Y. Keeneland September.
Half-brother to the modest 10f to 12f winner Ordained and the 1997 German 3-y-o winner Fly On Flash (both by Mtoto). The dam, a quite useful 3-y-o dual 12f winner, is out of the US Grade 1 10f Santa Barbara Handicap and Grade 1 9f Gamely Handicap winner Sisterhood (by Exclusive Native). (Maktoum Al Maktoum).

---

346 - PEACE SIGNAL (USA) b.f. Time For A Change - Peinture Bleue (Alydar).
Fourth foal.
Half-sister to the 3-y-o Pine Chip and to the outstanding 1997 3-y-o middle-distance colt Peinture Bleue (both by Nureyev), winner of the Prix de l'Arc de Triomphe, the French Derby, the Grand Prix de Paris and the Prix Greffulhe. The dam won the Grade 2 12f Long Island Handicap in the USA and the listed 10f Prix Charles Laffitte at Longchamp and is a half-sister to the US Grade 3 winner Provins and the French Group 3 winner Parme. The second dam, Petroleuse (by Habitat), won the listed 6f Blue Seal Stakes (at 2 yrs) and the Group 3 8.5f Princess Eliabeth Stakes and is a half-sister to the Oaks, Prix de Diane and King George VI and Queen Elizabeth Diamond Stakes winner Pawneese.

---

347 - PEACE TALK (FR) b.f. Sadler's Wells - Pampa Bella (Armos).

Sister to the 1997 Group 3 10.5f Prix de Flore winner Palme d'Or and to the top-class colt Pistolet Bleu (by Top Ville), winner of the Group 1 Criterium de Saint-Cloud (at 2 yrs), the Group 1 Grand Prix de Saint-Cloud, Group 2 Prix Hocquart, Group 2 Prix Noailles and Group 2 Grand Prix d'Evry. The dam, a very useful filly, won the Group 3 10.5f Prix Penelope and was third in both the Prix de Diane and the Prix Saint Alary. The second dam, Kendie (by Klairon), won a small race in France.

---

348 - RAUCOUS LAD b.c. Warning - Someone Special (Habitat).
May 9. 420,000Y. Tattersalls Houghton.
Half-brother to the smart Group 2 10.4f Dante Stakes and Group 3 1m Craven Stakes winner Alnasr Alwasheek (by Sadlers Wells), to the smart Group 2 Sun Chariot Stakes winner One So Wonderful (by Nashwan), the very useful 1993 2-y-o 7f Rockfel Stakes winner and Irish 1,000 Guineas, Nassau Stakes and Sun Chariot Stakes placed Relatively Special, the quite useful 6f winner All Time Great (by Night Shift) and the hurdles winner Someone Brave (by Commanche Run). The dam, a useful 7f winner and third in the Group 1 1m Coronation Stakes to Sonic Lady, is a half-sister to the top-class miler Milligram. The second dam, One in a Million (by Rarity), won the 1,000 Guineas and Coronation Stakes and is out of an unraced half-sister to Deep Run. (Maktoum Al Maktoum).

349 - REPLAY (IRE)   b.c. Sadler's Wells - Sequel (Law Society).
March 21. Third foal. 300,000Y. Tattersalls Houghton.
Brother to the 3-y-o Shalwar Kameez and to Family Tradition, a winner of 3 races from 7f to 14f including the listed Debutante Stakes and third in the Group 1 Prix Marcel Boussac. The dam was third over 1m and fourth over 12f in Ireland as a 3-y-o. She is a half-sister to I Will Follow (the dam of Rainbow Quest), Slightly Dangerous (the dam of Commander in Chief, Warning, Dushyantor, Deploy and Yashmak) and Idyllic (the dam of Scenic). The second dam, Where You Lead (by Raise a Native), won the Musidora Stakes and was second in the Oaks. (Sheikh Mohammed).

350 - ROYAL ARROW (USA)   b.c. Dayjur - Buy The Firm (Affirmed).
February 26. Fourth foal. $65,000Y. Keeneland September.
Half-brother to the 1997 US 3-y-o winner Storm Broker (by Storm Cat). The dam, a winner of 12 races in the USA including the Grade 1 9f Top Flight Handicap and the Grade 2 9f Long Look Handicap, is a half-sister to the Grade 1 San Felipe Handicap winner Image Of Greatness. The second dam, By The Hand (by Intentionally), is a winning half-sister to 5 winners including the Manhattan Handicap winner Shelter Bay. (Maktoum Al Maktoum).

351 - ROYAL LINE   b.c. Saint Estephe - Double Line (What A Guest).
February 17. FF620,000. Deauville August.
Half-brother to the 3-y-o Surehand (by Sanglamore). The dam is a placed half-sister to the French 1,000 Guineas winner Pearl Bracelet (herself dam of the US Grade 3 winner Fleur de Nuit), to the very useful 1m (at 2 yrs) and 10.3f winner Forest Buck and the very useful French 2-y-o 6f winner Sugar Walls. The second dam, Zirconia (by Charlottesville), was a useful winner of 3 races at up to 1m in France and was fifth in the 1,000 Guineas. (Sheikh Mohammed).

352 - SKIMMING (USA)   b.c. Nureyev - Skimble (Lyphard).
January 30.
The dam, a fairly useful 6f (at 2 yrs) and 10.4f winner here, subsequently won 7 stakes events in the USA. She is a sister to the fair 10f winner Flit and is closely related to the Grade 1 Washington Lassie Stakes winner Contredance, the listed Roses Stakes winner Old Alliance and to the dam of the Lanson Champagne Stakes winner Eltish. The second dam, Nimble Folly (by Cyane), is an unraced sister to the very useful 2-y-o Group 3 winner and Group 1 third Misgivings. (Khaled Abdulla).

353 - SPINAZZOLA (USA)   ch.f. Irish River - Spit Curl (Northern Dancer).
January 28. Sixth foal. IR210,000Y. Goffs Orby.
Half-sister to the winner of 9 races in the USA, Ditch Plains (by Cox's Ridge) and to 2 minor 3-y-o winners in the USA by Mr Prospector and Ogygian. The dam won the Grade 1 10f Alabama Stakes, was second in the Grade 1 12f Coaching Club American Oaks and is closely related to the US Grade 3 Seneca Handicap winner Diver. The second dam, Coiffure (by Sir Gaylord), won at 2 yrs in France and was second in the Group 3 10f Prix Chloe. (Sheikh Mohammed).

354 - STATE SECRET   b.f. Green Desert - It's In The Air (Mr Prospector).
April 12.
Half-sister to the 3-y-o Note Musicale (by Sadler's Wells), to the very useful 1994 3-y-o 7.6f and 10f winner Monaassabaat (by Zilzal), the very useful 1987 2-y-o Group 2 Criterium de Maisons-Laffitte winner Bitooh (by Seattle Slew), the quite useful 1993 3-y-o 10f winner Arkaan (by Nijinsky), the American 1m stakes winner Air Dancer (by Northern Dancer) and the French trained winners Try to Catch Me (by Shareef Dancer) and Sous Entendu (by Shadeed). The dam, a joint-champion 2-y-o filly in the USA, won from 6f to 10f and is out of the 2-y-o winner A Wind is Rising (by Francis S), herself a half-sister to the good racehorse and sire Native Royalty. (Maktoum Al Maktoum).

355 - SUMMER BREEZE   br.f. Rainbow Quest - Suntrap (Roberto).
March 19. Sixth foal.
Sister to the French trained 3-y-o Rainshack, to the high-class Grade 1 12f Rothmans International, Group 1 15.5f Prix Royal-Oak and Group 2 15f Prix Kergorlay winner Raintrap and the very smart Group 1 10f Criterium de Saint-Cloud and Group 2 12f Prix du Conseil de Paris winner Sunshack. The dam, a useful dual 7f winner at 2 yrs and third in the Group 3 Prix d'Aumale, is a half-sister to the Group 2 German winner Non Partisan and the Grade 3 Canadian stakes winner Jalaajel. The second dam, Sunny Bay (by Northern Bay), won 3 stakes events in the USA and was second in the Grade 1 Sorority Stakes. (Khaled Abdulla).

356 - THEATRIX
b.c. Theatrical - Sylph (Alleged).
April 8.

Half-brother to the very useful Group 2 12f Prix de Malleret winner Privity, the Group 3 9f Prix Saint Roman winner Zindari (both by Private Account), the quite useful 12f winner Mingus (by The Minstrel) and the fairly useful 10f and 10.5f winner Nesaah (by Topsider). The dam was a very useful winner of the Group 3 12f Princess Royal Stakes, is a sister to the Irish St Leger winner Leading Counsel and closely related to the very useful middle-distance stakes winner Present The Colors. The second dam, Society Column (by Sir Gaylord), was an 8.5f stakes winner and a half-sister to the triple US Grade 1 stakes winner Typecast (herself dam of the Japanese Group 1 winner Pretty Cast). (Khaled Abdulla).

357 - TREFULA (IRE)
b.f. Rainbow Quest - Trefoil (Kris).
March 12. First foal.

The dam was a very useful winner of 2 races including a listed event over 10.5f in France. She is a full or half-sister to numerous winners including the smart middle-distance winners Maysoon, Richard of York, Three Tails (dam of the high-class middle-distance colt Tamure) and Third Watch. The second dam, Triple First (by High Top), won the Group 2 10f Nassau Stakes and the Group 2 10f Sun Chariot Stakes. (Sheikh Mohammed).

358 - VALLEE DES REVES (USA)
b.f. Kingmambo - Venise (Nureyev).

Closely related to the French trained 3-y-o Viking's Cove (by Miswaki) and half-sister to the Group 2 9.3f Prix de l'Opera winner Verveine (by Lear Fan), the Group 2 1m Prix du Muguet winner Vetheuil (by Riverman) and the minor 3-y-o winner Vanishing Prairie (by Alysheba). The dam is an unplaced three-parts sister to the Mill Reef Stakes and Richmond Stakes winner Vacarme and a half-sister to the Prix Jacques le Marois winner Vin de France. The second dam, Virunga (by Sodium) won the 12f Prix de Malleret and is a half-sister to the Champion Stakes winner Vitiges.

359 - VICTORY CRY (IRE)
ch.f. Caerleon - Verveine (Lear Fan).
March 14. Second foal.

Half-sister to the French trained 3-y-o Vagabond (by Alzao). The dam was a smart winner of the Group 3 7f Prix du Calvados (at 2 yrs) and the Group 2 9.3f Prix de l'Opera and is a half-sister to the Group 2 1m Prix du Muguet winner Vetheuil. The second dam, Venise (by Nureyev), is an unraced three-parts sister to the Mill Reef Stakes winner Vacarme and a half-sister to the Prix Jacques le Marois winner Vin de France. The third dam, Virunga (by Sodium) won the 12f Prix de Malleret and is a half-sister to the Champion Stakes winner Vitiges.

360 - WAJINA
b.f. Rainbow Quest - Wajd (Northern Dancer).
April 17. Fourth foal.

Sister to the 3-y-o Nedawi and half-sister to the smart Group 3 12f Cumberland Lodge Stakes winner Wall Street (by Mr Prospector). The dam, a very smart filly, won the Group 2 12f Grand Prix d'Evry and the Group 3 12f Prix de Minerve, is closely related to the Group 1 Prix Lupin, Grade 1 Century Handicap, San Juan Capistrano Invitational Handicap and San Luis Rey Stakes winner Dahar and to the US Grade 2 winner Llandaff and a half-sister to the US Grade 1 winners Rivlia, Delegant and Dahlia's Dreamer. The second dam, Dahlia (by Vaguely Noble), was a brilliant and tough mare. She won 15 races, notably the King George VI and Queen Elizabeth Stakes (twice), the Benson and Hedges Gold Cup (twice), the Irish Oaks, Grand Prix de Saint-Cloud, Prix Saint-Alary, Man O'War Stakes, Washington D C International, Hollywood Invitational Handicap and the Canadian International Championship. (Sheikh Mohammed).

361 - WHITE QUARTZ (IRE)
gr.f. Sadler's Wells - Modiyna (Nishapour).
February 8. IR115,000Y. Goffs Orby.

Half-sister to the very smart 1997 3-y-o Group 1 12f Prix Vermeille winner Queen Maud (by Akarad), to the useful Irish 1m winner and Group 1 National Stakes second Manashar (by Doyoun), the Hong Kong listed winner Marwazi (by Darshaan) and minor winners by Lashkari, Shernazar and Shahrastani. The dam, a winner in France over 11.5f and listed-placed, is a half-sister to 9 winners including the Group 2 Prix du Conseil de Paris winner Marasali. The second dam, Monique (by Tanerko), won the 12.5f Prix de Royallieu. (Sheikh Mohammed).

362 - WHITE STAR (IRE)　　　　　b.f. Darshaan - White Star Line (Northern Dancer).

March 21.

Half-sister to the useful 1997 2-y-o 5f winner and Flying Childers Stakes third Titanic, to the smart Group 2 13.5f Prix de Pomone winner Whitehaven, the Irish 6f to 12f winner Whitesville (both by Top Ville), the quite useful dual 1m winner Puissant (by Nashwan), the Irish 10f winner Hill of Snow (by Reference Point), the useful 2-y-o 7f winner Native Wizard (by In Reality), the 1m winner Urjwan (by Seattle Slew), the 2-y-o 6f winner Lustre (by Halo) - both fairly useful - and minor winners by Sir Ivor and Exclusive Native. The dam won 9 races including three Grade 1 stakes events at up to 10f in the USA and is a half-sister to the Grade 2 stakes winner Fairway Fun (herself dam of several stakes winners), Trick Chick (dam of the Prix de Diane and Prix Vermeille winner Northern Trick and the US Grade 1 winner On The Sly), Day Line (dam of the CCA Oaks winner Magazine) and the Prix Morny winner Filiberto. The second dam, Fast Line (by Mr Buster), won at 2 yrs in the USA. (Sheikh Mohammed).

363 - WHITE TORNADO (IRE)　　　　　b.f. Warning - Whitehaven (Top Ville).

May 12. Fifth foal.

Half-sister to the French trained 3-y-o Copeland (by Generous). The dam, a smart filly, won the Group 2 13.5f Prix de Pomone at 3 yrs after winning over 1m as a juvenile, is a sister to the Irish 6f to 12f winner Whitesville and a half-sister to 5 winners including the useful 2-y-o 7f winner Native Wizard. The second dam, White Star Line (by Northern Dancer), won 9 races including 3 Grade 1 events from 8.5f to 10f in the USA and is a half-sister to Trick Chick (dam of the high-class filly Northern Trick and the US Grade 1 winner On the Sly), Day Line (dam of the Coaching Club of America Oaks winner Magazine), the Prix Morny winner Filiberto and the US Grade 2 winner and good broodmare Fairway Fun. (Sheikh Mohammed).

364 - WITHOUT FAIL　　　　　br.f. Warning - Javandra (Lyphard).

March 15. First foal.

The dam was placed twice in France and is a sister to Dancing Brave, winner of the 2,000 Guineas, the Derby, the King George VI and Queen Elizabeth Diamond Stakes and the Prix de l'Arc de Triomphe and to the top-class filly Jolypha, winner of the Prix de Diane and the Prix Vermeille and second in the Breeders Cup Classic and the Grade 1 Beverly Hills Handicap. The second dam, Navajo Princess (by Drone), a good winner of 16 races at up to 1m including the Grade 2 Molly Pitcher Handicap and the Grade 3 Falls City Handicap, is a sister to the stakes winner Passamaquoddy (herself dam of 5 winners) and a half-sister to the Grade 3 winner Soldier Boy.

365 - ZAPATEADO (IRE)　　　　　b.c. Exit To Nowhere - Serenad Dancer (Antheus).

February 17. Second foal. IR110,000Y. Goffs Orby.

The dam won and was listed placed over 10f in France and is a half-sister to 5 winners including the Italian Group 3 Premio Ambrosiano winner Charlo Mio. The second dam, Charlata (by Chaparral), won at 3 yrs in France and is a half-sister to 5 winners including the Prix Cleopatre winner Dourdan (dam of the Group winners Devalois and Dunphy). (Sheikh Mohammed).

366 - UNNAMED　　　　　b.c. Barathea - Overcall (Bustino).

April 5. IR150,000Y. Goffs Orby.

Half-brother to the 3-y-o Royal Request (by Royal Academy), to the Grade 2 American Derby winner and Italian and German Derby placed Overbury (by Caerleon), the fairly useful 1m and 10.2f winner Overruled (by Last Tycoon) and the Irish 12f and hurdles winner Call My Guest (by Be My Guest). The dam, a winning Irish middle-distance stayer, is a half-sister to 9 winners including the dam of the Melbourne Cup winner Vintage Crop. The second dam, Melodramatic (by Tudor Melody), was a very useful winner of 3 races and was placed in the Coronation Stakes.

367 - UNNAMED　　　　　ch.f. Gulch - Sabin (Lyphard).

March 5. $1,050,000. Keeneland July.

Closely related to the US stakes winner Al Sabin, to the minor US winner of 3 races Alster (both by Alydar), the US stakes-placed winner In Excelsis Deo (by Forty Niner) and minor winners in the USA by Conquistador Cielo and Easy Goer and half-sister to the US stakes winner Sabina (by Cox's Ridge). The dam won 18 races in the USA including the Grade 1 Yellow Ribbon Invitational and the Grade 1 Gamely Handicap and is a half-sister to the Musidora Stakes winner Fatah Flare and to the dam of the Group 3 C L Weld Park Stakes winner Asema. The second dam, Beaconaire (by Vaguely Noble), a stakes winner of 3 races at up to 10f in France, is a half-sister to the high-class filly Kittiwake (the dam of the excellent American filly Miss Oceana and grandam of the Coronation Stakes winner Magic of Life).

James Fanshawe

368 - FIRST FANTASY   b.f. Be My Chief - Dreams (Rainbow Quest).
March 4. First foal.

The dam, a quite useful 3-y-o 10.3f winner, is a half-sister to Jeune, winner of the Group 2 12f Hardwicke Stakes here and the Melbourne Cup in Australia and to the very useful Group 3 12f King Edward VII Stakes winner Beneficial. The second dam, Youthful (by Green Dancer), won over 12f at Longchamp and is a half-sister to 6 winners including the Group 2 13.5f Grand Prix de Deauville winner First Prayer and the Grade 3 9f Next Move Handicap winner Water Lily (herself dam of the Grade 1 Flamingo Stakes winner Talinum). (Aylesfield Farms Ltd).

Jimmy Fitzgerald

369 - MINILODGE (IRE)   ch.c. Grand Lodge - Mirea (The Minstrel).
January 28. FF550,000Y. Deauville August.

Half-brother to 4 winners in France including the dams of the listed winners Misbegotten and Magic Play. The dam won once at 2 yrs in France and is out of the unraced Mlle Vitesse (by Tom Rolfe), herself a half-sister to the Prix Morny winner Filiberto, the Alabama Stakes and Kentucky Oaks winner White Star Line and to the dam of the Prix Vermeille winner Northern Trick. *"A very settled colt with a great stride, he's a nice type and will be racing by mid-summer".*

370 - UNNAMED   b.c. Slip Anchor - Lady Norcliffe (Norcliffe).
March 3. 58,000Y. Tattersalls October.

Half-brother to the unplaced 1997 2-y-o Norski Lad (by Niniski), to the 1989 Irish 2-y-o 5f and 7f winner and listed-placed Shagudine (by Shadeed), the fair 1995 2-y-o 6f winner Kriscliffe (by Kris) and the modest 12f seller winner Lady St Lawrence (by Bering). The dam, a winner of 6 races at up to 11f in the USA including the Grade 2 Queen Charlotte Handicap, is a half-sister to 3 minor winners in the USA. The second dam, Mlle Patrice (by Southern Brook), is an unraced half-sister to 8 winners. (Marquesa de Moratella). *"A nice, mature two-year-old, he's a horse for the mid-summer over seven furlongs".*

Godolphin

The following two-year-olds are to be trained by either Saeed bin Suroor or David Loder. When I spoke to Simon Crisford in mid-April, the final decision had yet to be made. Here, however, is a selection of the best of the blue-blooded Godolphin two-year-olds.

371 - AFWAJ (USA)   b.br.c. Danzig - Orca (Southern Halo).
April 4. Third foal.

Closely related to the fairly useful 1996 2-y-o dual 6f winner Ikdam (by Dayjur). The dam won the Argentinian 1,000 Guineas. *"A nice, strong colt, Afwaj is going the right way. He's mature and working well at the moment"* Simon informs me.

372 - ALATTRAH (USA)   gr.f. Shadeed - Desirable (Lord Gayle).
April 23.

Sister to the 3-y-o Shaher and to the high-class and genuine filly Shadayid, winner of the 1,000 Guineas and the Prix Marcel Boussac and placed in the Coronation Stakes, the Sussex Stakes and the Queen Elizabeth II Stakes and half-sister to the very useful 1994 3-y-o listed 7f winner and Jersey Stakes third Dumaani (by Danzig), the fairly useful 1995 3-y-o dual 7f winner Azdihaar (by Mr Prospector) and the fairly useful 1993 4-y-o 10f winner Badie (by Blushing Groom). The dam won the Group 1 6f Cheveley Park Stakes and the 6f Princess Margaret Stakes, was third in the 1,000 Guineas and is a half-sister to the Irish Oaks winner Alydaress, the Cheveley Park winner Park Appeal and the very useful middle-distance colt Nashamaa. The second dam, Balidaress (by Balidar), won three races from 7f to 10f in Ireland. *"A backward filly, she won't be ready to run until the back-end".*

373 - BLUE SNAKE (USA)   b.c. Gone West - Dabaweyaa (Shareef Dancer).
March 7. Sixth foal.

Half-brother to the fairly useful 1997 2-y-o 5.7f winner Ascot Cyclone (by Rahy), to the very useful 1994 2-y-o 6f winner and Group 1 7f Prix de la Salamandre second Bin Nashwan (by Nashwan), the very useful 1m and 10f winner Magellan (by Hansel), the very useful 6f winner and Group 3 7f Supreme Stakes second Alanees (by Cadeaux Genereux) and the quite useful 1m winner Aneesati (by Kris). The dam was a smart winner of the 1m Atalanta Stakes and was placed in the 1,000 Guineas and the Kiveton Park Stakes. She is a half-sister to the Group 3 winning sprinter Bruckner, the 12f Galtres Stakes winner Ma Femme and the smart Hoover Fillies Mile and Nassau Stakes winner Acclimatise. The second dam, Habituee (by Habitat), won over 1m in France and was second in the Prix d'Aumale. *"A very nice colt, very athletic and with a good attitude, he'll be out by mid-summer if not earlier and is a promising individual".*

---

374 - FATINA
ch.f. Nashwan - Gharam (Green Dancer).
January 23.
Sister to the very useful 1997 3-y-o 10f winner Shaya, to the quite useful 1996 3-y-o 10.5f winner Naazeq (both by Nashwan) and half-sister to the fairly useful 1997 2-y-o 7f winner and Group 3 Prestige Stakes third Elshamms (by Zafonic). The dam, a very useful 2-y-o 6f winner, was third in the French 1,000 Guineas and is a half-sister to the US Grade 1 9f winner Talinum and the smart French middle-distance performer First Prayer. The second dam, Water Lily (by Riverman), was a very useful French 2-y-o and subsequently winner of the Grade 3 Next Move Handicap in the USA. *"A nice filly, she's doing everything right but won't be that early. She has a good look about her and may start over seven furlongs".*

---

375 - IFTITAH (USA)
ch.c. Gone West - Mur Taasha (Riverman).
January 25. First foal.
The dam, a very useful 7f and 1m winner, is a half-sister to several winners including the very promising 1997 2-y-o 6f listed winner Ikhteyaar. The second dam, Linda's Magic (by Far North), was a smart winner of the listed 7f John Of Gaunt Stakes and the listed 7f Criteion Stakes. *"This is a horse I like a lot. He looks a really nice sort, won't be too early, but is a quality two-year-old".*

---

376 - KAAREK
b.c. Zafonic - The Perfect Life (Try My Best).
February 10. Fourth foal.
Half-brother to the 1997 2-y-o 7f and 1m winner Rabah, to the 3-y-o 1m winner Muhtafel (both fairly useful) and the useful 2-y-o 6f winner and Cheveley Park Stakes third Najiya (all by Nashwan). The dam won the Group 3 5f Prix du Bois and the listed 7f Prix Imprudence and was second in the Group 2 Prix Robert Papin. She is a full sister to the top-class colt Last Tycoon (winner of the Grade 1 Breeders Cup Mile, the Group 1 Kings Stand Stakes and the Group 1 William Hill Sprint Championship) and is closely related to the very useful Group 2 6f Premio Melton and Group 3 6f Goldene Peitsche winner Astronef. The second dam, Mill Princess (by Mill Reef), won over 10f at 3 yrs in France and is a half-sister to the Irish Sweeps Derby winner Irish Ball and to the top-class broodmare Irish Bird (dam of the classic winners Assert, Bikala and Eurobird). *"A fine, big horse, he'll probably take time but does everything right and is a promising colt for the future".*

---

377 - MUTAFAWEQ (USA)
b.c. Silver Hawk - The Caretaker (Caerleon).
February 21. First foal. $310,000. Saratoga. Shadwell Stud.
The dam, a very useful filly and winner of the Cartier Million at 2 yrs and two listed events in Ireland over 7f and 1m at 3 yrs, is a half-sister to the US Grade 3 8.5f winner Go Honey Go and the useful Irish sprinter Fearless Lad. The second dam, Go Feather Go (by Go Marching), won over 5f at 2 yrs in Ireland and is a half-sister to numerous winners. *"This is a very nice colt and next year he'll be a smart middle-distance horse"* Simon tells me. *"He has enough speed to win as a two-year-old from mid-summer onwards and is a colt with a lot of potential".*

---

378 - PROSPECTS OF GLORY (USA)
b.c. Mr Prospector - Hatoof (Irish River).
January 24. First foal.
The dam, a high-class filly and winner of 7 races notably the 1,000 Guineas, the Champion Stakes and the Prix de l'Opera, is a half-sister to the French listed winners Fasateen and Insijaam. The second dam, Cadeaux d'Amie (by Lyphard), won over 1m at 2 yrs and 10f at 3 yrs in France, was third in the Group 3 Prix d'Aumale and is a half-sister to the Champion 2-y-o filly and Prix Vermeille winner Mrs Penny. *"A little bit behind the others at the moment, he's not done a lot but hopefully he'll still make a two-year-old later on. So far we're happy with him".*

379 - SARHAN (USA) b.br.c. Gone West - My Song For You (Seattle Song). May 7. Third foal. $1,700,000Y. Keeneland September.
Half-brother to the US stakes-placed winner Minister's Melody (by Deputy Minister). The dam, a winner of 4 races in the USA and placed in a minor stakes event, is closely related to the Champion US 2-y-o colt Capote and a half-sister to numerous winners including the Coronation Cup, Grand Prix de Paris and Hollywood Gold Cup winner Exceller. The second dam, Too Bald (by Bald Eagle), was a US stakes winner of 13 races. *"Sarhan could come to hand quite quickly as he's training very nicely and we like him a lot. He has a lot of presence and we'll probably start him over six furlongs".*

380 - TRANQUIL LIFE (USA) b.f. Dayjur - Sanctuary (Welsh Pageant). March 3.
Half-sister to the top class sprinter Sheikh Albadou (by Green Desert), winner of the Keeneland Nunthorpe Stakes, the Breeders Cup Sprint, the Haydock Park Sprint Cup and the Kings Stand Stakes, to the useful 14f and 2m winner Captain Jack (by Salse), the quite useful 5f to 6f winner Assignment and the minor Irish 2-y-o 5f winner Sawlah (both by Known Fact). The dam is an unraced half-sister to the good horses Little Wolf (Ascot Gold Cup), Smuggler (Yorkshire Cup), Camouflage (Royal Hunt Cup) and Disguise (Horris Hill Stakes) and to the dam of the Nell Gwyn Stakes winner Niche. The second dam, Hiding Place (by Doutelle), was a very useful winner of the Nell Gwyn Stakes and a half-sister to the Sussex Stakes winner Queen's Hussar. *"A very nice filly, she looks like she could be fairly early and we really like her".*

381 - ZA AAMAH (USA) ch.f. Mr Prospector - Roseate Tern (Blakeney). February 2. Fourth foal.
Sister to the useful listed 10f winner Siyadah and half-sister to the promising 1997 2-y-o 7f winner Fakhr (by Riverman). The dam, a very smart filly, won the Group 1 12f Yorkshire Oaks, the Group 2 12f Jockey Club Stakes and the Group 3 12f Lancashire Oaks, was second in the Epsom Oaks and third in the St Leger. She is a half-sister to several winners including Cerise Bouquet (dam of the smart 1996 2-y-o filly Red Camellia) and the high class middle distance colt Ibn Bey, winner of the Irish St Leger, the Gran Premio d'Italia, two Group 1 events in Germany and second in the Breeders Cup Classic. The second dam, Rosia Bay (by High Top), a useful 7.5f and 1m winner, is a half-sister to the top class Queen Elizabeth II Stakes and Budweiser Arlington Million winner Teleprompter and to the Group 3 Brigadier Gerard Stakes winner Chatoyant. *"A backward type, she'll take a lot of time but will be a very nice filly in the second half of the season".*

382 - UNNAMED gr.f. Rainbow Quest - Alruccaba (Crystal Palace). February 2. 360,000Y. Tattersalls Houghton.
Half-sister to the very smart 1996 Group 2 10f Nassau Stakes and Sun Chariot Stakes winner Last Second (by Alzao), to the very useful 1992 3-y-o Irish listed 14f winner and Irish Oaks third Arrikala, the useful 1993 Irish 3-y-o 12f listed winner Alouette (both by Darshaan) and minor winners by Niniski (2) and Slip Anchor. The dam, a quite useful 2-y-o 6f winner, is a half-sister to 3 minor winners out of the French 7f winner Allara (by Zeddaan) - herself a half-sister to the dams of Aliysa and Nishapour. *"A very nice filly, she won't be early but has plenty of quality and she'll be a middle-distance three-year-old".*

383 - UNNAMED b.f. Zafonic - Don't Rush (Alleged). April 25. Fifth living foal.
Half-sister to the the the fairly useful 1993 3-y-o 8.3f winner Reine de Neige (by Kris) and to the fair 1995 5-y-o dual 5f winner King of Show (by Green Desert). The dam, a fairly useful 3-y-o dual 12f winner, is a half-sister to four good winners in Seaside Attraction (Grade 1 Kentucky Oaks), Gorgeous (Grade 1 Hollywood Oaks and Grade 1 Ashland Stakes), the dual Canadian Grade 3 winner Key to the Moon and the Group 3 6f Princess Margaret Stakes winner Hiamm. The second dam, Kamar (by Key to the Mint), was a champion Canadian 3-y-o filly and a sister to the Grade 1 winner Love Smitten. *"We like this filly. She's very nice, has a good action and is doing everything we ask. We're pleased with her so far and she should be racing in mid-summer"* Simon explained.

384 - UNNAMED b.c. Sadler's Wells - Darara (Top Ville). March 31. 500,000Y. Tattersalls Houghton.
Brother to the Group 2 12.5f Prix Maurice de Neiuil winner Darazari, closely related to the minor French winner Dardjini (by Nijinsky) and half-brother to 4 winners including the listed 10.5f and 12f winner Dariyoun (by Sharastani) and the promising 1997 2-y-o 8.1f winner Kilimanjaro (by Shirley Heights). The dam, a top-class filly, won the Group 1 12f Prix Vermeille and the Group 3 10f Prix de Psyche and

is a half-sister to the Prix du Jockey Club winner Darshaan and the Group 2 Prix de Royallieu winner Dalara. The second dam, Delsy (by Abdos), won over 12f and was third in the Prix de Pomone. *"He'll take some time but he looks like a very nice colt for the future"*.

---

385 - UNNAMED
b.c. Barathea - Ela Romara (Ela Mana Mou).
May 1. Fifth foal.
Closely related to the smart 1994 3-y-o Group 2 12f King Edward VII Stakes winner Foyer (by Sadlers Wells). The dam was a high class winner of the Group 3 6f Lowther Stakes (at 2 yrs) and the Group 2 10f Nassau Stakes and is a half-sister to 7 winners including the very useful 10f colt Roman Gunner. The second dam, Romara (by Bold Lad, Ire), was a useful winner over 7f and 1m at 3 yrs and was fourth in the Irish 1,000 Guineas. *"This colt looks like she'll be a nice two-year-old from July onwards. A very promising colt"*.

---

386 - UNNAMED
b.c. Danzig - Elizabeth Bay (Mr Prospector).
First foal.
The dam was a smart winner of the Group 3 6.5f Prix Eclipse (at 2 yrs) and was placed in the Coronation Stakes, the Prix Jacques le Marois and the Prix de l'Opera. The second dam, Life At The Top (by Seattle Slew), won 9 races in the USA including the Grade 1 Ladies Handicap and the Grade 1 Mother Goose Stakes. *"A colt with a lot of quality in his pedigree, he'll be racing in July or August and seems to be a very well-made individual"*.

---

387 - UNNAMED
b.f. Danehill - Kerrera (Diesis).
February 26. Fifth living foal.
Half-sister to the useful 1997 2-y-o 6f winner Shmoose (by Caerleon), to the quite useful 7.1f winner Kerry Ring (by Sadler's Wells) and the French 1m to 10f winner Kerrier (by Nashwan). The dam was a smart filly and winner of 3 races over 6f including the Group 3 Cherry Hinton Stakes and the Sandy Lane Stakes. She was also placed in the 1,000 Guineas (second to Musical Bliss) and in the July Cup (fourth to Cadeaux Genereux) and is a half-sister to the very smart, game and genuine colt Rock City and to the very useful 1992 middle-distance 3-y-o colt Peto. The second dam, Rimosa's Pet (by Petingo), won the Group 3 Musidora Stakes and the Group 3 Princess Elizabeth Stakes. *"A strong-looking filly, she'll come to hand fairly early, has had a good winter in Dubai and I expect she'll be a miler next year"* Simon explained.

---

388 - UNNAMED
b.br.c. Silver Hawk - Music Lane (Miswaki).
February 7. First foal. $675,000. Keeneland September.
The dam, a minor winner at 4 yrs in the USA, is a half-sister to 8 winners including Hawkster (winner of three US Grade 1 events), the French listed winner Silver Kite and the Group 3 Prix de la Grotte winner and Irish Oaks third Silver Lane (all by Silver Hawk - the sire of this colt). The second dam, Strait Lane (by Chieftain), is an unraced half-sister to 2 stakes winners in the USA. *"A fine, big horse, he looks a nice horse for the future and is a two-year-old in the making for the second half of the season. Doing well at present, he's a good-moving colt and will be a middle-distance three-year-old"*.

---

389 - UNNAMED
ch.c. Zafonic - Princess Accord (D'Accord).
February 4. Third foal. 440,000Y. Tattersalls Houghton.
Half-brother to the useful 1997 9f winner Darcy (by Miswaki) and to the US winner of 4 races Rank and File (by Forty Niner). The dam, a smart winner of 5 races from 6f (at 2 yrs) to 9f including the listed October Stakes and the listed Darley Stakes, is a sister to the US Grade 1 Futurity Stakes and Grade 2 Saratoga Special Stakes winner Montreal Red and a half-sister to 5 winners. The second dam, Cohutta Princess (by Groton), won twice in the USA and is a half-sister to the US Grade 1 winners Fancy Naskra and Rose's Cantina. *"A speedily-bred colt, he'll definitely make a two-year-old and we're pleased with him"*.

---

390 - UNNAMED
ch.f. Rainbow Quest - Talented (Bustino).
January 17. First foal.
The dam, a very useful filly, won three races including the Group 2 10f Sun Chariot Stakes, was second in the Ribblesdale Stakes and is a half-sister to several winners. The second dam, Triple Reef (by Mill Reef), is an unraced half-sister to the smart middle-distance winners Maysoon, Richard of York, Three Tails (dam of the high-class middle-distance colt Tamure) and Third Watch. The third dam, Triple First (by High Top), won the Nassau Stakes and the Sun Chariot Stakes. *"Very much a three-year-old, she has a lot of scope and is a very attractive filly"*.

391 - UNNAMED

ch.f. Barathea - Welsh Love (Ela Mana Mou).
April 14. Sixth foal. IR950,000. Goffs Orby.
Closely related to the minor Irish 10f winner Catalyst (by Sadler's Wells) and half-sister to the high-class 1997 2-y-o Group 1 1m Grand Criterium winner Second Empire (by Fairy King), the very useful 7f (at 2 yrs) to 10f winner Ihtiram and the minor Irish 9f winner (both by Royal Academy). The dam, a minor Irish 3-y-o 12f winner, is a half-sister to the Coronation Stakes winner Flame of Tara (dam of the Group 1 winners Salsabil and Marju) and to the Lupe Stakes second Fruition (dam of the Breeders Cup Turf winner Northern Spur and the high-class stayer Kneller). The second dam, Welsh Flame (by Welsh Pageant), was a useful 3-y-o winner of 4 races at around 1m and a half-sister to the Musidora Stakes second Sofala - dam of the Doncaster Cup second Bourbon Boy. *"A nice filly, we're pleased with her at the moment and she should be out by mid-summer. She'll want at least a mile next year".*

John Gosden

392 - AESOPS (USA)

ch.c. Diesis - Affirmative Fable (Affirmed).
March 25. $300,000Y. Keeneland September.
Half-brother to 3 winners including the useful 1990 2-y-o Group 3 1m May Hill Stakes winner Majmu (by Al Nasr). The dam, a minor US 4-y-o winner at around 1m, is a half-sister to the Grade 3 Palomar Handicap winner Northern Fable. The second dam, Fairway Fable (by Never Bend), won 3 races including a minor stakes and was placed in two Grade 3 events. *"A colt that goes nicely, he's a tall, leggy colt with a good action".*

393 - ALOYSIA (USA)

ch.f. Diesis - Alyanaabi (Roberto).
April 18. Fourth foal. $100,000Y. Keeneland September.
Half-sister to the fair 1996 3-y-o dual 10f winner Seattle Alley (by Seattle Dancer). The dam, a fair 3-y-o 10f winner at Folkestone in 1990, is a half-sister to the US stakes winner Fairly Regal - herself dam of four US stakes winners including Present Value (Grade 2 Michigan One Mile and One-Eighth Handicap). The second dam, Fair (by Madara), won 7 races in Chile. (Sheikh Mohammed). *"A small filly with a galloping action and a nice temperament"* John tells me.

394 - ARBITRATION (IRE)

b.f. Bigstone - Final Decision (Tap On Wood).
January 31. Fifth foal. IR160,000Y. Goffs Orby.
Half-sister to the useful Group 2 1m Berlin Brandeburg Trophy and Group 3 1m Kilavullan Stakes winner Kill The Crab (by Petorius), to the useful 1996 2-y-o 6f winner and Group 1 National Stakes second Referendum, the modest 1993 2-y-o 5f winner Sweet Decision (both by Common Grounds) and a winner in Austria by Doulab. The dam, an Irish middle-distance winner, is a half-sister to 3 winners out of the unraced Her Review (by Reviewer). (Sheikh Mohammed). *"A filly with a quite excitable nature, she's an athletic type".*

395 - ARDENNES (USA)

ch.c. Woodman - Crockadore (Nijinsky).
February 20. Fourth foal. 400,000Y. Tattersalls Houghton.
Half-brother to the 1997 1m placed 2-y-o Golden Hawk (by Silver Hawk), to the 1996 Irish 2-y-o 6f winner Mynador (by Forty Niner) and the 1996 Irish 3-y-o 6f winner Shunaire (by Woodman). The dam won 5 races in Ireland and the USA including the Grade 2 12f Orchid Handicap and the Grade 3 11f Sheepshead Bay Handicap and is closely related to the Group 3 5f Meadow Meats Flying Five winner Flowing. The second dam, Flo Russell (by Round Table), was placed in the USA and is a half-sister to 10 winners including the Grade 3 winner Embassy Row and the stakes winner Knightly Belle - herself dam of the Grade 1 Sword Dancer Handicap winner Dr Root. *"A nice-moving colt that should be racing by late May".*

396 - BERTOLINI (USA)

b.c. Danzig - Aquilegia (Alydar).
February 9. First foal. $750,000. Keeneland July.
The dam, a winner of 8 races including the Grade 2 10f New York Handicap and the 9f Grade 3 Black Helen Handicap, is a sister to the US Grade 2 winner Aishah and the champion US 2-y-o filly Althea (herself dam of four stakes winners) and a half-sister to 12 winners including Grade 1 winners Ali Oop and Ketoh. The second dam, Courtly Dee (by Never Bend), won 4 races at up to 6f. (Sheikh Mohammed). *"A small colt, he shows a fair amount of speed and should be out in May".*

397 - CAVALRY QUEEN   ch.f. Cadeaux Genereux - Gunner's Belle (Gunner B).
January 22. 48,000Y. Tattersalls Houghton.
Sister to the very smart 1994 2-y-o filly Hoh Magic, winner of the Group 1 Prix Morny and the Group 3 Molecomb Stakes and to the Dubai winner Handsome Singer and half-sister to the quite useful 2-y-o 5f winner Gunmaster (by Precocious) and the fair 3-y-o 1m winner Gunner's Daughter (by Pharly). The dam, a modest 7f and 10f winner, is a half-sister to the very smart Prince Of Wales's Stakes winner Crimson Beau. The second dam, Crimson Belle (by Red God), won 3 times over 7f. (Sheikh Mohammed). *"Cavalry Queen looks an athletic type of filly. Quite speedy, she should be out in May".*

398 - CHARMES (USA)   b.br.c. Personal Hope - Double The Charm (Nodouble).
April 4. Fourth foal. $150,000Y. Keeneland September.
Half-brother to 2 winners including the US stakes winner and Grade 2 Louisville Budweiser Breeders Cup Stakes third Teewinot (by Vice Regent). The dam, a winner of 7 races including a minor stakes in the USA, is a half-sister to 8 winners out of the US 2-y-o winner Album (by Never Bend) - herself a half-sister to the smart US stakes winner Don B. (Sheikh Mohammed). *"This colt is small but moves nicely. He's ready to run but needs six furlongs".*

399 - COMPATIBLE (IRE)   b.c. Ela Mana Mou - Good Enough (Simply Great).
February 9. First foal. IR45,000Y. Goffs Orby.
The dam, a winner of 7 races in Scandinavia including the listed Norwegian 1,000 Guineas, is a half-sister to 6 minor winners. The second dam, Sally Gal (by Lord Gayle), won twice and was fourth in the Group 3 7f Park Stakes in Ireland. (Sheikh Mohammed). *"A tall colt that carries himself well and has a nice action. He's a staying sort and will want seven furlongs to begin with".*

400 - DETECTIVE   ch.c. Wolfhound - Ivoronica (Targowice).
February 8. 42,000Y. Houghton.
Half-brother to the 1997 1m placed 2-y-o Putuna (by Generous), to the useful sprinter Lochonica (by Lochnager), the fairly useful listed 2-y-o 6f winner Ivory Bride (by Domynsky), the fairly useful 7f (at 2 yrs) and 12f Bessborough Handicap winner Tykeyvor (by Last Tycoon), the quite useful 5f and 6f winner Diamond Appeal (by Star Appeal) and the fair 3-y-o 7.5f winner Ivordale (by Beldale Flutter). The dam, a fairly useful 2-y-o 5f winner, is a half-sister to 3 winners out of the minor US winner Lady Mickey (by Swaps), herself a half-sister to the dams of the the French Group 3 winners Prince Mab and Ruscelli. *"A tall colt that moves well. He's a bit weak at the moment and needs to strengthen"* explains the trainer.

401 - ELEGANT LADY   ch.f. Selkirk - Prompting (Primo Dominie).
February 5. Second foal. 53,000Y. Tattersalls October.
Half-sister to the 1997 German 2-y-o winner Sharp Domino (by Sharpo). The dam, a fair 2-y-o 5f winner and subsequently a winner in Switzerland, is a half-sister to the very useful Group 2 6f Moet and Chandon Rennen winner and Group 2 Mill Reef Stakes third Sharp Prod. The second dam, Gentle Persuasion (by Bustino), a fairly useful 2-y-o 6f winner, was placed in the Princess Margaret Stakes and the Rockfel Stakes. *"A nice filly in the making, Elegant Lady moves well and is very enthusiastic".*

402 - FLOWER STATE   b.c. Sabrehill - Flower Arrangement (Lomond).
April 4. Fourth foal. 100,000Y. Tattersalls October.
Half-brother to the 1994 Italian 2-y-o listed winner Armenian Dancer and to the minor 1996 Italian 2-y-o winner Ahary (both by Shavian). The dam is an unraced half-sister to 5 winners including the Kentucky Derby second Bold Arrangement and to the dam of the Group 3 Guardian Classic Trial winner Galitzin. The second dam, Arrangement (by Floribunda), is a placed half-sister to the Cheveley Park Stakes winner Lindsay. (Sheikh Mohammed). *"A nice colt this, he looks like he'll be a decent two-year-old and although he's had sore shins, he's got over it and should be out in May".*

403 - GALANTY SHOW   b.f. Danehill - Sacristy (Godswalk).
February 1. Fifth foal.
Sister to the useful 7f (at 2 yrs) to 9f winner Holtye (by Danehill) and half-sister to the minor 2-y-o 1m winner Laatansa (by Don't Forget Me). The dam, a plating class filly, was placed twice over 5f at 2 yrs and is a half-sister to the Irish Oaks winner Alydaress, to the Cheveley Park Stakes winner Desirable (dam of the 1,000 Guineas winner Shadayid) and the Cheveley Park Stakes and Moyglare Stud Stakes winner Park Appeal. The second dam, Balidaress (by Balidar), won 3 races from 7f to 10f in Ireland. (Khaled Abdulla). *"Hopefully a fairly early two-year-old, she's quite athletic and light on her feet".*

404 - GEORGETTE (USA) ch.f. Geiger Counter - Odori (The Minstrel).
April 29. First foal. IR50,000Y. Goffs Orby.
The dam is an unplaced half-sister to 5 winners including the Irish 2-y-o listed 6f Cherry Blossom Stakes winner Chinese Justice and the dam of the Champion Australian 2-y-o filly Isolda. The second dam, Taiwanese (by Giacometti), is a placed half-sister to 8 winners including the US stakes winner Northeastern. (Sheikh Mohammed). *"A filly that goes quite nicely, she'll be racing early on but will need her first run"*.

405 - GLAMIS (USA) b.c. Silver Hawk - Glaze (Mr Prospector).
May 8. $130,000. Keeneland September.
Brother to the minor US winner Verreaux and half-brother to Glassine (by Assert), a minor winner of 5 races in the USA. The dam, a winner of 3 races in the USA and second in a 6f stakes event at 2 yrs, is a half-sister to 4 winners including the dam of the US Graded stakes winners Fine N' Majestic and Electric Flash. The second dam, Round Pearl (by Round Table), won 10 races including a stakes event in the USA. (Sheikh Mohammed). *"Coming along well enough, he's still only cantering at the moment but should be ready by July"*.

406 - GOLD CAMP (USA) b.c. Mr Prospector - Dance Colony (Pleasant Colony).
March 28. Third foal. $300,000. Keeneland July.
Closely related to the 1997 US 3-y-o winner and Group 3 Busher Stakes second Gold Colony (by Forty Niner). The dam, a winner of 6 races including the Group 2 6.5f Astarita Stakes and the Group 2 6f Adirondack Stakes, is a half-sister to the US Grade 1 winners Another Review and No Review. The second dam, Dance Review (by Northern Dancer), won twice at 3 yrs and is a half-sister to the dam of the US Grade 1 winner Urbane. (Sheikh Mohammed). *"A bit weak at the moment, he's a light-framed colt and should be out by mid-summer"*.

407 - GUEST ISLAND (IRE) ch.c. Grand Lodge - Guest Room (Be My Guest).
March 16. Second foal. IR310,000Y. Goffs Orby.
Half-brother to the 3-y-o Gamine (by High Estate). The dam is an unraced half-sister to the top-class Oaks, St Leger and Yorkshire Oaks winner Sun Princess, the high-class middle-distance colt Saddlers Hall, the French listed winner Sundar, the very useful 1m and 10f winner Dancing Shadow (herself dam of the Princess Royal Stakes winner Dancing Bloom) and the dam of the Italian Group 1 winner Poluto. The second dam, Sunny Valley (by Val de Loir), won over 10.5f and 12f in France and is a half-sister to the dam of the high-class miler Then Again. (Sheikh Mohammed). *"Likely to be out by July, Guest Island is a nice-moving horse"*.

408 - HABUB (USA) b.c. Danzig - Cheval Volant (Kris S).
February 2. Fourth foal.
Half-brother to the 1m winners Amanah and Alrayyih (both by Mr Prospector). The dam won 5 races in the USA including the Hollywood Starlet Stakes and the Las Virgines Stakes (both Grade 1 1m events) and is a half-sister to the dual US Grade 3 winner Chaldea. The second dam, Flight (by Barachois), was unplaced in her only race, is a sister to the stakes placed winner of 5 races Pere Gedeon and a half-sister to 3 winners. (Hamdan Al Maktoum). *"A strong horse, his action has improved and although he'll take a little time, he should be racing by June or July"*.

409 - HALBERD (IRE) b.c. Barathea - Hanzala (Akarad).
April 25. IR120,000Y. Goffs Orby.
Half-brother to the 3-y-o Hanzanar (by Alzao), to the 1995 Irish 3-y-o listed 12f winner Hasainaya (by Top Ville) and to winners in France by Dancing Brave and Doyoun. The dam won three listed events in France at up to 12.5f and is a half-sister to the Italian Derby winner Houmayoun. The second dam, Halwah (by The Minstrel), won over 12.5f in France. (Sheikh Mohammed). *"Halberd has grown a lot, is a bit weak and needs to strengthen"*.

410 - KHARTOUM (IRE) ch.c. Common Grounds - Kayu (Tap On Wood).
April 3. Fourth foal. IR50,000Y. Goffs Orby.
Half-brother to the fair 1994 2-y-o 6.1f and subsequent Hong Kong winner Rich Victim (by Lapierre), to the minor 1995 Irish 2-y-o 7f winner Vincitore (by Petorius) and the Italian winner Acquaiura (by Astronef). The dam, an unraced twin, is a half-sister to 2 minor winners. The second dam, Ladytown (by English Prince), a minor Irish 3-y-o 10f winner, is a half-sister to the Irish St Leger winner M-Lolshan. (Sheikh Mohammed). *"A colt that's already been out, Khartoum needed the race and will come on for the run"* John explained.

411 - LIONHEARTED (IRE)　　　　　　　　br.c. Catrail - Quiche (Formidable).
February 27. Fifth living foal. IR200,000Y. Goffs Orby.
Half-brother to the 1997 7f placed 2-y-o Doraid (by Danehill), to the useful Irish sprint winner Symboli Kildare (by Kaldoun) and a winner in Japan by Dancehall. The dam, a quite useful 6f winner, is a half-sister to 3 winners. The second dam, La Galette (by Double Form), is an unplaced half-sister to 6 winners including the Group 2 Yorkshire Cup winner Bright Finish and the Group 3 St Simon Stakes winner Shining Finish. (Sheikh Mohammed). *"A big, strong horse, he's getting his act together now and will be a mid-season two-year-old".*

---

412 - MAIDEN'S BLUSH (USA)　　　　　　ch.f. Silver Hawk - Barmistress (Alydar).
May 15. Third foal. $240,000. Keeneland July.
The dam, a minor winner at 3 yrs in the USA, is a half-sister to Jet Ski Lady, winner of the Oaks and runner-up in both the Irish Oaks and the Yorkshire Oaks. The second dam, Bemissed (by Nijinsky), won 5 races including the Grade 1 8.5f Selima Stakes in the USA, was third in the Kentucky Oaks and is a half-sister to the very useful Group 2 12f Princess of Wales's Stakes winner Desert Team. The second dam, Bemis Heights (by Herbager), won 5 races in the USA including the Grade 3 9f Ruthless Stakes and is a half-sister to two Grade 3 winners. (Sheikh Mohammed). *"A small filly and slightly temperamental, she'll be relatively early - possibly late May".*

---

413 - MAMBRINO (USA)　　　　　　　b.c. Kingmambo - Dream Deal (Sharpen Up).
March 13. Sixth foal. $325,000. Keeneland July.
Closely related to a minor winner in the USA by Forty Niner and half-brother to the US Grade 1 8.5f Shuvee Handicap and Grade 2 8.5f Cotillion Handicap winner Clear Mandate (by Deputy Minister) and the US stakes-placed winner Dream Scheme (by Danzig). The dam won four races including the Grade 1 9f Monmouth Oaks, was placed in the Grade 1 Alabama Stakes and the Grade 1 Gazelle Handicap and is a half-sister to the top-class colt Creme Fraiche, winner of six Grade 1 events including the Belmont Stakes. The second dam, Likely Exchange (by Terrible Tiger), won 23 races including the Grade 1 Delaware Handicap. (Sheikh Mohammed). *"A well-balanced colt but his knees are a bit immature and he'll need some time".*

---

414 - MANCHURIA (IRE)　　　　　　　ch.c. Indian Ridge - Shih Ching (Secreto).
February 21. Fifth foal. IR200,000Y. Goffs Orby.
Brother to the 1997 Irish 9.5f winner Hayward and half-brother to the quite useful 3-y-o 1m winner Province (by Dominion), the German 7.5f and 9f winner Story Of Love (by Taufan) and a winner over hurdles by Squill. The dam is an unraced half-sister to 4 winners including the Grade 1 Spinster Stakes and Grade 1 Vanity Invitational Handicap winner Dontstop Themusic. The second dam, Yellow Serenade (by Graustark), is an unraced half-sister to 7 winners. (Sheikh Mohammed). *"A colt that's had sore shins but he's OK now, goes nicely and should be out in late May".*

---

415 - MENEER (USA)　　　　　　　b.br.c. Silver Hawk - Mrs West (Gone West).
January 29. Second foal. $170,000Y. Keeneland September.
The dam, a quite useful 2-y-o 6f and 7.5f winner here and in Italy, is a half-sister to 5 minor winners. The second dam, Mrs Hat (by Sharpen Up), won once at around 6f at 3 yrs in the USA, and is a half-sister to 5 winners out of a half-sister to Gorytus. (Sheikh Mohammed). *"A small colt, he'll probably start off in a six furlong maiden".*

---

416 - MUTAMAYYAZ (USA)　　　　　　b.c. Nureyev - Ajfan (Woodman).
April 14.
Half-brother to the quite useful 1997 2-y-o 7f winner Elsurur. The dam was a very useful winner of 3 races from 7f (at 2 yrs) to 1m and was third in the 1,000 Guineas. She is a half-sister to several winners including Space Cruiser, winner of the Windsor Castle Stakes. The second dam, Misinskie (by Nijinsky), was placed over 6f and 7f at 2 yrs and is a half-sister to the high-class sprinter/miler Clever Trick. (Hamdan Al Maktoum). *"A nice little horse, he has been coughing but hopefully he'll still make a two-year-old".*

---

417 - PEARL CROWN (USA)　　　　　　gr.f. Diesis - Peach Of It (Navajo).
February 24. Third foal. $150,000. Keeneland September.
Half-sister to the minor US stakes winner Affairwithpeaches (by Black Tie Affair). The dam won 15 races in the USA including the Grade 3 9f Sixty Sails Handicap and is a half-sister to 5 winners. The second dam, Best Of Peaches (by Best Of It), won 4 races including a stakes event in the USA. *"A tall, very backward filly, she'll not see the racecourse until the autumn".*

418 - PLEASING PROSPECT (USA)　　　　　b.f. Mr Prospector - Promising Girl (Youth).
March 10. $400,000. Keeneland July.
Sister to the very useful listed 10f Predominate Stakes and subsequent US Grade 2 9f American Handicap winner Man From Eldorado and half-brother to 2 winners including the useful 7f (at 2 yrs) and 8.2f winner and Group 3 Prix Chloe third Star Of The Future (by El Gran Senor). The dam, a stakes-placed winner at up to 1m in the USA, is a half-sister to the Grade 1 San Antonio Stakes and Grade 2 California Derby winner Beau's Eagle. The second dam, Beaufield (by Maribeau), won 4 races in the USA. (Sheikh Mohammed). *"Another filly for the back-end of the season".*

---

419 - SAIK (USA)　　　　　　　　　　br.f. Riverman - Close Comfort (Far North).

Closely related to the 5f and 6f winner Liffey River (by Irish River) and half-sister to the smart Group 3 10f Brigadier Gerard Stakes and Group 3 10f Scottish Classic winner Husyan, the quite useful 10f winner Thabit (both by Alleged) and the American stakes-placed winner Miss Waikiki (by Miswaki). The dam is an unraced half-sister to the champion French 2-y-o filly Ancient Regime (herself dam of 3 good winners in Crack Regiment, Rami and La Grande Epoque), to the Group 2 Prix Maurice de Gheest winner Cricket Ball and to the US stakes winners Olden and Mug Punter. The second dam, Caterina II (by Princely Gift), won the 5f Nunthorpe Stakes and is a half-sister to the Eclipse Stakes winner Scottish Rifle. (Sheikh Mohammed). *"A good mover, this filly has a nice way about her and she should be out by August or September".*

---

420 - SAMHAIN　　　　　　　　　　　　b.c. Salse - Stardyn (Star Appeal).
April 9. Fifth foal. 80,000Y. Tattersalls December.
Half-brother to the 3-y-o Young-Un, to the smart and genuine Group 3 7f Hungerford Stakes and Group 3 7f Prix du Palais-Royal winner Young Ern (both by Efisio), the quite useful 6f and 7f winner Scharnhorst (by Tacheron) and the poor 1m seller winner Crown Reserve (by Another Realm). The dam, a poor middle-distance placed handicapper, is a half-sister to 4 winners. The second dam, Northern Dynasty (by Breeders Deam), won over 1m at 3 yrs. (Sheikh Mohammed). *"A bit cheeky, Samhain has grown and strengthened and should be racing in May".*

---

421 - SHARP STEPPER　　　　　　　　　b.f. Selkirk - Awtaar (Lyphard).
February 7. First foal. 88,000Y. Tattersalls October.
The dam is a sister to the useful 2-y-o 6f and 7f winner Muhab and is closely related to the fair 3-y-o 7.1f winner Wali. The second dam, Magic Slipper (by Habitat), a useful 10f and 11.5f winner, is a half-sister to the classic winners Fairy Footsteps (1,000 Guineas) and Light Cavalry (St Leger). *"Sharp Stepper is a tall, leggy filly that moves well"* says John.

---

422 - SHEET MUSIC (IRE)　　　　　　　b.f. Sadler's Wells - Delage (Bellypha).
April 5. Second foal. IR130,000Y. Goffs Orby.
Half-sister to the 1997 German 4-y-o winner Doctor Biba (by Classic Music). The dam is an unraced half-sister to 5 winners including College Chapel (Prix Maurice de Gheest and Cork And Orrery Stakes). The second dam, Scarcely Blessed (by So Blessed), won the Group 3 5f King George Stakes and is out of the July Cup winner Parsimony (by Parthia). (Sheikh Mohammed). *"A typically backward Sadler's Wells two-year-old, but she does have a nice action".*

---

423 - SHOOGLE (USA)　　　　　　　　　ch.f. A.P.Indy - Dokki (Northern Dancer).
February 24. Fifth living foal.
Closely related to the Grade 1 9f Hollywood Oaks winner Sleep Easy (by Seattle Slew) and half-sister to the smart US 6f (at 2 yrs) to 8.5f winner Electrify (by Warning), the 1992 1m placed 2-y-o Karnak (by Shirley Heights) and the 1998 3-y-o Temper Lad (by Riverman), unplaced on his only start at 2 yrs. The dam is an unraced half-sister to the champion US colt Slew O'Gold - winner of seven Grade 1 events - and Coastal, winner of the Belmont Stakes. The second dam, Alluvial (by Buckpasser), is an unraced daughter of the champion US 3-y-o filly Bayou and a half-sister to the Santa Margarita Handicap winner Batteur. (Khaled Abdulla). *"A light-framed filly that will need time".*

---

424 - SNOOZY　　　　　　　　b.f. Cadeaux Genereux - Quiet Week-End (Town And Country).
March 3. Fifth foal. 100,000Y. Tattersalls October.
Half-sister to the fair 1997 2-y-o 6f winner Love Academy (by Royal Academy), to the fairly useful 1996 2-y-o 1m winner Home Alone (by Groom Dancer), to the useful 7.5f (at 2 yrs) and 10.5f winner Pleasant Surprise (by Cadeaux Genereux) and the fair 3-y-o 1m winner Tranquillity (by Night Shift). The dam, a

useful 2-y-o 6f and 7f winner, later won in the USA and is a half-sister to the Group 1 Moyglare Stud Stakes and Group 2 Falmouth Stakes winner Lemon Souffle and to Caramba - also winner of the Falmouth Stakes. The second dam, Melodrama (by Busted), was a useful 6f and 1m 3-y-o winner out of the Portland Handicap winner Matinee. *"A filly that moves well, but is a bit backward at the moment".*

425 - SWAN KNIGHT (USA)

b.c. Sadler's Wells - Shannkara (Akarad).
March 26. Second foal. $600,000. Keeneland July.

Closely related to the US stakes winner and Grade 3 placed Tekken (by Nureyev). The dam, a winner in France and the Grade 3 8.5f Nijana Stakes in the USA, is a half-sister to the Prix Vermeille winner Sharaya and the Grand Prix d'Evry winner Sharaniya. The second dam, Shanizadeh (by Baldric), was a useful French 6f and 1m winner. (Sheikh Mohammed). *"A good-looking horse with a good action, he's quite forward for a Sadler's Wells two-year-old and will hopefully be out by July".*

426 - TACTFUL REMARK (USA)

ch.c. Lord At War - Right Word (Verbatim).
March 14. $400,000. Keeneland July.

Brother to 3 winners in the USA including the stakes winner of 9 races and Grade 3 placed Words Of War and the 1997 US 2-y-o Grade 3 winner Ascutney and half-brother to 3 winners including the US stakes winner Word O'Ransom (by Red Ransom). The dam is a placed sister to the US stakes winner Spruce Song and a half-sister to the stakes winner Visto. The second dam, Oratorio (by Fleet Nasrullah), won at 3 yrs and is a half-sister to the dams of the US Grade 1 winners Danzig Connection and Pine Circle. (Sheikh Mohammed). *"A big horse with a good action and a good attitude to his work".*

427 - TEN KINGDOMS (USA)

b.c. Mr Prospector - Chinese Empress (Nijinsky).
January 19. First foal. $850,000. Keeneland July.

The dam, a winner of 5 races in the USA and third in a Grade 3 event over 8.5f on turf, is a half-sister to 5 winners including Possible Mate (winner of four Graded stakes and herself dam of the high-class filly Fairy Garden) and the dam of the US Grade 1 winner Prenup. The second dam, Execution (by The Axe II), is an unraced half-sister to the US Grade 3 winner Jacksboro. (Sheikh Mohammed). *"A tall colt who has outgrown his frame somewhat, he moves well and seems a nice type of two-year-old".*

428 - THREAT

br.c. Zafonic - Prophecy (Warning).
February 5. First foal.

The dam, a smart filly and winner of the Group 1 6f Cheveley Park Stakes, was second in the Group 3 7f Nell Gwyn Stakes at 3 yrs. The second dam, Andaleeb (by Lyphard), was a useful winner of 2 races including the Group 3 12f Lancashire Oaks and was fourth in the Group 1 Yorkshire Oaks. The third dam, Bag of Tunes (by Herbager), won the Grade 2 8.5f Kentucky Oaks and is a half-sister to the Santa Maria Handicap, Cork and Orrery Stakes and Diadem Stakes winner Swingtime. (Khaled Abdulla). *"A small colt - just like his mother - he's sharp and should be relatively early".*

429 - UNTOLD RICHES (USA)

b.f. Red Ransom - Asdaf (Forty Niner).
January 5. First foal. 205,000 Y. Houghton Tattersalls.

The dam, a modest 3-y-o 7f winner at Catterick, is a half-sister to the US stakes winners Graceful Minister and Burbank. The second dam, Cagey Exuberance (by Exuberant), won 18 races in the USA including the Grade 2 6.5f Astarita Stakes (at 2 yrs) and the Grade 3 7f First Flight Handicap. (Sheikh Mohammed). *"Untold Riches moves nicely but is a bit backward just now".*

430 - VELENI (IRE)

b.f. Doyoun - Vaison La Romaine (Arctic Tern).
April 18. IR52,000Y. Goffs Orby.

Closely related to the French listed 1m winner Queenemara and the minor French 2-y-o winner Campeon Basco (both by King Of Clubs) and half-sister to the very useful German Group 2 11f winner Vialli, the Champion Spanish filly and 6f to 11f winner La Strada (both by Niniski), the modest 8.2f winner Viva Verdi (by Green Desert) and a winner over hurdles by Kris. The dam, a useful 7.5f winner, was fourth in the Group 3 Prix Cleopatre and is a half-sister to 5 winners. The second dam, Victory Tune (by Dr Fager), won at 3 yrs in France and is a half-sister to 6 winners. (Sheikh Mohammed). *"A backward filly. One for the second half of the season".*

431 - WAHOO

br.c. Warning - Jubilee Trail (Shareef Dancer).
January 18. Fourth foal.

Brother to the useful 7f (at 2 yrs) and listed 1m Heron Stakes winner Peace Envoy and half-brother to the fairly useful 11.5f and 12f winner Welcome Parade (by Generous). The dam, a quite useful 10.4f winner, is a sister to the Swedish listed winner Green Turban and a half-sister to the Park Hill Stakes winner Rejuvenate, to the Group-placed winners Colorific, Meistersinger and Society Boy and to the dam of the Park Hill Stakes winner Casey. The second dam, Miss Petard (by Petingo), won the Group 2 12f Ribblesdale Stakes and is a half-sister to the dam of the triple Group 1 winner Pelder. (Khaled Abdulla). *"This colt has a good action, the right attitude and looks to be a very nice two-year-old"*.

Neil Graham

432 - HINDI

b.c. Indian Ridge - Tootsiepop (Robellino).
April 29. Sixth foal. 35,000Y. Tattersalls October.

Half-brother to the 1997 German 2-y-o winner El Maimoun (by Royal Academy) and to the poor Strength Of Vision (by Unfuwain), placed once over 1m. The dam won once in the USA, was placed 13 times and is a half-sister to 6 winners including Splendent (Group 2 Gimcrack Stakes) and Aim For The Top (Group 3 Premio Chiusura). The second dam, Sticky Habit (by Habitat), was a quite useful 1m and 10f winner and a half-sister to 7 winners including the Group 3 Mulcahy Stakes winner I've A Bee. (Hamdan Al Maktoum). *"A big, lengthy colt and a lovely mover with a good attitude, Hindi is still quite weak and is much more of a back-end two-year-old" says Neil.*

433 - SAMPAN

b.f. Elmaamul - Boathouse (Habitat).
April 30.

Half-sister to the smart middle-distance stayer Dry Dock (by High Line, to the useful 2-y-o 7f and 3-y-o 1m winner Showboat (by Warning) and the fairly useful 3-y-o 10.2f winner River Patrol (by Rousillon). The dam was a smart winner of 2 races, was third in the Sun Chariot Stakes and is a half-sister to the Oaks winner Bireme. The second dam, Ripeck (by Ribot), stayed 12f. (Hamdan Al Maktoum). *"A nice-moving filly, she has a good, long stride on her. Quite tall, she'll make a lovely middle-distance three-year-old".*

434 - TAWADUD

ch.f. Arazi - Cunning (Bustino).
March 22. Second foal.

Half-sister to the 3-y-o Natayig (by Fairy King), unplaced on her only start at 2 yrs. The dam, a smart filly, won four of her five races from 10.2f to 12f at 3 yrs including the Group 3 Princess Royal Stakes and the listed Galtres Stakes and was second in the Group 1 Prix Vermeille. The second dam, Vice Vixen (by Vice Regent), is an unraced half-sister to the useful Gallinule Stakes second Baltic Fox. (Hamdan Al Maktoum). *"A nice filly, the mare was very backward as a two-year-old but Tawadud is a very neat, well-made filly and she should win this year".*

435 - TRUMP STREET

b.f. First Trump - Pepeke (Mummy's Pet).
April 29. 18,500Y. Tattersalls October.

Half-sister to Walking Possession (by Faustus), a winner of 16 races including 5f events here and a listed event in Germany, to the 7f seller winner Castletown Count (by Then Again) and a winner in Norway by Indian Ridge. The dam, a fair 3-y-o 7f winner, is a half-sister to 6 minor winners. The second dam, Great Optimist (by Great Nephew), was a moderate middle-distance placed maiden. *"A lovely, sharp sort, Trump Street is showing speed at home and will definitely make his mark as a two-year-old, He'll begin his career at the end of May"* the trainer informs me.

Michael Grassick

436 - DRIOCHT (IRE)

ch.f. Catrail - Swallowcliffe (Caerleon).
March 11. Third foal. IR30,000Y. Goffs Orby.

Half-sister to the 3-y-o Ewan (by Indian Ridge) and to the modest 6f placed 2-y-o Seva (by Night Shift). The dam, a quite useful 2-y-o 6f winner, stayed 1m and is a half-sister to 5 winners including the smart sprinter Ya Malak. The second dam, La Tuerta (by Hot Spark), a fairly useful sprint winner of 3 races, is a half-sister to Cadeaux Genereux. (Mr M Duffy). *"Not a bad sort at all, she's quite a big, strong filly and will be running by mid-summer".*

437 - ELEGANT (IRE)

b.f. Marju - Braneakins (Sallust).
April 17.

Half-sister to the very useful, though temperamental, 1990 2-y-o 1m and 3-y-o 12f winner Peking Opera, to the 1994 Irish 3-y-o 10f to 14f winner Bryn Clovis (both by Sadler's Wells) and to the fair 1989 7f to 9f placed 3-y-o Akin to Fame (by Ahonoora). The dam, a winner of 3 races over 12f at 3 yrs in Ireland, is a half-sister to the Cheveley Park Stakes winners Park Appeal and Desirable (herself dam of Shadayid) and to the Irish Oaks winner Alydaress. The second dam, Balidaress (by Balidar), won 3 races from 7f to 10f in Ireland. (Mrs B Brannigan). *"A good, deep-bodied filly with plenty of scope, she'll be out from July onwards, possibly over six furlongs"*.

438 - PRIX NOBLE (FR)

b.f. Brief Truce - Viceroy Princess (Godswalk). February 6. FF300,000. Deauville August.

Half-sister to 4 winners including the useful Group 3 5f Molecomb Stakes winner and Flying Childers Stakes, Curragh Stakes and Norfolk Stakes placed Classic Ruler (by Dominion). The dam, a modest 2-y-o 7f seller winner, is a half-sister to 6 winners including the listed Marble Hill Stakes winner Black Country. The second dam, Black Crow (by Sea Hawk II), was a fair 9f and 12f winner and a half-sister to the Prix Foy winner Beeshi and the John Smith's Magnet Cup winner Chaumiere. (M G Hynes). *"A small, tough filly, Prix Noble will probably be my first two-year-old runner this year. She's a sprinting type"*.

439 - ROSE OF TARA (IRE)

ch.f. Generous - Flame Of Tara (Artaius). May 25.

Closely related to the very useful Group 3 10f Prix de Psyche and Irish 1,000 Guineas Trial winner Danse Royale (by Caerleon) and half-sister to numerous winners including the brilliant filly Salsabil, winner of the 1,000 Guineas, the Oaks, Irish Derby and Prix Vermeille, the high-class Group 1 St James's Palace Stakes winner Marju, the smart 1995 3-y-o dual 12f winner Song of Tara, the very useful 1989 3-y-o 10f and 10.5f winner Nearctic Flame (all by Sadler's Wells) and the 1995 2-y-o Group 3 6f Railway Stakes winner Flame of Athens (by Royal Academy). The dam won 8 races including the Group 2 1m Coronation Stakes and the Group 2 Pretty Polly Stakes and was second in the Champion Stakes. She is a half-sister to the useful dual 2-y-o 7f winner Blaze of Tara and to Fruition - dam of both the Breeders Cup Turf winner Northern Spur and the high-class stayer Kneller. The second dam, Welsh Flame (by Welsh Pageant), won 4 races at up to 1m and is a half-sister to the Musidora Stakes second Sofala - herself dam of the good stayer Bourbon Boy. (Miss P F O'Kelly). *"A filly with a lot of quality, she's the image of her sire. Strong, deep-bodied with a good temperament and not over-big, she's a late foal and a bit backward but has plenty of scope and depth" Michael tells me.*

440 - SHANTONAGH (IRE)

b.c. Darshaan - Lisana (Alleged). May 7. 70,000Y. Tattersalls December.

Half-brother to the French trained 3-y-o Liyana, to the very useful Group 3 12f Prix de Minerve winner Linnga (both by Shardari) and the French winner of 6 races Liyoun (by Shernazar), subsequently Grade 1 placed in the USA. The second dam, Licara (by Caro), won twice in France, was second in the Group 3 Prix Chloe and is a half-sister to the Group 1 winners Akiyda (Prix de l'Arc de Tromphe), Acamas (Prix du Jockey Club) and Akarad (Grand Prix de Saint-Cloud). (Mrs M Murtagh). *"A smashing colt, Shantonagh is very attractive and a good, easy mover. We might see him in June or July. A nice horse" says the trainer.*

441 - UNNAMED

b.f. Unfuwain - Alys (Blakeney). February 25. 52,000Y. Tattersalls October.

Half-sister to the 1992 German Group 2 1,000 Guineas winner Princess Nana (by Bellypha), to the Baden-Baden listed winner and Group 1 Prix du Cadran third Warfield (by Glint Of Gold), the triple German 3-y-o winner Assia (by Royal Academy) and the minor French and Belgian winner Windsor Herald (by Formidable). The dam won 4 races in France including the listed 1m Prix de Saint-Cyr and is a half-sister to 7 winners including the German listed winner Book Of Love. The second dam, Bessie Wallis (by Prince de Galles), won the listed 7f Houghton Stakes at 2 yrs. (Ricardo Sanz). *"A nice backward filly, she's good-looking and will want seven furlongs at least this year".*

442 - UNNAMED

b.f. St Jovite - Barleyabride (Blushing Groom). March 15. Third foal. 48,000Y. Tattersalls Houghton.

Half-sister to Robber Barron (by Track Barron) and Luvacat (by Storm Cat) - both minor winners in the USA. The dam, placed once in the USA at 3 yrs, is a sister to the Group 3 11f Premio Federico Tesio and Group 3 14f Premio Roma Vecchia winner Heart Of Groom and a half-sister to 4 winners. The second dam, Polar Bear (by Hoist The Flag), is an unraced daughter of the US Graded stakes winner Cold Comfort. (Mrs G Watt). *"An attractive, medium-sized filly, she's backward and will want seven furlongs in the second half of this season" explains Michael.*

443 - UNNAMED
b.c. Caerleon - Honorine (Blushing Groom).
May 14. IR32,000Y. Goffs Orby.
Half-brother to the Group 3 1m Premio Dormello winner Foolish Heart (by Fools Holme), to the fair 1996 3-y-o 12f winner Village King (by Roi Danzig), the fairly useful 9f and 10f winner Lord Bertie (by Roberto) and minor winners by Fools Holme, Roi Danzig and Temperance Hill. The dam, placed once in France over 1m, is a half-sister to 5 winners including the Group 3 10.5f Prix Corrida winner Echoes. The second dam, Equal Honor (by Round Table), won three races in the USA and was stakes-placed. (Mr G Canavan). *"Small and deep-bodied, she's a workmanlike filly that will start off at six furlongs in May or June".*

444 - UNNAMED
ch.f. Bluebird - Tanouma (Miswaki).
April 17. 52,000Y. Tattersalls Houghton.
Half-sister to the quite useful 1997 2-y-o 7f winner Marran (by Caerleon), to the very useful 8.2f (at 2 yrs), 10f and Group 2 13.3f Geoffrey Freer Stakes winner Azzilfi (by Ardross), the very useful Group 3 15f Coppa d'Oro di Milano winner Khamaseen (by Slip Anchor), the useful 1995 2-y-o 7f listed stakes winner Tamnia (by Green Desert), the fairly useful 10f winner Nawasib (by Warning) and the Swedish winner of 8 races Yamamah (by Siberian Express). The dam, a very useful 6f (at 2 yrs) and 7f winner, was third in the Group 3 7.3f Fred Darling Stakes and is a half-sister to 7 winners. The second dam, Diffusion (by Habitat), won two races including the Group 3 5f Prix d'Arenburg and was fourth in the Group 3 5f Prix du Petit Couvert. (Mr F O'Malley). *"A small, racy filly, she'll require good ground and should be ready to run by June or July".*

Rae Guest

445 - JUST DREAMS
ch.f. Salse - Pato (High Top).
February 28.
Sister to the high-class Group 1 St Leger and Group 1 Ascot Gold Cup winner Classic Cliche (by Salse) and half-sister to the smart Group 1 12f Prix Vermeille winner My Emma (by Marju), the quite useful 1993 2-y-o 6f and 7f winner Threatening (by Warning) and the minor 1m and 10.5f winner Cheeky Pot (by Petoski). The dam, a fairly useful 2-y-o 7f and triple 4-y-o 10f winner, is a sister to the very smart sprinter Crews Hill. The second dam, Patosky (by Skymaster), was a fairly useful winner of 4 races at up to 1m. (Matthews Breeding & Racing).

446 - MY FIRST
b.c. First Trump - Jubilee Song (Song).
April 30. 44,000Y. Tattersalls October.
Closely related to the Group 2 5f Prix du Gros-Chene winner Millyant (by Primo Dominie) and half-brother to the Group 2 5f Flying Childers Stakes and Group 3 5f Palace House Stakes winner Prince Sabo, the quite useful 8.2f to 10.4f winner Solo Artist (both by Young Generation), the fairly useful dual 6f winner My Cadeaux (by Cadeaux Genereux), the quite useful 2-y-o 5f winner Swellegant (by Midyan) and the 1990 Irish listed 2-y-o winner Bold Jessie (by Never So Bold) - herself dam of the Gimcrack Stakes winner Abou Zouz. The dam, a fair 3-y-o 5f winner, is a half-sister to 7 winners including the listed-placed Band On The Run and Shark Song. The second dam, Sylvanecte (by Silver Shark), was a fair 3-y-o 10f winner. (Mr C J Mills).

William Haggas

447 - FULL EGALITE
gr.c. Ezzoud - Milva (Jellaby).
April 20. 27,000Y. Tattersalls October.
Half-brother to the quite useful dual 6f winner Milagro (by King Of Spain), to the fair 1991 2-y-o 7f and subsequent Italian winner Miltiades (by Magic Mirror), the modest 1997 2-y-o 5f winner Mill End Quest (by King's Signet), the modest 14f winner Serious Time (by Good Times), the Italian winner Belong To Me (by Squill) and the 1997 French 3-y-o winner Yucatan (by Saint Andrews). The dam, a modest 3-y-o 6f winner, is a half-sister to 4 winners. The second dam, Cornflower (by Vilmorin), won at 2 yrs and was a fairly useful sprinter. (Mr S Hassiakos). *"I like this colt and he'll probably start over six furlongs by mid-season"* the trainer was telling me.

448 - FULL PITCH
ch.c. Cadeaux Genereux - Tricky Note (Song).
March 9. Sixth foal. 49,000Y. Tattersalls December.
Half-brother to the quite useful 1997 2-y-o 6f winner Composition (by Wolfhound), to the Irish 9f and 10f winner Ros Castle (by Reference Point) and a 3-y-o winner in Japan by Caerleon. The dam, a fairly

useful winner of 3 races including the listed National Stakes at Sandown, is a sister to the Group 3 Duke Of York Stakes winner Jester and a half-sister to 6 winners. The second dam, Trickster (by Major Portion), won over 5f and is a half-sister to 5 winners and to the dams of the useful winners Fayruz, Reesh and Tadwin. (Mr R Burton). *"Full Pitch is a nice colt, quite backward now, but when he strengthens he'll be a seriously nice horse. He'll be out by mid-summer and I don't think he'll be slow!"*

449 - FUTURE COUP (USA)
b.c. Lord At War - Holy Moly (Halo).
February 26. Sixth foal. $37,000Y. Keeneland September.
Brother to the minor US 2-y-o winner Holy Wish and half-brother to 2 other minor winners. The dam, a winner at 4 yrs in the USA, is a half-sister to the Grade 1 Hopeful Stakes winner Papal Power. The second dam, Papal Decree (Noble Decree), is a winning half-sister to the Irish Derby second and high-class sire Siver Hawk. (Mr M Brower). *"Future Coup had a problem earlier on and he's a little bit behind but he should be out by mid-summer. He definitely looks like a 2-y-o type".*

450 - HISTORIC (IRE)
b.c. Sadler's Wells - Urjwan (Seattle Slew).
March 11. Sixth foal. IR62,000Y. Goffs Orby.
Half-brother to the very useful 14f to 2m winner Jiyush (by Generous), to the fairly useful 10.3f winner Dawlah (by Shirley Heights) and the quite useful 1996 2-y-o 7f and subsequent US winner Bareeq (by Nashwan). The dam, a fairly useful 1m winner, is a half-sister to 9 winners including the Group 2 Prix de Pomone winner Whitehaven and the dam of the Italian Oaks winner Valley Of Gold. The second dam, White Star Line (by Northern Dancer), won the Alabama Stakes, the Delaware Oaks and the Kentucky Oaks (all Grade 1 events) and is a half-sister to 7 winners including the Prix Morny winner Filiberto and the dams of the Graded stakes winners Magazine, Fairway Flyer and Torsion. (Highclere Thoroughbred Racing Ltd). *"A backward colt, he has a good temperament but won't be ready to run until the back-end" William tells me.*

451 - KING OBERON (IRE)
b.c. Fairy King - Annenberg (Slip Anchor).
February 17. First foal. IR110,000Y. Goffs Orby.
The dam won 2 minor races in France at 2 and 3 yrs and is a half-sister to 2 winners including the French and US winner and Group 3 1m Prix Messidor placed River Of Light. The second dam, Boreale (by Bellypha), won the Group 3 1m Prix des Reservoirs, was second in the French 1,000 Guineas and is a half-sister to 6 winners including the dam of the Prix de la Salamandre and Prix Morny winner Princesse Lida. *"A very nice horse and sharp too. I'll be aiming him for the Gimcrack - a race I've always wanted to win".*

452 - PICTURE PUZZLE
b.f. Royal Academy - Cloudslea (Chief's Crown).
April 20. Second foal. 25,000Y. Tattersalls October.
The dam, a minor French 3-y-o winner, is closely related to the useful 10f and 12f winner and listed-placed Jagellon (by Danzig Connection). The second dam, Heavenlyspun (by His Majesty), is an unplaced half-sister to 8 winners including Folk Art (Grade 1 Oak Leaf Stakes), Mashaallah (Irish St Leger, Grosser Preis von Baden and Premio di Milano), the good US stakes winner Sportin' Life and the dams of the Group/Graded stakes winners Local Talent, Local Suitor, Connie's Gift and Court Hostess. (Mr M H Wilson). *"Quite backward but a lovely mover, she won't be seen out until September".*

453 - PINNACLE
b.f. Shirley Heights - Manhattan Sunset (El Gran Senor).
January 23. First foal. 80,000Y. Tattersalls Houghton.
The dam, a fair 2-y-o 7f winner at Newmarket, is a half-sister to 2 minor winners in the USA. The second dam, Mezimica (by Dewan), won over 10.5f in France and the Grade 3 8.5f Falls City Handicap in the USA and is a half-sister to the listed Pretty Polly Stakes winner Spiranthes. (Mrs B Bassett). *"Pinnacle is a very nice filly with a good temperament for a Shirley Heights. She's active and should be running by August over six or seven furlongs".*

454 - PREDOMINANT (USA)
ch.c. Sky Classic - Hard Knocker (Raja Baba).
January 27. $45,000Y. Keeneland September.
Half-brother to the minor US winners Proven Desire (by Green Dancer) and Deputy Mayor (by Deputy Minister). The dam is an unraced half-sister to the Irish St Leger, Gran Premio di Milano and Grosser Preis von Baden winner Mashaallah, to the US Grade 1 winner Folk Art and to the dam of the Prix Jean Prat winner Local Talent. The second dam, Homespun (by Round Table), won at 2 and 3 yrs in the USA. (Mr P Ellick). *"Predominant is a strong 2-y-o type that should be running in May and has the scope to improve".*

455 - WELCOME GIFT b.c. Prince Sabo - Ausonia (Beldale Flutter).
April 18. Fifth foal. IR37,000Y. Goffs Orby.
Half-sister to the Italian 3-y-o 9f winner Billy Corgan (by Last Tycoon). The dam is an unplaced sister to the French listed winner Battlement de Coeur and a half-sister to 4 winners including the Group 2 Laurent Perrier Champagne Stakes winner Young Runaway. The second dam, Mauritania (by The Brianstan), was placed four times at 3 yrs and is a half-sister to 9 winners including the very useful middle-distance performer Belper and the Musidora Stakes winner Lovers Lane. (Mr M H Wilson). *"This is a nice horse, uncomplicated and he'll be a mid-season type".*

456 - ZILARATOR (USA) b.c. Zilzal - Allegedly (Sir Ivor).
February 12. 100,000 Y. Tattersalls Houghton.
Half-brother to the smart gelding Per Quod (by Lyllos), a winner of three Group 3 races including the 13.4f Ormonde Stakes, to the US Grade 3 winner Suspect Terrain (by Corridor Key), the fair 1m to 2m winner Prosequendo (by Robellino) and the minor US winners Uncle Albie (by Opening Verse) and Shiitake (by Green Desert) - the latter also dam of the US Grade 1 winner Taking Risks. The dam is an unraced half-sister to the outstanding dual 'Arc' winner Alleged. The second dam, Princess Pout (by Prince John), was a US stakes winner of 13 races . (Dandy Racing Ltd). *"A backward colt that will have one or two runs at the back-end, Zilarator will make a nice staying horse next year. I like him very much".*

457 - UNNAMED b.c. Turtle Island - Lightino (Bustino).
May 17. Fifth foal. 31,000Y. Tattersalls October.
Closely related to the fair 1996 3-y-o 8.5f winner Alambar (by Fairy King). The dam was placed 5 times in Ireland and is a half-sister to 6 winners including the Group 1 Gran Premio d'Italia winner Welsh Guide. The second dam, Highland Light (by Home Guard), won 3 races and was a useful sprinter. (Dandy Racing Ltd). *"A late foal but he's done well and seems to like his work. Quite a nice horse and definitely a two-year-old".*

Ben Hanbury

458 - HAAFIZ (USA) b.c. Green Desert - Midway Lady (Alleged).
March 13.
Brother to the useful 1991 3-y-o 7f and 1m winner and Irish 1,000 Guineas third Umniyatee (by Green Desert) and half-brother to the 1998 3-y-o Abuljjood (by Marju) and the quite useful 1993 12f placed 3-y-o and subsequent Dubai winner Alasad (by Kris). The dam, a smart 2-y-o winner of the Group 1 Prix Marcel Boussac and Group 3 May Hill Stakes, trained on to become a high-class 3-y-o and winner of both the 1,000 Guineas and Oaks before an injury forced her into premature retirement. She is a half-sister to 5 winners including the very useful 11.8f listed winner Capias. The second dam, Smooth Bore (by His Majesty), won 2 stakes races at around 1m in the USA at 4 yrs. (Hamdan Al Maktoum). *"This is a very nice, sharp colt and a typical Green Desert in that he looks a quality horse. His head reminds me very much of his dam and I see him starting over six furlongs around August time"* Ben informs me.

459 - LUCKY RASCAL (IRE) b.br.c. Indian Ridge - Chesnut Tree (Shadeed).
March 2. Fourth foal. 60,000 Y. Tattersalls Houghton.
Half-brother to the 3-y-o North Cape (by Soviet Star) and to the 5.2f (at 2 yrs) and 1m placed Mayflower (by Midyan). The dam, a fairly useful 3-y-o 12f winner, is a half-sister to 4 winners including the dam of the Group 2 12f Ribblesdale Stakes winner Phantom Gold. The second dam, Expansive (by Exbury), a very useful winner of the Ribblesdale Stakes, is a sister to the Park Hill Stakes winner Example and a half-sister to the Lancashire Oaks winner Amphora. (Abdullah Ali).

460 - MISS SHEMA (USA) b.f. Gulch - Fire And Shade (Shadeed).
March 21. Fourth foal. 120,000Y. Tattersalls Houghton.
Half-sister to the French trained 3-y-o Guerre Et Paix (by Soviet Star), to the useful 1996 3-y-o 10f winner Freedom Flame (by Darshaan) and the fair middle-distance placed maiden Surtsey (by Nashwan). The dam, a fairly useful 2-y-o 6f winner, is a half-sister to 2 winners out of the very smart Group 3 Musidora Stakes winner Fatah Flare (by Alydar) - herself a half-sister to the dual US Grade 1 winner Sabin. The third dam, Beaconaire (by Vaguely Noble), a winner of 3 races at up to 10f in France, is a half-sister to the Grade 2 winner Kittiwake (dam of the multiple Grade 1 winner Miss Oceana, the Prix Jean Prat

winner Kitwood and the Grade 2 winner Larida - herself dam of the Coronation Stakes winner Magic of Life). (Abdullah Ali).

---

461 - MUTAMAKIN (USA) b.c. Red Ransom - Won't She Tell (Banner Sport).
April 13. $70,000Y. Keeneland September.

Half-brother to the US stakes winner and Grade 1 placed Dr Caton (by Seattle Slew), to the Group 3 Solario Stakes winner White Crown (by Secreto), the 2-y-o 6f winner Wind Cheetah (by Storm Cat) and the 11.8f winner Zuboon (by The Minstrel) - all at least useful. The dam won 9 races in the USA at up to 9f, including a minor stakes event, was fourth in a Grade 3 stakes and is a half-sister to the American Triple Crown winner Affirmed, to the stakes winners Love You Dear and Silent Fox and to She Won't Tell, the winning dam of the US Grade 1 stakes winner Senor Pete. The second dam, Won't Tell You (by Crafty Admiral), won 5 races. (Hamdan Al Maktoum).

---

462 - SUHAIL (IRE) b.c. Wolfhound - Sharayif (Green Desert).
May 23. Third foal.

Half-brother to the fair 1997 7f placed 2-y-o Ratiyya (by Mujtahid). The dam is an unraced sister to the useful 7f and 1m winner and Irish 1,000 Guineas third Umniyatee (herself dam of the useful winners Messhed and Jarah). The second dam, Midway Lady (by Alleged), was a high-class winner of the 1,000 Guineas, the Oaks, the Prix Marcel Boussac and the May Hill Stakes and is a sister to the very useful 10f winner Capias. The third dam, Smooth Bore (by His Majesty), was an American stakes winner at around 1m. (Hamdan Al Maktoum).

---

463 - TEBYAAN (USA) b.br.f. Silver Hawk - Umniyatee (Green Desert).
March 20. Fourth foal.

Half-sister to the useful 7f and 1m winner Jarah (by Forty Niner) and to the useful Messhed (by Gulch), a winner of three races over 7f. The dam was a useful 3-y-o winner of two races over 7f and 1m and was third in the Irish 1,000 Guineas. The second dam, Midway Lady (by Alleged), was a high-class winner of the 1,000 Guineas, the Oaks, the Prix Marcel Boussac and the May Hill Stakes and is a sister to the very useful 10f winner Capias. The third dam, Smooth Bore (by His Majesty), was an American stakes winner at around 1m. (Hamdan Al Maktoum).

---

464 - UPON A WISH b.br.c. Alzao - Imprecise (Polish Precedent).
March 7. First foal. 85,000Y. Tattersalls Houghton.

The dam, a modest 3-y-o 8.1f winner, is a half-sister to 5 winners including the high-class colt Shady Heights, a winner of 7 races from 6f to 10.5f, notably the Group 1 International Stakes (on the disqualification of Persian Heights) and second in both the Eclipse Stakes and the Phoenix Champion Stakes. The second dam, Vaguely (by Bold Lad, Ire), was a fairly useful 1m (at 2 yrs) and 10f winner. (Ahmed Ali).

Criquette Head

---

465 - AQUIRE NOT DESIRE (USA) ch.c. Woodman - Forladiesonly (Sovereign Dancer).
March 28. Third foal. $120,000. Keeneland September.

The dam, a US stakes winner of 11 races, is a half-sister to the US Grade 3 Cherry Hill Mile winner Dr. Bobby A and three other stakes winners. The second dam, Cricket Club (by Dr Fager), a minor US stakes winner, is a half-sister to the dam of the Group 3 Prestige Stakes winner Love Of Silver. (Maktoum Al Maktoum).

---

466 - CRYSTAL MAGICIAN ch.c. Cadeaux Genereux - Miss Temerity (Sharrood).
April 6. First foal. 130,000Y. Houghton.

The dam, placed from 7f to 9.4f at 3 yrs, is a half-sister to the Italian Group 3 winner and Diadem Stakes second Leap For Joy. The second dam, Humble Pie (by Known Fact), a fairly useful 2-y-o 6f winner, is a half-sister to 4 winners including the Prix Maurice de Gheest, Cork And Orrery Stakes and Greenlands Stakes winner College Chapel. (Maktoum Al Maktoum).

---

467 - ELEANOR'S PRIDE (FR) ch.f. Barathea - Escaline (Arctic Tern).
April 25. FF1,500,000. Deauville August.

Half-sister to the 1997 3-y-o listed 12f Prix de l'Avre winner Arabian King (by Arazi), to the French winner and Group 3 Prix de Guiche third East of Heaven (by Lyphard), the French winners Sans Escale (by Diesis) and Ensorcelles Moi (by Riverman) and the very useful maiden Kaheel (by Caro) - placed fourth in the Epsom Derby. The dam, a high-class winner of four races including the Group 1 10.5f Prix de Diane, is a half-sister to the Group 3 Premio Carla Porta winner Esdale and to the dam of the German Group 2 winner Royal Abjar. The second dam, Esdee (Hail to Reason), was placed over 10f in France. (Maktoum Al Maktoum).

468 - EMERALD PARK (USA)
b.c. Zilzal - Greenland Park (Red God).

Half-brother to the high-class filly Fitnah (by Kris), winner of the Prix Saint-Alary, the Prix Vanteaux, the Prix de la Nonette and the Prix du Prince d'Orange and to the minor French winner Falcon Eye (by Touching Wood). The dam was a high class filly herself, winning the Queen Mary Stakes, the Molecomb Stakes and the Cornwallis Stakes, is a sister to the Coventry Stakes winner Red Sunset and a half-sister to the unraced Mary Martin, herself dam of the very useful filly Marina Park. The second dam, Centre Piece (by Tompion), was placed once over 6f. (Maktoum Al Maktoum).

469 - FRANKLY FINE (IRE)
b.f. Fairy King - Melting Gold (Cadeaux Genereux).
March 7. First foal.
The dam, a very useful French 2-y-o 7f winner, was second in the Group 3 1m Prix de Sandringham at 3 yrs. The second dam, a fair 3-y-o 9f winner at Ayr, is a half-sister to the 2,000 Guineas and Queen Elizabeth II Stakes winner Shadeed. The second dam, Continual (by Damascus), won twice at up to 7f in the USA and is a sister to the dam of the outstanding Kentucky Derby and Belmont Stakes winner Swale. (Maktoum Al Maktoum).

470 - GOLD BUST
ch.f. Nashwan - Riviere d'Or (Lyphard).
May 12.
Closely related to the French-trained 3-y-o Or Bleu (by Rainbow Quest) and to the smart filly Gold Splash (by Blushing Groom), winner of the Group 1 1m Prix Marcel Boussac and the Group 1 1m Coronation Stakes. The dam, also a smart filly, won the Group 1 10f Prix Saint-Alary, the Group 3 1m Prix d'Aumale and the Group 3 9.2f Prix Vanteaux, is closely related to the Group 3 Prix du Lys winner Chercheur d'Or and the French 2,000 Guineas second Goldneyev. The second dam, Gold River (by Riverman), won the Prix de l'Arc de Triomphe, the Prix Jean Prat, the Prix du Cadran and the Prix Royal-Oak. (Wertheimer et Frere).

471 - IRISH PRIZE (USA)
b.c. Irish River - Cadeaux d'Amie (Lyphard).

Brother to the 1992 1,000 Guineas and Prix de l'Opera winner Hatoof (by Irish River) and half-brother to the Ed Dunlop trained 3-y-o Opera Queen (by Pleasant Colony), the dual 10f listed winner Insijaam (by Secretariat) and the 12f listed winner Fasateen (by Alysheba) - both trained in France. The dam, a winner over 1m at 2 yrs and 10f at 3 yrs in France, was third in the Group 3 1m Prix d'Aumale and is a half-sister to the Champion 2-y-o filly and Prix Vermeille and Prix de Diane winner Mrs Penny. The second dam, Tananarive (by Le Fabuleux), won 3 times at up to 14f in France and is a half-sister to the stakes winners Tahitian King and Tuxpan. (Maktoum Al Maktoum).

472 - MIDNIGHT FOXTROT
b.c. Kingmambo - Vana Turns (Wavering Monarch).
April 21. Fifth foal.
Closely related to the Group 2 9f Ohio Derby winner Petionville (by Seeking The Gold) and half-brother to the Grade 1 9f Kentucky Oaks and Group 3 9f California Derby winner Pike Place Dancer (by Seattle Dancer). The dam won 6 races including 2 stakes events and is a half-sister to 4 winners. The second dam, The Wheel Turns, won two Grade 3 races. (Maktoum Al Maktoum).

473 - NE COUPEZ PAS (USA)
b.c. Nureyev - Soundings (Nureyev).

Closely related to the French trained 3-y-o Sand Prospector, to the very useful 1992 Group 1 5.5f Prix Robert Papin winner Didyme (both by Dixieland Band), and half-brother to the high-class French 2,000 Guineas and Prix d'Ispahan winner and St James's Palace Stakes and Prix du Moulin placed Green Tune (by Green Dancer), the Group 1 6f Cheveley Park Stakes winner Pas de Reponse (by Danzig) and the 1996 3-y-o 1m listed winner Ecoute (by Manila). The dam won two races in the USA, is a sister to the very useful 5f and 6f winner Al Zawbaah and a half-sister to 5 other winners. The second dam, Ocean's Answer (by Northern Answer), won the Natalma Stakes and is closely related to Storm Bird. (Wertheimer et Frere).

474 - SALLIVERA b.f. Sillery - Mabrova (Prince Mab).
February 11. Fourth foal.
Half-sister to the high-class filly Kistena (by Miswaki), winner of 6 races including the Group 1 5f Prix
de l'Abbaye, Group 3 6f Prix de Meautry and Group 3 5f Prix de Seine-et-Oise and to Spend a Rubble
(by Spend A Buck), a minor winner of 4 races over 10f at 3 yrs in France. The dam, a winner over 7f
at 2 yrs in France and fourth in the Group 3 Prix des Reservoirs. The second dam, Makarova (by
Nijinsky), was a middle-distance winner of 3 races in France. (Wertheimer et Frere).

475 - TRAPEZINA b.f. Saumarez - Only Seule (Lyphard).
Fourth foal.
Sister to the Criquette Head trained 3-y-o Only Quest and half-sister to the high-class Group 1 7f Prix
de la Foret and Group 1 6.5f Prix Maurice de Gheest winner Occupandiste (by Kaldoun) and the useful
French 2-y-o 7.5f winner Lonely Tycoon (by Last Tycoon). The dam, a winner over 7.5f in France at 2
yrs, is closely related to the Irish 1,000 Guineas and Tripleprint Celebration Mile winner Mehthaaf and
the high-class 1997 Diadem Stakes winner Elnadim. The second dam, Elle Seule (by Exclusive Native),
won 3 races including the Group 3 1m Prix d'Astarte and is a half-sister to the Group/Grade 1 winners
Fort Wood, Hamas and Timber Country and to the group winners Northern Aspen, Colorado Dancer
and Mazzacano. (Wertheimer et Frere).

476 - VALNERINA b.f. Caerleon - Lady Capulet (Sir Ivor).
May 13. IR195,000Y. Goffs Orby.
Half-sister to the 3-y-o Lake Valentia (by Fairy King), to the very smart 1991 Irish 2-y-o El Prado, a
winner of 4 races including the Group 1 National Stakes and Group 2 Beresford Stakes, the 1992 Irish
2-y-o 7f and 3-y-o 14f winner Portrait Gallery and the 1993 Japanese 2-y-o winner Pia Tiara (all by
Sadler's Wells) and the high-class 1m Desmond Stakes winner and Irish Derby, Irish 2,000 Guineas
and Phoenix Champion Stakes placed Entitled (by Mill Reef). The dam won the 1977 Irish 1,000
Guineas on the first of her three outings, is a sister to the Royal Lodge Stakes winner Sir Wimborne
and a half-sister to the good American sire Drone. The second dam, Cap and Bells (by Tom Fool), was
a stakes-placed winner in the USA. (Mr G Oldham).

477 - ZIGGY GOLD (USA) b.c. Danzig - Gold Splash (Blushing Groom).
First foal.
The dam, a very smart filly, won the Group 1 1m Prix Marcel Boussac and the Group 1 1m Coronation
Stakes. The second dam, Riviere d'Or (by Lyphard), won the Group 1 Prix Saint-Alary, the Group 3
Prix d'Aumale and the Group 3 Prix Vanteaux. The third dam, Gold River (by Riverman), won the Prix
de l'Arc de Triomphe. (Wertheimer et Frere).

Lady Herries

478 - BELLADONIA b.f. Primo Dominie - Susquehanna Days (Chief's Crown).
April 11. Second foal. 40,000Y. Tattersalls October.
Half-sister to the quite useful 1997 2-y-o 6f winner Clef Of Silver (by Indian Ridge). The dam, a fair
3-y-o 1m and 8.2f winner, is a half-sister to several winners including Clare Bridge, (Group 3 Gilltown
Stud Stakes), Song Of Sixpence (listed Winter Hill Stakes) and Early Rising (dam of the St Leger
winner Silver Patriarch). The second dam, Gliding By (by Tom Rolfe), won over 6f on her only start, is
closely related to Key To The Mint (four Grade 1 wins in the USA) and a half-sister to the US Horse Of
The Year Fort Marcy and the Grade 1 winner Key To Content. (Mr D Oliver & Mrs J Oliver).

479 - BOLD FAIRY (IRE) b.c. Fairy King - Copsewood (Thatching).
January 21. First foal. 28,000Y. Tattersalls October.
The dam is an unplaced half-sister to the Group 3 Beresford Stakes and Group 3 Greenlands Stakes
winner Burden Of Proof (by Fairy King - the sire of this colt). The second dam, Belle Passe (by Be My
Guest), ran unplaced in two starts. (Major Gen. Guy Watkins & Sir William Purves).

480 - CELTIC FLING b.f. Lion Cavern - Celtic Ring (Welsh Pageant).
May 1. Fourth foal.
Half-sister to the outstanding colt and Champion 2-y-o Celtic Swing (by Damister), winner of the French
Derby and the Racing Post Trophy and second in the 2,000 Guineas and to the quite useful 1992 2-y-o
7f winner Cissbury Ring (by Jalmood). The dam, a fairly useful 10f and 12f winner, is out of the
twice-raced Pencuik Jewel (by Petingo), herself a half-sister to the Ascot Gold Cup winner Ragstone

and to the top-class broodmare Castle Moon (dam of the Group 1 winners Moon Madness and Sheriff's Star). (Angmering Park Stud).

481 - DISTANT MOON

b.c. Distant Relative - Moon Carnival (Be My Guest).
February 8. Second foal. 52,000Y. Tattersalls October.
Half-brother to the 3-y-o Malayan Moon (by Kris). The dam, a fair 3-y-o 11.6f and 12.5f winner, is a half-sister to 6 winners including Moon Madness (St Leger and Grand Prix de Saint-Cloud), Sheriff's Star (Coronation Cup and Grand Prix de Saint-Cloud) and Lucky Moon (Goodwood Cup). The second dam, Castle Moon (by Kalamoun), won from 1m to 13f, is a sister to the very smart middle-distance stayer Castle Keep and a half-sister to the Ascot Gold Cup winner Ragstone. (Mr G Ward). *"All five of these young horses are nice and Distant Moon is by far the most forward. He's exceptionally nice and should be running by June" Lady Herries tells me.*

482 - STAND ASIDE

b.c. In The Wings - Honourable Sheba (Roberto).
May 28. Fourth foal. 33,000Y. Tattersalls October.
Half-brother to the 3-y-o Master Caster (by Night Shift), unplaced twice at 2 yrs, to the quite useful 1995 2-y-o winner Crystal Falls (by Alzao) and the fair 1997 3-y-o 1m winner Olivo (by Priolo). The dam is an unraced half-sister to the US stakes winner Ells Noble Peace. The second dam, Honor Guard (by Vaguely Noble), was placed five times in France and the USA and is a half-sister to the high-class miler and sire Lear Fan and to the very smart colt Pirate Army. (Mr C Hardy).

Barry Hills

483 - BURMA BABY (USA)

ch.c. Woodman - Rangoon Ruby (Sallust).
April 14. $200,000Y. Keeneland September.
Half-brother to the smart Group 3 7f Jersey Stakes winner Gneiss (by Diesis), to the US stakes winner New Madrid (by Devil's Bag) and 2 minor winners in the USA by Alysheba and Vice Regent. The dam won 7 races including the Group 3 Baroda Stud Phoenix Sprint and was placed in a Grade 3 event in the USA. The second dam, Pretty Crier (by Town Crier), is a placed half-sister to the Sun Chariot Stakes and Child Stakes winner Duboff. (Maktoum Al Maktoum). *"A big horse, but not that backward, he'll be suited by seven furlongs eventually. A lovely stamp of a horse, he has a good temperament and shows a lot of promise" says Assistant Trainer Kevin Mooney. Barry has a number of other young horses in the Early Types section.*

484 - CALCUTTA

b.c. Indian Ridge - Echoing (Formidable).
February 21. IR60,000Y. Goffs Orby.
Half-brother to the fair 1995 dual 12f all-weather winner Sommersby (by Vision) and to the poor 1993 3-y-o 6f winner Buckski Echo (by Petoski). The dam, a fairly useful 2-y-o 5f winner, is out of the unraced Siren Sound (by Manado), herself a half-sister to 6 winners including the Irish listed winner Combine Harvester and the Child Stakes fourth Rule Britannia. (Mrs J M Corbett). *"Calcutta is a big horse, but he's a well-balanced type that does everything really well and I could see him being a fairly useful two-year-old".*

485 - CHESHIRE CAT (IRE)

b.f. Ezzoud - Riyda (Be My Guest).
March 7. Sixth foal. 62,000Y. Tattersalls Houghton.
Closely related to the Irish 1m and 9f winner Ridiya (by Last Tycoon) and half-sister to 3 winners including the useful 1997 triple 12f winner Ridaiyma (by Kahyasi) and the Irish 10f winner Riyama (by Doyoun). The dam, a useful 1m and 10f listed winner, is a half-sister to 5 winners including the Group 3 Royal Whip Stakes winner Rayeka and the dam of the Prix Hocquart winner Rifapour. The second dam, Rilasa (by St Paddy), a very useful winner in France, was third in the Group 3 9.5f Prix Vanteaux and is a half-sister to 3 winners including the Prix du Cadran second Hereas. (Mr C Wright). *"A scopey filly with a lot to like about her, Cheshire Cat is a good mover but she won't be ready to run until mid-summer" I was told.*

486 - CRAGGY MOUNTAIN

ch.c. Cadeaux Genereux - Jet Ski Lady (Vaguely Noble).
February 12. Third foal.
Half-brother to the minor 1997 Irish 3-y-o 12f winner Legaya (by Shirley Heights). The dam, a winner over 6f and 7f in Ireland at 2 yrs, won a 10f listed event at the Curragh and the Group 1 12f Epsom Oaks the following year. The second dam, Bemissed (by Nijinsky), a good American filly, won the Grade 1 Selima Stakes at 2 yrs, was third in the Kentucky Oaks and is a half-sister to the very useful

Group 2 12f Princess of Wales's Stakes winner Desert Team. (Maktoum Al Maktoum). *"A very big horse, Craggy Mountain has had a few setbacks and won't be on the racecourse until the back-end".*

487 - EAGLESHAM (IRE)
b.c. Barathea - High Hawk (Shirley Heights).
February 2.
Closely related to the top class middle distance colt In the Wings, winner of the Breeders Cup Turf, Coronation Cup, Grand Prix de Saint-Cloud and Prix du Prince d'Orange, to the smart 1993 3-y-o Group 2 10.5f Prix Greffulhe winner Hunting Hawk and the very useful 1994 3-y-o 10f and 11.5f winner Hawker's News (all by Sadlers Wells) and half-brother to the useful 3-y-o 10.4f and 4-y-o 10f winner Mohawk River (by Polish Precedent). The dam won 6 races from 10f to 14.5f including the Group 1 Premio Roma, Group 2 Ribblesdale Stakes, Group 2 Park Hill Stakes and Group 3 Prix de Royallieu and is a half-sister to the useful miler Heron's Hollow and to the dam of Infamy (Rothman's International, Sun Chariot Stakes, etc). The second dam, Sunbittern (by Sea Hawk II), a very useful 2-y-o 6f and 7f winner, was fourth in the Cheveley Park Stakes. (Sheikh Mohammed).

488 - GOLDEN SNAKE (USA)
b.c. Danzig - Dubian (High Line).
April 18.
Half-brother to the top-class filly Sayyedati, winner of the Cheveley Park Stakes and Moyglare Stud Stakes at 2 yrs, the 1,000 Guineas and Prix Jacques le Marois at 3 yrs and the Sussex Stakes at 5 yrs, to the 1990 2-y-o 6f winner Shihama (both by Shadeed) and the fair 1994 7f to 1m placed 3-y-o Tigwa (by Cadeaux Genereux). The dam, a smart filly, won over 7f at 2 yrs, 12f at 3 yrs and the Group 1 12f Premio Lydia Tesio at 4 yrs. She was also placed in the Epsom Oaks and Irish Oaks, and is a half-sister to the triple champion hurdler See You Then. The second dam, Melodina (by Tudor Melody), won the 5f Seaton Delaval Stakes at 2 yrs, a 10f event at 3 yrs when she was placed in the Ribblesdale Stakes and the Musidora Stakes, and was a half-sister to the Irish Oaks winner Celina. (Mohammed Obaida). *"Quite a tall horse and on the leg at the moment, he's just doing long canters but he's a very good mover and does everything easily. He needs time and probably won't run until August or September".*

489 - GRACIOUS PLENTY (IRE)
ch.f. Generous - Formide (Trempolino).
March 10. Third foal. IR44,000Y. Goffs Orby.
The dam, a minor French 2-y-o winner, is a sister to the Group 3 Prix de Flore second Suivez La and a half-sister to the Group 2 Beresford Stakes winner Victory Piper. The second dam, Arisen (by Mr Prospector), was a stakes winner of 6 races and a half-sister to the dual US Grade 3 winner Pair Of Deuces. (Mr E D Kessly). *"Not over-big but she's done very well. A good-moving filly, she's still backward at the moment".*

490 - GUNNER SAM
ch.c. Emarati - Minne Love (Homeric).
March 26. 20,000Y. Doncaster St Leger.
Brother to the fair dual 6f winner Brockton Flame and to the minor Irish 7f winner Live Coment and half-brother to the quite useful sprinter Micro Love (by Homeric), a winner of 7 races over 5f. The dam, a modest 2-y-o 6f winner, is a half-sister to 4 minor winners. The second dam, Late Love (by Great White Way), won twice at 2 yrs and was placed in the Flying Childers Stakes and the Gimcrack Stakes. (Mr R W Miller). *"A good mover but he's done nothing but grow and although I think he'll show us some speed one day, he's very much on the back burner for now".*

491 - HASTY WORDS (IRE)
b.f. Polish Patriot - Park Elect (Ahonoora).
February 9. Third foal. 36,000Y. Tattersalls Houghton.
Half-sister to the fairly useful 5f and 6f winner Katya (by Dancing Dissident) and the fair 2-y-o 5f winner Hyde Park (by Alzao). The dam won over 7f and 9f in Ireland at 3 yrs and is a half-sister to 3 winners. The second dam, Petite Realm (by Realm), a fairly useful 2-y-o dual 5f winner, was second in the Group 3 Mulcahy Stakes. (W J Gredley).

492 - HULA ANGEL (USA)
br.f. Woodman - Jode (Danzig).
March 19. Third foal. IR85,000Y. Goffs Orby.
Half-sister to the 1997 Irish 3-y-o 9f winner Jaunting (by Seattle Slew). The dam, a fair 2-y-o 6f winner here and in America at 3 yrs, is a sister to a US stakes-placed winner, is closely related to another and a half-sister to the Kentucky Derby winner Spend A Buck. The second dam, Belle de Jour (by Speak John), won a 6f claiming race in the USA. (Mr J R Fleming). *"This is a lovely two-year-old. She should be out by June, has a good temperament and is a classy-looking filly. She's doing extremely well and is a good mover".*

493 - KILTING　　　　　　　　　　　　　　ch.f. Nashwan - Balliasta (Lyphard).
　　　　　　　　　　　　　　　　　　　　　　　　　　　　March 3. Third foal.
Half-brother to High Atlas (by Shirley Heights), placed over 14f at 3 yrs on his only outing. The dam was unplaced on both her outings at 2 yrs in France but is a half-sister to the high-class middle-distance colt Sanglamore - winner of the French Derby and the Prix d'Ispahan - and the very useful listed 10f winner Opera Score. The second dam, Ballinderry (by Irish River), was a very useful winner of the Group 2 12f Ribblesdale Stakes, was third in the Yorkshire Oaks and is a half-sister to numerous good winners including Sharpman (placed in the French 2,000 Guineas and the French Derby), Mot d'Or (Prix Hocquart) and Lydian (Grosser Preis von Berlin and Gran Premio de Milano). (Khaled Abdulla).

---

494 - KIND SIR　　　　　　　　　　　b.c. Generous - Noble Conquest (Vaguely Noble).
　　　　　　　　　　　　　　　　　February 15. First foal. 65,000Y. Tattersalls Houghton.
The dam, a minor winner in France, is a half-sister to 6 winners including the Group 1 Prix de la Salamandre and Group 3 Prix du Bois winner Noblequest and the listed-placed Dance Quest (dam of the Group 2 winners Pursuit Of Love and Divine Danse). The second dam, Polyponder (by Barbizon), won 6 races including the Prix de la Porte Maillot, Prix de Saint-Georges, Prix du Gros-Chene and Prix du Petit Couvert (all Group 3 events). (Mr A D Shead). *"Kind Sir is a big horse that's done extremely well. He's not all that backward, has a lovely temperament and is a good mover. He'll probably start off at six furlongs".*

---

495 - MAYA COVE　　　　　　　　　　b.f. Caerleon - Shining Water (Kalaglow).
　　　　　　　　　　　　　　　　　　　　　　　　　　　February 12.
Sister to the high-class 1992 2-y-o Group 1 1m Grand Criterium and 3-y-o Group 2 10.4f Dante Stakes winner Tenby, to the useful 1996 2-y-o 7f and 1m winner River Usk and the very useful 1m (at 2 yrs) and 10f winner Bright Water, closely related to the promising 1997 2-y-o 1m winner Bristol Channel (by Generous) and half-sister to the very useful 1993 2-y-o 7f winner and Group 1 1m Racing Post Trophy second Bude (by Dancing Brave) and the quite useful 1993 4-y-o 9f and 10f winner Reflecting (by Ahonoora). The dam was a very useful winner of the Group 3 7f Solario Stakes and was placed in the Group 2 Park Hill Stakes. The second dam, Idle Waters (by Mill Reef), was a smart winner of 3 races including the Park Hill Stakes. (Khaled Abdulla). *"Maya Cove is a lovely filly with lots of class. She's only doing routine work at the moment but there's a lot to like about her. A really nice filly, she'll probably be suited by seven furlongs this season".*

---

496 - MISS UNIVERSE (USA)　　　　　gr.f. Warning - Reine d'Beaute (Caerleon).
　　　　　　　　　　　　　　　　　February 10. Fourth foal. 30,000Y. Tattersalls Houghton.
Half-sister to the useful German 7f (at 2 yrs) to 11f winner Silver Sign (by Shirley Heights) and to the fair 6f and 7f placed Silver Kristal (by Kris). The dam, a fairly useful 1m and 9f winner from her only starts, is a half-sister to 7 winners including the Group 3 May Hill Stakes winner Intimate Guest. The second dam, As You Desire Me (by Kalamoun), won 2 listed events in France over 7.5f and 1m and is a half-sister to the King Edward VII Stakes winner Classic Example. (Mrs J M Corbett). *"An unfurnished filly at present, she's just going to take a little time. We'll probably start her off over six furlongs and just gradually build her up".*

---

497 - MODEL GROOM (USA)　　　　　b.c. Dayjur - Model Bride (Blushing Groom).
　　　　　　　　　　　　　　　　　　　　　　　　　January 24. Fifth foal.
Half-brother to the useful 1995 3-y-o listed 1m winner Arabride (by Unfuwain) and the useful 1993 2-y-o 1m winner Mediterraneo (by Be My Guest). The dam is an unraced half-sister to the smart Queen Elizabeth II Stakes third Zaizafon (the dam of Zafonic) and to the unraced Modena (the dam of Elmaamul and Reams Of Verse). The second dam, Mofida (by Right Tack), was a very useful and tough filly, winning 8 of her 27 races at 2 and 3 yrs from 5f to 7.2f including the William Hill Trophy and the Playboy Bookmakers Trophy (both handicaps at York). (Khaled Abdulla). *"Model Groom is a big, unfurnished, long-striding horse. There's a lot to like about him but he needs a bit of time".*

---

498 - MOSS ROSE　　　　　　ch.f. Wolfhound - Champagne 'N Roses (Chief Singer).
　　　　　　　　　　　　　　　　　April 1. Second foal. 30,000Y. Tattersalls October.
The dam, a modest Irish 4-y-o 7f winner, was placed at up to 10f in England as a 3-y-o. The second dam, Pushoff (by Sauce Boat), won over 5f at 3 yrs and is a half-sister to the Group 3 winners Bluebook and Myself. (Mrs A D Bourne). *"Moss Rose is a nice filly that will probably want seven furlongs this year".*

499 - NIGHT VENTURE (USA)　　　　　　　　　　b.c. Dynaformer - Charming Ballerina (Caerleon).
March 28. Third foal. $300,000. Keeneland September.
The dam, a fairly useful winner of 2 races here at 2 yrs at around 7f, subsequently won 4 races in the USA. She is a sister to the Irish 12f winner Caerleon's Success (dam of the US Grade 1 winner Stuka) and a half-sister to the Group 1 Benson and Hedges Gold Cup winner Hawaiian Sound and the Group 3 Goodwood Cup winner Sonus. The second dam, Sound Of Success (by Successor), ran unplaced twice. (Maktoum Al Maktoum). *"Night Venture is quite backward and won't be ready to run until mid-season. A lovely horse, but very immature at the moment".*

500 - OCEANS FRIENDLY (USA)　　　　　　　　　b.f. Green Dancer - Sedra (Nebbiolo).
March 24. 72,000Y. Tattersalls Houghton.
Sister to the smart 12f King George V Handicap winner and St Leger fourth Samraan and half-sister to the useful 6f (at 2 yrs) and 7f winner Star Talent (by Local Talent), the fair 7f winner Sherjamal (by Raise a Native) and the Irish 7f and 1m winner Topper Up (by Sharpen Up). The dam was a smart winner of 6 races from 6f (at 2 yrs) to 10f including the listed Ebbisham Handicap, was second in the Group 2 Sun Chariot Stakes and is a half-sister to 6 winners. The second dam, Hispanica (by Whistling Wind), a quite useful 2-y-o 5f winner, is a half-sister to the Coventry Stakes winner Perdu. (W J Gredley).

501 - PROSPEROUS (IRE)　　　　　　　　　　ch.f. Generous - Amwag (El Gran Senor).
April 4. Third foal. IR26,000Y. Goffs Orby.
Half-sister to the quite useful 1997 3-y-o 12f winner Irsal (by Nashwan). The dam, a useful 3-y-o 1m listed winner at Sandown, is a half-sister to the smart St Leger third Istidaad. The second dam, Mazzei Mood (by Roberto), is a winning sister to the US Grade 3 winner Mystical Mood and a half-sister to the German Group 3 winner Maximilian. (Mrs R A Scarborough). *"Prosperous looks very much like the other Generous filly we have, Gracious Plenty. They are both nice two-year-olds that should be out by mid-season".*

502 - QUIET DIGNITY　　　　　　　　　　　b.f. Unfuwain - Docklands (On Your Mark).
May 4.
Half-sister to the 3-y-o Ija Najo (by Slip Anchor), to the useful 1987 12f listed Lingfield Oaks Trial winner Port Helene (by Troy) - herself dam of the Group 2 winner Helen of Spain, the 1992 German 3-y-o winner Desmona (by Rainbow Quest) and the fair 1996 4-y-o 7f and 1m winner Darcey Burrell (by Green Desert). The dam, a fair winner of 3 races as a 4-y-o at around a mile, is a half-sister to the 1,000 Guineas and Cheveley Park Stakes winner Night Off and to the dam of the Grade 1 winner Super Moment. The second dam, Persuader (by Petition), was a smart filly at up to 10f. (W J Gredley).

503 - QUIGLEYS POINT (IRE)　　　　　　　　b.c. Royal Academy - Remind Me (Riverman).
April 22. First foal. IR24,000Y. Goffs Orby.
The dam is an unraced sister to the Group 3 10f Prix de la Nonette winner River Nymph. The second dam, Fourteen (by Bellypha), is an unraced half-sister to 7 winners and to the unraced dam of the Australian Grade 1 winners Zabeel and Baryshnikov. (Mr J C Grant). *"A big, backward horse, he'll be nice one day. He has a good action but he's not going to be ready until the middle of the season".*

504 - RAINBOW STAGE (USA)　　　　　　　　b.f. Lear Fan - Certain Flair (Danehill).
January 6. First foal. IR110,000Y. Goffs Orby.
The dam is an unraced three-parts sister to the useful dual 1m winner Dawna and a half-sister to 4 winners including the very useful French middle-distance performer Ordinance. The second dam, Welsh Daylight (by Welsh Pageant), won twice over 12f in Ireland and is a half-sister to the dam of the smart Group 2 Moet & Chandon Rennen winner Muchea. (Mr R Bonnycastle). *"A lovely, big, scopey filly, Rainbow Stage is a beautiful mover and is showing all the right signs at the moment. A good mover, she should be out in the summer".*

505 - RAS SHAIKH (USA)　　　　　　　　　b.f. Sheikh Albadou - Aneesati (Kris).
February 10. Second foal.
Half-sister to the 1998 3-y-o winner Epsom Cyclone (by Rahy). The dam, a quite useful 1m winner, is a half-sister to several winners including the Prix de la Salamandre second Bin Nashwan, the 1m and 10f winner Magellan and the Supreme Stakes second Alanees - all very useful. The second dam, Dabaweyaa (by Shareef Dancer), was a smart winner of the 1m Atalanta Stakes, was placed in the 1,000 Guineas and the Kiveton Park Stakes and is a half-sister to the Group 3 winning sprinter Bruckner, the 12f Galtres Stakes winner Ma Femme and the smart Hoover Fillies Mile and Nassau Stakes winner

Acclimatise. (Mr Salem Bel Obaida). *"This is a very nice filly, rangy and showing all the right signs. She'll be out by June and should be one to follow"*.

506 - ROSES FROM RIDEY (IRE)
b.f. Petorius - Minnie Habit (Habitat).
January 25. Third foal. IR58,000Y. Goffs Orby.
Half-sister to the 1997 2-y-o 6f winner Child Prodigy (by Ballad Rock) and to the Irish 14f winner Blue Bit (by Bluebird) - both quite useful. The dam, an Irish 4-y-o 9f winner, is closely related to the Curragh Stakes and Railway Stakes winner Bermuda Classic - herself dam of the Coronation Stakes winner Shake The Yoke and the Phoenix Sprint Stakes winner Tropical. The second dam, Minnie Tudor (by Tudor Melody), won over 6f (at 2 yrs) and 1m in Ireland. (Mr R Bonnycastle). *"This filly's done really well but we won't rush her, she's just doing long canters now and won't be out before June"*.

507 - SHEER VIKING (IRE)
b.c. Danehill - Schlefalora (Mas Media).
April 26. First foal. 85,000Y. Tattersalls Houghton.
The dam won 6 races in Sweden and is a half-sister to 4 winners including the 1,000 Guineas winner and Irish 1,000 Guineas second Las Meninas. The second dam, Spanish Habit (by Habitat), is an unraced half-sister to 5 winners out of the Irish Group 2 Player-Wills Stakes winner Donna Cressida. (Mr R J Arculli). *"Sheer Viking isn't over-big but he should make a 2-y-o. He's just doing long canters and a bit of upsides work at the moment"*.

508 - SPANKER
ch.f. Suave Dancer - Yawl (Rainbow Quest).
May 7. Second foal.
Half-sister to the 3-y-o Genoa (by Zafonic), unplaced over 7f on her only outing at 2 yrs. The dam, a very useful winner of 2 races over 7f at 2 yrs including the listed Rockfel Stakes, was second in the 10f Lupe Stakes at 3 yrs before injuring herself in the Oaks. She is a half-sister to several winners including the fairly useful 2-y-o 7f winner Trireme. The second dam, Bireme (by Grundy), a top-class though lightly raced middle-distance filly, won the 1980 Oaks and Musidora Stakes and is a half-sister to numerous good horses including the Coronation Cup winner Buoy. (Mr R D Hollingsworth). *"This filly is on the leg at the moment, she needs to fill out a little and although we've done all the ground work with her she'll be given a break and brought back later on. I do think she'll be alright in time though"*.

509 - TROUBLE
b.c. Kris - Ringlet (Secreto).
April 13. Second foal. 21,000Y. Tattersalls December.
Half-brother to the 3-y-o Incepta (by Selkirk), unplaced over 7f on his only run at 2 yrs. The dam, a moderate 10f and 13f winner, is a half-sister to the Queen Elizabeth II Stakes and St James's Palace Stakes winner Sure Blade (by Kris - the sire of this colt) and to the Earl of Sefton Stakes winner Sure Sharp. The second dam, Double Lock (by Home Guard), won over 10f at 3 yrs, was third in the Nassau Stakes and is a sister to the listed Ebbisham Handicap winner Turn The Key. *"A backward horse, this is a nice enough colt but he's weak and needs a bit of time"*.

510 - TURAATH (IRE)
b.c. Sadler's Wells - Diamond Field (Mr Prospector).
March 7. Sixth foal. 200,000Y. Tattersalls Houghton.
Brother to the 1997 3-y-o Group 3 15f Prix Berteux winner New Frontier, closely related to the very useful 1993 3-y-o triple 6f winner Storm Canyon (by Storm Bird) and half-brother to the Dubai listed winner Wafayt (by Danehill). The dam, placed over 5f at 2 yrs, is a half-sister to 6 winners including the US Grade 1 9f Hollywood Derby winner Victory Zone. The second dam, Zonely (by Round Table), is a stakes-placed winner of 4 races at up to 1m in the USA and is a half-sister to the Observer Gold Cup winner Take Your Place and the Canadian International Championship winner Drumtop (herself the dam of the smart sire Topsider). (Hamdan Al Maktoum). *"Turaath is a lovely horse that will probably start off at six or seven furlongs. He has a good temperament and has done plenty of long work. A colt to look out for from July onwards"*.

511 - WEAVER OF WORDS
b.f. Danehill - Canadian Mill (Mill Reef).
February 24. Fourth living foal.
Half-sister to the smart Group 2 10f Nassau Stakes, Group 3 1m May Hill Stakes and Group 3 10.4f Musidora Stakes winner Hawajiss (by Kris). The dam, a 2-y-o 6f winner, was second the Group 1 Cheveley Park Stakes but did not train on. She is a half-sister to the Royal Lodge Stakes second Khozaam out of the Champion Canadian 2-y-o and 3-y-o filly Par Excellance (by L'Enjoleur). (Maktoum Al Maktoum). *"This filly has had a few setbacks but she's a big, strong type with a lot to like about her. She should be a nice filly from about mid-summer onwards"*.

512 - WILLIAMSHAKESPEARE (IRE)   b.c. Slip Anchor - Rostova (Blakeney).
April 9.
Brother to the top-class 1992 3-y-o filly User Friendly (by Slip Anchor), winner of the Oaks, the St Leger, the Irish Oaks and the Yorkshire Oaks and second to Subotica in the Prix de l'Arc de Triomphe and to the fair 13f to 20f winner Sea Freedom. The dam, a fairly useful winner of 4 races from 12f to 14f, is a half-sister to the very successful Italian filly Judd. The second dam, Poppy Day (by Soleil II), was placed over 5f at 2 yrs. (W J Gredley).

513 - ZEBRE   b.c. Ezzoud - Mountain Bluebird (Clever Trick).
January 14. Fifth foal. 27,000Y. Tattersalls October.
Half-brother to the useful 1995 3-y-o 14f winner and Group 2 15f Prix Hubert de Chaudenay third Anchor Clever (by Slip Anchor), to the modest 1993 2-y-o 6f winner Mockingbird (by Sharpo) and the minor French and US winner Middleberg (by Midyan). The dam, a quite useful 3-y-o 1m winner, is a half-sister to 4 winners. The second dam, Bluebell (by Town Crier), was a useful 2-y-o 6f and 7.3f winner.

John Hills

514 - CASINO ROYALE   b.c. Royal Academy - Sharata (Darshaan).
April 5. Fourth foal. 28,000Y. Tattersalls October.
Half-brother to the French trained 3-y-o Pharatta (by Fairy King), to the smart German Group 2 8.5f and Italian Group 2 1m winner Crimson Tide (by Sadler's Wells) and the useful Irish 9f to 14f winner Sharatan (by Kahyasi). The dam is an unraced half-sister to the Derby and Irish Derby winner Shahrastani. The second dam, Shademah (by Thatch), won 3 races from 7f to 8.2f and is a half-sister to the Grand Prix de Saint-Cloud winner Shakapour, the US Grade 1 Bowling Green Handicap winner Sharannpour and the dam of the Prix de Diane winner Shemaka. (Mr C Wright & Partners). *"A half-brother to Crimson Tide, he's a lovely colt but will take lots of time. He has a beautiful action and I like him a lot but might only give him the odd run at the end of the season. He's much more of a three-year-old type",* the trainer explained.

515 - CUBISM (USA)   b.c. Miswaki - Seattle Kat (Seattle Song).
April 4. Fourth foal.
Half-brother to the minor 1997 US 3-y-o winner Fonteyn (by Nureyev). The dam won twice at 4 yrs in the USA, is a sister to the Grade 2 Arlington Classic winner Whadjathink and a half-sister to 6 winners including the US stakes winner Explosive Kate. The second dam, Katerina The Great (by Great Nephew), won at 3 yrs in France and is a half-sister to the Prix Maurice de Gheest winner Girl Friend (dam of the Group 3 winner Comrade In Arms) and the Prix Imprudence winner Best Girl (dam of the Champion Stakes winner Tel Quel). (Mr K Y Lim). *"A very well-made colt, he looks like he could be a really speedy 2-y-o and is going as well as anything at the moment".*

516 - DOMINANT DANCER   ch.f. Primo Dominie - Footlight Fantasy (Nureyev).
February 15. First foal. 30,000Y. Tattersalls October.
The dam, a fair 3-y-o 7f winner, is out of the top-class Milligram (by Mill Reef), winner of the Group 1 Queen Elizabeth II Stakes, the Group 2 Coronation Stakes etc., and herself a half-sister to the Coronation Stakes second Someone Special (dam of the Group winners Alnasr Alwasheek and Relatively Special). The third dam, One In A Million (by Rarity), won the 1,000 Guineas and Coronation Stakes. (Mr L Godfrey & Partners). *"Quite a good-sized filly and quite level, she's already going nicely and will definitely make a 2-y-o. Her pedigree might just make her a bit above average. She could easily be out by May, has a good attitude and shows speed. In the top three or four of my fillies I'd say".*

517 - GARDENIA (IRE)   b.f. Sadler's Wells - Formulate (Reform).
April 28.
Closely related to a winner in Japan by Lomond and half-sister to 8 winners including the Group 2 10f Pretty Polly Stakes winner and Epsom Oaks second Game Plan (by Darshaan), the modest 1m winner Ripsnorter (by Rousillon), the 15.8f winner Almarreekh (by Glint Of Gold) and the 1997 Irish 2-y-o 7f winner Shahtoush (by Alzao). The dam was a very smart filly and winner of 4 races including the Group 3 Hoover Fillies Mile. The second dam, Tabulator (by Never Say Die), won twice at 3 yrs in France. (Abbott Racing Partners). *"A compact filly with a good attitude, Gardenia looks like she'll make a 2-y-o. She has natural ability and is very well-balanced at this stage for a filly bred the way she is".*

518 - GREENSTONE b.f. Green Desert - Mahabba (Elocutionist).
May 14. IR24,000Y. Goffs Challenge.
Closely related to the quite useful 1m (at 2 yrs) and 10.2f winner Convoy Point and to the 1995 Irish 3-y-o 1m to 10f winner Radomsko (both by Polish Precedent) and half-sister to the useful 1991 3-y-o 11.5f winner Finance Dancer (by Shareef Dancer), the Group 3 10f Premio Baggio winner Ready To Dance (by Wassl) and the minor 2-y-o winners Abraham (by Kris) and Sure To Win (by Sure Blade). The dam, a fair 3-y-o 12f winner, is a half-sister to the US stakes winner Icy Lassie. The second dam, Amphora (by Ragusa), won the Group 3 12f Lancashire Oaks and is a half-sister to the Ribblesdale Stakes winner Expansive and the Park Hill Stakes winner Example. (Mr D Caruth & Partners). *"Bound to make a two-year-old despite being a May foal, I'll take my time with her and probably bring her out over six furlongs in mid-summer" the trainer tells me.*

519 - KNIGHTHOOD b.c. Highest Honor - Picardy (Polish Precedent).
February 16. First foal. 52,000Y. Tattersalls October.
The dam, placed over 1m on the all-weather at 2 yrs on her only start, was retired due to injury. She is a half-sister to 4 winners out of the smart Group 1 Irish St Leger and Group 3 Brownstown Meld Stakes winner Opale (by Busted), herself a half-sister to 3 minor winners. (Highclere Thoroughbred Racing Ltd). *"A very likeable horse but he's had a slight setback and won't be ready to run until mid-summer at the earliest" says John.*

520 - MOUTON b.f. Dolphin Street - The Queen Of Soul (Chief Singer).
April 16. Fifth foal. 60,000Y. Tattersalls October.
Half-sister to the fairly useful 1997 2-y-o 5f and 6f winner Ella (by Brief Truce), the modest 1993 2-y-o 5f winner Domino Queen (by Primo Dominie) and the modest 6f placed 2-y-o Walhaanah (by High Estate), subsequently a winner in Barbados. The dam, a fair 5f and 6f winner, is a half-sister to the Group 3 Cherry Hinton Stakes winner Crime Of Passion and the Ayr Gold Cup winner Primula Boy. The second dam, Catriona (by Sing Sing), was a fairly useful 2-y-o winner of 3 races over 5f and a half-sister to 6 winners including the Dee Stakes winner Playboy Jubilee. *"A lovely, quality filly, she goes very easily and is a promising prospect".*

521 - NICELY gr.f. Bustino - Nichodoula (Doulab).
March 16. First foal. 26,000Y. Tattersalls October.
The dam, a modest 3-y-o 7f and 1m winner, is a half-sister to 7 winners including the Group 1 Juddmonte International Stakes and Group 3 Earl Of Sefton Stakes winner Terimon (by Bustino, the sire of this filly). The second dam, Nicholas Grey (by Track Spare), a useful 2-y-o 5f to 7f winner, was second in the Group 1 Italian Oaks. (Mrs Claire Smith). *"A gorgeous filly, I'm really pleased with her, she's got a beautiful action and is more forward than her pedigree suggests. Nevertheless, she's going to need time and I won't rush her. I do like her a lot".*

522 - ROYAL FLAME b.f. Royal Academy - Samnaun (Stop The Music).
March 13. Third foal. 25,000Y. Tattersalls Houghton.
Half-sister to the poor 7.5f placed Loxley's Girl (by Lahib). The dam is an unraced half-sister to the useful Group 2 German 1,000 Guineas winner Quebrada and the useful 2-y-o listed 6f winner Court. The second dam, Queen To Conquer (by King's Bishop), won 6 races including the Grade 1 Yellow Ribbon Invitational and the Grade 2 Ramona Handicap (twice) and is a half-sister to 5 winners including the dual US Grade 3 winner Bold Brat. (Mr W Coleman & Partners). *"Of all my fillies up to now, I suppose Royal Flame would be my favourite. She won't be out until the mid-summer but she's got a lot of quality about her, has a beautiful action and does everything really easily. I like her a lot".*

523 - RUN SILENT (IRE) b.c. Sadler's Wells - Fair Of The Furze (Ela Mana Mou).
May 9. IR90,000Y. Goffs Orby.
Brother to the fair 1997 3-y-o 10f winner Bel Canto and half-brother to the top class Group 1 12f Italian Derby winner and King George VI and Queen Elizabeth Diamond Stakes second White Muzzle (by Dancing Brave), the useful 1991 3-y-o Elfaslah, a winner of 3 races from 10f to 10.4f including a listed race in Ireland and the fair 1997 4-y-o 1m winner Alfahaal (both by Green Desert). The dam, a very useful winner of the Group 2 10f Tattersalls Rogers Gold Cup, is a half-sister to the listed stakes winners Majestic Role (in Ireland), Norman Style (in Germany), Supreme Commander and Proconsular (both in France). The second dam, Autocratic (by Tyrant), won over 5f at 2 yrs in Ireland. (Mr Freddy Bienstock & Partners). *"Run Silent came into the yard rather late. He's a lovely, big, quality colt with a beautiful action. I love him but he's going to need lots of time and middle-distances".*

524 - RUSSIAN RIDGE ch.c. Indian Ridge - Petronella (Nureyev).
March 2. First foal. 75,000Y. Tattersalls Houghton.
The dam is an unraced half-sister to 5 minor winners here and abroad. The second dam, Hitting Irish (by Irish Ruler), won 9 races in the USA including a minor stakes event and was Grade 3 placed over 7f and 8.5f. She is a half-sister to 7 winners out of the minor US winner Arbee Eye (by Irish Ruler). *"A big, strong colt, a beautiful mover and a pretty nice horse" says John.*

525 - TIME MILL b.c. Shirley Heights - Not Before Time (Polish Precedent).
February 19, Second foal. 110,000Y. Tattersalls Houghton.
Half-brother to the 3-y-o Time Loss (by Kenmare). The dam is an unraced sister to the Group 2 12f Jockey Club Stakes and listed 12f Godolphin Stakes winner Zinaad and to the Cheshire Oaks second By Charter and a half-sister to the Group 3 12f Jockey Club Stakes and Group 3 12f Princess Royal Stakes winner Time Allowed (by Sadler's Wells). The second dam, Time Charter (by Saritamer), was an exceptionally talented filly and winner of the Oaks, King George VI and Queen Elizabeth Diamond Stakes, Champion Stakes, Coronation Cup, Prix Foy and Sun Chariot Stakes. (Mr George Tong). *"A lovely, quality colt, he's very much for the end of the season and for next year. But he's got a beautiful action and has a lot of quality about him. A colt that does everything extremely easily, I'll start him over seven furlongs and at the moment of all my two-year-olds he's giving me the best feel".*

526 - ZULU DAWN b.c. El Gran Senor - Celtic Loot (Irish River).
April 12. Fifth foal. 68,000Y. Tattersalls Houghton.
Brother to the very promising 1997 2-y-o 1m winner Himself and the fairly useful 7f winner Don Bosio. The dam, a minor winner at around 1m in the USA at 4 yrs, is a half-sister to the US Grade 3 winner Nelson, the Japanese Stakes winner Chokai Carol and the Ribblesdale Stakes third Blushing Storm. The second dam, Witwatersrand (by Mr Prospector), won the Grade 3 9f Pucker Up Stakes on turf in the USA. (Mrs N Hubbard & Mrs J Magnier). *"Zulu Dawn is a likeable horse, a good mover with a lot of scope and size about him. Very much a second half of the season horse, he's still growing and whatever he does this year will be a bonus".*

Lord Huntingdon

527 - FICTITIOUS ch.f. Machiavellian - Trying For Gold (Northern Baby).
March 9. Sixth foal.
Sister to the smart Group 2 12f Ribblesdale Stakes and Group 2 13.3f Geoffrey Freer Stakes winner Phantom Gold (by Machiavellian) and half-sister to the 3-y-o Filigree (by Salse) and the fairly useful 2-y-o 1m winner Tempting Prospect (by Shirley Heights). The dam was a useful 12f and 12.5f winner at 3 yrs. The second dam, Expansive (by Exbury), won the Ribblesdale Stakes and is a sister to the Park Hill Stakes winner Example. (The Queen).

528 - FIRST FAMILY (IRE) b.c. Polish Precedent - Happy Kin (Bold Hitter).
March 27.
Half-brother to the 3-y-o Riding School (by Royal Academy), to the Group 1 1m William Hill Futurity Stakes and Group 3 10f Prix Gontaut-Biron winner Emmson (by Ela Mana Mou), the very useful 2-y-o 6f Veuve Cliquot Champagne Stakes winner Who Knows (by Known Fact), the very useful middle-distance stayer Family Friend (by Henbit), the useful 12f winner and Ormonde Stakes third League Leader, the quite useful 1995 3-y-o 12f winner Top Lady (both by Shirley Heights) and the quite useful 3-y-o 12f winner Little Sister (by Kris). The dam won from 6f to 8.5f in the USA. The second dam, the unraced Gay Niece (by Sir Gaylord), was out of a sister to Great Nephew. (Lord Weinstock).

Michael Jarvis

529 - ALRASSAM b.c. Zafonic - Lady Blackfoot (Prince Tenderfoot).
February 8. 265,0000Y. Tattersalls Houghton.
Half-brother to the Grade 1 9f Hollywood Derby winner and Prix Jean Prat third Labeeb, to the Grade 2 Arlington Handicap winner and Arlington Million second Fanmore (both by Lear Fan), the US stakes winner and Grade 1 placed Madame L'Enjoleur (by L'Enjoleur), the quite useful 1m to 13f winner Northern Graduate (by Northrop) and the minor 2-y-o winner Monasteroris (by Nnorthern Jove). The dam, a very useful Irish sprinter, won 2 races and was fourth in the Group 1 Phoenix Stakes. The second dam, Indian Graduate (by Chieftain II), won twice at 3 yrs. (Sheikh Ahmed Al Maktoum). *"A*

big, well-grown colt, he goes nicely but is immature and won't run until the autumn, probably over seven furlongs to begin with" Michael explains.

530 - ANTHEM
b.c. Saddlers Hall - Full Orchestra (Shirley Heights). March 4. Fifth foal. 105,000Y. Tattersalls Houghton.
Brother to the Italian trained 3-y-o Tempting Proposal and half-brother to the useful 6f (at 2 yrs) and 9f winner Rudimental (by Rudimentary), the quite useful 1995 2-y-o 5f winner First Fiddler (by Primo Dominie) and the modest 1m to 10f winner Music Maker (by Unfuwain). The dam, a quite useful 10f winner at 3 yrs, is a half-sister to 8 winners including the US Grade 3 winner Cat Attack and the dam of the German 2-y-o Group 2 winner Sharp Prod. The second dam, Harp Strings (by Luthier), was a very useful winner of 3 races at up to 9f. (Mohammed bin Hendi). *"A very big horse, he'll be an autumn two-year-old and will be much better next year".*

531 - COMPENSATION (IRE)
gr.c. Turtle Island - Fontenoy (Lyphard's Wish). February 2. First foal. 23,000Y. Tattersalls October.
The dam is an unplaced half-sister to 4 winners including the Group 3 6.5f Prix Eclipse and listed 7f Prix Djebel winner Diamada. The second dam, Flota Armada (by Sovereign Path), won the listed 7f Prix Imprudence and is a half-sister to 7 winners including the French listed winner Fleetsin. (Mr D Fisher). *"A strong colt, he looks quite precocious and will be suited by five furlongs in June to start with".*

532 - EL LAYTH (USA)
b.br.c. Dayjur - Gesedeh (Ela-Mana-Mou). April 15.
Closely related to the minor middle-distance placed 3-y-o Dubai Summer (Green Desert) and half-brother to the useful 1997 3-y-o 11.5f winner Elbaaha (by Arazi). The dam, a smart middle-distance filly, won the Group 3 10.5f Prix de Flore and the Pretty Polly Stakes and was placed in the Sun Chariot Stakes, the September Stakes, the Prince of Wales's Stakes and the Scottish Derby. She is a half-sister to the top-class middle-distance stayer Ardross. The second dam, Le Melody (by Levmoss), won both her starts over 7f and is a half-sister to the Irish 1,000 Guineas winner Arctique Royale - herself dam of the Group winners Modhish and Russian Snows - and to the Irish Oaks third Racquette (dam of the very useful French colts Grand Chelem and Splendid Moment). (Sheikh Ahmed Al Maktoum). *This colt had yet to enter the yard by mid-April.*

533 - EL MOBASHERR (USA)
b.c. Machiavellian - Sheroog (Shareef Dancer). March 7. Fourth foal.
Brother to the very useful 14f winner Sharaf Kabeer and half-brother to the 3-y-o Kabool (by Groom Dancer) and the 1997 Irish 3-y-o 12f winner Rain and Shine (by Rainbow Quest). The dam, a fair 3-y-o 1m winner, is a sister to the very smart Prix de Pomone winner Colorado Dancer, closely related to the Grade 1 Gamely Handicap winner Northern Aspen, the Group 1 Grand Prix de Paris winner Fort Wood and the Group 1 July Cup winner Hamas, and a half-sister to the Grade 1 Breeders Cup Juvenile winner Timber Country, the Goodwood Cup winner Mazzacano and the Prix d'Astarte winner Elle Seule - herself dam of the Irish 1,000 Guineas winner Mehthaaf. The second dam, Fall Aspen (by Pretense), won 8 races including the Grade 1 7f Matron Stakes. (Sheikh Ahmed Al Maktoum). *"A leggy colt (and thus very much like his dam), this is a well-grown, free-moving colt. A really nice type, he should be out by August or September" says Michael.*

534 - FALLACHAN (USA)
ch.c. Diesis - Afaff (Nijinsky). February 25. Fifth foal. $25,000Y. Keeneland September.
The dam, a modest 1m placed 3-y-o, is a half-sister to the 2,000 Guineas and Queen Elizabeth II Stakes winner Shadeed. The second dam, Continual (by Damascus), won twice at up to 7f and is out Continuation - herself a sister to the dam of Swale and a half-sister to the dam of Forty Niner. *"A strong, very well-grown two-year-old, he goes nicely and I feel he was very well-bought. He'll be out in August or thereabouts and should be suited by a mile eventually".* The name, incidentally, had yet to be confirmed by the American Jockey Club by mid-April.

535 - KEEBAAR
b.c. Shirley Heights - Historiette (Chief's Crown). February 7. Third foal. 145,000Y. Tattersalls Houghton.
Half-brother to the 3-y-o Antigua (by Selkirk). The dam is an unraced three-parts sister to the July Cup winner Polish Patriot. The second dam, Maria Waleska (by Filiberto), won 6 races including the Group 1 11f Italian Oaks and the Group 1 12f Gran Premio d'Italia. (Sheikh Ahmed Al Maktoum). *"A nice horse and a good-looking individual, we won't see him until late summer".*

536 - MAYL (IRE) b.f. Lion Cavern - Possessive Dancer (Shareef Dancer).
April 10. Fourth foal.

Half-sister to the 3-y-o Zeenah (by Machiavellian) and to the smart, though unreliable, Group 3 12f September Stakes winner Maylane. The dam was a smart winner of 5 races from 6f (at 2 yrs) to 12f including the Group 1 Irish Oaks and the Group 1 Italian Oaks. She is a half-sister to the moderate 3-y-o dual 1m winner Possessive Lady and to the 1994 2-y-o 6f winner Desert Courier. The second dam, Possessive (by Posse), is an unraced half-sister to 10 winners including the smart miler Long Row and the Norfolk Stakes winner Colmore Row. The third dam, Front Row (by Epaulette), won the Irish 1,000 Guineas. (Sheikh Ahmed Al Maktoum). *"A leggy, late-maturing type, he won't be ready until the autumn".*

---

537 - MORVINO b.c. Night Shift - Hard Task (Formidable).
April 21. Second foal. 40,000Y. Tattersalls October.

Half-brother to the unplaced 1997 2-y-o Reach For A Star (by Midyan). The dam, a quite useful 12.3f winner, is a half-sister to 4 winners including the smart middle-distance colt Midnight Legend. The second dam, Myth (by Troy), a fairly useful middle-distance winner of 3 races, is a half-sister to the dam of the very useful 1997 Cherry Hinton and Queen Mary Stakes placed Crazee Mental. (Thurloe Thoroughbreds III). *"A smallish colt but strong with it, I'll set him off over six furlongs in mid-summer".*

---

538 - NOUSHKEY b.f. Polish Precedent - Top Of The League (High Top).
April 18. 55,000Y. Tattersalls Houghton.

Half-sister to the German listed winner and Group 1 placed Chesa Plana, to the 1997 Irish 3-y-o 11f to 13f winner San Sebastian (both by Niniski), the Irish winner of 5 races at up to 2m Desert Squaw (by Commanche Run) and winners abroad by Chief Singer and Petoski. The dam, a quite useful 2-y-o 7f winner, is a half-sister to 3 winners. The second dam, Home And Away (by Home Guard), is an unraced half-sister to the Grade 1 Man O'War and Grade 1 Sunset Handicap winner Galaxy Libra, to the French Group 2 winner Garden Of Heaven and to the dam of the Group 1 Prix du Cadran winner Molesnes. (Sheikh Ahmed Al Maktoum). *"This is quite a nice filly, but she'll need time to develop".*

---

539 - PEBBLE MOON gr.c. Efisio - Jazz (Sharrood).
January 29. Second foal. 30,000Y. Tattersalls October.

Half-brother to the quite useful 7f and 9f placed (in two starts) Ninth Chord (by Alzao). The dam, a fair 7f (at 2 yrs) and 10f placed maiden, is a half-sister to 8 winners including the fairly useful 2-y-o 5f winner Chasing Moonbeams. The second dam, Rainbow's End (by My Swallow), won once at 2 yrs. (Mr John Sims). *"A well-grown colt with a good temperament, he'll be suited by six or seven furlongs this summer".*

---

540 - SWEET CHARITY (IRE) ch.f. Bigstone - Tolstoya (Northfields).
April 14. IR21,000Y. Goffs Orby.

Half-sister to the unplaced 1997 2-y-o Resurrection (by Midyan), to the very useful Ayr Gold Cup winner of Wildwood Flower (by Distant Relative), the quite useful 1m winner Zaretski (by Pursuit Of Love), the minor US stakes winner His Tern To Win (by Arctic Tern), the modest 2-y-o 10f winner Calling Jamaica (by Elmaamul) and the modest 2-y-o 5f and 6f winner Lear Leader (by Lear Fan). The dam won over 5f at 2 yrs in Ireland and is a half-sister to 4 winners. The second dam, Anna Karenina (by Princely Gift), won the 5f Prix d'Arenburg and is a half-sister to the Group 3 Prix Messidor winner Arosa (dam of the Group 2 Prix Greffulhe). (Mrs Christine Stevenson). *"A nice, racy type, he should be out by late spring and he seems to lean on the dam's side in that he looks like a sprinter".*

---

541 - TAWAG b.c. Shirley Heights - Albertville (Polish Precedent).
February 12. First foal.

The dam, a French listed 10f winner at 3 yrs, is a half-sister to the 1997 Dubai winner Tremel (by Trempolino) out of Sierra Roberta (by Don Roberto). *"A really well-developed horse, he goes nicely and is a lovely two-year-old. If he gets it together he could really go places".*

---

542 - TOUGH GUY (IRE) b.c. Namaqualand - Supreme Crown (Chief's Crown).
January 11. Fifth foal. 25,000Y. Tattersalls Houghton.

Half-brother to the fairly useful 2-y-o 8.2f winner Violet Crown (by Kefaah) and to the Irish 2-y-o 5f winner Daffodil Dale (by Cyrano de Bergerac). The dam is an unraced half-sister to 4 winners including the listed Sirenia Stakes second and subsequent US Grade 3 placed Wesaam. The second dam, Share The Fantasy (by Exclusive Native), won the Grade 1 6f Spinaway Stakes at 2 yrs in the USA and is a half-sister to the US Grade 2 winner Tokatee and the Grade 1 placed winner Northern Majesty. (Sqdrn-Ldr R A Milsom). *"Tough Guy is doing well. A small, sturdy colt, he looks like he'll make a nice two-year-old. He'll start over six furlongs in June"*.

William Jarvis

543 - AT MY COMMAND
ch.f. Barathea - Fly Don't Run (Lear Fan).
January 31. First foal. 38,000Y. Tattersalls Houghton.
The dam, a modest 10.2f placed 3-y-o, is a sister to the Italian Group 2 12f Premio Ellington winner Run Don't Fly and to the unraced dam of the Group winners Raah Algharb (Flying Childers Stakes) and Pharian (Lancashire Oaks). The second dam, Gantlette (by Run The Gantlet), a French 2-y-o 1m winner, is a half-sister to 10 winners including the US Grade 2 winner Loquacious Don and to the dam of the US Grade 1 winner Hostage. (Mr K P Snow). *"This filly is a chestnut whilst most of the Barathea's are bay. A sharp little filly, she'll be running in May, has a good attitude and is straightforward to train"*.

544 - BUCKLE (IRE)
b.f. Common Grounds - Maratona (Be My Guest).
February 15. IR47,000Y. Goffs Orby.
Half-sister to the minor US winners Aint Nothing, Arlington Eight, Vunderful (all by Saratoga Six), Be My Conquistador (by Conquistador Cielo), Brutal Battle (by Mr Prospector) and Winter Colony (by Pleasant Colony). The dam ran twice unplaced in France and is a half-sister to numerous good winners including the Fillies Triple Crown winner Oh So Sharp (dam of the Prix Saint-Alary winner Rosefinch) and the Nassau Stakes winner Roussalka. The second dam, Oh So Fair (by Graustark), won over 10f in Ireland. (Mr A Foster). *"Buckle has grown and lengthened since we've had her. She's uncomplicated and seems to be a mid-summer type of 2-y-o"* William has two other two-year-olds in the Early Types section.

545 - CRESSET
ch.c. Arazi - Mixed Applause (Nijinsky).
April 19.
Closely related to the modest 1997 12f placed 3-y-o Arletty (by Rainbow Quest) and half-brother to the high-class St James's Palace Stakes and Beefeater Gin Celebration Mile winner Shavian, the 1995 2-y-o 8.2f winner Censor, the 3-y-o 10f winner Tempering (both fairly useful) and the minor 3-y-o 10f winner Khandjar (all by Kris), the high-class Ascot Gold Cup winner Paean (by Bustino), the 1993 3-y-o dual 6f winner Press Gallery (by Carmelite House) and the 1987 2-y-o 6f and 3-y-o 1m winner Grand Tier (by Habitat) - both fairly useful. The dam, a useful winner of the 2-y-o 6f Sweet Solera Stakes, is a half-sister to the dam of the champion 2-y-o Be My Chief. The second dam, My Advantage (by Princely Gift) was a fairly useful sprinter and a half-sister to Lady Seymour - the dam of Marwell. (Lord Howard de Walden). *"A very weak and backward horse at the moment, Cresset is definitely more of a three-year-old type"*.

546 - HELEN'S DAY
ch.f. Grand Lodge - Swordlestown Miss (Apalachee).
March 3. 35,000Y. Tattersalls October.
Half-sister to the useful 2-y-o 1m winner and 3-y-o 10.3f placed Traikey (by Scenic), to the fairly useful 2-y-o 6f winner Quest Express (by Rudimentary), the winning stayers Sword Master (by Sayf El Arab) and Danger Baby (by Bairn) and to a winner in Macau by Sayf El Arab. The dam won over 7f at 2 yrs in Ireland and is a half-sister to 4 minor winners. The second dam, Marcia Royale (by Le Levenstell), won 4 races including the Anglesey Stakes and was graded-stakes placed in the USA. (Mrs W B Dearman & Mrs Bell). *"A backward filly but very easy moving, she'll be more of a back-end two-year-old but we quite like her"*.

547 - KATTEGAT
b.c. Slip Anchor - Kirsten (Kris).
March 13. Third foal.
Half-brother to the 3-y-o Urbanity (by Suave Dancer). The dam, a fair 3-y-o 12.2f winner, is a half-sister to 5 winners including the King George VI and Queen Elizabeth Diamond Stakes winner Petoski. The second dam, Sushila (by Petingo), won 2 races in France at around 1m and is out of Shenandoah, a sister to the French Derby winner Val de Loir and a half-sister to the Irish 1,000 Guineas and Oaks winner Valoris and the top-class broodmare Kalida, (dam of the French Derby winner Roi Lear and the Prix Saint Alary winner Lilika). (Lord Howard de Walden). *"A nice horse, I like Kattegat and he seems to show me that he could make up into a two-year-old suited by seven furlongs or a mile. He has a very good attitude and goes nicely"*.

548 - PEPPERDINE b.c. Indian Ridge - Rahwah (Northern Baby).
April 1. IR56,000Y. Goffs Orby.
Half-brother to the fair Locorotondo (by Broken Hearted), a winner of 5 races from 10f to 11f, to the 2-y-o 5f winner Caps Ninety Two, the 1997 2-y-o 1m winner Mystic Magic (both by Magical Wonder) and the 1m winner Gilling Dancer (by Dancing Dissident) - all three only modest. The dam, a fair 12f winner, is closely related to the Group 1 Moyglare Stud Stakes winner Flutter Away and a half-sister to 5 winners. The second dam, Flying Bid (by Auction Ring), won over 10f at 4 yrs in Ireland and is a sister to the Prix Robert Papin winner Maelstrom Lake. *"I like this horse. He's a well-grown, good-looking colt, has done nothing wrong and I loved him as a yearling. What we've seen of him so far we like. We'll probably start him over six furlongs".*

---

549 - PLURALIST b.c. Mujadil - Encore Une Fois (Shirley Heights).
February 27. First foal. 45,000Y. Tattersalls October.
The dam, a quite useful winner of four races from 11.9f to 16f, is a half-sister to the German Grade 3 winner Global Player. The second dam, Guest Performer (by Be My Guest), won the Group 3 7f Kiveton Park Stakes and is a sister to the US Grade 3 winner Sojourn. (The Pluralist Partnership). *"I like this colt. He's got a bit of speed and is a good-looking horse. What we've seen of him so far we like"* says the trainer.

---

550 - ROSE CROIX (USA) b.f. Chief's Crown - La Papagena (Habitat).
February 4.
Sister to the Champion 1993 2-y-o Grand Lodge (by Chief's Crown), winner of the Group 1 7f Dewhurst Stakes and the Group 1 1m St James's Palace Stakes and half-sister to the minor 1993 3-y-o 11.5f winner Rose Noble (by Vaguely Noble). The dam is an unraced half-sister to the very useful 3-y-o 7f and 1m winner Pamina, the very useful 3-y-o 11f and 12.5f winner Lost Chord and the useful 11f Scottish Derby winner Eagling. The second dam, Magic Flute (by Tudor Melody), won the Cheveley Park Stakes and the Coronation Stakes and was very smart at up to 1m. (Lord Howard de Walden). *"Not a very big filly, but quite sharp and she wants to please you. She'll be out early and the first objective will be to win a race with her. With her lovely pedigree she'll then have a chance at stud".*

---

551 - TYLER'S TOAST ch.c. Grand Lodge - Catawba (Mill Reef).
February 3.
Half-brother to the 1997 3-y-o 12f winner Catchable (by Pursuit Of Love), to the 1993 3-y-o 10f to 12f winner Licorne (by Sadlers Wells) and the 1994 3-y-o 12f winner Isle of Pines (by Kris) - all fairly useful. The dam, a useful 3-y-o 10.5f winner, is a half-sister to the useful 12f winner Kenanga and to Strigida, winner of the Ribblesdale Stakes - a race also won by the second dam, Catalpa (by Reform) and the third dam Ostrya. (Lady Howard de Walden). *William is really pleased with Tyler's Toast. "A lovely colt, very similar to his sire and although he may not turn out so good, he's a strong, good-looking horse that catches the eye. He's got a good attitude and we have high hopes for him".*

---

552 - VILLA WANDA ch.f. Grand Lodge - Gisarne (Diesis).
March 1. Second foal.
Half-sister to the 1997 unplaced 2-y-o Hastate (by Persian Bold). The dam, a useful winner of the listed 10f Lupe Stakes, is closely related to the listed 1m winner Incisive and a half-sister to several winners. The second dam, Fair Sousanne (by Busted), was a fair 6f and 10f placed maiden. (Lord Howard de Walden). *"Villa Wanda is backward at the moment (early April) but she moves well and is a good-sized filly".*

Mark Johnston

---

553 - ACICULA b.f. Night Shift - Crystal City (Kris).
February 2. Second foal. 52,000Y. Tattersalls Houghton.
The dam, a minor winner at 3 yrs in France, is out of the Group 1 12f Yorkshire Oaks and Group 3 Hoover Fillies Mile winner Untold (by Final Straw) - herself a half-sister to the Yorkshire Oaks winner Sally Brown, the Group 3 Waterford Candelabra Stakes winner Shoot Clear and the dual listed winner Mohican Girl. (Mr P Savill). *"A mature, speedy filly, Acicula began her career at Newmarket's Craven meeting".*

554 - ATLANTIC DESTINY   b.f. Royal Academy - Respectfully (The Minstrel).
April 23. 26,000Y. Tattersalls October.
Half-sister to the 1997 Irish 2-y-o 7f winner Make No Mistake (by Darshaan), to the Irish 10f and 2m winner Limbo Lady (by Theatrical) and the Irish 7f and 8.5f winner Robertolomy (by Roberto). The dam was unplaced on her only start and is a half-sister to 6 winners. The second dam, Treat Me Nobly (by Vaguely Noble), is an unraced half-sister to Be My Guest and to the dam of the US Grade 1 winner Ida Delia. (Atlantic Racing Ltd). *"A big and very attractive filly, she's going well and will run very soon"*.

555 - ATLANTIC PRINCE (IRE)   b.c. Fairy King - Idle Chat (Assert).
May 1. Second living foal. IR40,000Y. Goffs Orby.
Half-brother to the promising 1997 2-y-o 7.5f winner Central Committee (by Royal Academy). The dam was a fairly useful 8.2f winner at 2 yrs, was third in the listed Lingfield Oaks Trial and subsequently won twice in Australia. She is a half-sister to 3 winners including Musicale, winner of the Cherry Hinton, Fred Darling, Rockfel and Prestige Stakes (all Group 3 events). The second dam, Gossiping (by Chati), won in the USA and is a half-sister to the high-class sprinter Committed (herself dam of the US Grade 1 winner Pharma). (Atlantic Racing Ltd). *"Going extremely well, Atlantic Prince will be an early runner for the yard"*.

556 - COMPLIMENTARY PASS (IRE)   b.f. Danehill - Capo di Monte (Final Straw).
May 12. Fifth foal.
Closely related to the quite useful 1994 3-y-o dual 7f winner Daawe, to the fair 1991 3-y-o 1m winner Dafrah and the fair 1995 3-y-o 7f winner Dream Ticket (all by Danzig). The dam, a smart filly, won over 6f at 2 yrs, the 10f Pretty Polly Stakes and 10f Virginia Stakes at 3 yrs and subsequently the Grade 3 11f Vineland Handicap in the USA. She is a half-sister to the smart Group 1 12f Aral-Pokal winner and Epsom Oaks second Wind In Her Hair. The second dam, Burghclere (by Busted), won over 14f at 3 yrs, is closely related to the good colt Milford and a half-sister to the Group 2 Princess of Wales's Stakes winner Height of Fashion - herself dam of Nashwan and Unfuwain. (Maktoum Al Maktoum). *"Complimentary Pass is an active, attractive filly, yet to do any serious work"*.

557 - DOUBLE BAILEYS   b.c. Robellino - Thimblerigger (Sharpen Up).
April 27. 50,000Y. Tattersalls Houghton.
Brother to the 2,000 Guineas, Royal Lodge Stakes and Lanson Champagne Stakes winner Mister Baileys and half-brother to the fair winning stayer Cleavers Gate (by Touching Wood) and minor winners abroad by Distant Relative (2), Bold Lad (Ire), Vitiges and Nishapour. The dam, a modest 10f winner, is a half-sister to 3 minor winners. The second dam, Tender Annie (by Tenerani), won the 10f Ribblesdale Stakes, was third in the Oaks and is a half-sister to the dam of the Belmont Stakes second Ruritania. (The Double Baileys Partnership). *"A striking big colt, but nowhere near as mature as Mister Baileys was at the same stage. Very long striding and not yet ready to work with sharper types, he still has enough presence to make us feel that he could be a serious horse later in the year"*.

558 - HORMUZ (IRE)   b.c. Hamas - Balqis (Advocator).
February 18. 23,000Y. Tattersalls October.
Half-brother to the useful Libk (by Kalaglow) a winner of 6 races from 1m to 12f, to the 14f and 20f winner Haitham (by Wassl), the dual 6f winner Marha (by Shaadi), the 3-y-o 1m winner Sabayik (by Unfuwain), the 3-y-o 10.2f winner Shahaamh (by Reference Point) - all fairly useful -and the fair 2-y-o 6f and subsequent South African winner Dalalah (by Doyoun). The dam, a fairly useful winner of the Group 3 5f Premio Primi Passi at 2 yrs, is a sister to the US stakes winner Amazing Love and a half-sister to 7 winners including the dam of the US Graded stakes winners Slew The Dragon and Slew The Knight. The second dam, Bold But Baffled (by Bold And Brave), was an unplaced half-sister to 7 winners. (Brian Yeardley Continental Ltd). *"A big, strong, heavy colt, not yet in fast work " says Mark.*

559 - ICE   b.c. Polar Falcon - Sarabah (Ela Mana Mou).
February 20. Third foal. 50,000Y. Tattersalls October.
Brother to the fairly useful 1996 2-y-o dual 6f winner Cryhavoc. The dam, a quite useful 10f winner, is a half-sister to 3 winners including the very smart triple Group 2 1m winner Gothenburg. The second dam, Be Discreet (by Junius), won 5 races in France at up to 7f and is a half-sister to 9 winners including the US Grade 3 winner Kirov Premiere and the French Group 2 placed Theatre Critic. (Mr J David Abell). *"A very attractive, heavy, thick-set colt, he'll take some time to get fit"*.

560 - LOVE DIAMONDS (IRE) b.c. Royal Academy - Baby Diamonds (Habitat).
February 22. IR50,000Y. Goffs Orby.
Closely related to the US Grade 2 1m Sheridan Stakes winner Gem Master (by Green Dancer) and half-brother to the US Grade 3 9.5f Next Move Handicap winner Madame Adolphe (by Criminal Type), the useful middle-distance maiden Benzine (by Secreto), the US stakes-placed winner Perfect Gem (by Alydar), the minor US winner Turn Baby Turn (by Arctic Tern) and the Canadian winner Dabbiana (by Fappiano) - herself dam of the US Grade 3 winner Party Season. The dam, a 6f winner at 2 yrs in the USA, is a sister to the Group 3 Cornwallis Stakes winner Tatibah and a half-sister to the Grade 1 Widener Handicap winner Vertee (by Vertex). The second dam, Three Tees (by Tim Tam), won in the USA and is a half-sister to the dam of the US Grade 1 winner Hail The Pirates. (Mr M Doyle). *"A very attractive, strong, powerful colt".*

561 - LUMIERE DE MA VIE (USA) b.c. Ghazi - Ma Biche (Key To The Kingdom).
March 2. 22,000Y. Tattersalls October.
Half-brother to the 3-y-o Jahanamee (by Hansel), to the quite useful 1994 triple 7f winning 3-y-o Desert Symphony (by Mr Prospector), the quite useful 1993 3-y-o 7f and 1m winner Kassbaan (by Alydar), the minor French 9f winner Bedouin Veil and the minor French 10f winner Desert Crest (both by Shareef Dancer). The dam was a top-class filly and winner of the 1,000 Guineas, Prix de la Foret, Cheveley Park Stakes and Prix Robert Papin. The second dam, Madge (by Roi Dagobert), won once over 11f and is a half-sister to another Cheveley Park Stakes winner in Mige. (Mrs S Yeardley). *"This is a nice, big, strong colt - yet to do any fast work".*

562 - OPULENCE ch.f. Arazi - Janaat (Kris).
May 18. Second foal.
Half-sister to the very useful 1997 2-y-o Group 1 1m Gran Criterium winner Lend A Hand (by Great Commotion). The dam, a fair 3-y-o 12f winner, is a sister to the French 3-y-o listed 10.5f winner Trefoil and a half-sister to numerous winners including the smart middle-distance winners Maysoon, Richard of York, Three Tails (dam of the high-class middle-distance colt Tamure) and Third Watch. The second dam, Triple First (by High Top), won seven races including the Group 2 10f Nassau Stakes and the Group 2 10f Sun Chariot Stakes. (Maktoum Al Maktoum). *"Smallish and a little backward, but if she is anything like Lend A Hand she'll grow a lot through the year. Her one piece of fast work was quite satisfactory but she'll take a lot more time".*

563 - ROYAL REBEL b.c. Robellino - Greenvera (Riverman).
March 29. Third foal. 145,000Y. Tattersalls October.
Half-brother to the 3-y-o Dream Lover (by Pursuit Of Love). The dam was placed once in France and is a half-sister to 6 winners including the French listed winner and Group 2 5f Prix du Gros-Chene third Way West. The second dam, Greenway (by Targowice), won 3 races in France including the Group 3 5f Prix d'Arenburg and is a half-sister to the Group 3 Prix Messidor winner Gay Minstrel and to the dam of the French Group 1 winners Oczy Czarnie and Glaieul. ((Mr P Savill). *"A very attractive colt for later in the season, he is going very well but will not run over minimum trips".*

564 - SINGING WINDS (IRE) b.f. Turtle Island - Shamiyda (Sir Ivor).
April 25. 70,000Y. Tattersalls December.
Half-sister to the very useful Group 3 15f Prix de Letuce winner Shaiybara (by Kahyasi) and to the minor French winners Shamaya (by Doyoun) and Shanntabariya (by Sharnazar). The dam, a quite useful middle-distance placed maiden, is a half-sister to 3 winners including the Australian Grade 2 winner and Group 2 King Edward VII Stakes second Shantaroun. The second dam, Shannfara (by Zeddaan), won 3 times in France and was fourth in the Group 3 Prix de la Grotte. (Sheikh Mohammed). *"An attractive, deep-bodied filly. A little backward at the moment"* explained Mark.

565 - STOLEN TEAR (FR) ch.f. Cadeaux Genereux - Durrah (Nijinsky).
March 6.
Half-sister to the 1994 2-y-o 8.2f winner High Standard (by Kris), the 1994 3-y-o 10f winner Mowlaie (by Nashwan) - both fairly useful, the 1996 Irish 3-y-o 5f winner Durrah Green (by Green Desert) and the 1992 Irish 2-y-o 6f winner Short Visit (by Private Account). The dam, a fairly useful French 2-y-o 1m winner, is a sister to the Grade 2 stakes winner Number (dam of the very smart 1989 2-y-o Jade Robbery), is closely related to the top-class sire Nureyev and a half-sister to Fairy Bridge (the dam of Sadlers Wells, Fairy King and Tate Gallery) and Kilavea (the dam of Kiliniski). The second dam, Special

(by Forli), was an unplaced sister to Thatch. (Maktoum Al Maktoum). *"A big, strong, powerful filly. She'll require a bit more time".*

Gay Kelleway

566 - ANOTHER RAINBOW (IRE)
b.f. Rainbows For Life - Phylella (Persian Bold). March 15. Sixth foal. IR22,000Y. Goffs Orby.
Half-sister to the 3-y-o Nocturne (by Tenby), unplaced in one outing at 2 yrs, to the very useful Group 3 7f Nell Gwyn Stakes winner Reunion (by Be My Guest), the fair 4-y-o 1m to 11.9f winner Mono Lady (by Polish Patriot) and the Irish 2-y-o 6f winner Foravella (by Cadeaux Genereux). The dam won in France (over 10f) and in the USA, is a sister to the US stakes winner Karman Girl and a half-sister to 4 winners. The second dam, Tumblella (by Tumble Wind), won the listed 1m Gilltown Stud Stakes and is a half-sister to 7 winners. (Pot of Gold). *"A lovely filly, she looks the part, will start her career over five furlongs very soon and is entered in the Moyglare"* Gay tells me.

567 - BARON DE PICHON (IRE)
b.c. Perugino - Ariadne (Bustino). March 29. IR32,000Y. Goffs Orby.
Half-brother to 6 winners including the useful 1997 2-y-o 5f and 6f winner Another Fantasy (by Danehill), the fairly useful 1988 2-y-o 5f to 7f winner Denham Green (by Dominion), the fair 3-y-o 12f winner Cas-En-Bas (by Good Times) and the fair 6f and 7f all-weather winner Runnel (by Runnett). The dam, a quite useful 2m winner at 3 yrs, is a sister to the Group 1 Premio Lydia Tesio winner Stufida - herself grandam of the high-class sprinter Pivotal. The second dam, Zerbinetta (by Henry The Seventh), was a useful 2-y-o dual 5f winner. (The Money Men). *"A horse with a lot of potential, he'll need a run to put him right, is laid back in his work and does everything nicely".*

568 - FAIRY CONTESSA (IRE)
b.f. Fairy King - More Fizz (Morston). April 24. IR110,000Y. Goffs Challenge.
Closely related to a minor winner in Australia by Sadlers Wells and half-sister to the very smart colt River Falls (by Aragon), a winner of three races at 2 and 3 yrs including the Group 2 6f Gimcrack Stakes and third in the Group 1 Middle Park Stakes, to the useful 1997 2-y-o 1m winner Success And Glory (by Alzao), the fair 1991 3-y-o 6f and 7f winner Fizz Time (by Good Times) and a minor winner abroad by Chilibang. The dam won once over an extended 9f in France at 3 yrs and is a half-sister to the French middle-distance winner El Famoso and to the dams of the Group 3 winners Premier Cuvee and Deep Finesse. The second dam, Effervescence II (by Charlottesville), won twice over 10f in France and is a half-sister to the French 2,000 Guineas winner and leading sire Zeddaan. (The Money Men). *"Although I haven't done much with her, I can't knock her. She's doing all her work nicely, is entered in all the right races and I think she's got an engine".*

569 - JAGUAR
b.c. Barathea - Oasis (Valiyar). February 17. 72,000Y. Newmarket Breeze Ups.
Half-brother to the fair 7f winner White Settler (by Polish Patriot). The dam won twice over hurdles and is a half-sister to several winners including the smart two-year-old and sire Magic Ring. The second dam, Emaline (by Empery), won in France and was fourth in the Group 3 Prix Thomas Bryon. This colt was purchased at the Newmarket Breeze-ups in Mid April.

James Lenehan

570 - CADENZA (USA)
ch.f. Machiavellian - In The Groove (Night Shift). February 19.
Half-sister to the 3-y-o Incentive (by Rainbow Quest) and to the fairly useful 1995 2-y-o 5f and 6f winner Incarvillea (by Mr Prospector). The dam was a top-class middle-distance filly and won seven races, notably the Irish 1,000 Guineas, Juddmonte International, Dubai Champion Stakes and Coronation Cup - all Group 1 events. She is a half-sister to 4 winners, including the fairly useful miler Spanish Pine, out of the quite useful dual 12f winner Pine Ridge (by High Top) - herself out of the minor 12f and 14f winner Wounded Knee (by Busted). (Sheikh Mohammed).

571 - DEMURE
b.f. Machiavellian - Shy Princess (Irish River). March 30.
Half-sister to the Irish trained 3-y-o Abashed (by Fairy King), to the very smart colt Diffident (by Nureyev), winner of the Group 3 6f Diadem Stakes, the Group 3 6f Prix de Ris-Orangis and the listed 7f European

Free Handicap and to a winner in France and Malaysia by Groom Dancer. The dam, a smart French 2-y-o 7f winner and second in the Group 1 Prix Morny, won over 6f as a 3-y-o and is a half-sister to the Breeders Cup Mile winner Opening Verse, previously a smart colt in England when second in the Eclipse Stakes. The second dam, Shy Dawn (by Grey Dawn II), won no less than 19 races at up to 10f including five Grade 3 stakes and is a half-sister to 3 stakes winners. (Sheikh Mohammed).

---

572 - FORLORNA (IRE)
b.f. Nashwan - Royal Lorna (Val de l'Orne).
March 24. Sixth living foal.

Half-sister to the fair 1993 12f and 14f placed 3-y-o Darzee (by Darshaan) and to several unraced horses. The dam, a very useful 3-y-o, won three times in England over 10f and the Premio Bagutta in Milan over 1m. She is a half-sister to the Yorkshire Oaks winner Awaasif (herself dam of Oaks winner Snow Bride and thus granddam of Lammtarra), to the Florida Derby second Akureyri, the 1,000 Guineas second Konafa (dam of the Group 1 winners Hector Protector, Shanghai and Bosra Sham) and the unraced Royal Stance (dam of the very useful 1m to 10f colt Majuscule). The second dam, Royal Statute (by Northern Dancer), won over 5f at 2 yrs and is a half-sister to the dual Canadian champion handicap horse Dance Act. (Sheikh Mohammed).

---

573 - MOJAVE
b.c. Green Desert - Somfas (What a Pleasure).
February 13.

Closely related to the very useful Group 2 6f Mill Reef Stakes winner Russian Bond and the useful 6f listed winner Snaadee (both by Danzig) and half-brother to the very useful 2-y-o Group 3 9f Prix de Conde winner Cristofori (by Fappiano), the minor US 9f winner Brio Cielo (by Conquistador Cielo) and the useful dual 7f winner Adbass (by Northern Dancer). The dam, a stakes-placed winner of 4 races at up to 7f in the USA, is a half-sister to the Canadian Horse of the Year Fanfreluche, herself dam of the good winners L'Enjoleur, Montelimar and Medaille d'Or. The second dam, Ciboulette (by Chop Chop), won the 8.5f Maple Leaf Stakes in Canada and also bred the very useful sire Night Shift. (Sheikh Mohammed).

---

574 - ROSIA (IRE)
b.f. Mr Prospector - Rosefinch (Blushing Groom).
March 14. Second foal.

Half-sister to the quite useful 1997 3-y-o 10.5f placed Manuetti (by Sadler's Wells). The dam, a smart filly, ran seven times at 3 yrs and won twice over 10f including the Group 1 Prix Saint-Alary. She is a half-sister to the very useful 7.3f and 9f English winner and subsequent Grade 2 Long Island Handicap winner Shaima (by Shareef Dancer) and to the useful 7f and 8.3f winner Felitza (by Soviet Star). The second dam, Oh So Sharp (by Kris), was a top class filly and a winner of 7 races from 5f to 14.6f, notably the fillies Triple Crown (1,000 Guineas, Oaks and St Leger). She is a full or half-sister to 8 winners including the Coronation and Nassau Stakes winner Roussalka (herself dam of the good fillies Ristna and Gayane), the 1,000 Guineas second Our Home and the Jersey Stakes winner Etienne Gerard. (Sheikh Mohammed).

---

575 - TRUE ROMANCE
b.c. Rainbow Quest - First Kiss (Kris).
May 1.

Half-brother to the very useful 2-y-o 7.1f winner and Group 2 12f Great Voltigeur Stakes fourth Apprehension (by In The Wings), to the smart 1994 Group 1 1m Coronation Stakes winner Kissing Cousin (by Danehill) - previously placed at 2 yrs in the Fillies Mile and the May Hill Stakes, the fairly useful 1991 3-y-o dual 2m winner Shahi (by Sahhrastani) and the fair 1993 3-y-o 1m winner Colin Muset (by The Minstrel). The dam, a quite useful dual 10f winner at 3 yrs, is out of the 9f winner Primatie (by Vaguely Noble), herself a daughter of the Prix de Diane, Prix Vermeille and Prix Saint Alary winner Pistol Packer (by Gun Bow). (Sheikh Mohammed).

In addition to these beautifully-bred two-year-olds, David will also be training many of those listed under Godolphin.

David Loder

---

576 - ARABIAN MOON (IRE)
ch.c. Barathea - Excellent Alibi (Exceller).
May 16. 60,000Y. Tattersalls Houghton.

Half-brother to the 3-y-o Excellent Song (by Suave Dancer), to the very useful middle distance stayer Witness Box (by Lyphard), a winner of 6 races including the Northumberland Plate and placed in the Doncaster Cup and Goodwood Cup and the fairly useful 3-y-o 7f and 1m winner Efharisto (by Dominion).

The dam won three races from 10f to 12f in France and is closely related to the outstanding filly Dahlia (twice winner of the 'King George' and herself dam of three Grade 1 winners). The second dam, Charming Alibi (by Honey's Alibi), won 16 of 21 races in the USA including four stakes events. (Salem Suhail).

577 - ARAWAT PRINCE
ch.c. College Chapel - Alpine Symphony (Northern Dancer).
April 23. 35,000Y. Tattersalls Houghton.

Half-brother to the very useful 1996 Chester Vase winner High Baroque and the quite useful 1993 3-y-o 10f winner Dancing Heights (both by High Estate). The dam is an unraced half-sister to the Irish 2,000 Guineas winner Nikoli, the Waterford Crystal Mile winner Captain James and the Coronation Stakes winner Sutton Place. The second dam, Aliceva (by Alcide), won a 10f maiden and is a half-sister to the dam of Le Moss and Levmoss.

578 - BENENITRA
b.f. Indian Ridge - Benedicite (Lomond).
April 3. Second foal. 150,000Y. Tattersalls October.

Half-sister to the 3-y-o Scapula (by Elmaamul). The dam is an unraced half-sister to 5 winners including the Group 2 6.5f Prix Maurice de Gheest and Group 3 6f Cork and Orrery Stakes winner College Chapel and the listed-placed winner Humble Pie (herself dam of the Italian Group 3 winner Leap For Joy). The second dam, Scarcely Blessed (by So Blessed), won the Group 3 5f King George Stakes and is a half-sister to the listed Strensall Stakes winner Petty Purse. (Sheikh Mohammed).

579 - BERLIOZ
b.c. Dolphin Street - Biraya (Valiyar).
May 11. Fourth foal. 115,000Y. Tattersalls October. Lot 722.

Half-brother to the Swedish winner Mighty Aphrodite (by Tirol). The dam is an unraced half-sister to 2 winners out of Yldizlar (by Star Appeal) - a fair 2-y-o 7f winner and half-sister to 9 winners including Domynsky (US Grade 3 winner) and Petrullo (French Group 3 winner). (Sheikh Mohammed).

580 - BLUE MELODY (USA)
b.f. Dayjur - Blue Note (Habitat).
April 13.

Closely related to the smart Group 1 6f Middle Park Stakes and Group 2 7f Challenge Stakes winner Zieten, to the Group 1 6f Cheveley Park Stakes and Group 3 5f Queen Mary Stakes winner Blue Duster (both by Danzig) and the fairly useful 1997 2-y-o 7f winner Naughty Blue (by Danehill) and half-sister to the 1993 French 6f, 6.7f and listed 1m winner Slow Jazz (by Chief's Crown). The dam won 5 races from 5f to 7f in France including the Group 2 Prix Maurice de Gheest and the Group 3 Prix de le Porte Maillot. The second dam, Balsamique (by Tourangeau), won 7 races at up to 11.5f and 2 jumping events in France. (Sheikh Mohammed).

581 - BRAZILIAN MOOD (IRE)
b.c. Doyoun - Sea Mistress (Habitat).
April 12. 65,000Y. Tattersalls October.

Half-brother to the 3-y-o Laa Jadeed, unplaced on his only outing at 2 yrs, to the very useful Group 3 6f Greenlands Stakes winner Nautical Pet (both by Petorius) and half-brother to the Irish 9f and 14f winner Touching Moment (by Pennine Walk), the modest 7-y-o 6f winner Waders Dream (by Doulab) and the fair dual 1m winner Roi de la Mer (by Fairy King). The dam is an unraced half-sister to 2 minor winners. The second dam, Gilwanigan (by Captain's Gig), won twice and is a half-sister to the Irish Oaks winner Pampalina (herself the dam of the Irish 2,000 Guineas winner Pampapaul) and the Free Handicap winner Short Commons (dam of the Cork and Orrery Stakes winner He Loves Me). (Salem Suhail).

582 - CALANDO (USA)
b.f. Storm Cat - Diminuendo (Diesis).
April 9. Sixth living foal.

Closely related to the modest 1995 4-y-o Carpathian (by Danzig), a winner of 5 races at around 12f including on the all-weather. The dam, a top class, game and genuine filly, won all four of her juvenile races from 6f to 1m including the Hoover Fillies Mile and the Cherry Hinton Stakes. As a three year old she won the Epsom Oaks, Irish Oaks (in a dead-heat), Yorkshire Oaks and the Musidora Stakes and was officially rated the top racehorse of her generation in the 11f+ category. The second dam, Cacti (by Tom Rolfe), won at around 1m in the USA at 3 yrs and is out of the 8.5f Vanity Handicap winner Desert Love. (Sheikh Mohammed).

583 - COUNTERFEIT (IRE)
b.c. In The Wings - Bogus John (Blushing John).
March 23. First foal. 110,000Y. Tattersalls October.

The dam is an unraced half-sister to 3 winners in the USA, Germany and Italy. The second dam, Bogus (by Nijinsky), is an unraced half-sister to 6 winners including the US Grade 1 winners Tiller and Endear (herself dam of the dual Breeders Cup Mile winner Lure) and the Grade 2 winner Digress. (Sheikh Mohammed).

---

584 - COUNTLESS (USA)

b.c. Danzig - Priceless Pearl (Alydar).
March 23.
Closely related to the fairly useful dual 6f winner Pearl d'Azur (by Dayjur) and half-sister to Isla Del Rey (by Nureyev), a useful winner from 6f to 7f in Ireland, Dubai and at Lingfield. The dam, a useful 2-y-o 7f winner, is a sister to Saratoga Six and to the dam of the multiple US Grade 1 winner Lakeway and a half-sister to Dunbeath. The second dam, Priceless Fame (by Irish Castle), won twice over sprint distances and is a half-sister to Bold Forbes. (Sheikh Mohammed).

---

585 - CROWN OF TREES (USA)

b.br.c. Chief's Crown - Ribbonwood (Diesis).
March 10. First foal.
The dam, a fairly useful 2-y-o 6f winner, was second in the Group 3 Fred Darling Stakes and is a half-sister to the Champion American 3-y-o colt Risen Star, winner of the Belmont Stakes and the Preakness Stakes. The second dam, Ribbon (by His Majesty), won 9 races from 6f to 11f in the USA including the Group 3 Pucker Up Stakes and is a half-sister to the very useful 1m to 10f winner Polar Gap. (Sheikh Mohammed).

---

586 - ELBAZ (USA)

ch.c. Thorn Dance - Stuttering (Ack Ack).
April 6. 22,000Y. Tattersalls October.
Closely related to a winner in Germany by Lyphard and half-brother to the minor US winners V Vigors, Stutz Cat (both by Vigors), Says It Twice (by Ferdinand) and Hurrah Hurrah (by Rahy). The dam won 3 races in the USA including a minor stakes event and is a half-sister to 3 winners. The second dam, Call Me Madam (by Bold Ruler), won once in the USA and is a half-sister to the US Grade 1 Sorority Stakes winner Squander and the US Grade 2 winner Duty Dance. (Jaber Abdullah).

---

587 - FAIRY QUEEN (IRE)

b.f. Fairy King - Dedicated Lady (Pennine Walk).
January 28. Third foal. 85,000Y. Tattersalls October.
The dam, a winner over 5f and 6f (twice) at 2 yrs in Ireland and listed placed, is a half-sister to 4 winners including the Group 3 Prix de Flore third Silk Petal (herself dam of a listed winner). The second dam, Salabella (by Sallust), is a placed half-sister to the Irish St Leger and Grosser Preis von Baden winner M-Lolshan. (Maktoum Al Maktoum).

---

588 - GOOMBAYLAND

ch.c. Common Grounds - House Of Fame (Trempolino).
March 5. First foal. 45,000Y. Tattersalls October.
The dam is an unraced half-sister to 5 winners including the US stakes-placed winner Lady Turk (herself dam of the US Grade 1 placed Gun Flight). The second dam, Name And Fame (by Arts And Letters), won 3 races in the USA and is a half-sister to the top-class broodmare Oh So Fair (dam of the Fillies Triple Crown winner Oh So Sharp, the Coronation Stakes winner Roussalka and the Jersey Stakes winner Etienne Gerard etc.,).

---

589 - HOPEFUL HENRY

ch.c. Cadeaux Genereux - Fernlea (Sir Ivor).
First living foal. 48,000Y. Tattersalls October.
The dam, placed twice at 2 yrs over 5f including the listed Topaz Sprint Stakes, is a sister to the Irish winner and listed 7f Tyros Stakes second Strover. The second dam, Pampas (by Pampapaul), a winner of three races in Ireland and second in the Group 3 5f Ballyogan Stakes, subsequently won in the USA and was second in the Grade 3 8.5f Dahlia Handicap.

---

590 - HOUSTON TIME (USA)

ch.c. Rahy - Band (Northern Dancer).
January 18. Second foal. 140,000 Y. Tattersalls Houghton.
Brother to the very useful 1995 2-y-o Applaud, winner of 2 races including the Group 3 6f Cherry Hinton Stakes. The dam is a placed half-sister to 5 winners including the US Grade 3 9f New Orleans Handicap winner Festive. The second dam, Swingtime (by Buckpasser), won 9 races here and in the USA including the Grade 2 Santa Maria Handicap, the Group 3 Cork And Orrery Stakes, the Group 3 Diadem Stakes and the Grade 3 Las Palmas Handicap. Swingtime is a half-sister to 5 winners including the Grade 2 Kentucky Oaks winner Bag Of Tunes (herself dam of the Lancashire Oaks winner Prophecy) and Song Sparrow (dam of the US Grade 1 winner Cormorant). (Jaber Abdullah).

591 - INCHMARIO　　　　　　　　　　gr.c. Machiavellian - Indian Skimmer (Storm Bird).
February 2. Third living foal.
The dam was a top-class filly and winner of the Phoenix Champion Stakes, the Dubai Champion Stakes, the Prix d'Ispahan, the Prix de Diane and the Prix Saint-Alary. The second dam, Nobiliare (by Vaguely Noble), is an unraced sister to the dam of the US Grade 2 winner Country Pine and a half-sister to the dam of the US Grade 1 winner Missy's Mirage. The third dam, Gray Mirage, was a stakes winning half-sister to the Champion US filly Dark Mirage. (Sheikh Mohammed).

592 - KING MIDAS　　　　　　　　　b.c. Bluebird - Ellebanna (Tina's Pet).
March 21. Third foal. 90,000Y. Tattersalls October.
Half-brother to the fair 1997 2-y-o 7.1f winner Gift Of Gold (by Statoblest). The dam, a winner of three races over 5f, is a half-sister to 5 winners including the useful sprinters Bolshoi, Great Chaddington and Tod. The second dam, Mainly Dry (by The Brianstan), is an unraced half-sister to 4 winners including the dam of the Portland Handicap winner Swelter. (Maktoum Al Maktoum).

593 - LAST WARNING　　　　　　　　b.c. Warning - Dancing Crystal (Kris).
March 22. Sixth foal. 46,000Y. Tattersalls October.
Half-brother to the useful 1995 3-y-o 8.3f winner Krystallos (by Polish Precedent) and to minor winners abroad by Reference Point, Ajdal and Lycius. The dam was fourth over 6f and 7f and is a half-sister to 4 winners. The second dam, Lyric Dance (by Lyphard), won the listed 7f Free Handicap and is a half-sister to 10 winners. (Maktoum Al Maktoum).

594 - LOVE STORY (IRE)　　　　　　b.c. Green Desert - Takwim (Taufan).
February 9. Fourth foal. IR75,000Y. Goffs Orby.
Half-brother to the 3-y-o Jaballiyah (by Lahib) and to the Irish 7f (at 2 yrs) to 10f placed Tamani (by Unfuwain). The dam won four races from 5f (at 2 yrs) to 7f including the listed Barronstown Stud Gold Stakes and is a half-sister to 3 winners including the German listed winner Capwell. The second dam, Brush Away (by Ahonoora), is an unraced half-sister to 9 minor winners. (Maktoum Al Maktoum).

595 - MARRUBIUM (USA)　　　　　　b.f. Dixieland Band - Marillette (Diesis).
January 27. First foal.
The dam, a very smart winner of 5 races including the Group 3 1m May Hill Stakes and the Group 3 10.5f Musidora Stakes, is a sister to the very useful 8.2f and listed 9f winner Storm Trooper. The second dam, Stormette (by Assert), won over 12f in Ireland and is a half-sister to Storm Bird and to the Canadian Oaks winner Northernette. (Sheikh Mohammed).

596 - NOCCIOLA　　　　　　　　　　ch.f. Cadeaux Genereux - Norpella (Northfields).
January 14. Sixth foal. 70,000Y. Tattersalls Houghton.
Sister to the useful listed 6f (at 2 yrs) and listed 1m winner Ultimo Imperatore and half-sister to the fairly useful 2-y-o 6f winner and 1m placed Sugarfoot (by Thatching), the 2-y-o 7f winner Primus (by Primo Dominie), the 9f and 10f winner Carlito Brigante (by Robellino) and the 7f and 9f winner Floralia (by Auction Ring) - all three quite useful. The dam, a fairly useful 10f and 12f winner, is a half-sister to 5 winners. The second dam, Palmella (by Grundy), won over 10f and is a half-sister to Teenoso and Topsy.

597 - PILGRIM'S WAY (USA)　　　　b.f. Gone West - Marling (Lomond).
May 10.
Half-sister to the 1997 2-y-o 6f winner Half-Hitch (by Diesis) and the 1997 3-y-o 7.1f winner Moonshiner (by Irish River) - both quite useful. The dam, a high-class filly and winner of the Cheveley Park Stakes, the Queen Mary Stakes, the Irish 1,000 Guineas, the Coronation Stakes and the Sussex Stakes is a half-sister to the Irish 2,000 Guineas and Prix de l'Abbaye second Caerwent. The second dam, Marwell (by Habitat), a half-sister to the Mill Reef Stakes winner Lord Seymour, was a champion 2-y-o and 3-y-o filly and winner of the July Cup, the Prix de l'Abbaye, the Kings Stand Stakes and the Cheveley Park Stakes.

598 - PLUTOCRAT　　　　　　　　　b.c. Polar Falcon - Choire Mhor (Dominion).
May 2. 27,000Y. Tattersalls October.
Half-brother to the modest 1997 2-y-o 5f winner iris may (by Brief Truce), to the very useful 1997 3-y-o 5f winner Cathedral (by Prince Sabo), to the fair 11f all-weather winner Themeda (by Sure Blade) and the quite useful 1994 2-y-o 8.5f all-weather winner Legitimate (by Last Tycoon). The dam, a useful winner of three races over 6f at 2 yrs, is a half-sister to the Group 3 Prix de la Jonchere winner Soft

Currency and the listed winner Fawzi - both useful. The second dam, Little Loch Broom (by Reform), is a placed half-sister to the dams of the Group winners Ozone Friendly, Ardkinglass, Wiorno and Reprimand.

---

599 - PRECEDENCE (IRE)   b.f. Polish Precedent - Braiswick (King Of Spain).
February 3. Third foal.
Half-sister to the fair 1995 3-y-o 10.2f winner Prickwillow (by Nureyev). The dam, a very smart winner of the Group 1 E P Taylor Stakes and the Group 2 Sun Chariot Stakes, is a half-sister to the Group 3 11f September Stakes winner Percy's Lass. The second dam, Laughing Girl, (by Sassafras), won the 10f Lupe Stakes, was placed in the Oaks and the Park Hill Stakes and is a half-sister to the dams of Teenoso, Topsy, Give Thanks, Favoridge and Old Country. (Sheikh Mohammed).

---

600 - ROSIE DREAM (IRE)   ch.f. Cadeaux Genereux - Impudent Miss (Persian Bold).
April 23. 40,000Y. Tattersalls October.
Half-sister to the modest 1997 6f to 9f placed 2-y-o Constant Attention (by Royal Academy), to the useful 1992 2-y-o 7f winner and May Hill Stakes second Self Assured (by Ahonoora), the fairly useful 6f (at 2 yrs) to 7.6f winner King Al (by Indian King), the 1997 3-y-o 10f winner Enlisted (by Sadler's Wells), the 7f (at 2 yrs) and 1m winner Good Reference (by Reference Point) - both quite useful - and the minor French 3-y-o winner Impetuous (by Darshaan). The dam, a very useful Irish 2-y-o winner of 3 races from 5f to 1m including the listed Silken Glider Stakes, is a half-sister to the smart Group 3 6f Prix de Seine-et-Oise winner Sayyaf. The second dam, Pavello (by Crepello), won over 1m at 3 yrs and is a half-sister to the Brigadier Gerard Stakes winner Rymer. (Salem Suhail).

---

601 - SIR JACK   b.c. Distant Relative - Frasquita (Song).
March 18. 50,000Y. Tattersalls October.
Half-brother to the fairly useful 5f and 6f winner Johnny Staccato (by Statoblest) and the Scandinavian winner Rose Bunch (by Never So Bold). The dam is an unraced sister to the smart sprinter Jester and the listed 5f winner Tricky Note. The second dam, Trickster (by Major Portion), won over 5f and is a half-sister to the dam of the Group 3 6f Greenlands Stakes winner Reesh. (Lucayan Stud).

---

602 - SNOWKISSED (IRE)   b.c. Rainbow Quest - Awaasif (Snow Knight).
March 16.
Closely related to the high class filly Snow Bride, winner of the Epsom Oaks (awarded race), Musidora Stakes and Princess Royal Stakes and herself dam of the Derby, King George and 'Arc' winner Lammtarra, and to the useful middle-distance winner Habaayib (both by Blushing Groom), and half-brother to the fair 8.2f winner and subsequent US Grade 3 New Orleans Handicap winner Jarraar (by Mr Prospector) and the 2-y-o 7f and subsequent US winner Salaadim (by Seattle Slew). The dam won the Group 1 Yorkshire Oaks and the Group 1 Gran Premio del Jockey Club and is a half-sister to numerous winners including the high class American colt Akureyri and the 1,000 Guineas second Konafa (herself dam of the high class French 6f and 7f performer Proskona and grandam of Hector Protector, Shanghai and Bosra Sham). The second dam, Royal Statute (by Northern Dancer), a 2-y-o 5f winner, is a sister to the dual Canadian champion handicap horse Dance Act. (Sheikh Mohammed).

---

603 - SPIRIT WILLING (IRE)   b.f. Fairy King - Pro Patria (Petingo).
April 3.
Closely related to the fair dual 1m winner Wahem (by Lomond) and half-sister to the 1987 Epsom and Irish Oaks winner Unite (by Kris), the fair 1997 7f placed 2-y-o Pride Of Place (by Caerleon), the French listed 12f winner Liversan (by Sure Blade), the minor 3-y-o and hurdles winner Palletine (by African Sky) and to Point of Honour (by Kris) - the unplaced dam of the smart Group 2 Pretty Polly Stakes winner Del Deya. The dam won over 5f and 6f at 2 yrs and is a sister to the smart miler Patris. The second dam, Joyful (by Princely Gift), is a half-sister to Lady Seymour - dam of the top-class filly Marwell.

---

604 - TANASIE   b.f. Cadeaux Genereux - Tansy (Shareef Dancer).
February 21. First foal.
The dam was a fair 2-y-o 6f winner, is closely related to the top-class middle-distance colt Most Welcome and the useful middle-distance winner Top Guest and a half-sister to several winners including the useful middle-distance filly Bourbon Topsy. The second dam, Topsy (by Habitat), was a very smart winner of the Sun Chariot Stakes, the Prix d'Astarte and the Fred Darling Stakes and is a half-sister to the Derby winner Teenoso.

605 - UP AND ABOUT b.f. Barathea - Upend (Main Reef).
March 19. Sixth foal. 62,000Y. Tattersalls Houghton.
Half-sister to the 3-y-o Wave Racer (by Royal Academy), to the useful 10f and 10.5f winner Shortfall (by Last Tycoon) and the useful 1m (at 2 yrs) and 12f winner Al Azhar (by Alzao). The dam, a smart winner of 3 races from 10f to 12f including the Group 3 St Simon Stakes and the listed Galtres Stakes, was second in the Group 3 Princess Royal Stakes and is a half-sister to 5 winners (3 of them over hurdles) including the fairly useful 10f to 12f winner High Gait (herself dam of the high-class stayer and champion hurdler Royal Gait). The second dam, Gay Charlotte (by Charlottown), a winner over 7.5f at 2 yrs in Ireland and over 1m at 3 yrs in the USA, is out of the Irish Oaks winner Merry Mate.

Willie Muir

606 - SOUHAITE (FR) b.c. Salse - Parannda (Bold Lad, Ire).
March 29. FF450,000Y. Deauville August. 65,000Y. Wolverhampton Breeze-Up Sale.
Half-brother to 3 winners including the Group 1 Italian Oaks winner Shahmiad (by Alleged) and a winner over the jumps in France by Dreams To Reality. The dam won 3 races including the Group 3 1m Prix de Sandringham, was fourth in the French 1,000 Guineas and is a half-sister to the good mare Pollenka - grandam of the Irish Derby winner Winged Love. The second dam, Polana (by Botticelli), won twice at up to 1m and was listed placed in France. (Mrs Danita Winstanly). *"Souhaite is a really nice colt that shows speed with the five furlong horses, even though I think he'll be a seven furlong horse. He does everything right and has a super temperament. I think he'll be top-notch".* More two-year-olds trained by Willie Muir can be found in the Early Types section.

Jeremy Noseda

607 - AUSTIN POWERS b.c. Sadler's Wells - Guess Again (Stradavinsky).
April 1. 310,000Y. Tattersalls Houghton.
Closely related to the minor 3-y-o winner Heike (by Glenstal) and half-brother to the 1998 3-y-o Key To Coolcullen (by Royal Academy), the very useful 1994 Group 1 6f Phoenix Stakes winner Eva Luna, the Group 3 1m Futurity Stakes winner Cois Na Tine (both by Double Schwartz), the Irish 2-y-o 1m winner Genesco (by Salmon Leap) and the Irish 4-y-o 12f winner Direct Lady (by Fools Holme). The dam won over 1m at 3 yrs and is out of the Molecomb Stakes third Galka (by Deep Diver), herself a half-sister to the high-class sprinter Double Form and the Lupe Stakes winner Scimitarra.

608 - BERGAMO b.c. Robellino - Pretty Thing (Star Appeal).
March 3. Fifth foal. 40,000Y. Tattersalls October.
Half-brother to the poor 8.5f all-weather winner Rajah (by Be My Chief) and a 10f winner in Germany by Formidable. The dam, a quite useful winner of 7 races, was suited by 12f and was third in the listed Galtres Stakes. She is a half-sister to 5 winners out of the 3-y-o 10f winner Monkey Tricks (by Saint Crespin III), herself a half-sister to the Lancashire Oaks winner and Epsom Oaks second Maina.

609 - BOLD BLUE b.c. Bluebird - Evangola (Persian Bold).
April 7. Sixth foal. 72,000Y. Tattersalls Houghton.
Half-brother to the useful Irish 2-y-o listed 7f winner Wangola (by Waajib), to Persian Creek (by Treasure Kay), a winner of 3 races in Ireland at up to 7f and the quite useful 1994 2-y-o 6f winner Scenic Heights (by Scenic). The dam is an unraced half-sister to 2 winners including the Group 2 Sun Chariot Stakes fourth Gazelle d'Or. The second dam, Gazelle (by Tudor Music), is a placed half-sister to 4 minor winners.

610 - CATAPULT (IRE) ch.c. Catrail - Flimmering (Dancing Brave).
March 14. Second foal. 62,000Y. Tattersalls October.
Half-brother to the 1997 French 3-y-o winner Peak Of Joy (by Anshan). The dam is an unraced half-sister to 3 winners including the dam of the French listed winner River Cra. The second dam, Fatah Flare (by Alydar), a very smart filly and winner of the Group 3 Musidora Stakes is a half-sister to the dual US Grade 1 winner Sabin.

611 - DESARU (USA) b.br.c. Chief's Crown - Team Colors (Mr Prospector).
January 22. Third foal. $90,000. Keeneland September.
Half-brother to the minor US winner Mariner (by Seattle Dancer). The dam is an unraced half-sister to a stakes-placed winner in the USA. The second dam, Private Colors (by Private Account), won 3 races

in the USA and is a sister to the top-class and unbeaten American mare Personal Ensign (winner of eight Grade 1 events and herself dam of two Grade 1 winners) and to the dual Grade 1 winner Personal Flag.

612 - INDIAN WARRIOR
b.c. Be My Chief - Wanton (Kris).
March 24. 50,000Y. Tattersalls October.

Brother to the useful 2-y-o 5f winner Magongo and half-brother to the smart 1997 Irish 1,000 Guineas winner Classic Park (by Robellino), the 1997 US Grade 2 winner Rumpipumpy (by Shirley Heights), the useful 2-y-o 6f and subsequent US winner Wilde Rufo (by Sharrood) and a winner in Italy by Reprimand. The dam, a useful 2-y-o 5f winner and third in the Group 2 Flying Childers Stakes, is a half-sister to 8 winners including the smart listed St Hugh's Stakes winner and Group 2 Prix du Gros-Chene second Easy Option. The second dam, Brazen Faced (by Bold And Free), a quite useful 2-y-o 5f winner, is a half-sister to 8 winners including the Musidora Stakes winner Lovers Lane and the City And Suburban Handicap winner Belper.

613 - INKBERRY
ch.f. Cadeaux Genereux - Chatterberry (Aragon).
January 26. Second foal. 90,000Y. Tattersalls Houghton.

Half-sister to the quite useful 1997 2-y-o 5f winner Cloudberry (by Night Shift). The dam, a modest 2-y-o 5f winner, is a sister to the Group 3 Cornwallis Stakes and King George Stakes winner Argentum and a half-sister to 6 winners including the fair miler Eurodollar. The second dam, Silver Berry (by Lorenzaccio), is an unplaced half-sister to 6 winners including the Sun Chariot Stakes winner Cranberry Sauce (dam of the Child Stakes winner Sauceboat and thus grandam of the Group winners King of Hush and Dusty Dollar).

614 - LADY IN COLOUR
b.f. Cadeaux Genereux - Piffle (Shirley Heights).
May 5. Fifth foal. IR85,000Y. Goffs Orby.

Half-sister to the Grade 1 12f Hollywood Turf Cup and Group 3 1m Beresford Stakes winner Frenchpark, to the fairly useful 6f (at 2 yrs) and 10f winner Sayeh and the fair 2-y-o 1m all-weather winner Feather Bed (all by Fools Holme). The dam, a quite useful 12f winner, is a sister to the useful stayer El Conquistador and a half-sister to 4 winners. The second dam, Fiddle-Faddle (by Silly Season), is a winning half-sister to the Irish St Leger winner Mountain Lodge.

615 - MELBEN
b.c. Dolphin Street - Shapely Test (Elocutionist).
March 19. 70,000Y. Tattersalls October.

Closely related to Birchwood Sun (by Bluebird), a fair winner of 8 races at up to 1m and half-brother to the very useful Group 3 6f Greenlands Stakes winner Lidanna (by Nicholas), the Czech 1,000 Guineas winner Shapely Star (by Rusticaro) and 2 minor winners in Italy by Ela-Mana-Mou and Indian King. The dam won over 1m in Ireland and is a half-sister to a listed winner in Australia and to 3 minor winners in the USA. The second dam, Tillie Gray (by Majestic Prince), won 3 times in the USA and is a half-sister to the Group 1 Kings Stand Stakes winner Godswalk.

616 - MISTER POPPINS (IRE)
ch.c. Lahib - From The Rooftops (Thatching).
March 27. Third foal. 62,000Y. Tattersalls October.

The dam is an unraced half-sister to 4 minor winners here and abroad. The second dam, Say Yes (by Junius), won over 1m at 2 yrs in Ireland and is a half-sister to the Molecomb Stakes winner Hatta and to the dam of the US Grade 3 winner Casa Eire.

617 - MY OWN LOVELY LEE (IRE)
b.f. College Chapel - Pairc-Na-Lee (Fairy King).
March 31. First foal. IR75,000Y. Goffs Orby.

The dam is closely related to the 2-y-o Group 1 1m National Stakes winner and Irish 2,000 Guineas second Fatherland and to the Irish winner and Group 3 placed Lisaleen and a half-sister to the Irish listed winners Yeats and Golden Dome. The second dam, Lisadell (by Forli), won the Coronation Stakes and the Athasi Stakes and is a half-sister to Thatch and to the dam of Nureyev.

618 - MYSTIC SPRING
gr.f. Royal Academy - Secret Sunday (Secreto).
May 12. Third foal. IR32,000Y. Goffs Orby.

The dam, a minor Irish 12f winner, is a sister to the 2,000 Guineas and Group 2 7f Challenge Stakes winner Mystiko and a half-sister to 4 winners including the dam of the Group 1 Grand Criterium third Basim. The second dam, Caracciola (by Zeddaan), was placed four times in France at around 1m and is a half-sister to the French Group winners Calderina (Prix de Malleret) and Pasakos (Prix La Rochette).

619 - RAIN IN SPAIN
b.c. Unfuwain - Maria Isabella (Young Generation).
March 21. 40,000Y. Tattersalls October.
Brother to the useful Italian listed 10.5f Premio Minerva winner and Italian Oaks second Streisand and half-brother to the quite useful 10f to 12f 3-y-o winner Top Royal (by High Top), the fair 2-y-o 5f winner Solfegietto (by Music Boy) and the French 3-y-o 1m winner Domador (by Dominion). The dam is a French placed half-sister to 7 winners including the listed Deauville winner Party Doll (dam of the French dual Group 2 winner Titus Livius) and the useful French 2-y-o 6.5f winner Microcosme. The second dam, Midnight Lady (by Mill Reef), won once at 2 yrs and is a half-sister to the US Grade 2 winner Regal Bearing and to the dams of the Grade 1 winners Metamorphose (in the USA) and Super Sheila (in South Africa).

620 - SNOWY RANGE (USA)
b.br.f. Seattle Slew - November Snow (Storm Cat).
January 31. First foal. $400,000. Keeneland July.
The dam won 8 races in the USA including the Grade 1 7f Test Stakes and the Grade 1 10f Alabama Stakes and is a half-sister to the US stakes winner Lady Sorella. The second dam, Princess Alydar (by Alydar), is a placed half-sister to 4 stakes winners in the USA.

621 - TOKOLOSHE KING (IRE)
b.c. Fairy King - Belize Tropical (Baillamont).
April 28. Fourth foal. IR44,000Y. Goffs Challenge.
Half-brother to the 1995 Irish 2-y-o 6f winner and listed Silver Flash Stakes second Orange Walk (by Alzao) and to the fair 1997 3-y-o dual 7f all-weather winner Bogan (by Caerleon). The dam, a French 2-y-o 7.3f winner, is a half-sister to 7 winners including the Group 1 Dewhurst Stakes dead-heater Scenic, the Group 3 Prix Daphnis winner Silent Warrior and the Group 1 Grand Prix de Paris second Ithaki. The second dam, Idyllic (by Foolish Pleasure), is an unraced half-sister to the top-class broodmares I Will Follow (dam of Rainbow Quest) and Slightly Dangerous (dam of Commander In Chief, Warning, Dushyantor, Deploy, Yashmak, etc.,).

622 - VIBRANCE (IRE)
b.c. College Chapel - Shalara (Dancer's Image).
March 22. 37,000Y. Tattersalls October.
Half-brother to the useful listed 1m Prix Omnium winner Shayzari, to the fair 2-y-o 6f and 1m winner Out Run (both by Nishapour), the Irish 6f winner Majesterium (by Red Regent), the minor French and Swiss winner Lazim (by Red Sunset), the modest 2-y-o 5f all-weather winner Shanoora (by Don't Forget Me), the modest 2-y-o 6f winner Endearing (by Runnett) and a winner in Hong Kong by Petorius. The dam is an unraced half-sister to the very useful miler Shasavaan. The second dam, Shaara (by Sanctus II), is a placed half-sister to 6 winners.

623 - WANNABE GRAND
b.f. Danehill - Wannabe (Shirley Heights).
January 18. First foal. 60,000Y. Tattersalls October.
The dam, a quite useful 1m and 10f winner, is a half-sister to the very useful 5f and 6f winner and Group 1 Cheveley Park Stakes second Tanami. The second dam, Propensity (by Habitat), was a fairly useful 2-y-o 5f winner.

Aidan O'Brien

624 - AKUNA BAY (USA)
b.f. Mr Prospector - Dark Lomond (Lomond).
May 9. Fifth foal.
Half-sister to the very useful 7f winner (at 2 yrs) and Group 1 1m Prix Marcel Boussac, Group 1 12f Irish Oaks and Group 2 12f Ribblesdale Stakes placed Gothic Dream, and to 2 winners in Japan by Shirley Heights and Lomond. The dam, a very smart filly, won the Irish St Leger and the Curragh Pretty Polly Stakes and is a half-sister to the 12f Blandford Stakes winner South Atlantic. 2nd dam, Arkadina (by Ribot), was placed in the Epsom Oaks, Irish Oaks and Irish 1,000 gns, is a sister to the high class stayer Blood Royal and a half-sister to Mazaca - herself dam of 3 good winners in Gypsy Talk, Itsamaza and Trove.

625 - APOLLO VICTORIA
b.c. Sadler's Wells - Crystal Spray (Beldale Flutter).
June 1. Fifth living foal. 625,000Y. Tattersalls Houghton.
Half-brother to the promising 1997 1m placed 2-y-o Star Crystal (by Brief Truce), to the 1995 2-y-o Group 3 1m May Hill Stakes winner and Cheshire Oaks second Solar Crystal (by Alzao) and the Group 3 12f Lancashire Oaks winner and Yorkshire Oaks and Prix Vermeille placed State Crystal (by High Estate) - both very useful. The dam, a minor Irish 4-y-o 14f winner, is out of the unplaced - in one start

- Crystal Fountain (by Great Nephew), herself a half-sister to Royal Palace and Glass Slipper (dam of the classic winners Fairy Footsteps and Light Cavalry).

---

626 - ASPEN LEAVES (USA)
ch.f. Woodman - Fall Aspen (Pretense).

Sister to the Grade 1 Breeders Cup Juvenile and Grade 1 Champagne Stakes winner Timber Country and half-sister to numerous winners including the Grade 1 Gamely Handicap and Group 2 Prix d'Astarte winner Northern Aspen, the Group 1 July Cup winner Hamas, the Group 1 Grand Prix de Paris winner Fort Wood, the Prix d'Astarte winner Elle Seule (herself dam of the Irish 1,000 Guineas winner Mehthaaf), the Goodwood Cup winner Mazzacano and the Group 2 13.5f Prix de Pomone winner Colorado Dancer. The dam, Fall Aspen (by Pretense) - clearly one of the finest broodmares of recent times - won eight races notably the Grade 1 7f Matron Stakes.

---

627 - BAKER STREET
b.c. Dolphin Street - Joli's Girl (Mansingh).
April 9. 120,000Y. Tattersalls October.

Half-brother to the 3-y-o Imperial Prince, to the useful listed 8.5f Princess Elizabeth Stakes winner Joli's Princess (both by Prince Sabo) and the poor 13f and 14f winner Side Bar (by Mummy's Game). The dam, a quite useful 3-y-o 9f winner, stayed 12f and is a half-sister to 6 winners. The second dam, Jolimo (by Fortissimo), was a quite useful winner of 7 races from 12f to 18f.

---

628 - BLACK ROCK DESERT (USA)
b.c. Danzig - City Dance (Seattle Slew).
April 20. Third foal. $400,000. Keeneland July.

Half-brother to the Japanese stakes winner Toyo Seattle (by Deputy Minister). The dam won a stakes race in the USA and was second in the Grade 3 7f Comely Stakes. She is a sister to the dual Grade 1 winner Slew City Slew and a half-sister to the Grade 1 Ballerina Stakes third Dream Touch. The second dam, Weber City Miss (by Berkley Prince), won 17 races including the Grade 1 Beldame Stakes.

---

629 - BUGATTI REEF (USA)
b.c. Danzig - Watch Out (Mr Prospector).
May 9.

Half-brother to the US and Dubai winner Noraquilon (by Deputy Minister). The dam is a winning sister to the top-class mare Gold Beauty (Champion sprinter and the dam of Dayjur). The second dam, Stick To Beauty (by Illustrious), won the Busanda Stakes.

---

630 - CARAMBOLA
b.f. Danehill - Purchasepaperchase (Young Generation).
May 6. 330,000Y. Tattersalls Houghton.

Sister to the fair 1997 7f to 8.3f winner Purchasing Power and half-sister to the 7f (at 2 yrs) and smart Irish 1,000 Guineas winner Matiya (by Alzao), to the German winner of 3 races Sandanista (by Pharly), the Irish 1m winner Al Naayy (by Tate Gallery) and the fair 10f winner Never Explain (by Fairy King). The dam was a useful winner of three races including the listed 1m Atalanta Stakes and was second in the Group 1 Prix Saint-Alary. The second dam, Tin Goddess (by Petingo), was placed once at 3 yrs.

---

631 - COLISEUM
b.c. Sadler's Wells - Gravieres (Saint Estephe).
January 30. Second foal. IR260,000Y. Goffs Orby.

Half-brother to the 3-y-o Kananaskis (by Caerleon). The dam won 5 races in France and the USA including the Grade 1 9f Santa Ana Handicap and is a half-sister to 7 winners. The second dam, Gay Spring (by Free Round), won over 6f (at 2 yrs) and 6.5f in France and is a half-sister to the dam of the Group 2 Prix Noailles and Grade 2 Tidal Handicap winner Glaros.

---

632 - CUPID
ch.c. Generous - Idyllic (Foolish Pleasure).
April 13. 125,000Y. Tattersalls Houghton.

Closely related to Blue Paradise (by Caerleon), a minor winner in France and the USA and half-brother to the very smart colt Scenic, winner of the Group 1 7f Dewhurst Stakes (in a dead-heat) and fourth in the Champion Stakes, to the French winner and Group 1 Grand Prix de Paris second Ithaki, the minor French winners Well Away and Flabbergasted (all by Sadler's Wells), the Group 3 9f Prix Daphnis winner Silent Warrior (by Nashwan) and the minor French 2-y-o winner Belize Tropical (by Baillamont). The dam is an unraced half-sister to the Oaks second Slightly Dangerous (herself dam of Commander in Chief, Deploy, Dushyantor, Warning and Yashmak) and to I Will Follow (the dam of Rainbow Quest). The second dam, Where You Lead (by Raise a Native), won the Musidora Stakes and was second in the Oaks.

633 - GENGHIS KHAN (IRE) b.c. Sadler's Wells - Doff The Derby (Master Derby).
January 24.
Brother to the Irish 7f and 1m listed winner and 1,000 Guineas second Strawberry Roan and half-brother to the top-class colt Generous (by Caerleon), winner of the Derby, the Irish Derby, the King George VI and Queen Elizabeth Diamond Stakes and the Dewhurst Stakes, to the Irish Group 3 and US Grade 3 winner Wedding Bouquet (by Kings Lake), the US stakes winner Windy Triple K (by Jaklin Klugman) and the Japanese winners Osumi Tycoon (by Last Tycoon) and Matikanebenizakura (by Royal Academy). The dam is an unraced half-sister to the Prix Ganay winner Trillion (herself dam of the outstanding racemare Triptych). The second dam, Margarethen (by Tulyar), won 16 races in the USA at up to 9f including the Beverley Handicap (twice).

634 - HIGH KING b.c. Fairy King - Ploy (Posse).
February 21. Sixth foal. IR650,000Y. Goffs Orby.
Half-brother to the smart Group 1 1m Premio Parioli winner Poliuto (by Last Tycoon) and to the minor 7f to 2m winner Sir Norman Holt (by Ela-Mana-Mou). The dam, a fair 10f and 12f placed maiden, is a half-sister to the top class Oaks and St Leger winner Sun Princess (dam of the very smart colt Prince of Dance), the Group 1 Coronation Cup winner Saddlers Hall and the very useful 8f to 10f winning filly Dancing Shadow (dam of the French 1,000 Guineas third River Dancer). The second dam, Sunny Valley (by Val de Loir), won over 10.5f and 12f in France and is a half-sister to the dam of the high class miler Then Again.

635 - MOON DRAGON b.c. Sadler's Wells - Moonsilk (Solinus).
May 3. IR98,000Y. Goffs Orby.
Closely related to the 1995 Irish 2-y-o 1m winner Night Spell (by Fairy King) and to the minor 1m (at 2 yrs) and 10f winner Ilkomo (by Glenstal) and half-brother to the very smart 1994 Group 1 14.6f St Leger and Group 1 15.5f Prix Royal-Oak winner Moonax (by Caerleon), to the promising 1996 2-y-o 1m winner Moon River (by Mujtahid) and the dual Italian 3-y-o winner Wassilk (by Wassl). The dam was placed over 9f in France and is a half-sister to the 1,000 Guineas winner Nocturnal Spree and the Prix Saint-Alary winner Tootens (herself grandam of the useful 1994 2-y-o filly Jural). The second dam, Night Attire (by Shantung), was an unplaced sister to the smart middle-distance filly Setsu - herself dam of the Group 2 Premio Melton winner Tres Gate.

636 - PEACH OUT OF REACH b.f. Sadler's Wells - Cocotte (Troy).
May 7. 480,000Y. Tattersalls Houghton.
Sister to the 3-y-o Golden Dancer and to the useful 1997 3-y-o 10.3f winner Conon Falls and half-sister to the top-class colt Pilsudski (by Polish Precedent), winner of the Grade 1 12f Breeders Cup Turf, the Grade 1 12f Japan Cup, the Group 1 10f Grosser Preis von Baden, the Group 1 10f Coral-Eclipse Stakes etc., the fairly useful 7f and 1m winner Glowing Ardour (by Dancing Brave) and the modest 1m all-weather winner Red Cotton (by Soviet Star). The dam, a very useful 10.2f winner, was second in the Group 3 Prix de Psyche, fourth in the Group 2 10f Nassau Stakes and is a half-sister to the listed winner Gay Captain. The second dam, Gay Milly (by Mill Reef), was a fair 3-y-o 1m winner out of the Irish 1,000 Guineas winner Gaily.

637 - SAFFRON WALDEN b.c. Sadler's Wells - Or Vision (Irish River).
March 5. IR1,200,000Y. Goffs Orby.
Brother to the 1997 French 2-y-o Group 3 1m Prix des Reservoirs second Insight and half-brother to the very smart Group 1 7f Prix de la Foret, Group 2 6.5f Prix Maurice de Gheest and Group 3 6f Prix de Seine-et-Oise winner Dolphin Street, to the 1997 Irish 3-y-o 6f and 7f winner Grass Roots (both by Bluebird) and the minor French winners Tanalot (by Common Grounds) and Cult Classic (by Caerleon). The dam won over 5.5f and 7f at 2 yrs and the listed 7f Prix Imprudence at 3 yrs, and is a half-sister to the US stakes winners Dixie Fine and Nijinsky's Lover. The second dam, Luv Luvin' (by Raise a Native), won 2 races in the USA.

638 - STRAVINSKY b.c. Nureyev - Fire The Groom (Blushing Groom).
May 1. Second foal. $625,000. Keeneland July.
The dam, a smart winner of five races here at around 1m, subsequently won four times in the USA including the Grade 1 Beverly D Stakes and the Grade 2 Wilshire Handicap. She is a half-sister to the Group 1 6f Vernons Sprint Cup winner and useful sire Dowsing. The second dam, Prospector's Fire (by Mr Prospector), is a placed half-sister to the US stakes winners Royal And Regal (Grade 1 Florida Derby) and Regal And Royal.

639 - URBAN OCEAN ch.c. Bering - Urban Sea (Miswaki).
February 15. First foal. 230,00Y. Tattersalls Houghton.
The dam was a top-class filly and winner of 8 races from 1m (at 2 yrs) to 12f including the Group 1 Prix de l'Arc de Triomphe, the Group 2 Prix d'Harcourt, the Group 3 Prix Exbury and the Group 3 Prix Gontaut-Biron. She is a half-sister to 5 winners including the smart Allez Les Trois, winner of the Group 3 10.5f Prix de Flore. The second dam, Allegretta (by Lombard), a useful 2-y-o 1m and 9f winner and second in the Lingfield Oaks Trial, is a sister to the German St Leger winner Anno and a half-sister to the German Group 2 winner Anatas.

Charles O'Brien

640 - ALUMNA ch.c. College Chapel - Red Roman (Solinus).
April 27. IR38,000Y. Goffs Orby.
Half-brother to the Italian winner of 7 races Vasco-Rossi (by Salmon Leap) and to 2 winners in Scandinavia and Macau by Glenstal and Don't Forget Me. The dam, a quite useful 2-y-o 5f winner, is a half-sister to 4 minor winners here and abroad. The second dam, Danger Signal (by Red God), was a useful 2-y-o winner of 3 races over 5f and a half-sister to the 2,000 Guineas winner Roland Gardens.

641 - CANALETTO b.c. Royal Academy - Diavolina (Lear Fan).
February 4. Fifth foal. 225,000Y. Tattersalls October.
Half-brother to the useful Polish Spring (by Polish Precedent), a winner here and in the USA from 6f (at 2 yrs) to 8.5f including a listed event, to the 1997 French 3-y-o 10f winner Go Boldly (by Sadler's Wells) and the quite useful 1997 2-y-o 6f and 7f winner The Rich Man (by Last Tycoon). The dam, a French 10f winner at 3 yrs, is a half-sister to 7 winners including the French listed winner Droiture. The second dam, Diamond Spring (by Vaguely Noble), won once in France and is a half-sister to the dams of the US Grade 1 winners Another Review, No Review and Urbane.

642 - DONATUS (IRE) b.c. Royal Academy - La Dame Du Lac (Round Table).
April 28. IR85,000Y. Goffs Orby.
Brother to the useful 1997 listed 6f Silver Flash Stakes winner and Group 1 6f Prix Morny placed Heeremandi, closely related to to four winners by Nijinsky, namely the very useful Irish 2-y-o 6f to 7f winner Nazoo, the useful Irish 2-y-o 6f winner and French 1m winner Lake Como, the fairly useful Irish 2-y-o 6f to 1m winner Single Combat and the minor US winner La Confidence (herself dam of the multiple US Grade 1 winner Flawlessly). Also, half-brother to the useful 1993 3-y-o Chester 7f winner Lacotte (subsequently a triple US winner), the useful Irish 2-y-o 6f winner Miznah (both by Sadler's Wells) and the US five-time winner and Grade 2 second Magloire (by Exceller). The dam is an unraced half-sister to 9 winners including the Grade 1 winner and champion sire Halo, the top-class filly Tosmah, the stakes winners Maribeau and Father's Image and the minor winner Queen Sucree (herself dam of the Kentucky Derby winner Cannonade and grandam of two Grade 1 winners). The second dam, Cosmah (by Cosmic Bomb), won 9 races including the Astarita Stakes and is a half-sister to Natalma - the dam of Northern Dancer.

643 - FRANCHETTI b.c. Unfuwain - Lady Shipley (Shirley Heights).
February 11. Fifth foal. 62,000Y. Tattersalls October.
Half-brother to the unplaced 1997 2-y-o Shipley Glen (by Green Desert) and to the Spanish winner Alud (by Rousillon). The dam, a very useful 7f (at 2 yrs) and listed 10f Lupe Stakes winner, was placed in the Yorkshire Oaks, the Nassau Stakes and the Princess Royal Stakes. She is a half-sister to the listed winner Ellie Ardensky and to the unraced dam of the Solario Stakes winner Brave Act. The second dam, Circus Ring (by High Top), was unbeaten as a 2-y-o including in the Lowther Stakes and was the champion juvenile filly of 1981.

644 - HIGHWAY ONE ELEVEN (IRE) b.c. Polar Falcon - Finger Of Light (Green Desert).
April 22. First foal. 28,000Y. Tattersalls December.
The dam, a fairly useful 2-y-o 6f winner, stayed 7f and is a half-sister to 5 winners including the listed winners Lady Shipley and Ellie Ardensky and to the unraced dam of the Group 3 Solario Stakes and US Grade 3 winner Brave Act. The second dam, Circus Ring (by High Top), was a joint-champion 2-y-o filly and won 3 races at 2 yrs including the Group 2 Lowther Stakes.

645 - JEWEL IN THE CROWN (USA) b.f. Seeking The Gold - Christabelle (Northern Dancer).
March 7. $375,000. Keeneland July.
Half-sister to the 1995 Irish 3-y-o 12f winner Alisidora and to the fairly useful 1994 3-y-o 10f winner - stayed 14.8f - Caladesi (by Slip Anchor), the 2-y-o 6f winner Na-Ayim (by Shirley Heights) and the minor Belgian winner Christalaw (by Law Society). The dam was placed once at 2 yrs in Ireland and is a half-sister to the Group 3 Prix de Minerve winner I Will Follow (dam of Rainbow Quest), to the Group 3 Fred Darling Stakes winner Slightly Dangerous (dam of Commander in Chief, Warning, Deploy, Dushyantor and Yashmak) and to the unraced Idyllic (dam of Scenic). The second dam, Where You Lead (by Raise a Native), won the Group 3 Musidora Stakes and was second in the Epsom Oaks.

646 - PAGAN STREAMS br.c. Lion Cavern - Allegra (Niniski).
February 12. IR72,000Y. Goffs Orby.
Half-brother to the quite useful 1996 2-y-o 6f winner All Is Fair and the 1997 Italian 2-y-o winner Mia Robino (both by Selkirk). The dam, a fair 12f winner at 3 yrs, is a half-sister to 4 winners including the Nassau Stakes winner Last Second, the Irish Oaks third Arrikala and the Moyglare Stud Stakes third Alouette. The second dam, Alruccaba (by Crystal Palace), a quite useful 2-y-o 6f winner, is out of a half-sister to the dams of Aliysa and Nishapour.

647 - RIMBAUD ch.c. College Chapel - Soltura (Sadler's Wells).
May 2. Third foal. 38,000Y. Tattersalls Houghton.
Half-brother to the 3-y-o Alcadia and to the 1997 Irish 7f placed 3-y-o Zapata (both by Thatching). The dam is an unraced three-parts sister to the Grade 2 Del Mar Handicap winner Sword Dance and to the Irish winners and listed-placed Palais Rose and La Joyeuse (herself dam of the Group 3 Kilavullen Stakes winner Endless Joy). The second dam, Rosa Mundi (by Secretariat), won at 3 yrs and is a half-sister to 5 winners including the Group 1 National Stakes winner Fatherland.

648 - SAN ROCCO ch.c. Thatching - Oatfield (Great Nephew).
March 20. IR70,000Y. Goffs Orby.
Half-brother to the 1997 5f placed 2-y-o Alpen Wolf (by Wolfhound) and to 7 winners including the Group 3 11.5f Lingfield Derby Trial Stakes winner Munwar, the Irish 14f listed Curragh Cup, Bessborough Stakes and Old Newton Cup winner Hateel (both by Kalaglow) and Barley Bill (by Nicholas Bill), a winner of three races at around 1m at 3 yrs - all at least very useful. The dam was placed at 2 yrs and is a half-sister to 3 winners. The second dam, No Recall (by Tutankhamen), won at 2 yrs and is a half-sister to the Geoffrey Freer Stakes and Jockey Club Stakes winner High Line.

649 - WILD HEAVEN b.br.f. Darshaan - Mild Intrigue (Sir Ivor).
March 4. Sixth foal. IR36,000Y. Goffs Orby.
Closely related to the fairly useful 1997 3-y-o 13.4f to 2m winner High Intrigue (by Shirley Heights) and half-sister to the 1998 3-y-o Suaverof (by Suave Dancer) and the Italian winner of 5 races at up to 12f Mild Dancer (by Fairy King). The dam, a fairly useful 10f winner, is a half-sister to the useful listed 10f winner Grimesgill. The second dam, Mild Deception (by Buckpasser), won 3 races in the USA at up to 1m, is a half-sister to Arkadina (placed in 3 Irish classics), to the Queen's Vase and Jockey Club Cup winner Blood Royal, the Group 1 Joe McGrath Memorial Stakes winner Gregorian and the Grade 3 Test Stakes winner Ivory Wand (dam of the Group 1 winner Gold And Ivory).

650 - YOUNG AMERICAN (IRE) br.c. Hamas - Banana Peel (Green Dancer).
March 10. 40,000Y. Tattersalls December.
Half-brother to 7 winners including the French listed winner and Group 2 Prix de l'Opera second Balanka (by Alzao), the 1994 Irish 3-y-o 10f winner Bhavnagar (by Darshaan), the minor US winner Famous Fool (by Foolish Pleasure) and the 1991 Irish 3-y-o 14f winner Banour (by Arctic Tern). The dam, a winner of 2 races in the USA at 4 yrs, is a half-sister to 10 winners including the Group 3 Grand Prix de Vichy winner Bulington and the French listed winners Batman and Beaune (herself the dam of Bering). The second dam, Barbra (by Le Fabuleux), is a winning half-sister to 8 winners including Bourbon (Prix Royal-Oak).

John Oxx

651 - ANSAR b.c. Kahyasi - Anaza (Darshaan).
February 2. Fifth foal.
Half-brother to 4 winners including the very smart French Group 3 9.5f winner and French Derby third Astarabad (by Alleged) and the useful Irish winner, at up to 10f, Asmara (by Lear Fan). The dam won over 1m in France at 2 yrs. (H.H. Aga Khan). *"A bit backward perhaps, but I do think this a nice horse".*

652 - CANDARLI   ch.c. Polish Precedent - Calounia (Pharly).
February 17. Second foal.
The dam won over 10f at 3 yrs in Ireland and was third in the Ulster Derby. The second dam, Cadisa
(by Top Ville), was a fairly useful 11f winner. (H.H. Aga Khan). *"A very good-looking colt, Candarli will
improve with age and is a really nice horse".*

---

653 - COMPLEX   b.c. Nureyev - Colour Chart (Mr Prospector).
May 1. Fourth foal.
Brother to the 3-y-o Shade Dance and half-brother to the fairly useful 1996 2-y-o 6f winner Kumait and
the fair 1996 3-y-o 7f winner Chirico (both by Danzig). The dam was a very smart winner of the Group
2 9.2f Prix de l'Opera, Group 3 10f Prix de la Nonette and Group 3 1m Prix du Muguet and is a
half-sister to the very useful stayer Dance Spectrum. The second dam, Rainbow Connection (by Halo),
was a champion 2-y-o and 3-y-o filly in Canada and a half-sister to three other Canadian Grade 1
winners - Archdeacon, Hangin' on a Star and Mr Macho. (Sheikh Mohammed).

---

654 - DANSE CLASSIQUE   ch.f. Night Shift - Ballet Shoes (Ela Mana Mou).
IR61,000Y. Goffs Orby.
Half-sister to the 3-y-o Moonshadow (by Be My Guest). The dam, a fair 3-y-o dual 5f winner, is a
half-sister to the Irish 2,000 Guineas and Dubai Champion Stakes winner Spectrum and the useful
1996 3-y-o 1m winner Nash House. The second dam, River Dancer (by Irish River), was a smart
French winner over 5f (at 2 yrs) and the 1m Prix de la Calonne and was third in the French 1,000
Guineas. The third dam, Dancing Shadow (by Dancer's Image), a smart 1m to 10f winner, is a half-sister
to the top-class filly Sun Princess - herself dam of the high-class middle-distance colt Saddlers Hall.
(Mrs O'Reilly). *"A backward filly, but nice, she'll be an autumn type two-year-old".*

---

655 - EDABIYA   ch.f. Rainbow Quest - Ebaziya (Darshaan).
April 8.
Half-sister to the high-class 1997 3-y-o filly Ebadiyla (by Sadler's Wells), winner of the Irish Oaks and
the Prix Royal-Oak and to the 1998 3-y-o Enzeli (by Kahyasi). The dam won three listed races and
was third in the Group 2 12f Blandford Stakes. The second dam, Ezana (by Ela Mana Mou), won over
an exended 11f in France and is a half-sister to the French dual Group 3 winner Demia. (H.H. Aga
Khan). *"She'll take a bit of time, but she's a nice filly and should be out at the back-end of the season".*

---

656 - ELAINE   b.f. Common Grounds - Klarifi (Habitat).
May 17.
Half-sister to the 1997 Irish 7f placed 2-y-o Woodwin (by Woodman), to the very useful 7f and 1m
winner Tregaron (by Lyphard), the Irish middle-distance winner Ezy Koter (by Lomond), the quite useful
2-y-o 7f winner Kashteh (by Green Desert) and the dual hurdles winner Andermatt (by Top Ville). The
dam was a fairly useful winner of the 7f Ballycorus Stakes at 3 yrs and is a half-sister to the smart Irish
miler Captivator and the very useful 12f winners Eileen Jenny, Kasmayo and Bahamian - the latter also
dam of the Irish Oaks winner Wemyss Bight. The second dam, Sorbus (by Busted), was disqualified
after winning the Irish Oaks and was second in the Irish 1,000 Guineas, the Irish St Leger and the
Yorkshire Oaks. (G W Jennings). *"This is a nice filly, she might make a two-year-old and is fairly sharp".*

---

657 - KASOTA   b.f. Alzao - Kashka (The Minstrel).
April 10.
Half-sister to 6 winners including the smart filly Key Change, a winner of 4 races including the Group
1 12f Yorkshire Oaks, the minor Irish 10f winner Kazkar, the Irish middle-distance stayer Kakashda (all
by Darshaan) and the minor 3-y-o winners Sharkashka (by Shardari) and Quiet Counsel (by Law
Society). The dam, a winner over 12f at 3 yrs in France, is a half-sister to the Italian Group 3 winner
Karkisiya and to the dam of Kahyasi. The second dam, Kalkeen (by Sheshoon), was a very useful
winner of the listed 10f Prix de la Seine. (Lady Clague). *"Not very precocious, but she'll be a nice filly
in the second half of the year. She's medium-sized, very correct, strong and well-made".*

---

658 - LARBOREUS   b.c. Darshaan - Lypharita (Lightning).
January 25.
Half-brother to the French trained 3-y-o Balizac (by Arazi), to the quite useful 1991 3-y-o 7.6f and 1m
winner Swordstick (by Sure Blade) and the useful 1996 3-y-o 1m winner Polinesso (by Polish
Precedent). The dam was a high-class winner of the Group 1 10.5f Prix de Diane and was placed in
the Prix Vermeille and Prix Cleopatre. The second dam, Gracefully (by Lyphard), a minor 10f winner

in France, is a sister to the Prix Fille de l'Air third Model Girl (herself dam of the very useful 1m winners Arousal and In Focus) and a half-sister to the Group 3 Lingfield Oaks Trial second Grace Note (dam of the top-class middle-distance colt Belmez). (Sheikh Mohammed). *"A big, backward horse" John was telling me "but he's really nice and will be a late season two-year-old".*

---

659 - MANGWANA (USA)

b.f. Dehere - Yanuka (Pitcairn).
March 16. IR58,000Y. Goffs Orby.

Half-sister to the smart Group 2 6f Richmond Stakes, Group 3 6f Coventry Stakes and Group 3 7f Prix de Porte Maillot winner Dilum (by Tasso) and to the minor US sprint winner By Consensus (by Lydian). The dam, a very useful 2-y-o dual 6f winner, was third in the 1,000 Guineas and the Coronation Stakes and is a half-sister to the dam of the Italian Derby winner Welnor. The second dam, Strong Light (by Fortino II), was a useful winner of 4 races over 1m. (Mrs F G Wilson). *"A tallish, lengthy filly, she's bred for speed and I hope we'll see her over six furlongs in the summer. She has a bit of a stride to her".*

---

660 - MASSEY

b.br.c. Machiavellian - Massaraat (Nureyev).
March 14. Fourth foal.

Closely related to the French trained 3-y-o Massillon (by Mr Prospector). The dam, a French 3-y-o 7f listed winner, is a sister to the great filly Miesque, a winner of ten Group/Grade 1 races including the Breeders Cup Mile (twice), the 1,000 Guineas, the Prix Jacques le Marois (twice) and the Prix du Moulin - herself dam of the Group 1 winners Kingmambo and East of the Moon. The second dam, Pasadoble (by Prove It), won four races in France over 1m including two stakes events and is a half-sister to the Grade 1 Brooklyn Handicap winner Silver Supreme. (Sheikh Mohammed). *"Not a beauty, but she goes well and isn't a bad sort of filly. She's fairly big and needs to furnish".*

---

661 - PAMPITA (USA)

ch.f. Affirmed - Style N' Elegance (Alysheba).
January 29. First foal. IR34,000Y. Goffs Orby.

The dam was placed at 2 yrs in the USA and is a half-sister to 11 winners including the Irish 1,000 Guineas winner Trusted Partner and the Group 2 Premio Legnano winner Easy To Copy. The second dam, Talking Picture (by Speak John), won 6 races in the USA at up to 7f including the Grade 1 Spinaway Stakes and the Grade 1 Matron Stakes. (Mrs F G Wilson). *"A nice filly, Pampita should make a two-year-old in the second half of the year. A good sort and a good mover" the trainer informs me.*

---

662 - PAZIENZA (IRE)

b.f. Arazi - Park Appeal (Ahonoora).
April 29.

Half-sister to the 3-y-o Sherwood (by Thatching), to the very smart miler Cape Cross (by Green Desert) - disqualified after winning the Group 2 Tripleprint Celebration Mile, the useful 1990 2-y-o 7f winner Pastorale (by Nureyev), the fair 3-y-o 8.2f winner Arvola and the 12.5f listed stakes placed Lord of Appeal (both by Sadlers Wells). The dam, a high-class 2-y-o filly in 1984, won four 6f races including the Group 1 Cheveley Park Stakes and the Group 1 Moyglare Stud Stakes. She is a sister to the Group 3 9f Ballymacoy Stakes winner Nashamaa and a half-sister to the Irish Oaks and Ribblesdale Stakes winner Alydaress, the Cheveley Park Stakes winner Desirable - herself dam of the 1,000 Guineas winner Shadayid - and to the dam of the dual Group 3 winner Bin Ajwaad. The second dam, Balidaress (by Balidar), won three races from 7f to 10f in Ireland. (Sheikh Mohammed). *"A bit light, she's not a strong filly but is a very good mover. She's one for the late summer".*

---

663 - REMURIA (USA)

b.f. Theatrical - Reloy (Liloy).
May 22.

Closely related to the useful 1994 2-y-o 5f and listed 6f Firth of Clyde Stakes winner Loyalize (by Nureyev) and to the useful 1996 2-y-o 6f winner Reliquary (by Zilzal) and half-sister to the Irish-trained 3-y-o Loyal Deed (by Alleged), to the minor American winner Periscopic (by Secreto) and the fair 6f to 8.2f placed maiden Dimakya (by Dayjur). The dam was a smart winner of the Group 3 10.5f Prix de Royaumont, was second in the Group 1 12f Prix Vermeille and went on to win two Grade 1 events in the USA. She is a half-sister to the very useful French performers En Calcat and Roi Guillaume and to the smart French 1m winner Reine Imperiale. The second dam, the top-class filly Rescousse (by Emerson), won the Prix de Diane and was second in the Prix de l'Arc de Triomphe behind San San. (Sheikh Mohammed). *"Remuria is a very nice filly. She arrived at the yard quite late and is backward. A nice three-year-old prospect".*

664 - RIVANA b.f. Green Desert - My Potters (Irish River).
March 7. Fourth foal.
Half-sister to the 1997 Irish 2-y-o 7f winner Winona (by Alzao), to the minor 1995 Irish 2-y-o 1m winner Western Seas (by Caerleon) and to Carlisle Bay (by Darshaan), a winner over 6f in Ireland at 2 yrs in 1996 and third in the Group 3 7f Bord Gais Killavullan Stakes. The dam, an Irish 3-y-o 1m handicap winner, is a half-sister to numerous winners including the champion US sprinter My Juliet, the good middle-distance colt Lyphard's Special and the 2-y-o 6f Blue Seal Stakes winner New Trends. The second dam, My Bupers (by Bupers), was placed at 3 yrs. (Lady Clague). *"Although she's bred to be a two-year-old, she's had a slight setback and is smallish. A nice, sharp filly for the summer"*.

665 - ROYAL PARTNERSHIP b.c. Royal Academy - Go Honey Go (General Assembly).
May 8. Fifth foal. IR40,000Y. Goffs Orby.
Closely related to the 1997 dual 3-y-o 12f winner Western Chief (by Caerleon) and half-brother to the Japanese winner Gaily Flash (by Danehill) and Sweet Supposin (by Posen), a quite useful all-weather performer and winner of 13 races at up to 12f. The dam, a winner of 5 races in France and the USA including the Grade 3 8.5f Suwannee River Handicap, is a half-sister to the Irish listed winners The Caretaker and Feathers Lad. The second dam, Go Feather Go (by Go Marching), won over 5f at 2 yrs in Ireland. (Mr & Mrs R Schroff). *"A light-framed, backward horse, he's not a bad sort and a good mover. Another autumn type two-year-old"*.

666 - SAXON PRINCE (IRE) b.c. Darshaan - Sorbus (Busted).
April 19. IR52,000Y. Goffs Orby.
Closely related to the very useful listed 12f winner Kasmayo (by Slip Anchor) and half-brother to the Irish trained 3-y-o Beldarian (by Last Tycoon), the very useful Irish and Italian 12f winner and Irish Oaks third Eileen Jenny (by Kris), the very useful Lingfield Oaks Trial winner Bahamian (by Mill Reef and herself dam of the smart filly Wemyss Bight), the good Irish miler Captivator (by Artaius), the useful Irish 7f winner Klarifi and the useful middle-distance stayer West China (by Habitat). The dam was disqualified after winning the Irish Oaks and was second in the Irish 1,000 Guineas, the Irish St Leger and the Yorkshire Oaks. The second dam, Censorship (by Prince John), won over 1m in the USA and is a half-sister to the Santa Anita Derby winner Four-and-Twenty. (Sheikh Mohammed). *"A backward horse, he's small and not a two-year-old type. A good mover though"*.

667 - STRATEGIC b.c. Caerleon - Game Plan (Darshaan).
April 6. Fifth foal.
Half-brother to the modest 1997 7f placed 2-y-o Night Vigil (by Night Shift), to the fairly useful Irish 10f and 12f winner Power Play (by Nashwan). The dam was a smart winner of the Group 2 10f Pretty Polly Stakes at the Curragh, was second in the Epsom Oaks to Salsabil and is a half-sister to four minor winners. The second dam, Formulate (by Reform), was a very smart 2-y-o winner of the Hoover Fillies Mile and the Waterford Candelabra Stakes and was second in the 10f Lupe Stakes at 3 yrs. (Sheikh Mohammed). *"Strategic is quite a nice horse and a good mover. He'll be running in the second half of the season, is medium-sized, clean limbed and quite well forward"*.

668 - SUPERIORITY (USA) ch.c. Arazi - Outstandingly (Exclusive Native).
February 22.
Half-brother to the smart Group 2 1m Falmouth Stakes and Group 3 1m Prix de Sandringham winner Sensation (by Soviet Star), to the quite useful 1992 dual 10f 3-y-o winner Avice Caro (by Caro) and the US winner and Grade 2 8.5f placed Outlasting (by Seattle Slew). The dam was the champion American 2-y-o filly of 1984 and won the Grade 1 Breeders Cup Juvenile Fillies Stakes and the Grade 1 8.5f Hollywood Starlet Stakes. She is closely related to the Grade 3 9f Miss Grillo Stakes winner Loveliest (by Affirmed) and a half-sister to the fair 3-y-o 11f winner Wace. The second dam, La Mesa (by Round Table), a minor winner at 4 yrs in the USA, is out of a half-sister to the Horse of the Year Buckpasser. (Sheikh Mohammed). *"An autumn type two-year-old, he's quite reasonable and I'm happy enough with him"* says John.

669 - TANNHAUSER (IRE) b.c. Sadler's Wells - Tarsila (High Top).
February 26.
Half-brother to the smart Group 2 10.5f Dante Stakes winner Torjoun, to the very useful Group 2 10f Pretty Polly Stakes winner Takarouna (both by Green Dancer), the quite useful 2 m Northumberland Plate winner Tamarpour (by Sir Ivor) and the hurdles winner Torkabar (by Vaguely Noble). The dam, a winner over 1m and 9f, is a sister to Top Ville. The second dam, Sega Ville (by Charlottown), won the

Group 3 10.5f Prix de Flore and is out of the French 1,000 Guineas winner La Sega. (Sheikh Mohammed). *"A nice sort of horse but very much a three-year-old type".*

670 - TWIZZLE (IRE)
ch.f. Arazi - Twyla (Habitat).
March 23.
Closely related to the Irish trained 3-y-o Twilight Tango and to the very useful 7f and 1m (at 2 yrs) and Group 3 12.3f Dalham Chester Vase winner Twist and Turn and half-sister to the fair 13f winner High Pyrenees (by Shirley Heights). The dam, a useful dual 6f winner, is a sister to the smart 1983 2-y-o sprinter Defecting Dancer. The second dam, Running Ballerina (by Nijinsky), won over 6f at 2 yrs and is a half-sister to the dam of Persian Bold and to a number of good winners including Dominion Day, Northern Tavern, Padroug and Sir Penfro. (Sheikh Mohammed). *"Twizzle is a nice filly. She's fairly sharp and should make a two-year-old by June".*

671 - WINDWARD ROCK (USA)
ch.c. Woodman - Windmill Point (Storm Bird).
April 3. Third foal. $150,000. Keeneland September.
Half-brother to the 1997 US 3-y-o winner Stormy Temper (by Conquistador Cielo). The dam is an unplaced sister to the Cherry Hinton Stakes winner Storm Star (herself the dam of a US Grade 3 winner) and a half-sister to 5 winners including the dam of the Grade 1 Breeders Cup Juvenile Fillies winner Flanders. The second dam, Cinegita (by Secretariat), won the Grade 3 7f Railbird Stakes in the USA. (Sheikh Mohammed). *"A nice horse that might well be running by June over six furlongs".*

Jonathan Pease

672 - CONGO
b.c. Kris - Land Of Ivory (The Minstrel).
March 14.
Closely related to the French trained 3-y-o Ashkirk (by Selkirk) and half-brother to the useful 1990 2-y-o Group 1 7f National Stakes and 4-y-o 7f and 1m winner Heart of Darkness (by Glint of Gold) and to the quite useful 1995 3-y-o triple 10f winner Silently (by Slip Anchor). The dam, a very useful filly, won over 7f at 2 yrs, 1m at 3 yrs, was disqualified after winning the 8.5f Princess Elizabeth Stakes and was placed in the Prix Cleopatre and Lupe Stakes. She is a half-sister to the high-class middle-distance colt Gold and Ivory. The second dam, Ivory Wand (by Sir Ivor), was a smart winner of up to 1m and is a half-sister to Arkadina (placed in three classics and dam of the Irish St Leger winner Dark Lomond), the Queen's Vase and Jockey Club Cup winner Blood Royal, the top-class US filly Truly Bound and the high-class middle-distance colt Gregorian. (George Strawbridge).

673 - GOOD JOURNEY (USA)
ch.c. Nureyev - Chimes Of Freedom (Private Account).
April 27. Fourth foal.
The dam, a smart filly, won the Group 1 6f Moyglare Stud Stakes and the Group 3 6f Cherry Hinton Stakes at 2 yrs, prior to winning the Group 1 1m Coronation Stakes and the Group 2 1m Child Stakes in her second season. She is a half-sister to the very useful 2-y-o 6f listed Firth of Clyde Stakes winner and Cheveley Park Stakes second Imperfect Circle (herself dam of the top-class miler Spinning World) and to the useful 3-y-o 10.3f winner Binkhaldoun. The second dam, Aviance (by Northfields), was a very useful winner of the Group 1 6f Heinz 57 Phoenix Stakes and is out of the 7f and 1m winner Minnie Hauk, herself a sister to the smart winners Gielgud, Malinowski and Monroe and a half-sister to the US Grade 1 Kentucky Oaks winner Blush With Pride and the top-class broodmare Sex Appeal - dam of El Gran Senor and Try My Best. (The Niarchos Family).

674 - MOJAVE MOON (USA)
ch.c. Mr Prospector - East Of The Moon (Private Account).
April 25. First foal.
The dam was a high-class filly and winner of the French 1,000 Guineas, the Prix de Diane and the Prix Jacques le Marois. She is a half-sister to the top-class miler Kingmambo and the smart Group 3 6f Prix de Ris-Orangis winner Miesque's Son. The second dam, Miesque (by Nureyev), was a great filly and possibly the best miler of the Eighties. She won ten Group or Grade 1 events including the Breeders Cup Mile (twice), the Prix Jacques le Marois (twice), the 1,000 Guineas, the French 1,000 Guieas and the Prix du Moulin. (The Niarchos Family).

675 - MOONLIGHT'S BOX (USA)
b.f. Nureyev - Coup de Genie (Mr Prospector).
February 2. First foal.
The dam was a smart winner of the Group 1 6f Prix Morny and the Group 1 7f Prix de la Salamandre and was third in the 1,000 Guineas. She is a sister to the Champion 2-y-o Machiavellian and a half-sister

to the high-class miler Exit To Nowhere and the smart miler Hydro Calido. The second dam, Coup de Folie (by Halo), won the Group 3 1m Prix d'Aumale at 2 yrs and is out of an unraced half-sister to Northern Dancer. (The Niarchos Family).

676 - RANGOON RUBY (USA)   b.f. Kingmambo - Imperfect Circle (Riverman).
April 28. Third foal.
Half-sister to the French trained 3-y-o Ring Of Fire and to the top-class miler Spinning World (both by Nureyev), winner of the Breeders Cup Mile, the Irish 2,000 Guineas, the Prix du Moulin and the Prix Jacques le Marois (twice). The dam was a very useful 2-y-o winner of the listed 6f Firth of Clyde Stakes, was second in the Cheveley Park Stakes and subsequently won over 7f at 3 yrs. She is a half-sister to the very smart filly Chimes of Freedom, winner of the Coronation Stakes, the Moyglare Stud Stakes and the Child Stakes and to the useful 10.3f winner Binkhaldoun. The second dam, Aviance (by Northfields), won the 6f Heinz "57" Phoenix Stakes at 2 yrs and is out of the 7f and 1m winner Minnie Hauk (by Sir Ivor), herself a sister to Malinowski, Gielgud and Monroe (all at least smart) and a half-sister to the dual US Grade 1 winner Blush With Pride and the top-class broodmare Sex Appeal (dam of Try My Best and El Gran Senor). (The Niarchos Family).

Kevin Prendergast

677 - DARIOLE (IRE)   b.c. Priolo - Dance Land (Nordance).
March 5. Second foal. IR48,000Y. Goffs Orby.
The dam is an unraced sister to the Italian listed 10f winner Lifting and a half-sister to the listed Kingsclere Stakes winner and Queen Mary Stakes third Easy Landing and to the dam of the Zetland Stakes winner Upper Strata (herself dam of the Prix de la Salamandre winner Lord Of Men). The second dam, Land Ho (by Primera), is an unraced half-sister to the Group 3 Oaks Trial winner Lucent and to the grandam of Sonic Lady. (Mrs O'Reilly). *"A good-sized, good-looking horse, Dariole will be a nice two-year-old from mid-summer onwards and from six to seven furlongs"*. Kevin also has two of his young horses in the Early Types section.

678 - FANUS   b.c. Cadeaux Genereux - Sawlah (Known Fact).
February 4. Sixth living foal.
The dam, an Irish 2-y-o 5f winner, is a half-sister to the top-class sprinter Sheikh Albadou, winner of the Breeders Cup Sprint. The second dam, Sanctuary (by Welsh Pageant), is an unraced half-sister to Little Wolf and Smuggler. *"This fellow is a strong colt and really looks like a two-year-old type. One to follow, I think"* says his trainer.

679 - MUDAA-EB   br.c. Machiavellian - Alkaffeyah (Sadler's Wells).
March 3. Third foal.
Half-brother to the quite useful 1996 2-y-o 6f winner Kharir (by Machiavellian). The dam is an unraced sister to the 1995 3-y-o listed 11.9f Galtres Stakes winner and Group 1 Prix Vermeille third Larrocha and a half-sister to the outstanding middle-distance stayer Ardross and the Pretty Polly Stakes winner Gesedeh. The second dam, Le Melody (by Levmoss), won both her starts, over 7f and 10f, and is a half-sister to the Irish 1,000 Guineas winner Arctique Royale (herself dam of the Group winners Modhish and Russian Snows), to the Irish Oaks third Racquette (dam of the smart French colts Grand Chelem and Splendid Moment) and to the dam of the Queen Anne Stakes winner Alflora. (Hamdan Al Maktoum). *"A backward horse, he'll probably have just the one run at the back-end"*.

680 - SARRAAF (IRE)   ch.c. Perugino - Blue Vista (Pennine Walk).
February 12. 64,000Y. Tattersalls October.
Half-brother to the modest 1996 2-y-o 7f winner Smugers (by Masterclass). The dam is an unraced half-sister to 6 winners including the smart sprinter Polykratis. The second dam, Blue Persian (by Majority Blue), won 3 races including the listed 5f St Hugh's Stakes at 2 yrs and is a half-sister to the Group 3 Henry II Stakes winner Saronicos. (Hamdan Al Maktoum).

681 - TARFAA (IRE)   b.c. Night Shift - Robinia (Roberto).
April 5. Fourth foal. IR155,000Y. Goffs Orby.
Half-brother to the 12.3f Ulster Harp Derby winner and Group 3 Royal Whip Stakes second I'm Supposin (by Posen) and the fairly useful 7f and 1m winner Paonic (by Exactly Sharp). The dam, a fairly useful 2-y-o 7f winner, is a half-sister to 5 winners here and in the USA. The second dam, Royal Graustark (by Graustark), won 7 races at up to 7f in the USA and is a half-sister to the Grade 2 Lexington Stakes

winner Royal Roberto. (Hamdan Al Maktoum). *"A big horse and a really nice type, I can see him running by the mid-summer over six furlongs".*

Sir Mark Prescott

682 - BAHRAIN (IRE)
ch.c. Lahib - Twin Island (Standaan).
March 17. Fourth foal. 75,000Y. Tattersalls Houghton.
Half-brother to the smart Tagula (by Taufan), winner of the Group 1 6f Prix Morny, the Group 3 6f July Stakes and the Group 3 7f Supreme Stakes and third in the French 2,000 Guineas. The dam ran once unplaced and is a half-sister to the Group 3 C.L. Weld Park Stakes winner Jolly Saint (herself dam of the Breeders Cup Mile winner Da Hoss). The second dam, Jolly Widow (by Busted), was unraced. (Prince Fahd Salman). Sir Mark has three other two-year-olds in the Early Types section.

683 - BEMUSE
b.f. Forzando - Barsham (Be My Guest).
February 7. 36,000Y. Tattersalls October.
Half-sister to the very useful 1996 2-y-o listed 1m winner Falkenham (by Polar Falcon), to the fairly useful 10f and 10.3f winner Jameel Asmar (by Rock City), the quite useful dual 1m winner Redisham (by Persian Bold) and the modest 15.4f winner Guestwick (by Blakeney). The dam, a fairly useful 10f winner, is a half-sister to 6 minor winners out of the 3-y-o 12f and 13.3f winner Bodham (by Bustino) - herself a daughter of a half-sister to Blakeney and Morston.

684 - CARABINE (USA)
gr.f. Dehere - Carraciola (Zeddaan).
March 19.
Half-sister to the 1991 2,000 Guineas, Group 2 7f Challenge Stakes and listed 7f European Free Handicap winner Mystiko, to the minor 3-y-o winner Secret Sunday (both by Secreto), the French 8.5f winner Mer Belle (by Far North) and minor winners in the USA by Topsider and Far North. The dam was placed in France at around 1m and is a half-sister to the Prix de Mallerett winner Calderina and the Prix de la Rochette winner Pasakos. The second dam, Cendres Bleues (by Charlottesville), was a smart middle-distance filly in Italy and a half-sister to the high-class Italian colts Claude and Crivelli. (Miss K Rausing).

685 - COVER GIRL (IRE)
ch.f. Common Grounds - Peace Carrier (Doulab).
April 14. Third foal. 20,000Y. Tattersalls October.
Half-sister to the 3-y-o Peace Paradise (by Pips Pride) and the modest 7f all-weather winner Hever Golf Charger (by Silver Kite). The dam was placed over 12f in Ireland and is a half-sister to the useful Irish sprinter Sandhurst Goddess (dam of the Molecomb Stakes and Anglesey Stakes winner Lady Alexander). The second dam, Paradise Bird (by Sallust), won twice at 2 yrs. (The Speculators). *"Quite an attractive filly, she should be a nice type in the mid-summer, probably starting over six furlongs".*

686 - DREAMING
b.f. Polar Falcon - Dream Baby (Master Willie).
January 26. Second foal. 33,000Y. Tattersalls October.
Sister to the fair 1997 2-y-o 7f winner Only In Dreams. The dam, unplaced in her only start, is a half-sister to 9 winners including the dual Italian Group 3 1m winner Rosa de Caerleon. The second dam, Carose (by Caro), was placed four times in France and is a half-sister to 7 winners including Noir Et Or (Grand Prix d'Evry, Prix du Conseil du Paris etc.,) and Apple Tree (four Group 1 wins including the Coronation Cup and the Turf Classic). (Cheveley Park Stud). *"Quite a tall and leggy filly, she won't be out until June".*

687 - EYEBALLS OUT
b.c. Polar Falcon - Jacquelina (Private Account).
February 3. First foal. 23,000Y. Tattersalls October.
The dam, a modest 8.1f placed 3-y-o, is a half-sister to the very useful 6f winner Zarani Sidi Anna. The second dam, Emmaline (by Affirmed), won twice at up to 9f in the USA, including a stakes event and is a half-sister to the Grade 1 winners Bates Motel and Hatim. (John Brown & Megan Dennis).

688 - INDIAN BAZAAR (IRE)
ch.c. Indian Ridge - Bazaar Promise (Native Bazaar).
February 26. Fifth foal. IR130,000Y. Goffs Orby.
Brother to the useful 1995 3-y-o Cheyenne Spirit, winner of 7 races including a listed event over 6f, to the fair 1995 2-y-o 6f winner Charwelton and the modest 1994 3-y-o 8.5f and 10f winner Indian Express. The dam is an unplaced sister to the very useful sprinter Crofthall. The second dam, Woodland Promise (by Philemon), is an unplaced half-sister to 6 winners. (Eclipse Thoroughbreds). *"Indian Bazaar is a decent horse but a backward type that won't run until the autumn".*

126

689 - MOLYNEUX b.c. Marju - Mahasin (Danzig).
February 12. Third foal. IR65,000Y. Goffs Orby.
Half-brother to the quite useful 1997 3-y-o 7f winner Musharak (by Mujtahid) and to the promising 1997 1m placed 2-y-o Elhayq (by Nashwan). The dam, a fairly useful 3-y-o 7f and 1m winner, is closely related to the Group 1 1m Wm Hill Futurity winner Al Hareb and the 10f La Coupe de Maisons-Laffitte winner Dr Somerville and a half-sister to 5 winners including the useful Irish horses Cerussite, Meringue, Rising and Snowtop. The second dam, Icing (by Prince Tenderfoot), was a very useful 2-y-o winner from 5f to 1m including the Argos Star Fillies Mile. (Mr A Speelman). *"A big, strong horse, Molyneux will be running from mid-season onwards and although he may be a two-year-old, he'll probably be better next year".*

---

690 - MOON SHOT gr.c. Pistolet Bleu - La Luna (Lyphard).
March 11. Sixth foal. 120,000Y. Tattersalls October.
Half-brother to the very useful 1996 2-y-o 7f winner and Group 3 Musidora Stakes third Etoile (by Kris) and to winners in France and Germany by Reference Point, Kaldoun and Slip Anchor. The dam, a winner over 9f at 3 yrs in France, is a sister to the Group 3 Prix Daphnis winner and smart sire Bellypha and a half-sister to the Prix Eugene Adam winner Bellman and the Peruvian Grade 1 winner Run And Deliver. The second dam, Belga (by Le Fabuleux), won over 9f in France. (Eclipse Thoroughbreds). *"A very good-looking colt, he's quite backward and will take time. A middle-distance horse next year".*

---

691 - SOVEREIGN ABBEY (IRE) b.f. Royal Academy - Elabella (Ela Mana Mou).
March 16. Fifth foal. 50,000Y. Tattersalls Houghton.
Half-sister to the 1997 6f placed 2-y-o Golden Reprimand (by Reprimand), to the useful sprinter Espartero (by Ballad Rock), a winner of three races here and in the USA and the 1994 3-y-o 12f seller winner Typographer (by Never So Bold). The dam is an unraced half-sister to 4 minor winners. The second dam, Annabella (by Habitat), won once at 2 yrs and is a half-sister to the Mecca-Dante Stakes winner and Irish Derby second Lucky Sovereign and the listed winner Flashy (herself dam of the Italian Group 2 winner Feu De Guerre). The third dam, Sovereign (by Pardao), was the champion 2-y-o filly of 1967 and won 5 races including the Coronation Stakes. (Mr G S Shropshire). *"A tall, leggy filly, she'll want seven furlongs this autumn".*

---

692 - SWAGGER ch.c. Generous - Widows Walk (Habitat).
January 28. 52,000Y. Tattersalls Houghton.
Half-brother to the 3-y-o Green For Go (by Green Desert), to the fairly useful 10f and 12f all-weather winner Rainbow Walk (by Rainbow Quest) and the quite useful dual 10f winner Sadler's Walk (by Sadler's Wells). The dam ran once unplaced and is a half-sister to 6 winners including Art Of War, winner of the listed Sirenia Stakes. The second dam, On The House (by Be My Guest), won the 1,000 Guineas and the Sussex Stakes. (Mr G Moore).

---

693 - THE BALTIC ch.c. Emarati - Harold's Girl (Northfields).
April 29. 20,000Y. Tattersalls October.
Half-brother to the useful 1997 3-y-o listed 1m winner Jafn (by Sharpo), to the useful 6f to 10f (including German Group 3 event) winner Tout Est Permis (by Pyjama Hunt), the French 2-y-o winners Childe Harold (by Mummy's Pet) and River Maiden (by Riverman) and another winner in France by Ti King. The dam, a French 2-y-o 6f winner, is a half-sister to 3 winners including the listed 1m winner Mirbeau. The second dam, Naughty Marcia (by Connaught), won twice in France and was third in the Group 3 Prix de Minerve. (Lord Swaythling). *"A very big horse that needs plenty of time, he won't be out until late summer".*

---

694 - TREASURY ch.f. Generous - Atlantic Flyer (Storm Bird).
March 27. Third foal. 135,000Y. Tattersalls Houghton.
Sister to the fairly useful 1996 3-y-o 7.9f winner Van Gurp. The dam, a useful 2-y-o 6f winner, is a half-sister to 6 winners here and abroad. The second dam, Euphrosyne (by Judger), won 10 races at up to 13f including the Grade 2 Long Island Handicap and the Grade 3 Knickerbocker Handicap and is a half-sister to 5 winners. (Cheveley Park Stud).

---

695 - WHITE TRUFFLE (USA) ch.f. Dehere - Familiar (Diesis).
February 24. Fifth foal. IR135,000Y. Goffs Orby.
Half-sister to the minor US 2-y-o winner Familiar Trick (by Clever Trick). The dam, a fairly useful 3-y-o 1m winner, is a half-sister to the high-class Prix du Moulin winner and Epsom Oaks second All At Sea,

to the smart French dual Group 3 winner Over The Ocean, the US stakes winner Full Virtue and the listed 10f winner Quandary. The second dam, Lost Virtue (by Cloudy Dawn), is an unraced half-sister to the US Grade 2 winner Anti-Lib and to the dam of the US 2-y-o Grade 2 winner Tiffany Ice. (Faisal Salman).

Lynda Ramsden

696 - SILVER GYRE (IRE)   b.f. Silver Hawk - Kraemer (Lyphard).
April 7. 45,000Y. Tattersalls Houghton.
Half-sister to the minor 1992 French 3-y-o winner Glenarff (by Irish River) and to the modest 1995 3-y-o 17.2f winner Kriva (by Reference Point). The dam won 4 races in France and the USA including the listed 8.5f Bay Meadows Oaks and is a half-sister to the high-class Prix du Rond-Point and Prix d'Astarte winner Shaanxi. The second dam, Rich And Riotous (by Empery), won once over 1m in France and is a daughter of the Italian Oaks winner Carnauba. (Mrs Joan L. Egan). *Jack and Lynda have several more two-year-olds among the 'Early Types'. Silver Gyre is "a nice filly with a touch of class about her. She should be out by July, probably over six furlongs".*

697 - AFRICAN VISION   b.c. Mtoto - Sibley (Northfields).
April 26. 23,000Y. Tattersalls October.
Half-brother to the 3-y-o Merry Mary (by Magic Ring), to the Spanish Group 3 12f and French listed winner King Cobra (by Ardross) and the very useful 1m winner and Group 2 10f Prix Eugene Adam second Acharne (by Pharly). The dam won over 10f in France and is out of the Lingfield Oaks Trial winner and Oaks third Suni (by Crepello). (Mr M J Simmonds). *"A backward colt that will need a trip, he won't see a racecourse before mid-summer".* Most of Lynda's two-year-olds are in the Early Types section.

J de Roualle

698 - MARIE D'ISLAND (FR)   b.f. Turtle Island - Pick Marie (Shadeed).
March 16. Fourth foal. FF550,000. Deauville August.
The dam is an unraced half-sister to the Group 1 Prix Marcel Boussac winner Mary Linoa, the French listed winner Ming Dynasty and the very useful 10f to 11.5f winner Tapis Rouge. The second dam, Marie Noelle (by Brigadier Gerard), won 7 races in France and the USA and was second in the Group 3 1m Prix des Reservoirs and is a half-sister to the Prix Ganay winner Marildo. (K-H Eng).

699 - MIKHAEL   ch.f. Arazi - Scimitarra (Kris).
January 16. Sixth foal.
Half-sister to the quite useful 1991 2-y-o 7f and 3-y-o 8.2f winner Deserve (by Green Desert). The dam, a very useful filly, won over 6f and 7.2f at 2 yrs prior to winning the Lupe Stakes at 3 yrs. On her only subsequent outing she was favourite for the Epsom Oaks and took the lead two furlongs out only to break a cannon bone. Almost certainly she would have finished second to the eventual winner Unite. Scimitarra is a half-sister to the top class sprinter Double Form, to the very useful 5f to 1m winner Gradiva and the dam of the Group 1 Phoenix Stakes winner Eva Luna. The second dam, Fanghorn (by Crocket), was placed in the French 1,000 Guineas. (Hakam Zakaria).

700 - OLINKA (USA)   b.f. Wolfhound - Optimistic Lass (Mr Prospector).

Half-sister to the French trained 3-y-o Sweet Victory (by Polish Precedent), to the top-class 1989 3-y-o filly Golden Opinion (by Slew O'Gold), winner of the Group 1 1m Coronation Stakes, Group 3 1m Prix du Rond-Point etc, and placed in the French 1,000 Guineas and July Cup, to the quite useful 1996 3-y-o 10f winner Opal Jewel (by Sadler's Wells) and the fair 1995 3-y-o 7f all-weather winner Joyful (by Green Desert). The dam, a winner over 6f at 2 yrs, was a smart 3-y-o winner of the Group 2 10f Nassau Stakes and the Group 3 10.5f Musidora Stakes. The second dam, Loveliest (by Tibaldo), was a very useful winner at up to 10.5f in France and 9f in the USA and is a half-sister to the US Grade 1 winner Arbees Boy. (Haras de la Perelle).

701 - QUEEN OF NORWAY (USA)   ch.f. Woodman - Qena (The Minstrel).
January 28. Second foal. 130,000Y. Tattersalls Houghton.
Closely related to the 3-y-o Western Lady (by Gone West). The dam won at 2 yrs in France and is a half-sister to 6 winners including the US Grade 1 Demoiselle Stakes winner Only Queens (herself dam

of the US dual Grade 1 winner Tactile). The second dam, Queens Only (by Marshua's Dancer), won 4 races from 6f to 1m in the USA. (K-H Eng).

Jean-Claude Rouget

702 - AIDAMON (USA)   b.c. Affirmed - Black Tulip (Fabulous Dancer).
Fifth foal.
Half-brother to the 3-y-o Tulipe Noire, to the Group 2 12.5f Prix de Royallieu, Group 2 12f Ribblesdale Stakes, Group 2 12f Premio Legnano and Group 3 10.5f Prix Penelope winner Tulipa (both by Alleged) and the German Group 3 winner Devil River Peek (by Silver Hawk). The dam won 7 races in France, including 2 listed events, from 10f to 12f and was Grade 2 placed over 12f in the USA. The second dam, Saimore, won 6 races in Italy. (Ecurie I M Fares).

703 - CRUELLE (USA)   ch.f. Irish River - Company (Nureyev).
Fifth foal.
Half-sister to the minor French 2-y-o winners Catalane and Cout Contact (both by Septieme Ciel) - the latter also a winner at 3 yrs. The dam won once as a 2-y-o at Longchamp and was fourth in the Group 3 5f Prix d'Arenburg. She is a sister to the very useful sprinter King's Signet, is closely related to the good sprinter Sicyos and a half-sister to the 2-y-o Group 3 6.5f Prix Eclipse winner Radjhasi. The second dam, Sigy (by Habitat), a champion French 2-y-o filly, won the Group 1 5f Prix de l'Abbaye de Longchamp and is a half-sister to another good broodmare in Sonoma (dam of the Group 3 winner Funambule and the listed winner Sarmatie). (N Radwan).

704 - JAPAN EXILE   b.f. Arazi - Terre de Feu (Busted).

Half-sister to the top class colt Subotica (by Pampabird), winner of the Prix de l'Arc de Triomphe, the Grand Prix de Paris, the Prix Ganay (all Group 1 events) and the Group 2 Prix Niel. The dam won over 1m and 10f at 3 yrs in France and is a half-sister to the listed Prix de Gouvieux winner Force de Frappe. The second dam, Ludivine (by Luthier), won one race in France and is a half-sister to the Group 2 Prix Hocquart and Group 2 Prix Dollar winner Margouillat. (J F Gribomont).

Alain de Royer-Dupre

705 - BEHRANI (IRE)   b.c. Linamix - Behera (Mill Reef).
April 10. Sixth foal.
Half-brother to the French 3-y-o Behrajan (by Arazi) and to the very useful Group 3 15.5f Prix Berteaux winner Bayrika (by Kahyasi). The dam won the Group 1 10f Prix Saint-Alary and the Group 3 10.5f Prix Penelope and was second in the Prix de l'Arc de Triomphe. The second dam, Borushka (by Bustino), won the Park Hill Stakes. (H.H. Aga Khan).

706 - DABARPOUR (IRE)   b.br.c. Alzao - Dabara (Shardari).
March 23.
The dam, a French 3-y-o listed winner, is a half-sister to numerous winners including the top-class French Derby winner Darshaan (by Shirley Heights), the top-class Prix Vermeille winner Darara (by Top Ville), the smart Group 2 12.5f Prix de Royallieu winner Dalara (by Doyoun) and the useful 12f and listed 16f winner Daraydan. The dam won over 12f and was third in the Prix de Pomone. The second dam, Kelty (by Venture VII), was unraced. (H H Aga Khan).

707 - DOUNINE   b.f. Kaldoun - Flabbergasted (Sadler's Wells).
April 15. Second foal.
The dam won once at 3 yrs in France and is a sister to Scenic, winner of the Group 1 Dewhurst Stakes (in a dead-heat) and placed in the Group 1 St James's Palace Stakes and Champion Stakes, and a half-sister to 4 winners including the Group 3 9f Prix Daphnis winner Silent Warrior. The second dam, Idyllic (by Foolish Pleasure), is an unraced half-sister to the outstanding broodmare Slightly Dangerous (dam of Commander in Chief, Warning, Deploy and Dushyantor) and to I Will Follow - herself the dam of Rainbow Quest. (Mme Marlene Brody).

708 - HAPPY ROSE (IRE)   gr.f. Linamix - Indian Rose (General Holme).
February 8.
The dam was a high class winner of three middle-distance races at 3 yrs, notably the Group 1 Prix Vermeille and the Group 3 Prix Cleopatre. She is a half-sister to the Group 1 Prix Ganay winner Vert

Amande, the Group 1 Grand Prix de Paris winner Le Nain Jeune, to two other good winners in Mulberry and Woolskin, and to the French middle-distance winner Featherhill - dam of the top class Group 1 Prix Lupin winner Groom Dancer. The second dam, Lady Berry (by Violon d'Ingres), won the Prix Royal-Oak. (Baron Guy de Rothschild).

Alec Stewart

709 - ADHALATNI
ch.f. Wolfhound - Ameerat Jumaira (Alydar).
January 21. Third foal.

The dam was placed once over 10.3f at 3 yrs, from four starts, is a sister to the Irish 2-y-o 7f and minor US 1m stakes winner Charmante and a half-sister to the top class miler Zilzal. The second dam, French Charmer (by Le Fabuleux), won five races at 3 yrs including the Grade 2 Del Mar Oaks and is a half-sister to the dams of the Group/Grade 1 winners Awe Inspiring, Culture Vulture and Polish Precedent. (Sheikh Ahmed Al Maktoum). *"This is a very, very attractive filly, big and with a beautiful stride" Alec was telling me. "Slightly unfurnished, she's likely to be better in the second half of the season, but she has a very impressive action".*

710 - AFREET
ch.c. Kris - Cambara (Dancing Brave).
April 17. Second foal.

Half-brother to the 3-y-o Beyond Reach (by Darshaan). The dam was a useful winner of three 1m events at 3 yrs and is a half-sister to the good French 6f to 1m winner Pluralisme, to the very useful 10f Virginia Stakes winner Singletta, the very useful 11f Grand Prix Prince Rose winner Classic Tale, the useful 1m winners Only and Cambrian and to the 10f winner Ghislaine - herself dam of the high-class miler Markofdistinction. The second dam, Cambretta (by Roberto), won over 9f in Ireland at 3 yrs, is a sister to the high-class middle-distance colt Critique and a half-sister to the dam of the 1992 Derby winner Dr Devious. (Sheikh Ahmed Al Maktoum). *"He's on the small side, but is a good-moving horse and I'd expect him to be running by mid-summer" says Alec.*

711 - ALFATH (USA)
ch.c. Diesis - Lady Express (Soviet Star).
January 13. Second foal. 280,000Y. Tattersalls Houghton.

The dam, a winner at 3 yrs in France, is a half-sister to a listed winner in Japan. The second dam, Park Express (by Ahonoora), won 5 races including the Group 1 10f Phoenix Champion Stakes, the Group 2 10f Nassau Stakes and the Group 3 12f Lancashire Oaks. She is a half-sister to 6 winners including the listed 6f Firth of Clyde Stakes winner Myra's Best. (Sheikh Hamdan Al Maktoum). *"Alfath is a very good mover, has a nice attitude and is a likeable individual. He should certainly run this year, but not before the second half of the season".*

712 - BALWAT ALZAMAAN (IRE)
ch.f. Lycius - Balwa (Danzig).
April 20. Fourth foal.

Closely related to the 3-y-o Balaitini (by Lion Cavern) and half-sister to the modest 1996 3-y-o 12f winner Laazim Afooz (by Mtoto). The dam, a useful winner over 5f (twice) and 7f, is closely related to the very useful 7f (at 2 yrs) to 12f winner Azzaam. The second dam, Princess Oola (by Al Hattab), won 5 races including a stakes event over 8.5f, was second in a Grade 3 stakes and is a half-sister to the champion US filly Althea, to the Grade 1 stakes winners Ali Oop and Ketoh, the US Grade 2 winners Aishah, Aquilegia and Twining and to the unraced dam of Green Desert. Third dam, the clearly exceptional broodmare Courtly Dee (by Never Bend), won 4 races at up to 6f. (Sheikh Ahmed Al Maktoum). *"This filly does look precocious, she's a little bit naughty, but she moves rather well and there's a lot to like about her. I think she'll have bags of speed and that she'll make a nice 2-y-o".*

713 - DEHOUSH (USA)
ch.c. Diesis - Dream Play (Blushing Groom).
February 15. 110,000Y. Tattersalls Houghton.

Half-brother to 7 winners including the US Grade 3 12f winner Party Cited (by Alleged), the very useful 7f to 10.1f winner Amid Albadou (by Sheikh Albadou), the fairly useful Irish 10f winner Salmon River, the quite useful 1996 3-y-o 11.8f and 11.9f winner Ragsak Jameel (both by Northern Baby), the US stakes-placed winner Milwaki (by Miswaki) and the fair 3-y-o 7f winner The Dawn Trader (by Naskra). The dam, a winner of 2 races in the USA at 2 yrs at up to 9f, is a half-sister to the US stakes winner and Grade 1 placed Irish Fighter. The second dam, Go On Dreaming (by Dewan), won 16 races in the USA including a minor stakes and is a half-sister to 11 winners including the Grade 1 placed Costly Dream (herself dam of the Lanson Champagne Stakes winner Treboro). (Sheikh Ahmed Al Maktoum).

"Dehoush is a nice horse and a very good mover. He enjoys his work, is a medium-sized, good sort of colt and he's going to be a 2-y-o alright".

---

714 - DOOWALEY (IRE)

br.c. Sadler's Wells - Dwell (Habitat). February 12. Fifth foal. 100,000Y. Tattersalls Houghton.

Closely related to the 1997 German 3-y-o winner Dwings (by In The Wings) and half-brother to the Hong Kong listed winner Quick Action (by Alzao) and the Austrian winner King Leon (by Caerleon). The dam, a fairly useful 3-y-o 1m winner, is a half-sister to the dam of the very useful gelding Cap Juluca. The second dam, Wink (by Forli), won twice at 2 yrs and is a half-sister to the US Grade 2 winner Glow. (Sheikh Ahmed Al Maktoum). *"A big, somewhat backward horse and mentally quite immature at the moment. But he's attractive and out of a good mare I trained myself. This colt definitely shows me more speed than any other Sadler's Wells horse I've had before - though I haven't had that many! I like him and he's a colt to look out for in the late summer".*

---

715 - HYPERACTIVE (IRE)

b.c. Perugino - Hyannis (Esprit du Nord). January 30. Second foal. 25,000Y. Tattersalls October.

Half-brother to the Italian 3-y-o Trissi (by Distinctly North). The dam is an unraced half-sister to the French listed 12f winner Hasanati. The second dam, Heracleia (by Kenmare), a placed half-sister to 8 winners in France and the USA, is out of a half-sister to the French Derby winner Crystal Palace. (Racing For Gold). *"This is a nice little horse. Quite mature, I would imagine he'd be one of the first of my two-year-olds to run - probably towards the end of May. He looks a quick type"* Alec was telling me.

---

716 - INDIGO BAY (IRE)

b.c. Royal Academy - Cape Heights (Shirley Heights). March 26. Fourth foal. 100,000Y. Tattersalls October.

Half-brother to the 1995 Italian 2-y-o winner Capetown (by Tibullo). The dam, a winner of 3 races at 3 yrs in Italy, is a sister to the French listed winner Dazzling Heights and a full or half-sister to 5 other winners. The second dam, Cape Chestnut (by Bustino), won once at 3 yrs and is a half-sister to the US Grade 2 winner Colway Rally. (Clare Hall Racing Ltd). *"An exceptionally nice horse. Very well grown, a very good-moving horse and physically quite mature. Mentally he's still a big baby however, and although I like him a lot he won't be out earlier than the late summer. But he's a very nice sort of horse".*

---

717 - KOLLEYA (IRE)

b.c. Royal Academy - Samya's Flame (Artaius). May 1. Sixth foal.

Half-brother to the fair 1993 3-y-o 12f winner Raneen Alwatar and to 4 disappointing animals. The dam, a useful 3-y-o 9f and 10f winner is a sister to the very smart filly Flame of Tara (herself dam of the top class filly Salsabil and the St James's Palace Stakes winner Marju) and a half-sister to the Lupe Stakes second Fruition (dam of the high class stayer Kneller). The second dam, Welsh Flame (by Welsh Pageant), a useful winner of 4 races at around 1m, is out of a lightly raced half-sister to the Derby winner Parthia. (Sheikh Ahmed Al Maktoum). *This colt had yet to enter training in early April.*

---

718 - PITTODRIE (IRE)

b.br.c. Petardia - Evictress (Sharp Victor). March 28. First foal. 20,000Y. Tattersalls October.

The dam was placed three times from 6f (at 2 yrs) to 1m in Ireland and is a half-sister to three minor winners in the USA and one in Italy. The second dam, Nurse Jo (by J O Tobin), ran twice unplaced in the USA and is a half-sister to the dual US Grade 1 winner Love Sign, the Irish and Italian Oaks winner Melodist and the US Grade 2 winner Fatih. (Racing For Gold). *"This really is a nice horse. He looks quite mature although I've had to go quite slowly with him because his knees were slightly open during the winter months. A nice horse with a sweet temperament and a very good mover. I'm pleased with him".*

---

719 - RAJI

b.c. Green Desert - Cancan Madame (Mr Prospector). May 9.

Closely related to the fairly useful 1995 3-y-o 7f winner Tarhhib (by Danzig) and half-sister to the high-class colt Dancehall (by Assert), winner of the Group 2 11f Prix Noailles, the Group 2 12f Prix Hocquart and the Group 3 9f Prix de Conde and to the French 11f winner Can Do Madame (by Trempolino). The dam, a minor US 3-y-o 9f winner, is out of the unraced Wild Madame (by Le Fabuleux), herself a half-sister to the dam of the Grade 2 $500,000 earner Fast Gold and to the smart US turf filly Mademoiselle Ivor. (Hamdan Al Maktoum). *"A very backward colt in early April, he won't be seen out for quite some time".*

720 - TARJOU b.f. Marju - Azm (Unfuwain).

April 14. First foal. 65,000 Y. Tattersalls Houghton.

The dam was unplaced on her only start, over 1m at 3 yrs. She is a half-sister to the Group 1 Middle Park Stakes winner Balla Cove, to the Irish listed winners Blasted Heath and Tribal Rite and the US stakes winner Burning Issue. The second dam, Coven (by Sassafras), won four races in Ireland at 3 yrs from 6f to 10f and is a half-sister to 4 winners including the French listed winner Interdit. (Sheikh Ahmed Al Maktoum). *"A very small filly but otherwise she's been no problem. I trained the dam who never ran at 2 yrs, but I think this filly will run this year. She will need a bit of time however".*

Michael Stoute

721 - ALL OUR HOPE (USA) b.f. Gulch - Knoosh (Storm Bird).

April 19. Sixth foal.

Sister to the fairly useful 10f winner Rocky Oasis and half-sister to the fair 10f placed maiden Ranosh (by Rahy). The dam, a winner over 7f on her only start as a 2-y-o, was a very useful winner of three listed races at 3 yrs including the 12f Glorious Stakes at Goodwood and the 12f Galtres Stakes at York. The second dam, Fabulous Salt (by Le Fabuleux), a fairly useful winner of the 1m Masaka Stakes and third in the 10f Playboy Pretty Polly Stakes at 3 yrs, won in the USA at 4 yrs and is a half-sister to the 1m Senorita Stakes winner Ballare - herself dam of the US stakes winner Balladry and the Group 3 Kiveton Park Stakes winner Gold Seam. (Maktoum Al Maktoum).

722 - ALTICHIERO b.c. Polish Precedent - Anna Matruschka (Mill Reef).

March 4.

Half-brother to the very smart 1996 3-y-o Group 2 12.5f Prix de Royallieu and Group 2 12f Prix du Conseil de Paris winner Annaba (by In The Wings), to the very useful Group 2 12f Park Hill Stakes winner Anna of Saxony (by Ela Mana Mou), the fairly useful Andrassy (by Ahonoora) a winner of 6 races here and in the USA and the minor 1995 German 3-y-o winner Anna d'Autriche. The dam is an unraced half-sister to the German Group 3 winner Anno Luce and to the dam of the very smart middle-distance colt Annus Mirabilis. The second dam, Anna Paola (by Prince Ippi), won the German Oaks. (Sheikh Mohammed).

723 - ARCHITECT b.c. Grand Lodge - Olean (Sadler's Wells).

March 19. Sixth foal. IR95,000Y. Goffs Orby.

Half-brother to the 1997 Irish 2-y-o 7f winner Retention (by Statoblest), to the Italian winner of 6 races Purple Cap and the Irish 10f and 11f winner Two Shonas (both by Persian Heights). The dam is an unplaced half-sister to 4 winners. The second dam, Osmunda (by Mill Reef), won over 10f at 3 yrs in Ireland, was fourth in the Group 2 10f Pretty Polly Stakes and is a half-sister to the Beresford Stakes winner Icelandic and the Sun Chariot Stakes winner Snow.

724 - AUGURY b.f. Warning - Phyliel (Lyphard).

March 26.

Third foal. The dam, a quite useful 2-y-o 6f winner, is closely related to the smart Grade 2 9f Citation Handicap and Group 3 1m Prix Messidor winner Jeune Homme (by Nureyev). The second dam, Alydariel (by Alydar), a minor winner of three races in the USA including a minor stakes event at around 1m, is a half-sister to the top-class Breeders Cup Mile and July Cup winner Royal Academy and to the dual US Grade 2 winners Pancho Villa and Terlingua (the latter also dam of the Grade 1 winner and high-class sire Storm Cat).

725 - AUSPICIOUS b.f. Shirley Heights - Blessed Event (Kings Lake).

January 26.

Brother to the smart 1994 Group 2 11.9f Great Voltigeur Stakes winner Sacrament (by Shirley Heights) and half-brother to the useful 1997 2-y-o dual 7f winner Confirmation (by Polar Falcon) and the 1991 2-y-o 7f winner Blessed Honour (by Ahonoora). The dam was a very useful winner of the listed 10f Ballymacoll Stud Stakes at 3 yrs and was placed in the Yorkshire Oaks, Champion Stakes, Ribblesdale Stakes, Curragh Pretty Polly Stakes and Sun Chariot Stakes. She is a half-sister to 4 minor winners out of the German Group 2 11f Preis der Diana winner Friedrichsruh (by Dschingis Khan).

726 - BEAT ALL (USA) b.br.c. Dynaformer - Spirited Missus (Distinctive).

February 29. $280,000Y. Keeneland September.

Half-brother to 8 winners including the US Grade 3 8.5f Boiling Springs Handicap winner Darby Shuffle (by Darby Creek Road) and the minor US winners Walsh (by Seattle Slew), Greensboro (by Raja Baba) and Swingtown (by Slew O'Gold). The dam, a stakes-placed winner of 3 races in the USA, is a half-sister to 10 winners. The second dam, Missus Beau (by Bolero), was a minor winner of 4 races in the USA. (Saheed Suhail).

727 - BLUE RIBBON (IRE)
b.c. Bluebird - Sweet Justice (Law Society). March 31. Fourth foal. IR50,000Y. Goffs Orby.
Half-brother to the 3-y-o Darina (by Danehill) and to 2 winners in Italy by Be My Guest and Bob Back. The dam won in France at 3 yrs and is a half-sister to 7 winners including the US stakes winner Princess Ivor. The second dam, Hilo Girl (by Pago Pago), won twice and was fourth in the Group 2 10f Nassau Stakes and is a half-sister to 6 winners including the top-class middle-distance colt Ragusa and the Musidora Stakes winner Ela Marita (dam of the Group 2 Pretty Polly Stakes winner Mariel).

728 - BOMBALLERINA (IRE)
b.f. Barathea - Tribal Rite (Be My Native). February 15. 160,000Y. Tattersalls Houghton.
Half-sister to the useful 1997 2-y-o 6f and 1m winner and listed-placed Silent Tribute (by Lion Cavern), to the fair 12.3f winner Danesrath (by Danehill) and the fair Irish 6f and 7f winner Scalp (by Thatching). The dam, a fairly useful Irish 2-y-o listed 6f and 3-y-o 10f winner, is a half-sister to the Middle Park Stakes winner Balla Cove and the US stakes winner Burning Issue and the Irish listed winner Blasted Heath. The second dam, Coven (by Sassafras), won 4 races at 3 yrs.

729 - CAPTAIN BLIGH
b.c. Green Desert - Hyabella (Shirley Heights). May 14. Fourth foal. 250,000Y. Tattersalls Houghton.
Half-brother to the quite useful 1997 3-y-o 1m winner Summer Dance (by Sadler's Wells). The dam, a very useful filly, won three races over 1m at 3 yrs including the listed Atalanta Stakes and the listed Ben Marshall Stakes and is a half-sister to the high-class Prince of Wales's Stakes winner Stagecraft. The second dam, Bella Colora (by Bellypha), won four races including the Group 3 7f Waterford Candelabra Stakes at 2 yrs and the Group 2 9.2f Prix de l'Opera at 3 yrs and is a half-sister to the Irish Oaks winner Colorspin - herself dam of the top-class middle-distance colt Opera House.

730 - CLOUDY SKY (USA)
b.c. Sadler's Wells - Dancing Shadow (Dancer's Image). February 18.
Brother to the very useful filly Dancing Bloom, a winner over 6f (at 2 yrs) and the Group 3 12f Princess Royal Stakes (at 4 yrs) and second twice in the Group 1 Yorkshire Oaks and half-sister to the good French 2-y-o 5f winner and 1,000 Guineas third River Dancer (by Irish River and herself dam of the Champion Stakes winner Spectrum), the 1993 2-y-o 7f winner Ballerina (by Dancing Brave) and the minor French 2-y-o winner Entracte (by Henbit). The dam, a very useful filly, won over 1m and 10f including the Sean Graham Fillies Stakes and is a half-sister to the top-class Oaks winner Sun Princess and the high-class middle-distance colt Saddlers Hall. The second dam, Sunny Valley (by Val de Loir), won over 10.5f and 12f in France and is a half-sister to the dam of the high-class miler Then Again. (Lord Weinstock).

731 - DARAWAD (IRE)
b.c. Bluebird - Dawala (Lashkari). April 21. Third foal.
Half-brother to the 3-y-o Darwasha (by Robellino) and to the useful 1997 3-y-o 10.2f and 13.3f winner Darapour (by Fairy King). The dam, a minor winner in France over 12f, is closely related to the top-class French Derby winner Darshaan and a half-sister to numerous winners including the top-class Prix Vermeille winner Darara and the Prix de Royallieu winner Dalara. The second dam, Delsy (by Abdos), won over 12f and was third in the Prix de Pomone. (H H Aga Khan).

732 - EMILY'S LUCK CHARM (USA)
b.br.c. Lear Fan - Emily's Charm (Dom Alaric). February 12. Sixth foal. $80,000Y. Keeneland September.
Half-brother to 3 winners including Colonel Mosby (by Deputy Minister), a winner of 11 races in the USA. The dam won once at 2 yrs in Canada, was placed in listed events over 7f and 8.5f and is a half-sister to 4 winners including the Canadian Grade 3 winner Cool Halo. The second dam, Slight Deception (by Northern Dancer), is an unraced sister to the Grade 2 winner Diana Dance and a half-sister to the Champion Canadian 2-y-o filly Deceit Dancer. (Maktoum Al Maktoum).

733 - ENTIKAA (IRE)
b.c. Sadler's Wells - Miranisa (Habitat). May 2. Sixth foal. IR340,000Y. Goffs Orby.
Half-brother to the 1997 2-y-o Twister (by Royal Academy) and to the French winner and listed placed Marishaan (by Darshaan). The dam is an unplaced half-sister to the French listed winner Mabira and

a half-sister to the French 1,000 Guineas and Prix Robert Papin winner Masarika (dam of the Group winner Massyar and Madjaristan). The second dam, Miss Melody (by Tudor Melody), a smart 2-y-o 5f winner, was third in the Molecomb Stakes. (Hamdan Al Maktoum).

---

734 - FAIRY FLAME

b.f. Fairy King - Favoridge (Riva Ridge).
February 4.
Half-sister to the quite useful 1992 2-y-o 5f to 6.5f winner Falsoola (by Kris) and to the modest dual 3-y-o 1m winner Vote in Favour (by General Assembly). The dam won four races from 5f to 1m including the Group 3 Nell Gwyn Stakes and is a half-sister to the Queen Mary Stakes winner Amaranda. The second dam, Favoletta (by Baldric II), won the Irish 1,000 Guineas and is a half-sister to the dams of numerous good horses, notably Teenoso, Topsy, Ashayer, Braiswick and Give Thanks. (Sheikh Mohammed).

---

735 - FANTASTIC LIGHT (USA)

b.c. Rahy - Jood (Nijinsky).
February 13. Third foal.
Half-brother to the 3-y-o Wanice (by Mr Prospector). The dam ran just twice but was quite useful, being placed over 7f at 2 yrs and over 10f at 3 yrs. She is a half-sister to the Grade 1 Ashland Stakes and Grade 1 Hollywood Oaks winner Gorgeous, the Grade 1 Kentucky Oaks winner Seaside Attraction (herself dam of the Cherry Hinton Stakes winner Red Carnival), the Canadian dual Grade 3 winner Key to the Moon and the Group 3 Princess Margaret Stakes winner Hiamm. The second dam, Kamar (by Key to the Mint), was a champion Canadian 3-y-o filly and is a sister to the Grade 1 winner Love Smitten and a half-sister to the US stakes winners Dancing on a Cloud and Stellarette (dam of the Grade 1 winner Cuddles). (Maktoum Al Maktoum).

---

736 - FLAMING QUEST

b.c. Rainbow Quest - Nearctic Flame (Sadler's Wells).
March 9. Fifth foal.
Brother to the very useful 1996 2-y-o 7f winner Happy Valentine, closely related to the very useful Group 3 14f Budweiser Guiness Curragh Cup winner Blushing Flame (by Blushing Groom) and half-brother to the 1997 3-y-o Candescent (by Machiavellian). The dam was a very useful winner of two of her five races, over 10f and 10.5f at 3 yrs and was third in the Group 2 12f Ribblesdale Stakes. She is a sister to the top-class Irish Derby, Prix Vermeille and 1,000 Guineas winner Salsabil, closely related to the Prix de Psyche winner Danse Royale and a half-sister to the high-class St James's Palace Stakes winner Marju. The second dam, Flame of Tara (by Artaius), won eight races including the Group 2 Coronation Stakes and the Group 2 Pretty Polly Stakes at the Curragh, was second in the Champion Stakes and is a half-sister to the Lupe Stakes second Fruition - herself dam of the Tote Ebor, Doncaster Cup and Jockey Club Cup winner Kneller and of the Breeders Cup Turf winner Northern Spur. (Cheveley Park Stud).

---

737 - FLORAL RAJ

ch.c. Indian Ridge - Spring Daffodil (Pharly).
March 27. Fourth foal. 150,000Y. Tattersalls Houghton.
Half-brother to the 3-y-o Pantar (by Shirley Heights), unplaced twice at 2 yrs, and to the Irish 1m winner Lower The Tone (by Phone Trick). The dam, a fairly useful winner of 6 races in Ireland and the USA including the Group 3 1m Matron Stakes, is a half-sister to the Australian Grade 1 12f winner Dance The Day Away and to the unraced dam of the US Grade 2 winner Golden Pond. The second dam, Daffodil Day (by Welsh Pageant), ran twice unplaced and is a half-sister to the high-class middle-distance colt Connaught and the St James's Palace Stakes winner Court Sentence.

---

738 - FORTIFY

b.f. Machiavellian - Talon d'Aiguille (Big Spruce).
March 11.
Sister to the 1994 2-y-o 6f winner Deceive (by Machiavellian) and half-sister to the 1994 3-y-o 1m winner Decant (by Rousillon). The dam, a winner at 3 yrs in France and third in the Group 3 10.5f Prix de Flore, is a half-sister to the high-class French filly Proskona and to the smart Prix Chloe winner Korveya - herself dam of the classic winners Bosra Sham, Hector Protector and Shanghai. The second dam, Konafa (by Damascus), a winner over 7f at 2 yrs and second in the 1,000 Guineas, is a half-sister to the Yorkshire Oaks winner Awaasif (dam of the Oaks winner Snow Bride and thus grandam of Lammtarra), to the high-class American colt Akureyri and the unraced Royal Stance - dam of the Group 3 winners Majuscule and Royal Cielo.

739 - FORT WILLIAM b.c. Ezzoud - Lovely Noor (Fappiano).
May 5. Sixth foal. 37,000Y. Tattersalls Houghton.
Half-brother to the French trained 3-y-o Formidable Noor (by Efisio), to the very useful 1m to 12f winner Medaille Militaire (by Highest Honor) and the fairly useful 1995 2-y-o 7f winner Wahiba Sands (by Pharly). The dam, a minor 3-y-o winner at around 1m in the USA, is a half-sister to 3 winners. The second dam, Love's Dream (by Rheingold), is an unplaced half-sister to the 1,000 Guineas winner Fairy Footsteps and the St Leger winner Light Cavalry.

740 - GREETINGS b.f. Rainbow Quest - Kissing Cousin (Danehill).
February 22. First foal.
The dam was a smart filly and winner of four races including the Group 1 1m Coronation Stakes. The second dam, First Kiss (by Kris), a quite useful 3-y-o 10f winner, is a half-sister to the smart 1m winner Miller's Mate. The third dam, Primatie (by Vaguely Noble), is a winning daughter of the top-class filly Pistol Packer. (Sheikh Mohammed).

741 - HANDOVER THECASH (USA) b.c. Red Ransom - Ambigua (Alydar).
February 7. First foal. $100,000Y. Keeneland September.
The dam, placed at 3 yrs in the US, is a half-sister to the useful 1997 3-y-o 12f November Handicap winner Sabadilla. The second dam, Jasmina (by Forli), won 6 races in the US including a stakes event and is a half-sister to the top-class miler Polish Precedent. (Maktoum Al Maktoum).

742 - HEARTWOOD (USA) ch.f. Woodman - Good Example (Crystal Glitters).
January 30. Third foal. $160,000Y. Keeneland September.
Half-sister to the minor US winner Southern Letters (by Capote). The dam won 3 races in France including the Group 3 1m Prix des Reservoirs at 2 yrs. The second dam, the French 2-y-o placed Divona (by Nodouble), is a half-sister to the US Grade 2 winner Grey Beret, to the Group 2 Criterium de Maisons-Laffitte winner Rapide Pied and the US stakes winners Alleged Jr. and Joli Vert. (Sheikh Mohammed).

743 - HIGHEST PEAK (USA) ch.c. Mt Livermore - Disconiz (Northern Dancer).
March 4. $85,000Y. Keeneland September.
Closely related to the Group 1 Heinz "57" Phoenix Stakes winner Digamist, to the fairly useful 3-y-o 1m winner Fly To The Moon, the modest 3-y-o 6.1f winner Jumaira Star (all by Blushing Groom) and minor winners in France, Italy and the USA. The dam, a very smart stakes winner of 7 races at up to 12f including the Grade 3 Princess Stakes, is a half-sister to the English listed 10f and US Grade 3 9f winner Conquering Hero. The second dam, Codorniz (by Cockrullah), was a stakes winner in Venezuela. (Maktoum Al Maktoum).

744 - IMPRESARIO b.c. Sadler's Wells - Exclusive Order (Exclusive Native).
April 16.
Brother to the 1997 2,000 Guineas winner and Derby fourth Entrepreneur, to the smart 1995 Cheshire Oaks winner and Epsom Oaks second Dance a Dream and the very useful 1994 3-y-o middle-distance listed winner Sadler's Image and half-brother to 5 winners including the promising 1997 2-y-o 7f winner Exclusive (by Polar Falcon), the useful 7f and 1m winner Mizaaya (by Riverman) and the useful French winner at up to 1m Irish Order (by Irish River). The dam won 4 races in France including the Group 2 6.5f Prix Maurice de Gheest and the Group 3 7f Prix de la Porte Maillot. The second dam, Bonavista (by Dead Ahead), won 3 races in the USA and was stakes-placed. (Cheveley Park Stud).

745 - ISCAN (IRE) b.c. Caerleon - Idraak (Kris).
February 12. Third foal.
Half-brother to the French trained 3-y-o Illyria (by Nashwan) and to the fairly useful 1m (at 2 yrs in 1996) and 11.9f winner Idrica (by Rainbow Quest). The dam is a placed half-sister to the high-class filly Snow Bride, winner of the Epsom Oaks (awarded race), Musidora Stakes and Princess Royal Stakes and herself dam of the Derby, King George and 'Arc' winner Lammtarra, to the useful middle-distance winner Habaayib (both by Blushing Groom) and the fair 8.2f winner and subsequent US Grade 3 New Orleans Handicap winner Jarraar (by Mr Prospector). The second dam, Awaasif (by Snow Knight), won the Group 1 Yorkshire Oaks and the Group 1 Gran Premio del Jockey Club and is a half-sister to numerous winners including the high-class American colt Akureyri, the 1,000 Guineas second Konafa (herself dam of the high-class French 6f and 7f performer Proskona and grandam of Hector Protector, Shanghai and Bosra Sham) and the unraced Royal Stance (dam of the very useful 1m to 10f colt Majuscule and the US Grade 3 winner Royal Cielo). (Sheikh Mohammed).

746 - KENTISH LAD ch.c. Caerleon - Jaljuli (Jalmood).
April 17. Fifth foal. IR150,000Y. Goffs Orby.
Half-brother to a winner in Japan by Persian Bold. The dam, a very useful 2-y-o 5f and 6f winner, was placed in the Cheveley Park, Rockfel, Lowther and Princess Margaret Stakes and is a half-sister to the top-class Coronation Stakes, Coral-Eclipse Stakes and Irish 1,000 Guineas winner Kooyonga. The second dam, Anjuli (by Northfields), is an unraced half-sister to the 2,000 Guineas winner Roland Gardens.

747 - LEDHAM (USA) ch.c. Diesis - First Tracks (Alleged).
April 27. Third foal. $185,000Y. Keeneland September.
The dam, placed at 2 and 4 yrs in the USA, is out of the Irish 3-y-o 7f winner Snowdonia (by Alydar), herself a half-sister to the US Grade 1 winner Scoot and the Group 2 Beresford Stakes winner Gold Crest. The third dam, Northernette (by Northern Dancer), a champion Canadian filly, is a sister to Storm Bird. (Saheed Suhail).

748 - LONESOME b.f. Night Shift - Pine Ridge (High Top).
February 12.
Sister to the fair middle-distance placed maiden Curzon Street and to the top class filly In the Groove, winner of the Champion Stakes, Juddmonte International Stakes, Irish 1,000 Guineas and Coronation Cup and half-sister to the useful 5f to 1m winner Spanish Pine (by King of Spain), the quite useful 3-y-o 7f winner Awesome Venture (by Formidable), the fair 3-y-o 12f winner Pineapple (by Superlative) and the minor American winner Stripped Pine (by Sharpo). The dam won two minor races at 3 yrs over 12f. The second dam, Wounded Knee (by Busted), won two small races over 12f and 14f.

749 - MENDELSSOHN (USA) b.c. Polish Precedent - Secret Obsession (Secretariat).
March 4. Sixth foal. 68,000Y. Tattersalls Houghton.
Half-brother to the fair 1997 2-y-o 6f winner Obsessed, to the fair 7f winner Storm Nymph (both by Storm Bird), the useful 2-y-o 6f winner and Group 3 10.4f Musidora Stakes third Obsessive (by Seeking The Gold) and a minor 2-y-o winner in the USA by Woodman. The dam, a fairly useful 10f winner, is a half-sister to 6 winners including the Group 2 12f King Edward VII Stakes winner Beyton. The second dam, Ann Stuart (by Lyphard), is an unraced half-sister to the Champion US filly Chris Evert (dam of the Grade 1 winner Six Crowns), the US stakes winner All Rainbows (dam of the Kentucky Derby winner Winning Colors) and to the dams of Two Timing (winner of the Prince Of Wales's Stakes) and Missed The Storm (winner of the Grade 1 Test Stakes). (Cheveley Park Stud).

750 - MESSENGER MISS (USA) b.f. Danehill - Foreign Courier (Sir Ivor).
March 21.
Closely related to the high class colt and sire Green Desert, a winner of 5 races from 5f to 7f including the Group 1 Norcros July Cup, the Vernons Sprint Cup, the European Free Handicap and the Flying Childers Stakes, to the useful 2-y-o 6f winners Kissogram Girl, Yousefia and Blue Ocean (all four by Danzig) and to the fairly useful 2-y-o 5f winner Moumayaz (by Nureyev) and half-brother to the 5f winner Lillah Darak (by Shadeed). The dam is an unraced half-sister to 13 winners, notably the Grade 1 winners Althea (herself dam of the US Grade 3 winner Destiny Dance), Ali Oop and Ketoh, and the Grade 2 winners Aishah, Aquilegia and Twining. The second dam, Courtly Dee (Never Bend), won four races at up to 6f. (Maktoum Al Maktoum).

751 - MR GROOM (IRE) b.c. Indian Ridge - One Wild Oat (Shareef Dancer).
March 6. First foal. 74,000Y. Tattersalls Houghton.
The dam, a modest 7f placed 2-y-o before winning in France at 3 yrs, is a half-sister to 9 winners including the Australian Grade 1 winner Marooned and the dam of the Prix de Pomone and John Porter Stakes winner Whitewater Affair. The second dam, Short Rations (by Lorenzaccio), won at 2 yrs in Italy and is a half-sister to the Cork And Orrery Stakes and Hungerford Stakes winner He Loves Me. (Saheed Suhail).

752 - MUKHTAAL b.c. Machiavellian - On The House (Be My Guest).
April 16. 120,000Y. Tattersalls Houghton.
Brother to the very useful listed 6f Sirenia Stakes winner Art of War (by Machiavellian), to the useful 3-y-o 7f winner Domus (by Kalaglow), the fairly useful 7f winners St Radegund (by Green Desert) and Castel Rosselo (by Rousillon) and the fair 3-y-o dual 12f and 14f winner Upper House (by Shirley Heights). The dam was a high-class winner of 4 races from 5f to 1m including the 1,000 Guineas and

the Sussex Stakes. The second dam, Lora (by Lorenzaccio), was unplaced and is closely related to the high-class sprinter D'Urberville and to the dam of the champion sprinter Habibti. (Hamdan Al Maktoum).

---

753 - NABONASSAR

ch.c. Lion Cavern - Negligent (Ahonoora).
April 30. Third foal.

Brother to the very promising 1997 2-y-o 7f winner Asad and half-brother to the useful 1995 2-y-o 7f winner Shawanni (by Shareef Dancer). The dam, a champion 2-y-o filly, won the 7f Rockfel Stakes at 2 yrs and was third in the 1,000 Guineas behind Salsabil on the first of her three outings at 3 yrs. She is a sister to the dual 2-y-o 6f winner and 1,000 Guineas fourth Ala Mahlik and a half-sister to the very useful 22.2f Queen Alexandra Stakes winner Ala Hounak and the useful 1m and 10f winner Zalon. The second dam, Negligence (by Roan Rocket), was placed once over 10f at 3 yrs and is a half-sister to the dams of the very useful sprinter Governor General and the smart French 10f performer Galunpe. (Sheikh Mohammed).

---

754 - POP QUEEN

ch.f. Nashwan - Pick Of The Pops (High Top).
April 6. Sixth foal. 370,000Y. Tattersalls Houghton.

Half-sister to the 3-y-o Paganini (by Polish Precedent), to the useful 1996 2-y-o 8.2f winner Fascinating Rhythm (by Slip Anchor) and the useful 10f and 10.3f winner Migwar (by Unfuwain). The dam, a very useful 2-y-o 7f winner, was second in the Group 2 Hoover Fillies Mile and is a half-sister to 3 winners. The second dam, Rappa Tap Tap (by Tap on Wood), won the listed 6f Blue Seal Stakes and is a half-sister to the Prix de l'Opera winner Bella Colora (the dam of Stagecraft, Hyabella and Balalaika), the Irish Oaks winner Colorspin (the dam of Opera House) and the Irish Champion Stakes winner Cezanne.

---

755 - PROKOFIEV (USA)

b.br.c. Nureyev - Aviara (Cox's Ridge).
March 5. Second foal. 215,000Y. Tattersalls Houghton.

Half-brother to the 3-y-o Trampolo (by Trempolino). The dam, a minor winner in France, is a half-sister to 4 winners including the US stakes winner Spectacular Bev and the dam of the Queen's Vase winner Stelvio and also to the placed Connecting Link (dam of the US Grade 1 winner Link River). The second dam, Bev Bev (by Nijinsky), won twice in France and is a half-sister to the Group 1 winners Ajdal, Formidable and Flying Partner and to the Group 3 winner Fabuleux Jane - herself the grandam of Arazi.

---

756 - RAIN GOD

b.c. Rainbow Quest - Mystic Goddess (Storm Bird).
February 20. Second foal. 100,000Y. Tattersalls Houghton.

Closely related to a 3-y-o in Japan by Nashwan. The dam was a fairly useful winner of the listed 7f Sweet Solera Stakes at 2 yrs and was placed in the Queen Mary Stakes, the Cherry Hinton Stakes and the Rockfel Stakes. She is a half-sister to the smart Group 1 Gran Criterium winner Sanam and to the South African Grade 2 winner Shaybani. The second dam, Rose Goddess (by Sassafras), is an unraced half-sister to 8 winners including Czenia (dam of three German Group winners). (Cheveley Park Stud).

---

757 - RED TIARA (USA)

br.f. Mr Prospector - Heart of Joy (Lypheor).
March 12. Second foal. $950,000. Keeneland July.

The dam won in 10 races in England and the USA including the Grade 2 Palomar Handicap and the Group 3 Nell Gwyn Stakes and was second in the Irish 1,000 Guineas. She is a half-sister to several winners including two minor US stakes winners. The second dam, Mythographer (by Secretariat), is a placed half-sister to the Grade 1 United Nations Handicap winner Acaroid.

---

758 - RIVER SAINT (USA)

ch.f. Irish River - Imagining (Northfields).
April 15. $525,000. Keeneland July.

Half-sister to 4 winners including the Champion US 3-y-o filly Serena's Song (by Rahy), a winner of 18 races (eleven of them Grade 1 stakes), to the US 2-y-o Grade 3 8.5f Golden Rod Stakes winner Vivid Imagination (by Raise A Man) and the minor US 4-y-o winner My Imagination (by Easy Goer). The dam, a minor winner of 2 races at 4 yrs in the USA, is a half-sister to the US Grade 3 winner and Grade 1 placed Alabama Nana. The second dam, Image Intensifier (by Dancer's Image), won at 3 yrs in Ireland.

759 - RUSSIAN REBEL ch.f. Machiavellian - Russian Royal (Nureyev).
April 3. Fifth foal.
Sister to the French trained 3-y-o Queen Catherine and half-sister to the useful 1996 2-y-o 7f winner and Group 3 1m May Hill Stakes third Gretel (by Hansel) and to a winner in Dubai by Bering. The dam was a useful winner over 6f at 2 yrs and 7f at 3 yrs and was placed in the Jersey Stakes, the Fred Darling Stakes, the Supreme Stakes and the Beeswing Stakes. She is a half-sister to numerous winners here and in the USA including the very useful, though lightly raced, 1987 3-y-o 9f winner Incinderator (by Northern Dancer). The second dam, Princess Karenda (by Gummo), won 6 races including the Grade 1 9f Hollywood Oaks and the Grade 1 9f Santa Margarita Invitational Handicap and is a half-sister to the Grade 3 8.3f Post-Deb Stakes winner Big Puddles, herself dam of the Graded stakes winners Thunder Puddles and Always Run Lucky. (Sheikh Mohammed).

760 - SAPPHIRE TRIO b.c. Bluebird - Triode (Sharpen Up).
May 10. Fifth foal. 150,000Y. Tattersalls Houghton.
Half-brother to the fairly useful 1996 2-y-o 6f winner Blane Water (by Lomond) and to a winner in Germany by Storm Bird. The dam, a useful 1m winner and placed in the Group 3 Premio Bagutta and the listed Oak Tree Stakes, is a half-sister to 2 minor winners. The second dam, Triple Tipple (by Raise A Cup), won 10 races here and in the USA including the Grade 2 8.5f Wilshire Handicap and the listed 7f Strensall Stakes and was second in the Grade 1 Gamely Handicap.

761 - SEABOUND b.f. Prince Sabo - Shore Line (High Line).
February 14.
Half-sister to the high-class dual Group 1 1m Juddmonte Stakes winner Soviet Line (by Soviet Star) and the useful middle-distance peformers Mamdooh (by Green Desert) and South Shore (by Caerleon). The dam, a very useful 7f winner, was fourth in the Oaks and is a sister to the Group 2 winners Ancholia and Quay Line (grandam of the Oaks winner Pure Grain). The second dam, Dark Finale (by Javelot), won at up to 12f in Ireland.

762 - SECRET'S OUT b.c. Danzig - Queena (Mr Prospector).
March 29. Fourth foal. $775,000. Keeneland July.
The dam, a winner of 10 races in the USA including the 9f Ruffian Handicap, the 1m Maskette Stakes and the 7f Ballerina Stakes, is a sister to the Grade 1 Ashland Stakes winner Chic Shirine (herself dam of the US Grade 2 winners Waldoboro and Tara Roma). The second dam, Too Chic (by Blushing Groom), won the Grade 1 Maskette Stakes in the USA.

763 - SHAFTESBURY b.c. Sadler's Wells - Surmise (Alleged).
May 18. Sixth foal. IR275,000Y. Goffs Orby.
Closely related to the Italian winner of 7 races and 5f listed-placed Flagpole (by Be My Guest) and half-brother to the fair 1997 7f placed 2-y-o Palmetto Bay (by Royal Academy). The dam, a fair 3-y-o 7f winner, is a half-sister to 6 winners including the Group 2 Gimcrack Stakes winner Splendent and the Group 3 7f Premio Chiusura and listed Princess Elizabeth Stakes winner Aim For The Top. The second dam, Sticky Habit (by Habitat), was a quite useful 1m and 10f winner and a half-sister to 7 winners including the Group 3 Mulcahy Stakes winner I've A Bee.

764 - SIEGE b.c. Indian Ridge - Above Water (Reference Point).
February 7. First foal. 100,000Y. Tattersalls Houghton.
The dam, unplaced on both her outings in France, is closely related to the Group 2 Lanson Champagne Vintage Stakes second Golden Wave and a half-sister to 7 other winners including the Group 1 Yorkshire Oaks winner Hellenic - herself dam of the Group 3 Ormonde Stakes winner Election Day. The second dam, Grecian Sea (by Homeric), won once in France, was fourth in the Group 3 7f Prix du Calvados and is a half-sister to 8 winners including Sailor's Mate (Group 3 Meld Stakes).

765 - SIKASSO (USA) b.br.c. Silver Hawk - Silken Doll (Chieftain).
January 7. $300,000. Keeneland September.
Brother to the very useful 7f (at 2 yrs) to 12f winner and Group 1 1m Racing Post Trophy third Juyush and half-brother to the Champion Canadian 2-y-o filly Silken Cat (by Storm Cat), the US stakes-placed winner Raven Red, the minor US winner Chief Appeal (both by Valid Appeal) and 2 other minor winners by Meadowlake and In Reality. The dam won 4 races in the USA at up to 9f including a minor stakes event and is a half-sister to the US Grade 1 Turf Classic winner Turk Passer. The second dam, Insilca (by Buckpasser), was unraced. (Sheikh Mohammed).

766 - SONINKE b.f. Machiavellian - Sonic Lady (Nureyev).
February 8.
Half-sister to the 3-y-o Lady Icarus (by Rainbow Quest), to the very useful Hazaam, winner of four races from 7f to 1m at 3 yrs including the Group 3 Supreme Stakes and the very useful Group 3 1m Prix de la Jonchere winner Sharman (both by Blushing Groom). The dam was a top-class miler and won 8 races, notably the Irish 1,000 Guineas, the Coronation Stakes, the Sussex Stakes and the Prix du Moulin - all Group 1 events. She was rated fourth in the International Classifications - in front of Highest Honor, Sure Blade, Baiser Vole, Flash of Steel and Then Again. The second dam, Stumped (by Owen Anthony), was a smart winner of 4 races from 6f to 1m including the Child Stakes. (Sheikh Mohammed).

767 - SUMOOD b.f. Rainbow Quest - Bella Ballerina (Sadler's Wells).
February 4. First foal. 150,000Y. Tattersalls Houghton.
The dam, a quite useful 3-y-o 9f winner, is a sister to the high-class Group 2 10f Prince of Wales's Stakes and Group 3 10f Brigadier Gerard Stakes winner Stagecraft and the useful 1997 4-y-o listed 9f winner Balalaika and a half-sister to the very useful dual 3-y-o 1m listed stakes winner Hyabella. The dam, Bella Colora (by Bellypha), won four races including the Group 2, 9.2f Prix de l'Opera and the Group 3, 7f Waterford Candelabra Stakes and was a very close third in the 1,000 Guineas. She is a half-sister to the Irish Oaks winner Colorspin (herself dam of the top-class middle-distance colt Opera House), to the Irish Champion Stakes winner Cezanne and the very useful filly Rappa Tap Tap. (Hamdan Al Maktoum).

768 - TELECASTER (IRE) ch.c. Indian Ridge - Monashee (Sovereign Dancer).
May 5. Third foal. 38,000Y. Tattersalls October.
The dam is an unraced daughter of Empress Express (by Sovereign Dancer), an unplaced half-sister to 7 winners including the high-class broodmare Royal Dilemma (dam of the good winners Silver Fling, Silverdip, Imperial Fling and Imperial Dilemma).

769 - THESEUS b.c. Danehill - Graecia Magna (Private Account).
April 10.
Closely related to the smart 7f to 7.9f winner Thourios and to the modest 10f to 12f winner Thaleros (both by Green Desert) and half-brother to the quite useful 1995 3-y-o 10f winner Polydamus and the fairly useful 2-y-o 1m winner and 10f placed 3-y-o Akamantis (by Kris). The dam was a very useful winner over 7f at 2 yrs and the Group 3 12f Lancashire Oaks and was second in the Group 2 12f Ribblesdale Stakes. The second dam, Dancing Peach (by Nijinsky), is an unraced daughter of the very smart 1973 2-y-o Fleet Peach.

770 - TIME SAVED b.f. Green Desert - Time Charter (Saritamer).
June 6.
Sister to the very useful 7.9f winner Illusion and half-sister to the 3-y-o Generous Terms (by Generous), the very useful Group 3 12f Princess Royal Stakes winner Time Allowed (by Sadlers Wells), the very useful Group 3 12f Jockey Club Stakes winner Zinaad and the useful 7f winner (at 2 yrs) and Cheshire Oaks second By Charter (both by Shirley Heights). The dam was an exceptionally talented filly and winner of the Oaks, the King George VI and Queen Elizabeth Diamond Stakes, the Champion Stakes, the Coronation Cup, the Prix Foy and the Sun Chariot Stakes. The second dam, Centrocon (by High Line), won 4 races including the Lancashire Oaks and is a sister to the high-class horses Nicholas Bill and Centroline.

771 - WOOD POUND (USA) b.br.c. Woodman - Poundzig (Danzig).
February 6. First foal. $200,000. Keeneland July.
The dam is an unraced half-sister to Goodbye Halo, winner of no less than seven Grade 1 events in the USA, and to the US stakes winner Rampaging Native. The second dam, Pound Foolish (by Sir Ivor), is an unraced half-sister to the US Grade 3 winner Serious Spender and to the Houghton Stakes winner and King Edward VII Stakes second Russian Roubles.

James Toller

772 - BUN ALLEY b.c. Be My Guest - Neptunalia (Slip Anchor).
February 7. First foal. 50,000Y. Tattersalls Houghton.
The dam, a fair 3-y-o 12f winner, is a half-sister to 3 winners including the very smart Group 1 Gran Criterirm and Group 2 Dante Stakes winner Glory Of Dancer. The second dam, Glory Of Hera (by

Formidable), a useful 2-y-o sprinter, is a half-sister to 4 winners including the Group 1 Heinz "57" Phoenix Stakes second So Directed. (Duke Of Devonshire). *"I like Bun Alley a lot" says James. "He's a strong sort, not too precocious, needs plenty of work and I may start him in June over at least six furlongs".*

773 - NULLI SECUNDUS

b.c. Polar Falcon - Exclusive Virtue (Shadeed).
April 10. Third foal. 80,000Y. Tattersalls Houghton.
Brother to the quite useful 8.2f (at 2yrs) and 10f placed Dancing Debut and half-brother to the fairly useful 1997 2-y-o 8.2f winner Virtuous (by Exit To Nowhere). The dam, a fairly useful 2-y-o 7f winner, stayed 12f and is a half-sister to 7 winners including the 1997 2,000 Guineas winner and Derby fourth Entrepreneur, the smart 1995 Cheshire Oaks winner and Epsom Oaks second Dance a Dream and the very useful 1994 3-y-o middle-distance listed winner Sadler's Image. The second dam, Exclusive Order (by Exclusive Native), won the Group 2 6.5f Prix Maurice de Gheest and the Group 3 7f Prix de la Porte Maillot. (Duke Of Devonshire). *"A backward colt, he's a nice horse but has grown a lot since we bought him and we won't run him until the back-end".*

774 - UMBRIAN GOLD (IRE)

b.f. Perugino - Golden Sunlight (Ile de Bourbon).
February 20. 20,000Y. Tattersalls October.
Half-sister to the quite useful 1997 3-y-o 1m and 10f winner Ile Distinct (by Dancing Dissident), the fair 5f to 8.5f winner Broctune Gold (by Superpower), the modest 1996 3-y-o 10f all-weather winner Posen Gold (by Posen) and winners abroad by Auction Ring and Dominion. The dam is an unraced half-sister to the Lincoln Handicap winner King's Glory and the Racing Post Trophy third Marcham. The second dam, Dazzling Light (by Silly Season), won the listed 1m Ebbisham Handicap and is a half-sister to the Lockinge Stakes winner Welsh Pageant. (Mrs R W Gore-Andrews). *Umbrian Gold is "a nice sort of filly, not very early but she has plenty of scope and will be one to watch in the second half of the year over six furlongs or more".* James has another two-year-old in the next section of this book.

Mark Tompkins

775 - INTENSITY

b.c. Bigstone - Brillante (Green Dancer).
April 10. 40,000Y. Tattersalls October.
Half-brother to the modest middle-distance stayer Arc Bright (by Trempolino) - winner of 7 races, to the US winner of 3 races Jodi's Dad (by Devil's Bag), the dual German winner Lirango (by Sure Blade), the French 2-y-o winner Bazilia (by Mr Prospector) and the Norwegian winner Arinaga (by Warning). The dam won the listed 11f Prix de la Seine and is a half-sister to 7 winners including Bellman (Group 2 Prix Eugene Adam), Bellypha (Group 3 Prix Daphnis) and the Peruvian Grade 1 winner Run And Deliver. The second dam, Belga (by Le Fabuleux), won over 9f in France. (Mr J Lovat). *"This is a really nice, strong colt. Look out for him in mid-summer over six or seven furlongs".* Mark has several other young horses in the Early Types section of the book.

776 - IT'S OUR SECRET (IRE)

ch.c. Be My Guest - Lady Dulcinea (General).
April 17. IR38,000Y. Goffs Challenge.
Half-brother to 2 winners in Italy by Petorius and River Falls and to a hurdles winner by Nordico. The dam won 5 races in the USA and Peru and is a half-sister to Fremanche - dam of the Group 2 Blandford Stakes winner Royal Ballerina and the Sun Chariot Stakes and Nassau Stakes winner Free Guest (herself dam of the Fillies Mile winner and Oaks second Shamshir). The second dam, La Manche (by Sideral), won 3 races in Argentina. (Mrs M Barwell). *"This colt will be running in May, probably over six furlongs and he'll definitely get a mile later on. He's a strong, short-coupled two-year-old type"* Mark was telling me.

777 - MASONIC (IRE)

ch.c. Grand Lodge - Winning Heart (Horage).
April 22. Second foal. IR48,000Y. Goffs Orby.
Half-brother to the 3-y-o Winning Saint (by St Jovite). The dam won 4 races in Ireland at up to 10f and is a half-sister to 2 minor winners. The second dam, Silver Heart (by Yankee Gold), won 3 races in Ireland including 1m McDonagh Handicap and is a half-sister to 5 winners. (Mrs Beryl Lockey). *"A backward colt with plenty of scope, he looks a typical Grand Lodge and will start off over six or seven furlongs in August".*

Marcus Tregoning

778 - ASLEY (IRE)

b.c. Danehill - Ausherra (Diesis).
March 8. Fourth foal. IR85,000Y. Goffs Orby.
Half-brother to the 3-y-o My Way (by Marju) and to the very useful 1996 2-y-o 1m winner and 12f placed 3-y-o Yorkshire (by Generous). The dam, a very useful filly, won the listed 12f Lingfield Oaks

Trial, is a sister to the useful middle-distance colt Royal Scimitar and a half-sister to 7 other winners. The second dam, Princess Of Man (by Green God), won the Group 3 Musidora Stakes. (Sheikh Ahmed Al Maktoum). *"We like this colt and he's certainly one to watch. He'll be out in May, probably over six furlongs, and shows speed"* the trainer tells me.

779 - DONTBETONME
ch.f. Kris - Reveuse du Soir (Vision).
February 1. Third foal. 120,000Y. Tattersalls Houghton.
Half-sister to the French trained 3-y-o Panfilo (by Thatching). The dam won once in France at 2 yrs and is a half-sister to 7 winners including the French 1,000 Guineas and Prix de la Foret winner Danseuse du Soir and the listed winners Don Corleone and Dana Springs. The second dam, Dance By Night (by Northfields), won twice over 7f at 2 yrs. (Sheikh Mohammed). *"This filly is full of quality and though not very early, she'll be out in mid-summer over six furlongs. A good-topped filly, she has inherited the precocity of Kris".*

780 - ELHIDA (IRE)
ch.f. Mujtahid - Nouvelle Star (Luskin Star).
May 23.
Sister to the useful 1996 2-y-o 6f winner and Group 3 July Stakes second Juwwi and half-sister to the 7f winner Sariah (by Kris). The dam won from 5f to 8.2f in Australia including a Grade 2 event and was the Champion older filly at 4 yrs. (Hamdan Al Maktoum). *"Elhida looks an early type, is a super mover and has plenty of speed"* Marcus was telling me.

781 - EL NAHRAWAN (USA)
b.br.c. Red Ransom - Woodja (Woodman).
April 18. First foal. $235,000Y. Keeneland September.
The unraced dam is a three-parts sister to a stakes winner in Japan and to the US winner and Grade 3 placed Choctaw Ridge and a half-sister to the Cherry Hinton Stakes winner Storm Star (herself dam of the US Grade 3 winner Dodge) and the dam of the Grade 1 Breeders Cup Juvenile Fillies winner Flanders. The second dam, Cinegita (by Secretariat), won the Grade 3 7f Railbird Stakes in the USA. (Hamdan Al Maktoum). *"A good-looking horse and a good mover, he's well forward in his programme and works well. The type to want six furlongs or more this year".*

782 - JERYAAN (IRE)
b.c. Fairy King - Moonshine Lake (Kris).
January 22. First foal.
The dam, a quite useful 3-y-o 12.3f winner, is a sister to the high-class Group 3 Diadem Stakes winner Shining Steel and to the smart Swet Solera Stakes and Lupe Stakes winner Moon Cactus (herself dam of the Oaks winner Moonshell). The second dam, Lady Moon (by Mil Reef), won three races from 11f to 12.3f and is out of the Oaks third Moonlight Night. (Sheikh Ahmed Al Maktoum). *"We like this colt particularly well. He has a wonderful temperament and a smooth, easy action for such a big-topped colt".*

783 - KAFI (USA)
b.c. Gulch - Nonoalca (Nonoalco).
April 7. $250,000Y. Keeneland September.
Brother to the 2-y-o Grade 1 6.5f Hopeful Stakes winner Great Navigator, closely related to the English 6f and subsequent US winner Nucleon (by Mr Prospector) and half-brother 5 winners including the French 7.5f to 12f and US stakes winner Narghile (by Foolish Pleasure), the French 10.5f winner Narmada (by Blushing Groom) and the minor US winner Hidden Promise (by Blushing John). The dam, a very smart filly, won 3 races including the Group 3 1m Prix de la Grotte and the Group 3 1m Prix des Reservoirs and was second in the French 1,000 Guineas. The second dam, Madina (by Beau Prince II), won the Prix Morny and was second in the Prix de la Salamandre. (Hamdan Al Maktoum).

784 - LIONNE
b.f. Darshaan - Percy's Lass (Blakeney).
April 2. Fourth living foal.
Half-sister to the very useful 1m to 10f winner Blue Lion (by Lomond) and to the quite useful 9f and 10.5f placed Lion Tower (by Soviet Star). The dam was a very useful winner from 6f (at 2 yrs) to 11.5f including the Group 3 September Stakes and is a half-sister to the E.P. Taylor Stakes winner Braiswick. The second dam, Laughing Girl (by Sassafras), won the 10f Lupe Stakes and is a half-sister to the dams of Teenoso, Topsy, Give Thanks, Ashayer, Favoridge and Old Country. (Sheikh Mohammed). *"Lionne needs time. She's done nothing wrong and is a good mover but won't be out until the back-end".*

785 - MOUTAHDEE (IRE)
b.c. Alzao - Ah Ya Zein (Artaius).
April 29. 68,000Y. Tattersalls October.
Half-brother to the French 3-y-o Apatride (by Polish Patriot), to the fairly useful 7.6f and 10f winner Najm Mubeen (by Last Tycoon) and the minor French winners Seen Running and Sharon Doll (both

by Shahrastani). The dam, winner of the listed 10f Grand Prix de Marseille, is a half-sister to 7 winners out of the minor 3-y-o winner Come True (by Nasram II). (Sheikh Ahmed Al Maktoum). *"A terrific mover and a strapping horse, he's well forward and would want six or seven furlongs as a two-year-old".*

---

786 - QANDIL (USA)
ch.c. Riverman - Confirmed Affair (Affirmed).
May 20. Sixth foal. $160,000Y. Keeneland September.
Half-brother to the US stakes winner This One's For Us (by Cox's Ridge) and to a minor 3-y-o winner in the USA by Nureyev. The dam, a stakes-placed winner of 5 races in the USA, is a half-sister to the US Grade 2 winner Angel Island (herself dam of Sharrood) and to the unraced dam of the US Grade 1 winner Jolie's Halo. The second dam, Who's To Know (by Fleet Nasrullah), won 5 races including a stakes event. (Hamdan Al Maktoum).

---

787 - QUESTUARY (IRE)
b.f. Rainbow Quest - Pelf (Al Nasr).
April 21.
Half-sister to the French trained 3-y-o Pelfre (by Suave Dancer), to the quite useful 1995 2-y-o 9f winner House of Riches (by Shirley Heights) and the fair 1994 13.8f 3-y-o winner Referential (by Reference Point). The dam, a 7f winner at 3 yrs in Italy, is a half-sister to the good broodmares Crown Treasure (dam of Glint of Gold and Diamond Shoal), Carefully Hidden (dam of Enscone) and Frontonian (dam of I Want to Be). The second dam, Treasure Chest (by Rough n Tumble) was a very useful stakes winner over 6.5f and 1m. (Sheikh Mohammed). *"Not very big, Questuary more than makes up for her lack of size with guts and determination and she's not missed a day's exercise. She'll do well as a two-year-old".*

---

788 - RUSKIN WALK
b.f. Machiavellian - Air Distingue (Sir Ivor).
April 28.
Sister to the very smart 1995 French 2,000 Guineas winner Vettori (by Machiavellian) and half-sister to the quite useful 1996 7f placed 2-y-o Chivalric (by Arazi), the French 9f to 10f winner Stage Manner (by In the Wings), the 3-y-o 10f winners Lodestar (by Rainbow Quest) and Decided Air (by Sure Blade) and the minor 1993 3-y-o 9f winner Livonian (by Kris). The dam won the Group 3 1m Prix d'Aumale, was second in the Nassau Stakes and third in the Prix de Diane and is a half-sister to the smart French 2-y-o Eastern Dawn. The second dam, Euryanthe (by Nijinsky), an unraced sister to the Irish St Leger and dual US Group 1 winner Caucasus, is closely related to the champion Canadian turf horse One For All and a half-sister to both the Musidora Stakes winner Last Feather and the dam of Run the Gantlet. (Sheikh Mohammed).

---

789 - SAIF MAJROUR
b.c. Darshaan - Garconniere (Gay Mecene).
February 10. 90,000Y. Tattersalls Houghton.
Half-brother to the Italian listed winner Giselle Penn (by Cozzene), to the French 3-y-o winner and listed Prix Yacowlef third Pretty Davis (by Trempolino) and minor winners in Italy by Ballad Rock, Sadler's Wells and Stalwart. The dam ran unplaced twice in France and is a half-sister to the Group 1 Gran Criterium winner Grease and the Group 3 Criterium Nazionale winner Godot. The second dam, Greedy Of Gain (by Habitat), won 4 races in Italy including a listed event and is a half-sister to Godzilla (dam of the Group 1 placed Ernani, Observation Post and Phydilla). (Sheikh Ahmed Al Maktoum).

---

790 - TAANIS (USA)
b.f. Dayjur - Ra'a (Diesis).
January 25. Fourth foal.
Sister to the 3-y-o Musafi (placed over 6f on his only outing last year) and half-sister to the quite useful 6f winner Awayil (by Woodman). The dam was a useful winner of five races over 5f and 6f including a listed event at Newmarket. The second dam, Shicklah (by The Minstrel), was a useful 5f and 6f winner at 2 yrs. (Hamdan Al Maktoum). *Marcus, when assistant trainer to Major Dick Hern, was associated with this filly's sire Dayjur and says "I feel very fortunate to have Taanis who seems to have inherited some of Dayjur's speed".*

---

791 - TABAREEH (IRE)
b.c. Marju - Rosia Bay (High Top).
February 3.
Half-brother to the to the high class middle distance colt Ibn Bey (by Mill Reef), a winner of 10 races including the Irish St Leger, the Gran Premio d'Italia and the Geoffrey Freer Stakes and second in the Breeders Cup Classic, to the smart filly Roseate Tern (by Blakeney), winner of the Yorkshire Oaks, the Lancashire Oaks and the Jockey Club Stakes, the fairly useful 10f winner Masharik (by Caerleon), the fairly useful 14f and 14.6f winner Barakat (by Bustino), the fair 14f winner Barraak (by El Gran Senor)

and a minor 2-y-o 5f winner by Mummy's Pet. The dam, a useful 7.5f and 1m winner, is a half-sister to the top class Queen Elizabeth II Stakes and Budweiser Arlington Million winner Teleprompter. The second dam, Ouija (by Silly Season), was a useful dual 1m winner at 3 yrs. (Hamdan Al Maktoum).

---

792 - THURAYYA
ch.f. Nashwan - Elfaslah (Green Desert).
March 16. Fourth foal.

Half-sister to the useful 1997 2-y-o 7f winner and Group 2 1m Royal Lodge Stakes second Almutawakel (by Machiavellian) and the fairly useful 7f (at 2 yrs) and 10f winner (in Dubai) Mawjud (by Mujtahid). The dam, a useful winner of three races from 10f to 10.4f at 3 yrs including a listed event at the Curragh, is a half-sister to the Group 1 12f Italian Derby winner and 'King George' second White Muzzle. The second dam, Fair of the Furze (by Ela Mana Mou), a very useful winner of four races including the Group 2 10f Tattersalls Rogers Gold Cup, was second in the Pretty Polly Stakes and is a half-sister to the listed stakes winners Majestic Role (in Ireland), Norman Style (in Germany) and Proconsular (in France). (Hamdan Al Maktoum).

---

793 - YEGGDAR
ch.c. Rudimentary - Raffle (Balidar).
April 17. 45,000Y. Tattersalls October.

Half-brother to the fair 1997 2-y-o 5f winner Centre Court (by Second Set), to the useful winner of 4 races at around 7f Rasan (by Dominion), the fair 2-y-o 5f winner Solo Prize (by Chief Singer) and the poor 14f to 2m winner Top Prize (by High Top). The dam, a quite useful 3-y-o 5.8f winner, is a half-sister to the the good sprinters Mummy's Pet, Parsimony and Arch Sculptor. The second dam, Money For Nothing (by Grey Sovereign), won 3 races over 5f. (Sheikh Ahmed Al Maktoum).

Peter Walwyn

---

794 - AL NAKHLAH (USA)
b.f. Sheikh Albadou - Magic Slipper (Habitat).
March 9.

Half-sister to the useful 1994 2-y-o 6f and 7f winner Muhab (by Lyphard), to the fair gelding Wali (by Lomond) a winner of four races at around 7f, the quite useful 1992 3-y-o 7f winner Ahbab (by Ajdal) and the modest 1997 3-y-o 12f winner Atnab (by Riverman). The dam, a useful 10f and 11.5f winner, is a half-sister to the 1,000 Guineas winner Fairy Footsteps and to the St Leger winner Light Cavalry. The second dam, Glass Slipper (by Relko), a useful 13.3f winner at 3 yrs and second in the Musidora Stakes, is a half-sister to Royal Palace. (Hamdan Al Maktoum).

Dermot Weld

---

795 - ALL TO EASY
b.f. Alzao - Easy To Copy (Affirmed).
April 22.

Sister to the 1992 Irish 3-y-o 7f and 1m winner Easy Definition and half-sister to the 1998 3-y-o Two-Twenty-Two (by Fairy King), the 1992 Irish 3-y-o 1m winner Clear Procedure (by The Minstrel) and the 1996 Irish 2-y-o listed 6f winner Desert Ease (by Green Desert). The dam was a useful winner of 5 races from 1m to 12f in Ireland and Italy including the Group 2 Premio Legnano and subsequently performed well in Graded stakes company in America. She is a sister to the Irish 1,000 Guineas winner Trusted Partner, to the useful Irish listed 2-y-o 6f winner Low Key Affair and the useful 7f and 9f winner Epicure's Garden. The second dam, Talking Picture (by Speak John), the champion American filly of 1973, won at up to 7f. (Moyglare Stud Farm). *"A big filly and a really nice type, All to Easy will be one to follow in the second half of the season. She's one of my best two-year-olds and I expect her to be decent. She just could be well named!"* Dermot explained.

---

796 - ANAMARA (IRE)
b.f. Fairy King - Guanhumara (Caerleon).
March 22. Second foal. 40,000Y. Tattersalls October.

Sister to the unplaced 1997 2-y-o Greeba. The dam is an unplaced half-sister to the Champion sprinter and high-class sire Cadeaux Genereux (by Young Generation) and to the dam of the listed winning sprinters Ya Malak and Dominio. The second dam, Smarten Up (by Sharpen Up), a smart winning sprinter, won the Group 3 Temple Stakes and was second in the William Hill Sprint Championship. (Mrs O'Reilly). *"A sharp filly, she'll be out in May over five furlongs and will want good ground. There isn't a lot of her, but she's has ability and goes well"*

797 - BLEND OF PACE (IRE)　　　　　　b.f. Sadler's Wells - Trusted Partner (Affirmed).
February 3.
Brother to the Irish 12f winner Archive Footage, closely related to the Irish 9f winner Brave Raider (by Dixieland Band) and half-sister to the Irish 7f winner Trust In Luck (by Nashwan) and the Irish 2-y-o 6f winner Act Of Defiance (by Caerleon). The dam, a very useful filly, won both her 2-y-o races including the Group 3 7f C.L. Weld Park Stakes and next season won the Irish 1,000 Guineas and was second in the Mount Coote Matron Stakes at the Curragh. She is a sister to the useful middle distance performers Easy to Copy and Epicure's Garden and to the useful 1993 2-y-o Low Key Affair. The second dam, Talking Picture (by Speak John), was the top American 2-y-o filly of 1973 and won at up to 7f. (Moyglare Stud Farm). *"A lovely big filly, but she'll take time and is more of a three-year-old"* Dermot was telling me.

798 - COREUX NOIR (IRE)　　　　　　b.c. Be My Guest - Sanndila (Lashkari).
March 12. Second foal. IR45,000Y. Goffs Orby.
The dam, a winner from 12f to 2m in Ireland, is a half-sister to 6 winners including the Fred Darling Stakes fourth Sansiya. The second dam, Santalina (by Relko), won the listed 12f Prix Joubert and is a half-sister to the Grand Prix de Paris and Puma Preis von Europa winner Sumayr. (Michael J Smurfit). *"A staying type, he won't be ready until the autumn over seven furlongs and a mile".*

799 - FADHEL (USA)　　　　　　b.c. Zilzal - Nice Life (Sportin' Life).
February 25. Second foal. IR130,000Y. Goffs Orby.
Half-brother to the 1997 Italian 2-y-o winner Boxter (by Eastern Echo). The dam, a winner of 4 races in the USA, is a half-sister to 4 winners including the US Grade 3 Tremont Stakes winner Eternal Flight. The second dam, Nice And Sharp (by Blade), a US stakes winner of 6 races, was second in the Grade 2 8.5f Ashland Stakes. (Hamdan Al Maktoum). *"A nice, quality horse, he'll be out from July onwards and is a very nice colt that will make a two-year-old".*

800 - HALYCON　　　　　　b.c. Diesis - Happy Gal (Habitat).
April 28. 32,000Y. Tattersalls Houghton.
Half-brother to the 3-y-o Wiston Cheese (by Cryptoclearance), to the very smart Group 2 15f Prix Hubert de Chaudenay and Group 3 15f Prix du Lutece winner Tarator (by Green Dancer) and to winners in the USA and Mexico by Alleged and Graustark. The dam, a French 3-y-o 9.5f winner, is a half-sister to 6 winners. The second dam, Love And Care (by Ballymoss), won once at 2 yrs and is a half-sister to the Nell Gwyn Stakes winner Gently out of the Gimcrack Stakes winner Be Careful. (Peter Wetzel). *"A bit backward, this horse will take time but he's a nice colt that will be suited by a mile this year".*

801 - HIP POCKET (IRE)　　　　　　b.c. Sadler's Wells - Ebony And Ivory (Bob Back).
April 20. Second foal. 50,000Y. Tattersalls October.
Half-sister to a 3-y-o by Shernazar. The dam, a winner of 3 races from 10f to 12f at 3 yrs in Ireland, is a half-sister to 5 winners including Fenny Rough, winner of the listed Oak Tree Stakes here and the Grade 2 Las Palmas Handicap in the USA. The second dam, Geraldville (by Lord Gayle), was an Irish middle-distance winner of 3 races. (Michael Watt). *"A fine, big horse and a very imposing individual, he won't be seen out until the autumn but will make a good three-year-old".*

802 - ISLAND ESCAPE (IRE)　　　　　　b.f. Turtle Island - Clear Procedure (The Minstrel).
March 4. Second foal. IR38,000Y. Goffs Orby.
The dam, a winner over 1m in Ireland at 3 yrs, is a half-sister to 4 winners including the Irish listed Round Tower Stakes winner Desert Ease and to the unraced dam of the US Grade 2 winner Dixieland Gold. The second dam, Easy To Copy (by Affirmed), was a useful winner of 5 races from 1m to 12f in Ireland and Italy including the Group 2 Premio Legnano and subsequently performed well in Graded stakes company in America. She is a sister to the Irish 1,000 Guineas winner Trusted Partner, to the useful Irish listed 2-y-o 6f winner Low Key Affair and the useful 7f and 9f winner Epicure's Garden. (Mrs O'Reilly). *"A sweet filly with a lot of quality, I'll start her over six furlongs but she should get seven this year. I like her".*

803 - LA SERINA (IRE)　　　　　　b.f. Royal Academy - Hi Bettina (Henbit).
March 19. IR130,000Y. Goffs Orby.
Half-ister to the useful Group 2 7f Premio Melton Mmemorial Tudini winner Fred Bongusto, to the useful 1997 2-y-o 5f winner Atlantic Viking (both by Danehill), the 1994 Irish 2-y-o 5f winner and Group 3 Anglesey Stakes third High Charger, the German 2-y-o 6f winner Dolour (both by Last Tycoon) and the

modest 6f (at 2 yrs) to 1m winner Legal Flair (by Law Society). The dam, a fairly useful Irish sprinter, won twice, was second in the Group 3 Debutante Stakes in Ireland and is a half-sister to the Group 3 Norfolk Stakes winner Marouble. The second dam, Pitmarie (by Pitskelly), won four sprint races (including two listed events) in Ireland. (Thomas McDonagh). *"A medium-sized filly with a lot of quality, she should make a two-year-old and be on the racecourse by June or July. I think she'll be suited to six or seven furlongs to start" says Dermot.*

804 - MAFAATIN (IRE)
ch.f. Royal Academy - Aquitaine (Nureyev).
February 20. First foal. 130,000 Y. Tattersalls Houghton.
The dam, a minor 3-y-o winner in France, is a half-brother to the A. Fabre trained 3-y-o Arnaqueur (by Miswaki) and to the Group 3 1m Prix de Chenes (at 2 yrs) and Group 2 10f Prix Greffulhe winner Along All (by Mill Reef). The dam won the Prix de l'Arc de Triomphe, the Prix Vermeille, the Turf Classic, the Washington D.C. International and the Rothmans International and is a half-sister to the very useful miler Abala. The second dam, Agujita (by Vieux Manoir), won the Group 3 10.5f Prix de Royaumont. (Hamdan Al Maktoum).

805 - MUS-IF
b.c. Lahib - Navajo Love Song (Dancing Brave).
February 2. Second foal. FF350,000. Deauville August.
Half-brother to the 3-y-o Jet Fortuna (by Midyan). The dam is an unplaced half-sister to 3 minor winners in France. The second dam, Marquina (by Posse), won over 10.5f in France and is a half-sister to the French listed winners Fabulous Queen, Fabulous Teaser, Kopelman and Quemora. (Hamdan Al Maktoum). *"This is one of my nicest colts. He's a lengthy, attractive, quality colt I expect will run first over seven furlongs around September time".*

806 - PRINCE VALIANT
b.c. Be My Chief - Countess Olivia (Prince Tenderfoot).
February 29. 105,000Y. Tattersalls Houghton.
Brother to the very smart filly Donna Viola, a winner of 11 races here and abroad including the Grade 1 Yellow Ribbon Handicap, the Grade 1 Gamely Handicap and the Group 2 Prix de l'Opera, to the modest 1992 2-y-o 5f winner Juliet Bravo (by Glow), the modest 1992 5-y-o triple 7f winner Coral Flutter (by Beldale Flutter) and the Italian winner of 3 races Golden Olivia (by Petong). The dam, a fair 7f (at 2 yrs) and 10f winner, is a half-sister to 8 minor winners out of Coralivia (by Le Levenstell), a winner over 12f in Ireland. (Peter Wetzel). *"An interesting horse, he's a fine, big colt with a nice action. He's still growing but he'll make a two-year-old by the end of May. A top-of-the-ground horse".*

807 - RAGHDAN (USA)
ch.c. Diesis - High Sevens (Master Willie).
January 21. Third foal. 100,000Y. Tattersalls Houghton.
Brother to the fair 1996 2-y-o 7f winner Impulsif and to the fair 1997 2-y-o 7f placed Gunzells. The dam, a quite useful 2-y-o 6f winner, is a half-sister to the smart Group 3 Lingfield Derby Trial winner Munwar and the smart Irish middle-distance listed winner Hateel. The second dam, Oatfield (by Great Nephew), was placed at 2 yrs. (Hamdan Al Maktoum).

808 - RIVER CANYON (IRE)
b.c. College Chapel - Na-Ammah (Ela Mana Mou).
March 30. Second foal. IR70,000Y. Goffs Orby.
Half-brother to the 3-y-o Beseeching (by Hamas). The dam, a winner of 3 races at 3 yrs in Ireland including a listed event over 14f, is a half-sister to 3 winners including the Queen Anne Stakes, Sea World International Stakes and Premio Emilio Turati winner (all Group 2 events) Alflora. The second dam, Adrana (by Bold Lad), won her only start (over 5f at 2 yrs) and is a half-sister to the top-class middle-distance stayer Ardross and to the Group 3 winner Gesedeh and to the listed winners Larrocha and Karol. (Lord Philip Harris). *"An interesting colt this, as he's by a sprinter and out of a staying mare. A very strong horse, he goes very nicely and I suspect he'd want six or seven furlongs this season from August onwards" says the trainer.*

809 - RIVER GORGE
b.c. Magic Ring - Zinzi (Song).
March 27. 60,000Y. Tattersalls October.
Half-brother to the 3-y-o Pussy Galore (by Pursuit Of Love), to the very useful sprinter Sarcita, a winner of 6 races including the Portland Handicap, the modest 5f winner El Arz (both by Primo Dominie) and a winner in Hong Kong by Midyan. The dam won over 5f at 4 yrs in Ireland and is a half-sister to 4 winners including the Irish listed winner Checker Express. The second dam, Checkerberry (by Connaught), won over 1m and is a half-sister to the Sun Chariot Stakes winner Cranberry Sauce (dam of the Child Stakes winner Sauceboat and thus grandam of the Group winners Kind Of Hush and Dusty Dollar).

(Lord Philip Harris). *"A sharp colt, he'll be my first two-year-old to run. A good-actioned sort, he'd want good ground".*

810 - RIVER PLATE (USA)

ch.c. Jade Hunter - Cockney Lass (Camden Town).
March 30. $32,000Y. Keeneland September.
Half-brother to the minor 1996 Irish 4-y-o 7f and 9f winner Rockny (by Theatrical). The dam won 9 races in Ireland including the Group 2 10f Tattersalls Rogers Gold Cup. The second dam, Big Bugs Bomb (by Skymaster), won 5 races in England and Ireland and is a half-sister to the dam of the Tote Cesarewitch winner Kayudee. (Lord Philip Harris). *"A strong, good-sized, sharp colt, he certainly looks like a two-year-old. He'll be out in June or July and will prefer top of the ground".* The name River Plate, incidentally, had yet to be confirmed when the book was published.

811 - ROYAL COMMAND (IRE)

b.c. Green Desert - Elegance in Design (Habitat).
May 21.
Half-brother to the 1997 Irish 2-y-o 8.5f winner Hibernian Rhapsody (by Darshaan). The dam, a useful 2-y-o 6f and 3-y-o listed 6f winner, is a sister to the high-class Group 2 1m Coronation Stakes winner Chalon (herself dam of the Prix Ganay and Prix d'Ispahan winner Creator) and a half-sister to the good Irish 1m to 10f winner Executive Perk and the useful middle-distance performer Costly Lesson. The second dam, Areola (by Kythnos), was a very useful 2-y-o winner of three 5f events including the Phoenix Stakes. (Moyglare Stud Farm). *"A bit more backward than one might expect, but this is a nice colt that will make a two-year-old by September or October. One to follow".*

812 - RYAN'S BRIEF

b.c. Brief Truce - Too Shy (Top Ville).
March 29. Second foal. 80,000Y. Tattersalls Houghton.
Half-brother to a 3-y-o in Italy by Rainbows For Life. The dam is an unplaced half-sister to 5 winners including Sharaya (Group 1 Prix Vermeille), Sharaniya (Group 2 Grand Prix d'Evry) and Shannkara (Grade 3 Nijana Stakes in the USA). The second dam, Shanizadeh (by Baldric II), was a useful French 6f and 1m winner. (Mr C McHale). *"A colt for the second half of the season".*

813 - TALIGHTA (IRE)

b.f. Barathea - Morcote (Magical Wonder).
April 23. First foal. 48,000Y. Tattersalls Houghton.
The dam, a very useful winner of the Group 3 7f C L Weld Park Stakes at 2 yrs and fourth in the Irish 1,000 Guineas, is a half-sister to 4 winners including the very useful listed 7f Leopardstown 1,000 Guineas Trial winner and US Grade 1 placed Miami Sands. The second dam, Madame du Barry (by Wollow), is a placed half-sister to the French St Leger winner Mersey and the Prix Saint-Alary winner Muncie. (Michael J Smurfit). *"A small filly,Talighta will beat more expensive ones alright. She needs to grow but she's a good-actioned filly and I like her".*

814 - WIMBLEDON

b.c. Second Set - Rarely Irish (Irish Tower).
February 12. Sixth foal. 78,000Y. Tattersalls October.
Brother to the 3-y-o Rarely Set and half-brother to the German winners My Happy Guest (by Be My Guest) and Romantiker (by Pennine Walk). The dam, a minor Irish 4-y-o 9f winner, is a half-sister to 10 winners including the Hoover Fillies Mile second Exclusively Raised. The second dam, The Rarest (by Rarity), won once at 3 yrs, was second in the National Stakes at the Curragh and is a half-sister to the Jersey Stakes winner Ashleigh. (Prince Fahd Salman).

815 - ZILIO

ch.c. Zilzal - Tesio's Love (Tom Rolfe).
May 27. IR46,000Y. Goffs Orby.
Half-brother to the US stakes winner Cat Affair (by Storm Cat) and a minor 2-y-o winner in the USA by Family Doctor. The dam is an unplaced half-sister to 6 winners including the Grade 1 Santa Ana Handicap winner Anna Reunion (by Cresta Rider). The second dam, Love For Life (by Forli), is a placed half-sister to 5 winners. (Mrs O'Reilly). *"Backward now, but he's a quality colt and will be one to watch out for from mid-summer onwards".*

816 - UNNAMED

ch.f. Indian Ridge - Across The Ice (General Holme).
March 24. Third foal. 68,000Y. Tattersalls Houghton.
Half-sister to the French 3-y-o Glissando (by In The Wings). The dam, a minor French 3-y-o winner, is a half-sister to 5 winners including Northern Premier (Group 3 Prix de la Grotte and Group 3 Prix de la Porte Maillot). The second dam, Madame Premier (by Raja Baba), won 4 races in the USA including a minor stakes and was fourth in the Grade 1 Spinaway Stakes. (Michael J Smurfit). *"Very correct, this will be a nice filly over six furlongs in mid-summer".*

817 - UNNAMED   ch.g. Perugino - Perfect Chance (Petorius).
February 5. Fourth foal. IR21,000Y. Goffs Challenge.
Half-brother to the poor 5f (at 2 yrs) to 11f placed Perfect Bertie (by Cyrano de Bergerac). The dam, a
quite useful 7f winner, is out of the useful Irish 2-y-o 7f winner Perfect Line (by Rarity), herself a
half-sister to Deep Run and to the dam of One In A Million. (Mr A McManus). *"This gelding really looks
like a quality individual. He goes well, should be out by June and has the Goffs Challenge race as his
target".*

818 - UNNAMED   b.br.c. Green Dancer - Subtle Expression (Slew O'Gold).
February 5. First foal. $100,000Y. Keeneland September.
The dam is an unplaced half-sister to 4 winners including the US stakes winner Palm Reader and the
listed 10f James Seymour Stakes second Nadeed. The second dam, Palmistry (by Forli), won 6 races
including stakes events over 6.5f and 8.5f and is a half-sister to 8 winners notably the French Derby
winner and top-class sire Caerleon and the Grade 1 Secretariat Stakes winner Vision. (Michael J
Smurfit). *"Quite a nice colt, he's more forward than some Green Dancers and will run in the mid-summer".*

819 - UNNAMED   b.f. Royal Academy - Trojan Crown (Trojan Fen).
February 11. Second living foal. IR70,000Y. Goffs Orby.
Half-sister to the 3-y-o Prince Of Troy (by Pursuit Of Love). The dam, a fairly useful winner of 2 races
over 7f at 2 yrs including the listed Sweet Solera Stakes, is a half-sister to 4 winners. The second dam,
Crown Witness (by Crowned Prince), a winner of 6 races and a fairly useful miler, is a half-sister to 9
winners including the dams of the Melbourne Cup and Irish St Leger winner Vintage Crop and the
American Derby winner Overbury. (Michael J Smurfit). *"A real quality filly, she's big and will take some
time - probably the autumn - but she'll make a fine three-year-old".*

Sean Woods

820 - HIGH TATRA (IRE)   b.c. Polish Patriot - Bouffant (High Top).
April 23. 23,000Y. Tattersalls October.
Brother to the 3-y-o Seductive Song, to the fair 5f (at 2 yrs) to 10f winner Smart Boy and the German
winner Mutassariff and half-brother to the quite useful 9.9f winner Sahil and the plating-class 2-y-o 6.9f
winner Fanfan (both by Taufan). The dam was placed four times in Ireland at 3 yrs and is out of the
Group 3 12f Lingfield Oaks Trial winner Lucent (by Irish Ball) - herself a daughter of the July Cup winner
Lucasland. (Mr W J P Jackson & Mr R Norton). *"A nice type of horse, High Tatra is a big, straightforward
colt and I think he'll be suited by middle-distances next year"* Sean tells me.

821 - KNOCKHOLT   b.c. Be My Chief - Saffron Crocus (Shareef Dancer).
March 4. Second foal. IR27,000Y. Goffs Orby.
The dam, a minor 12f and 13f winner in Ireland, is a half-sister to the US stakes winner and Grade 2
placed Colchis Island. The second dam, Bright Crocus (by Clev Er Tell), won the Group 3 1m May Hill
Stakes at 2 yrs here, the Grade 3 Fair Grounds Oaks in the USA and was second in the Grade 1
Kentucky Oaks. (Mr R Crawley). *"A very strong individual, she'll want six or seven furlongs this summer
but will be campaigned with her three-year-old career in mind".*

822 - LEAVE IT TO ME   b.f. College Chapel - Enaam (Shirley Heights).
March 18. Fourth foal. 26,000Y. Doncaster St Leger.
Half-sister to the useful 1997 2-y-o 6f winner Linden Heights (by Distinctly North) and the modest and
ungenuine 1996 3-y-o 1m winner Linda's Joy (by Classic Secret). The dam, a moderate 1m to 10f
placed 3-y-o, is a half-sister to 2 minor winners abroad. The second dam, Elzaahirah (by Irish Ball),
won 6 races abroad and is a half-sister to Irish Oaks winner Give Thanks. (Mr J Sanchez). *"A forward
two-year-old, he looks quite nice, will be out in May and shows speed".*

823 - PRINCE EMAN   b.c. Primo Dominie - Carolside (Music Maestro).
January 30.
Brother to the minor 2-y-o 5f winner Oh Whataknight and half-brother to several winners including the
useful 1m to 9f winner Eton Ld (by Never So Bold) and the quite useful 7f winner Summer Queen (by
Robellino). The dam was a very useful 2-y-o 5f winner. *"A very powerful, good-moving horse, he'll
make a two-year-old alright".*

824 - TOMOE GOZEN (IRE) b.f. Brief Truce - Deelish (Caerleon).
February 11. First foal. IR34,000Y. Goffs Orby.
The dam, a winner over 11f in Ireland at 3 yrs, is out of the unraced Mayfair Madam (by Hello Gorgeous), herself a half-sister to 9 winners including the Group 3 Royal Whip Stakes winner Beyond The Lake and the listed-placed Tree Of Knowledge (dam of the Irish Derby and Breeders Cup Turf winner Theatrical). (Mr M Simpson). *"This filly just oozes class. She'll be suited by six or seven furlongs this year and I'm really getting excited about her. She should win this year but I won't press her too hard as a two-year-old".*

825 - TRANSITION (IRE) b.c. Brief Truce - Six Penny Express (Bay Express).
April 12. 27,000Y. Tattersalls October.
Half-brother to the very useful 1995 2-y-o Irish listed 5f winner Nashcash (by Nashamaa), the fair 1997 2-y-o 6f winner Madame Claude (by Paris House), the Irish 10f winner Copper and Steel (by Wolverlife) and the 2-y-o 5f winners Miss Amy Lou (by Gallic League) and Tannerrun (by Runnett). The dam was placed at 3 yrs in Ireland and is a half-sister to 4 winners including the Group 2 Hardwicke Stakes winner Charlie Bubbles. The second dam, Sixandahalf (by Thirteen of Diamonds), won once at 3 yrs. (Broadgate III Partnership). *"He's had a slight setback but I do feel that Transition will make up into a nice type of horse".*

Geoff Wragg

826 - BALISADA ch.f. Kris - Balnaha (Lomond).
February 10. Second foal.
Half-sister to the 3-y-o Forest Call (by Wolfhound). The dam, a modest 3-y-o 1m winner, is a sister to Inchmurrin (a very useful winner of the Child Stakes and herself dam of the very smart and tough colt Inchinor), is closely related to the very useful 1m winner Guest Artiste and a half-sister to the Mill Reef Stakes winner Welney. The second dam, On Show (by Welsh Pageant), won over 10f and was second in the November Handicap. (Mr A E Oppenheimer).

827 - CASSANDRA GO (IRE) gr.f. Indian Ridge - Rahaam (Secreto).
April 3. Fourth foal. 200,000Y. Tattersalls Houghton.
Half-sister to the smart Group 3 6f Coventry Stakes winner and Irish 2,000 Guineas second Verglas (by Highest Honor) and to Persian Secret (by Persian Heights), a fairly useful 2-y-o 6f winner here and subsequently a French listed winner. The dam, a fairly useful 3-y-o 7f winner, is a half-sister to 8 winners including the Prix Thomas Bryon winner and French 2,000 Guineas third Glory Forever. The second dam, Fager's Glory (by Mr Prospector), is an unraced half-sister to 5 winners including the US Grade 3 stakes winner Perfect Parade. (Mr A E Oppenheimer).

828 - DESDEMONA (IRE) b.f. Lahib - Tragic Point (Tragic Role).
March 10. First foal. 33,000Y. Tattersalls October.
The dam won over 1m at 2 yrs in Ireland and was third in the Group 3 1m Killavullan Stakes. The second dam, North Queen (by Northfields), was a useful 6f and 7f winner and a half-sister to the US Grade 2 winner Electric Society and the Doncaster Cup second Bourbon Boy (subsequently a Grade 3 winner in Australia). (Cheveley Park Stud).

829 - DOWNLAND b.c. Common Grounds - Boldabsa (Persian Bold).
February 18. Sixth foal. IR115,000Y. Goffs Orby.
Brother to the useful 1994 2-y-o listed 6f winner Painted Madam, to Double Eight, a fair winner of 2 races at around 12f at 3 yrs in 1997 and the 1993 Irish 2-y-o 1m winner Oliver Messel. The dam, a fairly useful Irish 9f and 10f winner, is a half-sister to 5 winners out of Absaroka (by Prince Tenderfoot), a winner at 3 yrs in France and third in the Group 3 Prix Cleopatre. (Mollers Racing).

830 - ISLAND HOUSE (IRE) ch.c. Grand Lodge - Fortitude (Last Tycoon).
February 19. First foal. FF750,000. Deauville August.
The dam, a winner of 4 minor races in France, is a half-sister to the Group 2 Prix Jean Prat winner Rachmaninov and to the listed winner Reine Wells. The second dam, Rivoltade (by Sir Ivor), is an unraced half-sister to the French 1,000 Guineas winner Riverqueen. (Mollers Racing).

831 - KITTIWAKE b.f. Barathea - Gull Nook (Mill Reef).
March 15. 300,000Y. Tattersalls Houghton.
Closely related to the very useful Group 3 14f Premio Roma winner and Group 1 Yorkshire Oaks fourth Spring and to the minor 3-y-o 12.2f winner Tanz (both by Sadlers Wells) and half-sister to the top-class

colt Pentire (by Be My Guest), winner of the King George VI and Queen Elizabeth Diamond Stakes and the Irish Champion Stakes etc., and to the fairly useful 1m to 10f winner Smart Generation (by Cadeaux Genereux). The dam, a smart filly, won over 10.5f at 3 yrs and was second in the Group 2 12f Ribblesdale Stakes. She is a sister to the useful 3-y-o 12f winner Primrose Valley, closely related to the Group 3 12f Princess Royal Stakes winner Banket and a half-sister to the Group 3 13.5f Ormonde Stakes winner Mr Pintips. The second dam, Bempton (by Blakeney), was placed four times at up to 11f and is a half-sister to Shirley Heights. (Gestut Schlenderhan).

---

832 - LAMZENA (IRE)

b.f. Fairy King - Ezana (Ela Mana Mou).
March 14. 60,000Y. Tattersalls Houghton.

Half-sister to Erzadjan (by Kahyasi), a winner of three races at around 12f in Ireland at 3 yrs and to Ebaziya (by Darshaan), a winner from 7f (at 2 yrs) to 12f in Ireland including three listed events and herself dam of the Irish Oaks winner Ebadiyla. The dam, a winner in France at 3 yrs over 11.5f, is a half-sister to 5 winners including the Group 3 Prix de Flore and Group 3 Prix Penelope winner Demia. The second dam, Evisa (by Dan Cupid), was unraced. (Mr Roy Bracher).

---

833 - MISS SIDDONS (IRE)

ch.f. Royal Academy - White Water (Pharly).
May 9. Sixth foal. IR54,000Y. Goffs Orby.

Half-sister to the 3-y-o Rafting (by Darshaan), to the very useful Italian Group 3 1m winner Lear Water (by Lear Fan) and 3 minor winners in France by Irish River, Lear Fan and Saint Estephe. The dam won 10 races in France from 6.5f to 11.5f, including a listed event, and is a half-sister to the French listed winners Sovereign Water and Gulf Water and to the French Derby fourth Bellwater. The second dam, Paddle (by Jim French), won twice and was fourth in the Prix de Diane and is a half-sister to the high-class French filly Dunette. (Mrs Rebecca Philipps).

---

834 - OUTCRY

b.f. Caerleon - In Full Cry (Seattle Slew).
January 23. Second foal.

The dam, a winner of 2 races in the USA and Grade 2 placed, is a half-sister to the top-class miler Posse, to the Grade 3 winner Late As Usual and to the dam of the Italian Group 2 winner Lonely Bird. The second dam, In Hot Pursuit (by Bold Ruler), was a top 2-y-o filly in the USA. (Mr A E Oppenheimer).

---

835 - REPEAT WARNING

b.f. Warning - Reprocolor (Jimmy Reppin).
April 24.

Sister to the 3-y-o Global Warning and half-sister to the high-class Group 1 10f Irish Champion Stakes winner Cezanne (by Ajdal), the Irish Oaks winner Colorspin (by High Top) - dam of the top-class colt Opera House, the Group 2 Prix de l'Opera and Group 3 Waterford Candelabra Stakes winner Bella Colora (by Bellypha) - dam of the smart colt Stagecraft, to the useful 6f to 1m winner Rappa Tap Tap (by Tap on Wood), the fair 9f winner Colorful Ambition (by Slip Anchor) and the unraced dam of the very useful 7f and 1m winner Torch Rouge. The dam was a very useful winner of the 12f Lingfield Oaks Trial and the 12f Lancashire Oaks. The second dam, Blue Queen (by Majority Blue), was an unplaced half-sister to the high-class sprinter Sandford Lad. (Lancen Farm Partnership).

---

836 - SLOANE

ch.c. Machiavellian - Gussy Marlowe (Final Straw).
May 3. Third foal.

Half-brother to the 3-y-o Nadine (by Arazi). The dam, a smart filly, won the Group 3 10.5f Musidora Stakes and the 10f Pretty Polly Stakes, was third in the Group 1 1m Coronation Stakes and is a half-sister to a minor 10.6f winner. The second dam, Lady Lorelei (by Derring Do), was a useful winner of 4 races from 5f (at 2 yrs) to 1m. (Mrs John Van Geest).

---

837 - SOSSUS VLEI

b.c. Inchinor - Sassalya (Sassafras).
February 24. 90,000Y. Tattersalls Houghton.

Half-brother to 12 winners including the high class 7f Jersey Stakes and Challenge Stakes winner Sally Rous (by Rousillon), the high-class Group 1 Prix d'Ispahan winner Sasuru, the quite useful 2-y-o 6f winner Tzu'mu (both by Most Welcome), the Welsh Derby winner Assemblyman (by General Assembly), the 7f and 7.5f winner Bold Indian (by Bold Lad, Ire), the 6f and 14f winner The Faraway Tree (by Suave Dancer), the 12f winner Chauve Souris (by Beldale Flutter) - all four very useful - and the useful Schweppes Golden Mile Handicap winner Little Bean (by Ajdal). The dam won over 10f in Ireland and is a half-sister to the smart colts Beau Sham and Lafontaine. The second dam, Valya (by Vandale), won 3 races including the 13.5f Prix de Pomone. (Mr A E Oppenheimer).

838 - SWALLOW FLIGHT (IRE)   b.c. Bluebird - Mirage (Red Sunset).
April 20. Fourth foal. IR62,000Y. Goffs Orby.
Half-brother to a 2-y-o winner in Germany by Thatching. The dam, a sprint winner of 2 listed events in
Germany, is a half-sister to 5 winners including a Group 3 winner in Scandinavia. The second dam,
Another Way (by Wolverlife), is a placed half-sister to 8 winners. (Mollers Racing).

839 - TALIBAN (IRE)   b.c. Bigstone - Aunt Hester (Caerleon).
April 30. Fifth foal. 180,000Y. Tattersalls October.
Half-brother to the 1997 German 3-y-o winner First Wings (by In The Wings) and to the modest 6f (at
2 yrs) and 8.3f winner Samaka Hara (by Taufan). The dam, a modest 2-y-o 5f winner, is closely related
to the smart Group 3 9f Prix Daphnis winner L'Irresponsable. The second dam, Lady Hester (by Native
Prince), won over 5f and 6f in Ireland. (Mollers Racing).

840 - TURNTABLE (IRE)   b.f. Dolphin Street - Sharp Circle (Sure Blade).
January 25. Third foal. 72,000Y. Tattersalls October.
Half-sister to the 1997 3-y-o 7f all-weather seller winner Compact Disc (by Royal Academy). The dam,
a quite useful 3-y-o 1m winner, is a half-sister to 6 winners including the Coventry Stakes winner and
useful sire Red Sunset and the Queen Mary Stakes winner Greenland Park (dam of the Prix Saint-Alary
winner Fitnah). The second dam, Centre Piece (by Tompion), was placed fourth once over 6f and is a
half-sister to 6 winners. (Cheveley Park Stud).

THE EARLY TYPES

Jack Berry and Barry Hills have both chalked up over 100 2-y-o wins in the past three seasons; Hills leads the 2-y-o prize money table for the same period

This section of the book is primarily concerned with precocious two-year-olds - most of them specifically suggested by the trainers themselves. The majority will have been early foals and will already have shown enough to suggest a successful season is in the offing. Others may be slightly later-developing types, perhaps even by middle-distance stallions, which the trainers are nonetheless enthusiastic about. Naturally, those trainers well-known for producing fast, early sorts - Jack Berry, Richard Hannon, Mick Channon and Brian Meehan for example - are strongly represented.

Eric Alston

Eric has suggested three fillies which he feels will certainly be good enough to win this year. "Damalis, a big filly, ran a terrific race first time out. She'll probably want seven furlongs eventually". Diletto is "a sharp two-year-old that was unlucky in running first time out, but will put that right" and Record Time "will be out in May over five furlongs. She's quite a lengthy filly, but sharp nonetheless.

841 - DAMALIS (IRE)
b.f. Mukaddamah - Art Age (Artaius).
April 3. IR5,000Y. Goffs Challenge.
Half-sister to the quite useful Doncaster Spring Mile winner Artful Dane (by Danehill), to the quite useful 2-y-o 6f winner Naked Poser (by Night Shift) and the modest 2-y-o 5f winner Happy Tycoon (by Polish Patriot). The dam is an unraced half-sister to 9 winners out of the 2-y-o winner and Group 2 Phoenix Stakes second Pepi Image (by National). (Liam Ferguson).

842 - DILETTO (IRE)
b.f. Mujadil - Avidal Park (Horage).
April 25. IR3,000Y. Goffs Challenge.
Half-sister to the fair 1997 1m all-weather winner Projectvision (by Roi Danzig), the modest 12f winner Real Popcorn and the Italian winner of 12 races Rosso Fiorentino (both by Jareer). The dam, a fair 2-y-o 5f winner, is out of the quite useful 2-y-o 6f winner Debutina Park (by Averof), herself a half-sister to the Italian Derby winner Don Orazio. (Liam Ferguson).

843 - RECORD TIME
ch.f. Clantime - On The Record (Record Token).
February 27. 14,000Y. Doncaster St Leger.
Sister to the useful 1994 2-y-o listed 5f Harry Rosebery Trophy winner Lago di Varano and half-sister to the fair 6f and 7f winner Sky Music (by Absalom). The dam, a fair 5f winner, is a half-sister to 3 minor winners. The second dam, Bella Travaille (by Workboy), was a 5f sprinter and won 6 races. (Peter Onslow).

David Arbuthnot.

David's two-year-olds this year include these two promising youngsters. Pawsible is "a decent sort of filly, neat and racy. She should be out over six furlongs on good ground in May". Price of Passion is "big, active and strong. A sprinting-type filly, I'd expect her to be out at the end of April over five furlongs, though she might get a mile next year". Both filles are being aimed at the Weatherbys Sprint.

844 - PAWSIBLE
b.f. Mujadil - Kentucky Wildcat (Be My Guest).
April 27. Sixth foal. 10,000Y. Tattersalls October.
Half-sister to the 3-y-o Safe Sharp Jo (by Case Law), to the fairly useful 2-y-o 5f and 6f winner and listed Firth of Clyde Stakes placed Randonneur (by Red Sunset) and the quite useful 5f winner of 7 races here and abroad Two Moves In Front (by Ballad Rock). The dam, a modest 7f (at 2 yrs) and 15.8f placed maiden, is a half-sister to 6 minor winners abroad. The second dam, Formosanta (by Believe It), is a placed half-sister to the Group 3 Cherry Hinton Stakes winner Turkish Treasure (dam of the Norfolk Stakes winner Magic Mirror).

845 - PRICE OF PASSION
b.f. Dolphin Street - Food Of Love (Music Boy).
April 19. Third foal. 29,000Y. Doncaster St Leger.
Half-sister to the quite useful 1997 2-y-o 5f and 6.5f winner Branston Berry (by Mukaddamah). The dam, a very useful sprinter, won 6 races and was placed in the Group 3 King George Stakes. The second dam, Shortbread (by Crisp And Even), was a useful 7f winner here and later won over 12f in Norway. (Noel Cronin).

Alan Bailey

Carequick and Bodfari Times are the two suggested by Cheshire handler Alan Bailey. He informs me they are both good two-year-olds and that they have both worked with, and beaten, older horses. Carequick is "quite strong, compact and will start off at five furlongs but will get further". Bodfari Times is "a tallish, angular filly that is sharp and will also be best over five furlongs to start". He plans to take one of these fillies to Chester and the other to York (both in May).

846 - BODFARI TIMES
ch.f. Clantime - Tendency (Ballad Rock).
January 30. Fifth foal. 11,000Y. Doncaster St Leger.
Sister to the 3-y-o Clancy and half-sister to the fairly useful 6f to 8.7f all-weather winner Le Sport (by Dowsing) and the poor 7f all-weather seller winner Dowdency. The dam, a fair 4-y-o 6f winner, is out of the unraced Clover Hollow (by Wolver Hollow), herself a half-sister to the Irish Silken Glider Stakes winners Ballet Francais and French Score.

847 - CAREQUICK
ch.f. Risk Me - Miss Serlby (Runnett).
March 9. 7,200Y. Doncaster St Leger.
Sister to the 2-y-o dual 5f winner Risk Me's Girl and half-sister to the 2-y-o 5f and 6f winner Left Stranded (by Governor General) - both quite useful. The dam, a modest 5f placed maiden, is out of the fairly useful 2-y-o 6f winner Sarasingh (by Mansingh).

Jack Banks

Jack and I have sorted out these three two-year-olds of his that should be visiting the winner's enclosure this year. Havana is "a really nice filly that will be out by June or July over six furlongs. She is a filly with a lot of presence". Lion Cub "will be campaigned in France as well as in England, because of the owner's premiums. A lovely, big horse, but still immature and still growing in mid-April". Jack also suggested Rose of Mooncoin - "a nice filly with a lovely temperament, she's showing a bit of speed".

848 - HAVANA
b.f. Dolphin Street - Royaltess (Royal and Regal).
March 16. IR28,000Y. Goffs Challenge.
Closely related to the fair 6f placed 2-y-o Blue Tess (by Bluebird), subsequently a winner of 5 races in the USA and half-sister to the 1997 unplaced 2-y-o Hunt Hill (by High Estate) and the useful 1989 2-y-o 6f winner Makbul (by Fairy King). The dam is an unraced sister to the winner and Phoenix Stakes placed Regaltess and a half-sister to the Moyglare Stud Stakes winner Daness. The second dam, Devil's Drink (by Red God), was unplaced. (E Carter).

849 - LION CUB (IRE)
b.c. Catrail - Lightly Dancing (Groom Dancer).
April 26. First foal. FF280,000. Deauville August.
The dam, a winner at 3 yrs in France, is a half-sister to the Group 2 Prix de Pomone winner Light The Lights, the Group 3 Fille de l'Air winner Liastra and the Group 3 Royal Whip Stakes winner Last Light. The second dam, Lighted Glory (by Nijinsky), won the Group 3 Prix de Flore and is a half-sister to the Prix Kergorlay winner King Luthier and to the dams of Cool (Grade 1 Manhattan Handicap) and the Group 2 winners Mountain Kingdom and Paris House.

850 - ROSE OF MOONCOIN (IRE)
b.f. Brief Truce - Sharp Deposit (Sharpo).
March 21. Third foal.
Half-sister to the quite useful 2-y-o 6f winner Fly Tip (by Bluebird) and to the 1997 Italian 2-y-o winner Come Va Va (by Tenby). The dam is an unraced half-sister to the Ebor Handicap winner Deposki. The second dam, Deposit (by Thatch), was placed at 2 yrs before winning in the West Indies and is a half-sister to the Sweet Solera Stakes winner Lucayan Princess - herself dam of the high-class Italian Derby winner Luso and the Gallinule Stakes winner Needle Gun.

David Barron

Among David's nicer two-year-olds this year are the colts Court Thirteen and Northern Svengali. Court Thirteen is "quite a nice, strong colt. He'll be out in May over five furlongs". Northern Svengali is "a colt that will pay to follow. Smallish, very strong and powerfully built, he would prefer fast ground and is a typical sprinter".

851 - COURT THIRTEEN
b.c. Petong - Madam Bold (Never So Bold).
February 25. Fifth foal. 32,000Y. Doncaster St Leger.
Half-brother to the fair 1997 2-y-o 7f winner Miss Vivien (by Puissance), to the fair 1994 2-y-o 5f winner Rigsby (by Fools Holme) and the Swedish 6f winner Bold Risk (by Midyan). The dam is an unraced

half-sister to one winner. The second dam, Sophisticated Lady (by Habitat), ran unplaced once and is a sister to the top-class sprinter Sigy (dam of two French Group winners and the listed winner King's Signet) and the Prix du Gros-Chene winner Sonoma (dam of the French Group 3 winner Funambule). (Peter Savill).

852 - NORTHERN SVENGALI (IRE)
b.c. Distinctly North - Trilby's Dream (Mansooj).
April 17. First foal. 10,000Y. Tattersalls Fairyhouse.
The dam is an unraced half-sister to one winner out of the dual Irish winner and Group 3 Moyglare Stud Stakes third Little Trilby (by Tyrant) - herself a half-sister to 4 winners including the dam of the Derby third Shearwalk and the Ribblesdale Stakes third Santiki. (Timothy Cox).

Michael Bell

Michael's suggestions for likely two-year-old winners this year are as follows. Automatic is "a big, scopey horse, not that sharp but he's done well physically, has a good temperament and is potentially a nice horse. I'll probably start him off over six furlongs". Bratby is "not going to be as early as I thought, but he has a high cruising speed, looks very promising and will start off at six furlongs. One of the nicer ones". Exit is "very much liked by everyone in the yard. A very powerful mover, he could start off in a six furlong maiden in mid-May at Newmarket. One to follow". Hoh Steamer is "going well and looks early. He should be out at the Guineas meeting, is very sound and looks to have gears. A sharp colt, he'll start over five furlongs". Housemaster is "a big, long-striding horse that has done well physically. Very athletic, he's a nice horse and will probably be suited by seven furlongs this year". Prairie Wolf is "strong and mature and possibly better than his dam who won for me. He'll be a mid-summer two-year-old over seven furlongs". Schnitzel is "a strong filly, will probably want seven furlongs and is a filly we all like". Michael has another two horses in the Premier Section.

853 - AUTOMATIC
b.c. Clantime - Gentle Gypsy (Junius).
April 25. 27,000Y. Doncaster St Leger.
Half-brother to the modest dual 5f winner Indian Crystal (by Petong), to the minor US winner Nabeela (by Belfort) and to Coconut Johnny (by King Of Spain), a modest winner of three races here over 5f and of 17 races on the continent. The dam, a fairly useful 2-y-o 5f winner, is a half-sister to 5 winners including the Easter Stakes winner Regiment. The second dam, Rossaldene (by Mummy's Pet), won once at 2 yrs. (Billy Maguire).

854 - BRATBY (IRE)
b.c. Distinctly North - Aridje (Mummy's Pet).
April 14. 33,000Y. Tattersalls October.
Half-brother to the useful 1987 2-y-o 5f and 6f winner Lust Of Power, to the moderate triple 7f winner Lust Of Love (both by Sallust) and the very useful steeplechaser Fragrant Dawn (by Strong Gale). The dam, a quite useful 2-y-o 5f winner, is a half-sister to 3 minor winners. The second dam, Derrede (by Derring-Do), is an unraced half-sister to the good sprinter Singing Bede. (Mr C M Watt).

855 - EXIT
b.f. Exbourne - Meteoric (High Line).
January 30. 30,000Y. Tattersalls October.
Half-sister to the French 1993 3-y-o 10f winner From Afar (by Riverman), to the 1997 3-y-o 10.2f winner Meteor Strike (by Lomond) and winners in the USA and Denmark by Topsider. The dam, a useful sprinter, won 2 races and was second in the Group 3 Waterford Candelabra Stakes. She is a half-sister to 8 winners including the US Grade 2 Arcadia Handicap winner Tychonic and the Group 2 William Hill Sprint Championship second Fine Edge. The second dam, Metair (by Laser Light), won 7 races and was a game sprinter.

856 - HOH STEAMER
b.c. Perugino - Dane's Lane (Danehill).
April 28. Second foal. IR30,000Y. Goffs Orby.
The dam is an unraced half-sister to 4 winners including the Group 1 Premio Parioli third War Brave. The second dam, Kizzy (by Dancer's Image), won the listed Kilruddery Stakes and is a half-sister to the Group 3 Lingfield Oaks Trial winner Heaven Knows. (Mr D F Allport).

857 - HOUSEMASTER (IRE)
b.c. Rudimentary - Glenarff (Irish River).
February 17. Third foal. 72,000Y. Tattersalls Houghton.
Half-brother to the 1997 French 3-y-o winner Vic River (by Old Vic). The dam, a minor winner at 3 yrs in France, is a half-sister to 2 minor winners. The second dam, Kraemer (by Lyphard), a half-sister to the French Group 2 Prix d'Astarte winner Shaanxi, won four races in France and the USA including

the listed 8.5f Bay Meadows Oaks and was second in the Grade 2 9f Del Mar Oaks. (Hoghclere Thoroughbred Racing Ltd).

858 - PRAIRIE WOLF ch.c. Wolfhound - Bay Queen (Damister).
March 26. First foal.
The dam, a quite useful 9.9f to 11.1f winner, is out of the quite useful 1m winner Be My Queen (by Be My Guest), herself a daughter of a half-sister to the Derby second Cavo Doro. (Bernard Warren).

859 - SCHNITZEL (IRE) b.f. Tirol - Good Reference (Reference Point).
February 8. Second foal. 18,500Y. Tattersalls October.
Half-sister to the fair 1997 6f and 1m placed 2-y-o Good Catch (by Last Tycoon). The dam, a quite useful 7f (at 2 yrs) and 1m winner is a half-sister to 4 winners including the Group 3 May Hill Stakes second Self Assured. The second dam, Impudent Miss (by Persian Bold), won the Group 3 Silken Glider Stakes and is a half-sister to the smart sprinter Sayyaf. (Mrs G Rowland-Clark).

Jack Berry

Jack's two-year-olds began the season in fine form and it looks like he's in for a banner year. All of the following should enter the winner's enclosure this year - if they've not already done so! Ace of Parkes is "a good colt, a full-brother to My Melody Parkes and he's certainly worth a mention. Quite a sharp horse, he'll win this year". Angie Baby is "a nice little filly that just got beaten a head on her first outing. Certain to win". Conwy Lodge "took a bit of time coming to hand but he'll do alright later on". Cyclone Flyer is "by the good first-season sire College Chapel. This filly is really nice, wouldn't be far off her first run and I think she's got a future". Desert Darling is "certainly the best-bred horse I've got. She's ready to run and is a lovely, sharp filly". Done And Dusted is "one of my Up And At 'Em two-year-olds which have come on leaps and bounds just lately. This filly is a nice, big, strong sort and she'll be racing soon". Fair Cestrian "injured himself when he slipped in the yard which put him back a bit, but he's over it and is going to win races". Glanwydden "will probably get at least seven furlongs this year. He's a really nice horse in the making". Input "was our biggest disappointment of the year so far when she was beaten first time. She's so fast at home that I think she'll bounce back". Karisal is "a really nice filly from a family I know well and she's flying at the moment". Key To Dooks is "a good sort and he's going awfully well. He's not far off a run". Laurel Prince "is out of that wonderful mare Laurel Queen. Not an early type, but he's a nice colt and he'll give his owners a lot of fun". Mamma's F-C. "will have already run before this book is published. She's a sharp sort and I'm expecting a good run from her". Miss Grapette is "going exceptionally well at the moment and we'll be finding a race for her soon. She's a lovely filly with a nice attitude and she has a lot going for her". Principality is "a really good colt that was unlucky in the Brocklesby before winning at Newcastle. I'm pleased with him". Queensland Star "won on his debut at Newmarket for Alex Ferguson and he'll go on to win more races". Risk One Farthing is "fit and raring to go. She'll win races alright". Rosselli is "from a family I know well. I think this colt has got a real future. A beautiful-looking horse, he's got all the hallmarks of a real racehorse and is the nearest thing to Mind Games (also by Puissance) that I've seen". Smokin "got away badly from a flag start on his first run. He needed the experience of a race and, to me, is a winner without a penalty". Speedy James is "without doubt the best two-year-old I've seen so far this season. A really good sort, with speed to burn, he's got Royal Ascot written all over him". Stavanger "was odds-on when beaten first time out at Lingfield. He's better than that and I'm quite hopeful he'll win us some races". Zaragossa is "a very fast filly, very similar to my 1997 two-year-old Salamanca. Very sharp, she's a bit temperamental but she can really run and has a future".

860 - ACE OF PARKES b.c. Teenoso - Summerhill Spruce (Windjammer).
March 18.
Brother to the useful dual 5f winner and Moyglare, Lowther and Queen Mary Stakes placed My Melody Parkes and half-brother to the useful mare Lucky Parkes, a winner of 13 races over 5f, the 4-y-o 6f winner Bella Parkes (by Tina's Pet) and to a winner in Holland by Jupiter Island. The dam, a fair winner of a 6f seller at 3 yrs, is out of the unraced Sharper Still (by Sharpen Up). (Mr J Heler).

861 - ANGIE BABY b.f. Puissance - Hyde Princess (Touch Paper).
May 9. Sixth foal. 4,800Y. Doncaster St Leger.
Half-sister to the fair 1997 6f and 7f placed 2-y-o Durham Flyer (by Deploy) and to the modest 5f winner of 4 races The Fed (by Clantime). The dam, a fair sprint winner of 3 races at 2 yrs, is out of the minor Canadian 2-y-o winner and subsequent Irish hurdles winner Wild Elk Inn (by Briartic). (The Cooper Group).

862 - CONWY LODGE (IRE)   b.c. Lahib - Alriyaah (Shareef Dancer).
March 8. Third foal. IR40,000Y. Goffs Orby.
Half-brother to the 1994 2-y-o 5f winner Rotherfield Park (by High Estate) and the 1996 7f 3-y-o winner Mirani (by Danehill) - both modest all-weather winners. The dam, a fair 2-y-o 5f winner, is a half-sister to 4 minor winners out of the unraced Sharpina (by Sharpen Up), herself a half-sister to 4 winners including the US stakes winner Sorayah. (Lord Mostyn).

863 - CYCLONE FLYER   br.f. College Chapel - Mainly Dry (The Brianstan).
March 14. 23,000Y. Tattersalls October.
Half-sister to the unplaced 1997 2-y-o Bolshaya (by Cadeaux Genereux), to the useful sprinters Bolshoi (by Royal Academy), Great Chaddington (by Crofter) and Tod (by Petorius), the fair 5f winners Ellebanna (by Tina's Pet) and Robin's Arrow (by Jalmood) and the fair dual 6f winner Teetotaller (by Taufan). The dam is an unraced half-sister to 4 winners including the dam of the Portland Handicap winner Swelter. The second dam, Sunny Spell (by Vigo), was placed once at 2 yrs and is a half-sister to a Grade 2 winner in Australia. (Mr Reg Leah).

864 - DESERT DARLING   b.f. Green Desert - Habibti (Habitat).
March 16.
Sister to the Irish 1994 2-y-o 5f winner Desert Lily (by Green Desert) and half-sister to the 6f and 7f placed 3-y-o Woodbury Lad (by Woodman) and the dual 6f placed 2-y-o Reem Albaraari (by Sadlers Wells) - all fair performers. The dam, a brilliant sprinter, won the July Cup, the William Hill Sprint Championship, Prix de l'Abbaye and Kings Stand Stakes (all Group 1 events) and the Group 2 Vernons Sprint Cup. She also finished fourth, promoted to third, in the 1,000 Guineas and is a half-sister to the useful Irish sprinter Knesset and to Eight Carat, dam of two Grade 1 winners in Australia and New Zealand. The second dam, Klairessa (by Klairon), won once at just under 6f, is a sister to the good sprinter D'Urberville and is closely related to Lora, herself dam of the 1,000 Guineas winner On the House. (Lucayan Stud).

865 - DONE AND DUSTED (IRE)   ch.f. Up And At 'Em - Florentink (The Minstrel).
March 19. 8,000Y. Doncaster St Leger.
Half-sister to the 1997 Irish 7f placed 2-y-o Shalazar, to the Irish listed 10f winner Cheering News (both by Shernazar), the fairly useful 2-y-o 7f winner Guaranteed Bonus (by Darshaan) and the minor US winners Fluorishing Style (by Shardari) and Occasional Dream (by Hello Gorgeous). The dam is an unraced half-sister to 6 minor winners. The second dam, Gala Lil (by Spring Double), was a stakes winner of 5 races in the USA and was placed in three Graded stakes events. (Chris & Antonia Deuters).

866 - FAIR CESTRIAN (IRE)   b.c. Petardia - Fair Chance (Young Emperor).
March 30. 12,000Y. Goffs Challenge.
Half-brother to the fairly useful 2-y-o 5f winner Gold Futures (by Fayruz), the fair 2-y-o 5f winner Imp Express (by Mac's Imp), the Irish 3-y-o 1m winner Burella (by Burslem), the Irish middle-distance and hurdles winner Lolshan (by Montelimar) and 2 winners abroad by Fayruz and Cajun. The dam, an Irish 2-y-o 5f and 7f winner, is a half-sister to 3 winners in Germany. The second dam, Fair Martial (by Martial), won in Germany and is a half-sister to 5 winners. (J & J R Littler).

867 - GLANWYDDEN   ch.c. Grand Lodge - Brush Away (Ahonoora).
February 9. IR32,000Y. Goffs Orby.
Half-brother to the fairly useful 1989 Irish 3-y-o 7f listed winner Takwim (by Taufan), to the German listed winner Capwell (by Celestial Storm), the fair 1993 3-y-o 6f and 1m winner Mr Vincent (by Nishapour) and the modest 1990 2-y-o dual 5f winner Go Tally-Ho (by Gorytus). The dam is an unraced half-sister to 9 winners including the US listed winner Fawlty Towers and the Musidora Stakes third Princess Genista. The second dam, Queen Of The Brush (by Averof), won at 3 yrs and is a half-sister to the Italian Derby winner Old Country. (Lord Mostyn).

868 - INPUT   ch.f. Primo Dominie - Putout (Dowsing).
March 1. Second foal. 14,000Y. Tattersalls October.
Half-sister to the fair 1997 6f placed 2-y-o Bedevilled (by Beveled). The dam, a fair 3-y-o 5f winner, is a half-sister to the Group 3 6f Prix de Meautry winner Pole Position. The second dam, Putupon (by Mummy's Pet), a fairly useful 2-y-o 5f winner, is a half-sister to the good horses Jupiter Island (Japan Cup), Pushy (Queen Mary Stakes) and Precocious (Gimcrack Stakes). (Furnace Mill Partnership).

869 - KARISAL (IRE) b.f. Persian Bold - Pasadena Lady (Captain James).
May 28. IR30,000Y. Goffs Orby.
Half-sister to the useful sprinter Palacegate Episode, a winner of 11 races here and abroad including a Group 3 race in Italy and numerous listed events, to the fair sprinter Another Episode (both by Drumalis), a winner of 11 races and second in the Group 3 Molecomb Stakes, to the useful sprinter Palacegate Jack (by Neshad), also a winner of 11 races including listed events and to the fair sprinter Sports Post Lady (by M Double M), a winner of four 5f events. The dam is an unraced half-sister to 5 minor winners out of the 3-y-o winner Gliding Gay (by Hill Gail) - herself a half-sister to the Prix Gladiateur winner Alciglide and the Irish Oaks fourth All Saved. (Mrs Joan Hawkins).

870 - KEY TO DOOKS (IRE) b.c. Up And At 'Em - Global Princess (Transworld).
April 20. 38,000Y. Doncaster St Leger.
Half-brother to the fairly useful 1995 Irish 3-y-o 8.5f winner Kates Choice (by Taufan), to the minor French winners Market Review (by Theatrical) and Flamingo Lolita (by Imperial Frontier), the minor US winners Get Katz (by Deputy Minister) and Small Diamond (by Diamond Shoal) and the Austrian winner Purple Penny (by Pennine Walk). The dam was placed twice in the USA and is a half-sister to 6 winners and to My Bupers - dam of the September Stakes winner Lyphard's Special and the US Grade 2 winner My Juliet (herself dam of the US Grade 1 winners Stella Madrid and Tis Juliet). The second dam, Princess Revoked (by Revoked), won 8 races in the USA. (Mr Reinhard Fabricus).

871 - LAUREL PRINCE b.c. Reprimand - Laurel Queen (Viking).
January 28. First foal.
The dam, a fair 6f to 1m filly, was tough and genuine. She won no less than 22 races and is a half-sister to several winners. The second dam, Prima Bella (by High Hat), was a fair stayer. (Laurel Racing Club).

872 - MAMMA'S F-C (IRE) ch.f. Case Law - Wasaif (Lomond).
March 18. IR5,000Y. Tattersalls Fairyhouse.
The dam, a fair 3-y-o 7f winner, is a half-sister to 3 winners including the Group 3 Diadem Stakes winner Cool Jazz. The second dam, Amber Fizz (by Effervescing), ran once unplaced and is a half-sister to 9 winners including the US stakes winner and Grade 1 placed Groton High. (Mr J K Brown & Partners).

873 - MISS GRAPETTE (IRE) b.f. Brief Truce - Grapette (Nebbiolo).
April 24. IR17,000Y. Goffs Challenge.
Half-sister to the useful sprint winner of 8 races Gorinsky (by Gorytus), to the modest 2-y-o dual 7f winner Shall We Go (by Shalford), the minor Irish 9f winner Twenty Twenty (by Vision) and to winners in Italy and Hong Kong by Taufan and Thatching. The dam, a minor Irish 10f and hurdles winner, is a half-sister to 9 winners. The second dam, Great Aunt (by Great Nephew), won at 2 yrs. (Nan Robertson & Mr J Berry).

874 - PRINCIPALITY b.c. College Chapel - Desert Palace (Green Desert).
March 16. Third foal. IR26,000Y. Fairyhouse September.
The dam, a minor 3-y-o 5f winner in Ireland, is a half-sister to 3 winners out of the fairly useful 3-y-o 8f and 9f winner Gatchina (by Habitat) - herself a half-sister to the top-class middle-distance colt Kalaglow and the Ribblesdale Stakes winner Armarama. (Coolmore Stud).

875 - QUEENSLAND STAR (IRE) b.c. College Chapel - Zenga (Try My Best).
April 6. 17,000Y. Tattersalls October.
Half-brother to the 1997 unplaced 2-y-o All Our Blessings (by Statoblest), to the useful Group 3 7f Nell Gwyn Stakes winner A-To-Z (by Ahonoora) and the Swiss winner Ancient Air (by Thatching). The dam, a winner of 4 races in Italy and listed-placed, is a half-sister to 7 winners including Night In Town, a winner of 17 races including a listed event at Ascot. The second dam, Dusky Evening (by Chamier), was unraced. (Mr Alex Ferguson).

876 - RISK ONE FARTHING ch.f. Risk Me - Farinara (Dragonara Palace).
May 14. 3,200Y. Doncaster St Leger.
Half-sister to the fair all-weather 6f (at 2 yrs) and 7f winner Miss Offset (by Timeless Times) and the fairly useful 2-y-o dual 5f winner Croft Imperial (by Crofthall) - subsequently a winner of five more races at 7 and 8 yrs. The dam is an unraced half-sister to 4 winners here and abroad. The second dam, Faridina (by Sky Gipsy), was a useful soft-ground 5f winner of 6 races and a half-sister to 8 winners. (Mr A N Brooke Rankin).

877 - ROSSELLI b.c. Puissance - Miss Rossi (Artaius).
April 9. 32,000Y. Tattersalls October.
Half-brother to the useful Dancing Music (by Music Boy), a winner of five races over 5f including a listed event in Ireland, to the useful Heather Bank (by Nordance), a winner of four races over 6f, the fair 4-y-o 6f winner Rossini Blue (by Music Boy) - subsequently a winner in Italy - and the Irish sprint winner Lyndon's Linnet (by Prince Sabo). The dam is an unraced half-sister to 5 winners including a listed winner in Japan. The second dam, Trail (by Thatch), is an unraced half-sister to 6 winners. (T G Holdcroft and Mr J Berry).

878 - SMOKIN (IRE) b.c. Magic Ring - Casbah Girl (Native Bazaar).
April 22. 30,000Y. Doncaster St Leger.
Half-brother to the 3-y-o Le Genereux (by Cadeaux Genereux), to the useful 2-y-o listed 5f Roses Stakes and 4-y-o listed Tipperary Sprint winner Sabre Rattler (by Beveled), the useful 5f to 7f winner Mister Bloy (by Dowsing) - subsequently a winner in Dubai - and the 6f seller winner Cashtal Queen (by Ballacashtal). The dam, a quite useful 6f and 7f winner at 3 yrs, is a sister to a winner and a half-sister to another. The second dam, Avengeress (by Aggressor), was a fair winner at up to 13.8f and a hslf-sister to the Ascot Stakes winner Delmere. (H Hughes & D Bloy).

879 - SPEEDY JAMES ch.c. Fayruz - Haraabah (Topsider).
February 22. Sixth foal. 21,000Y. Tattersalls October.
Half-brother to the useful sprinter and winner of 6 races Double Quick (by Superpower), and to the quite useful 5f and 6f winner Top Of The Form (by Masterclass). The dam, a useful 5f to 7f winner, is a half-sister to 3 winners out of the French winner Marie de Sarre (by Queen's Hussar), herself a half-sister to the Group 2 Grand Prix de Deauville winner Dom Alaric. (Lucayan Stud).

880 - STAVANGER (IRE) b.c. Distinctly North - Card Queen (Lord Gayle).
April 20. 55,000Y. Doncaster St Leger.
Brother to the 1996 Irish 2-y-o Distinctly West, winner of 3 races at around 7f and half-brother to winners in France, Italy and Spain by Salmon Leap, Cure The Blues and Le Moss. The dam is an unraced half-sister to 6 winners including the Group 2 Grand Prix de Deauville winner Card King - placed in twelve Group 1 events. The second dam, Nantua (by Again), was an unraced sister to the good Argentinian horses Imbroglio and Karachi. (Chris & Antonia Deuters).

881 - ZARAGOSSA gr.f. Paris House - Antonia's Folly (Music Boy).
March 26. First foal. 10,000Y. Doncaster October.
The dam, a modest 2-y-o 5f winner, stayed 6f and is a half-sister to several minor winners. The second dam, Royal Agnes (by Royal Palace), was a fair 14f winner and a half-sister to the smart two-year-old All Systems Go. (Slatch Farm Stud).

James Bethell

James feels that his two-year-olds this season are as nice a bunch as he's had. Fearby Cross is "a nice colt that was coughing but should be out by the end of May. Quite a stocky colt, he is well put together with plenty of bone". Grizelda is "a very nice filly and in fairly strong work now. Chester or York in May would be two possibilities for her. She's certainly going the right way". Rich Dominion is "a very early colt. I quite like him and he wouldn't want any further than six furlongs".

882 - FEARBY CROSS b.c. Unblest - Two Magpies (Doulab).
March 20. Second foal. 22,000Y. Tattersalls October.
Half-brother to the modest 1997 5f placed 2-y-o Dangerman (by Pips Pride). The dam won 4 races in Ireland from 7f to 10f and is out of the unraced Captive Audience (by Bold Lad, Ire), herself a half-sister to 6 minor winners here and abroad. (Clarendon Thoroughbred Racing).

883 - GRIZELDA (IRE) gr.f. Bluebird - Phazania (Tap On Wood).
April 7. Sixth foal. 22,000Y. Tattersalls October.
Half-sister to the unplaced 1997 Irish trained 2-y-o Grey Lightning (by Brief Truce), to the quite useful 2-y-o 5f winners Future Prospect (by Marju) and Il Caravaggio (by Tate Gallery), the Irish 2-y-o 6f winner Dick Ching (by Dance of Life) and a winner in Sweden by Priolo. The dam won 3 races in Ireland from 6f to 1m and is a half-sister to 6 winners including the Irish listed winner Muffutys. The second dam, Contrail (by Roan Rocket), is a placed half-sister to 9 winners including the English and Irish Oaks winner Blue Wind. (Mrs Catherine Corbett).

884 - RICH DOMINION ch.c. First Trump - Tiszta Sharok (Song).
January 24. 16,000Y. Doncaster St Leger.
Half-brother to the quite useful 2-y-o dual 6f winner Akalim, the Irish 9f and 10f winner Petofi (both by Petong), the quite useful 3-y-o 6f winner Rosebud (by Indian Ridge) - subsequently Grade 3 placed in the USA, the minor 2-y-o 6f winner Peter Rowley (by Absalom) and the poor 1m winner Flood's Hot Stuff (by Chilibang). The dam ran just twice, winning over 5f at 2 yrs, and is a half-sister to 2 minor winners. The second dam, Tin Tessa (by Martinmas), won as a 2-y-o at Bath and is a half-sister to 3 winners. (Mrs J E Vickers).

Gerard Butler

Gerard has several other two-year-olds in the Premier Section. Of these slightly earlier types, he says "Captain Chris is a nice sort and a big, strong, tough horse. He has a good way of going, is the type to do well this season and also improve later on. Compton Aviator is a nice horse with a very nice way of going, he'll start over six furlongs in mid-summer".

885 - CAPTAIN CHRIS ch.c. Magic Ring - Alpine Pass (Head For Heights).
February 21. First foal.
The dam, a minor winner at 3 yrs in Ireland, subsequently won a number of listed events in Sweden. (Mr M Berger).

886 - COMPTON AVIATOR ch.c. First Trump - Rifada (Ela Mana Mou).
March 17. Third living foal. 16,000Y. Tattersalls December.
Half-brother to the smart Group 2 12f Prix Hocquart winner Rifapour (by Shahrastani) and to the minor 4-y-o and hurdles winner Rifawan (by Cox's Ridge). The dam was a useful winner over 12f and a half-sister to 5 winners including the Group 3 Royal Whip Stakes winner Rayseka. The second dam, Rilasa (by St Paddy), won once in France and was third in the Group 3 Prix Vanteaux. (Mr E Penser).

Henry Candy

Henry has three other two-year-olds in the Premier Section. He feels that Secret Treasure is "a strong filly with a nice attitude. She shows a bit of speed and should start over five furlongs in June".

887 - SECRET TREASURE b.f. Dilum - Surprise Surprise (Robellino).
February 28. Third foal.
The dam won her only 2-y-o race over 7.1f at Chepstow, was a fairly useful second over 10f at 3 yrs and is a half-sister to 4 minor winners. The second dam, Fair and Wise (by High Line), a fair winner of 3 races and suited by 14f, is a sister to the Warren Stakes third High Beacon and a half-sister to 9 winners. (Mrs A Dixon).

Mick Channon

Kingsdown Stables in Upper Lambourn houses some particularly nicely-bred two-year-olds and Mick was pleased to discuss them with me. Bint Allayl is "a lovely filly with plenty of size and scope. She should be out in May and will certainly make a 2-y-o". Druridge Bay is "a lovely colt, quite mature and he'll be running in May. He'd be suited by further than five furlongs and might even get a mile later on". Forty Forte is a "lovely horse that will be running quite early. I'll start him off over five furlongs but he'll probably be better over seven. Certainly a 2-y-o type". Franco Mina "got no sort of run at all first time out and he's certainly better than that. A nice colt, he'll have no problem getting seven furlongs this year". Josr Algarhoud is "fairly backward and only doing cantering work but he's a lovely horse that's doing everything right". Lokomotiv "is a nice colt who shows all the right signs. He'll be running in May and be suited by six or seven furlongs later on". Maidaan is "a lovely big horse that canters nicely, has the right attitude and looks great. He needs a bit of time but I'm pleased with him". Maureena is "a lovely filly that's done nothing but grow so far. I'll probably start her off at six furlongs and she should be a nice filly this autumn". Paula's Joy "is a nice little filly that moves well, she'll be ready to run in May and should make a 2-y-o". Ranaan "is a very nice 2-y-o, he'll probably be running from the end of May onwards, goes well and is a nice horse all round". Raneen Nashwan is "a lovely horse that needs time. He canters well but won't be out until the back-end". Robergerie is a colt "we probably won't see on the racecourse until August but he's going the right way and is a decent horse". Royal Origine "is doing everything right, he'll come to hand early and in May we should see a different horse.

I like him". Shakieyl is a "lovely, big horse that's gone the right way. He needs a bit of time but he's done everything right and is a lovely mover. He could be a proper horse". Top Star "won't be ready until about June but he'll make a 2-y-o alright and moves well". The Waajib - Esquire Lady colt "does all his work nicely and he'll be running in May". Finally, Mick's first Sadler's Wells horse, Wedoudah, is "a nice, big filly that needs plenty of time".

---

888 - BINT ALLAYL
b.f. Green Desert - Society Lady (Mr Prospector). January 19. First living foal.
The dam, a fair 6f and 7f placed 2-y-o, is a sister to a minor winner and a half-sister to several others including the useful French 2-y-o 5.5f winner Kentucky Slew. The second dam, La Voyageuse (by Tentam), won 26 races races in Canada where she was a Champion filly. (Sheikh Ahmed Al Maktoum).

---

889 - DRURIDGE BAY (IRE)
b.c. Turtle Island - Lady Of Shalott (Kings Lake). March 5. Sixth foal. 45,000Y. Tattersalls October.
Half-brother to the 3-y-o Blue Zola (by Alzao), to the useful 5f winner Meliksah (by Thatching), the fair 7f winner Knight Of Shalot and the 1m seller winner Irrepressible (both by Don't Forget Me). The dam, a modest 1m placed maiden, is a half-sister to 6 winners including the King Edward VII Stakes and Princess Of Wales's Stakes winner Head For Heights. The second dam, Vivante (by Bold Lad, Ire), a quite useful 3-y-o 6f winner, is a half-sister to 9 winners and to the dam of the Wokingham Handicap winner Le Johnstan. (Mr Martin St Quinton).

---

890 - FORTY FORTE
b.c. Pursuit Of Love - Cominna (Dominion). April 18. Fifth foal. 40,000Y. Tattersalls October.
Half-brother to the 3-y-o Caprioara (by Sharpo), to the quite useful 1994 2-y-o 6f winner Prima Cominna (stayed 7f at 3 yrs) and the modest 1996 3-y-o 2m winner Go With The Wind (both by Unfuwain). The dam is an unraced sister to the Group 2 Richmond Stakes winner and useful sire Primo Dominie and a half-sister to the Group 1 Phoenix Stakes winner Swan Princess. The second dam, Swan Ann (by My Swanee), won once at 3 yrs over 6f. (Mr Martin St Quinton).

---

891 - FRANCO MINA (IRE)
b.c. Lahib - Play The Queen (King Of Clubs). February 28. Fourth foal. IR41,000Y. Goffs Orby.
Half-brother to the quite useful 2-y-o 6f winner Salty Jack (by Salt Dome), the fair 1997 2-y-o 6f all-weather winner Oh Never Again and the Swedish winner Windy Walkie (both by Ballad Rock). The dam, a winner over 7f in Ireland at 3 yrs, is out of the Group 2 Coronation Stakes and Group 3 Athasi Stakes winner Orchestration (by Welsh Pageant), herself a half-sister to the Group 2 Prix d'Harcourt winner Welsh Term. (Maygain Ltd).

---

892 - JOSR ALGARHOUD (IRE)
b.c. Darshaan - Pont-Aven (Try My Best). February 22. Third foal. 160,000Y. Tattersalls Houghton.
Brother to the fairly useful 2-y-o 7f winner Pommard and half-brother to the 1998 French-trained 3-y-o Saint Marine (by Kenmare). The dam, a half-sister to 3 winners, was a very useful winner of 3 races including the Group 3 5f Prix de Saint-Georges and was second in the French 1,000 Guineas. The second dam, Basilia (by Frere Basile), is a placed half-sister to the Italian Group 2 winner Bold Apparel and the French listed winner Cedrico. (Sheikh Ahmed Al Maktoum).

---

893 - LOKOMOTIV
b.c. Salse - Rainbow's End (My Swallow). February 24. 34,000Y. Tattersalls October.
Brother to the minor French 2-y-o winner Plein de Couleurs and half-brother to the very useful 1993 2-y-o 6f and 7f winner Carmot (by Cadeaux Genereux), the useful 6f and 7.6f winner Finian's Rainbow (by Relkino), the 2-y-o 5f winner Chasing Moonbeams, the 2-y-o 7f winner Varnish (by Final Straw) - both quite useful, the fairly useful stayer Cap de Mond (by Troy), the fair 2m winner Storm Cloud (by High Line), the fair 1m to 10f winner Coltrane (by Dominion) and the modest 2-y-o 7.5f and 1m winner Elfin Laughter (by Alzao). The dam, a quite useful 2-y-o 6f winner, is out of Pantomime (by Silly Season), a useful winner of 3 races at up to 1m. (Allevemento La Nuova Sbarra SRL).

---

894 - MAIDAAN
b.c. Midyan - Panache Arabelle (Nashwan). February 24. First foal. 210,000Y. Tattersalls Houghton.
The dam, unplaced on her only start, is a half-sister to the Group 2 10f Prince Of Wales's Stakes winner Stagecraft and the listed winners Hyabella and Balalaika. The second dam, Bella Colora (by Bellypha), won the Group 2 Prix de l'Opera and is a half-sister to the Irish Champion Stakes winner Cezanne and

to the Irish Oaks winner Colorspin (dam of the King George VI and Queen Elizabeth Diamond Stakes winner Opera House). (Sheikh Ahmed Al Maktoum).

895 - MAUREENA
ch.f. Grand Lodge - Inshad (Indian King). March 18. Sixth foal. 25,000Y. Tattersalls October.
Half-sister to the fairly useful 1994 3-y-o 7f and 1m winner and listed-placed Mareha (by Cadeaux Genereux). The dam, a quite useful 6f and 7f winner, is a sister to the winner and listed-placed Sweeping and a half-sister to 7 winners. The second dam, Glancing (by Grundy), won the Group 3 5f Prix d'Arenburg and is a half-sister to the Middle Park Stakes winner Bassenthwaite and to the dam of the Prix de l'Abbaye winner Keen Hunter. (Mrs Maureen Buckley).

896 - PAULA'S JOY
b.f. Danehill - Pernilla (Tate Gallery). February 8. Second foal. 21,000Y. Tattersalls October.
Half-sister to the 3-y-o Zarzi (by Suave Dancer). The dam, a useful winner of the Group 3 7f Concorde Stakes and second in the Group 3 6f Greenlands Stakes, is a half-sister to 4 winners including the Queen Alexandra Stakes winner Easy To Please (herself dam of the Irish dual listed winner Azra). The second dam, Clonsella Lady (by High Top), won over 8.5f in France and is a half-sister to 4 minor winners. (Mr John Breslin).

897 - RANAAN (IRE)
ch.c. Brief Truce - Ma Minti (Mummy's Pet). April 2. 26,000Y. Tattersalls October.
Half-brother to the modest 5f and 6f winner Apres Huit (by Day Is Done) and to minor winners in Italy by Classic Music, Final Straw and Prince Sabo. The dam, a modest 3-y-o 5f winner, is out of the US winner of 2 races Tartagine (by Blue Tom), herself a half-sister to 7 winners. (Ahmed Al Shafar).

898 - RANEEN NASHWAN
b.c. Nashwan - Raneen Alwatar (Sadler's Wells). January 17. Second foal.
Half-brother to the 3-y-o Aneen Alkamanja (by Last Tycoon). The dam, a quite useful 3-y-o 12f winner, is out of the useful 3-y-o 9f and 10f winner Samya's Flame (by Artaius) - herself a sister to the top-class broodmare Flame of Tara (dam of Salsabil and Marju) and a half-sister to Fruition (dam of the Breeders Cup Turf winner Northern Spur and the high-class stayer Kneller). (Sheikh Ahmed Al Maktoum).

899 - ROBERGERIE
b.c. Robellino - Daisy Grey (Nordance). April 9. 20,000Y. Tattersalls October.
Half-brother to the 3-y-o Rafeef (by Salse) and to the 1997 Italian 3-y-o winner Grey Oak (by Batshoof). The dam, a 4-y-o 7f seller winner, is a half-sister to the dam of the top-class sprinter Lochsong. The second dam, Great Grey Niece (by Great Nephew), was placed once at 2 yrs. (Mr R M Brehaut).

900 - ROYAL ORIGINE (IRE)
b.c. Royal Academy - Belle Origine (Exclusive Native). April 23. IR35,000Y. Goffs Orby.
Half-brother to the 3-y-o Smart (by Last Tycoon), to the very smart Group 1 6f Haydock Park Sprint Cup winner Lavinia Fontana (by Sharpo) and the minor 3-y-o winner Ceide Dancer (by Alzao). The dam, a minor French 3-y-o 9.5f winner, is a half-sister to 9 winners including the French listed winners My Volga Boatman and Bel Sorel. The second dam, Belle Sorella (by Ribot) was a useful 12f winner and a sister to the champion 2-y-o Ribofilio. (Maygain Ltd).

901 - SHAKIEYL (IRE)
b.c. Grand Lodge - Frill (Henbit). February 10. Sixth foal. 38,000Y. Tattersalls October.
Half-brother to the 3-y-o Chapel Lane (by Selkirk), to the minor French 2-y-o 6f and 7f winner Lady Frill (by Standaan) and the quite useful 1997 3-y-o 12.5f to 17.2f winner Sudest (by Taufan). The dam, a minor Irish 3-y-o 12f winner, is a half-sister to 8 winners including the high-class miler Pitcairn (the sire of Ela Mana Mou), the Blandford Stakes winner Valley Forge and the Irish 1m and 10f winner Dingle Bay - herself dam of the high-class stayer Assessor. The second dam, Border Bounty (by Bounteous), a very useful middle-distance stayer, was second in the Park Hill Stakes and the Yorkshire Oaks. (Mr A Merza).

902 - TOP STAR (IRE)
b.c. Thatching - Decadence Star (High Estate). February 27. First foal. 41,000Y. Doncaster St Leger.
The dam, a winner at 2 yrs in France, is a half-sister to 4 winners including the listed 5f Scarborough Stakes winner and Group 1 Prix de l'Abbaye second Mistertopogigo (by Thatching - the sire of this

colt). The second dam, Decadence (by Vaigly Great), is an unplaced sister to the high-class sprinter Hallgate. (Stephen Crown).

903 - WEDOUDAH (IRE)
b.f. Sadler's Wells - Salvora (Spectacular Bid).
March 10. 80,000Y. Tattersalls Houghton.
Closely related to the modest 2-y-o 6f and subsequent Brazilian listed winner Special Gallery and to the minor French winner Valsora (both by Tate Gallery) and half-sister to the Grade 1 Yellow Ribbon Invitational winner Aube Indienne (by Bluebird), the French listed 10.5f winner Raisonnable, the minor French winner Spenderella (both by Common Grounds) and the French winner of 13 minor races Fuente Mayor (by Ti King). The dam won over 10f in France and is a half-sister to the US stakes winner Smackover Creek and to the dams of the Australian triple Grade 1 winner Flying Spur and the US Grade 2 winner Fit To Lead. The second dam, Grand Luxe (by Sir Ivor), is a stakes winner of 10 races in Canada and the USA and a half-sister to the Grade 1 winners L'Enjoleur, La Voyageuse and Medaille d'Or. (Sheikh Ahmed Al Maktoum).

904 - UNNAMED
b.c. Waajib - Esquire Lady (Be My Guest).
April 25. IR34,000Y. Fairyhouse September.
Half-brother to the modest dual 6f winner Tara's Girl (by Touching Wood), to the Italian winner of 4 races Mamacita (by Alzao) and the German 2-y-o winner Ellore (by Don't Forget Me). The dam, a winner over 1m and 9.5f in Ireland at 3 yrs, is out of the 3-y-o winner and Group 3 Cherry Hinton Stakes third La Mia Raggazza (by Alcide), herself a half-sister to 8 winners including the Coronation Stakes winner Lucyrowe and the dam of the Oaks Trial winner Suni. (Tim Corby).

Luca Cumani

Most of the Bedford House two-year-olds can be found in the Premier Section, but here are three horses I felt were likely to be quite early. Luca tells me that Don Quixote is "a good-looking horse, mature enough to be running by June or July. I'll probably start him off over six furlongs". Sarpedon "should win as a 2-y-o. He's quite strong and forward and should be running by June, probably over six furlongs". Victory Spin is "not one of my more expensive purchases, but he's a fairly typical 2-y-o type and ought to win a race or two this year".

905 - DON QUIXOTE
b.c. Waajib - Maimiti (Goldhill).
May 6. IR160,000Y. Goffs Orby.
Brother to the useful 5f listed Rous Stakes winner My-Oh-My and half-brother to the 1997 Irish 6f placed 2-y-o Galahad (by Alzao) and the minor Irish 8.3f winner Fletcher's Bounty (by Glenstal). The dam is an unplaced half-sister to the useful Irish sprinter Title Roll, winner of the Group 3 King George Stakes. The second dam, Tough Lady (by Bay Express), was a fairly useful 2-y-o 6f winner. (Mr M Tabor and Mrs J Magnier).

906 - SARPEDON (IRE)
ch.c. Be My Chief - Sariza (Posse).
March 4.
Half-brother to the quite useful 8.5f winner Aratos (by Night Shift), to the fair 1997 7f and 1m placed Selfish (by Bluebird) and to a number of disappointing animals. The dam was placed in all her five races - from 6f to 1m - at 3 yrs and is a half-sister to the useful dual 12f winner Double Dagger. The second dam, Tolmi (by Great Nephew), was a high-class winner of the Coronation Stakes and is a half-sister to the champion 2-y-o Tromos, the Irish Derby winner Tyrnavos and the Middle Park Stakes winner Tachypous. (Mr L Marinopoulos).

907 - VICTORY SPIN
ch.c. Beveled - Victoria Mill (Free State).
January 25. Sixth foal. 15,000Y. Doncaster St Leger.
Half-brother to the French 10f and 10.5f winner Victory Mill (by Ron's Victory) and to the 1997 unplaced 2-y-o Nordic Pirjo (by Nordico). The dam, a modest 10f placed 3-y-o, is a half-sister to 3 minor winners. The second dam, Island Mill (by Mill Reef), a fair winning stayer, is a half-sister to 14 winners including the French Group 3 winners Silicon Lady and Silicon Bavaria and to the unplaced dam of the Grand Prix de Paris winner Risk Me. (Mrs Luca Cumani).

Mick Easterby

Now housing a fabulous collection of well-bred two-year-olds, the Mick Easterby yard must be looking forward to the season with relish. Cut The Deck is "a strong, decent colt that will be running in May, possibly over the minimum trip". Hit the Beach is "a big strong horse that will also be quite early. He'll start off in May, probably over six furlongs". Loughanlea was "due to start his career at the end of April. He's a tough colt that will start over five furlongs but may be more suited by six". Mick also has a number of two-year-olds in the Premier Section.

908 - CUT THE DECK   b.c. First Trump - Kantikoy (Alzao).
February 6. First foal. 22,000Y. Tattersalls October.
The dam is an unraced half-sister to the Group 3 12 St Simon Stakes winner Kithanga. The second dam, Kalata (by Assert), was unplaced on her only start and is a half-sister to the Italian Group 3 winner Karkisiya and to the dams of the Derby winner Kahyasi, the Yorkshire Oaks winner Key Change and the Prix Cleopatre winner Kalajana. (Mr I Bray).

909 - HIT THE BEACH   b.c. Turtle Island - Malacca (Danzig).
January 15. First foal. 31,000Y. Tattersalls October.
The dam is an unraced half-sister to a minor winner in the USA. The second dam, Leyali (by Habitat), a useful 7f winner, was placed in the listed Sceptre Stakes and the listed Grand Metropolitan Stakes and is a half-sister to the good sprinter Hanu. (Mr I Bray).

910 - LOUGHANLEA (USA)   b.c. Salt Lake - Moment Of Flight (My Favourite Moment).
February 5. First foal. IR47,000Y. Goffs Orby.
The dam is an unraced half-sister to 5 winners including the French listed-placed Primevere (dam of the Prix du Moulin, Prix Jacques le Marois and Prix Jean Prat winner Priolo). The second dam, Spring Is Sprung (by Herbager), ran once unplaced in the USA and is a half-sister to the US Grade 2 winner Flitalong. (MP Burke's 5th Family Settlement).

Tim Easterby

Tim has some beautifully-bred young horses this year. Four of them can be found in the Premier Section of this book. Amongst his earlier types, Dram Time is "a nice, good-bodied, sensible colt who should be suited by five or six furlongs". Flanders is "a nice, sharp filly. We like her at the moment and she'll be reasonably early. A five furlong type, she's good-bodied and a good moving filly". Tierworker "has done very well physically, is a very good mover and will be a mid-summer two-year-old. We all like him".

911 - DRAM TIME   b.c. Clantime - Chablisse (Radetzky).
May 12. Fifth foal. 21,000Y. Doncaster St Leger.
Brother to the 6f (at 2 yrs) and 7f winner Dummer Golf Time and to the 5.9f (at 2 yrs) to 7f winner Parfait Amour and half-brother to the 7f (at 2 yrs) to 10f winner Ooh Ah Cantona (by Crofthall) - all fair performers. The dam, a fair 10f to 12f winner, is a half-sister to the dam of the smart and tough racemare Branston Abby. The second dam, Late Idea (by Tumble Wind), won once at 3 yrs. (Mrs Jennifer Pallister).

912 - FLANDERS   b.f. Common Grounds - Family At War (Explodent).
February 7. Third foal. 21,000Y. Doncaster St Leger.
Sister to the 1997 Irish 7f placed 2-y-o Bismarck and to the quite useful 1996 3-y-o 6f winner Disputed. The dam, a fair 2-y-o 5f winner, is a half-sister to 4 winners abroad. The second dam, Sometimes Perfect (by Bold Bidder), was a minor winner at around 6f at 2yrs in the USA and is a half-sister to the very useful French winners Gain and Tiger Run, and to the German Group 3 winner Krotz. (Mrs Jean Connew).

913 - TIERWORKER   b.c. Tenby - On The Tide (Slip Anchor).
January 29. First foal. IR34,000Y. Goffs Orby.
The dam, a fair 3-y-o 1m winner, is a half-sister to 8 winners including the high-class Gimcrack Stakes winner Rock City and the smart Cherry Hinton Stakes winner Kerrera. The second dam, Rimosa's Pet (by Petingo), was a very useful winner from 6f to 10.5f including the Group 3 Musidora Stakes and the Group 3 Princess Elizabeth Stakes. (MP Burke's 5th Family Settlement).

David Evans

David's two-year-olds have been a bit slower to come to hand than usual this year, he was telling me. Three to watch out for in the next few weeks are - Paper Flight, "a filly that returned with a temperature after she ran at Doncaster, she'll get better as the season progresses and is sharp enough to win as a two-year-old", Slightly Dusty "a small filly but very sharp, she'll stay at least six furlongs" and Tryardia-On-Again "a big filly that definitely has a win in her, she'll also get six furlongs".

914 - PAPER FLIGHT   gr.f. Petong - Tissue Paper (Touch Paper).
February 21. 3,000Y. Tattersalls December.
Half-sister to four winners including the useful German 1m listed winner Hoh Express and the quite useful 7f and 1m winner Mo-Addab (both by Waajib). The dam, a fairly useful winner of three 5f events

in Ireland at 2 yrs, is a half-sister to 3 winners including the French listed winner Tuberosa. The second dam, Tacora (by Cernobbio), was a Champion filly in Spain. (Mrs E A Dawson).

915 - SLIGHTLY DUSTY
b.f. Deploy - Dusty's Darling (Doyoun).
February 10. Second foal. 10,500Y. Doncaster St Leger.
Half-sister to the quite useful 1997 2-y-o dual 5f winner Filey Brigg (by Weldnaas). The dam is an unplaced half-sister to a winner in Austria. The second dam, Proserpina (by Shafaraz), is an unplaced half-sister to 5 winners including the dam of the top-class sprinter/miler Chief Singer. (Mr D Maloney).

916 - TRYARDIA-ON-AGAIN
ch.f. Petardia - Trysinger (Try My Best).
March 13. First foal. IR5,500Y. Tattersalls Fairyhouse.
The dam is an unraced half-sister to 6 winners including the Coventry Stakes fourth Run With The Wind and the Curragh Stakes third Fast As Light. The second dam, Song Beam (by Song), won twice at 3 yrs. (Men Behaving Badly).

Les Eyre

The Hambleton House stables of Les Eyre have been one of the success stories of recent years and Les has indicated that these four young horses can carry on the good work. Amaranth is "a grand stamp of a colt that needs a little time to furnish. Six furlongs in June should be his starting point". Decoded is "a lovely, big horse that will be out by the end of May, probably over six furlongs. A really nice type". Rainbow View is "a strapping big horse that really could be anything. He'll be racing by June and 1m will be his trip next year". Roonah Quay is "a very forward colt with a bit of class and will be suited by seven furlongs later on this season. He's owned by Andy Dodd, the manager of the rock band Simply Red".

917 - AMARANTH
b.c. Mujadil - Zoe's Delight (Hatim).
April 28. Third foal. Doncaster Breeze Ups.
The dam is an unraced half-sister to 2 minor winners. The second dam, Amendola (by Amen), won 4 races in France including over the jumps and is a half-sister to 7 winners including the French 10f listed winner Leontine.

918 - DECODED
ch.c. Deploy - Golden Panda (Music Boy).
March 18. Fifth foal. 16,500Y. Doncaster St Leger.
Half-brother to the modest 2-y-o 6f winner Pandiculation (by Statoblest), to the French 2-y-o 1m winner Star Of China (by Celestial Storm) and a winner in Hungary by Vague Shot. The dam, a fair 3-y-o 8.2f winner, is a half-sister to 7 winners including the fairly useful 6f and 7f winner Payroll. The second dam, Sarsgrove (by Hornbeam), was a fair 12f winner and a half-sister to 9 winners including the dam of the Royal Lodge Stakes winner Gairloch. (Mr A G Watson).

919 - RAINBOW VIEW
b.g. Rainbows For Life - L'Anno d'Oro (Habitat).
February 4. Fourth foal. 5,500Y. Tattesalls October.
Half-brother to the fairly useful 1995 2-y-o 6f winner Lacryma Cristi (by Green Desert). The dam is an unplaced sister to the top-class sprinter Habibti and a half-sister to the Ballyogan Stakes winner Knesset and to the outstanding Australasian broodmare Eight Carat - dam of no less than five Grade 1 winners. The second dam, Klairessa (by Klairon), won once at just under 6f, is a sister to the Norfolk Stakes winner D'Urberville and a half-sister to the dam of the 1,000 Guineas winner On The House.

920 - ROONAH QUAY
b.f. Soviet Lad - Piney Lake (Sassafras).
February 11. 8,000Y. Doncaster St Leger.
Half-sister to the 3-y-o Di Matteo (by Emarati) and to 8 winners here and abroad including the fair 2-y-o 6f winner Cafe Noir (by Comedy Star) and the modest 6f all-weather winner Mariposa Lily (by Forzando). The dam, a modest 1m and 10f placed maiden, is a half-sister to 10 winners including the Group 3 Prix Foy winner Beeshi and the John Smith's Magnet Cup winner Chaumiere. The second dam, Cafe au Lait (by Espresso), was a fairly useful winner of 3 races and stayed 12f. (Mr A Dodd).

Martin Fetherston-Godley

Martin has two interesting candidates here. Langan's Figurine is "quite a nice filly that shows speed. She looks very much like her mother and will be out in May over five furlongs". Promises To Keep "has grown a fair bit since I got him and won't be as early as I expected. A very strong, very attractive colt with a fair bit of scope, he's stuffy at the moment and needs plenty of work".

921 - LANGAN'S FIGURINE
b.f. Petardia - Cree's Figurine (Creetown).
February 17. Sixth foal. 22,000Y. Doncaster St Leger.
Half-sister to the useful sprinter Royal Figurine (by Dominion Royale), a winner of 9 races including a listed event at Newmarket and to the modest 1991 2-y-o 5f seller winner Early Morning Lady (by The Noble Player), subsequenly a winner in Germany. The dam, a modest 2-y-o 5f winner, is a half-sister to 2 minor winners. The second dam, Figurehead (by Seaepic), is an unplaced half-sister to the dams of the St James's Palace Stakes winner Persian Heights and the Nunthorpe Stakes winner Blue Cashmere. (Craig Pearman & Partners).

922 - PROMISES TO KEEP
gr.c. Petong - Miss Taleca (Pharly).
February 24. Third foal. 25,000Y. Doncaster St Leger.
Half-brother to the fair 5f and 6f winner Croeso Cynnes (by Most Welcome). The dam ran twice unplaced before being retired due to an injury. She is a half-sister to 4 winners including Kyoei Keyman (Grade 1 placed in Japan) and the fairly useful sprinter Love Legend, a winner of 13 races including the Portland Handicap. The second dam, Sweet Emma (by Welsh Saint), a smart Irish two-year-old, won 3 races including the Group 1 6f Heinz "57" Phoenix Stakes and was fourth in the Coronation Stakes. (Kennet House Partnership).

Sally Hall

Sally was pleased to suggest these three two-year-olds for inclusion in the book. Gravy Boat is "quite a sharp colt that goes nicely and will be suited by six furlongs to begin with". Otterington Girl is "on the tall side, but goes well and will start at five furlongs" and Darras Sky is "small, compact and will be a two-year-old. He'll start over five furlongs".

923 - DARRAS SKY
ch.c. Clantime - Sky Music (Absalom).
March 23. First foal.
The dam, a fairly useful 3-y-o 6f and 7f winner, was second in the Bunbury Cup at 4 yrs and is out of the fair sprinter On The Record (by Record Token). (Skylark Partnership).

924 - GRAVY BOAT (IRE)
b.c. River Falls - Newstreet Princess (Head For Heights).
April 6. Second foal. 7,800Y. Doncaster St Leger.
The dam, a minor 3-y-o winner in Ireland, is a half-sister to 2 winners. The second dam, La Loie Fuller (by Rheffic), was placed in France and is a full or half-sister to 4 winners including the dam of 3 listed winners in France. (Miss Betty Duxbury).

925 - OTTERINGTON GIRL
b.f. Noble Patriarch - Bidweaya (Lear Fan).
February 15. First foal.
The dam, a winner of 2 moderate events over 1m, is a half-sister to the Gimcrack Stakes winner Chilly Billy and to the fairly useful 1m and 8.3f winner Weaver Bird. The second dam, Sweet Snow (by Lyphard), won over 10.5f in France and is out of the Kentucky Oaks winner Sun And Snow. (Mrs Joan Hodgson).

Richard Hannon

Richard had yet to ask his two-year-olds any serious questions when we spoke in early April. All those listed have the potential to be decent horses, but perhaps the ones we should really look out for as the season progresses are Gold Academy, Learned Friend, Patron Saint, Red Delirium and Wallace.

926 - AMAZING DREAM (IRE)
b.f. Thatching - Aunty Eileen (Ahonoora).
February 14. IR31,000Y. Fairyhouse September.
Half-sister to the quite useful 1995 2-y-o 6f winner Astuti (by Waajib), to Moving Image (by Nordico) a modest winner of four races over 5f, the South African winner of 9 races Just Do It Joey (by Glenstal) and the fair 1991 2-y-o dual 6f winner Ambitious Venture (by Gorytus) - subsequently a winner of 10

races in Italy. The dam is an unraced half-sister to 6 winners including the smart sprinter Lugana Beach. The second dam, Safe Haven (by Blakeney), is an unplaced half-sister to 15 winners, notably Mtoto. (Mrs P Jubert).

---

927 - BAHAMIAN BANDIT
b.c. First Trump - Sound Of The Sea (Windjammer).
February 29. IR44,000Y. Goffs Orby.

Half-brother to the quite useful 5f and 6f all-weather winner Princely Sound (by Prince Sabo), to the fair 2-y-o dual 5f winner Endless Wave (by Indian Ridge) and the Irish 2-y-o 5f and 6f winner Cu Na Mara (by Never So Bold) - subsequently a winner in Italy. The dam was a fairly useful winner at up to 7f and is a half-sister to 7 minor winners. The second dam, Running Cedar (by Bryan), won twice in the USA and is a half-sister to three Graded stakes winners in the USA including the grandam of the Oaks winner Jet Ski Lady. (Lucayan Stud).

---

928 - BELLA LOUPA
b.f. Wolfhound - Quay Line (High Line).
April 14. 24,000Y. Tattersalls December.

Half-sister to the useful 2-y-o 1m winner Known Line (by Known Fact), to the fairly useful 14f winner Harbour Island (by Rainbow Quest), the fair 14.6f winner Mill Line (by Mill Reef and herself dam of the Irish and Yorkshire Oaks winner Pure Grain), the winning stayer Coleridge (by Bellypha), the quite useful 14f winner Purple Splash (by Ahonoora), the modest 12f winner Newquay (by Great Nephew) and a winner in Jersey by Young Generation. The dam, a smart filly, won the Group 2 Park Hill Stakes and is a sister to the Group 2 Premio Dormello winner Ancholia and the listed winners High Finale and Trade Line. The second dam, Dark Finale (by Javelot), won 3 races at up to 12f in Ireland. (Major A M Everett).

---

929 - CABARET QUEST
ch.c. Pursuit Of Love - Cabaret Artiste (Shareef Dancer).
April 12. Second foal. IR32,000Y. Goffs Orby.

Half-brother to the fair 1997 2-y-o 7f winner Misalliance (by Elmaamul). The dam is an unraced daughter of the placed Zuaetreh (by Raise A Native) - a half-sister to the US stakes winner Border Cat. (Thurloe Thoroughbreds III).

---

930 - CAPPELLA (IRE)
br.f. College Chapel - Mavahra (Mummy's Pet).
April 6. IR24,000Y. Goffs Challenge.

Half-sister to the fairly useful 5f (at 2 yrs) and 7f winner Queenfisher (by Scottish Reel), to the quite useful 5f and 6f winner Shout Fore, the Irish 5f winner Courier (both by Petong) and the fair 5f winner Indiahra (by Indian Ridge). The dam, a fairly useful 5f and 6f winner, is a half-sister to 5 winners including the dam of the Beeswing Stakes winner Savahra Sound. The second dam, Avahra (by Sahib), was a very useful winner of 3 races and stayed 6f. (Thurloe Thoroughbreds III).

---

931 - CASTILIAN (IRE)
b.c. Priolo - Hertford Castle (Reference Point).
March 28. First foal. 56,000Y. Tattersalls Houghton. Resold 53,000Y. December Sales.

The dam is an unplaced half-sister to four minor winners here and abroad. The second dam, Forest Flower (by Green Forest), was the Champion 2-y-o filly of 1986 and won 5 races including the Irish 1,000 Guineas, the Mill Reef Stakes, the Cherry Hinton Stakes and the Queen Mary Stakes. The third dam, Leap Lively (by Nijinsky), won the Hoover Fillies Mile and the Lingfield Oaks Trial. (Mr J C Smith).

---

932 - CYBINKA
ch.f. Selkirk - Sarmatia (Danzig).
January 24. Second foal.

Sister to the 1997 3-y-o Poleaxe, unplaced in both her starts. The unraced dam is closely related to the smart Group 2 Forte Mile winner Rudimentary and a half-sister to the champion miler and sire Kris, the champion 2-y-o Diesis, the good winners Keen and Presidium and to Pris - herself dam of the smart Prince of Wales's Stakes winner Perpendicular. The second dam, Doubly Sure (by Reliance II), was placed over 12f and is out of the Royal Lodge Stakes winner Soft Angels. (Lady Howard de Walden).

---

933 - DANAMALA
b.f. Danehill - Carmelized (Key To The Mint).
April 25. Second foal. 90,000Y. Tattersalls Houghton.

Closely related to the 3-y-o Abi (by Chief's Crown). The dam, a winner in the USA, is a half-sister to 4 minor winners. The second dam, Carmelize (by Cornish Prince), a winner of 6 races and second in the Grade 3 Sheephead Bay Handicap, is a half-sister to the top-class US filly Chris Evert (dam of the Grade 1 winner Six Crowns and thus grandam of Chief's Crown) and the dams of numerous other stakes winners incuding Winning Colors (Kentucky Derby), Two Timing (Prince Of Wales's Stakes), Missed The Storm (Grade 1 Test Stakes) and Beyton (King Edward VII Stakes). (T Ananda Krishnan).

934 - DEMOCRACY (IRE)

ch.c. Common Grounds - Inonder (Belfort). January 31. Second foal. 40,000Y. Tattersalls October.

Brother to the fairly useful 1997 2-y-o 5f to 7.5f winner Chips. The dam is an unplaced daughter of Rainfall (by Relko), a winning middle-distance stayer and a half-sister to the John Smith's Magnet Cup winner Air Trooper. (Highclere Thoroughbred Racing Ltd).

935 - DESCANT

b.f. Bluebird - Dubai Lady (Kris). April 8. 45,000Y. Tattersalls Houghton.

Half-sister to the smart 8.1f to 10.1f winner and Group 1 Coral-Eclipse fourth Ela Aristokrati (by Danehill). The dam, a fair middle-distance placed maiden, is a half-sister to 6 winners including the Group 3 Diomed Stakes and Grade 3 All American Handicap winner Bluegrass Prince. The second dam, Amata (by Nodouble), won 3 races in France and the USA and is a half-sister to the Group 3 Princess Royal Stakes winner Trillionaire. (Royal Ascot Racing Club).

936 - GOLD ACADEMY (IRE)

b.c. Royal Academy - Soha (Dancing Brave). March 19. Third foal. 140,000Y. Tattersalls October.

Closely related to the 3-y-o Free Spirit (by Caerleon) and half-brother to the fair 1996 2-y-o 5f and 6f winner Without Friends (by Thatching). The dam, a modest 12f placed 3-y-o, is out of the Italian Oaks winner Paris Royal (by Mill Reef), herself a half-sister to the Irish 2,000 Guineas winner Northern Treasure and the Athasi Stakes winner Etoile de Paris (dam of the Yorkshire Oaks winner Only Royale). (George Teo).

937 - GOLDEN FORCE

b.c. Forzando - Silverlocks (Sharrood). January 18. First foal. 22,000Y. Tattersalls October.

The dam was a fairly useful winner of 6 races from 6f (at 2 yrs) to 10f and is a half-sister to 3 winners including the fairly useful Philidor. The second dam, Philgwyn (by Milford), is a placed half-sister to the very smart sprinter Primo Dominie, the Phoenix Stakes winner Swan Princess and the 2,000 Guineas Trial winner Poyle Crusher. (George Teo).

938 - GOLDEN PRINCE (IRE)

gr.c. Polish Patriot - Cathryn's Song (Prince Tenderfoot). April 16. 55,000Y. Tattersalls October.

Half-brother to the 2-y-o dual 7f all-weather winner and useful hurdler Indefence (by Conquering Hero), the 5f (at 2 yrs) to 10.8f winner Katy's Lad (by Camden Town), the 7.5f to 9.4f winner Wentbridge Lad (by Coquelin) - all fair performers - and the modest 6f to 8f winner Stairway To Heaven (by Godswalk). The dam is an unraced half-sister to 5 winners out of Tell Katty (by Le Levenstell), a winner of 3 races in Ireland. (George Teo).

939 - GRAND VIEW

ch.c. Grand Lodge - Hemline (Sharpo). March 24. Fifth foal. 23,000Y. Tattersalls October.

Half-brother to the quite useful 1997 3-y-o 11.6f winner Heart Of Armor (by Tirol) and to the modest 1993 3-y-o 6f all-weather winner Pirates Gold (by Vaigly Great). The dam, a fair 3-y-o 7f winner, is out of the useful listed Galtres Stakes winner and Group 2 Park Hill Stakes second Ma Femme (by Bustino), herself a half-sister to the Nassau Stakes winner Acclimatise, the Irish Group 3 winner Bruckner and the 1,000 Guineas second Dabaweyaa. (Mr I Wight & Mrs D Wight).

940 - LEADING LIGHT (IRE)

ch.c. College Chapel - Valiant Friend (Shahrastani). March 6. Second foal. IR22,000Y. Fairyhouse September.

Half-sister to the quite useful 1997 2-y-o 6.1f winner King Darius (by Persian Bold). The dam ran twice unplaced in France and is a half-sister to 3 minor winners there. The second dam, Salva (by Secretariat), is an unraced half-sister to the Group 2 Geoffrey Freer Stakes winner Valinsky, the Grade 2 Del Mar Oaks winner Savannah Dancer and the listed Pretty Polly Stakes winner Val's Girl. (Mr I Wight & Mrs D Wight).

941 - LEARNED FRIEND (IRE)

ch.c. College Chapel - Caring (Crowned Prince). February 9. IR33,000Y. Goffs Orby.

Half-brother to Bishop's Ring (by Northfields), winner of 9 races here and in the USA including the listed 12f Old Newton Cup. The dam is an unraced half-sister to 9 winners including the Italian listed winners Greedy Of Gain (dam of the Group 1 Gran Criterium winner Grease) and Godzilla (dam of the French dual Group 3 winner Phydilla and the Irish Derby second Observation Post). (Mr J C Smith).

---

942 - LETHAL HOPE
b.c. Mujtahid - Vian (Far Out East).
March 17. 40,000Y. Tattersalls October.
Half-brother to the useful 2-y-o dual 5f winner Wavian (by Warning), to the 1997 6f and 7f placed 2-y-o Chocolate (by Brief Truce), the 2-y-o 8.3f winner Hindsight (by Don't Forget Me) and the 2-y-o 1m winner Ansillo (by Rousillon) - all three fair performers. The dam is an unraced half-sister to 10 winners including the Nassau Stakes and Musidora Stakes winner Optimistic Lass (herself dam of the Coronation Stakes winner Golden Opinion). The second dam, Loveliest (by Tibaldo), a half-sister to the US Grade 1 stakes winner Arbees Boy, was a very useful winner at up to 10.5f in France and 9f in the USA. (Saleh Al Homeizi).

---

943 - LITTLE GEM
b.f. Night Shift - Um Lardaff (Mill Reef).
January 18. Fifth foal.
Half-sister to the very promising 1997 2-y-o 7f winner Fantasy Island (by Zafonic) and to the fairly useful 6.9f (at 2 yrs) and 10f winner Expensive Taste (by Cadeaux Genereux). The dam, a winner over 11f and 12f at 3 yrs in France, is a sister to the Derby winner and high-class sire Shirley Heights and a half-sister to the good mare Bempton - dam of the Group 3 winners Mr Pintips and Banket and of the Group 2 winner Gull Nook (herself dam of the very useful filly Spring). The second dam, Hardiemma (by Hardicanute), was a quite useful 3-y-o 11f winner, after winning over 7f at 2 yrs. (Mohammed Suhail).

---

944 - MY PETAL
b.f. Petong - Najariya (Northfields).
March 9. 24,000Y. Doncaster St Leger.
Half-sister to the useful Nominator (by Nomination), a winner of 6 races including the listed 7f Somerville Tattersall Stakes, to the poor 13f winner Longcroft, the German winner Come On Ken (both by Weldnaas) and the Hong Kong winner Big Apple (by Auction Ring). The dam is an unraced half-sister to the Cherry Hinton Stakes winner and Coronation Stakes third Nasseem (dam of the Heron Stakes winner Neshad) and to the dam of the Princess Royal Stakes winner Narwala. The second dam, Noureen (by Astec), is an unraced half-sister to the Prix Dollar winner Tajubena. (Mrs P R Jubert).

---

945 - PATRON SAINT
b.c. Primo Dominie - Tender Loving Care (Final Straw).
February 20. 30,000Y. Tattersalls October.
Half-brother to the fairly useful 1990 2-y-o 7f winner Noble Destiny (by Dancing Brave) and to 6 disappointing animals. The dam, a useful 2-y-o 7f winner and placed in the Group 3 May Hill Stakes, is a half-sister to 9 winners including the useful 2-y-o's Satinette and Silk Pyjamas. The second dam, Silk Stocking (by Pardao), won the listed 7f Strensall Stakes and is a half-sister to the Palace House Stakes winner Shiny Tenth. (Royal Ascot Racing Club).

---

946 - POLISH FALCON
b.c. Polish Patriot - Marie de Fresnaye (Dom Racine).
April 12. Third foal. 32,000Y. Tattersalls October.
Half-brother to a placed 2-y-o in France by Fijar Tango. The dam is an unraced half-sister to the Group 2 Prix de Pomone winner Marie de Litz and to the dam of the Ladbroke Sprint Cup winner Polar Falcon. The second dam, Mohair (by Blue Tom), is an unraced half-sister to 7 winners including the Prix Vermeille second Percale (herself dam of the Prix Vermeille winner Paysanne). (Absal A M Everett).

---

947 - RED DELIRIUM
b.c. Robellino - Made Of Pearl (Nureyev).
April 1. IR88,000Y. Goffs Orby.
Half-brother to the useful 1997 2-y-o 7f winner and Group 3 1m May Hill Stakes second Flawless (by Warning), to the fairly useful 10f winner Seek The Pearl (by Rainbow Quest) and the minor 12f winner Cultured (by Saint Cyrien). The dam, a useful French 7f listed winner, is a half-sister to 4 winners. The second dam, Mother Of Pearl (by Sir Gaylord), won twice in France and was second in the Group 3 Prix de la Grotte. (Mr Terry Neill).

---

948 - QUICKSTEP
ch.f. Salse - Short And Sharp (Sharpen Up).
March 19. 25,000Y. Tattersalls October.
Half-sister to the quite useful 1997 2-y-o 6f and 7f winner Golden Fortune (by Forzando), to the quite useful 1991 3-y-o 7f winner Step High (by Dominion) and winners in Italy by Night Shift and Young Generation. The dam was placed over 6f and 7f at 2 yrs and is a half-sister to 6 winners including the

Coventry Stakes third Stay Sharp. The second dam, Brevity (by Pindari), was a fair 2-y-o 7f winner and a half-sister to the listed winner and Derby fourth Shotgun. (Lady Tennant).

---

949 - RED MAY   b.br.f. Persian Bold - Stay That Way (Be My Guest).
                                                      February 23. IR40,000Y. Goffs Orby.
Half-sister to the German 3-y-o Susi Wong (by Selkirk), to the 1997 Irish 1m winner Delirious Moment (by Kris), the 1994 Irish 8.5f winner Devastating Storm (by Shernazar) and a minor winner in the USA by Maelstrom Lake. The dam is an unraced sister to the useful 12f winner and Coronation Cup fourth Costly Lesson and a half-sister to the high-class Coronation Stakes winner Chalon (dam of the Prix Ganay and Prix d'Ispahan winner Creator), the Group 3 Ballymacoy Stakes winner Executive Perk and the Irish listed winner Elegance In Design (dam of the Irish Oaks winner Dance Design). The second dam, Areola (by Kythnos), won 3 races in Ireland including the Phoenix Stakes. (Mr Terry Neill).

---

950 - SAILING SHOES (IRE)   b.c. Lahib - Born To Glamour (Ajdal).
                                                      February 19. Second foal. IR30,000Y. Goffs Orby.
Half-brother to the 3-y-o Tarbaan (by Nashwan). The dam, a winner over 6f at Leopardstown at 2 yrs, is a half-sister to 9 winners including the French listed winner North Haneena. The second dam, the French winner Haneena (by Habitat), was fourth in the Cheveley Park Stakes and is a half-sister to the Jersey Stakes winner Gwent. (Mrs Caroline Parker).

---

951 - NEELA (IRE)   ch.f. Bluebird - Scammony (Persian Bold).
                                                      April 5. First foal. 130,000Y. Tattersalls Houghton.
The dam ran once unplaced and is a sister to the Irish 7f winner and Group 3 Park Stakes placed Persian Polly - herself the dam of the top-class sprinter Lake Coniston. The second dam, Polyester Girl (by Ridan), won once at 4 yrs and is a half-sister to 9 winners including the Group 2 Gran Criterium winner Northern Spring and the dam of the Group 3 Palace House Stakes winner Perion. (T Ananda Krishnan).

---

952 - SKY OF HOPE (FR)   b.c. Zieten - Rain Or Shine (Nonoalco).
                                                      April 4. FF310,000. Deauville August.
Half-brother to the quite useful 1989 2-y-o 7f winner Rail d'or, to the French winner of 4 races at around 10f Brin d'Or (both by Brustolon), the French 7f winner and listed-placed Rain or Zino (by Zino) and the minor French winner of 3 races Miss Flora (by Fioravanti). The dam is an unraced half-sister to 5 winners including the smart sprinter and Group 3 Prix d'Arenburg winner Reasonable. The second dam, Reno (by Pronto), was a minor winner in the USA and a half-sister to the Grade 1 winner Green Hills and the Grade 2 winner Morgaise. (Lucayan Stud).

---

953 - THUNDER DRAGON (IRE)   b.c. Zieten - Kiryaki (Secretariat).
                                                      February 28. Second foal. IR53,000Y. Goffs Orby.
Half-brother to the German-trained 3-y-o Revelin (by Goldneyev). The dam is a placed sister to the high-class Group 2 Prix de l'Opera winner Athyka (herself dam of the US and French Group 3 winner Atticus). The second dam, Princesse Kathy (by Luthier), won twice in France, was listed-placed and is a half-sister to the dam of the Prix Lupin winner Cudas. (Lucayan Stud).

---

954 - TIN DRUM (IRE)   b.c. Roi Danzig - Triumphant (Track Spare).
                                                      February 20. IR37,000Y. Goffs Orby.
Half-brother to the high-class 10f filly Timarida (by Kalaglow), winner of the Group 1 Irish Champion Stakes, the Group 1 Dallymayr-Preis and the Grade 1 Beverly D Stakes, to the fair winner of 7 races at up to 10f Double Entendre (by Dominion), the Irish 2-y-o 7f winner Timiniya (by Kahyasi), the Irish 2-y-o 6f winner Tirhala (by Chief Singer), the 10f seller winner Fresh From Victory (by Hotfoot) and the placed Heaven High (dam of the listed winners Miss Sacha and Pinta). The dam, a fairly useful 7.6f winner, is a half-sister to the Group 1 Benson and Hedges Gold Cup winner Relkino. The second dam, Pugnacity (by Pampered King), was a smart winner of 8 races including the Lowther Stakes, the Falmouth Stakes and the King George Stakes. (Michael Pescod).

---

955 - VINTAGE PRIDE   ch.f. Pips Pride - Vieux Carre (Pas de Seul).
                                                      February 16. Fifth foal. 23,000Y. Doncaster St Leger.
Half-sister to the modest 1996 2-y-o 5f to 7f winner Contravene and to the German 4-y-o winner John's Law (both by Contract Law). The dam is an unplaced half-sister to 6 minor winners here and abroad. The second dam, Two's Company (by Sheshoon), won a listed event over 11f in France and is a half-sister to 5 winners. (P Adams, M Grant & W Hawkings).

956 - WALLACE　　　　　　　　　　　　　　ch.c. Royal Academy - Masskana (Darshaan).
April 27. Second foal. IR50,000Y. Goffs Orby.
Half-brother to the French trained 3-y-o Guinevere. The dam a minor winner of 3 races in France, is a half-sister to the US Grade 3 Arcadia Handicap winner Madjaristan and the Group 2 Gallinule Stakes winner Massyar. The second dam, Masarika (by Thatch), won the French 1,000 Guineas and the Prix Robert Papin. (Mr J A Lazzari).

957 - WHY WORRY NOW (IRE)　　　　　ch.f. College Chapel - Pretext (Polish Precedent).
February 20. First foal. IR38,000Y. Goffs Orby.
The dam was placed once in France at 3 yrs and is a half-sister to 4 winners including the US Grade 2 1m and Group 3 1m Prix Quincey winner Bon Point. The second dam, Twixt (by Kings Lake), won over 7f in France and is a half-sister to the Group 2 Maurice de Gheest winner Interval, to the Grade 2 La Prevoyante Handicap winner Interim and to the dam of the Hoover Fillies Mile winner Invited Guest. (Mr N Hayes).

958 - WILD THING　　　　　　　　　　　b.c. Never So Bold - Tame Duchess (Saritamer).
February 28. 21,000Y. Doncaster St Leger.
Half-brother to the unplaced 1997 2-y-o Muji (by Safawan), to the modest 7f winner Duke Of Dreams (by Efisio) and minor winners abroad by Another Realm and Efisio (2). The dam,a fair 6f placed 2-y-o, stayed 10f and is a half-sister to the smart sprinter Son Of Shaka. The second dam, Pink Garter (by Henry The Seventh), won once at 2 yrs. (Mr J Palmer-Brown).

Patrick Haslam

Patrick believes he has four nice two-year-olds here. Air of Esteem is "a good-looking colt that will be out in mid-summer over six furlongs". Per Chance is "a nice, strong, good-looking colt that will also start over six furlongs". Maybe Special is "a big, workmanlike colt that should be ready for York in May. He'll be even better next year" and the Anshan colt Fiori "will start over six furlongs and stay seven later on. Bigger and scopier than his brother Prince Ashleigh, he'll still make up into a nice two-year-old".

959 - AIR OF ESTEEM　　　　　　　　　　b.c. Forzando - Shadow Bird (Martinmas).
April 8. Third foal. 29,000Y. Doncaster St Leger.
Half-brother to the fairly useful 2-y-o 6f winner and listed 10f Zetland Stakes third Shadow Lead (by Midyan). The dam, a fair winner of 5 races and best around 12f, is a half-sister to the French listed winner and Coronation Cup fourth Punishment. The second dam, In The Shade (by Bustino), was a fairly useful winner of 4 races from 12f to 14.8f and is a half-sister to the listed Festival Stakes winner and Group 2 Celebration Mile second Flashfoot. (Middleham Park Racing).

960 - MAYBE SPECIAL　　　　　　　　　b.c. Then Again - With Love (Be My Guest).
February 17. First foal. 16,000Y. Tattersalls October.
The dam, unplaced over 10.5f on her only outing at 3 yrs, is a half-sister to 7 winners including the smart Dewhurst Stakes third Genghiz. The second dam, Royal Caprice (by Swaps), won 3 races in the USA at up to 1m and is a half-sister to 9 winners including the dam of the US Grade 1 winner King's Swan. (Mr L Buckley).

961 - PER CHANCE　　　　　　　　　　　ch.c. Perugino - Irish Hope (Nishapour).
ch.c. May 9. Third foal. 22,000Y. Doncaster St Leger.
Half-brother to the Italian winner of 5 races Grey Hope (by Double Schwartz). The dam won 8 races in Italy and is a half-sister to 6 winners here and abroad. The second dam, Miss Moat (by Dike), won once in France and is a half-sister to the dam of the Group 2 Pretty Polly Stakes winner Happy Bride and the Group 2 Blandford Stakes winner Topanoora.

962 - FIORI　　　　　　　　　　　　　　　　b.c. Anshan - Fen Princess (Trojan Fen).
April 22. Third foal.
Brother to the fair 1997 7f and 1m placed 2-y-o Prince Ashleigh and half-brother to the 1996 2-y-o 7f and subsequent minor US 1m stakes winner Ben's Ridge (by Indian Ridge). The dam was a modest 15f winner at 4 yrs. The second dam, Cenerentola (by Caro), was a very useful 1m winner in France. (Mr S Dinsmore).

Barry Hills

Most of Barry's young horses are in the Premier Section, but here are four expected to be earlier than most. "Bodfari Muka is a good-moving horse who will be out early. He's quite a nice horse". Dangerous Dancer is "not over-big, but she'll definitely be a two-year-old. She goes well, is pleasing us at the moment and has potential. She'll probably start over six furlongs in May". Makebelieve Island is "a smallish, compact horse that does his work really well. Both our Namaqualand colts look to be nice horses. I expect Makebelieve Island to be ready for Newmarket's Craven meeting". Yellow Ribbon is "quite a sharp filly that goes very well. She's a bit wintry in her coat at the moment but shows promise and she'll be an early type".

---

963 - BODFARI MUKA (IRE)

ch.c. Mukaddamah - Precious Egg (Home Guard).
March 13. IR28,000Y. Goffs Challenge.

Half-brother to the 6f winners Easter Glory (by Dalsaan) and Fox Path (by Godswalk), to a winner over hurdles and a winner in Hong Kong (both by Crofter). The dam is a poor half-sister to the Group 3 6f Cork and Orrery Stakes winner Kearney. The second dam, Gilded Egg (by Faberge II), won 3 races over 6f and 7f in Ireland. (Bodfari Stud Ltd).

964 - DANGEROUS DANCER

b.f. Warning - Silabteni (Nureyev).
February 12. First foal. 21,000Y. Doncaster St Leger.

The dam is an unraced three-parts sister to the top-class filly Indian Skimmer, winner of the Champion Stakes, Irish Champion Stakes, Prix de Diane, Prix d'Ispahan and Prix Saint-Alary. The second dam, Nobiliare, (by Vaguely Noble), is an unraced half-sister to the dam of the US Grade 1 winners Missy's Mirage and Classy Mirage. (Mr S Crown).

965 - MAKEBELIEVE ISLAND (IRE)

b.c. Namaqualand - Zalamera (Rambo Dancer).
March 7. First foal. IR45,000Y. Goffs Orby.

The dam, a poor maiden, was placed once over 12f at 3 yrs and is a half-sister to 7 winners including the dam of the Group 1 National Stakes winner Definite Article. The second dam, My Candy (by Lorenzaccio), was placed once at 2 yrs and is a half-sister to the Ballymoss Stakes and Royal Whip Stakes winner Candy Cane. (Mr A D Shead).

966 - YELLOW RIBBON (IRE)

b.f. Hamas - Busker (Bustino).
April 30. Sixth foal. 24,000Y. Tattersalls October.

Closely related to the 1993 Italian 2-y-o winner Dox (by Roi Danzig) and half-sister to the quite useful 1995 2-y-o 6f winner Singing Patriarch (by Marju), the German 3-y-o winner Bluehende Heide (by Sharrood) and the poor 3-y-o 6f winner Prime Property (by Tirol). The dam ran twice unplaced at 2 yrs and is a half-sister to 7 winners including the Queen's Vase winner Arden and the French listed winner Kerulen. The second dam, Kereolle (by Riverman), is a placed half-sister to the top-class broodmare Miss Manon - dam of 5 stakes winners including the Group winners Mot D'Or, Lydian and Ballinderry (herself dam of the French Derby winner Sanglamore). (Mr A N Foster).

William Jarvis

William has suggested these two youngsters for this section. Concerning Gold Crystal, he explained "I like this horse. I thought he was going to be my first two-year-old runner until he had a slight setback and we've had to back off him a bit. From what we've seen he should give the owner some fun this year". "I also like Ingenious. He's sharp, has plenty of speed and could be a nice horse. We were just beginning to get a bit excited about him until he disappointed in the soft at Kempton". Most of William's representatives in this book are in the Premier Section.

---

967 - GOLD CRYSTAL

b.c. Fayruz - Lightning Laser (Monseigneur).
March 17. Sixth foal. 24,000Y. Doncaster St Leger.

Brother to the fairly useful 1995 Irish 2-y-o 5f and 6f winner Kingsandvagabonds and to the fair 1997 3-y-o 7f all-weather and 1998 1m winner Mozambique and half-brother to the fair Morocco, a winner of 8 races at up to 1m and the Italian 3-y-o winner L'Irriducibile (both by Cyrano de Bergerac). The dam, a moderate 2-y-o 7f winner, is a half-sister to 3 winners out of the French 3-y-o winner Spring Bride (by Auction Ring), herself a sister to the smart 2-y-o Highest Bidder and a half-sister to the US Grade 2 winner Peregrinator.

968 - INGENIOUS
b.c. Zieten - Siddon Pretty (Darshaan).
January 26. First foal. 23,000Y. Tattersalls October.
The dam won at 4 yrs in Germany and is a half-sister to 4 winners here and abroad. The second dam, Miss Siddons (by Cure The Blues), is an unplaced half-sister to the Irish Oaks winner Princess Pati and the Great Voltigeur Stakes winner Seymour Hicks. The third dam, Sarah Siddons, won the Irish 1,000 Guineas and the Yorkshire Oaks. (Noodles Racing).

Mark Johnston

Renowned for its high-class winners at both ends of the spectrum, from precocious two-year-olds to top-class stayers, Kingsley House in Middleham is sure to demand plenty of respect again this year. Not surprisingly, most of Mark's young horses are in the Premier Section, but here's what he has to say about my choices for earlier types. Branston Max "is a nice, lazy type of colt that has yet to do any fast work". Forum Girl is "a very strong, mature filly, going very well and will run soon". Spitzbergen is "an attractive, racy colt - about to commence fast work". Turtle "is a sharp, racy type and is due to run in April". The Dayjur - Humility filly is "nice, big and strong - going very nicely" and finally the "Sheikh Albadou - Urbacity filly has yet to do any fast work".

969 - BRANSTON MAX
b.c. Turtle Island - Tuxford Hideaway (Cawston's Clown).
April 11. 35,000Y. Tattersalls Houghton.
Half-brother to the 3-y-o Fetherolf (by Wolfhound), to the very useful and tough mare Branston Abby (by Risk Me), a winner of 24 races at up to 7f including numerous listed events, to the fairly useful 2-y-o dual 5f winner Branston Jewel (by Prince Sabo), the fairly useful 2-y-o 6f and 7f winner Big Blow (by Last Tycoon), the moderate 2-y-o 6f winner Glowing Dancer (by Glow) and the Danish winner of four races Chance Me (by Risk Me). The dam, a useful sprinter, won two races at 2 yrs and is a half-sister to 4 winners out of the minor 3-y-o winner Late Idea (by Tumble Wind). (Mr J David Abell).

970 - FORUM GIRL
b.f. Sheikh Albadou - Brava (Arratos).
January 23. 25,000Y. Tattersalls October.
Half-sister to the US stakes winner Simply Brave, to the French winner and listed placed Belle Brava (both by El Baba), the minor US winners Rara Avis (by Hawkster), Bravo Brava (by Rio Carmelo) and Forest Gumpett (by Green Forest) and the French winner of 4 races Seattle Savour (by Seattle Song). The dam won twice in Germany and is a half-sister to 8 winners there including the dual listed winner Bueno. The second dam, Brigida (by Priamos), won the Group 3 Schwarzgold-Rennen at Dusseldorf. (Mr J Conroy).

971 - SPITZBERGEN
ch.c. Polar Falcon - Soba (Most Secret).
April 20. 20,000Y. Tattersalls Houghton.
Half-brother to the useful 1994 2-y-o 6f winner French Gift (by Cadeaux Genereux), to the fairly useful 7.6f winner Water Well (by Sadler's Wells), the quite useful 7f and 12f winner Gold Dust (by Golden Fleece), the fair 5f and 6f winner Sobering Thoughts (by Be My Guest), the modest 10.3f winner Soba Up (by Persian Heights), the modest 14f all-weather winner Love and Kisses (by Salse) and a winner in Belgium by Caerleon. The dam, a high-class and tough sprinter, won 13 races including the Group 3 King George Stakes. The second dam, Mild Wind (by Porto Bello), was an unplaced half-sister to 4 minor winners. (Brian Yeardley Continental Ltd).

972 - TURTLE
b.c. Turtle Island - Kate Marie (Bering).
April 2. Second foal. 21,000Y. Tattersalls October.
Half-brother to the French-trained 3-y-o Fibonacci (by Alzao). The dam, a winner of 3 races in France and third in a listed event over 10f at Longchamp, is a half-sister to 3 winners. The second dam, Brigade Speciale (by Posse), won twice in France including a listed event over 1m at Maisons-Laffitte and is a half-sister to the Group 2 Royal Lodge Stakes winner Gairloch. (Mr M J Pilkington).

973 - UNNAMED
b.br.f. Dayjur - Humility (Cox's Ridge).
April 6. Second foal. $28,000Y. Keeneland September.
The dam, a winner of 3 races in France, is a half-sister to the US winner and Grade 2 placed Shy Minstrel. The second dam, Shy Bride (by Blushing Groom), won 5 races including a minor stakes in the USA, is a half-sister to the Somerville Tattersall Stakes winner Imperial Frontier and is out of the French Group 3 winner Hartebeest (herself a half-sister to the US Grade 1 winners Musical Lark and Spark Of Life). (Mr J S Morrison).

974 - UNNAMED b.f. Sheikh Albadou - Urbacity (Fappiano).
January 28. $19,000Y. Keeneland September.
Half-sister to 7 winners including the US stakes winner Viv (by Houston) and the US stakes-placed winners Urbanity (by Superbity), Track City Girl (by Track Barron) and Trafalgar Eight (by Lyphard's Wish). The dam is an unraced half-sister to the US stakes winner of 14 races Jeblar. The second dam, City Girl (by Lucky Debonair), won the Grade 3 8.5f Alcibiades Stakes at 2 yrs and is a half-sister to the Champion handicap mare and dual Grade 1 winner Proud Delta. (Mr & Mrs G Middlebrook).

Geoff Lewis

Geoff feels that his two-year-olds this year are a slightly later maturing bunch and that, on average, they'll need six furlongs to start with. Commonwealth is "a grand horse that should be out by the end of May. A big, powerful horse, he enjoys his work and has a future as a three-year-old". Fast And Neat is "a lovely horse with a good action and attitude". Latch Lifter is what Geoff calls his 'Charles Bronson' - not very pretty but he'll make lots of money! "A horse with a good action, I've entered him for the Heinz "57" Phoenix Stakes. Also entered for that race is Royal Playboy - "not very big, but strong and doing everything right, he's a grand horse that will definitely make a two-year-old". Manzoni "looks like he's going to be speedier than his pedigree would suggest. He's built like a two-year-old, is a tough little horse with great conformation and is very likeable". The Dolphin Street colt Neptune is "a lovely, big horse but more of an autumn type two-year-old" and finally the unnamed Cyrano de Bergerac colt is "a lovely big horse, very imposing and he'll be suited by ten furlongs next year".

975 - COMMONWEALTH (IRE) b.c. Common Grounds - Silver Slipper (Indian Ridge).
April 4. Second foal. IR£60,000Y. Goffs Orby.
Half-brother to a 3-y-o in Germany by Pips Pride. The dam, a modest dual 7f seller winner at 2 yrs, is closely related to the useful Group 3 Tetrarch Stakes winner Irish Memory and a half-sister to 6 winners. The second dam, Irish Isle (by Realm), was a modest 3-y-o 1m winner and a half-sister to 7 winners including the dam of the Prix Robert Papin winner Maelstrom Lake. (Highclere Thoroughbred Racing Ltd).

976 - FAST AND NEAT ch.c. Soviet Lad - Stop The Cavalry (Relko).
March 14. 22,000Y. Doncaster St Leger.
Brother to the Irish 2-y-o 5f and 6f winner Liprandi and half-brother to 2 minor winners in Italy and the USA by Auction Ring and Try My Best and to the quite useful Group 3 1m May Hill Stakes placed maiden Super Serena (by Taufan). The dam is an unraced half-sister to 4 winners including the Palace House Stakes winner Brave Lad. The second dam, Social Bee (by Galivanter), won 3 races.

977 - LATCH LIFTER b.c. Prince Sabo - Thevetia (Mummy's Pet).
April 26. Sixth foal. 27,000Y. Doncaster St Leger.
Half-brother to the fair 1997 2-y-o 5f winner Out Like Magic (by Magic Ring), to the useful 7f and 7.9f winner In Like Flynn (by Handsome Sailor), the modest 6f all-weather winner Cool Tactician (by Petong) and the modest 6f (at 2 yrs) and 8.2f winner Mac Kelty (by Wattlefield). The dam, a modest 6f placed maiden, is a half-sister to 7 winners including the Coronation Stakes fourth Moogie. The second dam, Cape Chestnut (by Bustino), was a quite useful 1m winner and a half-sister to the US Grade 2 winner Colway Rally. (Mr David Barker).

978 - MANZONI b.c. Warrshan - Arc Empress Jane (Rainbow Quest).
January 5. First foal. 23,000Y. Doncaster St Leger.
The dam is an unraced half-sister to two winners including the quite useful 1996 3-y-o Aerleon Jane. The second dam, An Empress (by Affirmed), a winner of two Grade 3 events in the USA over 8.5f and second in the Grade 1 Hollywood Oaks, is out of the champion Venezuelan filly Blondy. (Mr David Barker).

979 - NEPTUNE b.c. Dolphin Street - Seal Indigo (Glenstal).
April 16. Third foal. 35,000Y. Tattersalls Houghton.
Half-brother to a 3-y-o in Japan by Lion Cavern. The dam, a fairly useful winner of 5 races over middle-distances, is a half-sister to the Italian winner and Group 3 placed Campalto and to the winner and listed Oaks Trial fourth Gorgeous Dancer. The second dam, Simply Gorgeous, (by Hello Gorgeous), is an unraced half-sister to the Irish Oaks, Lancashire Oaks, Musidora Stakes and Lingfield Oaks Trial winner Give Thanks. (Highclere Thoroughbred Racing Ltd).

980 - ROYAL PLAYBOY　　　　ch.c. Clantime - First Play (Primo Dominie).
January 26. First foal. 24,000Y. Doncaster St Leger.
The dam, a modest 3-y-o 6f winner, is out of the quite useful School Concert (by Music Boy), a winner of four races over 6f and a full or half-sister to 7 winners including the French dual Group 3 winning sprinter Kind Music. (Lucayan Stud).

Peter Makin

Here are three youngsters Peter will be aiming at the winner's enclosure this year. Avanti is "a nice colt that has just started working upsides other horses. A two-year-old type, he's a nice, strong colt". Belisha Beacon is "a typical Warning in that she won't be early. She's a backward, quality filly that won't be rushed but should be out by mid-season". Truth Seeker is "a very nice, mature young horse. A big, strong two-year-old, he'll hopefully be out in May but wouldn't want firm ground".

981 - AVANTI　　　　gr.c. Reprimand - Dolly Bevan (Another Realm).
March 15. Fifth foal. 20,000Y. Doncaster St Leger.
Half-brother to the useful Oggi, a winner of 6 races at up to 6f and to the fairly useful Pengamon (both by Efisio), a winner of 4 races at up to 1m. The dam a 2-y-o 6f seller winner, is a half-sister to Pips Pride, a winner of 6 races including the Group 1 6f Heinz "57" Phoenix Stakes. The second dam, Elkie Brooks (by Relkino), was a quite useful 6f placed 2-y-o. (Dr Carlos Stelling).

982 - BELISHA BEACON　　　　b.f. Warning - Kindergarten (Trempolino).
April 17. First foal. 22,000Y. Tattersalls December.
The dam won two races at 2 yrs in France including the Group 3 1m Prix d'Aumale and was second in the Group 1 1m Prix Marcel Boussac and is a half-sister to 3 winners. The second dam, Children's Corner (by Top Ville), won over 1m (at 2 yrs) and 9f in France, was third in the Group 3 Prix des Reservoirs and is a sister to the dam of the Irish Derby winner Winged Love. (Bakewell Bloddstock Ltd).

983 - TRUTH SEEKER　　　　b.c. Wolfhound - Swame (Shirley Heights).
April 18. Second foal. 52,000Y. Tattersalls Houghton.
Half-brother to the 3-y-o Algunnaas (by Red Ransom). The dam won three races in the USA and is a half-sister to 3 winners including the Grade 3 Athenia Handicap winner High Browser. The second dam, Browser (by Nijinsky), is an unraced half-sister to the Group 3 Gladness Stakes winner Rose Reef, the Lupe Stakes winner Golden Bowl, the US Grade 1 placed Rokeby and to the dam of the US Grade 2 winner Rockamundo. The third dam, Rose Bowl (by Habitat), was a half-sister to Ile de Bourbon and won 6 races including the Champion Stakes. (Mr P Wragg).

Kevin McAuliffe

Kevin feels that these four two-year-olds are probably his best at this early stage of the season. Swampy is "a nice horse with a good attitude that goes extremely well. He has a good way about him, will be out in May and will be suited by five or six furlongs this year". Thames Dancer is "a very nice horse. Not leggy and backward like a lot of young Green Dancer horses, he's definitely a two-year-old type and will be out in May". Riverdance "goes well, is a nice horse and very much a sprint type. Six furlongs would be his maximum". Hill Storm "is also an early type. His sire is an influence for speed and this colt will be suited by six furlongs this year. A mature colt, he has a tough attitude".

984 - HILL STORM　　　　b.c. Mukaddamah - Brockley Hill Lass (Alzao).
April 12. First foal. 21,000Y. Tattersalls October.
The dam was unplaced on her only start (over 7f at 2 yrs) and is a half-sister to 5 winners including the Group 2 Laurent Perrier Champagne Stakes third Handstand. The second dam, Moorland Chant (by Double Jump), won once in France over 9f. (Mr E D Kessly).

985 - RIVERDANCE (IRE)　　　　ch.c. College Chapel - Valmarana (Danzig Connection).
February 24. First foal. 37,000Y. Tattersalls October.
The dam, a minor Irish 3-y-o 12f winner, is closely related to Baltic Fox, a winner in both Ireland and the USA and second in the Group 2 Gallinule Stakes and the Grade 2 Nassau County Handicap. The second dam, Super Foxe (by Blood Royal), is an unraced half-sister to 4 winners including the French listed winner and Prix de la Foret fourth Lichine. (Gallagher Equine Ltd).

986 - SWAMPY   b.c. Second Set - Mystery Lady (Vaguely Noble).
                                              April 29. IR24,000Y. Goffs Challenge.
Closely related to the quite useful 9f and 10f winner Conspicuous (by Alzao) and half-brother to the
Group 2 10f Premio Lydia Tesio winner and US Grade 1 Ramona Handicap third Pourquoi Pas (by
Nordico) and the minor US winner of 14 races Marty's Smarty (by Smarten). The dam ran unplaced
twice in the USA and is a half-sister to 6 winners. The second dam, Our Dancing Girl (by Solo Landing),
won the Group 2 6f Schuylerville Stakes at 2 yrs in the USA and is a half-sister to the dam of the triple
US Grade 1 winner Island Whirl. (Gallagher Equine Ltd).

987 - THAMES DANCER (USA)   ch.c. Green Dancer - Hata (Kaldoun).
                                        April 1. Third foal. 33,000Y. Tattersalls October.
Half-brother to the minor US 1996 3-y-o winner Going To The Well (by Antheus) and to a winner over
jumps in France by Trempolino. The dam was placed five times in France and is a half-sister to 7
winners including the listed winner and Group 1 Prix Robert Papin third Harifa. The second dam,
Hamada (by Habitat), won the Group 3 Prix de la Porte Maillot and the Group 3 Prix de Sandringham
and is a half-sister to the dam of the Derby winner Erhaab. (Mr J S Dunningham).

Brian Meehan

*Watch out for the two-year-olds from Brian Meehan's Upper Lambourn yard this year. Our discussion
at the yard brought out these particularly nice types. Annapurna "should be ready to have a run out in
May and she's a decent sort", Aquamarina "is a nice filly, slightly backward but I don't think she'll take
long", Arctic Char "is slightly backward due to an injury and won't be out before July", Blue Laser is "a
nice sharp horse and he'll be suited by five or six furlongs in May". The French-bred colt Challenges
is "a lovely colt that's just started working and he'll be a good one to follow from the middle of May
onwards". Dramatize "is a gelding I had in mind for the Brocklesby Stakes until he got a temperature.
By some time in May I think he'll be a sharp two-year-old". Gypsy Rose Lee "will be a nice six furlong
filly from June onwards", Indiana Legend is "a good sort of horse by Indian Ridge. He's had a touch of
sore shins so we'll have to wait with him a bit, but he should be out in late May". Jade Tiger is "very
sharp and will be running in late April". Maxime is "a nice sort of filly that will be suited by five or six
furlongs and be out quite soon". Polish Girl is "a mid-summer type with a lot of class. She'll get six
furlongs well and is a good sort for the future". Santisima "is a Grand Lodge filly that is just starting to
do well. She's a lovely filly". Sarah's Song "wouldn't take long before she's ready. She's working well".
September Harvest is "a nice horse that was laid out for a while. I've brought him back now and he
shouldn't take long. I'd expect him to be suited to a Newbury maiden in the middle of May". Susan's
Pride "is a good five furlong type. I'm hoping he's an Ascot type so he should be out before the end of
May". Tumbleweed Glen "will probably want six furlongs and he'll be ready as soon as those races
start". Tumbleweed Quartet "is a big, weak two-year-old. A nice horse with a lot of class. He'll be out
in June or July". The unnamed Pips Pride - Aubretia colt is "a lovely horse, quite tall but not backward.
He'll be a May two-year-old" and the unnamed Puissance - Aryaf colt is "a nice 2-y-o, a half-brother to
Mind Games but quite big and backward at the moment".*

988 - ANNAPURNA   b.br.f. Brief Truce - National Ballet (Shareef Dancer).
                                        March 10. Third foal. 44,000Y. Tattersalls October.
Half-sister to the very useful 1997 2-y-o Name Of Love (by Petardia), a winner of 3 races over 7f
including the Group 3 Rockfel Stakes and the listed Oh So Sharp Stakes. The dam is an unraced
half-sister to 7 winners including the listed winners Broken Wave, Guarde Royale, Clifton Chapel and
Saxon Maid. The second dam, Britannia's Rule (by Blakeney), won the Lupe Stakes and was third in
the Oaks. (Thurloe Thoroughbreds).

989 - AQUAMARINA   b.f. Dolphin Street - Galapagos (Pitskelly).
                                           April 8. Fourth foal. 9,000Y. Tattersalls October.
Half-sister to the German 3-y-o winner Little Dame (by Prince Rupert) and the Irish trained 3-y-o Blue
Booby (by Mac's Imp). The dam was placed in Ireland at 3 and 4 yrs and is a half-sister to 5 winners
including the useful sprinter Love Legend. The second dam, Sweet Emma (by Welsh Saint), won the
Group 1 5f Heinz "57" Phoenix Stakes. (Mr J Blackshaw).

990 - ARCTIC CHAR   br.f. Polar Falcon - Breadcrumb (Final Straw).
                                        February 20. 32,000Y. Tattersalls October.
Sister to the quite useful 1997 2-y-o 7f winner Arctic Air and half-sister to the useful 1990 2-y-o 5f and
6f winner Heard A Whiser (by Bellypha), the 1993 3-y-o 7f winner Khubza (by Green Desert) and the

1994 3-y-o 8.3f winner Midnight Snack (by Night Shift) - both quite useful. The dam, a very useful 6f and 7f winner, is a half-sister to the Group 2 Prix Maurice de Gheest winner and July Cup second College Chapel. The second dam, Scarcely Blessed (by So Blessed), won 3 races including the Group 3 King George Stakes. (Miss G Abbey).

991 - BLUE LASER (IRE)
b.c. Mujtahid - Dazzling Fire (Bluebird).
February 1. Second foal. IR31,000Y. Goffs Orby.
The dam, a modest 3-y-o 11.7f winner, is a half-sister to 6 winners including the fairly useful dual 2-y-o 6f winner Sotoboy. The second dam, Fire Flash (by Bustino), is a placed half-sister to the Lincoln Handicap winner King's Glory. The third dam, Dazzling Light (by Silly Season), was a smart half-sister to Welsh Pageant. (Miss J Semple).

992 - CHALLENGES (FR)
b.c. Zieten - La Toscanella (Riverton).
March 21. Sixth foal. FF210,000Y. Deauville August.
Half-brother to 2 minor winners in France by Kadrou and Leading Counsel and to a winner in Spain by Kadrou. The dam is an unraced half-sister to 4 winners out of the minor French winner Tirnova (by Silver Shark). (Mr J Gutkin).

993 - DRAMATIZE (IRE)
ch.g. Great Commotion - Silk Cord (Sallust).
March 6. Second foal. 9,500Y. Doncaster St Leger.
The dam was placed several times in Ireland from sprint to middle-distances and is a half-sister to 2 minor winners. The second dam, Silk Rein (by Shantung), won once at 3 yrs and is a half-sister to the outstanding middle-distance colt Troy. (Mr N Attenborough).

994 - GIPSY ROSE LEE (IRE)
b.f. Marju - Rainstone (Rainbow Quest).
February 17. Third foal. IR36,000Y. Goffs Orby.
Half-sister to the 3-y-o Yatahed (by Mujtahid), unplaced on his only start at 2 yrs and to the Italian 2-y-o 1m winner Holes In The Grass (by Be My Guest). The dam, placed twice over 1m on the all-weather, won in Belgium and is a half-sister to the Group 3 Cornwallis Stakes and Group 3 Norfolk Stakes winner Magic Ring. The second dam, Emaline (by Empery), won over 7f at 2 yrs in France and is a half-sister to the dam of the listed Criterium d'Evry winner Firm Friend. (Mrs K J Crangle).

995 - INDIANA LEGEND (IRE)
ch.c. Indian Ridge - Mardi Gras Belle (Masked Dancer).
April 16. Sixth foal. IR21,000Y. Goffs Challenge.
Half-brother to the 3-y-o Aquarela (by Shirley Heights). The dam, a modest maiden, was placed at up to 12f and is a half-sister to the 2 winners including the dam of a stakes winner in the USA. The second dam, Sun Piper(by Sea Bird II), is an unplaced half-sister to 3 minor winners. (The Two's Company Partnership).

996 - JADE TIGER
ch.c. Lion Cavern - Precious Jade (Northfields).
April 5. 45,000Y. Tattersalls Houghton.
Closely related to the Italian winner of 4 races Precious Dame (by Damister) and half-brother to the Group 1 Premio Vittorio di Capua winner Just a Flutter, the modest 2-y-o 6f winner Jadebelle (both by Beldale Flutter), the Group 1 Premio Roma winner Slicious (by Slip Anchor), the fair 7f and 1m winner Glowing Jade (by Kalaglow), the modest 5f winner Bold Gem (by Never So Bold) and the 2-y-o 5f seller winner Diamond Sky (by Absalom). The dam, a modest 4-y-o 7f winner, is a half-sister to 5 winners. The second dam, Love Letter (by Gratirude), was a fairly useful sprint winner. (Mr F Wilson).

997 - MAXIME
b.f. Mac's Imp - Ludovica (Bustino).
April 12. IR36,000Y. Tattersalls Fairyhouse.
Closely related to the Irish trained 3-y-o Terrahawk (by Imp Society) and half-sister to the useful 1995 7.5f to 1m winner Weet-A-Minute (by Nabeel Dancer), the Italian winner of 5 races Ombre Rosse (by Jareer) and the modest 1990 2-y-o Where's Carol (by Anfield), a winner of 4 races over 6f an the all-weather. The dam is an unraced half-sister to 6 winners out of Lorelene (by Lorenzaccio), a winner of 4 races and second in the Ebor Handicap.

998 - POLISH GIRL
b.f. Polish Precedent - Stack Rock (Ballad Rock).
March 19. First foal. 54,000Y. Tattersalls Houghton.
The dam was a very useful winner of 9 races from 5f to 1m including the listed Hopeful Stakes and was second in the Group 1 Prix de l'Abbaye. She is a half-sister to 3 minor winners out of the fair 1m to 10f winner One Better (by Nebbiolo). (Mr F Wilson).

999 - SANTISIMA ch.f. Grand Lodge - Ship's Twine (Slip Anchor). January 21. First foal.

The dam, a poor 1m and 10f placed maiden, is a half-sister to the very smart Group 2 9.8f Prix Dollar winner and Champion Hurdler Alderbrook, the smart Group 3 1m Minstrel Stakes winner Restructure and the very useful 6f (at 2 yrs) and 10f winner Native Twine. The second dam, Twine (by Thatching), is an unraced half-sister to the listed winners Tea House (dam of the Australian Grade 1 winner Danish and the good chaser Sybillin) and Academic (also third in the Grade 1 San Juan Capistrano Handicap).

1000 - SARAH'S SONG (IRE) b.f. Warning - Two And Sixpence (Chief's Crown). January 16. Third foal. 20,000Y. Tattersalls October.

Half-sister to the 1997 unplaced 2-y-o La Galleria (by Royal Academy) and the German placed Tairoon (by Reprmand). The dam was a fair 3-y-o winner over 17f and is a half-sister to the US stakes winner Evening Highlight. The second dam, Candlelight Service (by Blushing Groom), is an unraced half-sister to 5 winners. (Mrs Susan Roy).

1001 - SEPTEMBER HARVEST (USA) ch.c. Mujtahid - Shawgatny (Danzig Connection). March 18. Second foal. IR28,000Y. Goffs Orby.

Half-brother to the 3-y-o Noble Charger (by Cadeaux Genereux). The dam, a winner over 9f in Ireland at 2 yrs, is a sister to the Group 3 Desmond Stakes winner Star of Gdansk and a half-sister to the US Grade 3 winner W D Jacks and the US stakes winner Empress Jackie (dam of the Princess Margaret Stakes winner Tajannub). The second dam, Star Empress (by Young Emperor), won 3 races in the USA and is a half-sister to the grandam of the Graded stakes winners and sires Mt Livermore, Magical Wonder and Salt Dome. (Mr J Dunningham).

1002 - SUSAN'S PRIDE (IRE) b.c. Pips Pride - Piney Pass (Persian Bold). April 10. 60,000Y. Tattersalls October.

Brother to the fair 1997 6f placed 3-y-o Easter Ogil and half-brother to the fairly useful winner of 17 races at up to 1m Allinson's Mate (by Fayruz), the quite useful 2-y-o 7f winner Woosie, the fair 2-y-o 5f and 6f winner Mountview (both by Montekin) and the modest 2-y-o 7f winner Pass The Key (by Treasure Kay). The dam won over 8.5f in Ireland at 2 yrs and is a half-sister to 7 winners. The second dam, Big Bertha (by Herbager), is a placed half-sister to 6 winners. (Mrs Susan Roy).

1003 - TUMBLEWEED GLEN (IRE) ch.c. Mukaddamah - Mistic Glen (Mister Majestic). February 20. First foal. 30,000Y. Tattersalls October.

The dam, a winner twice over hurdles, is a half-sister to 3 winners including the Irish listed-placed sprinter Wolverglen. The second dam, Northern Glen (by Northfields), is an unraced half-sister to the Molecomb Stakes winner Pert Lassie (herself dam of the Australian Grade 2 winner Cheeky Trot). (The Fifth Tumbleweed Partnership).

1004 - TUMBLEWEED QUARTET b.c. Manila - Peggy's String (Highland Park). February 25. Fifth foal. 31,000Y. Tattersalls October.

Half-brother to 3 minor winners in the USA by Badger Land, Seattle Song and Sportin' Life. The dam is an unraced half-sister to 6 winners including the Group 3 Queen Mary Stakes winner and Group 1 July Cup third Gwydion. The second dam, Papamiento (by Blade), is a placed half-sister to the Grade 1 Suburban Handicap winner Twice Worthy and to the Grand Prix de Paris winner Armistice III. (The Tumbleweed Partnership).

1005 - UNNAMED b.c. Puissance - Aryaf (Vice Regent). April 23.

Brother to the high-class sprinter Mind Games, winner of the Group 2 Temple Stakes (twice), the Norfolk Stakes and the Palace House Stakes and to the 2-y-o 1m winner Able Fun (by Double Schwartz). The dam is an unplaced half-sister to 4 winners including the Group 2 Tripleprint Celebration Mile third Peartree House. The second dam, Fashion Front (by Habitat), is an unraced half-sister to the Horris Hill Stakes winner Long Row and the Norfolk Stakes winner Colmore Row. (Mr T Hyde).

1006 - UNNAMED ch.c. Pips Pride - Aubretia (Hatchet Man). March 16. 20,000Y. Doncaster St Leger.

Brother to the 1997 Italian 2-y-o winner and listed placed Aupride and half-brother to Charming Gift (by Petorius), a modest winner of three races over 1m. The dam, a quite useful 2-y-o 7f winner, is a half-sister to 4 winners including the Group 3 Lingfield Oaks Trial second Rockfest - herself dam of the Group 3 Lancashire Oaks winner Rainbow Lake. The second dam, Rock Garden (by Roan Rocket), a quite useful 3-y-o 1m winner, is a half-sister to the Group 3 Greenham Stakes winner Glen Strae. (Mr J McCarthy).

Willie Muir

Willie Muir's Lambourn stables house a number of nice young horses this year. Willie was particularly pleased with the following - Buona Sera is "a lovely Marju colt that will be out by the end of May. He shows enough speed for five furlongs but he might be better over six". Inflite is "a horse I just hope will be ready for Royal Ascot. He'll be a really good horse, shows plenty of ability and should be a five or six furlong type". Kanz Wood "looks a really good sort and he could go on to be anything". Loch Fyne "is very speedy, goes well and I'd like her to have one or two runs before the Queen Mary Stakes at Royal Ascot. I couldn't say enough about her - I like her a lot". Mowgli is "rather like his half-brother Averti before him in that he shows me the right attitude and ability already, even though I won't campaign him before the summer months". Parkside is "a nice, speedy colt but a backward type, he will be a 2-y-o at the end of the summer". Thrust "will definitely be a 2-y-o. He's very sharp and quite early. I think he's got a lot of ability and again, I would hope he'd be good enough for Royal Ascot" and finally, Tiger Grass "is a nice horse that goes well but he won't be seen out for some time yet". William also has a two-year-old in the Premier Section of this book.

1007 - BUONA SERA
b.c. Marju - Blueberry Walk (Green Desert).
March 14. First foal. 20,000Y. Tattersalls December.
The dam is an unraced sister to the listed 2m George Stubbs Stakes winner Hawait Al Barr and a half-sister to 2 winners. The second dam, Allegedly Blue (by Alleged), won once at 3 yrs, was placed in the Park Hill Stakes and the Princess Royal Stakes and is a full or half-sister to 4 winners including the dam of the Queen Anne Stakes winner Allied Forces. (Fayzad Thoroughbred Ltd).

1008 - INFLITE
b.c. Indian Ridge - Nightitude (Night Shift).
February 7. First foal. 55,000Y. Tattersalls October.
The dam, a fairly useful 2-y-o 5f winner and placed over 6f, became unreliable at 3 yrs. She is a half-sister to 7 winners including the useful 1985 2-y-o 7f winner Normanby Lass. The second dam, Rectitude (by Runnymede), was a useful winner of 3 races at up to 8.5f. (V S Fleet).

1009 - KANZ WOOD
ch.c. Woodman - Kanz (The Minstrel).
February 16.
Half-brother to the 3-y-o Kanz Pride (by Lion Cavern), to the useful 1991 3-y-o 10.5f and 12f winner Kansk (by Top Ville), the minor 1994 Irish 2-y-o 8f winner Treasurer (by Darshaan) and the quite useful 1989 2-y-o 6f winner Peterhouse (by Habitat). The dam, winner of the Group 3 8.5f Princess Elizabeth Stakes and second in the Yorkshire Oaks, is closely related to the very useful Gold Treasure and a half-sister to the dams of the good horses Ensconse, I Want To Be, Media Starguest, Diamond Shoal and Glint of Gold. The second dam, Treasure Chest (by Rough n' Tumble), was a very useful stakes winner over 6.5f and 1m. (Mr D J Deer).

1010 - LOCH FYNE
b.f. Ardkinglass - Song's Best (Never So Bold).
March 8. Fifth foal. 25,000Y. Doncaster St Leger.
Half-sister to the fair 1997 5f placed 2-y-o Percy-P and the useful 1994 2-y-o 5f and 6f winner Lennox Lewis. The dam is an unraced sister to the listed winner and Group 3 Phoenix Flying Five second Tadwin (herself dam of the Queen Mary Stakes winner Nadwah) and a half-sister to the Group 3 6f Greenlands Stakes and Group 3 5f Palace House Stakes winner Reesh. The second dam, Song's Jest (by Song), is an unraced half-sister to 6 winners including the dam of the sprinters Jester and Tricky Note. (Mr D J Deer).

1011 - MOWGLI
b.c. Wolfhound - Imperial Jade (Lochnager).
April 15.
Half-brother to the 3-y-o Imperial Envoy (by Zafonic) and to several winners including the very useful Averti, winner of the Group 3 5f King George Stakes. The dam, a useful sprinter, was a sister to the Greenlands Stakes, Palace House Stakes and Temple Stakes winner Reesh and a half-sister to the useful Diadem Stakes placed Tadwin (herself dam of the Queen Mary Stakes winner Nadwah). The second dam, Songs Jest (by Song), is an unraced half-sister to the dams of the smart sprinters Jester and Fayruz. (Mr D J Deer).

1012 - PARKSIDE b.c. Common Grounds - Warg (Dancing Brave).
February 3. Second foal. 28,000Y. Tattersalls October.
Half-brother to the useful 1997 2-y-o 6f winner Marksman (by Marju). The dam is an unraced half-sister to the very promising 1997 2-y-o 7f winner Fantasy Island and to the fairly useful 7f (at 2 yrs) and 10f winner Expensive Taste. The second dam, Um Lardaff (by Mill Reef), a winner over 11f and 12f at 3 yrs in France, is a sister to the Derby winner and high-class sire Shirley Heights and a half-sister to the very good mare Bempton - dam of the Group 3 winners Banket and Mr Pintips and of the Group 2 winner Gull Nook (herself dam of the top-class colt Pentire). (Parkside Partnership).

1013 - THRUST br.c. Prince Sabo - La Piaf (Fabulous Dancer).
April 26. Second foal. 32,000Y. Doncaster St Leger. 50,000Y. Doncaster 2-y-o Sale.
Half-sister to the French trained 3-y-o Mister Eric (by Miswaki). The dam won 6 races in France and the USA including a stakes event over 1m on turf and is a half-sister to 3 winners. The second dam, Loon (by Kaldoun), won 4 races in France including the listed 12f Prix de la Porte de Passy. (Mrs H Levy).

1014 - TIGER GRASS (IRE) gr.c. Ezzoud - Rustic Lawn (Rusticaro).
February 23. Sixth foal. FF450,000. Deauville August.
Half-brother to the quite useful 1m to 10f winner Silver Groom by Shy Groom) and to the modest 1996 8.5f placed 2-y-o High Extreme (by Danehill). The dam is an unraced half-sister to 3 winners and to the dam of the Lockinge Stakes winner Broken Hearted. The second dam, Ash Lawn (by Charlottesville), is a winning sister to the Hardwicke Stakes winner Selhurst and a half-sister to the Derby winner Royal Palace and to Glass Slipper (dam of the classic winners Fairy Footsteps and Light Cavalry). (Mr M Caddy).

Jeremy Noseda

The majority of Jeremy's two-year-olds in the book can be found in the Premier Section. Here are some that are likely to be slightly earlier.

1015 - CALYPSO (IRE) b.c. Turtle Island - Music Of The Night (Blushing Groom).
May 10. IR30,000Y. Goffs Challenge.
Closely related to the 1996 Irish 3-y-o 5f winner Antithesis (by Fairy King) and half-brother to the 1997 2-y-o Moonlit (by Tirol), the quite useful 6f (at 2 yrs) to 12f winner At Liberty (by Danehill), the poor 10f winner Master Copy and the Swiss winner Melodic Sound (both by Bluebird). The dam is an unraced half-sister to 9 winners including the German and Swedish Group 1 winner and Champion Stakes second Prima Voce. The second dam, Que Mona (by Ribot), won over 6f in the USA and is a daughter of the Oaks winner Monade.

1016 - SONG 'N DANCE MAN b.c. Prince Sabo - Born To Dance (Dancing Brave).
February 19. Third foal. 66,000Y. Tattersalls October.
Brother to the 3-y-o Marweh and half-brother to the 6f placed Marengo (by Never So Bold). The dam, a fair 3-y-o 8.1f winner, is a half-sister to 6 winners including the dam of the Richmond Stakes winner Contract Law. The second dam, Oh So Bold (by Better Bee), won twice in the USA and is a half-sister to 11 winners including the Irish Derby winner Law Society, the US Grade 2 winner Strike Your Colors and the Lingfield Derby Trial winner Legal Bid.

1017 - TINDLELITE b.c. Cyrano de Bergerac - Plie (Superlative).
April 2. Fifth foal. 21,000Y. Doncaster St Leger.
Half-brother to the modest 2-y-o 7f all-weather winner Red Simba (by Absalom) and to a winner in Scandinavia by Sayf El Arab. The dam, a fair 2-y-o 5.8f winner, stayed 1m and is a half-sister to 2 minor winners. The second dam, La Pirouette (by Kennedy Road), was a fair 3-y-o 7f winner.

1018 - TOMASEAN b.c. Forzando - Bunny Gee (Last Tycoon).
February 27. First foal. 25,000Y. Tattersalls October.
The dam, unplaced in six outings at 2 and 3 yrs, is out of the quite useful 3-y-o 12f winner Mountain Isle (by Shirley Heights) - herself a half-sister to 7 winners.

1019 - TOUCH OF LOVE　　　　　　　　　　b.c. Pursuit Of Love - Nitouche (Scottish Reel).
January 20. Second foal. 25,000Y. Tattersalls October.
Half-brother to the poor 1997 1m placed 2-y-o Thecomebackking (by Mystiko). The dam, a modest 5f
(at 2 yrs) and 7f winner, is a half-sister to 2 winners. The second dam, Loredana (by Grange Melody),
was a modest 7f and 1m winner and a half-sister to 3 winners.

Kevin Prendergast

*Here are two young horses Kevin feels will be early. Institutrice is "a tidy filly. Quite sharp, she'll be
running in May" and Pipe Dream is "a sharp, muscular, sprint type two-year-old". Kevin has six
particularly well-bred two-year-olds in the Premier Section.*

1020 - INSTITUTRICE (IRE)　　　　　　b.f. College Chapel - Miss Turnberry (Mummy's Pet).
March 24. IR23,000Y. Fairyhouse September.
Half-sister to the Irish listed 10f winner Cheviot Amble (by Pennine Walk) and the Irish listed 6f winner
(at 2 yrs) Alalja (by Entitled). The dam, a winner of 2 races in Ireland and placed in the Group 3 C L
Weld Park Stakes at Phoenix Park, is a half-sister to 3 winners. The second dam, Pleasure Boat (by
Be Friendly), won at 2 yrs and is out of the Yorkshire Oaks second Blue Galleon. (Mrs O'Reilly).

1021 - PIPE DREAM　　　　　　　　　　b.c. King's Signet - Rather Warm (Tribal Chief).
May 15. 26,000Y. Doncaster St Leger.
Half-brother to the 2-y-o 6f winner Prince Emilio (by Prince Sabo), the triple 10f winner Woodurather,
the 2-y-o 7f winner Rather Touching (both by Touching Wood), the 3-y-o 7f winner Rather Homely (by
Homing), the 6f to 7.6f winner Sparky Lad (by Hot Spark) - all fair performers - and the modest 1997
11.6f winner Blush (by Gildoran). The dam, a useful winner of 3 races at up to 7.6f at 2 yrs, is out of
the fairly useful Reddish (by Red God), a winner of 3 races at up to 6f at 2 yrs. (Mr F Hardy & Mr N
Wilson).

Sir Mark Prescott

*Most of Sir Mark's representatives in this book are in the Premier Section. Of the earlier types, he says
- "Hidden Magic should be out by June, probably over five furlongs and is quite a nice colt". Magic
Light is "a good-looking horse, he'll be an early type and on pedigree at least will probably be a sprinter".
Rajmata is "a nice looking filly, if a bit light, and she'll be an early, sprint type".*

1022 - HIDDEN MAGIC　　　　　　　　b.c. Magic Ring - Magic Milly (Simply Great).
March 12. Fourth foal. 35,000Y. Tattersalls October.
Half-brother to the fairly useful 1997 2-y-o 5f winner Batswing (by Batshoof), to the useful listed 5f
Harry Rosebery Trophy and listed 5f Field Marshal Stakes winner Westcourt Magic (by Emarati) and
the 6f (at 2 yrs) to 10.8f winner Folly Finesse (by Joligeneration). The dam, a modest 2-y-o 1m winner,
is out of the fairly useful 2-y-o dual 7f winner Supreme Fjord (by Targowice). (Platinum Syndicate Ltd).

1023 - MAGIC LIGHT (IRE)　　　　　　　b.c. Dilum - Wynona (Cyrano de Bergerac).
March 23. First foal. 38,000Y. Tattersalls October.
The dam, a fairly useful 2-y-o dual 7f winner, is a half-sister to the very useful Group 3 Ballyogan
Stakes winner Anzio (by Hatim). The second dam, Highdrive (by Ballymore), is an unplaced half-sister
to 6 minor winners. (Mr H D Kelly).

1024 - RAJMATA (IRE)　　　　　　　　br.f. Prince Sabo - Heart Of India (Try My Best).
February 27. First foal. 25,000Y. Tattersalls October.
The dam is an unraced half-sister to 6 winners including the useful sprinters Bolshoi, Great Chaddington
and Tod. The second dam, Mainly Dry (by The Brianstan), is an unraced half-sister to 4 winners
including the dam of the Portland Handicap winner Swelter. (Mrs C R Philipson).

Lynda Ramsden

*Capitalist is "a colt we all like quite a bit. He's forward and will be running in May over five furlongs".
Regarding the cleverly named Elvis Reigns, Jack says "I like this colt a lot. A bit backward at the
moment, he'll be out in June and is a nice type". Kinlano is "a nice, big colt that will be out in
mid-summer", whilst Preposition is a "stocky little colt that is going quite well and will be out in May".
Prince Consort "is backward and growing all the time. He'll be out around July time" and Riverblue
"may not be very big but he's a nice colt that will probably start over five furlongs in June". Jack and
Lynda have two more horses in the Premier Section.*

1025 - CAPITALIST   b.c. Bigstone - Pinkie Rose (Kenmare).
March 12. Third foal. 31,000Y. Tattersalls October.
Half-brother to the modest 1997 7f placed 2-y-o Spree Rose (by Dancing Spree). The dam won over 12f in France and is a half-sister to 2 other minor winners. The second dam, Rose Bonbon (by High Top), won over 13f in France and is a half-sister to the French Group 1 winners Le Nain Jaune, Indian Rose and Vert Amande and to the dam of the Prix Lupin winner Groom Dancer. (Platinum Syndicate Ltd).

1026 - ELVIS REIGNS   b.c. Rock City - Free Rein (Sagaro).
February 10. 31,000Y. Doncaster St Leger.
Half-brother to 7 winners by Red Sunset including the quite useful 1994 2-y-o 7f winner Chance Bid, the fair 3-y-o 10f winner Ice Magic, the fair 3-y-o 1m and 8.2f winner Sunset Reins Free, the moderate 1993 2-y-o 5f winner Hiltons Travel, the modest 3-y-o 7f and 4-y-o 1m winner Perdition and the modest La Reine Rouge - a winner of three 12f events on the all-weather. The dam is an unraced half sister to one winner on the flat and another over hurdles. The second dam, Silk Rein (by Shantung), won at 3 yrs and is a half-sister to the outstanding colt Troy, winner of the Derby, the King George, the Irish Derby etc., and to the Prince of Wales's Stakes winner Admetus. (Bernard Hathaway).

1027 - KINLANO   b.c. Cyrano de Bergerac - Kinlacey (Aragon).
April 1. Second foal. 37,000Y. Doncaster St Leger.
Half-brother to the fairly useful 1997 2-y-o 5f and 6f winner Islamabad (by Petong). The dam, a fair 7f and 7.5f winner, is a half-sister to 3 winners. The second dam, Mimika (by Lorenzaccio), was a quite useful 2-y-o 5f winner. (Bernard Hathaway).

1028 - PREPOSITION   b.c. Then Again - Little Emmeline (Emarati).
April 15. First foal. 21,000Y. Doncaster St Leger.
The dam, a 2-y-o 5f seller winner, is a half-sister to 3 winners including the listed Roses Stakes winner Dealers Wheels. The second dam, Hyacine (by High Line), was placed at up to 12f and is a sister to Capricorn Line, a winner of 5 races and second in the Group 1 Gran Premio di Milano. (Bernard Hathaway).

1029 - PRINCE CONSORT   b.c. Clantime - Miss Petella (Dunphy).
May 17. Sixth foal. 31,000Y. Doncaster St Leger.
Half-brother to the fair 1997 2-y-o 5f winner Suivez la Trace (by Shalford), the quite useful 7f (at 2 yrs) to 11.4f winner Traceability (by Puissance) and the modest 1996 2-y-o winner Full Traceability (by Ron's Victory). The dam is an unplaced half-sister to 5 winners including the Group 2 Prix d'Astarte and Group 3 Child Stakes winner Meis-El-Reem. The second dam, Tavella (by Petingo), was a useful 2-y-o 6f winner. (Peter Savill).

1030 - RIVERBLUE   b.c. Bluebird - La Riveraine (Riverman).
March 18. First foal. 23,000Y. Tattersalls October.
The dam was a quite useful 3-y-o 11.5f and 11.8f winner. The second dam, La Romaria (by Vaguely Noble), was placed once in France from 3 starts and is out of a winning half-sister to the outstanding broodmare Slightly Dangerous (dam of Commander In Chief, Warning, Deploy, Dushyantor and Yashmak) and to the dams of Rainbow Quest and Scenic. (Mrs Joan L Egan).

James Toller

James has three other two-year-olds in the Premier Section and he feels that Frankincense could also be quite useful early on. In fact, he seems to like all his two-year-olds this year. Frankincense is "a horse for the first half of the season and although I haven't worked him seriously yet, he looks quite sharp".

1031 - FRANKINCENSE (IRE)   gr.c. Paris House - Mistral Wood (Far North).
March 1. Fourth foal. IR21,000Y. Goffs Challenge.
Brother to the 1997 Irish 8.5f placed 2-y-o Gay Paree. The dam is an unplaced half-sister to 7 winners including the US stakes winner Jolly Mariner and the Old Newton Cup winner Glide Path. The second dam, Jolly Polka (by Nice Dancer), is an unraced half-sister to the Canadian stakes winner Jansum Regal (herself dam of the Champion Canadian 2-y-o and dual Grade 1 winner Dauphin Fabuleux). (Duke Of Devonshire).

182

Mark Tompkins

Mark has a good number of nice young horses this year, some of which are in the Premier Section. His earlier types include Batanta "a tall, scopey filly with the ability and maturity to start over six furlongs in June", Big Chief "a nice, big colt I bred myself. He'll be quite early and could be anything", Fadmoor "a pretty sharp colt. He's strong and short-coupled and he'll be out in May over six furlongs", Mega "a big, strong filly that goes well and will probably start over six furlongs in mid-season", Mensa "a nice colt, he's a big, strong individual and again the plan would be to start him over six furlongs in mid-summer" and finally Seven Stars "a sharp and early two-year-old, he's a nice strong horse with a bit of scope. He has the pace for five furlongs but will get further".

1032 - BATANTA
br.f. Bob's Return - Atlantic Air (Air Trooper).
April 24. 10,200Y. Tattersalls Autumn.
Half-sister to the 1997 Italian 2-y-o winner of four races Plan Maison (by Thowra), to the quite useful 7f to 8.3f winner Mullitover (by Interrex), the modest 2-y-o 5f winner Domino Dancing (by Lidhame) and winners abroad by Ballacashtal and Weldnaas. The dam won twice in Italy and is a half-sister to 3 minor winners. The second dam, Atlantica (by Tulyar), is an unraced half-sister to 6 winners. (Alison Ruggles).

1033 - BIG CHIEF
ch.c. Be My Chief - Grove Daffodil (Salt Dome).
March 31. First foal.
The dam, a quite useful filly, won over 7f at 2 yrs and was fourth in the Group 3 10.4f Musidora Stakes. She is a half-sister to several winners including the 1m and 10f winner Shannon Express. The second dam, Tatisha (by Habitat), won over 1m in France and is a half-sister to the high-class sprinter Green God. (P H Betts (Holdings) Ltd).

1034 - FADMOOR (IRE)
ch.c. Mujtahid - Gingerly (Ferdinand).
February 13. First foal. IR32,000Y. Goffs Orby.
The dam, a modest 7f placed 2-y-o, is a half-sister to 7 winners including the French listed winner and Prix Jean Prat third Blackwater and the useful 1997 3-y-o 10f winner Running Stag. The second dam, Fruhlingstag (by Orsini), won in France and was second in the French 1,000 Guineas. (P J M Racing).

1035 - MEGA (IRE)
b.f. Petardia - Gobolino (Don).
May 14. IR26,000Y. Goffs Challenge.
Half-sister to 5 winners including the Italian listed winner Don Fayruz (by Fayruz), the quite useful dual 1m winner Golden Ace (by Archway) and the Irish winner of 7 races on the flat and over hurdles Bolino Star (by Stalker). The dam, a winner over 7f at 2 yrs in Ireland, is a full or half-sister to 4 winners. The second dam, Broccoli (by Welsh Saint), won over 6f at 2 yrs and once over hurdles in Ireland. (Mystic Meg Ltd).

1036 - MENSA
ch.c. Rudimentary - Musianica (Music Boy).
April 28. Fourth foal. IR39,000Y. Goffs Orby.
Half-brother to the fairly useful 1994 3-y-o 7f winner Dime Time (by Midyan), to the quite useful 6f to 9.4f winner Barrel Of Hope (by Distant Relative) and the modest 1997 3-y-o 5f winner Pizicato (by Statoblest). The dam, a fairly useful 2-y-o 6f winner, is out of the Italian winner of 7 races Penny Bianca (by My Swallow). (Beryl Lockey).

1037 - SEVEN STARS
b.c. Rudimentary - Carlton Glory (Blakeney).
February 27. 11,000Y. Tattersalls October.
Brother to the 3-y-o Vittoria and half-brother to the modest 1m all-weather winner Molly Music, to a winner in Norway (both by Music Boy) and the poor 11f to 15.8f winner Reach For Glory (by Reach). The dam is an unplaced half-sister to the Group 3 7f Prix de la Porte Maillot winner Gosport. The second dam, Greek Gift (by Acropolis), is an unplaced half-sister to 8 winners including the dam of the high-class sprinter and sire Music Boy. (The Magnificent Seven).

Peter Walwyn

Peter suggested these three as likely candidates for success as two-year-olds. Awwaliya is "a nice, big filly, that will probably start over six furlongs", By The Glass is "on the small side, but a colt that should be running soon" and Rainbow Romeo "looks like he's a sharp colt and he too will be out quite early". Peter has another two-year-old in the Premier Section.

1038 - AWWALIYA
b.f. Distant Relative - El Rabab (Roberto).
March 28. Third foal.
Half-sister to the 1997 2-y-o 6f winner Filfilah (by Cadaux Genereux) and the 1996 2-y-o 5f and 6f winner Marathon Maid (by Kalaglow) - both quite useful. The dam, a fair 2-y-o 1m winner, was placed

over 11.5f at 3yrs and is a half-sister to the US stakes winner Russian Tango. The second dam, Brave Raj (by Rajab), won the Breeders Cup Juvenile Fillies and was the champion American 2-y-o filly of 1986. (Hamdan Al Maktoum).

1039 - BY THE GLASS   b.c. Ardkinglass - Mia Fillia (Formidable).
                                                       March 12. Third foal. 15,500Y. Tattersalls October.
Half-brother to the poor 7f all-weather placed Death By Chocolate (by Sayf El Arab). The dam, a modest 10f placed maiden, is a half-sister to 5 winners including the listed St Hugh's Stakes winner Glory of Hera - herself dam of the Gran Criterium and Dante Stakes winner Glory Of Dancer. The second dam, As Blessed (by So Blessed), won twice at 2 yrs and was fourth in the Queen Mary Stakes.

1040 - RAINBOW ROMEO (IRE)   br.c. Rainbows For Life - Splendid Chance (Random Shot).
                                                                                          February 11.
Half-brother to the Group 2 6f Mill Reef Stakes winner Luqman (by Runnett), to the French listed winner Splendid Day (by Day Is Done) and winners abroad by Bluebird, Great Commotion, Runnett, Precocious and Taufan. The dam won at 3 yrs in Ireland over 10f and also won over hudles. The second dam, Splendid Star (by Star Gazer), was an unplaced half-sister to 6 winners including the very useful miler Tack On. (Mr Eric Perry).

STALLION
REFERENCE

Fairy King (top) and first-season sire Grand Lodge

This section deals with the sires of the two-year-olds housed in the Premier Section of the book. The reference numbers given with each stallion are the numbers of their chosen two-year-old representatives. Please take note of the fascinating statistical information provided in tabular form by Timeform in this book. These tables can be of great value when evaluating a stallion's ability to sire winners.

Amongst the stallions listed in this section are the best stallions of America and Europe. Horses like the American sires Danzig, Gone West, Lyphard, Mr Prospector, Nureyev, Riverman, Seattle Slew, Seeking The Gold, Storm Cat and Woodman. The top European sires include Caerleon, Danehill, Fairy King, Rainbow Quest, Sadler's Wells and last year's Champion first season sire Zafonic.

Each year we see a new batch of sires with their first runners. This season, the exciting young stallions with offspring racing for the first time include Barathea, Catrail, College Chapel, Dolphin Street, Ezzoud, First Trump, Grand Lodge, Perugino and Turtle Island.

Unless otherwise indicated, the races mentioned in each stallion profile are Group or Grade 1 events.

AFFIRMED
1975 Exclusive Native - Won't Tell You (Crafty Admiral).
(193, 661, 702)
Racing record: 22 wins in the USA, notably the Triple Crown (Kentucky Derby, Preakness Stakes and Belmont Stakes) and eleven other Grade 1 races. Horse of the Year and Champion at 2, 3 and 4 yrs. Stud record: Best winners include Affidavit, Bint Pasha (Prix Vermeille, Yorkshire Oaks), Charlie Barley, Claude Monet, Flawlessly (Matriarch Stakes, Beverly Hills Handicap, Ramona Handicap, Beverly D Stakes, etc), Buy The Firm (Top Flight Handicap), Easy to Copy, Firm Stance (Top Flight Handicap), Low Key Affair, One From Heaven (Selene Stakes, Canadian Oaks), Peteski (Breeders Stakes, Queens Plate, Prince of Wales Stakes - Canada), Regal State (Prix Morny), Tibullo (Gran Criterium), Trusted Partner (Irish 1,000 Guineas) and Zoman (Budweiser International, Prix d'Ispahan).

ALLEGED
1974 Hoist the Flag - Princess Pout (Prince John).
(200, 255, 316)
Racing record: 9 wins, notably the Prix de l'Arc de Triomphe (twice), the Group 2 Gallinule Stakes and the Group 2 Great Voltigeur Stakes. Champion 3-y-o colt. Stud record: Best winners include Always Earnest (Prix du Cadran), Fiesta Gal (Coaching Club American Oaks), Flemensfirth (Prix Lupin), Hours After (French Derby), Law Society (Irish Derby), Leading Counsel (Irish St Leger), Legal Case (Champion Stakes), Midway Lady (1,000 gns and Oaks), Milesius (Manhattan Handicap), Miss Alleged (Breeders Cup Turf), Muhtarram (Phoenix Champion Stakes), Shantou (St Leger), Sir Harry Lewis (Irish Derby) and Strategic Choice (Irish St Leger & Gran Premio de Milano).

ALZAO
1980 Lyphard - Lady Rebecca (Sir Ivor).
(160, 167, 464, 657, 706, 785, 795)
Racing record: 4 wins from 1m to 12f. Stud record: Best winners include Alcando (Beverly Hills Handicap), Alpride (Yellow Ribbon Invitational), Bobzao, Capricciosa (Cheveley Park Stakes), Last Second, Matiya (Irish 1,000 Guineas), Pass The Peace (Cheveley Park Stakes), Second Set (Sussex Stakes), Unblest and Wind In Her Hair (Aral-Pokal). Standing at Coolmore Stud in Ireland. 1998 fee: IR15,000 Gns (Oct 1st).

A P INDY
1989 Seattle Slew - Weekend Surprise (Secretariat).
(85, 423)
Racing record: 8 wins from 6.5f (at 2 yrs) to 12f, notably the Belmont Stakes, the Breeders Cup Classic, the Santa Anita Derby and the Hollywood Futurity. Horse Of The Year. Champion 3-y-o colt. Stud record: First runners in 1996. Sire of the US Grade 2 winner Pulpit and the Grade 3 winner Accelerator. A P Indy is a half-brother to another American classic winner in Summer Squall (Preakness Stakes). He is inbred 4x3 to Bold Ruler and represents a complete outcross for the preponderance of Northern Dancer line mares. Standing at Lane's End Farm, Kentucky. $75,000 (live foal, Sept 1st).

ARAZI
1989 Blushing Groom - Danseur Fabuleux (Northern Dancer).
(74, 96, 127, 294, 330, 332, 434, 545, 562, 662, 668, 670, 699, 704)
Racing record: 9 wins from 5f to 8.5f, notably the Prix de la Salamandre, the Prix Morny, the Grand Criterium and the Breeders Cup Juvenile. Champion 2-y-o. The size of Arazi's sensational victory in the 1991 Breeders Cup Juvenile at Churchill Downs was of Hollywood proportions and although he failed subsequently to prove himself a wonder horse, he was still a high-class 3-y-o and winner of the

Ciga Prix du Rond-Point. Stud record: First runners in 1996. A very disappointing sire so far, his chief earner in Britain is the useful handicapper Apache Star. Standing at Three Chimneys Farm, Lexington, Kentucky.

BARATHEA   1990 Sadler's Wells - Brocade (Habitat).
(31, 79, 91, 197, 199, 206, 213, 214, 224, 272, 273, 366, 385, 391, 409, 467, 487, 543, 569, 576, 605, 728, 813, 831)
Racing record: 5 wins from 7f to 1m, notably the Breeders Cup Mile and the Irish 1,000 Guineas. Stud record: First runners 1998. Standing at Rathbarry Stud, Ireland. 1998 fee: IR17,000 Gns (Oct 1st).

BE MY CHIEF   1987 Chief's Crown - Lady Be Mine (Sir Ivor).
(368, 612, 806, 821)
Racing record: Won 6 races at 2 yrs from 6f to 1m notably the Racing Post Trophy. Stud record: Best performers include Donna Viola (Yellow Ribbon Handicap, Gamely Handicap), Flying Squaw, Dances With Dreams, Indian Light, Magongo. Standing at The National Stud, Newmarket. 1998 fee: £3,500 (Oct 1st).

BE MY GUEST   1974 Northern Dancer - What a Treat (Tudor Minstrel).
(144, 338, 772, 776, 798)
Racing record: 4 wins from 6f to 8.5f including the Waterford Crystal Mile and the Blue Riband Trial. Stud record: Best performers include the Group winners Anfield, Astronef, Double Bed, Free Guest, Go and Go, Invited Guest, Intimate Guest, Luth Enchantee, Most Welcome, Media Starguest, Northern Treat, Pelder and Pentire. Standing at Coolmore Stud in Ireland. IR6,000 Gns (Oct 1st).

BERING   1983 Arctic Tern - Beaune (Lyphard).
(230, 299, 639)
Racing record: 5 wins from 8.5f to 12f notably the Prix du Jockey Club, the Group 2 Prix Hocquart and the Group 2 Prix Noailles. Stud record: Best winners include Matiara (French 1,000 Guineas), Glorosia (Fillies Mile), Pennekamp (2,000 Guineas), Peter Davies (Racing Post Trophy), Steamer Duck (Gran Criterium) and the Group/Graded Stakes winners Break Bread, Beau Sultan, Salmon Ladder, Signe Divin, Serrant, Special Price and Vertical Speed. Standing at the Haras du Quesnay. 1998 fee: 100,000 FF. (Oct 1st).

BIEN BIEN   1989 Manila - Stark Winter (Graustark).
(45)
Racing record: Four Grade 1 wins in the USA - the Hollywood Turf Cup, Hollywood Turf Cup Handicap, San Juan Capistrano Invitational and the San Luis Rey Stakes. Stud record: First crop now two-year-olds. 1998 fee: $10,000 (live foal, Nov 1st).

BIGSTONE   1990 Last Tycoon - Batave (Posse).
(394, 540, 775, 839)
Racing record: 6 wins from 7f to 9f including the Prix d'Ispahan, Prix de la Foret, Queen Elizabeth II Stakes and Sussex Stakes. Stud record: First crop now two-year-olds. 1998 fee: IR8,000 Gns (Oct 1st).

BLUEBIRD   1984 Storm Bird - Ivory Dawn (Sir Ivor).
(8, 71, 195, 288, 444, 592, 609, 727, 731, 760, 838)
Racing record: 4 wins from 5f to 6f including the Group 1 Kings Stand Stakes. Stud record: Best performers include Dolphin Street (Prix de la Foret), Lake Coniston (July Cup), Aube Indienne (Yellow Ribbon Invitational), Blue Siren, Delilah, Fly To The Stars, Harbour Master and the Australasian Grade 1 winners Race Master, Flitter and Happiness. 1998 fee: IR10,000 Guineas (Oct 1st).

BRIEF TRUCE   1989 Irish River - Falafel (Northern Dancer).
(175, 438, 812, 824, 825)
Racing record: 4 wins from 6f to 10f notably the St James's Palace Stakes and the Group 2 Gallinule Stakes and placed in the Breeders Cup Mile, the Irish 2,000 Guineas, the Prix du Moulin and the Queen Elizabeth II Stakes. Rated the top 3-y-o colt over a mile, three pounds below the filly Marling, in the International Classifications. Stud record: His first two-year-olds ran last year. Eight winners including the useful Hopping Higgins. Standing at Coolmore Stud in Ireland. 1998 fee: IR6,500 Gns (Oct 1st).

BUSTINO 1979 Busted - Ship Yard (Doutelle).
(189, 521)
Racing record: 5 wins notably the Coronation Cup, the St Leger and the Group 2 Great Voltigeur Stakes. Stud record: Best winners include Easter Sun (Coronation Cup), Paean (Ascot Gold Cup), Stufida (Premio Lydia Tesio), Terimon (Juddmonte International) and the Group 2 winners Borushka, Bustomi, Dish Dash, Height of Fashion and Talented.

CADEAUX GENEREUX 1985 Young Generation - Smarten Up (Sharpen Up).
(48, 118, 196, 218, 221, 236, 246, 247, 266, 315, 397, 424, 448, 466, 486, 565, 589, 596, 600, 604, 613, 614, 678)
Racing record: 7 wins from 5f to 7f notably the July Cup, the William Hill Sprint Championship, the Group 3 Van Geest Criterion Stakes and the Group 3 Diadem Stakes. Champion sprinter. Stud record: Best winners include Bahamian Bounty (Middle Park Stakes), Bijou d'Inde (St James's Palace Stakes), Embassy (Cheveley Park Stakes), Hoh Magic (Prix Morny), Land of Dreams, Monaassib and Warning Shadows. Standing at Whitsbury Manor Stud in Hampshire. 1998 fee: £15,000 (live foal).

CAERLEON 1980 Nijinsky - Foreseer (Round Table).
(94, 123, 153, 155, 178, 301, 359, 443, 476, 495, 667, 745, 746, 834)
Racing record: 4 wins from 6f to 12f notably the Prix du Jockey Club and the Benson and Hedges Gold Cup. Stud record: 18 individual Group or Grade 1 winners including Auriette (Gamely Handicap), Generous (Derby, Irish Derby, King George VI and Queen Elizabeth Diamond Stakes), Grape Tree Road (Grand Prix de Paris), In a Tiff (Italian Derby), Kostroma (Beverly D Stakes, Yellow Ribbon Invitational, Santa Barbara Handicap), Lady Carla (Oaks), Moonax (St Leger), Only Royale (Yorkshire Oaks), Shake The Yoke (Coronation Stakes) and Tenby (Grand Criterium).

CATRAIL 1990 Storm Cat - Tough As Nails (Majestic Light).
(70, 116, 188, 317, 411, 436, 610)
Racing record: 6 wins from 6f to 7f including the Group 2 Challenge Stakes, the Group 2 Prix Maurice de Gheest and the Group 3 Diadem Stakes. Stud record: First crop now two-year-olds. Standing at the Irish National Stud. 1998 fee: IR£7,000 (Oct 1st).

CHIEF'S CROWN 1982 Danzig - Six Crowns (Secretariat).
(550, 585, 611)
Racing record: Won 12 races - notably eight Grade 1 stakes - including the Breeders Cup Juvenile, the Travers Stakes, the Cowdin Stakes and the Blue Grass Stakes. Stud record: Best winners include the Epsom Derby winner Erhaab, the champion 2-y-o colts Grand Lodge (Dewhurst Stakes, St James's Palace Stakes) and Be My Chief (Racing Post Trophy), Chief Honcho (Brooklyn Handicap), the Australian Grade 1 winner Azzaam, Ampulla (Grade 2 Long Island Handicap), Crowned (Grade 2 Delaware Handicap), Halesia (Group 2 Prix de Royallieu) and Key of Luck (a high-class horse in Dubai).

COLLEGE CHAPEL 1990 Sharpo - Scarcely Blessed (So Blessed).
(12, 53, 67, 149, 577, 617, 622, 640, 647, 808, 822)
Racing record: 5 wins from 6f to 7f including the Group 2 Prix Maurice de Gheest and the Group 3 Cork & Orrery Stakes. Stud record: First crop now two-year-olds. 1998 fee: IR4,500 Gns. (Oct 1st).

COMMON GROUNDS 1985 Kris - Sweetly (Lyphard).
(173, 182, 225, 410, 544, 588, 656, 685, 829)
Racing record: 2 wins including the Group 1 7f Prix de la Salamandre. Stud record: Best performers include Earl Of Barking (Hollywood Turf Handicap), Artema, Astudillo, Fallow, Golden Arches, Rich Ground and Three For Fantasy. Standing at Morristown Lattin Stud, Ireland. 1998 fee: IR8,000 (Oct 1st).

COZZENE 1980 Caro - Ride The Trails (Prince John).
(51)
Racing record: 10 wins from 6f to 9f including the Breeders Cup Mile. Stud record: Best performers include Alphabet Soup (Breeders Cup Classic), Environment Friend (Eclipse Stakes), Tikkanen (Turf Classic) and Star Of Cozzene (Man O'War Stakes). Standing at Gainesway Farm, Lexington, Kentucky. 1998 fee: $30,000 (live foal).

CRYPTOCLEARANCE 1984 Fappiano - Naval Orange (Hoist The Flag).
(113)
Racing record: 12 wins from 6f to 10f including the Grade 1 Florida Derby. Stud record: Best performers include Strategic Maneuver (Spinaway Stakes), Traitor (Futurity Stakes) and Crypto Star. Standing at Vinery Stud, Midway, Kentucky. 1998 fee: $30,000 (live foal, Nov 1st).

DANEHILL 1986 Danzig - Razyana (His Majesty).
(36, 38, 68, 69, 142, 198, 238, 387, 403, 507, 511, 556, 623, 630, 750, 769, 778)
Racing record: 4 wins from 6f to 7f including the Ladbroke Sprint Cup at Haydock Park and the Group 3 Cork and Orrery Stakes. Stud record: Best winners include Alriffa, Ardana, Danehill Dancer (Heinz 57 Phoenix Stakes and National Stakes), Danish (Keeneland Queen Elizabeth II Challenge Cup), Desert King (Irish 2,000 Guineas, Irish Derby and National Stakes), Hill Hopper, Indian Jones, Kissing Cousin (Coronation Stakes), Restructure and numerous Australian Grade 1 winners including Danarani, Danewin, Danzero, Flying Spur, Joie Denise, Merlene and Nothin Leica Dane. Certainly the most successful of dual hemisphere sires, Danehill has been a champion sire in Australia several times. Standing at Coolmore Stud in Ireland. 1998 fee: IR35,000 Gns (Oct 1st).

DANZIG 1977 Northern Dancer - Pas de Nom (Admiral's Voyage).
(106, 292, 327, 371, 386, 396, 408, 477, 488, 584, 628, 629, 762)
Racing record: 3 wins from 3 starts in the USA from 5.5f to 6f. Stud record: Best winners in the US include the Grade 1 winners Adjudicating, Chief's Crown, Contredance, Dance Smartly, Danzig Connection, Langfuhr, Pine Bluff, Polish Navy, Stephan's Odyssey and Versailles Treaty. In Europe, his best include the Group 1 winners Anabaa, Danehill, Dayjur, Green Desert, Hamas, Maroof, Pas de Reponse, Petit Loup, Polish Patriot, Polish Precedent, Polonia and Shaadi. Standing at Claiborne Farm, Kentucky.

DARSHAAN 1981 Shirley Heights - Delsy (Abdos).
(251, 362, 440, 649, 658, 666, 784, 789)
Racing record: 5 wins from 1m to 12f, notably the Prix du Jockey Club, the Group 2 Criterium de Saint-Cloud, the Group 2 Prix Hocquart and the Group 2 Prix Greffulhe. Stud record: Best winners include Aliysa, Arzanni, Grand Plaisir, Hellenic (Yorkshire Oaks), Key Change (Yorkshire Oaks), Kotashaan (multiple Grade 1 wins including the Breeders Cup Turf), Mark Of Esteem (2,000 Guineas, Queen Elizabeth II Stakes) and Zayyani. Standing at the Gilltown Stud in County Kildare. 1998 fee: IR£20,000 (Oct 1st).

DAYJUR 1987 Danzig - Gold Beauty (Mr Prospector).
(143, 186, 204, 258, 285, 295, 304, 329, 350, 380, 497, 532, 580, 790)
Racing record: 7 wins from 5f to 6f notably the Keeneland Nunthorpe Stakes, the Ladbroke Sprint Cup and the Ciga Prix de l'Abbaye. Champion European Racehorse. Stud record: Best performers include Hayil (Middle Park Stakes) and the Group winners Asfurah, Millstream, Tipsy Creek and With Fascination. Standing at Shadwell Farm, Lexington, Kentucky. 1998 fee: $20,000 (live foal).

DEHERE 1991 Deputy Minister - Sister Dot (Secretariat).
(136, 194, 312, 659, 684, 695)
Racing record: 6 wins from 5f to 8.5f including the Grade 1 Champagne Stakes and the Grade 1 Hopeful Stakes. Champion 2-y-o colt. Stud record: First crop now two-year-olds. 1998 fee: $40,000 (Oct 1st).

DIESIS 1980 Sharpen Up - Doubly Sure (Reliance II).
(49, 87, 279, 309, 392, 393, 417, 534, 711, 713, 747, 800, 807)
Racing record: Champion 2-y-o in 1982. Winner of 3 races notably the Dewhurst Stakes and the Middle Park Stakes. Stud record: Best winners include Diminuendo (Oaks, Irish Oaks, Yorkshire Oaks), Elmaamul (Coral-Eclipse Stakes, Phoenix Champion Stakes), Halling (Coral-Eclipse Stakes (twice), International Stakes (twice), Prix d'Ispahan), Husband (Rothmans International), Keen Hunter (Prix de l'Abbaye), Knifebox (Premio Roma), Daggers Drawn, Marillette, Rootentootenwooten (Demoiselle Stakes) and Sabrehill. Standing at Mill Ridge Farm, Lexington, Kentucky. 1998 fee: $30,000 (live foal, Sept 1st).

DISTANT RELATIVE 1986 Habitat - Royal Sister II (Claude).
(26, 237, 481, 601)
Racing record: 8 wins from 6f to 1m including the Prix du Moulin and the Sussex Stakes. Stud record: Best winners include the Group winners Bin Rosie and Germane, the listed winner My Branch and the

useful handicapper Wildwood Flower. Standing at Whitsbury Manor Stud in Hampshire. 1998 fee: £5,000 (Oct 1st).

DIXIELAND BAND 1980 Northern Dancer - Mississippi Mud (Delta Judge).
(3, 259, 264, 595)
Racing record: 8 wins including the Grade 2 9f Pennsylvania Derby and the Grade 2 9f Massachusetts Handicap. Stud record: Best winners include Bedeviled (Grade 2 Razorback Handicap), Del Mar Dennis (Grade 2 San Bernardino Handicap), Devoted Brass (Grade 2 Swaps Stakes), Didyme (Group 2 Prix Robert Papin), Dixie Brass (Metropolitan Handicap), Dixeland Brass (Grade 2 Fountain Of Youth Stakes), Drum Taps (Ascot Gold Cup) and Spinning Round (Ballerina Stakes). Standing at Lane's End Farm, Lexington, Kentucky. 1998 fee: $60,000 (live foal, Sept 1st).

DOLPHIN STREET 1990 Bluebird - Or Vision (Irish River).
(520, 579, 615, 627, 840)
Racing record: 5 wins from 6f to 7f including the Group 1 Prix de la Foret and the Group 2 Prix Maurice de Gheest. Stud record: First crop now yearlngs. 1998 fee: IR5,000 Gns (Oct 1st).

DOYOUN 1985 Mill Reef – Dumka (Kashmir II).
(263, 430, 581)
Racing record: Won the 2,000 Guineas and placed in the Derby, the Waterford Crystal Mile and the Champion Stakes. Stud record: Best winners include Daylami (Poule d'Essai des Poulains), Manntari (National Stakes), Adaiyka (Group 3 Prix Chloe), Dalara (Group 2 Prix de Royallieu) and numerous listed winners including Khaytada and Sheraka. Standing at Gilltown Stud in Ireland. 1998 fee: IR7,000 Guineas.

DYNAFORMER 1985 Roberto - Andover Way (His Majesty).
(499, 726)
Racing record: 7 wins from 7f to 12f including the Grade 2 Florida Derby and the Grade 2 Discovery Handicap. Stud record: Best winners include the US Grade 3 winners Blumin' Affair, Old Chapel and Rabiadella. Standing at Three Chimneys Farm, Lexington, Kentucky. 1998 fee: $20,000 (live foal, Sept 1st).

EFISIO 1982 Formidable - Eldoret (High Top).
(11, 539)
Racing record: 8 wins from 6f to 1m including the Group 1 Premio Emilio Turati, the Group 2 Premio Chiusura, the Group 3 Challenge Stakes and the Group 3 Horris Hill Stakes. Stud record: Best winners include Hever Golf Rose (Prix de l'Abbaye), Pips Pride (Phoenix Stakes), Casteddu, Tomba and Young Ern. Standing at Highclere Stud. 1998 fee: £7,000 (Oct 1st).

ELA MANA MOU 1976 Pitcairn - Rose Bertin (High Hat).
(399)
Racing record: 10 wins from 6f to 12f notably the King George VI and Queen Elizabeth Stakes and the Eclipse Stakes. Stud record: Best winners include Almaarad (Aral Pokal and three Australian Grade 1 wins), Double Trigger (Ascot Gold Cup), Emmson (William Hill Futurity Stakes), Eurobird (Irish St Leger), Natski (AJC Metropolitan Handicap - Australian Grade 1), Snurge (St Leger, Rothmans International and Gran Premio di Milano), Sumayr (Grand Prix de Paris) and the Group 2 winners Double Eclipse, Ela Romara, Fair Of The Furze, Grecian Urn, O'Connor, The Little Thief and Trivial Pursuit. Standing at Simmonstown Stud, Co. Kildare, Ireland. 1998 fee: IR6,000 Gns (Oct 1st).

EL GRAN SENOR 1981 Northern Dancer - Sex Appeal (Buckpasser).
(192, 265, 526)
Racing record: 7 wins notably the 2,000 Guineas, the Irish Sweeps Derby and the Dewhurst Stakes. Champion 2-y-o and 3-y-o colt. Stud record: Best winners include the English and Irish 2,000 Guineas winner Rodrigo de Triano and the King George winner Belmez, followed by Al Hareb (William Hill Futurity Stakes), George Augustus (Tattersalls Rogers Gold Cup), Le Triton (Prix Jean Prat) and the American Grade 1 winners Corrazona, Helmsman, Lit de Justice, Morgana, Senor Tomas and Toussaud. Standing at Ashford Stud in Kentucky. 1998 fee: $20,000 (Oct 1st).

ELBIO 1987 Precocious - Maganyos (Pioneer).
(16)
Racing record: 9 wins from 5f to 6f including the Group 2 Kings Stand Stakes (twice) and the Group 2 Goldene Peitsche. Stud record: First two-year-olds ran in 1997. Sire of 4 minor winners. Standing at Ennistown Stud, Ireland. 1998 fee: IR1,750 Gns (Oct 1st).

ELMAAMUL 1987 Diesis - Modena (Roberto).
(278, 307, 433)
Racing record: 5 wins from 7f to 10f including the Group 1 Eclipse Stakes and the Group 1 Phoenix Champion Stakes. Stud record: Best winners include Ashbal, Dankeston, Mawwal and Muhtathir. Standing at Eagle Lane Farm, Newmarket. 1998 fee: £3,500 (October 1st).

EMARATI 1986 Danzig - Bold Example (Bold Lad, USA).
(490, 693)
Racing record: Placed twice. Stud record: Best progeny include Emerging Market and Westcourt Magic. Standing at The National Stud. 1998 fee: £3,000 (October 1st).

EXIT TO NOWHERE 1988 Irish River - Coup de Folie (Halo)
(219, 291, 365)
Racing record: 4 wins including the Prix Jacques le Marois, the Group 3 Prix Thomas Bryon, Prix du Muguet and the Group 3 Prix Edmond Blanc. Stud record: From just two crops, the best of his 27 individual winners is Shaka (Criterium de Saint-Cloud). Standing at Haras de Fresnay-le-Buffard. 1997 fee: 55,000FF (Oct 1st).

EZZOUD 1989 Last Tycoon - Royal Sister II (Claude).
(28, 447, 485, 513, 739)
Racing record: 6 wins from 7f to 10f & 85f yds, notably the Juddmonte International (twice) and the Eclipse Stakes. Stud record: First crop now two-year-olds. Standing at Sandringham Stud. 1998 fee: £6,000 (live foal).

FAIRY KING 1982 Northern Dancer - Fairy Bridge (Bold Reason).
(65, 146, 168, 171, 212, 217, 344, 451, 469, 479, 555, 568, 587, 603, 621, 634, 734, 782, 796, 832)
Racing record: Ran once, unplaced. Stud record: Best winners include Fairy Heights (Fillies Mile), Helissio (Prix de l'Arc de Triomphe, Grand Prix de Saint-Cloud, Prix Lupin), Kool Kat Katie (E P Taylor Stakes), Pharaoh's Delight (Phoenix Stakes), Princely Heir (Phoenix Stakes), Revoque (Prix de la Salamandre, Grand Criterium), Prince Arthur (Premio Parioli), Second Empire (Grand Criterium) and Turtle Island (Irish 2,000 Guineas). Standing at Coolmore Stud in Ireland. 1998 fee: IR50,000 Gns (Oct 1st).

FIRST TRUMP 1991 Primo Dominie - Valika (Valiyar).
(86, 148, 183, 435, 446)
Racing record: 5 wins over 6f including the Middle Park Stakes and the Group 2 Richmond Stakes. Stud record: First crop now two-year-olds. Standing at The National Stud. 1998 fee: £4,000 (October 1st).

FORMIDABLE 1975 Forli - Native Partner (Raise a Native).
(297)
Racing record: 8 wins from 6f to 1m including the Middle Park Stakes and the Group 2 Mill Reef Stakes. Stud record: Best progeny include Efisio (Group 1 Premio Emilio Turati), Forzando (Grade 1 Metropolitan Handicap) and the Group winners Chilibang, Secret Form, Formidable Flight, Kerita, Premiere Cuvee and Reasonable.

FORTY NINER 1985 Mr Prospector - File (Tom Rolfe)
(90)
Racing record: Winner of 11 of his 19 races from 6f to 10f including the Champagne Stakes, the Futurity Stakes, the Travers Stakes and the Haskell Invitational Stakes. Stud record: Best winners include Editor's Note (Belmont Stakes), Nine Keys (Apple Blossom Handicap), Gold Fever (NYRA Mile Handicap) and the US Graded stakes winners Roar and End Tree. Sadly, we are unlikely to see many of his runners in Europe in the future as Forty Niner now stands in Japan.

FORZANDO   1981 Formidable - Princely Maid (King's Troop).
(683)
Racing record: 12 wins from 6f to 9f including the Grade 1 Metropolitan Handicap and the Group 2 Premio Melton. Stud record: Best progeny include Easycall, Great Deeds and Up And At 'Em. Standing at Throckmorton Court Stud. 1998 fee: £2,000 (no foal, no fee).

GEIGER COUNTER   1982 Mr Prospector - Thong (Nantallah).
(404)
Racing record: 2 wins over 6 furlongs. Stud record: Best progeny include the Australasian Grade 1 winners Raratonga Treaty and Minegold.

GENEROUS   1988 Caerleon - Doff the Derby (Master Derby).
(84, 181, 280, 439, 489, 494, 501, 632, 692, 694)
Racing record: European Champion 3-y-o. Won the Derby, the Irish Derby, the King George VI and Queen Elizabeth Diamond Stakes and the Dewhurst Stakes. Stud record: Best performers include the French Group winners Radevore and Tenuous, the Queens Vase winner Windsor Castle, the US Grade 3 winner Worldly Ways and the Select Stakes winner Fahris. Now standing in Japan.

GHAZI   1989 Polish Navy - Port Damascus (Damascus).
(561)
Racing record: 6 wins from 7f to 10f including the Grade 1 Secretariat Stakes. Stud record: First crop now two-year-olds.

GONE WEST   1970 Mr Prospector - Secrettame (Secretariat).
(80, 110, 121, 130, 132, 150, 284, 336, 373, 375, 379, 597)
Racing record: 6 wins notably the Grade 1 9f Dwyer Stakes, the Grade 2 1m Gotham Stakes and the Grade 2 1m Withers Stakes. Stud record: Best winners include the champion 2-y-o and 3-y-o Zafonic (2,000 Guineas, Prix Morny, Prix de la Salamandre and Dewhurst Stakes), Da Hoss (Breeders Cup Mile), West by West (Nassau County Handicap), Link River (John A. Morris Handicap), the European Group winners Aboline, Dance Parade, Dazzle, Lassigny, Raah Algharb, Royal Abjar, Tamayaz, West Man and Zamindar and the US Graded Stakes winners Mr Greeley, Old Tascosa and Supremo. Standing at Mill Ridge Farm in Lexington, Kentucky. $100,000 (live foal)

GRAND LODGE   1991 Chief's Crown - La Papagena (Habitat).
(32, 33, 43, 126, 154, 174, 208, 245, 369, 407, 546, 551, 552, 723, 777, 830)
Racing record: Won 4 races from 6f to 1m including the Dewhurst Stakes and the St James's Palace Stakes. Champion European Two-Year-Old of 1993. Stud record: First crop now two-year-olds. Standing at Coolmore Stud. 1998 fee: IR10,000 Gns (Oct 1st).

GREAT COMMOTION   1986 Nureyev - Alathea (Lorenzaccio).
(203)
Racing record: 4 wins from 6f to 1m including the Group 3 Cork and Orrery Stakes and the Group 3 Beeswing Stakes. Second in the Irish 2,000 Guineas and the July Cup. Stud record: From three crops, sire of Deadly Dudley (Group 2 Criterium des Deux Ans) and the French listed winner Xianlang. Standing at Damastown Stud, County Kildare, Ireland.

GREEN DANCER   1972 Nijinsky - Green Valley (Val de Loir).
(25, 202, 500, 818)
Racing record: 4 wins notably the Observer Gold Cup, the French 2,000 Guineas and the Prix Lupin. Stud record: His best colts include Suave Dancer (Prix de l'Arc de Triomphe, Prix du Jockey Club, Irish Champion Stakes), Greinton (three Grade 1 wins in the USA), Green Tune (French 2,000 Guineas and Prix d'Ispahan), the US Grade 1 winners Vilzak and Senor Pete, the European Group 2 winners Cadoudal, Lovely Dancer, Tarator and Torjoun, the Doncaster Cup winner Canon Can and the Italian Group 1 winning 2-y-o Will Dancer. Among his best fillies are the Group/Grade 1 winners Aryenne (dam of the Derby winner Quest For Fame), Fantastic Look, First Waltz, Market Booster, Maximova and Northern Emerald. Standing at Gainesway Farm in Kentucky.

GREEN DESERT   1983 Danzig - Foreign Courier (Sir Ivor).
(124, 129, 250, 303, 354, 458, 518, 573, 594, 664, 719, 729, 770, 811)
Racing record: 5 wins from 5f to 7f including the July Cup, the Vernons Sprint Cup and the Flying Childers Stakes. Stud record: Best winners include Owington (July Cup), Sheikh Albadou (Breeders

Cup Sprint, Keeneland Nunthorpe Stakes, Haydock Park Sprint), Greenlander (Prix Robert Papin), Gabr (Group 2 Sandown Mile), Redden Burn (Group 2 Grosser Preis von Dusseldorf) and numerous Group 3 winners including Absurde, Ardkinglass, Christmas Gift (in the USA), Desert Shot, Desert Style, Magic Ring, Mint Crisp, Mojave, Shahid and Tropical. Standing at the Shadwell Stud, Norfolk. 1997 fee: £25,000 (live foal).

GULCH
1984 Mr Prospector - Jameela (Rambunctious).
(326, 367, 460, 721, 783)
Racing record: 13 wins (including seven Grade 1 stakes) from 5f to 9f, notably the Breeders Cup Sprint, the Metropolitan Handicap (twice) and the Wood Memorial. Champion sprinter at 4 yrs in the USA. Stud record: Best winners include the Group/Grade 1 winners Great Navigator (Hopeful Stakes), Harayir (1,000 Guineas), Thunder Gulch (Kentucky Derby, Belmont Stakes, Travers Stakes and Florida Derby), Torrential (Prix Jean Prat) and Wallenda (Super Derby). Standing at Lane's End Farm, Kentucky. 1998 fee: $60,000 (live foal, Sept 1st).

HAMAS
1989 Danzig - Fall Aspen (Pretense).
(10, 558, 650)
Racing record: 5 wins from 5f to 1m including the July Cup and the Group 3 Duke of York Stakes. Stud record: A second season sire, Hamas has sired the winners of 22 runners from his first crop including the Firth of Clyde Stakes winner Regal Revolution. Hamas is a half-brother to the Group/Grade 1 winners Timber Country, Fort Wood and Northern Aspen. Standing at Derrinstown Stud in Ireland. 1997 fee: IR4,000 Guineas (Oct 1st).

HERMITAGE
1988 Storm Bird - Fairy Bridge (Bold Reason).
(133, 235, 241)
Racing record: Unraced. Stud record: A three-parts brother to Sadler's Wells and Fairy King, Hermitage had his first runners in 1996 and they included the smart Somerville Tattersall Stakes and Predominate Stakes winner Grapeshot. 1998 fee: $5,000 (live foal, Nov 1st).

HIGHEST HONOR
1983 Kenmare - High River (Riverman).
(519)
Racing record: 4 wins from 7f to 9f 55yds. Stud record: Best progeny include Medaaly (Racing Post Trophy), Admise (Oak Tree Turf Club Championship), the Group 2 winners Erminius, Gothland and Dadarissime and the Group 3 winners Baroud d'Honneur, Verglas, Take Risks and Go Between. Standing at Haras du Quesnay. 1998 fee: 100,000 FF. (Oct 1st).

IN THE WINGS
1986 Sadler's Wells - High Hawk (Shirley Heights).
(482, 583)
Racing record: 7 wins from 6f to 12f notably the Breeders Cup Turf, the Coronation Cup and the Grand Prix de Saint-Cloud. Stud record: Best winners (from just four crops) include Singspiel (Japan Cup, Canadian International Stakes), Winged Love (Irish Derby), Annaba (Group 2 Prix de Royallieu) and the Group/Grade 3 winners Central Park, Irish Wings and Thief Of Hearts. Standing at the Ragusa Stud, Kildare, Ireland. 1997 fee: IR£15,000 (Oct 1st).

INCHINOR
1990 Ahonoora - Inchmurrin (Lomond).
(837)
Racing record: 5 wins from 6f to 7f 64 yds. Stud record: Second crop sire. Sire of the winners of 7 races. Standing at Woodland Stud, Newmarket. 1998 fee: £3,000 (no foal, no fee). Oct 1st.

INDIAN RIDGE
1985 Ahonoora - Hillbrow (Swing Easy).
(73, 223, 244, 268, 275, 414, 432, 459, 484, 524, 548, 578, 688, 737, 751, 764, 768, 818, 827)
Racing record: 5 wins from 5f to 7f notably the Group 2 Kings Stand Stakes, the Group 3 Duke of York Stakes and the Group 3 Jersey Stakes. Stud record: Best winners include Compton Place (July Cup), Ridgewood Pearl (Irish 1,000 Guineas, Coronation Stakes, Prix du Moulin, Breeders Cup Mile), Definite Article (National Stakes) and the Group winners Indian Rocket, Blomberg, Handsome Ridge, Ridgewood Ben, Tumbleweed Ridge, Fumo di Londra and Island Magic. Standing at the Irish National Stud. 1997 fee: IR30,000 Guineas.

IRISH RIVER
1976 Riverman - Irish Star (Klairon).
(112, 164, 165, 205, 335, 341, 353, 471, 703, 758)
Racing record: A top-class miler and winner of 7 Group 1 races in France - the Grand Criterium, the Prix de la Salamandre, the Prix Morny (all at 2 yrs), the French 2,000 Guineas, the Prix d'Ispahan, the

Prix Jacques le Marois and the Prix du Moulin. Stud record: His nine Group or Grade 1 winners are Brief Truce (St James's Palace Stakes), Exit to Nowhere (Prix Jacques le Marois), Hatoof (1,000 Guineas and Beverly D Stakes), Leariva (Budweiser International), Mashkour (San Juan Capistrano Handicap), Navarone (Oak Tree Invitational), Orban (Premio Roma), Paradise Creek (Arlington Million, Manhattan Stakes and Hollywood Derby) and Seven Springs (Prix Morny and Prix Robert Papin). Standing Gainesway Farm, Lexington, Kentucky. 1998 fee: $35,000 (live foal).

JADE HUNTER
1984 Mr Prospector - Jadana (Pharly).
(810)
Racing record: 6 wins from 6f to 10f including the Grade 1 Gulfstream Park Handicap and the Grade 1 Donn Handicap. Stud record: Best performers include Stuka (Santa Anita Handicap), Diazo (Strub Stakes), Jade Flush (Grade 2 Rare Perfume Handicap). Standing at Brookside Farms, Kentucky.

KAHYASI
1985 Ile de Bourbon - Kadissya (Blushing Groom).
(651)
Racing record: 5 wins from 1m to 12f notably the Derby and the Irish Derby. Stud record: Best winners include the Group winners Vereva (Prix de Diane), Bayrika, Massyar, Shaiybara, Shamadara and Shemaran. Standing at Gilltown Stud in Ireland. 1998 fee: IR£5,000 (Oct 1st).

KALDOUN
1975 Caro - Katana (Le Haar).
(707)
Racing record: Won 5 races from 5f to 1m and was placed in the Prix Edmond Blanc, the Prix Perth and the Prix du Palais Royal (all Group 3 events). Stud record: Best winners include Occupandiste (Prix de la Foret and Prix Maurice de Gheest), Mercalle (Prix du Cadran), La Koumia (Gamely Handicap) and the French Group winners Kadounor, Cardoun, Kaldounevees, Balleroy, Kadrou and Varxi. 1998 fee: FF90,000 (Oct 1st).

KINGMAMBO
1990 Mr Prospector - Miesque (Nureyev).
(18, 19, 41, 77, 339, 358, 413, 472, 676)
Racing record: 5 wins from 6f to 1m notably the French 2,000 Guineas, the Prix du Moulin and the St James's Palace Stakes. Stud record: A son of the world's most successful living sire and of the great racemare Miesque, Kingmambo's first runners appeared last year. Standing at Lane's End Farm, Kentucky.

KNOWN FACT
1977 In Reality - Tamerett (Tim Tam).
(104)
Racing record: Won the 2,000 Guineas (upon the disqualification of Nureyev), the Middle Park Stakes and the Queen Elizabeth II Stakes. Stud record: Best winners include the outstanding miler and good young sire Warning, So Factual (Nunthorpe Stakes), the high class miler Markofdistinction, the Group 3 Prix de Porte Maillot winner Nidd, the dual Sagaro Stakes winner Teamster, the July Stakes winner Bold Fact, the Grade 2 Delaware Handicap winner Night Fax and the Breeders Cup Juvenile second Itsali'lknownfact. Known Fact stands at Juddmonte Farm in Kentucky.

KRIS
1976 Sharpen Up - Doubly Sure (Reliance II).
(59, 111, 509, 672, 710, 779, 826)
Racing record: 14 wins from 6f to 1m notably the 2,000 Guineas, the Sussex Stakes and the St James's Palace Stakes. Twice Champion European Miler. Stud record: Best winners include Common Grounds (Prix de la Salamandre), Fitnah (Prix Saint-Alary), Flash of Steel (Irish 2,000 Guineas), Oh So Sharp (1,000 Guineas, Oaks, St Leger), Rafha (Prix de Diane), Shamshir (Brent Walker Fillies Mile), Shavian (St James's Palace Stakes), Sudden Love (E P Taylor Stakes), Unite (Oaks, Irish Oaks), Single Empire (Italian Derby) and numerous Group 2 winners including Sure Blade. Standing at the Plantation Stud, Newmarket. 1997 fee: £15,000 (no foal, no fee. Oct 1st).

LAHIB
1988 Riverman - Lady Cutlass (Cutlass).
(253, 256, 616, 682, 805, 828)
Racing record: 3 wins, notably the Queen Elizabeth II Stakes and the Group 2 Queen Anne Stakes. He was also second in the Dubai Champion Stakes and the Prix Jacques le Marois. Stud record: These are his third crop of two-year-olds. His numerous winners to date include the Group 3 Horris Hill Stakes winner La-faah. Standing at Derrinstown Stud in Ireland. 1997 fee: IR5,000 Guineas (Oct 1st).

LEAR FAN   1981 Roberto - Wac (Lt. Stevens).
                                                              (345, 504, 732)
Racing record: 5 wins from 7f to 1m notably the Prix Jacques le Marois and the Group 2 Laurent Perrier Champagne Stakes. Stud record: Best winners include Casual Lies, Corrupt, Fanmore, Fantastic Fellow, Glaieul (Criterium de Saint-Cloud), Labeeb (Hollywood Derby), Loup Solitaire (Grand Criterium), Ryafan (Prix Marcel Boussac and three US Grade 1 wins), Run Don't Fly, Sikeston (Gran Criterium, Premio Ribot, Premio Parioli, etc), Verveine and Windsharp (San Luis Rey Stakes). Standing at Gainesway Farm, Lexington, Kentucky. 1998 fee: $20,000 (live foal).

LINAMIX   1987 Mendez - Lunadix (Breton).
                                                                  (705, 708)
Racing record: 4 wins over 1m including the French 2,000 Guineas and the Group 3 Prix de Fontainebleau. Stud record: Best performers include Miss Satamixa (Prix Jacques le Marois) and the Group winners Clodora, Diamond Mix, Housamix, Fragrant Mix and Walk On Mix. Standing at Haras du Val Henry. 1998 fee: FF150,000 (Oct 1st).

LION CAVERN   1989 Mr Prospector - Secrettame (Secretariat).
                                            (5, 66, 105, 480, 536, 646, 753)
Racing record: 5 wins from 6f to 7f including the Grade 2 True North Handicap, the Group 3 Horris Hill Stakes and the Group 3 Greenham Stakes. Stud record: A full brother to the highly successful stallion Gone West, Lion Cavern's first crop were 2-y-o's of 1997 and he sired the winners of 19 races. Standing at Dalham Hall Stud, Newmarket. 1997 fee: £10,000 (Oct 1st).

LORD AT WAR   1980 General - Luna de Miel (Con Brio).
                                                                  (426, 449)
Racing record: Won 10 races in Argentina including three Grade 1 events. Stud record: Sire of numerous minor stakes winners and the Grade 1 Queen Elizabeth Challenge Cup winner La Gueriere. Standing at Gainesway Farm, Lexington, Kentucky. 1998 fee: $20,000 (live foal)

LYCIUS   1988 Mr Prospector - Lypatia (Lyphard).
                                                                       (712)
Racing record: 2 wins over 6f and 7f including the Middle Park Stakes and placed in six other Group 1 races. Stud record: With three crops racing he has sired three Group winners - Hello (Gran Criterium), Aylesbury and Media Nox - and the useful performers Ivan Luis and Miss Universal. Standing at the Ragusa Stud, Co. Kildare, Ireland. 1997 fee: IR£8,000 (Oct 1st).

LYPHARD   1969 Northern Dancer - Goofed (Court Martial).
                                                                   (76, 147)
Racing record: 6 wins notably the Prix Jacques le Marois and the Prix de la Foret. Stud record: Best winners include the European Group 1 winners Three Troikas (Prix de l'Arc de Triomphe), Riviere d'Or (Prix Saint-Alary), Dancing Maid (French 1,000 Guineas), Ensconse (Irish 1,000 Guineas), Pearl Bracelet (French 1,000 Guineas), Monteverdi (Dewhurst Stakes), Durtal (Cheveley Park Stakes), Jolypha (Prix Vermeille), Reine de Saba (Prix Saint-Alary), Ski Paradise (Prix du Moulin), the good French racehorses and sires Pharly, Al Nasr and Esprit du Nord and the American Grade 1 winners Au Point, Dahar, Ends Well, Lyphard's Wish, Rainbows For Life, Sabin and Sangue. Best of all are the 1986 3-y-o colts Dancing Brave (European champion) and Manila (champion U.S. turf horse).

MACHIAVELLIAN   1987 Mr Prospector - Coup de Folie (Halo).
                (20, 328, 527, 533, 570, 571, 591, 660, 679, 738, 752, 759, 766, 788, 836)
Racing record: 4 wins from 6f to 7f notably the Prix de la Salamandre and the Prix Morny. Stud record: With just four crops racing, his best winners have been Vettori (French 2,000 Guineas), Rebecca Sharp (Coronation Stakes), Phantom Gold (Group 2 Ribblesdale Stakes and Geoffrey Freer Stakes), Kahal (Group 2 Challenge Stakes), Majorien (Group 2 Prix du Conseil de Paris), the Group 3 winners Sinyar, Titus Livius, Whitewater Affair and Kokuto Julian, the listed winners Art of War, Don Michelotto, Luminoso, Philanthrop, Sharaf Kabeer and Vittelozzi. Standing at Dalham Hall Stud, Newmarket.

MAGIC RING   1989 Green Desert - Emaline (Empery).
                                                                       (809)
Racing record: 3 wins including the Group 3 Cornwallis Stakes and the Group 3 Norfolk Stakes. Stud record: His first runners appeared last year and among his numerous winners were Merlin's Ring

(Group 3 Prix Eclipse) and Crazee Mental (placed in the Queen Mary, the Cherry Hinton and the Cheveley Park). Standing at Whitsbury Manor Stud in Hampshire. 1998 fee: £4,500 (Oct 1st).

MAJESTIC LIGHT   1973 Majestic Prince - Irradiate (Ribot).
(179)
Racing record: won 11 races, notably the Swaps Stakes, the Man O'War Stakes, the Haskell Handicap and the Monmouth Invitational Handicap. Stud record: Best winners include Lacovia (Prix de Diane, Prix Saint-Alary), the champion Japanese filly and sprinter Nishino Flower, Solar Splendor (Turf Classic), Lite Light (four Grade 1 wins in the USA), Christiecat (Flower Bowl Handicap), Prince True (San Juan Capistrano Handicap and San Luis Rey Stakes), Wavering Monarch (Haskell Invitational), Collins (Selima Stakes), Hidden Light (Santa Anita Oaks), War (Blue Grass Stakes) and the $1.6 million winner Simply Majestic. 1998 fee: $10,000.

MANILA   1983 Lyphard - Dona Ysidra (Le Fabuleux).
(187)
Racing record: 12 wins including five Grade 1 Stakes, notably the Breeders Cup Turf. Stud record: Best winners include Bien Bien (Hollywood Turf Cup Handicap), Time Star (Italian Derby), Great Palm (Premio Presidente della Repubblica) and the Group/Grade 2 winners Montjoy, Manilaman and Star of Manila. Standing at Lane's End Farm, Kentucky.

MARJU   1988 Last Tycoon - Flame of Tara (Artaius).
(233, 437, 689, 720, 791)
Racing record: 3 wins including the St James's Palace Stakes and the Group 3 Craven Stakes and placed second in the Derby. Stud record: A very successful young sire, Marju sired two Group 1 winners in his first crop - My Emma (Prix Vermeille) and Sil Sila (Prix de Diane). His other winners since include the Italian Group 3 winner Della Scala and the listed winner Hattab. Standing at Derrinstown Stud in Ireland. 1997 fee: IR10,000 Guineas (Oct 1st).

MIDYAN   1984 Miswaki - Country Dream (Ribot).
(226)
Racing record: 3 wins from 6f to 7f including the Group 3 Jersey Stakes. Stud record: Best winners include Alhijaz (four Group 1 wins in Italy) and the Group winners Accento, Beauchamp Hero, Central City, Les Boyer and Tioman Island. Standing at Haras du Thenney. 1998 fee: 30,000FF. (Oct 1st).

MISWAKI   1978 Mr Prospector - Hopespringseternal (Buckpasser).
(93, 262, 515)
Racing record: 6 wins notably the Prix de la Salamandre and placed in the Prix Morny and the Dewhurst Stakes. Stud record: Best winners include Black Tie Affair (Breeders Cup Classic), Kistena (Prix de l'Abbaye), Misil (Premio Roma), Papal Power (Hopeful Stakes), Playlist (Canadian Oaks), Urban Sea (Prix de l'Arc de Triomphe), Waki River (Criterium de Saint-Cloud), the Australian Grade 1 winner Umatilla and numerous other Group/Graded stakes winners including Abou Zouz, Allied Forces, Balawaki, Diligence, Hurricane State, Le Belvedere, Midyan, Miswaki Tern and Whakilyric (the dam of Hernando). Standing at Walmac International Farm in Kentucky. 1998 fee: $35,000 (live foal).

MR PROSPECTOR   1970 Raise a Native - Gold Digger (Nashua).
(97, 117, 243, 286, 378, 381, 406, 418, 427, 574, 624, 674, 757)
Racing record: 7 wins notably the 6f Whirlaway Stakes and the 6f Gravesend Handicap. Stud record: His multitude of Group/Grade 1 winners include Distant View (Sussex Stakes), Ravinella (1,000 Guineas, French 1,000 Guineas), Rhythm (Breeders Cup Juvenile Stakes, Travers Stakes), It's in the Air (Vanity Handicap, Alabama Stakes), Eillo (Breeders Cup Sprint), Kingmambo (French 2,000 Guineas, St James's Palace Stakes), Tank's Prospect (Preakness Stakes) and Ta Rib (French 1,000 Guineas). He has also proved an exceptional sire of sires, particularly through his sons Conquistador Cielo, Fappiano, Forty Niner, Gone West, Gulch, Jade Hunter, Machiavellian, Miswaki, Seeking the Gold and Woodman. Standing Claiborne Farm, Kentucky.

MT LIVERMORE   1981 Blushing Groom - Flama Ardiente (Crimson Satan).
(743)
Racing record: 11 wins from 6f to 1m including the Grade 2 Carter Handicap and Grade 2 Fall Highweight Handicap. Stud record: Best winners include Housebuster (three US Grade 1 wins), Eliza (Champion US 2-y-o filly), the US Grade 1 winners Mt Sassafras and Peaks And Valleys, the Canadian Grade 1

winner Humpty's Hoedown and the US Grade 2 winners Blushing Julian and Greek Costume. Standing at Gainesway Farm, Lexington, Kentucky. 1998 fee: $50,000 (live foal).

MTOTO
1983 Busted - Amazer (Mincio).
(697)

Racing record: 8 wins notably the King George VI and Queen Elizabeth Diamond Stakes, the Coral-Eclipse Stakes (twice) and the Group 2 Prince of Wales's Stakes (twice). He was also placed twice in the Prix de l'Arc de Triomphe. Stud record: Best winners include Shaamit (Derby), Celeric (Ascot Gold Cup), Presenting (Geoffrey Freer Stakes), Arbatax (Group 2 Prix Hocquart), Mousse Glacee (Group 3 Prix des Reservoirs), Maylane (Group 3 September Stakes), Cap Juluca (Cambridgeshire Handicap) and the Classic placed Book At Bedtime and Crown Of Light. Standing at the Aston Upthorpe Stud in Oxfordshire. 1998 fee: £10,000 (Oct 1st).

MUJADIL
1988 Storm Bird - Vallee Secrete (Secretariat).
(549)

Racing record: 3 wins including the Group 3 Cornwallis Stakes. Stud record: From two crops racing, sire of the listed winners Bay Prince and Craigievar and the Molecomb Stakes second Connemara. Standing at Rathasker Stud, Naas, Ireland. 1998 fee: IR£4,000 (Oct 1st).

MUJTAHID
1988 Woodman - Mesmerize (Mill Reef)
(257, 780)

Racing record: 3 wins including the Group 2 Gimcrack Stakes and the Group 3 July Stakes. Champion British 2-y-o of 1990. Stud record: After just two crops of runners Mujtahid has proved himself a useful sire of 2-y-o's. His best winners include Mubhij (Group 3 Cornwallis Stakes), Boojum (listed Radley Stakes), Grand Lad and Juwwi. Standing at Derrinstown Stud, Co. Kildare, Ireland. 1998 fee: IR5,000 Guineas. (Oct 1st).

MUKADDAMAH
1988 Storm Bird - Tash (Never Bend).
(138)

Racing record: 4 wins from 6f to 8.5f incuding the Group 2 John Roarty Memorial International and the Group 3 Lanson Champagne Vintage Stakes. Stud record: His first runners appeared last year. To February this year they included the winners of 23 races in the UK. Standing at Rathbarry Stud. 1998 fee: IR4,000 Gns (Oct 1st).

MYSTIKO
1988 Secreto - Caracciola (Zeddaan).
(162)

Racing record: 4 wins from 6f to 1m including the 2,000 Guineas and the Challenge Stakes. Stud record: From 2 crops racing, sire of the winners of 23 races (to February this year). 1998 fee: £2,000 (special live foal).

NAMAQUALAND
1990 Mr Prospector - Namaqua (Storm Bird).
(542)

Racing record: 4 wins from 6f to 8.5f including a US Grade 3 event. Stud record: First crop now two-year-olds. Standing at Rathbarry Stud. 1998 fee: IR4,000 Gns (Oct 1st).

NASHWAN
1986 Blushing Groom - Height of Fashion (Bustino).
(17, 82, 172, 254, 269, 293, 310, 324, 374, 470, 493, 572, 754, 792)

Racing record: 6 wins from 7f to 12f notably the 2,000 Guineas, the Derby, the Coral-Eclipse Stakes and the King George VI and Queen Elizabeth Diamond Stakes. Champion 3-y-o colt. Stud record: Best winners include Aqaarid (Fillies Mile), Swain (King George VI and Queen Elizabeth Diamond Stakes), Wandesta (Santa Barbara Handicap and Santa Ana Handicap), the Grade 2 Diana Handicap winner Didina, the Group 2 Sun Chariot Stakes winner One So Wonderful and the Group 3 winners Bint Salsabil, Bint Shadayid, Myself and Silent Warrior. Standing at the Nunnery Stud in Norfolk.

NIGHT SHIFT
1980 Northern Dancer - Ciboulette (Chop Chop).
(180, 283, 311, 319, 537, 553, 654, 681, 748)

Racing record: Minor winner over 6f in the USA. Stud record: Best winners include Creaking Board (Starlet Stakes), In The Groove (Juddmonte International, Champion Stakes, Irish 1,000 Guineas and Coronation Stakes), Listening (Hollywood Oaks), Nicolotte (Premio Vittorio di Capua and Group 2 Queen Anne Stakes), the Group winners Eveningperformance, Just Happy, Northern Goddess,

Struggler and Time Gentlemen and the smart Midnight Legend. Standing at Coolmore Stud in Ireland. 1998 fee: IR12,500 Guineas (Oct 1st).

NORTHERN FLAGSHIP   1986 Northern Dancer - Native Partner (Raise A Native).
(46)
Racing record: Placed twice from 4 starts. Stud record: A brother of Ajdal and a half-brother to Formidable, his best winners include Polaris Flight (Criterium de Saint-Cloud), the German Group 3 winner Macanal and several US stakes winners.

NUREYEV   1977 Northern Dancer - Special (Forli).
(23, 131, 137, 333, 352, 416, 473, 638, 653, 673, 675, 755)
Racing record: Ran three times. Won the 7f Prix Djebel and the 7.5f Prix Thomas Bryon and was disqualified from first place in the 2,000 Guineas. Stud record: His Group/Grade 1 winners include Alwuhush, Annoconnor, Atticus, Flagbird, Kitwood, Mehthaaf, Miesque, Pattern Step, Peintre Celebre, Polar Falcon, Reams of Verse, Sonic Lady, Soviet Star, Spinning World, Stately Don, Theatrical, Vilikaia, Wolfhound and Zilzal. Standing at Walmac International Farm in Lexington, Kentucky.

PERSONAL HOPE   1990 Storm Bird - All The Years (Alydar).
(398)
Racing record: 4 wins from 6f to 9f including the Grade 1 Santa Anita Derby. Stud record: His first crop were two-year-olds of 1997. Standing at Ashford Stud in Kentucky. 1998 fee: $7,500 (Oct 1st).

PERUGINO   1991 Danzig - Fairy Bridge (Bold Reason).
(1, 61, 567, 680, 715, 774, 817)
Racing record: One win over 6f at 2 yrs. Stud record: Closely related to Sadler's Wells, Fairy King and Tate Gallery. His first crop are now two-year-olds. 1998 fee: IR4,000 Gns (Oct 1st).

PETARDIA   1990 Petong - What a Pet (Mummy's Pet).
(718)
Racing record: 4 wins from 5f to 7f including the Group 2 Laurent Perrier Champagne Stakes and the Group 3 Coventry Stakes. Stud record: His first crop were two-year-olds of 1997 and included the Group 3 Cornwallis Stakes winner Halmahera and the Group 3 Rockfel Stakes winner Name of Love. Standing at the Tally-Ho Stud in Ireland. 1998 fee: IR3,500 (Oct 1st).

PETORIUS   1981 Mummy's Pet - The Stork (Club House).
(506)
Racing record: 6 wins from 5f to 6f including the Group 3 Cornwallis Stakes and the Group 3 Temple Stakes. Stud record: Best progeny include the Group winners Sapieha, Kill The Crab, Nautical Pet and Eichtercua and the listed winner Forest Cat. Standing at Tara Stud, Co. Meath, Ireland. 1998 fee: IR£2,000 (Oct 1st).

PIPS PRIDE   1990 Efisio - Elkie Brooks (Relkino)
(4, 7, 134)
Racing record: 6 wins from 5f to 6.5f including the Group 1 Heinz "57" Phoenix Stakes. Stud record: His first two-year-olds appeared last year and include the useful Cortachy Castle.

PISTOLET BLEU   1988 Top Ville - Pampa Bella (Armos).
(690)
Racing record: Winner of the Group 1 Criterium de Saint-Cloud, the Group 1 Grand Prix de Saint-Cloud, the Group 2 Prix Noailles and the Group 2 Prix Hocquart. Stud record: With two crops racing, his only black-type performer to date is the Group 3 placed Deflagration. Standing at the Haras d'Etreham. 1998 fee: FF35,000 (Oct 1st).

PLEASANT COLONY   1978 His Majesty - Sun Colony (Sunrise Flight).
(140)
Racing record: 6 wins notably the Kentucky Derby, the Preakness Stakes, the Wood Memorial Stakes and the Woodward Stakes. Stud record: His US Grade 1 winners include Colonial Affair, Colonial Waters, Pleasant Tap, Pleasant Stage, Pleasant Variety, Roanoke, Shared Interest and Sir Beaufort, whilst in Europe his outstanding performer is the Irish Derby and King George VI and Queen Elizabeth Diamond Stakes winner St Jovite. Standing at Buckland Farm in Lexington, Kentucky. 1998 fee: $60,000 (live foal).

POLAR FALCON 1987 Nureyev - Marie d'Argonne (Jefferson).
(559, 598, 644, 686, 687, 773)
Racing record: 5 wins notably the Group 1 6f Haydock Park Sprint Cup, the Group 2 1m Lockinge Stakes and the Group 3 1m Prix Edmond Blanc. Stud record: From three crops racing, the sire of Pivotal (Group 1 Nunthorpe Stakes and Group 2 Kings Stand Stakes), Red Camellia (Group 3 Prestige Stakes), the listed winners Falkenham and Just Ice, and the Fillies Mile third Exclusive. Standing at the Cheveley Park Stud, Newmarket. 1998 fee: £10,000 (October 1st).

POLISH PATRIOT 1988 Danzig - Maria Waleska (Filiberto).
(491, 820)
Racing record: Won 5 races including the July Cup and the Group 3 Cork and Orrery Stakes. Stud record: Best winners include Gothenberg (Group 2 Sea World International Stakes) and the listed winners Samara, Dungeon Master and Recondite.

POLISH PRECEDENT 1986 Danzig - Past Example (Buckpasser).
(14, 220, 314, 528, 538, 599, 652, 722, 749)
Racing record: 7 wins notably the Prix Jacques le Marois and the Prix du Moulin. Stud record: Best winners include Pilsudski (Breeders Cup Turf, Eclipse Stakes, Champion Stakes and Grosser Preis von Baden), Predappio, Pure Grain (Irish Oaks and Yorkshire Oaks), Red Route and Riyadian. Standing at Dalham Hall Stud, Newmarket. 1997 fee: £20,000 (Oct 1).

PRIMO DOMINIE 1982 Dominion - Swan Ann (My Swanee).
(176, 478, 516, 823)
Racing record: 6 wins including the Group 2 Richmond Stakes, the King George Stakes, the Coventry Stakes and the July Stakes (all Group 3 events). Stud record: Best winners include First Trump (Middle Park Stakes), Le Magister (Grade 1 Highlander Stakes, Woodbine), the Group 2 winners Arranvanna, Lara's Idea and Millyant and the Peruvian Grade 1 winner Dalnamein. Standing at Cheveley Park Stud in Newmarket. 1997 fee: £7,000 (Oct 1st).

PRINCE SABO 1982 Young Generation - Jubilee Song (Song).
(455, 761)
Racing record: 4 wins over 5f including the Group 2 Flying Childers Stakes and the Group 3 Palace House Stakes. Stud record: Best winners include: Princely Hush (Group 2 Mill Reef Stakes), Tippett Boy (Group 3 Norfolk Stakes), the listed winners Easy Option, Joli's Princess, Sea Gazer and Sipsi Fach and the Group 3 placed Cathedral and Maid For Walking. Standing at Cheveley Park Stud, Newmarket. 1998 fee: £4,500 (Oct 1st).

PRIOLO 1987 Sovereign Dancer - Primevere (Irish River).
(27, 677)
Racing record: 6 wins from 7f to 9f including the Prix Jacques le Marois, Prix Jean Prat and Prix du Moulin. Stud record: From three crops racing, his best progeny have been Brilliance (Prix Saint-Alary), Priory Belle (Moyglare Stud Stakes) and the Group 2 Prix Jean de Chaudenay winner Flyway. Standing at Corbally Stud, Co. Kildare, Ireland. 1998 fee: IR6,000 Gns (Oct 1st).

PROJECT MANAGER 1985 Ahonoora - Beparoejojo (Lord Gayle).
(37, 42)
Racing record: Won 3 races at 2 and 3 yrs from 7f to 10f including the Group 2 Gallinule Stakes. Stud record: His first runners appeared in 1994 and although he has sired a number of winners, none have been of any great consequence.

PUISSANCE 1986 Thatching - Girton (Balidar).
(64, 83)
Racing record: 3 wins over 6f including the Group 3 Greenlands Stakes. Stud record: Sire of the winners of over 100 races, by far the best being the high-class sprinter Mind Games. Standing at Bearstone Stud. 1998 fee: £3,000 (Oct 1st FFR).

PURSUIT OF LOVE 1989 Groom Dancer - Dance Quest (Green Dancer).
(107, 163)
Racing record: 4 wins including the Group 2 6.5f Prix Maurice de Gheest and the Group 3 7f Kiveton Park Stakes and placed in the July Cup, the 2,000 Guineas and the Dewhurst Stakes. Stud record: From two crops racing, sire of the winners of over 40 races including the listed winners Basse Besogne

and Head Over Heels and the Dewhurst Stakes second Musical Pursuit. Standing at the Plantation Stud, Newmarket. 1998 fee: £7,000 (no foal, no fee) (Oct 1st).

RAHY 1985 Blushing Groom - Glorious Song (Halo).
(2, 184, 252, 590, 735)

Racing record: 6 wins from 6f to 8.5f including the Grade 2 Bel Air Handicap and the listed Bonusprint Sirenia Stakes. Stud record: Best winners include Exotic Wood (Go For Wand Stakes), Serena's Song (Haskell Invitational and Oak Leaf Stakes) and the Group/Graded Stakes winners Applaud, Mariah's Storm, Miss Ra He Ra, Raphane and Raw Gold. 1998 fee: $50,000 (live foal, Sept 1st). Standing at Three Chimneys Farm, Kentucky.

RAINBOW QUEST 1981 Blushing Groom - I Will Follow (Herbager).
(88, 103, 109, 119, 169, 170, 207, 210, 227, 228, 232, 248, 260, 277, 340, 355, 357, 360, 382, 390, 575, 602, 655, 736, 740, 756, 767, 787)

Racing record: 6 wins from 7f to 12f including the Prix de l'Arc de Triomphe and the Coronation Cup. Placed in six other Group 1 races. Stud record: The leading British-based sire, Rainbow Quest's Group 1 winners are Armiger (Racing Post Trophy), Bright Generation (Italian Oaks), Knight's Baroness (Irish Oaks), Quest For Fame (Derby, Hollywood Turf Handicap), Raintrap (San Juan Capistrano Handicap), Rothmans International, Prix Royal-Oak), Sakura Laurel (Tenno Sho, Japan), Saumarez (Prix de l'Arc de Triomphe, Grand Prix de Paris), Sought Out (Prix du Cadran), Special Quest (Criterium de Saint-Cloud), Spectrum (Champion Stakes and Irish 1,000 Guineas), Sunshack (Coronation Cup, Prix Royal-Oak and Criterium de Saint-Cloud) and Urgent Request (Santa Anita Handicap). Standing at Banstead Manor Stud, Newmarket. 1998 fee: £40,000 (Oct 1st).

RAINBOWS FOR LIFE 1988 Lyphard - Rainbow Connection (Halo).
(566)

Racing record: 15 wins from 6f to 10f including 5 Grade 3 events in Canada. Champion two-year-old and older horse in Canada. Stud record: His first foals were two-year-olds in 1997. 1998 fee: IR4,000 Gns (Oct 1st).

RED RANSOM 1987 Roberto - Arabia (Damascus).
(201, 261, 429, 461, 741, 781)

Racing record: 2 wins, over 5f and 6f, from three outings. Stud record: Best peformers include Bail Out Becky (Del Mar Oaks), the Group/Grade 2 winners Sri Pekan, Trail City and Wandering Star, the Grade 3 winners Petrouchka and Upper Noosh and the very useful listed winner Intikhab. Standing at the Vinery Stud in Kentucky. 1998 fee: $35,000 (live foal).

REPRIMAND 1985 Mummy's Pet - Just You Wait (Nonoalco).
(9)

Racing record: 6 wins from 6f to 9f including the Group 2 Gimcrack Stakes, the Group 2 Forte Mile and the Group 3 Earl Of Sefton Stakes. Stud record: Best winners include Fard (Middle Park Stakes), Deep Finesse (Group 3 Palace House Stakes) and the US listed winner Royal Rebuke. Standing at the National Stud, Newmarket. 1998 fee: £2,500 (Oct 1st).

RIVERMAN 1969 Never Bend - River Lady (Prince John).
(22, 135, 270, 290, 419, 786)

Racing record: 5 wins notably the French 2,000 Guineas and the Prix d'Ispahan. Stud record: Consistently one of the world's best stallions, Riverman's best performers over the years have included the English trained Bahri, Dowsing, Kingfisher Mill, Lahib and Rousillon, the French trained Detroit, Gold River, Houseproud, Irish River, Loup Sauvage, Policeman, River Lady, River Memories and Triptych and the US trained Latin American, River Special and Rivlia. Riverman is also the broodmare sire of many Group 1 winners including Bosra Sham, Carnegie, Hector Protector, Helen Street, Saint Cyrien and Spinning World. Standing at Gainesway Farm in Lexington, Kentucky.

ROBELLINO 1978 Roberto - Isobelline (Pronto).
(242, 557, 563, 608)

Racing record: 5 wins including the Group 2 Royal Lodge Stakes and the Group 3 Seaton Delaval Stakes. Stud record: Best winners include Mister Baileys (2,000 Guineas), Classic Park (Irish 1,000 Guineas), Tot Ou Tard (Group 2 Grand Prix d'Evry), Street Rebel (Group 3 Greeenlands Stakes), Holly Golightly (Group 3 Prix Chloe), Faustus (Group 3 Greenham Stakes) and Local Herbert (Premio Lazio). Standing at Littleton Stud in Hampshire. 1998 fee: £5,000 (Oct 1st. No foal, no fee).

ROYAL ACADEMY 1987 Nijinsky - Crimson Saint (Crimson Satan).
(125, 139, 152, 211, 322, 325, 343, 452, 503, 514, 522, 554, 560, 618, 641, 642, 665, 691, 716, 717, 803, 804, 819, 833)
Racing record: 4 wins notably the Breeders Cup Mile and the July Cup. Placed in the Irish 2,000 Guineas and the Ladbroke Sprint Cup. Stud record: Champion first-season sire in 1994. Best winners include Sleepytime (1,000 Guineas), Ali-Royal (Sussex Stakes), Carmine Lake (Prix de l'Abbaye), Oscar Schindler (Irish St Leger) and the Group winners Centaine, Equal Rights, Flame of Athens, Painter's Row and Truth Or Dare.

RUDIMENTARY 1988 Nureyev - Doubly Sure (Reliance II).
(793)
Racing record: 4 wins from 1m to 10f including the Group 2 Forte Mile and the listed Main Reef Stakes. Stud record: Best performers include the listed Harry Rosebery Trophy winner Conspiracy, the Group 3 Prix du Bois third Alberelle and the Cambridgeshire second Rudimental. Standing at Cheveley Park Stud in Newmarket. 1998 fee: £6,000 (Oct 1st).

SABREHILL 1990 Diesis - Gypsy Talk (Alleged).
(75, 402)
Racing record: 1 win over 10f. Second in Group 1 Juddmonte International. Retired injured. Stud record: His first two-year-olds appeared in 1997 and his winners to date include Eco Friendly (Group 3 Prix Saint-Roman) and Alboostan (listed Stardom Stakes). Standing at Stetchworth Park Stud, Newmarket. 1998 fee: £3,000 (Oct 1st).

SADDLERS' HALL 1988 Sadler's Wells - Sunny Valley (Val de Loir).
(530)
Racing record: 6 wins from 10f to 13f 89yds including the Coronation Cup, the King Edward VII Stakes and the Princess of Wales's Stakes. Stud record: Best progeny (from two crops) include the St Leger winner Silver Patriarch, the Italian listed winner Madler and the useful 10f winner Silence Reigns. Standing at Cheveley Park Stud, Newmarket. 1998 fee: £7,500 (Oct 1st).

SADLER'S WELLS 1981 Northern Dancer - Fairy Bridge (Bold Reason).
(30, 72, 120, 141, 145, 151, 156, 157, 177, 216, 289, 302, 308, 323, 347, 349, 361, 384, 422, 425, 450, 510, 517, 523, 607, 625, 631, 633, 635, 636, 637, 669, 714, 730, 733, 744, 763, 797, 801)
Racing record: Winner of the Irish 2,000 Guineas, the Phoenix Champion Stakes and the Coral-Eclipse. Placed in the French Derby and the King George. Stud record: Group or Grade 1 winners include Barathea, Carnegie, Dance Design, Entrepreneur, In the Wings, Intrepidity, King's Theatre, Moonshell, Northern Spur, Old Vic, Opera House and Salsabil. Standing at Coolmore Stud in Ireland. 1998 fee: IR125,000 Gns (Oct 1st).

SAINT ESTEPHE 1982 Top Ville - Une Tornade (Traffic II).
(351)
Racing record: 4 wins including the Coronation Cup, the Group 2 Prix Maurice de Nieuil and the Group 2 Prix d'Harcourt. Stud record: Best winners include the Group/Grade 1 winners Blended, Gravieres and Pigeon Voyageur. 1998 fee: FF25,000 (Oct 1st).

SALSE 1985 Topsider - Carnival Princess (Prince John).
(56, 231, 420, 445, 606)
Racing record: 8 wins including the Group 1 Prix de la Foret, the Group 2 Bisquit Cognac Stakes and three Group 3 races. Stud record: Best winners include Air Express (Queen Elizabeth II Stakes), Bianca Nera (Moyglare Stud Stakes), Classic Cliche (St Leger), Lemon Souffle (Moyglare Stud Stakes), Luso (Italian Derby, Aral Pokal, Hong Kong International Vase) and Spout (Group 3 Lancashire Oaks and Group 3 John Porter Stakes). Standing at Side Hill Stud in Newmarket. 1998 fee: £17,500 (Oct 1st).

SAUMAREZ 1987 Rainbow Quest - Fiesta Fun (Welsh Pageant).
(475)
Racing record: 5 wins, notably the Prix de l'Arc de Triomphe and the Grand Prix de Paris. Stud record: Best winners include the French Group 2 winners Stretarez, Silver Fun and Steward and the French Group 3 winners Luna Mareza and Maroussie. Standing at the Haras du Quesnay in France. 1998 fee: FF60,000 (Oct 1st).

SCENIC   1986 Sadler's Wells - Idyllic (Foolish Pleasure).
(47)
Racing record: Won the Dewhurst Stakes (in a dead-heat) and the Group 3 William Hill Scottish Classic.
Stud record: Best winners include the Australian Grade 1 winners Lochrae, Shame and Blevic, the
Italian 1,000 Guineas winner Beauty to Petriolo and the useful 1997 2-y-o Speedfit Too.

SEATTLE SLEW   1974 Bold Reasoning - My Charmer (Poker).
(620)
Racing record: Outstanding racehorse. 14 wins, notably the American Triple Crown. Stud record: His
Group/Grade 1 winners include A P Indy, Slew O' Gold, Swale, Capote, Landaluce, Slew City Slew,
Life At The Top, Tsunami Slew, Adored, Slewpy, Lakeway, Seattle Song and Septieme Ciel. 1998 fee:
$100,000 (live foal, Sept 1st).

SECOND SET   1988 Alzao - Merriment (Go Marching).
(215, 298, 814)
Racing record: 3 wins from 7f to 1m 40yds including the Group 1 Sussex Stakes. Stud record: His first
crop were two-year-olds in 1997 and his winners include the Group placed Heed My Warning and
Evening Set. Standing at Gestut Zoppenbroich, Germany. 1998 fee: DM12,000 (Oct 1st).

SEEKING THE GOLD   1985 Mr Prospector - Con Game (Buckpasser).
(40, 229, 645)
Racing record: 8 wins from 6f to 10f, notably the Grade 1 Dwyer Stakes and the Grade 1 Super Derby.
Stud record: Best winners include the champion fillies and multiple Grade 1 winners Heavenly Prize
and Flanders, the Canadian Grade 1 winner Squire Jones, the US Graded Stakes winners At The Half,
Petionville, Secret Savings and Seeking Regina, the smart French Group 2 winning sprinter Spain
Lane and the very useful John of Gaunt Stakes winner Mutakddim. Standing at Claiborne Farm in
Kentucky. 1998 fee: $125,000.

SELKIRK   1988 Sharpen Up - Annie Edge (Nebbiolo).
(13, 122, 128, 158, 401, 421)
Racing record: 6 wins including the Queen Elizabeth II Stakes, the Lockinge Stakes, the Beefeater Gin
Celebration Mile and the Challenge Stakes. Stud record: From 2 crops racing, Selkirk has sired the
Group 2 Prix Eugene Adam winner Kirkwall, the Group 3 Lancashire Oaks winner Squeak, the Group
3 Prix de Sandringham winner Orford Ness and the listed winners Entice, Hidden Meadow and Trans
Island. Standing at Lanwades Stud in Newmarket. 1998 fee: £15,000 (Oct 1st).

SHADEED   1982 Nijinsky - Continual (Damascus).
(372)
Racing record: 4 wins notably the 2,000 Guineas and the Queen Elizabeth II Stakes. Stud record: Best
winners include Sayyedati (1,000 Guineas, Prix Jacques le Marois, Sussex Stakes, Cheveley Park
Stakes and Moyglare Stud Stakes), Shadayid (1,000 Guineas and Prix Marcel Boussac), the Canadian
and US Grade 1 winner Alydeed, the Brazilian Grade 1 winner Indian Hope, the very useful English
winners Nadwah (Queen Mary Stakes), Satin Flower (Jersey Stakes) and Splendent (Gimcrack Stakes)
and the US Graded Stakes winners Citadeed and Infamous Deed. Standing at Gainesborough Farm
in Kentucky. 1998 fee: $5,000 (Oct 1st).

SHAREEF DANCER   1980 Northern Dancer - Sweet Alliance (Sir Ivor).
(54)
Racing record: 3 wins including the Irish Derby. Stud record: Best winners include Glory Of Dancer
(Gran Criterium and Group 2 Dante Stakes), Possessive Dancer (Irish and Italian Oaks), Dancer Mitral
(Group 2 Premio Parioli), Rock Hopper (seven Group wins including the Group 2 Hardwicke Stakes),
Shaima (Grade 2 Long Island Handicap), Kazoo (Group 2 German 1,000 Guineas), Colorado Dancer
(Group 2 Prix de Pomone) and Spartan Shareef (Group 3 September Stakes). 1998 fee: £5,000 (Oct
1st, special live foal).

SHEIKH ALBADOU   1988 Green Desert - Sanctuary (Welsh Pageant).
(274, 505, 794)
Racing record: 6 wins including the Group 1 Keeneland Nunthorpe Stakes, the Group 1 Haydock Park
Sprint and the Grade 1 Breeders Cup Sprint. Stud record: From 2 crops racing, sire of the 10f winner
and Group 3 placed Amid Albadou and the 7f winner Tayseer (both useful), along with several other
minor winners. 1998 fee: $5,000 (Oct 1st).

SHIRLEY HEIGHTS   1975 Mill Reef - Hardiemma (Hardicanute).
                                 (108, 185, 453, 525, 535, 541, 725)
Racing record: Won 6 races including the Derby, the Irish Sweeps Derby, the Royal Lodge Stakes and the Dante Stakes. Stud record: His best colts have been the top class French Derby winner Darshaan, the equally talented Epsom Derby winner Slip Anchor and Arcadian Heights, Elegant Air, Head For Heights, High Estate, Perpendicular, Sacrament and Shady Heights. His best fillies have been the Group 1 winners High Hawk (the dam of In the Wings), Infamy and Valley of Gold.

SILLERY   1988 Blushing Groom - Silvermine (Bellypha).
                                                              (474)
Racing record: 7 wins from 1m to 10f including the Group 1 Prix Jean Prat and the Group 2 Prix Dollar. Stud record: With 2 crops racing, sire of the French listed winners Saralea and Yxenery and the Group placed Silic and Now Attention. Standing at Haras du Quesnay. 1998 fee: FF50,000 (Oct 1st).

SILVER HAWK   1979 Ribot - Gris Vitesse (Amerigo).
                          (234, 267, 287, 377, 388, 405, 412, 415, 463, 696, 765)
Racing record: 3 wins including the Group 3 Craven Stakes and the Intercraft Solario Stakes and placed in both the Derby and the Irish Derby. Stud record: His best performers include the 1997 Derby winner Benny The Dip, the Group or Grade 1 winners Lady in Silver (Prix de Diane), Magnificent Star (Yorkshire Oaks), Memories of Silver (Queen Elizabeth II Invitational), Hawkster (Secretariat Stakes, Oak Tree Invitational and Norfolk Stakes), Silver Ending (Pegasus Handicap), Hawk Attack (Secretariat Stakes), Red Bishop (San Juan Capistrano Handicap), Platinum Blonde (Natalma Stakes) and Zoonaqua (Oak Leaf Stakes). Other good American performers of his include the graded stakes winners Silver Medallion, Dansil, Silver Wizard and Silver Ray. In Europe, quite apart from those already mentioned he is the sire of Fahal (Rose of Lancaster Stakes), Silver Wisp (Jockey Club Stakes), Silver Wedge (Queens Vase), Silver Lane (Prix de la Grotte), the smart German horse Devil River Peek and the St Leger second Minds Music. Standing at the Airdrie Stud in Kentucky.

SKY CLASSIC   1987 Nijinsky - No Class (Nodouble).
                                                              (454)
Racing career: 15 wins notably the Rothmans International, the Turf Classic, the Cup And Saucer Stakes and the Canadian Maturity Stakes. Second in the Breeders Cup Turf and the Arlington Million. Stud record: His first two-year-olds ran in 1996 and he has sired a good number minor winners. 1998 fee: $15,000 (live foal, Oct 1st).

SLIP ANCHOR   1982 Shirley Heights - Sayonara (Birkhahn).
                                            (15, 24, 370, 512, 547)
Racing record: 4 wins including the Derby, the Group 3 Lingfield Derby Trial and the listed Heathorn Stakes. Second in the Champion Stakes, the Group 2 Jockey Club Stakes and the Group 3 September Stakes. Stud record: Best winners include User Friendly (Oaks, Irish Oaks and St Leger), L'Hermine (Sword Dancer Handicap), Posidonas (Gran Premio d'Italia), Slicious (Premio Roma), the Group 2 Great Voltigeur Stakes winner Stowaway, the Group 2 Ribblesdale Stakes winner Third Watch and the Group 3 winners Kaliana, Khamaseen, Safety in Numbers, Three Cheers and Up Anchor. Standing at Newmarket's Plantation Stud. 1998 fee: £8,000 (no foal, no fee, Oct 1st).

ST JOVITE   1989 Pleasant Colony - Northern Sunset (Northfields).
                                                          (39, 442)
Racing record: Won 6 races notably the King George VI and Queen Elizabeth Diamond Stakes (beating Saddlers Hall and Opera House) and the Irish Derby (beating his Epsom Derby conqueror Dr Devious). He was also precocious enough to win the Group 3 Anglesey Stakes and the Group 3 Futurity Stakes as a two-year-old. Stud record: His second crop were two-year-olds in 1997. His best performers include the US Graded Stakes placed Divine Insight and several listed placed horses. Standing at Kentucky's Payson Stud.

STORM BIRD   1978 Northern Dancer – South Ocean (New Providence).
                                                          (306, 334)
Racing record: Champion 2-y-o of 1980 and winner of 5 races including the Dewhurst Stakes. Stud record: Best winners include Balanchine (Oaks and Irish Derby), Classy Mirage (Ballerina Handicap), Indian Skimmer (French Oaks and Champion Stakes), Summer Squall (Preakness Stakes), Bluebird (Kings Stand Stakes), Prince of Birds (2,000 Guineas), Magical Wonder (Pris Jean Prat), Personal

Hope (Santa Anita Derby), Pacific Squall (Hollywood Oaks) and the Young America Stakes winner and top-class sire Storm Cat. Other nice horses by Storm Bird to have won in Europe include Mujadil, Mukaddamah, Ocean Ridge, Stonehatch, Storm Star and Wharf. Standing at Kentucky's Ashford Stud where his fee is private.

STORM CAT 1983 Storm Bird - Terlingua (Secretariat).
(34, 276, 582)

Racing record: 4 wins from 6f to 8.5f notably the Grade 1 Young America Stakes. Stud record: His best winners to date include Tabasco Cat (Preakness Stakes and Belmont Stakes), Sardula (Kentucky Oaks and Hollywood Starlet Stakes), November Snow (Alabama Stakes and Test Stakes), Harlan (Vosburgh Stakes), Missed the Storm (Test Stakes), Mistle Cat (Premio Vittorio di Capua), Desert Stormer (Breeders Cup Sprint), Hennessy (Hopeful Stakes), the Group 2 Challenge Stakes winner Catrail and the Grade 2 stakes winner and $1.47 million earner Mountain Cat. Storm Cat stands at Overbrook Farm in Lexington, Kentucky. His 1997 fee was $150,000.

SUAVE DANCER 1988 Green Dancer - Suavite (Alleged).
(63, 114, 508)

Racing record: Winner of five of his nine starts including the Prix de l'Arc de Triomphe, the Irish Champion Stakes and the French Derby. Stud record: His second crop were two-year-olds of 1997. His winners to date include the Group 3 Prix de la Nonette winner Dust Dancer, the Italian listed winner Classem Ducere, the very useful The Faraway Tree and the promising 1997 2-y-o Craigsteel. Standing at The National Stud in Newmarket. 1998 fee: £7,500 (no foal, no fee, Oct 1st).

SUNDAY SILENCE 1986 Halo - Wishing Well (Understanding).
(99)

Racing record: 9 wins from 6f to 10f, notably the Breeders Cup Classic, the Californian Stakes, the Kentucky Derby, the Preakness Stakes, the Santa Anita Derby and the Super Derby - all Grade 1 events. Stud record: Retired to stud in Japan in 1991 and sire of numerous stakes winners there.

TENBY 1990 Caerleon - Shining Water (Kalaglow).
(29, 161, 239, 249)

Racing record: 5 wins from 7f to 10.5f including the Grand Criterium and the Group 2 Dante Stakes. Stud record: First runners appeared last year and his numerous winners included the listed winners Mijana and Tenbyssimo. Now at stud in Japan.

THATCHING 1975 Thatch - Abella (Abernant).
(282, 648)

Racing record: Won four races including the July Cup, the Group 3 Cork and Orrery Stakes and the Group 3 Duke Of York Stakes. Stud record: Best winners include Danseuse du Soir (French 1,000 Guineas and Prix de la Foret), Tirol (English and Irish 2,000 Guineas), Fitzwilliam Place (Gamely Handicap and Beverly Hills Handicap) and the Group winners Revelation, Wiganthorpe, Aberuschka, Shalford and Archway. Quite a number of his sons are now stallions themselves. Standing at Castle Hyde Stud in Ireland. 1998 fee: IR5,000 Guineas (Oct 1st).

THEATRICAL 1982 Nureyev - Tree of Knowledge (Sassafras).
(356, 662)

Racing record: 10 wins from 8.5f to 12f - including six Grade 1 races in the USA - notably the Breeders Cup Turf, the Turf Classic and the Man O'War Stakes. Stud record: Best winners include the Group/ Grade 1 winners Broadway Flyer (Sword Dancer Invitational), Dahlia's Dreamer (Flower Bowl Invitational), Duda (Matrirach Stakes), Geri (Oaklawn Handicap), Golden Treat (Santa Anita Oaks), Hishi Amazon (Champion Japanese 2-y-o filly), Madeleine's Dream (French 1,000 Guineas), Marchand de Sable (Criterium de Saint-Cloud), Pharma (Santa Ana Handicap), Portland Player (Victoria Derby), Vaudeville (Secretariat Stakes) and Zagreb (Irish Derby).

THORN DANCE 1986 Northern Dancer - Barb's Bold (Bold Forbes).
(191, 586)

Racing record: 2 wins, over 6f and 7f, and listed placed. Stud record: From 4 crops racing, best winners include General Monash (Group 2 Prix Robert Papin) and the minor US stakes winner Thorn Tree. Standing at Jonabell Farm.

TIME FOR A CHANGE 1981 Damascus - Resolver (Reviewer).
(346)
Racing record: 5 wins from 7f to 9f including the Grade 1 Flamingo Stakes and the Grade 3 Everglades Stakes. Stud record: Best performers include the US Grade 1 winners Fly So Free and Technology, the Grade 2 winners Changing Ways, Iron Gavel, Living Vicariously, Thirst For Peace, Transient Friend and Why Change and the Group 3 Prix de Flore winner Tamise.

TREMPOLINO 1984 Sharpen Up - Trephine (Viceregal).
(44, 55, 115)
Racing record: Winner of four races including the Prix Lupin, the Prix Niel and most notably the Prix de l'Arc de Triomphe. Stud record: Best winners include Dernier Empereur (Champion Stakes), Germany (Grosser Preis von Baden), the US Grade 2 winners Talloires and Trempoli, the European Group 3 winners Arkadian Hero, For Valour, Neuilly and Triarius, the US Graded Stakes winners Cox Orange, Summer Ensign and Hidden Trick, the 6f colt Blue Goblin and the 12f colt Kalabo - both very useful. Trempolino stands at Gainesway Farm, Kentucky at a fee of $15,000 (live foal).

TURTLE ISLAND 1991 Fairy King - Sisania (High Top).
(52, 159, 305, 318, 320, 457, 531, 564, 698, 802)
Racing record: 6 wins from 5f to 1m including the Irish 2,000 Guineas, the Heinz "57" Phoenix Stakes and the Group 2 Gimcrack Stakes. Stud record: First crop now two-year-olds. Standing at Coolmore Stud in Ireland. 1998 fee: IR7,000 Guineas (Oct 1st).

UNFUWAIN 1985 Northern Dancer - Height of Fashion (Bustino).
(21, 81, 441, 502, 619, 643)
Racing record: Won 6 races including the Group 2 Princess of Wales's Stakes and the Group 3 Jockey Club Stakes. Stud record: Best performers include the Champion 1995 2-y-o Alhaarth (winner of the Dewhurst Stakes), Bolas (Irish Oaks), Mamlakah (Group 3 May Hill Stakes), the German Group 3 winner Alpha City, the Oaks second Mezzogiorno, the Chesham Stakes winner Shamikh and the 1998 Derby hopeful Gulland. Standing at the Nunnery Stud in Norfolk. 1998 fee: £10,000 (Oct 1st).

WARNING 1985 Known Fact - Slightly Dangerous (Roberto).
(35, 50, 57, 89, 92, 95, 101, 166, 348, 363, 364, 431, 496, 593, 724, 835)
Racing record: 8 wins including the Queen Elizabeth II Stakes, the Sussex Stakes, the Queen Anne Stakes and, at 2 yrs, the Richmond Stakes and the Laurent Perrier Champagne Stakes. Stud record: Best winners include Piccolo (Keeneland Nunthorpe Stakes), Prophecy (Cheveley Park Stakes), Annus Mirabilis (Japanese Grade 2 winner), the Group 2 winners Charnwood Forest, Decorated Hero, Torch Rouge and Bishop of Cashel and the Group 3 winners Armando Carpio, Averti, Beat of Drums, Inzar, Scarlet Plume and Zelding. Sadly, Warning now stands in Japan.

WOLFHOUND 1989 Nureyev - Lassie Dear (Buckpasser).
(209, 240, 296, 321, 400, 462, 498, 700, 709)
Racing record: Won 6 races from 5f to 7f, notably the Hazlewood Foods Sprint Cup at Haydock Park, the Prix de la Foret and the Group 3 Diadem Stakes. Stud record: First crop were two-year-olds of 1997 and were not as successful as expected. The 6f winner and listed placed Special Treat was his chief money earner. Standing at Dalham Hall Stud in Newmarket. 1998 fee: £10,000 (Oct 1st).

WOODMAN 1983 Mr Prospector - Playmate (Buckpasser).
(6, 60, 271, 300, 313, 395, 465, 483, 492, 626, 671, 701, 742, 771)
Racing record: A high class Irish 2-y-o in 1985, Woodman won two Group 3 races - the 6.3f Anglesey Stakes and the 1m Ferrans Futurity Stakes - but failed to train on. Stud record: Best winners include Bosra Sham (Fillies Mile, 1,000 Guineas and Champion Stakes), Gay Gallanta (Cheveley Park Stakes), Hansel (Belmont Stakes and Preakness Stakes), Hector Protector (Champion 2-y-o and winner of the French 2,000 Guineas, the Prix Jacques le Marois, etc.), Mahogany Hall (Whitney Handicap), Timber Country (Champion 2-y-o and winner of the Breeders Cup Juvenile, the Preakness Stakes etc.), Andromaque (Group 2 Prix de l'Opera), Bahhare (Group 2 Laurent Perrier Champagne Stakes), Kathie's Colleen (Grade 2 Monmouth Oaks), Mujtahid (Group 2 Gimcrack Stakes and Group 3 July Stakes), Woodland Melody (Group 3 Prix du Calvados) and Woodborough (Group 3 Anglesey Stakes). Standing at the Ashford Stud in Kentucky. 1998 fee: $75,000 (Oct 1st).

ZAFONIC
1990 Gone West - Zaizafon (The Minstrel).
(58, 78, 98, 100, 102, 190, 222, 337, 342, 376, 383, 389, 428, 529)

Racing record: Won 5 races from 6f to 1m notably the 2,000 Guineas, the Dewhurst Stakes, the Prix de la Salamandre and the Prix Morny. European Champion 2-y-o and 3-y-o. Stud record: Champion first season sire in 1997, his two-year-olds included the Champion juvenile Xaar and the useful Alharir, Bodyguard, Elshamms and Miss Zafonic. Standing at Banstead Manor Stud, Cheveley, Newmarket. 1998 fee: £30,000 (Oct 1st).

ZILZAL
1986 Nureyev - French Charmer (Le Fabuleux).
(62, 281, 331, 456, 468, 799, 815)

Racing record: 5 wins from 6 races notably the Sussex Stakes, the Queen Elizabeth II Stakes, the Group 3 Jersey Stakes and the Group 3 Criterion Stakes. Champion European 3-y-o miler. Stud record: Best winners include Always Loyal (French 1,000 Guineas), Among Men (Group 2 Tripleprint Celebration Mile), Nero Zilzal (Group 3 Prix Exbury), Ocean Queen (Grade 3 Bay Meadows Breeders Cup Derby), Shaanxi (Group 2 Prix du Rond-Point), Zilzal Zamaan (Group 3 Ormonde Stakes), the listed winner Monaassabaat and the smart colts Faithful Son and Kammtarra. Standing at Lanwades Stud, Newmarket. 1998 fee: £10,000 (live foal).

RACING TRENDS

Two key races – the Cherry Hinton (left, won by Asfurah last year) is 'a stepping stone to stardom', while the Sunday Conditions Stakes (Mudeer) has 'an exceptional record for a non-pattern race'

Among the countless numbers of two-year-old races run each season, a select few seem to produce the type of winner that carries on improving and does well the following season. Some of these races are more obvious than others - the Dewhurst Stakes for instance - but there are some surprises. Just as important, there are some two-year-old Group races which should be avoided when compiling lists of horses to follow. For example, the last eight winners of the Group 2 Mill Reef Stakes have won just one race between them as three-year-olds, the same total amassed by the last nine winners of Ireland's Group 3 Beresford Stakes. The Group 2 Richmond Stakes has fared little better - of the last eight winners only Dilum managed to win as a three-year-old. This section then, is the result of my research into a great number of two year old races to discover those that have proved most fruitful in pinpointing future three year old stars. Using the formbook - and with a watchful eye on their pedigrees - one ought to find a significant number of the very best of this year's classic generation.

Over the past few years these races have thrown up the classic winners Pennekamp, Mister Baileys, Rodrigo de Triano and Zafonic (all 2,000 Guineas), Bosra Sham, Harayir, Sayyedati, Zafonic (1,000 Guineas), Marling (Irish 1,000 Guineas), Culture Vulture (French 1,000 Guineas), Dr Devious, Lammtarra (Derby), Desert King (Irish 1,000 Guineas and Irish Derby), Reams Of Verse (Oaks), Celtic Swing (French Derby), Silver Patriarch and Bob's Return (St Leger), along with a multitude of other group race winners.

In the tables, the figure in the third column indicates the number of wins recorded as a three-year-old, with GW signifying a Group race winner at that age. The first race under examination is the Lowther Stakes, an event which has produced no less than nine individual three-year-old Group winners since 1980.

The horses listed below are the winners of the featured races in 1997 (Midnight Line actually won two of them). Anyone looking for horses to follow in the Group and Classic events of this season might well want to bear them in mind. Those in bold text are, I feel, particularly worthy of attention.

Amabel	Daggers Drawn	**King of Kings**	Setteen
Asfurah	**Duck Row**	Midnight Line	Trigger Happy
Bahr	**Embassy**	Mudeer	Wenda
Bintang	**Fantasy Island**	Quiet Assurance	**Xaar**
Cape Verdi	Glorosia	Rabah	
Central Park	**Haami**	Saratoga Springs	

Lowther Stakes
York, 6 furlongs, August.

1980	Kittyhawk	1
1981	Circus Ring	0
1982	Habibti	4 GW
1983	Prickle	0
1984	Al Bahathri	3 GW
1985	Kingscote	0
1986	Polonia	3 GW
1987	Ela Romara	1 GW
1988	Miss Demure	0
1989	Dead Certain	1 GW
1990	Only Yours	2 GW
1991	Culture Vulture	1 GW
1992	Niche	2 GW
1993	Velvet Moon	1
1994	Harayir	4 GW
1995	Dance Sequence	0
1996	Bianca Nera	0
1997	Cape Verdi	

The list of Lowther Stakes winners is impressive, including as it does the 1,000 Guineas heroine Harayir, the respective French and Irish 1,000 Guineas winners Culture Vulture and Al Bahathri, and the top-class sprinters Habibti and Polonia. Cape Verdi only just scraped home in this race before disappointing in the Cheveley Park Stakes. She appeals most strongly as the type of filly to improve as a three-year-old however and I expect her to win a good race or two this season. To start with the 1,000 Guineas would do nicely!

Dewhurst Stakes
Newmarket, 7 furlongs, October.

1980	Storm Bird	0
1981	Wind and Wuthering	0 (2,000 Gns 2nd)
1982	Diesis	0
1983	El Gran Senor	2 GW
1984	Kala Dancer	0
1985	Huntingdale	0
1986	Ajdal	4 GW
1987	ABANDONED	
1988	Prince of Dance &	1 (DISQ)
	Scenic (dead-heat)	1
1989	Dashing Blade	2 GW
1990	Generous	3 GW

1991 Dr Devious   2 GW
1992 Zafonic   1 GW
1993 Grand Lodge   1 GW
1994 Pennekamp   2 GW
1995 Alhaarth   1 GW
1996 In Command   0
1997 Xaar

In Command let the side down last season when he proved himself a sub-standard Dewhurst winner. The list of colts above him here makes impressive reading, with Derby winners Generous and Dr Devious, champion sprinter Ajdal and the Guineas winners Pennekamp, Zafonic and El Gran Senor outstanding. As far as Xaar is concerned, I expect him to emulate the last three by winning the 2,000 Guineas. A top-class 2-y-o, he will have no trouble getting a mile and ten furlongs should also be within his reach.

Zetland Stakes
Newmarket, 10 furlongs, November.

1980 Krug   0
1981 Paternoster Row   0
1982 John French   1 GW
1983 High Debate   0
1984 Ulterior Motive   2 GW
1985 Highland Chieftain 2 GW
1986 Grand Tour   0
1987 Upper Strata   Non-runner
1988 Mamaluna   1 GW
1989 Rock Hopper   1 GW
1990 Matahif   0
1991 Bonny Scot   2 GW
1992 Bob's Return   3 GW
1993 Double Trigger   1 GW
1994 Double Eclipse   1
1995 Gentilhomme   0
1996 Silver Patriarch   2 GW
1997 Trigger Happy

Silver Patriarch won last year's St Leger after finishing runner-up in the Derby. Previous winners of this race include the good four-year-olds Double Eclipse and Rock Hopper, Bob's Return (the second St Leger winner in this list) and the Ascot Gold Cup winner Double Trigger - surely the most notable of them all. Trigger Happy is closely related to the high-class middle-distance colt Snurge, but his forte should be as a stayer.

Laurent Perrier Champagne Stakes
Doncaster, 7 furlongs, September.

1980 Gielgud   Non-runner
1981 Achieved   1 GW
1982 Gorytus   0
1983 Lear Fan   2 GW

1984 Young Runaway   2 GW
1985 Sure Blade   3 GW
1986 Don't Forget Me   2 GW
1987 Warning   3 GW
1988 Prince of Dance   0
1989 ABANDONED
1990 Bog Trotter   2 GW
1991 Rodrigo de Triano   4 GW
1992 Petardia   1
1993 Unblest   1 GW
1994 Sri Pekan   Non-runner
1995 Alhaarth   1 GW
1996 Bahhare   0
1997 Daggers Drawn

Despite the odd disappointing year, this race continues to be of major importance as far as the following season's big 3-y-o races are concerned. Rodrigo de Triano and Don't Forget Me won both the English and Irish 2,000 Guineas and Warning was arguably the most talented of them all. Daggers Drawn put up a most discouraging performance in the Dewhurst Stakes and it is to be hoped that he will find his true form once again this season. If he does, then another Group race should fall to him - probably at distances no more than seven furlongs.

Coventry Stakes
Royal Ascot, 6 furlongs, June.

1980 Recitation   2 GW
1981 Red Sunset   0
1982 Horage   1 GW
1983 Chief Singer   3 GW
1984 Primo Dominie   1 GW
1985 Sure Blade   3 GW
1986 Cutting Blade   1
1987 Always Fair   1 GW
1988 High Estate   1
1989 Rock City   2 GW
1990 Mac's Imp   0
1991 Dilum   2 GW
1992 Petardia   1
1993 Stonehatch   Non-runner
1994 Sri Pekan   Non-runner
1995 Royal Applause   1
1996 Verglas   0
1997 Harbour Master

This race has proved a little disappointing in the last five seasons, but previously it's record for throwing up high-class horses was excellent. Perhaps the best amongst those listed is Jeff Smith's popular sprinter/miler Chief Singer. Harbour Master has reportedly been sold to race abroad.

Cheveley Park Stakes
Newmarket, 6 furlongs, October.

1980	Marwell	5 GW
1981	Woodstream	0
1982	Ma Biche	3 GW
1983	Desirable	0
1984	Park Appeal	0
1985	Embla	1
1986	Forest Flower (Disq)	1 GW
1987	Ravinella	4 GW
1988	Pass the Peace	0
1989	Dead Certain	1 GW
1990	Capricciosa	Non-runner
1991	Marling	3 GW
1992	Sayyedati	2 GW
1993	Prophecy	0
1994	Gay Gallanta	0
1995	Blue Duster	1
1996	Pas de Reponse	2 GW
1997	Embassy	

Arguably unlucky when finishing a close second to Cape Verdi in the Lowther Stakes, Embassy gained her revenge in this race. A very smart and genuine filly, if she stays a mile it will take a good filly to lower her colours in the 1,000 Guineas. If she doesn't stay, then expect her to perform with credit in the season's major sprint races.

Cherry Hinton Stakes
Newmarket, 6 furlongs, July.

1980	Nasseem	1
1981	Travel On	0
1982	Crime of Passion	0
1983	Chapel Cottage	0
1984	Top Socialite	1 GW
1985	Storm Star	0
1986	Forest Flower	1 GW
1987	Diminuendo	4 GW
1988	Kerrera	1
1989	Chimes of Freedom	2 GW
1990	Chicarica	0
1991	Musicale	1 GW
1992	Sayyedati	2 GW
1993	Lemon Souffle	1 GW
1994	Red Carnival	0
1995	Applaud	0
1996	Dazzle	1
1997	Asfurah	

There have been some top-notch winners of this event in the period under review, notably the 3-y-o Group 1 winners Forest Flower, Diminuendo, Chimes of Freedom and Sayyedati. A daughter of Dayjur, I doubt Asfurah staying a mile in the highest company, but a successful sprinting campaign beckons her this year.

Washington Singer Stakes
Newbury, 6 furlongs, August.

1980	Poldhu	1
1981	Custer	0
1982	Horage	1 GW
1983	Trojan Fen	2 GW
1984	Khozaam	0
1985	Faustus	2 GW
1986	Deputy Governor	0
1987	Emmson	0
1988	Prince of Dance	1 (DISQ)
1989	Karinga Bay	1 GW
1990	Heart of Darkness	0
1991	Rodrigo de Triano	4 GW
1992	Tenby	2 GW
1993	Colonel Collins	0
1994	Lammtarra	3 GW
1995	Mons	0
1996	State Fair	0
1997	Bahr	

As can be seen from the table, this race quite often provides us with Group or Classic pointers and in that regard Lammtarra and Rodrigo de Triano were outstanding. I was quite impressed with Bahr's performance in winning this race and I certainly expect her to continue her winning ways this year. A mile will prove no problem and she just might run a big race in the Oaks.

Lanson Champage Stakes
Goodwood, 7 furlongs, July.

1980	Church Parade	1
1981	Treboro	0
1982	All Systems Go	0
1983	Trojan Fen	2 GW
1984	Petoski	2 GW
1985	Faustus	2 GW
1986	Don't Forget Me	2 GW
1987	Undercut	0
1988	High Estate	1
1989	Be My Chief	0
1990	Mukaddamah	1 GW
1991	Dr Devious	2 GW
1992	Maroof	1
1993	Mister Baileys	1 GW
1994	Eltish	0
1995	Alhaarth	1 GW
1996	Putra	0
1997	Central Park	

All in all, this race is very informative in terms of sorting out future stars, with the classic winners Don't Forget Me, Dr Devious and Mister Baileys and the King George winner Petoski standing out. Central Park was a major disappointment in the Dewhurst Stakes when he surely failed to show his true form. He will win more races and will stay at least a mile.

National Stakes
Curragh, 1 mile, September.

1980	Storm Bird	0
1981	Day Is Done	0
1982	Glenstal	1 GW
1983	El Gran Senor	3 GW
1984	Law Society	2 GW
1985	Tate Gallery	0
1986	Lockton	3
1987	Caerwent	2
1988	Classic Fame	1 GW
1989	Dashing Blade	2 GW
1990	Heart Of Darkness	0
1991	El Prado	0
1992	Fatherland	0
1993	Manntari	1
1994	Definite Article	1
1995	Danehill Dancer	1 GW
1996	Desert King	3 GW
1997	King Of Kings	

Through his wins in the Irish 2,000 Guineas and the Irish Derby, Desert King has brought this race back into the limelight following a relatively disappointing run. Trainer Aidan O'Brien will be hoping King Of Kings can emulate his stable companion Desert King this season. On his bare form he needs to improve considerably to win a classic, but he is highly thought of at Ballydoyle. A son of Sadler's Wells, King Of Kings should certainly improve enough to win an important race or two.

Racing Post Trophy
Doncaster, 8 furlongs, October.

1980	Beldale Flutter	2 GW
1981	Count Pahlen	1 GW
1982	Dunbeath	0
1983	Alphabatim	3 GW
1984	Lanfranco	2 GW
1985	Bakharoff	1 GW
1986	Reference Point	5 GW
1987	Emmson	0
1988	Al Hareb	0
1989	Be My Chief	0
1990	Peter Davies	0
1991	Seattle Rhyme	0
1992	Armiger	1 GW
1993	King's Theatre	2 GW
1994	Celtic Swing	2 GW
1995	Beauchamp King	1 GW
1996	Medaaly	0
1997	Saratoga Springs	

Despite a disappointing five-year period in the middle of this table, the Racing Post Trophy seems to have regained its former status as an important classic pointer. Trainer Aidan O'Brien has a number of high-class colts and Saratoga Springs is reportedly to be trained for the Kentucky Derby. He improved throughout 1997 and can continue to do so this year and win good races.

Sandown Futurity Conditions Stakes
September, 1m.

1980	Obrovac	0
1981	ABANDONED	
1982	Magic Rarity	Non-runner
1983	Forest of Dean	2
1984	Lord Grundy	1
1985	Dancing Brave	6 GW
1986	Reference Point	5 GW
1987	Albadr	1
1988	Mired	0
1989	Elmaamul	3 GW
1990	Generous	3 GW
1991	King's Loch	1
1992	Geisway	1
1993	Overbury	1 GW
1994	Dreamer	0
1995	Inchrory	Raced abroad
1996	Barnum Sands	1
1997	Setteen	

Most of these previous winners managed to win as a 3-y-o and four of them - Dancing Brave, Reference Point, Elmaamul and Generous - were top-class. Now with Godolphin, Setteen may not be a name on everyone's lips, but he is a useful colt and one to watch out for in races of a mile or more.

Blue Seal Stakes
Ascot, 6 furlongs, September.

1980	Petroleuse	1 GW
1981	Dancing Rocks	1 GW
1982	Khaizaraan	0
1983	Rappa Tap Tap	1
1984	Dafayna	2 GW
1985	Sonic Lady	6 GW
1986	White Mischief	0
1987	New Trends	0
1988	Ensconse	2 GW
1989	Alwathba	0
1990	Crystal Gazing	1 GW
1991	Misterioso	0
1992	Queens View	1
1993	Tablah	0
1994	Marha	1
1995	Polska	0
1996	Lochangel	0
1997	Wenda	

This race is due for a change of fortune - the past six fillies having disappointed as 3-y-o's. Wenda finished last in the Rockfel Stakes but is surely better than that. She is no Sonic Lady or

Ensconse (previous Blue Seal Stakes winners) but should win another race this year. Her campaign started off well with a second in the Fred Darling Stakes.

Soham House Stakes
Newmarket, 8 furlongs, October.

1980	Video Tape	0
1981	Dudley Wood	4
1982	Coming and Going	0
1983	Sassagras	0
1984	Verdance	2
1985	Dancing Brave	6 GW
1986	Pillar of Wisdom	0
1987	Kahyasi	4 GW
1988	Warrshan	2 GW
1989	Belmez	4 GW
	(Carlsburg Stakes)	
1990	Polish King	0
1991	Hill Glitter	0
1992	Shaiba	1
1993	King of Naples	1
1994	Pipe Major	1 GW
1995	Believe Me	0
1996	River Usk	0
1997	Rabah	

This race had a great period in the late Eighties with winners like Dancing Brave, the top-class colts Kahyasi and Belmez and the dual Group winner Warrshan. A well-bred colt, Rabah is not in their class, but he is a distinctly useful colt and will win again at around a mile or ten furlongs this season.

Sunday Conditions Stakes (formerly the Mornington Stakes)
Ascot, 7 furlongs, September.

1980	Centurius	1 GW
1981	General Anders	0
1982	By Decree	0
1983	Donzel	0
1984	Tour d'Or	0
1985	Zahdam	1 GW
1986	Ajdal	4 GW
1987	Sheriff's Star	2 GW
1988	Shaadi	3 GW
1989	Shavian	2 GW
1990	Big Blow	Non runner
1991	Assessor	2 GW
1992	Inchinor	3 GW
1993	Mutakddim	3
1994	Wijara	1
1995	Story Line	0
1996	Kahal	2 GW
1997	Mudeer	

As a precursor to better things, this event has an exceptional record for a non-pattern race.

Previous winners include the Champion sprinter Ajdal and the high-class colts Inchinor, Sheriff's Star, Shaadi and Shavian. Kahal too, proved himself a very smart colt towards the end of last season. Last year's winner, the beautifully-bred colt Mudeer, went on to finish second in the Racing Post Trophy. He will stay at least ten furlongs this year and can surely win again.

May Hill Stakes
Doncaster, 8 furlongs, September.

1980	Exclusively Raised	0
1981	Height of Fashion	2 GW
1982	Bright Crocus	Non runner
1983	Satinette	0
1984	Ever Genial	2 GW
1985	Midway Lady	2 GW
1986	Laluche	0
1987	Intimate Guest	1
1988	Tessla	0
1989	Rafha	3 GW
1990	Majmu	0
1991	Midnight Air	0
1992	Marillette	1 GW
1993	Hawajiss	2 GW
1994	Mamlakah	0
1995	Solar Crystal	0
1996	Reams of Verse	2 GW
1997	Midnight Line	

Henry Cecil has a superb record in this race. He was on the mark in 1996 with the subsequent Oaks winner Reams of Verse and Midnight Line kept up the tradition in 1997. Although she may not be absolutely top-class, she seems sure to continue to make her presence felt in Group company as a 3-y-o. She will stay ten furlongs, perhaps twelve, and it will be fascinating to see just how good she really is. We may not have seen the best of her yet.

Fillies Conditions Race
Newbury, 7 furlongs, September.

1980	NO RACE	
1981	NO RACE	
1982	Salvinia	1
1983	Mahogany	1 GW
1984	Dubian	1
1985	Mill On The Floss	1
1986	Milligram	3 GW
1987	Andaleeb	1 GW
1988	Samaza	0
1989	Free At Last	1 (In USA)
1990	Fragrant Hill	1
1991	Freewheel	1
1992	Sueboog	1 GW
1993	Balanchine	2 GW
1994	Musetta	1

1995	Wild Rumour	0
1996	Etoile	0
1997	Amabel	

Races at around a mile will probably suit Amabel this year. A daughter of the good American sire Silver Hawk, she doesn't appear to be a high-class filly, but listed or possibly Group 3 events may not be beyond her. The brilliant fillies Balanchine and Milligram stand out in this group.

Haynes, Hanson and Clark Stakes
Newbury, 8 furlongs, September.

1980	Shergar	5 GW
1981	Super Sunrise	1 GW
1982	Polished Silver	0
1983	Rainbow Quest	1 GW
1984	Northern River	0
1985	My Ton Ton	0
1986	Thameen	1
1987	Unfuwain	3 GW
1988	Star Shareef	0
1989	Tanfith	0
1990	Prince Russanor	1
1991	Zinaad	1
1992	Pembroke	1
1993	King's Theatre	2 GW
1994	Munwar	2 GW
1995	Mick's Love	1
1996	King Sound	1
1997	Duck Row	

Shergar, Rainbow Quest, Unfuwain and King's Theatre are a hard act to follow and it will be surprising if Duck Row is as good as they were. Nonetheless, he is a distinctly promising colt and can win more races over ten furlongs or more. His disappointing run in the Horris Hill Stakes should be discounted.

Fillies Mile
Ascot, 8 furlongs, September.

1980	Leap Lively	1 GW
1981	Height of Fashion	2 GW
1982	Acclimatise	1 GW
1983	Nepula	0
1984	Oh So Sharp	4 GW
1985	Untold	1 GW
1986	Invited Guest	1 GW
1987	Diminuendo	4 GW
1988	Tessla	0
1989	Silk Slippers	0
1990	Shamshir	0
1991	Midnight Air	0
1992	Ivanka	0
1993	Fairy Heights	0
1994	Aqaarid	1 GW
1995	Bosra Sham	3 GW
1996	Reams of Verse	2 GW

1997	Glorosia

A desperately poor run for this race was halted by Aqaarid who won the Fred Darling Stakes and was placed in the 1,000 Guineas. Bosra Sham and Reams of Verse did much more than that. In fact Bosra Sham's performances were outstanding and certainly bear comparison with that of the Fillies Triple Crown heroine Oh So Sharp. Glorosia should relish distances of ten furlongs or more and the Oaks is a distinct possibility.

Prestige Stakes
Goodwood, 7 furlongs, August.

1980	Fairy Footsteps	2 GW
1981	Stratospheric	0
1982	Flamenco	0
1983	Shoot Clear	0
1984	Bella Colora	2 GW
1985	Asteroid Field	1
1986	Invited Guest	1 GW
1987	Obeah	0
1988	Life At The Top	0
1989	Moon Cactus	1 GW
1990	Jaffa Line	0
1991	Musicale	1 GW
1992	Love Of Silver	0
1993	Glatisant	0
1994	Pure Grain	3 GW
1995	Bint Shadayid	0
1996	Red Camellia	0
1997	Midnight Line	

The winners of this race are inevitably tried in top company as 3-y-o's. Going by the results, it seems they are either destined to win at least one more Group race or else nothing at all. Midnight Line, who also won the May Hill Stakes last year, was a May foal and there may yet be further improvement in her. If so, then more Group races over middle-distances would seem to be on the cards.

Moorestyle Convivial Stakes
York, 6 furlongs, August.

1980	Sweet Pleasure	0
1981	Rebollino	0
1982	Diana's Pet	0
1983	Double Schwartz	2
1984	Local Suitor	0
1985	Sit This One Out	0
1986	Bali Magic	1
1987	Brilliant Bay	0
1988	Danehill	3 GW
1989	In The Groove	4 GW
1990	Jallad	0
1991	Great Palm	1 GW
1992	Revelation	1 GW

1993	Owington	3 GW
1994	Green Perfume	0
1995	Desert Boy	0
1996	Indiscreet	1
1997	Bintang	

Since 1988 the winners of this race have included the high-class sprinters Double Schwartz and Owington, the very smart ten furlong colt Great Palm and, best of all, the cracking eight to twelve furlong filly In The Groove. Green Perfume and Desert Boy were also very useful 3-y-o's, despite failing to win at that age (Green Perfume actually won three races as a 4-y-o and Desert Boy was disqualified after winning the Prix Eugene Adam). Bintang is by the high-class miler Soviet Star and out of an Ahonoora mare. As such, he'll probably be suited by distances up to a mile. He can win again.

Girton Maiden
Newmarket, 7 furlongs, August.

1980	Clear Verdict	0
1981	Hayakaze	1
1982	Alligatrix	0
1983	Rainbow Quest	1 GW
1984	Koffi	0
1985	Stage Hand	0
1986	Roman Gunner	1
1987	Sheriff's Star	2 GW
1988	Lady Shipley	1
1989	Marienski	0
1990	Shamshir	0
1991	First Century	1
1992	Emperor Jones	1 GW
1993	Innishowen	0
1994	Classic Cliche	2 GW
1995	Even Top	1 GW
1996	Yalaietanee	1 GW
1997	Fantasy Island	

An intriguing maiden this, with the four-year-old dual Group 1 winners Rainbow Quest and Sheriff's Star, the St Leger and Gold Cup winner Classic Cliche and the smart colts Emperor Jones and Even Top catching the eye. The Zafonic colt, Fantasy Island, failed to reappear after winning this race impressively in 1997, but if all is well with him he is surely a colt of some potential. Now with Godolphin, I would expect him to stay ten furlongs without a problem and he is certainly a most interesting three-year-old.

Somerville Tattersall Stakes
Newmarket, 7 furlongs, September/October.

1980	Spark Of Life	1
1981	Wind and Wuthering	0
1982	Polished Silver	0

1983	Round Hill	0
1984	Damister	3 GW
1985	Truely Nureyev	0
1986	Imperial Frontier	1
1987	Salse	5 GW
1988	Opening Verse	1
1989	Free At Last	1 (in USA)
1990	Peter Davies	0
1991	Tertian	0
1992	Nominator	0
1993	Grand Lodge	1 GW
1994	Annus Mirabilis	1
1995	Even Top	1 GW
1996	Grapeshot	1
1997	Haami	

The bare figures in this table don't really tell the whole story, for there are some very good horses here. The Group winners speak for themselves but Opening Verse, Free At Last and Annus Mirabilis all went on to win good races abroad whilst Wind and Wuthering was second in the 2,000 Guineas. On breeding, one would expect Haami to stay at least ten furlongs, but the speed he showed in this race has me doubting that somehow. Potentially a high-class horse, there are surely some Group races to be won with him this year.

Westley Maiden Stakes
Newmarket, 7 furlongs, September.

1980	Kings Glory	1
1981	Simply Great	1 GW
1982	DIV 1 Tolomeo	1 GW
	DIV 2 Mandelstam	0
1983	Chelkov	0
1984	Profess	0
1985	DIV 1 Cromwell Park	1
	DIV 2 Illumineux	0
1986	DIV1 Pollenate	0
	DIV 2 Tweeter	0
1987	DIV 1 Doyoun	2 GW
	DIV 2 Charmer	0
1988	DIV 1 Pirate Army	1
	DIV 2 Observation Post	0
1989	DIV 1 Mukddaam	1
	DIV 2 Cutting Note	0
1990	DIV 1 Environment Friend	2 GW
	DIV 2 Sapieha	0
1991	DIV 1 Modernise	0
	DIV 2 Pursuit of Love	3 GW
1992	DIV 1 Placerville	2 GW
	DIV 2 Barathea	1 GW
1993	Darnay	0
1994	DIV 1 Painter's Row	1 GW
	DIV 2 Smart Alec	Non-runner
1995	Astor Place	1
1996	Mashhaer	0

1997 Quiet Assurance

Despite Quiet Assurance proving himself a very useful colt last year, he does seem some way short of classic material. I suspect that unless he races abroad, listed events will be just about his limit. Even so, that does mean he is good enough to win more races. This race really came into its own in 1987 when Doyoun went on to capture the 2,000 Guineas at the expense of Charmer. Subsequently, Environment Friend won the Eclipse, Placerville the Prince of Wales's Stakes, Pursuit of Love a Group 3 event in France before just getting pipped in the July Cup, Barathea won the Breeders Cup Mile and Painter's Row the Craven Stakes. Not a bad record for a 2-y-o maiden!

TIMEFORM STATISTICAL REVIEW

The following tables are extracted from the 'Timeform Statistical Review' which provides detailed and innovative statistics on hundreds of trainers and sires, including a written analysis of about a hundred top performers by Timeform's team of experts. The tables selected here relate only to achievements with two-year-olds.

The 'Timeform Statistical Review' includes an important development on the mass of previous racing statistics in its extensive use of Timeform Ratings which are internationally renowned as the most accurate measure of a horse's racing merit. The median Timeform Ratings are a measure of average ability.

		Strike rate %	Wins-Runs	Strike rate % first time	Wins-Runs	Strike rate % second time	Wins-Runs	Stable 2-y-o median rtg
1	H. R. A. Cecil	38	86-229	36	41-114	41	26-63	87
2	N. J. H. Walker	33	1-3	50	1-2	0	0-1	53
3	Saeed bin Suroor	32	35-111	33	17-51	29	9-31	93
4	D. R. Loder	27	75-279	26	32-121	29	22-76	80
5	D. Burchell	25	1-4	0	0-2	100	1-1	39
6	M. C. Pipe	22	4-18	22	2-9	20	1-5	55
7	J. F. Bottomley	21	3-14	0	0-3	33	1-3	53
8	P. W. Chapple-Hyam	20	61-301	18	20-110	26	23-88	84
	L. M. Cumani	20	41-205	13	11-83	28	17-60	80
10	J. H. M. Gosden	19	62-334	8	12-150	31	28-91	76
	J. A. R. Toller	19	11-59	17	3-18	7	1-15	71
12	B. W. Hills	18	101-554	13	24-179	21	29-140	78
	Sir Mark Prescott	18	61-340	10	9-94	20	16-82	69
14	P. F. I. Cole	17	92-543	20	33-169	16	22-137	78
	J. L. Dunlop	17	105-621	10	19-195	20	33-167	76
	M. R. Stoute	17	54-324	13	19-146	18	16-89	78
17	I. A. Balding	16	45-286	4	4-99	21	15-71	71
	R. Charlton	16	30-191	11	8-71	13	7-52	76
19	R. W. Armstrong	15	17-111	5	2-40	12	3-26	76
	J. Berry	15	129-877	13	21-159	14	20-145	61
	Mrs J. Cecil	15	8-55	14	3-21	0	0-11	68
	M. Johnston	15	112-752	11	20-189	17	29-174	70
	D. Morley	15	20-133	10	4-41	13	5-38	76
	A. C. Stewart	15	7-46	17	5-29	9	1-11	71
	Mrs L. Stubbs	15	5-34	8	1-12	25	2-8	49

1	H. R. A. Cecil	21	M. A. Jarvis	3	Miss Gay Kelleway	1
	P. W. Chapple-Hyam	21	G. Lewis	3	G. G. Margarson	1
3	J. L. Dunlop	16	J. A. R. Toller	3	K. McAuliffe	1
4	B. W. Hills	15	P. T. Walwyn	3	B. A. McMahon	1
	D. R. Loder	15	25 M. Bell	2	B. R. Millman	1
6	J. H. M. Gosden	13	M. R. Channon	2	Mrs J. R. Ramsden	1
7	P. F. I. Cole	12	B. Hanbury	2	A. C. Stewart	1
	Saeed bin Suroor	12	M. H. Tompkins	2	W. G. M. Turner	1
9	R. Hannon	9	G. Wragg	2	J. W. Watts	1
	M. Johnston	9	30 J. Berry	1	S. P. C. Woods	1
	M. R. Stoute	9	M. Blanshard	1		
12	I. A. Balding	8	R. Boss	1		
	L. M. Cumani	8	N. A. Callaghan	1		
14	Sir Mark Prescott	7	R. Charlton	1		
15	C. E. Brittain	5	J. L. Eyre	1		
	E. A. L. Dunlop	5	N. A. Graham	1		
17	B. J. Meehan	4	D. Haydn Jones	1		
	D. Morley	4	J. W. Hills	1		
19	R. W. Armstrong	3	A. P. Jarvis	1		
	Major W. R. Hern	3	W. Jarvis	1		

Sires by Timeform 2-y-o median ratings in Britain 1994-97
For sires with at least 15 two-year-old runners

		Median Rating	C & G Median	No. Colts & Geldings	Fillies Median	No. Fillies	No. Horses	Winners	Wins	Win Money
1	Zafonic (USA)	94	97	7	81	8	15	9	11	£168,145
2	Danzig (USA)	87	87	16	86	16	32	19	28	£336,374
3	Nashwan (USA)	86	86	22	83	18	40	19	29	£272,216
4	Mr Prospector (USA)	84	81	12	87	17	29	14	21	£162,064
5	Machiavellian (USA)	83	87	21	81	15	36	17	20	£102,459
6	El Gran Senor (USA)	82	84	20	76	11	31	15	17	£168,572
	Gone West (USA)	82	85	15	81	13	28	14	20	£191,520
	Silver Hawk (USA)	82	83	21	77	11	32	10	15	£151,380
9	Dixieland Band (USA)	81	85	12	81	3	15	5	6	£45,421
	Warning	81	81	49	80	33	82	36	50	£225,499
11	Dayjur (USA)	80	83	12	80	24	36	20	28	£253,582
	Generous (IRE)	80	83	29	69	20	49	15	23	£183,720
	Nureyev (USA)	80	84	14	72	14	28	9	15	£183,125
	Storm Bird (CAN)	80	93	6	69	9	15	7	7	£26,405
15	Diesis	79	80	33	72	17	50	21	27	£213,500
16	Caerleon (USA)	78	81	30	74	27	57	18	23	£190,924
17	Alleged (USA)	77	78	17	65	6	23	4	4	£16,092
	Brief Truce (USA)	77	78	9	76	13	22	4	4	£13,802
	Kris	77	79	31	75	21	52	17	19	£88,147
	Lear Fan (USA)	77	77	18	77	6	24	8	10	£43,259
	Red Ransom (USA)	77	78	23	70	5	28	12	18	£157,941
	Riverman (USA)	77	78	15	73	13	28	7	9	£38,518
23	Danehill (USA)	76	76	58	72	34	92	30	38	£153,390
	Green Desert (USA)	76	77	59	76	40	99	37	49	£266,060
	Known Fact (USA)	76	80	13	71	7	20	7	9	£54,065
	Marju (IRE)	76	79	26	67	13	39	16	18	£78,624
	Woodman (USA)	76	71	27	78	30	57	16	21	£318,390
	Zilzal (USA)	76	77	17	74	10	27	9	12	£53,143
29	Fairy King (USA)	75	78	37	67	36	73	27	36	£182,530
	Sadler's Wells (USA)	75	83	38	72	32	70	17	19	£177,473
31	Darshaan	74	75	22	72	7	29	9	10	£41,173
	Groom Dancer (USA)	74	75	18	70	9	27	8	11	£52,624
	In The Wings	74	71	18	74	14	32	7	9	£84,710
	Lahib (USA)	74	79	7	68	14	21	9	11	£70,842
	Royal Academy (USA)	74	79	37	69	31	68	26	30	£160,429
	Selkirk (USA)	74	76	15	66	20	35	14	19	£97,896
	Shaadi (USA)	74	81	12	71	19	31	17	18	£80,465
	Wolfhound (USA)	74	78	8	70	13	21	5	6	£22,861
39	Alzao (USA)	73	75	57	71	44	101	39	44	£211,958
	Arazi (USA)	73	76	11	70	7	18	4	6	£23,457
	Cadeaux Genereux	73	72	30	73	29	59	21	30	£339,429
	Indian Ridge	73	80	41	67	26	67	21	33	£191,649
	Lion Cavern (USA)	73	79	11	68	11	22	7	9	£30,148
	Shadeed (USA)	73	73	12	80	5	17	4	6	£47,374
45	Pursuit of Love	72	76	20	71	11	31	9	13	£62,273
	Rainbow Quest (USA)	72	72	23	72	24	47	12	13	£53,769

		Median Rating	C & G Median	No. Colts & Geldings	Fillies Median	No. fillies	No. Horses	Winners	Wins	Win Money
47	Last Tycoon	71	80	21	67	37	58	22	28	£108,340
	Lycius (USA)	71	75	25	66	18	43	16	21	£95,816
	Mujtahid (USA)	71	72	27	69	25	52	22	29	£136,908
	Polish Precedent (USA)	71	76	22	65	12	34	8	10	£57,610
	Shirley Heights	71	73	30	71	31	61	16	19	£87,451
52	Mtoto	70	73	19	63	20	39	11	13	£66,126
	Night Shift (USA)	70	71	45	69	50	95	28	38	£240,125
	Salse (USA)	70	72	33	65	40	73	21	25	£147,543
55	Mujadil (USA)	69	65	15	70	20	35	19	35	£134,622
	Thatching	69	69	30	70	15	45	16	23	£82,450
57	Scenic	68	73	19	66	13	32	6	8	£40,636
	Soviet Star (USA)	68	76	19	66	22	41	7	9	£42,756
	Unfuwain (USA)	68	70	19	67	24	43	12	18	£278,177
60	Distant Relative	67	66	26	69	30	56	20	25	£139,964
	Pips Pride	67	70	14	65	10	24	7	7	£21,353
	Polar Falcon (USA)	67	76	25	63	28	53	20	28	£150,189
	Primo Dominie	67	77	38	64	43	81	33	43	£162,761
	Saddlers' Hall (IRE)	67	72	7	64	19	26	6	7	£29,110
65	Damister (USA)	66	68	9	63	17	26	5	7	£116,456
	Emarati (USA)	66	71	28	60	26	54	19	32	£121,066
	Persian Bold	66	67	33	63	19	52	10	16	£109,623

Sires by 2-y-o's rated Timeform 100+ in Britain 1995-97

1 Green Desert (USA)	11	
2 Danzig (USA)	10	
3 Diesis	9	
Nashwan (USA)	9	
Royal Academy (USA)	9	
6 Warning	8	
7 Caerleon (USA)	7	
8 Cadeaux Genereux	6	
Mr Prospector (USA)	6	
Woodman (USA)	6	
11 Fairy King (USA)	5	
Gone West (USA)	5	
13 Alzao (USA)	4	
Danehill (USA)	4	
Dayjur (USA)	4	
El Gran Senor (USA)	4	
Generous (IRE)	4	
Indian Ridge	4	
Lycius (USA)	4	
Machiavellian (USA)	4	
Mujtahid (USA)	4	
Polar Falcon (USA)	4	
Salse (USA)	4	
Selkirk (USA)	4	
Silver Hawk (USA)	4	

Zafonic (USA)	4
27 Bering	3
Common Grounds	3
Darshaan	3
Distant Relative	3
Dixieland Band (USA)	3
Groom Dancer (USA)	3
Lear Fan (USA)	3
Miswaki (USA)	3
Nureyev (USA)	3
Rainbow Quest (USA)	3
Robellino (USA)	3
Sadler's Wells (USA)	3
Soviet Star (USA)	3
Storm Bird (CAN)	3
Unfuwain (USA)	3
42 Be My Chief (USA)	2
Dancing Dissident (USA)	2
Deploy	2
Distinctly North (USA)	2
Elmaamul (USA)	2
Forty Niner (USA)	2
Forzando	2
Great Commotion (USA)	2
Hansel (USA)	2
Highest Honor (FR)	2

In The Wings	2
Irish River (FR)	2
Known Fact (USA)	2
Kris	2
Kris S (USA)	2
Law Society (USA)	2
Magic Ring (IRE)	2
Mt Livermore (USA)	2
Persian Bold	2
Petardia	2
Polish Precedent (USA)	2
Primo Dominie	2
Prince Sabo	2
Rahy (USA)	2
Red Ransom (USA)	2
Reprimand	2
Sabrehill (USA)	2
Scottish Reel	2
Shadeed (USA)	2
Shareef Dancer (USA)	2
St Jovite (USA)	2
Then Again	2
Tirol	2
Trempolino (USA)	2
Waajib	2

Sires by winning 2-y-o's percentage in Britain 1994-97
For sires with at least 10 two-year-old winners

		Winning Horse %	Horses	Winners	Wins	Runs	Wins/Runs %	Median Rtg
1	Anita's Prince	65	17	11	15	106	14	59
2	Danzig (USA)	59	32	19	28	92	30	87
3	Dayjur (USA)	56	36	20	28	96	29	80
4	Shaadi (USA)	55	31	17	18	116	16	74
5	Mujadil (USA)	54	35	19	35	243	14	69
6	Lugana Beach	52	25	13	20	131	15	60
7	Gone West (USA)	50	28	14	20	75	27	82
8	El Gran Senor (USA)	48	31	15	17	81	21	82
	Mr Prospector (USA)	48	29	14	21	61	34	84
	Nashwan (USA)	48	40	19	29	91	32	86
11	Machiavellian (USA)	47	36	17	20	84	24	83
12	Tragic Role (USA)	44	25	11	13	104	13	59
	Warning	44	82	36	50	256	20	81
14	Elmaamul (USA)	43	37	16	22	144	15	63
	Red Ransom (USA)	43	28	12	18	90	20	77
16	Diesis	42	50	21	27	122	22	79
	Mujtahid (USA)	42	52	22	29	187	16	71
18	Marju (IRE)	41	39	16	18	145	12	76
	Polish Patriot (USA)	41	46	19	26	211	12	63
	Primo Dominie	41	81	33	43	344	13	67
21	Selkirk (USA)	40	35	14	19	92	21	74
22	Alzao (USA)	39	101	39	44	344	13	73
	Imp Society (USA)	39	28	11	14	147	10	61
	Komaite (USA)	39	46	18	25	219	11	61
	Timeless Times (USA)	39	56	22	35	356	10	54
26	Ballad Rock	38	39	15	17	132	13	65
	Efisio	38	84	32	52	383	14	59
	Last Tycoon	38	58	22	28	190	15	71
	Polar Falcon (USA)	38	53	20	28	165	17	67
	Royal Academy (USA)	38	68	26	30	200	15	74
	Soviet Lad (USA)	38	29	11	14	149	9	56
32	Fairy King (USA)	37	73	27	36	228	16	75
	Green Desert (USA)	37	99	37	49	277	18	76
	Lycius (USA)	37	43	16	21	140	15	71
	Sharpo	37	49	18	22	196	11	65
36	Cadeaux Genereux	36	59	21	30	174	17	73
	Distant Relative	36	56	20	25	225	11	67
	Thatching	36	45	16	23	151	15	69
39	Emarati (USA)	35	54	19	32	265	12	66
	Mazilier (USA)	35	49	17	26	300	9	54
	Statoblest	35	84	29	40	345	12	61
42	Pharly (FR)	34	35	12	14	138	10	64
	Rudimentary (USA)	34	35	12	14	146	10	61
44	Aragon	33	58	19	24	243	10	58
	Danehill (USA)	33	92	30	38	286	13	76
	Dowsing (USA)	33	36	12	21	154	14	61
	Kris	33	52	17	19	129	15	77

Sires by number of wins in Britain 1997—Two-year-olds

	Sire	Wins	Horses	Wnrs	1997 2-y-o Median Rating		Sire	Wins	Horses	Wnrs	1997 2-y-o Median Rating
1	Mujadil (USA)	22	21	11	71		Paris House	10	15	6	50
2	Warning	16	28	11	82		Petong	10	24	8	62
3	Greensmith	14	6	4	61	23	Ballad Rock	9	13	8	69
4	Diesis	13	14	9	96		Elmaamul (USA)	9	18	7	63
	Efisio	13	21	8	63		Last Tycoon	9	17	8	79
	Statoblest	13	24	8	66		Lion Cavern (USA)	9	22	7	73
7	Petardia	12	34	7	51		Polar Falcon (USA)	9	19	8	70
8	Alzao (USA)	11	30	10	72		Rambo Dancer (CAN)	9	15	8	53
	Cadeaux Genereux	11	14	7	71		Risk Me (FR)	9	36	6	40
	Forzando	11	13	8	67	30	Danehill (USA)	8	19	7	82
	Mukaddamah (USA)	11	8	4	63		Danzig (USA)	8	8	7	102
	Nashwan (USA)	11	9	6	92		Don't Forget Me	8	11	5	59
	Zafonic (USA)	11	15	9	94		Green Desert (USA)	8	21	6	72
14	Beveled (USA)	10	26	7	49		Hamas (IRE)	8	7	3	71
	Common Grounds	10	22	6	63		High Estate	8	13	5	69
	Distinctly North (USA)	10	19	8	64		Inchinor	8	13	4	60
	Fairy King (USA)	10	31	8	69		Komaite (USA)	8	16	8	62
	Generous (IRE)	10	19	7	79		Magic Ring (IRE)	8	21	7	62
	Mujtahid (USA)	10	16	7	72		Royal Academy (USA)	8	16	7	74
	Night Shift (USA)	10	36	10	70		Selkirk (USA)	8	19	6	67

Sires by number of wins in Britain 1994-97—Two-year-olds

	Sire	Wins	Horses	Wnrs	2-y-o Median Rating		Sire	Wins	Horses	Wnrs	2-y-o Median Rating
1	Efisio	52	84	32	59	27	Mujtahid (USA)	29	52	22	71
2	Warning	50	82	36	81		Nashwan (USA)	29	40	19	86
3	Green Desert (USA)	49	99	37	76		Reprimand	29	82	22	60
4	Alzao (USA)	44	101	39	73	30	Danzig (USA)	28	32	19	87
	Prince Sabo	44	92	29	60		Dayjur (USA)	28	36	20	80
6	Primo Dominie	43	81	33	67		Last Tycoon	28	58	22	71
	Risk Me (FR)	43	135	30	48		Polar Falcon (USA)	28	53	20	67
8	Statoblest	40	84	29	61		Rock City	28	73	22	59
9	Distinctly North (USA)	39	74	23	59	35	Diesis	27	50	21	79
10	Beveled (USA)	38	78	23	57		Forzando	27	54	17	58
	Danehill (USA)	38	92	30	76	37	Mazilier (USA)	26	49	17	54
	Night Shift (USA)	38	95	28	70		Polish Patriot (USA)	26	46	19	63
13	Fairy King (USA)	36	73	27	75	39	Distant Relative	25	56	20	67
	Midyan (USA)	36	81	24	62		Komaite (USA)	25	46	18	61
15	Mujadil (USA)	35	35	19	69		Salse (USA)	25	73	21	70
	Petong	35	91	24	55	42	Aragon	24	58	19	58
	Timeless Times (USA)	35	56	22	54		Be My Chief (USA)	24	62	17	61
18	Common Grounds	34	65	21	63	44	Caerleon (USA)	23	57	18	78
19	Indian Ridge	33	67	21	73		Generous (IRE)	23	49	15	80
	Presidium	33	60	18	53		Thatching	23	45	16	69
21	Emarati (USA)	32	54	19	66	47	Clantime	22	68	14	49
	Rambo Dancer (CAN)	32	77	23	53		Elmaamul (USA)	22	37	16	63
23	Fayruz	31	60	17	62		Sharpo	22	49	18	65
24	Cadeaux Genereux	30	59	21	73		Taufan (USA)	22	55	17	65
	Puissance	30	68	20	58		Tirol	22	46	14	65
	Royal Academy (USA)	30	68	26	74						

Sires by win prize money in Britain 1997—Two-year-olds

	Sire	£	Wins	Chief Earner	
1	Cadeaux Genereux	£339,429	30	Embassy	£99,552
2	Danzig (USA)	£336,374	28	Blue Duster	£136,414
3	Woodman (USA)	£318,390	21	Gay Gallanta	£103,289
4	Waajib	£317,548	21	Royal Applause	£172,529
5	Petong	£309,184	35	Blue Iris	£157,202
6	Prince Sabo	£299,757	44	Maid For Walking	£98,804
7	Unfuwain (USA)	£278,177	18	Alhaarth	£177,559
8	Nashwan (USA)	£272,216	29	Aqaarid	£105,405
9	Green Desert (USA)	£266,060	49	Tamarisk	£30,157
10	Distinctly North (USA)	£256,688	39	Miss Stamper	£78,471
11	Dayjur (USA)	£253,582	28	Hayil	£68,785
12	Night Shift (USA)	£240,125	38	Nightbird	£50,514
13	Warning	£225,499	50	Mudeer	£15,609
14	Diesis	£213,500	27	Daggers Drawn	£85,041
15	Alzao (USA)	£211,958	44	Al Azhar	£21,844
16	Bering	£209,628	6	Glorosia	£96,768
17	Reprimand	£201,710	29	Fard	£106,212
18	Efisio	£196,443	52	For Old Times Sake	£24,247
19	Indian Ridge	£191,649	33	Indian Rocket	£54,125
20	Gone West (USA)	£191,520	20	Dance Parade	£41,576
21	Caerleon (USA)	£190,924	23	Cape Verdi	£49,420
22	Generous (IRE)	£183,720	23	Teapot Row	£82,737
23	Nureyev (USA)	£183,125	15	Reams of Verse	£112,506
24	Fairy King (USA)	£182,530	36	Queen Sceptre	£22,956
25	Forzando	£181,395	27	Easycall	£86,750
26	Sadler's Wells (USA)	£177,473	19	In Command	£90,505
27	El Gran Senor (USA)	£168,572	17	Saratoga Springs	£110,086
28	Zafonic (USA)	£168,145	11	Xaar	£117,674
29	Primo Dominie	£162,761	43	Brandon Magic	£16,688
30	Mr Prospector (USA)	£162,064	21	Dance Sequence	£40,521
31	Taufan (USA)	£161,184	22	Brief Glimpse	£76,536
32	Royal Academy (USA)	£160,429	30	Painter's Row	£28,643
33	Red Ransom (USA)	£157,941	18	Sri Pekan	£99,141
34	Common Grounds	£154,761	34	Fallow	£26,036
35	Danehill (USA)	£153,390	38	Willow Dale	£13,726
36	Silver Hawk (USA)	£151,380	15	Benny The Dip	£78,672
37	Polar Falcon (USA)	£150,189	28	Red Camellia	£34,855
38	Salse (USA)	£147,543	25	Bianca Nera	£49,677
39	Sharpo	£146,334	22	Grazia	£69,250
40	Statoblest	£143,598	40	Bliss	£13,901
41	Risk Me (FR)	£142,515	43	Circa	£17,570
42	Distant Relative	£139,964	25	My Branch	£42,803
43	Mujtahid (USA)	£136,908	29	Mubhij	£36,819
44	Midyan (USA)	£135,092	36	Inchrory	£13,395
45	Mujadil (USA)	£134,622	35	Classy Cleo	£18,209
46	Highest Honor (FR)	£134,475	5	Medaaly	£105,638
47	Puissance	£132,006	30	Mind Games	£33,825
48	Beveled (USA)	£127,797	38	In Good Faith	£14,227
49	Deploy	£127,147	17	Mons	£78,644

INDEX TO HORSES

Two Year Olds of 1998 – Index To Horses

Two Year Olds of 1998 – Index To Horses

Two Year Olds of 1998 – Index To Horses

Two Year Olds of 1998 – Index To Horses

Two Year Olds of 1998 – Index To Horses

INDEX TO DAMS

Two Year Olds of 1998 – Index To Dams

Two Year Olds of 1998 – Index To Dams

Two Year Olds of 1998 – Index To Dams